WORD
BIBLICAL
COMMENTARY

Editorial Board

Volumes

*forthcoming as of 2014
**in revision as of 2014

47A WORD BIBLICAL COMMENTARY

Hebrews 1-8

WILLIAM L. LANE

General Editors: David A. Hubbard, Glenn W. Barker
Old Testament Editor: John D. W. Watts
New Testament Editor: Ralph P. Martin

ZONDERVAN
ACADEMIC

ZONDERVAN ACADEMIC

Hebrews 1-8, Volume 47A
Copyright © 1991 by Thomas Nelson, Inc

Previously published as *Hebrews 1-8*.

Formerly published by Thomas Nelson, now published by Zondervan, a division of HarperCollins*Christian Publishing*.

Requests for information should be addressed to:
Zondervan, 3900 *Sparks Dr. SE, Grand Rapids, Michigan 49546*

This edition: ISBN 978-0-310-52179-2

The Library of Congress has cataloged the original edition as follows:
Library of Congress Control Number: 2005295211

Printed in the United States of America
22 23 24 25 26 27 28 29 30 /TRM/ 20 19 18 17 16 15 14 13 12 11 10

To
the Memory of My Mentors
Glenn W. Barker
a commanding presence in the classroom
a creative theologian
and a man radiant for God
who fashioned me as a teacher
and taught me to delight in Scripture
and
Ned B. Stonehouse
a commanding presence in the forum
an engaging teacher
and a man valiant for faith
who encouraged me to be a commentator
and taught me to listen to the text

EDITOR'S NOTE

For the convenience of the reader, page numbers for both volumes of this commentary on Hebrews (47A and 47B) are included in the Contents. Page numbers for the volume in hand are printed in boldface type, while those for the other volume are in lightface.

In addition, all of the front matter from Vol. 47A but the *Introduction* has been repeated in Vol. 47B so that the reader may have abbreviations, bibliography, and other pertinent information readily at hand.

Contents

Editorial Preface

The launching of the *Word Biblical Commentary* brings to fulfillment an enterprise of several years' planning. The publishers and the members of the editorial board met in 1977 to explore the possibility of a new commentary on the books of the Bible that would incorporate several distinctive features. Prospective readers of these volumes are entitled to know what such features were intended to be; whether the aims of the commentary have been fully achieved time alone will tell.

First, we have tried to cast a wide net to include as contributors a number of scholars from around the world who not only share our aims, but are in the main engaged in the ministry of teaching in university, college, and seminary. They represent a rich diversity of denominational allegiance. The broad stance of our contributors can rightly be called evangelical, and this term is to be understood in its positive, historic sense of a commitment to Scripture as divine revelation, and to the truth and power of the Christian gospel.

Then, the commentaries in our series are all commissioned and written for the purpose of inclusion in the *Word Biblical Commentary.* Unlike several of our distinguished counterparts in the field of commentary writing, there are no translated works, originally written in a non-English language. Also, our commentators were asked to prepare their own rendering of the original biblical text and to use those languages as the basis of their own comments and exegesis. What may be claimed as distinctive with this series is that it is based on the biblical languages, yet it seeks to make the technical and scholarly approach to a theological understanding of Scripture understandable by—and useful to—the fledgling student, the working minister, and colleagues in the guild of professional scholars and teachers as well.

Finally, a word must be said about the format of the series. The layout, in clearly defined sections, has been consciously devised to assist readers at different levels. Those wishing to learn about the textual witnesses on which the translation is offered are invited to consult the section headed *Notes.* If the readers' concern is with the state of modern scholarship on any given portion of Scripture, they should turn to the sections of *Bibliography* and *Form/Structure/Setting.* For a clear exposition of the passage's meaning and its relevance to the ongoing biblical revelation, the *Comment* and concluding *Explanation* are designed expressly to meet that need. There is therefore something for everyone who may pick up and use these volumes.

If these aims come anywhere near realization, the intention of the editors will have been met, and the labor of our team of contributors rewarded.

General Editors: *David A. Hubbard*
Glenn W. Barker †
Old Testament: *John D. W. Watts*
New Testament: *Ralph P. Martin*

Author's Preface

When the invitation arrived to contribute the volume on Hebrews in the Word Biblical Commentary, I was advancing some preliminary studies toward a monograph on the christology of Hebrews. That research had made me alert to the distinctiveness and richness of the writer's understanding of Jesus and redemption, and to the depth of his pastoral concern for a community in crisis. I welcomed the opportunity to immerse myself in the text and the discussion it had prompted. I was convinced that I would be able to advance both projects in tandem. I had forgotten that an invitation to prepare a comprehensive commentary, especially on a document as complex and richly textured as Hebrews, is an invitation to humiliation. You never know enough. Confidence outstrips competence. And then confidence can falter.

When I took my place at the table among those who were vigorously engaged in the discussion of the text, I quickly realized that it was presupposed that all the participants were linguistically competent. They were speaking at least eleven Western European languages. And to make matters worse, there was no consensus among them. They all claimed to have listened to the text, but they had a tendency not to listen to each other or to learn from one another. The writing of a commentary is often an exercise in discrimination of the relative merits among competing arguments and opinions. Responsible interpretation is never a private affair. The writing of a commentary is a collaborative event. There is no autonomy of insight.

I have frequently had to disengage myself from the discussion of the text within the academy and simply to sit before the text itself, learning again how to listen to the text both in its detail and its totality. The past twelve years have been devoted to a sustained dialogue with the text in order to sharpen my ability to listen responsibly. I have just as frequently returned to the discussion prompted by the text because listening is not accomplished in isolation. Some of my colleagues have grown impatient while waiting for this commentary. When they ask me what I have been doing, I respond that I have been dismantling the mufflers erected between me and the text.

The task of a commentator is not only to organize and summarize the discussion of the text but to contribute to that discussion in a substantial way. For one who makes a theological commitment to the authority of the text in its canonical form, that is a demanding task. One cannot make facile decisions and then move on. At stake is the determination of the meaning of a text of ultimate significance and the expression of that meaning in a clear modern idiom that is faithful to the original and that communicates its intention forcefully to a contemporary reader. I have sought to contribute to the discussion of the text by introducing lesser-known participants in the discussion as well as by my own synthetic response to the text. Undergirding the commentary presented here is the conviction that commitment to the claims of the text is the essential condition for creative exegetical insight.

I have been encouraged and instructed by those who have prepared commentaries, especially O. Michel and C. Spicq, monographs, dissertations, and articles.

They have stimulated me to look at the text from different angles of vision. It has been a high privilege to interact with so many gifted scholars who have sought to interpret the witness of Hebrews. The divergence in their conclusions was an incentive to a fresh investigation of the text. I am especially indebted to those who called my attention to unpublished dissertations on Hebrews and who frequently assisted me by securing them for me. I was in the Netherlands when H. W. Attridge's commentary on Hebrews in the Hermeneia series became available, and regrettably I enjoyed access to it only when this commentary was in its final stage.

A major problem in the preparation of a commentary is that concentration on issues of a textual, grammatical, syntactical, rhetorical, or theological nature within a unit of text can foster a fragmented perception of the unit as a whole, just as concentration upon an individual section can interfere with the discernment of the document as a whole. A serious problem in making use of a commentary is that the concerns of the commentator in an individual section can direct the attention to the details of the text but divert it from the flow of the statement within the section and the document as a whole. In this commentary readers will be advised to read the *Introduction* to each of the five major divisions discerned in Hebrews before consulting the commentary on a particular section. This will allow the pastoral thrust of the document, as opposed to the section, to be grasped. When turning to individual sections, it will be helpful to read first the *Explanation* for an overview of the section before consulting the commentary on individual units of the text.

This commentary has been prepared for professional colleagues and seminary students, but also for pastors and teachers in the churches. I have sought to expose myself to the significant work that has been done on Hebrews in any Western European language in order to make that research accessible to those who work primarily in English. This has been a labor of love for the Church. This commentary will provide a resource for determining the state of scholarship on Hebrews. It will also seek to advance the claims of the text for unwavering commitment to God, who continues to speak decisively in his Son to a culture not unlike that to which Hebrews was addressed, one that appears to lack order, structure, and meaning.

Hebrews has acquired a reputation for being formidable and remote from the world in which we live. Consequently, it has been neglected in the liturgy and preaching of the churches, in the curriculum of seminaries, and in the devotional reading of the laity. There has been no dearth of commentaries, monographs, dissertations, and articles on Hebrews. In the course of my own research, I have come to appreciate that significant descriptive phrase from the computer age, "informational overload." But Hebrews tends to remain unappreciated and unused in the classroom, the pulpit, and the pew.

Ironically, Hebrews is a call for ultimate certainty and ultimate commitment. James Olthuis has described Hebrews as a "certitudinal Book": it concerns itself with the issue of certainty by confronting ultimate questions about life and death with ultimate realities. Its presentation of the way in which God responds to the human family as one who speaks, creates, covenants, pledges, calls, and commits himself is intended to breathe new life into men and women who suffer a failure of nerve because they live in an insecure, anxiety-provoking society. Hebrews participates in the character of Scripture as gift. It is a gift the Church sorely needs.

My debts to others are large, but not easy to define. I am especially indebted to the two mentors who did so much to train me for scholarship, to whose memory this volume is dedicated. A number of graduate students have assisted me in my research: Robert Herron, Kern Trembath, Joseph Causey, Paul Schmidgall, Bedford Smith, Jack Thomas, Bill Bailey, Alan Carter, David Wornam, Michael Card, Brian Yorton, Chris Steward, Pat Cely, Greg Salyer, Roy Swisher, and Alan Lewis. To each of them I express my appreciation. I owe a special debt of gratitude to my colleagues Joe Trafton and Jim Davis, with whom I discussed decisions to which I felt driven by the text, but for which I could find no other support. The writing of a commentary is happily a collegial experience. I am grateful to Robert Hanna of Seminario Evángelico in Maracay, Aragua, Venezuela, who responded to my grammatical questions and kindly presented me with a prepublication copy of his helpful *Grammatical Aid.*

Access to the splendid collection and the ideal setting for scholarship at Tyndale House in Cambridge, England, first in 1981, and then again in 1988 and 1989, was indispensable to the beginning of my research and to its completion. A year spent at the Institute for Ecumenical and Cultural Research in Collegeville, MN, in 1981-82, and the warm support of the director, Dr. Robert Bilheimer, made it possible for me to draft the commentary on the first eight chapters of Hebrews. A year spent in community in Amsterdam in 1988-89, with the men and women of Youth With A Mission, made it possible to return to the task of completing the commentary in a supportive environment and to sharpen my perspective through engagement in mission. I am appreciative of the careful editing of the manuscript by Dr. R. P. Martin and Dr. L. A. Losie, and for those on the editorial staff at Word Books who have seen the manuscript through the press.

My deepest debt is to my wife, Brenda, who believed in me when I felt inadequate to the task and who has been a source of constant encouragement. We talked at length about the problems presented by the text with which I was wrestling. Her ability to ask instinctively the right questions consistently pointed me in the direction of a solution. She has rejoiced in the completion of every section of the commentary and typed the bulk of the manuscript. I especially appreciate the counsel she gave me one day on a slip of paper tucked in with my work sheets: "The commentary is the Lord's. Do it in his strength!" I also appreciate the commitment to the project of my daughter, Debra Gensheimer, who completed the typing of the manuscript and the preparation of the copy for the publisher. I would be remiss if I did not mention the gracious hospitality of Dr. and Mrs. Ben Burgoyne, who made available to me a portion of their home in an exquisite setting where I was able to prepare the pages for the Introduction without distraction.

The writing of this commentary has been an act of love and devotion to God and to the Church. May it serve the Church and the guild well by directing attention to the remarkable gift we possess in the discourse that we call Hebrews.

July 12, 1991   WILLIAM L. LANE
School of Religion
Seattle Pacific University
Seattle, Washington

Abbreviations

A. General Abbreviations

A	Codex Alexandrinus
ad	comment on
Akkad.	Akkadian
א	Codex Sinaiticus
act	active
adj	adjective
adv	adverb
aor	aorist
Ap. Lit.	Apocalyptic Literature
Apoc.	Apocrypha
Aq.	Aquila's Greek Translation of the OT
Arab.	Arabic
Aram.	Aramaic
B	Codex Vaticanus
bo	Bohairic
C	Codex Ephraemi Syri
c.	*circa*, about
cent.	century
cf.	*confer*, compare
chap(s).	chapter(s)
cod., codd.	codex, codices
conj	conjunction
consec	consecutive
contra	in contrast to
D	Codex Bezae
dittogr	dittography
DSS	Dead Sea Scrolls
ed.	edited by, editor(s)
e.g.	*exempli gratia*, for example
et al.	*et alii*, and others
ET	English translation
EV	English Versions of the Bible
f., ff.	following (verse or verses, pages, etc.)
fem	feminine
frag.	fragments
FS	*Festschrift*, volume written in honor of
ft.	foot, feet
fut	future
gen	genitive
Gk.	Greek
hap. leg.	*hapax legomenon*, sole occurrence
haplogr	haplography

Heb.	Hebrew
Hitt.	Hittite
ibid.	*ibidem*, in the same place
id.	*idem*, the same
i.e.	*id est*, that is
impf	imperfect
ind	indicative
inf	infinitive
infra	below
in loc.	*in loco*, in the place cited
lat	Latin
lit.	literally
loc. cit.	the place cited
LXX	Septuagint
masc	masculine
mg.	margin
MS(S)	manuscript(s)
MT	Masoretic text (of the Old Testament)
n.	note
n.d.	no date
Nestle[26]	E. & E. Nestle (ed.), *Novum Testamentum Graece*[26], rev. by K. Aland et al.
NHC	Nag Hammadi Codex
no.	number
nom	nominative
n.s.	new series
NT	New Testament
obj	objective, object
obs.	obsolete
OG	Old Greek
OL	Old Latin
o.s.	old series
OT	Old Testament
p., pp.	page, pages
pace	with due respect to, but differing from
//	parallel(s)
par.	paragraph, parallel(s)
pass	passive
passim	elsewhere
pf	perfect
pl	plural
poss	possessive
prep	preposition

Pseudep.	Pseudepigrapha	Theod.	Theodotion
ptcp	participle	TR	Textus Receptus
Q	Quelle ("Sayings" source for the Gospels)	tr.	translator, translated by
		UBSGNT	The United Bible Societies Greek NT
q.v.	*quod vide*, which see		
rev.	revised, reviser, revision	Ugar.	Ugaritic
Rom.	Roman	UP	University Press
sa	Sahidic	u.s.	*ut supra*, as above
Sam.	Samaritan recension	v, vv	verse, verses
sc.	*scilicet*, that is to say	viz.	*videlicet*, namely
Sem.	Semitic	Vg	Vulgate
sg	singular	*v.l.*	*varia lectio*, alternative reading
subj	subjective, subject		
Sumer.	Sumerian		
s.v.	*sub verbo*, under the word	vol.	volume
sy	Syriac	x	times (2x = two times, etc.)
Symm.	Symmachus		
Tg.	Targum		

Note: The textual notes and numbers used to indicate individual manuscripts are those found in the apparatus criticus of *Novum Testamentum Graece*, ed. E. & E. Nestle, rev. K. Aland et al., 26th ed. (Stuttgart: Deutsche Bibelgesellschaft, 1979). This edition of the Greek NT is the basis for the *Translation* sections.

B. Abbreviations for Translations and Paraphrases

AmT	Smith & Goodspeed, *The Complete Bible, An American Translation*	Moffatt	J. Moffatt, *A New Translation of the Bible* (NT 1913)
		NAB	*The New American Bible*
ASV	American Standard Version of Revised Version (1901)	NASB	*The New American Standard Bible*
AV	Authorized Version = KJV	NCV	New Century Version
Basic	*The New Testament in Basic English*	NEB	*The New English Bible*
		NIV	The New International Version (1978)
Beck	W. F. Beck, *The New Testament in the Language of Today*		
		NJB	*New Jerusalem Bible* (1985)
		Phillips	J. B. Phillips, *The New Testament in Modern English*
GNB	*Good News Bible* = Today's English Version		
JB	*Jerusalem Bible*	RSV	Revised Standard Version (NT 1946, OT 1952, Apoc. 1957)
JPS	Jewish Publication Society, *The Holy Scriptures*		
KJV	King James Version (1611) = AV	RV	Revised Version, 1881–85
		TEV	Today's English Version
Knox	R. A. Knox, *The Holy Bible*		

C. Abbreviations of Commonly Used Periodicals, Reference Works, and Serials

AB	Anchor Bible	*Aeg*	*Aegyptus*
ACR	*Australasian Catholic Record*	AEPHE	*Annuaire de l'École pratique des Hautes Études*
ACW	Ancient Christian Writers		

AER	American Ecclesiastical Review	BAG	W. Bauer, W. F. Arndt, and
AIPHO	Annuaire de l'Institute de		F. W. Gingrich, Greek-
	Philologie et d'Histoire		English Lexicon of the NT
	Orientales		(1957)
AJBA	Australian Journal of Biblical	BAGD	W. Bauer, W. F. Arndt, F.
	Archaeology		W. Gingrich, and F. W.
AJBI	Annual of the Japanese		Danker, Greek-English
	Biblical Institute		Lexicon of the NT (1979)
AJPh	American Journal of Philoso-	BASOR	Bulletin of the American
	phy		Schools of Oriental
AJT	American Journal of Theology		Research
ALBO	Analecta lovaniensia	BBB	Bonner biblische Beiträge
	biblica et orientalia	BDF	F. Blass, A. Debrunner, and
ALGHJ	Arbeiten zur Literatur und		R. W. Funk, A Greek
	Geschichte des		Grammar of the NT
	hellenistischen	BenM	Benediktinische Monatsschrift
	Judentums		zur Pflege religiösen und
ALUOS	Annual of Leeds University		geistigen Lebens
	Oriental Society	BeO	Bibbia e oriente
AnBib	Analecta biblica	BETL	Bibliotheca ephemeridum
Ang	Angelicum		theologicarum
Angelos	Angelos: Archiv für		lovaniensium
	neutestamentliche	BETS	Bulletin of the Evangelical
	Zeitgeschichte und		Theological Society
	Kulturkunde	BFCL	Bulletin des Facultés
ANRW	Aufstieg und Niedergang der		Catholìques de Lyon
	römischen Welt	BFCT	Beiträge zur Förderung
Anton	Antonianum		christlicher Theologie
Anvil	Anvil	BGBE	Beiträge zur Geschichte
APOT	R. H. Charles (ed.),		der biblischen Exegese
	Apocrypha and	BHK	R. Kittel, Biblia hebraica⁷
	Pseudepigrapha of the Old	Bib	Biblica
	Testament	BibLeb	Bibel und Leben
ARG	Archiv für	BibOr	Biblica et orientalia
	Reformationsgeschichte	BibRev	Biblical Review
ASem	Asbury Seminarian	BibTh	Biblical Theology
AsiaJT	Asia Journal of Theology	BIOSCS	Bulletin of the International
ASNS	Annuaire de la societé Nathan		Organization for
	Söderblom		Septuagint and Cognate
AsSeign	Assemblées du Seigneur		Studies
ASTI	Annual of the Swedish	BIRBS	Bulletin of the Institute for
	Theological Institute		Reformation Biblical
ATh	L'Année Théologique		Studies
	Augustinienne	BJRL	Bulletin of the John Rylands
ATR	Anglican Theological Review		University Library of
AusBR	Australian Biblical Review		Manchester
AUSS	Andrews University Seminary	BLit	Bibel und Liturgie
	Studies	BR	Biblical Research
BA	Biblical Archaeologist	BSac	Bibliotheca Sacra

BT	*The Bible Translator*	EAJT	*East Asia Journal of Theology*
BTB	*Biblical Theology Bulletin*	EBib	*Études bibliques*
BU	Biblische Untersuchungen	EE	*Estudios Eclesiásticos*
Burg	*Burgense*	EEv	*Études Evangéliques*
BV	*Biblical Viewpoint*	EKKNT	Evangelisch-Katholischer Kommentar zum Neuen Testament
BVC	*Bible et vie chrétienne*		
BW	*The Biblical World*		
BZ	*Biblische Zeitschrift*	Enc	*Encounter*
BZNW	Beihefte zur *ZNW*	ErJb	*Eranos Jahrbuch*
CB	*Cultura bíblica*	ERT	*Evangelical Review of Theology*
CBQ	*Catholic Biblical Quarterly*		
CBQMS	Catholic Biblical Quarterly—Monograph Series	EstBib	*Estudios bíblicos*
		EstFran	*Estudios Franciscanos*
		ETL	*Ephemerides theologicae lovanienses*
CCER	*Cahiers du Cercle Ernest-Renan*		
		ETR	*Études théologiques et religieuses*
CentBibQ	*Central Bible Quarterly*		
CGTC	Cambridge Greek Testament Commentaries	EuA	*Erbe und Auftrage: Benediktinische Monatsschrift*
Chr	*Christus*		
CJT	*Canadian Journal of Theology*	EV	*Esprit et Vie*
ClBib	Clarendon Bible	EvJ	*Evangelical Journal*
CleM	*Clergy Monthly*	EvMz	*Evangelische Missionszeitschrift*
ClRev	*The Classical Review*		
CMech	*Collectanea Mechliniensia*	EvQ	*Evangelical Quarterly*
CNT	Commentaire du Nouveau Testament	EvT	*Evangelische Theologie*
		Exp	*Expositor*
Coll	*Colloquium*	ExpTim	*Expository Times*
CollTh	*Collectanea Theologica*	FGNK	Forschungen zur Geschichte des neutestamentlichen Kanons und der altkirchlichen Literatur
ConNT	*Coniectanea neotestamentica*		
CQR	*Church Quarterly Review*		
CrozQ	*Crozer Quarterly*		
CSion	Cahiers Sioniens		
CSEL	Corpus scriptorum ecclesiasticorum latinorum	FM	*Faith and Mission*
		FRLANT	Forschungen zur Religion und Literatur des Alten und Neuen Testaments
CTJ	*Calvin Theological Journal*		
CTM	*Concordia Theological Monthly*	FV	*Foi et Vie*
		GBTh	Gegenwartsfragen biblischer Theologie
CTom	*Ciencia Tomista*		
CurrThMiss	*Currents in Theology and Mission*	GCS	Griechischen christlichen Schriftsteller
CV	*Communio Viatorum*	GJ	*Grace Journal*
DACL	*Dictionnaire d'archéologie chrétienne et de liturgie*	GOTR	*Greek Orthodox Theological Review*
DBSup	*Dictionnaire de la Bible, Supplément*	Greg	*Gregorianum*
		GThT	*Gereformeered Theologisch Tijdschrift*
Div	*Divinitas*		
DivThom	*Divus Thomas*	GTJ	*Grace Theological Journal*

GL	*Geist und Leben*	*JSNT*	*Journal for the Study of the*
HBK	Herders Bibel Kommentar		*New Testament*
HDR	Harvard Dissertations in	JSNTSup	JSNT Supplement Series
	Religion	*JSOT*	*Journal for the Study of the*
Her	*Hermathena*		*Old Testament*
Hermes	*Hermes: Zeitschrift für*	*JSS*	*Journal of Semitic Studies*
	klassische Philologie	*JTSB*	*Jahrbuch der theologischen*
HeyJ	*Heythrop Journal*		*Schule Bethel*
HibJ	*Hibbert Journal*	*JTS*	*Journal of Theological*
Hist	*Historia*		*Studies*
HKNT	Handkommentar zum	*Jud*	*Judaism*
	Neuen Testament	*KD*	*Kerygma und Dogma*
HNT	Handbuch zum Neuen	KNT	Kommentar zum Neuen
	Testament		Testament
HNTC	Harper's NT Commentar-	LCC	Library of Christian
	ies		Classics
HTR	*Harvard Theological Review*	LCL	Loeb Classical Library
HUCA	*Hebrew Union College Annual*	LD	Lectio divina
IB	*Interpreter's Bible*	*LexTQ*	*Lexington Theological*
IBS	*Irish Biblical Studies*		*Quarterly*
ICC	International Critical	*LPGL*	G. W. H. Lampe, *Patristic*
	Commentary		*Greek Lexicon*
IDB	G. A. Buttrick (ed.),	*LQHR*	*London Quarterly and*
	Interpreter's Dictionary of		*Holborn Review*
	the Bible	LSJ	Liddell-Scott-Jones, *Greek-*
IEJ	*Israel Exploration Journal*		*English Lexicon*
IlRev	*Iliff Review*	*LV*	*Lumière et Vie*
Int	*Interpretation*	*LQ*	*Lutheran Quarterly*
It	*Itala*	*MCM*	*Modern Churchman*
ITQ	*Irish Theological Quarterly*	*Mel Theol*	*Melita Theologica*
JAC	Jahrbuch für Antike und	MeyerK	H. A. W. Meyer,
	Christentum		*Kritisch-exegetischer*
JBL	*Journal of Biblical Literature*		*Kommentar über das Neue*
JBR	*Journal of Bible and Religion*		*Testament*
JDT	*Jahrbuch für deutsche Theologie*	*MGWJ*	*Monatsschrift für Geschichte*
JETS	*Journal of the Evangelical*		*und Wissenschaft des*
	Theological Society		*Judentums*
JHS	*Journal of Hellenic Studies*	MM	J. H. Moulton and G.
JJS	*Journal of Jewish Studies*		Milligan, *Vocabulary of*
JNES	*Journal of Near Eastern*		*the Greek Testament*
	Studies	MNTC	Moffatt NT Commentary
JPTh	*Jahrbücher für protestantische*	*MPTh*	*Monatsschrift für Pastoral*
	Theologie		*Theologie*
JQR	*Jewish Quarterly Review*	*MQR*	*Methodist Quarterly Review*
JRS	*Journal of Roman Studies*	MTS	Münchener theologische
JSJ	*Journal for the Study of*		Studien
	Judaism in the Persian,	*MTZ*	*Münchener theologische*
	Hellenistic and Roman		*Zeitschrift*
	Period	*Mus*	*Muséon*

NAWG	Nachrichten der Akademie der Wissenschaften in Göttingen	PG	J. Migne, *Patrologia graeca*
		PRS	*Perspectives in Religious Studies*
NBl	*New Blackfriars*	PSB	*Princeton Seminary Bulletin*
NC	*Nineteenth Century*	PTR	*Princeton Theological Review*
NedTTs	*Nederlands theologisch Tijdschrift*	QuartRev	*Quarterly Review*
		RAC	*Reallexikon für Antike und Christentum*
Neot	*Neotestamentica*		
NewDocs	*New Documents Illustrating Early Christianity*, ed. G. H. R. Horsley	RB	*Revue biblique*
		RBén	*Revue bénédictine*
		RCB	*Revista de cultura bíblica*
NGWG	*Nachrichten der Gesellschaft der Wissenschaften zu Göttingen*	RDT	*Revue Diocésaine de Tournai*
		RefRev	*The Reformed Review*
		REJ	*Revue des études juives*
NIBC	New International Biblical Commentary	ResQ	*Restoration Quarterly*
		RevExp	*Review and Expositor*
NICNT	New International Commentary on the New Testament	*RevistB*	*Revista bíblica*
		RevistCal	*Revista Calasancia*
		RevistCatT	*Revista Catalana de Teologia*
NIDNTT	*New International Dictionary of New Testament Theology*	*RevQ*	*Revue de Qumran*
		RevRéf	*Revue Réformee*
NJDT	*Neue Jahrbücher für Deutsche Theologie*	*RevScRel*	*Revue des sciences religieuses*
		RGG	*Religion in Geschichte und Gegenwart*
NKZ	*Neue kirchliche Zeitschrift*		
NorTT	*Norsk Teologisk Tidsskrift*	RHPR	*Revue d'histoire et de philosophie religieuses*
NovT	*Novum Testamentum*		
NovTSup	Novum Testamentum, Supplements	RHR	*Revue de l'histoire des religions*
		RivB	*Revista biblica*
NPNF	Nicene and Post-Nicene Fathers	RNT	Regensburger Neues Testament
NRT	*La nouvelle revue théologique*	RPLHA	*Revue de Philologie de Littérature et d'Histoire Anciennes*
NTD	Das Neue Testament Deutsch		
NThS	*Nieuwe Theologische Studiën*	RSPT	*Revue des sciences philosophiques et théologiques*
NTS	*New Testament Studies*		
NTStud	*The New Testament Student*		
NTTS	New Testament Tools and Studies	RSR	*Recherches de science religieuse*
		RTP	*Revue de théologie et de philosophie*
OCD	*Oxford Classical Dictionary*		
OGI	*Orientis Graeci Inscriptiones Selectae*, ed. W. Dittenberger	RTR	*Reformed Theological Review*
		SacDoc	*Sacra Doctrina*
		Sal	*Salesianum: Pontificio ateneo salesiano*
OLZ	*Orientalische Literaturzeitung*		
OPTT	*Occasional Papers in Translation and Textlinguistics*	SB	Sources bibliques
		SBFLA	*Studii Biblici Franciscani Liber Annuus*
OTS	*Oudtestamentische Studiën*	SBLASP	Society of Biblical Literature Abstracts and Seminar Papers
PCSBR	*Papers of Chicago's Society of Biblical Research*		

SBLDS	SBL Dissertation Series	TCh	*The Churchman*
SBLMS	SBL Monograph Series	TD	*Theology Digest*
SBLSCS	SBL Septuagint and Cognate Studies	TDNT	G. Kittel and G. Friedrich (ed.), *Theological Dictionary of the New Testament*
SBT	Studies in Biblical Theology		
SC	Sources chrétiennes		
ScC	*Scuola cattolica: Revista di scienze religiose*	TF	*Theologische Forschung*
		TGl	*Theologie und Glaube*
ScEccl	*Sciences ecclésiastiques*	ThBullMDC	*Theological Bulletin: McMaster Divinity College*
Schol	*Scholastik*		
ScEs	*Science et Esprit*	ThEduc	*Theological Educator*
Scr	*Scripture*	Th	*Theology*
ScrHier	*Scripta hierasolymitana*	Theol(A)	*Theologia*
SE	*Studia Evangelica*	THKNT	Theologischer Handkommentar zum Neuen Testament
SEÅ	*Svensk exegetisk årsbok*		
Sem	*Semitica*		
Serv	*Servitium*	ThEv	*Theologica Evangelica*
SJT	*Scottish Journal of Theology*	ThRev	*Theological Review*
SNT	Studien zum Neuen Testament	ThViat	*Theologia Viatorum*
		TLZ	*Theologische Literaturzeitung*
SNTSMS	Society for New Testament Studies Monograph Series	TNTC	Tyndale New Testament Commentaries
		TPQ	*Theologisch-Praktische Quartalschrift*
SNTU	Studien zum Neuen Testament und seiner Umwelt, Series A	TRev	*Theologische Revue*
		TRu	*Theologische Rundschau*
SP	*Studia Patristica*	TS	*Theological Studies*
SPAW	Sitzungsberichte der preussischen Akademie der Wissenschaften	TSK	*Theologische Studien und Kritiken*
		TToday	*Theology Today*
SPB	Studia postbiblica	TTZ	*Trierer theologische Zeitschrift*
SpTod	*Spirituality Today*	TU	Texte und Untersuchungen
SR	*Studies in Religion/Sciences religieuses*		
		TY	*Tantur Yearbook*
ST	*Studia theologica*	TynBul	*Tyndale Bulletin*
STK	*Svensk teologisk kvartalskrift*	TZ	*Theologische Zeitschrift*
Str-B	[H. Strack and] P. Billerbeck, *Kommentar zum Neuen Testament*	UCB	Die Urchristliche Botschaft
		USQR	*Union Seminary Quarterly Review*
StudBibTh	*Studia Biblica et Theologica*	VC	*Vigiliae christianae*
StudNeot	Studia neotestamentica, Studia	VD	*Verbum domini*
		VL	Vetus Latina
SUNT	Studien zur Umwelt des Neuen Testaments	VoxEv	*Vox Evangelica*
		VS	Verbum salutis
SWJT	*Southwestern Journal of Theology*	VSpir	*Vie spirituelle*
		VT	*Vetus Testamentum*
TBei	*Theologische Beiträge*	VTSup	Vetus Testamentum, Supplements
TBl	*Theologische Blätter*		
TBT	*The Bible Today*	WesThJ	*Wesleyan Theological Journal*

WMANT	Wissenschaftliche Monographien zum Alten und Neuen Testament	ZKT	*Zeitschrift für Katholische Theologie*
		ZNW	*Zeitschrift für die neutestamentliche Wissenschaft*
Wor	*Worship*		
WTJ	Westminster Theological Journal	ZRGG	*Zeitschrift für Religions- und Geistesgeschichte*
WUNT	Wissenschaftliche Untersuchungen zum Neuen Testament	ZST	*Zeitschrift für systematische Theologie*
		ZTK	*Zeitschrift für Theologie und Kirche*
WW	*Word and World*		
ZAW	*Zeitschrift für die alttestamentliche Wissenschaft*	ZWT	*Zeitschrift für wissenschaftliche Theologie*
		ZZ	*Zeichen der Zeit*

D. Abbreviations for Books of the Bible, the Apocrypha, and the Pseudepigrapha

OLD TESTAMENT

Gen	1 Sam	Esth	Lam	Mic
Exod	2 Sam	Job	Ezek	Nah
Lev	1 Kgs	Ps(Pss)	Dan	Hab
Num	2 Kgs	Prov	Hos	Zeph
Deut	1 Chr	Eccl	Joel	Hag
Josh	2 Chr	Cant	Amos	Zech
Judg	Ezra	Isa	Obad	Mal
Ruth	Neh	Jer	Jonah	

NEW TESTAMENT

Matt	1 Cor	1 Thess	Philem	1 John
Mark	2 Cor	2 Thess	Heb	2 John
Luke	Gal	1 Tim	Jas	3 John
John	Eph	2 Tim	1 Pet	Jude
Acts	Phil	Titus	2 Pet	Rev
Rom	Col			

APOCRYPHA

1 Kgdms	1 Kingdoms	Wis	Wisdom of Solomon	Sus	Susanna
2 Kgdms	2 Kingdoms			Bel	Bel and the Dragon
3 Kgdms	3 Kingdoms	Sir	Ecclesiasticus (Wisdom of Jesus the son of Sirach)		
4 Kgdms	4 Kingdoms			Pr Man	Prayer of Manasseh
1 Esd	1 Esdras				
2 Esd	2 Esdras			1 Macc	1 Maccabees
Tob	Tobit	Bar	Baruch	2 Macc	2 Maccabees
Jdt	Judith	Ep Jer	Epistle of Jeremy	3 Macc	3 Maccabees
Add Esth	Additions to Esther	S Th Ch	Song of the Three Children (or Young Men)	4 Macc	4 Maccabees
4 Ezra	4 Ezra				

E. Abbreviations of the Names of Jewish, Pseudepigraphical, and Early Patristic Books

Adam and Eve	*Life of Adam and Eve*	*Gos. Pet.*	*Gospel of Peter*
Apoc. Abr.	*Apocalypse of Abraham* (1st to 2nd cent. A.D.)	*Gos. Thom.*	*Gospel of Thomas*
		Prot. Jas.	*Protevangelium of James*
2–3 Apoc. Bar.	Syriac, Greek *Apocalypse of Baruch*	*Barn.*	*Barnabas*
		1–2 Clem.	*1–2 Clement*
Asc. Isa.	*Ascension of Isaiah*	*Did.*	*Didache*
Apoc. Mos.	*Apocalypse of Moses*	*Diogn.*	*Diognetus*
As. Mos.	(See *T. Mos.*)	*Herm. Man.*	Hermas, *Mandates*
Apoc. Elijah	*Apocalypse of Elijah*	*Sim.*	*Similitudes*
1–2–3 Enoch	Ethiopic, Slavonic, Hebrew *Enoch*	*Vis.*	*Visions*
		Ign. Eph.	Ignatius, *Letter to the Ephesians*
Ep. Arist.	*Epistle of Aristeas*		
Jub.	*Jubilees*	*Magn.*	*Letter to the Magnesians*
Mart. Isa.	*Martyrdom of Isaiah*	*Phld.*	*Letter to the Philadelphians*
Odes Sol.	*Odes of Solomon*	*Pol.*	*Letter to Polycarp*
Pss. Sol.	*Psalms of Solomon*	*Rom.*	*Letter to the Romans*
Sib. Or.	*Sibylline Oracles*	*Smyrn.*	*Letter to the Smyrnaeans*
T. 12 Patr.	*Testaments of the Twelve Patriarchs*	*Trall.*	*Letter to the Trallians*
		Jos., Ag. Ap.	Josephus, *Against Apion*
T. Abr.	*Testament of Abraham*	*Ant.*	*The Jewish Antiquities*
T. Judah	*Testament of Judah*	*J. W.*	*The Jewish War*
T. Levi	*Testament of Levi*, etc.	*Life*	*The Life*
		Mart. Pol.	*Martyrdom of Polycarp*
Apoc. Pet.	*Apocalypse of Peter*	*Pol. Phil.*	Polycarp, *Letter to the Philippians*
Apost. Const.	*Apostolic Constitutions*		
Gos. Eb.	*Gospel of the Ebionites*	*Iren. Adv.*	Irenaeus, *Against*
Gos. Eg.	*Gospel of the Egyptians*	*Haer.*	*All Heresies*
Gos. Heb.	*Gospel of the Hebrews*	*Tert. De*	Tertullian, *On the*
Gos. Naass.	*Gospel of the Naassenes*	*Praesc. Haer.*	*Proscribing of Heretics*

F. Abbreviations of Names of Dead Sea Scrolls and Related Texts

CD	Cairo (Genizah text of the) Damascus (Document)	1QapGen	*Genesis Apocryphon* of Qumran Cave 1
Hev	Naḥal Ḥever texts	1QH	*Hôdāyôt* (*Thanksgiving Hymns*) from Qumran Cave 1
Mas	Masada texts		
Mird	Khirbet Mird texts	1QIsaᵃ,ᵇ	First or second copy of Isaiah from Qumran Cave 1
Mur	Wadi Murabbaʿat texts		
P	Pesher (commentary)	1QpHab	*Pesher on Habakkuk* from Qumran
Q	Qumran		
1Q, 2Q, 3Q, etc.	Numbered caves of Qumran, yielding written material; followed by abbreviation of biblical or apocryphal book	1QM	*Milḥāmāh* (*War Scroll*)
		1QS	*Serek hayyaḥad* (*Rule of the Community, Manual of Discipline*)
QL	Qumran literature	1QSa	Appendix A (*Rule of the Congregation*) to 1QS

1QSb	Appendix B (*Blessings*) to 1QS	4QTestim	*Testimonia* text from Qumran Cave 4
3Q15	Copper Scroll from Qumran Cave 3	4QTLevi	*Testament of Levi* from Qumran Cave 4
4QFlor	*Florilegium* (or *Eschatological Midrashim*) from Qumran Cave 4	4QPhyl	Phylacteries from Qumran Cave 4
4QMess ar	Aramaic "Messianic" text from Qumran Cave 4	11QMelch	*Melchizedek* text from Qumran Cave 11
4QPrNab	Prayer of Nabonidus from Qumran Cave 4	11QtgJob	*Targum of Job* from Qumran Cave 11

G. Abbreviations of Targumic Material

Tg. Onq.	*Targum Onqelos*	*Tg. Ps.-J.*	*Targum Pseudo-Jonathan*
Tg. Neb.	*Targum of the Prophets*	*Tg. Yer. I*	*Targum Yerušalmi I**
Tg. Ket.	*Targum of the Writings*	*Tg. Yer. II*	*Targum Yerušalmi II**
Frg. Tg.	*Fragmentary Targum*	*Yem. Tg.*	*Yemenite Targum*
Sam. Tg.	*Samaritan Targum*	*Tg. Esth. I, II*	*First or Second Targum of Esther*
Tg. Isa.	*Targum of Isaiah*		
Pal. Tgs.	*Palestinian Targums*		
Tg. Neof.	*Targum Neofiti I*	*optional title	

H. Abbreviations of Other Rabbinic Works

ʾAbot R. Nat.	*ʾAbot de Rabbi Nathan*	*Pesiq. R.*	*Pesiqta Rabbati*
ʾAg. Ber.	*ʾAggadat Berešit*	*Pesiq. Rab Kah.*	*Pesiqta de Rab Kahana*
Bab.	*Babylonian*	*Pirqe R. El.*	*Pirqe Rabbi Eliezer*
Bar.	*Baraita*	*Rab.*	*Rabbah* (following abbreviation for biblical book: *Gen. Rab.* = *Genesis Rabbah*)
Der. Er. Rab.	*Derek Ereṣ Rabba*		
Der. Er. Zuṭ.	*Derek Ereṣ Zuṭa*		
Gem.	*Gemara*	*Sem.*	*Semahot*
Kalla	*Kalla*	*Sipra*	*Sipra*
Mek.	*Mekilta*	*Sipre*	*Sipre*
Midr.	*Midraš*; cited with usual abbreviation for biblical book; but *Midr. Qoh.* = *Midraš Qohelet*	*Sop.*	*Soperim*
		S. ʿOlam Rab.	*Seder ʿOlam Rabbah*
		Talm.	*Talmud*
		Yal.	*Yalqut*
Pal.	*Palestinian*		

I. Abbreviations of Orders and Tractates in Mishnaic and Related Literature

Sources of tractates are indicated as follows: *m.* (Mishnah), *t.* (Tosepta), *b.* (Babylonian Talmud), and *y.* (Jerusalem Talmud).

ʾAbot	*ʾAbot*	*Beṣa*	*Beṣa* (= *Yom Tob*)
ʿArak.	*ʿArakin*	*Bik.*	*Bikkurim*
ʿAbod. Zar.	*ʿAboda Zara*	*B. Meṣ.*	*Baba Meṣiʿa*
B. Bat.	*Baba Batra*	*B. Qam.*	*Baba Qamma*
Bek.	*Bekorot*	*Dem.*	*Demai*
Ber.	*Berakot*	*ʿEd.*	*ʿEduyyot*

ʿErub.	*ʿErubin*	*Ohol.*	*Oholot*
Giṭ.	*Giṭṭin*	*ʿOr.*	*ʿOrla*
Ḥag.	*Ḥagiga*	*Para*	*Para*
Ḥal.	*Ḥalla*	*Peʾa*	*Peʾa*
Hor.	*Horayot*	*Pesaḥ.*	*Pesahim*
Ḥul.	*Ḥullin*	*Qinnim*	*Qinnim*
Kelim	*Kelim*	*Qidd.*	*Qiddušin*
Ker.	*Keritot*	*Qod.*	*Qodašin*
Ketub.	*Ketubot*	*Roš. Haš.*	*Roš Haššana*
Kil.	*Kilʾayim*	*Sanh.*	*Sanhedrin*
Maʿaś.	*Maaʿśerot*	*Šabb.*	*Šabbat*
Mak.	*Makkot*	*Šeb.*	*Šebiʿit*
Makš.	*Makširin (= Mašqin)*	*Šebu.*	*Šebuʿot*
Meg.	*Megilla*	*Šeqal.*	*Šeqalim*
Meʿil.	*Meʿila*	*Sota*	*Sota*
Menaḥ.	*Menahot*	*Sukk.*	*Sukka*
Mid.	*Middot*	*Taʿan.*	*Taʿanit*
Miqw.	*Miqwaʾot*	*Tamid*	*Tamid*
Moʿed	*Moʿed*	*Tem.*	*Temura*
Moʿed Qaṭ.	*Moʿed Qatan*	*Ter.*	*Terumot*
Maʿaś. Š.	*Maʿaśer Šeni*	*Tohar.*	*Toharot*
Našim	*Našim*	*T. Yom*	*Tebul Yom*
Nazir	*Nazir*	*ʿUq.*	*ʿUqsin*
Ned.	*Nedarim*	*Yad.*	*Yadayim*
Neg.	*Negaʿim*	*Yebam.*	*Yebamot*
Nez.	*Neziqin*	*Yoma*	*Yoma (= Kippurim)*
Nid.	*Niddah*	*Zabim*	*Zabim*
		Zebaḥ	*Zebahim*
		Zer.	*Zeraʿim*

J. Abbreviations of Nag Hammadi Tractates

Acts Pet. 12 Apost.	*Acts of Peter and the Twelve Apostles*	*Exeg. Soul*	*Exegesis on the Soul*
Allogenes	*Allogenes*	*Gos. Eg.*	*Gospel of the Egyptians*
Ap. Jas.	*Apocryphon of James*	*Gos. Phil.*	*Gospel of Philip*
Ap. John	*Apocryphon of John*	*Gos. Thom.*	*Gospel of Thomas*
Apoc. Adam	*Apocalypse of Adam*	*Gos. Truth*	*Gospel of Truth*
1 Apoc. Jas.	*First Apocalypse of James*	*Great Pow.*	*Concept of our Great Power*
2 Apoc. Jas.	*Second Apocalypse of James*	*Hyp. Arch.*	*Hypostasis of the Archons*
Apoc. Paul	*Apocalypse of Paul*	*Hypsiph.*	*Hypsiphrone*
Apoc. Pet.	*Apocalypse of Peter*	*Interp. Know.*	*Interpretation of Knowledge*
Asclepius	*Asclepius 21–29*	*Marsanes*	*Marsanes*
Auth. Teach.	*Authoritative Teaching*	*Melch.*	*Melchizedek*
Dial. Sav.	*Dialogue of the Savior*	*Norea*	*Thought of Norea*
Disc. 8–9	*Discourse on the Eighth and Ninth*	*On Bap. A*	*On Baptism A*
		On Bap. B	*On Baptism B*
Ep. Pet. Phil.	*Letter of Peter to Philip*	*On Bap. C*	*On Baptism C*
Eugnostos	*Eugnostos the Blessed*	*On Euch. A*	*On the Eucharist A*
		On Euch. B	*On the Eucharist B*
		Orig. World	*On the Origin of the World*

Paraph. Shem	*Paraphrase of Shem*	*Thom. Cont.*	*Book of Thomas the Contender*
Pr. Paul	*Prayer of the Apostle Paul*	*Thund.*	*Thunder, Perfect Mind*
Pr. Thanks	*Prayer of Thanksgiving*	*Treat. Res.*	*Treatise on Resurrection*
Prot. Jas.	*Protevangelium of James*	*Treat. Seth*	*Second Treatise of the Great*
Sent. Sextus	*Sentences of Sextus*		*Seth*
Soph. Jes. Chr.	*Sophia of Jesus Christ*	*Tri. Trac.*	*Triparite Tractate*
Steles Seth	*Three Steles of Seth*	*Trim. Prot.*	*Trimorphic Protennoia*
Teach. Silv.	*Teachings of Silvanus*	*Val. Exp.*	*A Valentinian Exposition*
Testim. Truth	*Testimony of Truth*	*Zost.*	*Zostrianos*

Commentary Bibliography

Andriessen, P., and **Lenglet, A.** *De Brief aan de Hebreeën.* Roermond: Roman and Zonen, 1971. **Aquinas, T.** "Ad Hebraeos." In *Super Epistolas S. Pauli Lectura.* Ed. R. Cai. Turin/Rome: Marietti, 1953. **Attridge, H. W.** *A Commentary on the Epistle to the Hebrews.* Hermeneia. Philadelphia: Fortress, 1989. **Barclay, W.** *The Epistle to the Hebrews.* Daily Study Bible. Philadelphia: Westminster, 1957. **Bénétreau, S.** *L'Épître aux Hébreux.* Vol. 1. Commentaire Evangélique de la Bible 10. Vaux-sur-Seine: ÉDIFAC, 1989. **Bleek, F.** *Der Brief an die Hebräer, erläutert durch Einleitung, Uebersetzung und fortlaufenden Kommentar.* 2 vols. in 3. Berlin: Dümmler, 1828–40. **Bonsirven, J.** *Saint Paul, Épître aux Hébreux.* 2nd ed. VS 12. Paris: Beauchesne, 1953. **Bose, W. P. du.** *High Priesthood and Sacrifice: An Exposition of the Epistle to the Hebrews.* New York: Longmans, Green, 1908. **Bourke, M. M.** *The Epistle to the Hebrews.* Englewood Cliffs, NJ: Prentice Hall, 1990. **Bowman, G. M.** *Don't Let Go! An Exposition of Hebrews.* Phillipsburg: Presbyterian & Reformed, 1982. **Bowman, J. W.** *Hebrews.* Richmond: Knox, 1962. **Braun, H.** *An die Hebräer.* HNT 14. Tübingen: Mohr, 1984. **Bristol, L. O.** *Hebrews: A Commentary.* Valley Forge, PA: Judson, 1967. **Brown, R.** *Christ above All: The Message of Hebrews.* Downers Grove, IL: Inter-Varsity Press, 1982. **Bruce, A. B.** *The Epistle to the Hebrews, The First Apology for Christianity: An Exegetical Study.* 2nd ed. Edinburgh: Clark, 1899. **Bruce, F. F.** *The Epistle to the Hebrews.* NICNT. Grand Rapids: Eerdmans, 1964. **Buchanan, G. W.** *To the Hebrews.* AB 36. Garden City, NY: Doubleday, 1972. **Calvin, J.** *The Epistle of Paul the Apostle to the Hebrews.* Tr. W. B. Johnston. Grand Rapids: Eerdmans, 1963. **Casey, J.** *Hebrews.* Dublin: Veritas Publications, 1980. **Caudill, R. P.** *Hebrews: A Translation with Notes.* Nashville: Broadman, 1985. **Chadwick, G. A.** *The Epistle to the Hebrews.* London: Hodder & Stoughton, n.d. **Chilstrom, H. W.** *Hebrews: A New and Better Way.* Philadelphia: Fortress, 1984. **Chrysostom, J.** "Homiliae xxxiv in Epistolam ad Hebraeos." *PG* 63 (1862) 9–256. ———. *Homilies on the Gospel of John and the Epistle to the Hebrews.* Tr. P. Schaff and F. Gardiner. NPNF 14. New York: Scribner's, 1889. **Corbishley, T.** *Good News in Hebrews: The Letter to the Hebrews in Today's English Version.* Cleveland: Collins & World, 1976. **Davidson, A. B.** *The Epistle to the Hebrews.* Edinburgh: Clark, 1882. **Davies, J. H.** *A Letter to Hebrews.* Cambridge Bible Commentary. Cambridge: UP, 1967. **Delitzch, F. J.** *Commentary on the Epistle to the Hebrews.* 2 vols. Tr. T. L. Kingsbury. Edinburgh: Clark, 1871–72. **Edwards, T. C.** *The Epistle to the Hebrews.* New York: A. C. Armstrong and Son, 1903. **Ellingworth, P.** and **Nida, E.** *A Translator's Handbook on the Letter to the Hebrews.* New York: United Bible Societies, 1983. **Evans, L. H.** *Hebrews.* The Communicator's Commentary 10. Waco, TX: Word, 1985. **Farrar, F. W.** *The Epistle of Paul the Apostle to the Hebrews.* CGTC. Cambridge: UP, 1894. **Feld, H.** *Der Hebräerbrief.* Beiträge der Forschung. Darmstadt: Wissenschaftliche Buchgesellschaft, 1985. **Gooding, D.** *An Unshakeable Kingdom: The Letter to the Hebrews for Today.* Grand Rapids: Eerdmans, 1989. **Graf, J.** *Der Hebräerbrief.* Freiburg i/B: Wagner, 1918. **Grässer, E.** *An die Hebräer: 1. Hebr 1–6.* EKKNT 17/1. Zürich: Benziger, 1990. **Gromacki, R. G.** *Stand Bold in Grace: An Exposition of Hebrews.* Grand Rapids: Baker Book House, 1984. **Grosheide, F. W.** *De Brief aan de Hebreeën en de Brief van Jakobus.* 2nd ed. Kampen: Kok, 1955. **Guthrie, D.** *The Letter to the Hebrews.* TNTC. Grand Rapids: Eerdmans, 1983. **Haering, T.** *Der Brief an die Hebräer.* Stuttgart: Calwer, 1925. **Hagner, D. A.** *Hebrews.* Good News Commentaries. San Francisco: Harper & Row, 1983. ———. *Hebrews.* NIBC 14. Peabody, MA: Hendrickson, 1990. **Hegermann, H.** *Der Brief an die Hebräer.*

THKNT 16. Berlin: Evangelische Verlangsanstalt, 1988. **Héring, J.** *L'Épître aux Hébreux.* CNT 12. Neuchâtel: Delachaux & Niestlé, 1954. [ET *The Epistle to the Hebrews.* Tr. A. W. Heathcote and P. J. Allcock. London: Epworth, 1970.] **Hewitt, T.** *The Epistle to the Hebrews.* TNTC. London: Tyndale Press, 1960. **Hillmann, W.** *Der Brief an die Hebräer.* Düsseldorf: Patmos, 1965. **Hollmann, G.** *Der Hebräerbrief.* Die Schriften des Neuen Testaments 3. Ed. W. Bousset and W. Heitmüller. 3rd ed. Göttingen: Vandenhoeck & Ruprecht, 1917. **Hudson, J. T.** *The Epistle to the Hebrews.* Edinburgh: Clark, 1937. **Hugedé, N.** *Le sacerdoce du Fils: Commentaire de l'Épître aux Hébreux.* Paris: Editions Fischbacher, 1983. **Hughes, P. E.** *A Commentary on the Epistle to the Hebrews.* Grand Rapids: Eerdmans, 1977. **Javet, J. J.** *Dieu nous parla: Commentaire sur l'Épître aux Hébreux.* Collection "L'Actualité Protestante." Neuchâtel/Paris: Delachaux & Niestlé, 1945. **Jewett, R.** *Letter to Pilgrims: A Commentary on the Epistle to the Hebrews.* New York: The Pilgrim Press, 1981. **Johnsson. W. G.** *Hebrews.* Knox Preaching Guides. Atlanta: John Knox, 1980. **Keil, K. F.** *Kommentar über den Brief an die Hebräer.* Leipzig: Deichert, 1885. **Kendrick, A. L.** *Commentary on the Epistle to the Hebrews.* Philadelphia: American Baptist, 1889. **Kent, H. A.** *The Epistle to the Hebrews, A Commentary.* Grand Rapids: Baker, 1972. **Ketter, P.** *Hebräerbrief, Jakobusbrief, Petrusbrief, Judasbrief: Übersetzt und erklärt.* HBK 16/1. Freiburg: Herder, 1950. **Kistemaker, S. J.** *Exposition of the Epistle to the Hebrews.* New Testament Commentary. Grand Rapids: Baker Book House, 1984. **Klijn, A. F. J.** *De Brief aan de Hebreeën.* Nijkerk: Callenbach, 1975. **Kuss, O.** *Der Brief an die Hebräer.* RNT 8/1. Regensburg: Pustet, 1966. **Lane, W. L.** *Call to Commitment: Responding to the Message of Hebrews.* Nashville: Nelson, 1985. **Lang, G. H.** *The Epistle to the Hebrews.* London: Paternoster, 1951. **Laubach, F.** *Der Brief an die Hebräer.* Wuppertal: Brockhaus, 1967. **Lenski, R. C. H.** *The Interpretation of the Epistle to the Hebrews and the Epistle of James.* Columbus, OH: Wartburg, 1946. **Lightfoot, N. R.** *Jesus Christ Today: A Commentary on the Book of Hebrews.* Grand Rapids: Baker, 1976. **Lünemann, G.** *Kritisch-exegetischer Handbuch über den Hebräerbrief.* MeyerK 13. Göttingen: Vandenhoeck & Ruprecht, 1878. **März, C.-P.** *Hebräerbrief.* Die neue echter Bibel, Neues Testament 16. Würzburg: Echter, 1989. **MacDonald, W.** *The Epistle to the Hebrews: From Ritual to Reality.* Neptune, NJ: Loizeaux, 1971. **McCaul, J. B.** *The Epistle to the Hebrews: A Paraphrastic Commentary with Illustrations from Philo, the Targums, the Mishna and Gemara, etc.* London: Longmans, Green, 1871. **Médebielle, A.** *Épître aux Hébreux: Traduite et commentée.* 3rd ed. SB 12. Paris: Letouzey et Ané, 1951. **Michel, O.** *Der Brief an die Hebräer.* 12th ed. MeyerK 13. Göttingen: Vandenhoeck & Ruprecht, 1966. **Moffatt, J.** *A Critical and Exegetical Commentary on the Epistle to the Hebrews.* ICC. Edinburgh: Clark, 1924. **Montefiore, H.** *A Commentary on the Epistle to the Hebrews.* HNTC. New York: Harper, 1964. **Morris, L.** *Hebrews.* Bible Study Commentary. Grand Rapids: Zondervan, 1983. **Nairne, A.** *The Epistle to the Hebrews.* CGTC. Cambridge: UP, 1917. ———. *The Epistle to the Hebrews.* Cambridge Bible for Schools and Colleges. Cambridge: UP, 1921. **Narborough, F. D. V.** *Epistle to the Hebrews.* Clarendon Bible. Oxford: Clarendon, 1930. **Neighbour, R. E.** *If They Shall Fall Away: The Epistle to the Hebrews Unveiled.* Miami Springs: Conlay & Schaettle, 1940. **Neil, W.** *The Epistle to the Hebrews.* 2nd ed. TBC. London: Black, 1959. **Newell, W. R.** *Hebrews: Verse by Verse.* Chicago: Moody Press, 1947. **Obiols, S.** *Epístoles de Sant Pau: Als Hebreus.* Montserrat: Monestir de Montserrat, 1930. **Owen, J.** *An Exposition of the Epistle to the Hebrews.* 7 vols. Edinburgh: Ritchie, 1812. **Pfitzner, V. C.** *Chi Rho Commentary on Hebrews.* Adelaide, S. Australia: Lutheran Publishing House, 1979. **Purdy, A. C.,** and **Cotton, J. H.** "The Epistle to the Hebrews." *IB* 11 (1955) 575–763. **Reisner, E.** *Der Brief an die Hebräer.* Munich: Beck, 1938. **Rendall, F.** *The Epistle to the Hebrews.* London: Macmillan, 1888. **Riggenbach, E.** *Der Brief an die Hebräer.* 3rd ed. KNT 14. Leipzig: Deichert, 1922. **Robinson, T. H.** *The Epistle to the Hebrews.* 8th ed. MNTC. London: Hodder & Stoughton, 1964. **Schierse, F. J.** *The Epistle to the Hebrews.* Tr. B. Fahy. London: Burns & Oates, 1969. **Schlatter, A.** *Der Brief an die Hebräer ausgelegt für Bibelleser.*

Stuttgart: Calwer, 1950. **Schneider, J.** *The Letter to the Hebrews.* Tr. W. A. Mueller. Grand Rapids: Eerdmans, 1957. **Schulz, D.** *Der Brief an die Hebräer.* Breslau: Holaufer, 1818. **Seeberg, A.** *Der Brief an die Hebräer.* KNT. Leipzig: Quelle & Meyer, 1912. **Smit, E.** *Die Brief aan die Hebreërs.* Pretoria: N. G. Kerkboekhandel Transval, 1982. **Smith, R. H.** *Hebrews.* Augsburg Commentary on the New Testament. Minneapolis: Augsburg, 1984. **Snell, A. A.** *New and Living Way: An Explanation of the Epistle to the Hebrews.* London: Faith, 1959. **Soden, H. von.** *Der Hebräerbrief.* 3rd ed. HKNT 3/2. Freiburg/Leipzig/Tübingen: Mohr, 1899. **Spicq, C.** *L'Épître aux Hébreux.* 2 vols. EBib. Paris: Gabalda, 1952–53. ———. *L'Épître aux Hébreux: Traduction, notes critiques, commentaire.* SB. Paris: Gabalda, 1977. **Stibbs, A. M.** *So Great Salvation: The Meaning and Message of the Letter to the Hebrews.* Exeter: Paternoster Press, 1970. **Strathmann, H.** *Der Brief an die Hebräer, übersetzt und erklärt.* 7th ed. NTD 9. Göttingen: Vandenhoeck & Ruprecht, 1963. **Strobel, A.** *Der Brief an die Hebräer.* NTD 9/2. Göttingen: Vandenhoeck & Ruprecht, 1975. **Stuart, M.** *A Commentary on the Epistle to the Hebrews.* 4th ed. Andover: W. F. Draper, 1876. **Teodorico, P.** *L'epistola agli Ebrei.* Torino/Rome: Marietti, 1952. **Theodoret.** *Interpretatio Epistulae ad Hebraeos.* PG 82. **Thompson, J. W.** *The Letter to the Hebrews.* Austin: Sweet, 1971. **Vaughan, C. J.** *The Epistle to the Hebrews.* London: Macmillan, 1890. **Weiss, B.** *Der Brief an die Hebräer.* 6th ed. MeyerK 13. Göttingen: Vandenhoeck & Ruprecht, 1897. **Westcott, B. F.** *The Epistle to the Hebrews: The Greek Text with Notes and Essays.* 3rd ed. London/New York: Macmillan, 1903. **Wettstein, J. J.** *Η ΚΑΙΝΗ ΔΙΑΘΗΚΗ: Novum Testamentum Graecum editionis receptae cum lectionibus variantibus Codicum MSS, editionum aliarum, versionum et patrum nec non commentario pleniore ex scriptoribus veteribus hebrais, graecis et latinis historiam et vim verborum illustrante.* Vol. 2. Amsterdam: Dommer, 1752. **Wickham, E. C.** *The Epistle to the Hebrews.* London: Methuen, 1910. **Williamson, R.** *The Epistle to the Hebrews.* London: Epworth, 1965. **Wilson, R. McL.** *Hebrews.* New Century Bible Commentary. Grand Rapids: Eerdmans, 1987. **Windisch, H.** *Der Hebräerbrief.* 2nd ed. HNT 14. Tübingen: Mohr, 1931.

Main Bibliography

Ahern, A. A. "The Perfection Concept in the Epistle to the Hebrews." *JBR* 14 (1946) 164–67. **Alexander, J. P.** *A Priest for Ever: A Study of the Epistle Entitled "To the Hebrews."* London: Clarke, 1937. **Alfaro, J.** "Cristo glorioso, revelador del Padre." *Greg* 39 (1958) 220–70. **Anderson, C. P.** "The Epistle to the Hebrews and the Pauline Letter Collection." *HTR* 59 (1966) 429–38. ———. "Hebrews among the Letters of Paul." *SR* 5 (1975–76) 258–66. ———. "The Setting of the Epistle to the Hebrews." Dissertation, Columbia University, 1969. ———. "Who Wrote 'The Epistle from Laodicea'?" *JBL* 85 (1966) 436–40. **Anderson, R.** *The Hebrews Epistle in the Light of the Types.* London: Nisbet, 1911. **Andriessen, P.** *En lisant l'Épître aux Hébreux: Lettre au R. P. A. Vanhoye, Professeur à l'Institute Biblique Pontifical sur l'interprétation controversée de certain passages.* Vaals: Abby St. Benedictusberg, 1977. ———. "L'Eucharistie dans l'Épître aux Hébreux." *NRT* 94 (1972) 269–77. **Appel, H.** *Der Hebräerbrief: Ein Schreiben des Apollos an Judenchristen der korinthischen Gemeinde.* Leipzig: Deichert, 1918. **Archer, G. L.,** and **Chirichigne, G.** *Old Testament Quotations in the New Testament.* Chicago: Moody, 1983. **Asting, R.** *Die Heiligkeit im Urchristentum.* FRLANT 29. Göttingen: Vandenhoeck & Ruprecht, 1930. **Atkinson, B. F. C.** *The Theology of Prepositions.* London: Tyndale, 1944. **Attridge, H. W.** "Paraenesis in a Homily (λόγος παρακλήσεως): The Possible Location of, and Socialization in, the 'Epistle to the Hebrews.'" *Semeia* 50 (1990) 211–26. **Aune, D.** *The New Testament in Its Literary Environment.* Philadelphia: Westminster, 1987. **Ayles, H. H. B.** *Destination, Date, and Authorship of the Epistle to the Hebrews.* London: Clay, 1899. ———. "The References to Persecution in the Epistle to the Hebrews." *Exp* 8th ser. 12 (1916) 69–74. **Badcock, F. J.** *The Pauline Epistles and the Epistle to the Hebrews in Their Historical Setting.* London: SPCK, 1937. **Bacon, B. W.** "The Doctrine of Faith in Hebrews, James and Clement of Rome." *JBL* 19 (1900) 12–21. **Baigent, J. W.** "Jesus as Priest: An Examination of the Claim that the Concept of Jesus as Priest May Be Found outside of the Epistle to the Hebrews." *VoxEv* 12 (1981) 33–44. **Ballarini, T.** "Il peccato nell 'epistola agli Ebrei.'" *ScC* 106 (1978) 358–71. **Barbel, J.** *Christos Angelos: Die Anschauung von Christus als Bote und Engel in der gelehrten und volkstümlichen Literatur des christlichen Altertums.* Bottrop: Postberg, 1941. **Barnes, A. S.** "St. Barnabas and the Epistle to the Hebrews." *HibJ* 30 (1931–32) 103–17. **Barrett, C. K.** "The Eschatology of the Epistle to the Hebrews." In *The Background of the New Testament and Its Eschatology.* Ed. W. D. Davies and D. Daube. Cambridge: Cambridge UP, 1954. **Barth, M.** "The Old Testament in Hebrews: An Essay in Biblical Hermeneutics." In *Current Issues in New Testament Interpretation.* Ed. W. Klassen and G. F. Snyder. New York: Harper & Row, 1962. **Bartlet, J. V.** "The Epistle to the Hebrews Once More." *ExpTim* 34 (1922–23) 58–61. **Bartlet, V.** "Barnabas and His Genuine Epistle." *Exp* 6th ser. 6 (1902) 28–30. ———. "The Epistle to the Hebrews as the Work of Barnabas." *Exp* 6th ser. 8 (1903) 381–96. **Barton, G. A.** "The Date of the Epistle to the Hebrews." *JBL* 57 (1938) 195–207. **Batdorf, I. W.** "Hebrews and Qumran: Old Methods and New Directions." *FS F. Wilbur Gingrich.* Ed. E. H. Barth and R. E. Cocroft. Leiden: Brill, 1972. **Bates, W. H.** "Authorship of the Epistle to the Hebrews Again." *BSac* 79 (1922) 93–96. **Batiffol, P.** "L'attribution de l'Épître aux Hébreux à S. Barnabé." *RB* 8 (1899) 278–83. **Beare, F. W.** "The Text of the Epistle to the Hebrews in p⁴⁶." *JBL* 63 (1944) 379–96. **Behm, J.** *Der Begriff Διαθήκη im Neuen Testament.* Berlin: Runge, 1912. **Berger, K.** *Exegese des Neuen Testaments: Neue Wege vom Text zur Auslegung.* 2nd ed. Heidelberg: Quelle & Meyer, 1984. **Bickerman, E. J.** "En marge de l'Écriture." *RB* 88 (1981) 19–41. **Bieder, W.** "Pneumatologische Aspekte im Hebräerbrief." In *Neues Testament und Geschichte.* FS O. Cullmann. Ed. H. Baltensweiler and B. Reicke. Tübingen: Mohr, 1972. **Biesenthal, J. H. R.** *Das Trostschreiben des Apostels Paulus an die Hebräer.* Leipzig: Fernau,

1878. **Bietenhard, H.** *Die himmlische Welt im Urchristentum und Spätjudentum.* WUNT 2. Tübingen: Mohr, 1951. **Black, D. A.** "The Problem of the Literary Structure of Hebrews." *GTJ* 7 (1986) 163–77. ———. *Linguistics for Students of New Testament Greek: A Survey of Basic Concepts and Applications.* Grand Rapids: Baker, 1988. **Black, M.** "The Christological Use of the Old Testament in the New Testament." *NTS* 18 (1971–72) 1–14. **Blass, F.** "Die rhythmische Komposition des Hebräers." *TSK* 75 (1902) 420–60. **Bligh, J.** *Chiastic Analysis of the Epistle to the Hebrews.* Heythrop: Athenaeum, 1966. ———. "The Structure of Hebrews." *HeyJ* 5 (1964) 170–77. **Bodelschwingh, F. V.** "Jesus der Mittler des Neuen Testaments nach dem Zeugnis des Hebräerbriefs." In *Lebendig und Frei:* Bethel bei Bielefeld: Anstalt Bethel, 1949. **Bolewski, H.** "*Christos Archiereus:* Über die Entstehung der hohepriesterlichen Wurdenamens Christi." Dissertation, Halle, 1939. **Bonnard, P.** "Actualité de l'Épître aux Hébreux." *FV* 62 (1963) 283–88. **Bonsirven, J.** "La sacerdoce et le sacrifice de Jésus-Christ après l'Épître aux Hébreux." *NRT* 71 (1939) 641–60, 769–86. **Bornhäuser, K.** *Empfänger und Verfasser des Briefes an die Hebräer.* BFCT 35/3. Gütersloh: Bertelsmann, 1932. **Borchet, L.** "A Superior Book: Hebrews." *RevExp* 82 (1985) 319–32. **Bornkamm, G.** "Das Bekenntnis im Hebräerbrief." *TBl* 21 (1942) 56–66. **Bover, J. M.** "La esperanza en la Epístola a los Hebreos." *Greg* 19 (1938) 110–20. ———. "Inspiración divina del redactor de la Epístola a los Hebreos." *EE* 14 (1935) 433–46. **Braun, H.** "Die Gewinnung der Gewissenheit in dem Hebräerbrief." *TLZ* 96 (1971) 321–30. ———. "Das himmlische Vaterland bei Philo und im Hebräerbrief." In *Verborum Veritas.* FS G. Stählin. Ed. O. Böcher and K. Haacker. Wuppertal: Brockhaus, 1970. **Bristol, L. O.** "Primitive Christian Preaching and the Epistle to the Hebrews." *JBL* 68 (1949) 89–97. **Brooks, W. E.** "The Perpetuity of Christ's Sacrifice in the Epistle to the Hebrews." *JBL* 89 (1970) 205–14. **Brown, J. V.** "The Authorship and Circumstances of 'Hebrews'—Again!" *BSac* 80 (1923) 505–38. **Brown, R.** "Pilgrimage in Faith: The Christian Life in Hebrews." *SWJT* 28 (1985) 28–35. **Bruce, F. F.** "Christianity under Claudius." *BJRL* 44 (1961–62) 309–26. ———. "Kerygma of Hebrews." *Int* 23 (1969) 3–19. ———. "Recent Contributions to the Understanding of Hebrews." *ExpTim* 80 (1969) 260–64. ———. "The Structure and Argument of Hebrews." *SWJT* 28 (1985) 6–12. ———. "'To the Hebrews' or 'To the Essenes'?" *NTS* 9 (1963) 217–32. **Brüll, A.,** ed. *Das samaritanische Targum zum Pentateuch.* 5 vols. Frankfurt: Kaufmann, 1874–79. **Buchanan, G. W.** "The Present State of Scholarship on Hebrews." In *Judaism, Christianity and Other Greco-Roman Cults.* FS Morton Smith. Ed. J. Neusner. Vol. 1. Leiden: Brill, 1975. **Büchel, C.** "Der Hebräerbrief und das Alte Testament." *TSK* 79 (1906) 508–91. **Büchsel, F.** *Die Christologie des Hebräerbriefs.* BFCT 27/2. Gütersloh: Bertelsmann, 1922. **Bullock, M. R.** "The Recipients and Destination of Hebrews." Dissertation, Dallas Theological Seminary, 1977. **Burch, V.** *The Epistle to the Hebrews: Its Sources and Its Message.* London: Williams & Norgate, 1936. ———. "Factors in the Christology of the Letter to the Hebrews." *Exp* 47 (1921) 68–79. **Burggaller, E.** "Das literarische Problem des Hebräerbriefes." *ZNW* 9 (1908) 110–131. ———. "Neue Untersuchungen zum Hebräerbrief." *TRu* 13 (1910) 369–81, 409–17. **Burns, D. K.** "The Epistle to the Hebrews." *ExpTim* 47 (1935–36) 184–89. **Burtness, J. H.** "Plato, Philo, and the Author of Hebrews." *LQ* 10 (1958) 54–64. **Burton, E. D.** *Syntax of the Moods and Tenses in New Testament Greek.* 3rd ed. Edinburgh: Clark, 1898. **Cabantous, J.** *Philon et l'Épître aux Hébreux ou essai sur les rapports del la christologie de l'Épître aux Hébreux avec la philosophie Judéo-Alexandrine.* Montauban: Granié, 1895. **Caird, G. B.** "The Exegetical Method of the Epistle to the Hebrews." *CJT* 5 (1959) 44–51. ———. *The Language and Imagery of the Bible.* London: Duckworth, 1980. **Cambier, J.** "Eschatologie ou héllenisme dans l'Épître aux Hébreux: Une étude sur μένειν et l'exhortation finale de l'épître." *Sal* 11 (1949) 62–96. [Reissued as ALBO 2/12. Bruges/Paris: Descles de Brouwer, 1949.] **Campbell, A. G.** "The Problem of Apostasy in the Greek New Testament." Dissertation, Dallas Theological Seminary, 1957. **Campbell, J. C.** "In a Son: The Doctrine of the Incarnation in the Epistle to the Hebrews." *Int* 10 (1956) 24–38. **Campbell, J. Y.** *Three New Testament Studies.* Leiden: Brill, 1965. **Campos, J.** "A Carta aos Hebreus como Apolo ã superasão de 'Certa

Religiosidade Popular.'" *RCB* 8 (1984) 122–24. **Carlston, C.** "Eschatology and Repentance in the Epistle to the Hebrews." *JBL* 78 (1959) 296–302. ———. "The Vocabulary of Perfection in Philo and Hebrews." In *Unity and Diversity in New Testament Theology.* FS G. E. Ladd. Ed. R. A. Guelich. Grand Rapids: Eerdmans, 1978. **Casey, R. P.** "The Earliest Christologies." *JTS* 10 (1959) 253–77. **Cason, D. V.** "*ΙΕΡΕΥΣ* and *ΑΡΧΙΕΡΕΥΣ* (and Related Contexts) in Hebrews: An Exegetical Study in the Greek New Testament." Dissertation, Southern Baptist Theological Seminary, 1931. **Castelvecchi, I.** *La homologia en la carta a los Hebreos: Estudio exegetico-teológico.* Montevideo: Pellegrini Impresares, 1964. **Cazelles, H.** et al. *Moïse, l'homme de l'alliance.* CSion 8:2–3–4. Paris/Tournai: Desclée, 1954. **Chapman, J.** "Aristion, Author of the Epistle to the Hebrews." *RBén* 22 (1905) 50–64. **Clarkson, M. E.** "The Antecedents of the High Priest Theme in Hebrews." *ATR* 29 (1947) 89–95. **Cleary, M.** "Jesus, Pioneer and Source of Salvation: The Christology of Hebrews 1–6." *TBT* 67 (1973) 1242–48. **Clements, R. E.** "The Use of the Old Testament in Hebrews." *SWJT* 28 (1985) 36–45. **Cody, A.** *Heavenly Sanctuary and Liturgy in the Epistle to the Hebrews: The Achievement of Salvation in the Epistle's Perspectives.* St. Meinrad, IN: Grail, 1960. **Collins, R. F.** *Letters That Paul Did Not Write: The Epistle to the Hebrews and the Pauline Pseudepigrapha.* Wilmington, DE: Glazier, 1988. **Combrink, H. J. B.** "Some Thoughts on the Old Testament Citations in the Epistle to the Hebrews." *Neot* 5 (1971) 22–36. **Conner, W. T.** "Three Theories of the Atonement." *RevExp* 43 (1946) 275–90. ———. "Three Types of Teaching in the New Testament on the Meaning of the Death of Christ." *RevExp* 43 (1946) 150–66. **Constable, T. L.** "The Substitutionary Death of Christ in Hebrews." Dissertation, Dallas Theological Seminary, 1966. **Coppens, J.** "Les affinités Qumrâniennes de l'Épître aux Hébreux." *NRT* 84 (1962) 128–41, 257–82. [Reissued as ALBO 4/1 (1962).] ———. "La portée messianique du Ps CX." *ETL* 32 (1956) 1–23. **Cothenet, E., LeFort, P., Prigent, P.,** and **Dussaut, L.** *Les écrits de Saint Jean et l'Épître aux Hébreux.* Paris: Desclée, 1984. **Cotterell, P.,** and **Turner, M.** *Linguistics and Biblical Interpretation.* Downers Grove, IL: Inter-Varsity, 1989. **Cox, W. L. P.** *The Heavenly Priesthood of Our Lord.* Oxford: Blackwell, 1929. **Craddock, F. B.** *The Pre-Existence of Christ in the New Testament.* Nashville: Abingdon Press, 1968. **Cullmann, O.** *The Christology of the New Testament.* Rev. ed. Philadelphia: Westminster, 1963. **Culpepper, R. H.** "The High Priesthood and Sacrifice of Christ in the Epistle to the Hebrews." *ThEduc* 32 (1985) 46–62. **Custer, S.** "Annotated Bibliography on Hebrews." *BV* 2 (1968) 45–68. **Dahms, J. V.** "The First Readers of Hebrews." *JETS* 20 (1977) 365–75. **Dalbert, P.** *Die Theologie der hellenistisch-jüdischen Missionsliteratur unter Ausschluss von Philo und Josephus.* TF 4. Hamburg: Evangelischer, 1954. **Daly, R. J.** "The New Testament Concept of Christian Sacrificial Activity." *BTB* 8 (1978) 99–107. **D'Angelo, M. R.** *Moses in the Letter to the Hebrews.* SBLDS 42. Missoula, MT: Scholars, 1979. **Daniélou, J.** "La session à la droite du Père." *SE* 1 (1959) 689–98. **Daube, D.** "Rabbinic Methods of Interpretation and Hellenistic Rhetoric." *HUCA* 22 (1949) 239–64. **Dautzenberg, G.** "Der Glaube in Hebräerbrief." *BZ* 17 (1963) 161–77. **Davies, J. H.** "The Heavenly Work of Christ in Hebrews." *SE* 4 (1968) 384–89. **Déaut, R. le.** "Apropos a Definition of Midrash." *Int* 25 (1971) 259–82. ———. *La nuit pascale.* Rome: Institute Biblique Pontificale, 1963. **Deichgräber, R.** *Gotteshymnus und Christushymnus in der frühen Christenheit: Untersuchungen zu Form, Sprache und Stil der frühchristlichen Hymnen.* SUNT 5. Göttingen: Vandenhoeck & Ruprecht, 1967. **Descamps, A.** "La Sacerdoce du Christ d'après l'Épître aux Hébreux." *RDT* 9 (1954) 529–34. ———. "La structure de l'Épître aux Hébreux." *RDT* 9 (1954) 333–38. **Dey, L. K. K.** *The Intermediary World and Patterns of Perfection in Philo and Hebrews.* SBLDS 25. Missoula, MT: Scholars, 1975. **De Young, J. C.** *Jerusalem in the New Testament.* Kampen: Kok, 1960. **Dibelius, F.** *Der Verfasser des Hebräerbrief: Eine Untersuchung zur Geschichte des Urchristentums.* Strassburg: Heitz & Mundel, 1910. **Dibelius, M.** "Der himmlische Kultus nach dem Hebräerbrief." In *Botschaft und Geschichte: Gesammelte Aufsätze II: Zum Urchristentum und zur hellenistischen Religionsgeschichte.* Tübingen: Mohr, 1956. [Reprinted from *TBl* 21 (1942) 1–11.] **Dickie, J.** "The Literary Riddle of the 'Epistle to the Hebrews.'" *Exp* 8th ser. 5 (1913) 371–78. **Díez Macho, A.** *Neophyte 1: Targum*

Palestinense MS de la Biblioteca Vaticana. 6 vols. Madrid/Barcelona: Consejo Superior de Investigaciones Cientificas, 1968–79. **Dimock, N.** *The Sacerdotium of Christ.* London: Longmans, Green, 1910. **Dinkler, E.** "Hebrews, Letter to the." *IDB* 2 (1962) 571–75. **Dobschütz, E. von.** "Rationales und irrationales Denken über Gott in Urchristentum: Eine Studie besonders zum Hebräerbrief." *TSK* 95 (1923–24) 235–55. **Dubarle, A. M.** "Rédacteur et destinataires de l'Épître aux Hébreux." *RB* 48 (1939) 506–29. **Dukes, J. G.** "Eschatology in the Epistle to the Hebrews." Dissertation, Southern Baptist Theological Seminary, 1956. **Dunbar, D. G.** "The Relation of Christ's Sonship and Priesthood in the Epistle to the Hebrews." Dissertation, Westminster Theological Seminary, Philadelphia, 1974. **Dupont, J.** "'Assis à la droite de Dieu': L'interpretation du Ps 110,1 dans le Nouveau Testament." In *Resurrexit: Actes du Symposium International sur la Résurrection de Jésus, Rome, 1970.* Ed. E. Dhanis. Rome: Vaticana, 1974. **Dussaut, L.** *Synopse structurelle de l'Épître aux Hébreux: Approche d'analyse structurelle.* Paris: Desclée, 1981. **Dyck, T. L.** "Jesus Our Pioneer: *APXHΓOΣ* in Heb. 2:5–18; 12:1–3, and Its Relation in the Epistle to Such Designations as *ΠΡΩΤΟΤΟΚΟΣ ΑΙΤΟΣ, ΠΡΟΔΡΟΜΟΣ, ΑΡΧΙΕΡΕΥΣ, ΕΓΓΥΟΣ, ΜΕΣΙΤΗΣ, ΠΟΙΜΗΝ* and to the Recurring Theme of Pilgrimage in Faith along the Path of Suffering Which Leads to Glory." Dissertation: Northwest Baptist Theological Seminary, 1980. **Eagar, A. R.** "The Authorship of the Epistle to the Hebrews." *Exp* 6th ser. 10 (1904) 74–80, 110–23. ———. "The Hellenistic Elements in the Epistle to the Hebrews." *Her* 11 (1901) 263–87. **Eccles, R. S.** "Hellenistic Mysticism in the Epistle to the Hebrews." Dissertation, Yale University, 1952. ———. "The Purpose of the Hellenistic Patterns in the Epistle to the Hebrews." In *Religions in Antiquity.* FS E. R. Goodenough. Ed. J. Neusner. Leiden: Brill, 1968. **Edgar, S. L.** "Respect for Context in Quotations from the Old Testament." *NTS* 9 (1962–63) 55–62. **Elbogen, I.** *Der jüdische Gottesdienst in seiner geschichtlichen Entwicklung.* 3rd ed. Frankfurt: Kaufmann, 1931. **Ellingworth, P.** "The Old Testament in Hebrews: Exegesis, Method and Hermeneutics." Dissertation, University of Aberdeen, 1977. **Ellis, E. E.** "Midrash, Targum and New Testament Quotations." In *Neotestamentica et Semitica.* FS Matthew Black. Ed. E. E. Ellis and M. Wilcox. Edinburgh: Clark, 1969. **English, E. S.** *Studies in the Epistle to the Hebrews.* Traveler's Rest, SC: Southern Bible House, 1955. **Etheridge, J. W.,** ed. *The Targums of Onkelos and Jonathan ben Uzziel on the Pentateuch.* London: Longmans, Green, 1962–65. **Fairhurst, A. M.** "Hellenistic Influence in the Epistle to the Hebrews." *TynBul* 7–8 (1961) 17–27. **Feld, H.** "Der Hebräerbrief: Literarische Form, religionsgeschichtlicher Hintergrund, theologische Fragen." *ANRW* 2.25.4 (1987) 3522–3601. ———. *Martin Luthers und Wendelin Steinbachs Vorlesungen über den Hebräerbrief: Eine Studie zur Geschichte der neutestamentlichen Exegese und Theologie.* Wiesbaden: Steiner, 1971. ———. "Die theologischen Hauptthemen der Hebräerbrief-Vorlesung Wendelin Steinbachs." *Augustiniana* 37 (1987) 187–252. **Fensham, F. C.** "Hebrews and Qumran." *Neot* 5 (1971) 9–21. **Fenton, J. C.** "The Argument in Hebrews." *SE* 7 (1982) 175–81. **Fernández, J.** "La teleíosis o perfección cristiana en la epistola a los Hebreos." *CB* 13 (1956) 251–59. **Feuillet, A.** "L'attente de la Parousie et du Jugement dans l'Épître aux Hébreux." *BVC* 42 (1961) 23–31. ———. "Les points de vue nouveaux dans l'eschatologie de l'Épître aux Hébreux." *SE* 2 (1964) 369–87. ———. *The Priesthood of Christ and His Ministers.* Garden City: Doubleday, 1975. **Field, F.** *Notes on the Translation of the New Testament.* Cambridge: Cambridge UP, 1899. **Field, J. E.** *The Apostolic Liturgy and the Epistle to the Hebrews.* London: Rivertons, 1882. **Filson, F. V.** "The Epistle to the Hebrews." *JBR* 22 (1954) 20–26. ———. *"Yesterday": A Study of Hebrews in the Light of Chapter 13.* SBT 2nd ser. 4. Naperville: Allenson, 1967. **Fiorenza, E. Schüssler** "Der Anführer und Vollender unseres Glaubens: Zum theologischen Verständnis des Hebräerbriefes." In *Gestalt und Anspruch des Neuen Testaments.* Ed. J. Schreiner. Würzburg: Echter, 1969. **Fitzer, G.** "Auch der Hebräerbrief legitimiert nicht eine Opfertodchristologie zur Frage der Intention des Hebräerbriefes und seiner Bedeutung für die Theologie." *KD* 15 (1969) 294–319. **Fitzmyer, J. A.** "The Use of Explicit Old Testament Quotations in Qumran Literature and in the New Testament." *NTS* 7 (1960–61) 297–333. **Floor, L.** "The General

Priesthood of Believers in the Epistle to the Hebrews." *Neot* 5 (1971) 72–82. **Fonseca, L. G. da.** "Διαθήκη—Foedus an testamentum?" *Bib* 8 (1927) 31–50, 161–81, 290–319, 418–41; 9 (1928) 26–40, 143–60. **Ford, J. M.** "The First Epistle to the Corinthians or the First Epistle to the Hebrews." *CBQ* 28 (1966) 402–16. ———. "The Mother of Jesus and the Authorship of the Epistle to the Hebrews." *TBT* 82 (1976) 683–94. **Forkman, G.** *The Limits of the Religious Community.* Lund: Gleerup, 1972. **Fransen, I.** "Jésus Pontife parfait du parfait sanctuaire (Épître aux Hébreux)." *BVC* 20 (1957) 262–81. ———. "Jesus, wahrer Hoherpriester des wahren Bundeszeltes." *BLit* 25 (1957–58) 172–82, 218–25, 261–69. **Friedrich, G.** "Beobachtungen zur messianischen Hohepriestererwartung." *ZTK* 53 (1956) 265–311. **Galinsky, G. K.** *The Herakles Theme.* Leiden: Brill, 1972. **Galot, J.** "Le sacrifice rédempteur du Christ selon l'Épître aux Hébreux." *EV* 89 (1979) 369–77. **Gamble, J.** "Symbol and Reality in the Epistle to the Hebrews." *JBL* 45 (1926) 162–70. **Gammie, J. G.** "A New Setting for Psalm 110." *ATR* 51 (1969) 4–17. ———. "Paraenetic Literature: Toward the Morphology of a Secondary Genre." *Semeia* 50 (1990) 41–77. **Gardiner, F.** "The Language of the Epistle to the Hebrews as Bearing upon Its Authorship." *JBL* 7 (1887) 1–25. **Garrard, L. A.** "The Diversity of New Testament Christology." *HibJ* 55 (1956–57) 213–22. **Gayford, S. C.** *Sacrifice and Priesthood.* 2nd ed. London: Methuen, 1953. **Gelin, A.** "Le sacerdoce du Christ d'après l'Épître aux Hébreux." In *Études sur le Sacrement de l'Ordre.* Lyon: LePuy, 1957. **Gemés, I.** "Alianca no Documento de Damasco e na Epístola aos Hebreus: Una contribuicão a questão: Qumran e as origens do Christianismo." *RCB* 6 (1969) 28–68. **Gifford, E. H.,** ed. *Eusebii Pamphilli Evangelicae Praeparationis.* 4 vols. Oxford: Oxford University, 1903. **Gilbert, G. H.** "The Greek Element in the Epistle to the Hebrews." *AJT* 14 (1910) 521–32. **Giversen, S.** "Evangelium Veritatis and the Epistle to the Hebrews." *ST* 13 (1959) 87–96. **Glaze, R. E.** "Introduction to Hebrews." *ThEduc* 32 (1985) 20–37. ———. *No Easy Salvation: A Careful Examination of Apostasy in Hebrews.* Nashville: Broadman, 1966. **Gnilka, J.** "Der Erwartung des messianisches Hohepriesters in den Schriften von Qumran und im Neuen Testament." *RevQ* 2 (1960) 395–426. **Goguel, M.** "La seconde géneration chrétienne." *RHR* 136 (1949) 31–57, 180–208. **Gooding, D.** *An Unshakeable Kingdom: Studies on the Epistle to the Hebrews.* Toronto: Everyday Publications, 1976. **Goodspeed, E. J.** "First Clement Called Forth by Hebrews." *JBL* 30 (1911) 157–60. ———. "The Problem of Hebrews." *JBR* 22 (1954) 122. **Goppelt, L.** *Typos: Die typologische Deutung des Alten Testaments im Neuen.* BFCT 2/43. Gütersloh: Bertelsmann, 1939. **Gordon, V. R.** "Studies in the Covenantal Theology of the Epistle to the Hebrews in Light of Its Setting." Dissertation, Fuller Theological Seminary, 1979. **Gornatowski, A.** *Rechts und Links im antiker Aberglauben.* Breslau: Nischkowsky, 1936. **Gotaas, D. S.** "The Old Testament in the Epistle to the Hebrews, the Epistle of James, and the Epistle of Peter." Dissertation, Northern Baptist Theological Seminary, 1958. **Gourgues, M.** *A la droite de Dieu: Résurrection de Jésus et actualisation du Psaume 110:1 dans le Nouveau Testament.* EBib. Paris: Gabalda, 1978. ———. "Lecture christologique du Psaume CX et fête de la Pentecôte." *RB* 83 (1976) 5–24. ———. "Remarques sur la 'structure centrale' de l'Épître aux Hébreux." *RB* 84 (1977) 26–37. **Graham, A. A. K.** "Mark and Hebrews." *SE* 4 (1968) 411–16. **Grass, K. K.** *Ist der Brief an die Hebräer an Heidenchristen gerichtet?* St. Petersburg: Köhne, 1892. **Grässer, E.** "Zur Christologie des Hebräerbriefes: Eine Auseinandersetzung mit Herbert Braun." In *Neues Testament und christliche Existenz.* FS H. Braun. Tübingen: Mohr, 1973. ———. "Die Gemeindevorsteher im Hebräerbrief." In *Vom Amt des Laien in Kirche und Theologie.* FS G. Krause. Ed. H. Schröer and P. G. Müller. Berlin: de Gruyter, 1982. 67–84. ———. *Der Glaube im Hebräerbrief.* Marburg: Elwert, 1965. ———. "Der Hebräerbrief 1938–1963." *TRu* 30 (1964) 138–236. ———. "Der historische Jesus im Hebräerbrief." *ZNW* 56 (1965) 63–91. ———. "Rechtfertigung im Hebräerbrief." In *Rechtfertigung.* FS E. Käsemann. Ed. J. Friedrich, W. Pöhlmann, and P. Stuhlmacher. Tübingen: Mohr, 1976. ———. "Das wandernde Gottesvolk zum Basismotiv des Hebräerbriefes." *ZNW* 77 (1986) 160–79. ———. *Texte und Situation.* Gütersloh: Mohn, 1973. **Greer, R. A.** "The Antiochene Exegesis of Hebrews."

Dissertation, Yale University, 1965. ————. *The Captain of Our Salvation: A Study in the Patristic Exegesis of Hebrews.* BGBE 15. Tübingen: Mohr, 1973. **Griffin, H.** "The Origin of the High Priestly Christology of the Epistle to the Hebrews." Dissertation, University of Aberdeen, 1978. **Grogan, G. W.** "The New Testament Interpretation of the Old Testament." *TB* 18 (1967) 54–76. **Grothe, J. F.** "Was Jesus the Priestly Messiah? A Study of the New Testament's Teaching of Jesus' Priestly Office against the Background of Jewish Hopes for a Priestly Messiah." Dissertation, Concordia Seminary, 1981. **Guthrie, D.** "The Epistle to the Hebrews." In *New Testament Introduction.* Vol. 3. Chicago: Inter-Varsity, 1962. **Guthrie, G. H.** "The Structure of Hebrews: A Textlinguistic Analysis." Dissertation, Southwestern Baptist Theological Seminary, 1991. **Gyllenberg, R.** "Die Christologie des Hebräerbriefes." *ZST* 11 (1934) 662–90. ————. "Die Komposition des Hebräerbriefs." *SEÅ* 22–23 (1957–58) 137–47. **Haering, T.** "Gedankengang und Grundgedanken des Hebräerbriefs." *ZNW* 18 (1917–18) 145–64. **Hagen, K.** *Hebrews Commenting from Erasmus to Beza 1516–1598.* BGBE 23. Tübingen: Mohr, 1981. ————. *A Theology of Testament in the Young Luther: The Lectures on Hebrews.* Leiden: Brill, 1974. **Hagner, D. A.** "Interpreting the Epistle to the Hebrews." In *The Literature and Meaning of Scripture.* Ed. M. A. Inch and C. H. Bullock. Grand Rapids: Baker, 1981. 217–42. ————. *The Use of the Old and New Testaments in Clement of Rome.* Leiden: Brill, 1973. **Hamerton-Kelly, R. G.** *Pre-Existence, Wisdom, and the Son of Man: A Study of the Idea of Pre-Existence in the New Testament.* SNTSMS 21. Cambridge: Cambridge UP, 1973. **Hammer, P.** "The Understanding of Inheritance ($\kappa\lambda\eta\rho\sigma\nu\sigma\mu\iota\alpha$) in the New Testament." Dissertation, Heidelberg University, 1958. **Hamp, V.** "Ps 110, 4b und die Septuaginta." In *Neues Testament und Kirche.* FS R. Schnackenberg. Ed. J. Gnilka. Freiburg: Herder, 1974. **Hanna, R.** *A Grammatical Aid to the Greek New Testament.* Vol. 2: *Romans to Revelation.* Hidalgo, Mexico: Saenz, 1979. **Hanson, A. T.** "Christ in the Old Testament according to Hebrews." *SE* 2 (1964) 393–407. ————. "The Gospel in the Old Testament according to Hebrews." *Theol* 52 (1949) 248–52. **Harder, G.** "Die Septuagintazitate des Hebräerbriefs: Ein Beitrag zum Problem der Auslegung des Alten Testaments." In *Theologia Viatorum.* Ed. M. Albertz. Munich: Kaiser, 1939. **Harnack, A.** "Probabilia über die Adresse und den Verfasser des Hebräerbriefs." *ZNW* 1 (1900) 16–41. **Harris, J. R.** "Menander and the Epistle to the Hebrews." *ExpTim* 44 (1932–33) 191. ————. "An Orphic Reaction in the Epistle to the Hebrews." *ExpTim* 40 (1928–29) 449–51. ————. "Side-Lights on the Authorship of the Epistle to the Hebrews." In *Side-Lights on New Testament Research.* London: Kingsgate, 1908. **Harrison, E. F.** "The Theology of the Epistle to the Hebrews." *BSac* 121 (1964) 333–40. **Harrison, M. P.** "Psalm 110 in the Epistle to the Hebrews." Dissertation, Southern Baptist Theological Seminary, 1950. **Harrop, C. K.** "The Influence of the Thought of Stephen upon the Epistle to the Hebrews." Dissertation, Southern Baptist Theological Seminary, 1955. **Harvill, J.** "Focus on Jesus: The Letter to the Hebrews." *SpTod* 37 (1985) 336–47. ————. "Focus on Jesus (Studies in the Epistle to the Hebrews)." *ResQ* 22 (1979) 129–40. **Hatch, E.,** and **Redpath, H. A.** *A Concordance to the Septuagint and the Other Greek Versions of the Old Testament.* 2 vols. Oxford: Clarendon, 1897. **Hatch, W. H. P.** "The Position of Hebrews in the Canon of the New Testament." *HTR* 29 (1936) 133–51. **Hay, D. M.** *Glory at the Right Hand: Psalm 110 in Early Christianity.* SBLMS 18. Nashville: Abingdon, 1973. **Heigl, B.** *Verfasser und Adresse des Briefes an die Hebräer: Eine Studie zur neutestamentlichen Einleitung.* Freiburg i/B: Wagner, 1905. **Henderson, M. W.** "The Priestly Ministry of Jesus in the Gospel of John and the Epistle to the Hebrews." Dissertation, Southern Baptist Theological Seminary, 1965. **Héring, J.** "Eschatologie biblique et idéalisme platonicien." In *The Background of the New Testament and Its Eschatology.* Ed. W. D. Davies and D. Daube. Cambridge: Cambridge UP, 1954. **Heris, C. V.** *The Mystery of Christ, Our Head, Priest and King.* Cork/Liverpool: Mercier, 1950. **Herrmann, L.** "L'épître aux (Laodicéens et l'apologie aux) Hébreux." *CCER* 15 (1968) 1–16. **Hession, R.** *From Shadow to Substance: A Rediscovery of the Inner Message of the Epistle to the Hebrews Centered around the Words "Let Us Go On."* Grand Rapids: Zondervan, 1977. **Higgins, A. J. B.** "The Priestly Messiah." *NTS* 13 (1967) 211–39. **Hill, D.** *Greek Words* *and Hebrew Meanings.* SNTSMS 5. Cambridge: Cambridge UP, 1967. **Hill, H. E.** "Messianic Expectation in the Targum of the Psalms." Dissertation, Yale University, 1955. **Hillmann, W.** "Glaube und Verheissung: Einführung in die Grundgedanken des Hebräerbriefes (10,32–13,25)." *BibLeb* 1 (1960) 237–52. ————. "Der Höhenpriester der künftigen Güter: Einführung in die Grundgedanken des Hebräerbriefes (4,14–10,31)." *BibLeb* 1 (1960) 157–78. ————. "Lebend und wirksam ist Gottes Wort: Einführung in die Grundgedanken des Hebräerbriefes (1,5–4,13)." *BibLeb* 1 (1960) 87–99. ————. "Das Wort der Mahnung: Einführung in die Grundgedanken des Hebräerbriefes." *BibLeb* 1 (1960) 17–27. **Hillmer, M. R.** "Priesthood and Pilgrimage: Hebrews in Recent Research." *ThBullMDC* 5 (1969) 66–89. **Hoekema, A. A.** "The Perfection of Christ in Hebrews." *CTJ* 9 (1974) 31–37. **Hoennicke, G.** "Der Hebräerbrief und die neuer Kritik." *NKZ* 29 (1918) 347–68. ————. "Die sittlichen Anschauungen des Hebräerbriefes." *ZWT* 45 (1902) 24–40. **Hofius, O.** *Katapausis: Die Vorstellung vom endzeitlichen Ruheort im Hebräerbrief.* WUNT 11. Tübingen: Mohr, 1970. ————. *Der Vorhang vor dem Thron Gottes: Eine exegetisch-religions-geschichtliche Untersuchung zu Hebräer 6,19f. und 10,19f.* WUNT 14. Tübingen: Mohr, 1972. **Holbrook, F. B.,** ed. *Issues in the Book of Hebrews.* Silver Spring, MD: Biblical Research Institute, 1989. **Holtz, T.** "Einführung in die Probleme des Hebräerbriefes." *ZZ* 23 (1969) 321–27. **Holtzmann, O.** "Der Hebräerbrief und das Abendmahl." *ZNW* 10 (1909) 251–60. **Hoppin, R.** *Priscilla, Author of the Epistle to the Hebrews and Other Essays.* New York: Exposition, 1969. **Horton, C. D.** "The Relationship of the Use of Tenses to the Message in the Epistle to the Hebrews." Dissertation, Southern Baptist Theological Seminary, 1953. **Hoskier, H. C.** *A Commentary on the Various Readings in the Text of the Epistle to the Hebrews in the Chester Beatty Papyrus P[46].* London: Quaritch, 1938. **Houlden, J. L.** "Priesthood in the New Testament and the Church Today." *SE* 5 (1968) 81–87. **Howard, G.** "Hebrews and the Old Testament Quotations." *NovT* 10 (1968) 208–16. **Howard, W. F.** "Studia Biblica, XIII: The Epistle to the Hebrews." *Int* 5 (1951) 80–91. **Hughes, G.** *Hebrews and Hermeneutics: The Epistle to the Hebrews as a New Testament Example of Biblical Interpretation.* SNTSMS 36. Cambridge: Cambridge UP, 1979. **Hughes, P. E.** "The Blood of Jesus and His Heavenly Priesthood in Hebrews." *BSac* 130 (1973) 99–109, 195–212, 305–14; 131 (1974) 26–33. ————. "The Christology of Hebrews." *SWJT* 28 (1985) 19–27. **Humphrey, J. F.** "The Christology of the Epistle to the Hebrews." *LQHR* 14 (1945) 425–32. **Hunt, B. P. W. S.** "The 'Epistle to the Hebrews': An Anti-Judaic Treatise?" *SE* 2 (1964) 408–10. **Hunter, A. M.** "Apollos the Alexandrian." In *Biblical Studies.* FS William Barclay. Ed. J. R. McKay and J. F. Miller. Philadelphia: Westminster, 1976. 147–56. **Hurst, L. D.** "Apollos, Hebrews, and Corinth: Bishop Montefiore's Theory Examined." *SJT* 38 (1985) 505–13. ————. "The Background and Interpretation of the Epistle to the Hebrews." Dissertation, Oxford University, 1981. [Published as *The Epistle to the Hebrews: Its Background of Thought.* SNTSMS 65. Cambridge: Cambridge UP, 1990.] ————. "Eschatology and 'Platonism' in the Epistle to the Hebrews." *SBLASP* (1984) 41–74. **Hutaff, M. D.** "The Epistle to the Hebrews: An Early Christian Sermon." *TBT* 99 (1978) 1816–24. **Huxhold, H. N.** "Faith in the Epistle to the Hebrews." *CTM* 38 (1967) 657–61. **Immer, K.** "Jesus Christus und die Versuchten: Ein Beitrag zur Christologie des Hebräerbriefes." Dissertation, Halle, 1943. **Jansen, A.** "Schwäche und Vollkommenheit des Hohepriesters Christus: Ein Beitrag zur Christologie des Hebräerbriefes." Dissertation, Gregorian Pontifical University, 1957. **Jeffrey, P. J.** "Priesthood of Christ in the Epistle to the Hebrews." Dissertation, University of Melbourne, 1974. **Johnson, S. L.** "Some Important Mistranslations in Hebrews." *BSac* 110 (1953) 25–31. **Johnsson, W. G.** "The Cultus of Hebrews in Twentieth-Century Scholarship." *ExpTim* 89 (1977–78) 104–8. ————. "Defilement and Purgation in the Book of Hebrews." Dissertation, Vanderbilt University, 1973. ————. "Issues in the Interpretation of Hebrews." *AUSS* 15 (1976–77) 169–87. ————. "The Pilgrimage Motif in the Book of Hebrews." *JBL* 97 (1978) 239–51. **Jones, C. P. M.** "The Epistle to the Hebrews and the Lucan Writings." In *Studies in the Gospels.* FS R. H. Lightfoot. Ed. D. E. Nineham. Oxford: Oxford University, 1957. **Jones, E. D.** "The Authorship of Hebrews xiii." *ExpTim*

46 (1934–35) 562–67. **Jones, P. R.** "The Figure of Moses as a Heuristic Device for Understanding the Pastoral Intent of Hebrews." *RevExp* 76 (1979) 95–107. **Kallenbach, W. D.** *The Message and Authorship of the Epistle "To the Hebrews."* St. Paul: Northland, 1938. **Käsemann, E.** *Das wandernde Gottesvolk: Eine Untersuchung zum Hebräerbrief.* 4th ed. FRLANT 55. Göttingen: Vandenhoeck & Ruprecht, 1961. [ET: *The Wandering People of God.* Tr. R. A. Harrisville and I. L. Sandberg. Minneapolis: Augsburg, 1984.] **Katz, P.** "The Quotations from Deuteronomy in Hebrews." *ZNW* 49 (1958) 213–23. **Keck, L. E.** "The Presence of God through Scripture." *LexTQ* 10 (1975) 10–18. **Kennedy, G. A.** *New Testament Interpretation through Rhetorical Criticism.* Chapel Hill, NC: University of North Carolina Press, 1984. **Kennedy, H. A. A.** "The Significance and Range of the Covenant-Conception in the New Testament." *Exp* 8th ser. 10 (1915) 385–410. **Kidner, D.** "Sacrifice—Metaphors and Meaning." *TynBul* 33 (1982) 119–36. **Kirkpatrick, E.** "Hebrews: Its Evangelistic Purpose and Literary Form." Dissertation, Southern Baptist Theological Seminary, 1941. **Kistemaker, S.** *The Psalm Citations in the Epistle to the Hebrews.* Amsterdam: Van Soest, 1961. **Kitchens, J. A.** "The Death of Jesus in the Epistle to the Hebrews." Dissertation, New Orleans Baptist Theological Seminary, 1964. **Klappert, B.** *Die Eschatologie des Hebräerbriefs.* Munich: Kaiser, 1969. **Knox, E. A.** "The Samaritans and the Epistle to the Hebrews." *TCh* 22 (1927) 184–93. **Knox, W. L.** "The Divine Hero Christology of the New Testament." *HTR* 41 (1948) 229–49. **Koester, H.** *Introduction to the New Testament.* Vol. 2: *History and Literature of Early Christianity.* Philadelphia: Fortress, 1982. **Koester, W.** "Platonische Ideenwelt und Gnosis im Hebräerbrief." *Schol* 4 (1956) 545–55. **Kögel, J.** "Der Begriff τελειοῦν im Hebräerbrief." In *Theologische Studien Martin Kähler dargebracht.* Leipzig: Deichert, 1905. **Kosmala, H.** *Hebräer, Essener, Christen: Studien zur Vorgeschichte der frühchristlichen Verkündigung.* SPB 1. Leiden: Brill, 1959. **Kuss, O.** "Über einige neuere Beiträge zur Exegese des Hebräerbriefes." *TGl* 42 (1952) 186–204. ⸺. "Der theologische Grundgedanke des Hebräerbriefes: Zur Deutung des Todes Jesu im Neuen Testament." *MTZ* 7 (1956) 233–71. ⸺. "Der Tod Jesu im Hebräerbrief." *MTZ* 7 (1956) 1–22. ⸺. "Zur Deutung des Hebräerbriefes." *TRev* 53 (1957) 247–54. ⸺. "Der Verfasser des Hebräerbriefes als Seelsorger." *TTZ* 67 (1958) 1–12, 65–80. **Lach, S.** "Les Ordonnances du culte Israélite dans la Lettre aux Hébreux." In *Sacra Pagina: Miscellanea Biblica Congressus Internationalis Catholici de Re Biblica.* Ed. J. Coppens, A. Descamps, and E. Massaux. Paris: Gabalda, 1959. **Laflamme, R.,** and **Gervais, M.,** eds. *Le Christ hier, aujourd'hui et demain: Colloque de Christologie tenu à l'Université Laval (21 et 22 mars 1975).* Quebec: l'Université Laval, 1976. **Lampe, G. W. H.** "Hermeneutics and Typology." *LQHR* 190 (1965) 17–25. ⸺. "Typological Exegesis." *Theol* 56 (1953) 201–8. **Lane, W. L.** "Hebrews: A Sermon in Search of a Setting." *SWJT* 28 (1985) 13–18. **Larcher, C.** *L'actualité chrétienne de l'Ancien Testament d'après le Nouveau Testament.* Rome: Institute Biblique Pontifical, 1962. **Larrañaga, V.** *L'Ascension de Notre-Seigneur dans le Nouveau Testament.* Rome: Institute Biblique Pontifical, 1938. **Larsson, E.** "Om Hebréerbrevets syfte." *SEÅ* 37–38 (1972–73) 296–309. **LaSor, W. S.** "The Epistle to the Hebrews and the Qumran Writings." In *The Dead Sea Scrolls and the New Testament.* Grand Rapids: Eerdmans, 1972. 179–90. **Laub, F.** *Bekenntnis und Auslegung: Die paränetische Funktion der Christologie im Hebräerbrief.* BU 15. Regensburg: Pustet, 1980. **Legg, J. D.** "Our Brother Timothy: A Suggested Solution to the Problem of Authorship of the Epistle to the Hebrews." *EvQ* 40 (1968) 220–23. **Lehne, S.** *The New Covenant in Hebrews.* JSNTSup 44. Sheffield: JSOT, 1990. **Leivestad, R.** *Christ the Conqueror: Ideas of Conflict and Victory in the New Testament.* New York: Macmillan, 1954. ⸺. "Jesus som forbillede ifølge Hebréerbrevet." *NorTT* 74 (1973) 195–206. **Leon, H. J.** "The Jews of Rome in the First Centuries of Christianity." In *The Teacher's Yoke.* FS H. Trantham. Ed. E. J. Vardaman and J. L. Garrett. Waco, TX: Baylor UP, 1964. **Leonard, W.** *The Authorship of the Epistle to the Hebrews.* London/Vatican: Polyglott, 1939. **Leschert, D.** "Hermeneutical Foundations of the Epistle to the Hebrews: A Study in the Validity of Its Interpretation of Some Core Citations from the Psalms." Dissertation, Fuller Theological Seminary, 1991. **Lewis, T. W.** "The Theological Logic in Hebrews 10:19–12:29

and the Appropriation of the Old Testament." Dissertation, Drew University, 1965. **Lewis, W. M.** "St. Paul's Defense before King Agrippa, in Relation to the Epistle to the Hebrews." *BW* 13 (1899) 244–48. **Lidgett, J. S.** *Sonship and Salvation: A Study of the Epistle to the Hebrews.* London: Epworth, 1921. **Lindars, B.** *New Testament Apologetic: The Doctrinal Significance of the Old Testament Quotations.* London: SCM, 1961. ———. "The Rhetorical Structure of Hebrews." *NTS* 35 (1989) 382–406. **Linss, W. C.** "Logical Terminology in the Epistle to the Hebrews." *CTM* 37 (1966) 365–69. **Linton, O.** "Hebréerbrevet och 'den historiske Jesus.'" *STK* 26 (1950) 335–45. **Loader, W. R. G.** "Christ at the Right Hand: Ps. cx. 1 in the New Testament." *NTS* 24 (1977–78) 199–217. ———. *Sohn und Hoherpriester: Eine traditionsgeschichtliche Untersuchung zur Christologie des Hebräerbriefes.* WMANT 53. Neukirchen/Vluyn: Neukirchener Verlag, 1981. **Loane, M. L.** "The Unity of the Old and New Testaments as Illustrated in the Epistle to the Hebrews." In *God Who is Rich in Mercy.* FS D. B. Knox. Ed. P. T. O'Brien and D. G. Peterson. Homebush West, NSW: Lancer, 1986. 255–64. **LoBue, F.** "The Historical Background to the Epistle to the Hebrews." *JBL* 75 (1956) 52–57. **Loew, W.** *Der Glaubensweg des Neuen Bundes: Eine Einführung in den Brief an die Hebräer.* UCB. Berlin: Akademie, 1941. **Loewerich, W. von.** "Zum Vertändnis des Opfergedankens im Hebräerbrief." *TBl* 12 (1933) 167–72. **Lohmann, T.** "Zur Heilsgeschichte des Hebräerbriefes." *OLZ* 79 (1984) 117–25. **Longacre, R. E.** *An Anatomy of Speech Notions.* Lisse, Belgium: de Ridder, 1976. ———. "Some Fundamental Insights of Tagmemics." *Language* 41 (1965) 66–76. ———. *Tagmemics.* Waco, TX: Word, 1985. **Longenecker, R. N.** *Biblical Exegesis in the Apostolic Period.* Grand Rapids: Eerdmans, 1975. **Louw, J. P.** *The Semantics of New Testament Greek.* Philadelphia: Fortress, 1982. **Luck, U.** "Himmlisches und irdisches Geschehen im Hebräerbrief: Ein Beitrag zum Problem des 'historischen Jesus' im Urchristentum." *NovT* 6 (1963) 192–215. **Lueken, W.** *Michael: Eine Darstellung und Vergleichung der jüdischen und der morgenländisch-christlichen Tradition vom Erzengel Michael.* Göttingen: Vandenhoeck & Ruprecht, 1898. **Lussier, E.** *Christ's Priesthood according to the Epistle to the Hebrews.* Collegeville, MN: Liturgical, 1975. **Luther, J. H.** "The Use of the Old Testament by the Author of Hebrews." Dissertation, Bob Jones University, 1977. **Luther, M.** *Vorlesungen über den Hebräerbrief.* Ed. E. Hirsch and H. Rückert. Berlin: de Gruyter, 1929. **Lyonnet, S.** "Bulletin d'exégèse paulinienne (V): Épître aux Hébreux." *Bib* 33 (1952) 240–57. ——— and **Sabourin, L.** *Sin, Redemption and Sacrifice.* AnBib 48. Rome: Pontifical Biblical Institute, 1970. **Maar, O.** "Philo und der Hebräerbrief." Dissertation, Vienna, 1964. **Mack, B. L.** *Logos und Sophia: Untersuchungen zur Weisheitstheologie im hellenistischen Judentum.* SUNT 10. Göttingen: Vandenhoeck & Ruprecht, 1973. ———. *Rhetoric and the New Testament.* Minneapolis, MN: Fortress, 1990. **MacKay, C.** "The Argument of Hebrews." *CQR* 168 (1967) 325–38. **MacNeil, H. L.** *The Christology of the Epistle to the Hebrews.* Chicago: Chicago University, 1914. **MacRae, G. W.** "Heavenly Temple and Eschatology in the Letter to the Hebrews." *Semeia* 12 (1978) 179–99. **Madsen, N. P.** *Ask and You Will Receive: Prayer and the Letter to the Hebrews.* St. Louis: CBP Press, 1989. **Maeso, D. G.** "Lengua original, autor y estilo de la epístola a los Hebreos." *CB* 13 (1956) 202–15. **Manson, T. W.** *Ministry and Priesthood: Christ's and Ours.* Richmond: John Knox Press, 1958. ———. "The Problem of the Epistle to the Hebrews." *BJRL* 32 (1949–50) 1–17. **Manson, W.** *The Epistle to the Hebrews: An Historical and Theological Reconsideration.* London: Hodder & Stoughton, 1951. **Marchant, G. J. C.** "Sacrifice in the Epistle to the Hebrews." *EvQ* 20 (1948) 196–210. **Marcos, J. R.** *Jesús de Nazaret y su glorificación: Estudio de la exegésis patrística de la formula "Sentado a la diestra de Dios" hasta el Concilio de Niceo.* Salamanca/Madrid: Instituto Superior de Pastoral, 1974. **Marshall, I. H.** *Kept by the Power of God: A Study of Perseverance and Falling Away.* London: Epworth, 1969. **Mauro, P.** *God's Apostle and High Priest.* New York: Revell, 1912. ———. *God's Pilgrims: Their Danger, Their Resources, Their Rewards.* Rev. ed. Boston: Hamilton Brothers, 1918. **Maxwell, K. L.** "Doctrine and Parenesis in the Epistle to the Hebrews, with Special Reference to Pre-Christian Gnosticism." Dissertation, Yale University, 1952. **Mayser, E.** *Grammatik der griechischen Papyri aus der Ptolemäerzeit, mit Einschluss der gleichzeitigen Ostraka und der in*

Äegypten verfassten Inschriften. 2 vols. Berlin/Leipzig: Teubner, 1906–34. **McCown, W. G.** "Holiness in Hebrews." *WesThJ* 16 (1981) 58–78. ———. *"Ο ΛΟΓΟΣ ΤΗΣ ΠΑΡΑΚΛΗΣΕΩΣ:* The Nature and Function of the Hortatory Sections in the Epistle to the Hebrews." Dissertation, Union Theological Seminary, Richmond, 1970. **McCullough, J. C.** "Hebrews and the Old Testament." Dissertation, Queen's University, Belfast, 1971. ———. "The Old Testament Quotations in Hebrews." *NTS* 26 (1979–80) 363–79. ———. "Some Recent Developments in Research on the Epistle to the Hebrews." *IBS* 2 (1980) 141–65. **McDonald, J. I. H.** *Kerygma and Didache: The Articulation and Structure of the Earliest Christian Message.* SNTSMS 37. Cambridge: Cambridge UP, 1980. **McGaughey, D. H.** "The Hermeneutic Method of the Epistle to the Hebrews." Dissertation, Boston University, 1963. **McNamara, M.** *The New Testament and the Palestinian Targum to the Pentateuch.* AnBib 27. Rome: Pontifical Biblical Institute, 1966. ———. *Targum and Testament: Aramaic Paraphrases of the Hebrew Bible, A Light on the New Testament.* Shannon: Irish UP, 1972. **McNicol, A. J.** "The Relationship of the Image of the Highest Angel to the High Priest Concept in Hebrews." Dissertation, Vanderbilt University, 1974. **McNicol, J.** "The Spiritual Value of the Epistle to the Hebrews." *BibRev* 15 (1930) 509–22. **McRay, J.** "Atonement and Apocalyptic in the Book of Hebrews." *ResQ* 23 (1980) 1–9. **Mealand, D. L.** "The Christology of the Epistle to the Hebrews." *MCM* 22 (1979) 180–87. **Méchineau, L.** *L'Epistola agli Ebrei secondo le risposte della Commissione Biblica.* Rome: Pontifical Biblical Commission, 1917. **Médebielle, A.** *L'Expiation dans l'Ancien Testament et Nouveau Testament.* 2 vols. Rome: Institut Biblique Pontifical, 1923. **Medico, M. dal.** *L'auteur de l'Épître aux Hébreux.* Rome: Pontifical Biblical Institute, 1914. **Meeter, H. H.** *The Heavenly High Priesthood of Christ.* Grand Rapids: Eerdmans-Sevensma, 1916. **Ménégoz, E.** *La théologie de l'Épître aux Hébreux.* Paris: Fischbacher, 1894. **Mercier, R.** "La Perfección de Cristo y de los Cristiános en la carta a los Hebreos." *RevistB* 35 (1973) 229–35. **Merle, G.** *La christologie de l'Épître aux Hébreux.* Montauban: Granié, 1877. **Metzger, B. M.** "The Formulas Introducing Quotations of Scripture in the NT and the Mishnah." *JBL* 70 (1951) 297–307. ———. *A Textual Commentary on the Greek New Testament: A Companion Volume to the United Bible Societies' Greek New Testament (third edition).* London/New York: United Bible Societies, 1971. **Michaelis, W.** *Zur Engelchristologie im Urchristentum.* GBTh 1. Basel: Maier, 1942. **Michel, O.** "Die Lehre von der christlichen Vollkommenheit nach der Anschauung des Hebräerbriefes." *TSK* 106 (1934–35) 333–55. **Mickelsen, A. B.** "Methods of Interpretation in the Epistle to the Hebrews." Dissertation, University of Chicago, 1950. **Miller, P. D.** *The Divine Warrior in Early Israel.* Cambridge, MA: Harvard UP, 1973. **Milligan, G.** "The Roman Destination of the Epistle to the Hebrews." *Exp* 4 (1901) 437–48. ———. *The Theology of the Epistle to the Hebrews with a Critical Introduction.* Edinburgh: Clark, 1899. **Milligan, W.** *The Ascension and Heavenly Priesthood of Our Lord.* London: Macmillan, 1891. **Minear, P. S.** "An Early Christian Theopoetic?" *Semeia* 12 (1978) 201–14. ———. *New Testament Apocalyptic.* Nashville: Abingdon, 1981. **Moe, O.** "Der Gedanke der allgemeinen Priestertums im Hebräerbrief." *TZ* 5 (1949) 161–69. ———. "Das Priestertum Christi im NT ausserhalb des Hebräerbriefs." *TLZ* 72 (1947) 335–38. **Moffatt, J.** "The Christology of the Epistle to the Hebrews." *ExpTim* 28 (1916–17) 505–8, 563–66; 29 (1917–18) 26–30. ———. *Jesus Christ the Same.* The Shaffer Lectures for 1940 in Yale University Divinity School. New York: Abingdon-Cokesbury, 1940. **Molero, X. R.** "El sacerdocio celeste de Cristo." *EstBib* 22 (1963) 69–77. **Monod, V.** *De titulo epistolae vulgo ad Hebraeos inscriptae.* Montalbani: Granié, 1910. **Mora, G.** *La Carta a los Hebreos como Escrito Pastoral.* Barcelona: Herder, 1974. ———. "Ley y sacrificio en la carta a los Hebreos." *RCB* 1 (1976) 1–50. **Morgenthaler, R.** *Statistik des neutestamentlichen Wortschatzes.* Zürich: Gotthelf, 1958. **Morin, J.** "L'Église dans l'Épître aux Hébreux." In *L'Église dans la Bible.* Paris/Bruges: Desclée de Brouwer, 1962. **Morris, L.** *The Apostolic Preaching of the Cross.* Grand Rapids: Eerdmans, 1955. **Moule, C. F. D.** "Commentaries on the Epistle to the Hebrews." *Theol* 61 (1958) 228–32. ———. *An Idiom-Book of New Testament Greek.* 2nd ed. Cambridge: UP, 1960. ———. "The Influence of Circumstances on the Use of Christological Terms." *JTS* n.s. 10 (1959)

247–63. ———. "The Influence of Circumstances on the Use of Eschatological Terms." *JTS* n.s. 15 (1964) 1–15. ———. *The Sacrifice of Christ.* Greenwich: Seabury Press, 1957. **Moulton, J. H.** *A Grammar of New Testament Greek: I. Prolegomena.* 3rd ed. Edinburgh: Clark, 1908. ——— and **Howard, W. F.** *A Grammar of New Testament Greek: II. Accidence and Word-Formation.* Edinburgh: Clark, 1920. **Moulton, W. F.,** and **Geden, A. S.** *A Concordance to the Greek Testament according to the Texts of Westcott and Hort, Tischendorf and the English Revizers.* 4th ed. Rev. H. K. Moulton. Edinburgh: Clark, 1963. **Moxnes, H.** *Theology in Conflict.* NovTSup 53. Leiden: Brill, 1980. **Müller, P. G.** *ΧΡΙΣΤΟΣ ΑΡΧΗΓΟΣ: Der religions-geschichtliche und theologische Hintergrund einer neutestamentlichen Christusprädikation.* Frankfurt a/M.: Lang, 1973. ———. "Die Funktion der Psalmzitate im Hebräerbrief." In *Freude an der Weisung des Herrn.* Ed. E. Haag and F. L. Hossfeld. Stuttgart: Katholisches Bibelwerk, 1986. 223–42. **Murray, J.** "The Heavenly, Priestly Activity of Christ." In *Collected Writings of John Murray.* Ed. I. Murray. Vol. 1. Edinburgh: Banner of Truth Trust, 1976. 44–58. ———. "Jesus the Son of God." In *Collected Writings of John Murray.* Vol. 4. Edinburgh: Banner of Truth Trust, 1982. 58–81. **Murray, R.** "Jews, Hebrews and Christians: Some Needed Distinctions." *NovT* 24 (1982) 194–208. **Nairne, A.** *The Epistle of Priesthood: Studies in the Epistle to the Hebrews.* Edinburgh: Clark, 1913. **Nakagawa, H.** "Christology in the Epistle to the Hebrews." Dissertation, Yale University, 1955. **Nash, R. H.** "The Notion of Mediator in Alexandrian Judaism and the Epistle to the Hebrews." *WTJ* 40 (1977) 89–115. **Nauck, W.** "Zum Aufbau des Hebräerbriefes." In *Judentum, Urchristentum, Kirche.* FS J. Jeremias. Ed. W. Eltester. BZNW 26. Giessen: Töpelmann, 1960. **Neeley, L. L.** "A Discourse Analysis of Hebrews." *OPTT* 3–4 (1987) 1–146. **Nellessen, E.** "Lateinische Summarien zum Hebräerbrief." *BZ* 14 (1970) 240–51. **Nestle, E.** "On the Address of the Epistle to the Hebrews." *ExpTim* 10 (1898–99) 422. **Neufeld, V. H.** *The Earliest Christian Confessions.* NTTS 5. Grand Rapids: Eerdmans, 1963. **Nicolau, M.** "El 'Reíno des Dios' en la carta a los Hebreos." *Burg* 20 (1979) 393–405. **Nicole, R.** "C. H. Dodd and the Doctrine of Propitiation." *WTJ* 17 (1955) 117–57. **Nida, E. A., Louw, J. P.,** et al. *Style and Discourse: With Special Reference to the Text of the Greek New Testament.* Cape Town: Bible Society, 1983. **Nikiprowetsky, V.** "La Spiritualisation des sacrifices et le cult sacrificial au Temple de Jérusalem chez Philon d'Alexandrine." *Sem* 17 (1967) 98–114. **Nissilä, K.** *Das Hohepriestmotiv in Hebräerbrief: Eine exegetische Untersuchung.* Helsinki: Oy Liitun Kirjapaino, 1979. **Nomoto, S.** "Herkunft und Struktur der Hohepriestervorstellung im Hebräerbrief." *NovT* 10 (1968) 10–25. ———. "Die Hohenpriester-Typologie im Hebräerbrief: Ihre traditionsgeschichtliche Herkunft und ihr religionsgeschichtlicher Hintergrund." Dissertation, Hamburg, 1965. **Norden, E.** *Agnostos Theos: Untersuchungen zur Formengeschichte religiöser Rede.* Leipzig: Teubner, 1913. **Oepke, A.** *Das neue Gottesvolk in Schrifttum, Schauspiel, bildender Kunst und Weltgestaltung.* Gütersloh: C. Bertelsmann, 1950. **Olson, S. N.** "Wandering but Not Lost." *WW* 5 (1985) 426–33. **Osborne, G.** "Soteriology in the Epistle to the Hebrews." In *Grace Unlimited.* Ed. C. Pinnock. Minneapolis: Bethany Fellowship, 1975. **Otto, C. W.** *Der Apostel und Hohepriester unseres Bekenntnis.* Leipzig: Deichert, 1861. **Oudersluys, R. C.** "Exodus in the Letter to the Hebrews." In *Grace upon Grace.* FS L. J. Kuyper. Ed. J. I. Cook. Grand Rapids: Eerdmans, 1975. 143–52. **Padolski, M. V.** *L'idée du sacrifice de la Croix dans l'Épître aux Hébreux.* Paris: Gabalda, 1935. **Padva, P.** *Les citations de l'Ancien Testament dans l'Épître aux Hébreux.* Paris: Danzig, 1904. **Parker, H. M., Jr.** "Domitian and the Epistle to the Hebrews." *IlRev* 36 (1979) 31–43. **Perdelwitz, R.** "Das literarische Problem des Hebräerbriefs: 1. Der literarische Charakter des Schreibens. 2. Der Verfasser. 3. Die Addressaten." *ZNW* 11 (1910) 59–78, 105–23. **Perdue, L. B.** "The Social Character of Paraenesis and Paraenetic Literature." *Semeia* 50 (1990) 5–39. **Perkins, D. W.** "A Call to Pilgrimage: The Challenge of Hebrews." *ThEduc* 32 (1985) 69–81. **Perowne, T. T.** *Our High Priest in Heaven.* 2nd ed. London: E. Stock, 1894. **Pevella, C. M.** "De justificatione secundum Epistolam ad Hebraeos." *Bib* 14 (1933) 1–21, 150–69. **Pérez, G.** "Autenticidad y canonicidad de la Carta a los Hebreos." *CB* 13 (1956) 216–26. **Perry, M.** "Method and Model in the Epistle to the Hebrews." *Theol* 77 (1974) 66–74. **Peterson, D. G.**

"An Examination of the Concept of 'Perfection' in the 'Epistle to the Hebrews.'" Dissertation, University of Manchester, 1978. [Published as *Hebrews and Perfection: An Examination of the Concept of Perfection in the "Epistle to the Hebrews."* Cambridge: Cambridge UP, 1982.] ———. "The Ministry of Encouragement." In *God Who Is Rich in Mercy.* FS D. B. Knox. Ed. P. T. O'Brien and D. G. Peterson. Homebush West, NSW: Lancer, 1986. 235–53. ———. "Towards a New Testament Theology of Worship." *RTR* 43 (1984) 65–73. **Pinto, L. di.** *Volontà di Dio e legge antica nell'Epistola agli Ebrei: Contributo ai fondementi biblici della teologia morale.* Naples: Gregorian, 1976. **Pittard, C. R.** "The Person and Work of Christ in the Epistle to the Hebrews." Dissertation, Southern Baptist Theological Seminary, 1926. **Plessis, P. J. du.** *ΤΕΛΕΙΟΣ: The Idea of Perfection in the New Testament.* Kampen: Kok, 1959. **Ploeg, J. van der.** "L'exégèse de l'Ancien Testament dans l'Épître aux Hébreux." *RB* 54 (1947) 187–228. **Plooij, D.** *Studies in the Testimony Book.* Amsterdam: Noord-Hollandsche, 1932. **Plumptre, E. H.** "The Writings of Apollos." *Exp* n.s. 1 (1885) 329–48, 409–35. **Pollard, E. B.** "Notes on the Old Testament Citations in the Epistle to the Hebrews." *CrozQ* 1 (1924) 447–52. **Powell, C. H.** *The Biblical Concept of Power.* London: Epworth, 1963. **Powell, D. L.** "Christ as High Priest in the Epistle to the Hebrews." *SE* 7 (1982) 387–99. **Pretorius, E. A. C.** "Christusbeeld en Kerkmodel in die Hebräerbrief." *ThEv* 15 (1982) 3–18. ———. "*Diathēkē* in the Epistle to the Hebrews." *Neot* 5 (1971) 37–50. **Prince, A.** "An Investigation into the Importance of Perseverance in the Christian Life as Presented in Five Warning Passages in Hebrews." Dissertation, Southwestern Baptist Theological Seminary, 1980. **Prümm, K.** "Das neutestamentliche Sprach- und Begriffsproblem der Vollkommenheit." *Bib* 44 (1963) 76–92. **Purdy, A. C.** "The Purpose of the Epistle to the Hebrews." *Exp* 8th ser. 19 (1920) 123–39. ———. "The Purpose of the Epistle to the Hebrews in the Light of Recent Studies in Judaism." In *Amicitiae Corolla.* Ed. H. G. Wood. London: University of London, 1933. **Quentel, J.** "Les destinataires de l'Épître aux Hébreux." *RB* 9 (1912) 50–68. **Rábanos, R.** "Sacerdocio de Melquisedec, sacerdocio de Aarón, sacerdocio de Cristo." *CB* 13 (1956) 264–75. **Rahlfs, A.,** ed. *Septuaginta: Id est Vetus Testamentum graece iuxta LXX interpretes.* 4th ed. 2 vols. Stuttgart: Württembergische Bibelanstalt, 1950. **Ramsay, W. M.** "The Date and Authorship of the Epistle to the Hebrews." In *Luke the Physician.* London: Hodder & Stoughton, 1908. **Rawlingson, A. E. J.** "Priesthood and Sacrifice in Judaism and Christianity." *ExpTim* 60 (1949) 116–21. **Reid, R.** "The Use of the Old Testament in the Epistle to the Hebrews." Dissertation, Union Theological Seminary, New York, 1964. **Rendall, F.** *Theology of the Hebrew Christians.* London: Macmillan, 1886. **Rendall, R.** "The Method of the Writer to the Hebrews in Using Old Testament Quotations." *EvQ* 27 (1955) 214–20. **Renner, F.** *An die Hebräer: Ein pseudepigraphischen Brief.* Münsterschwarz: Vier-Türme, 1970. **Rice, G. E.** "Apostasy as a Motif and Its Effect on the Structure of Hebrews." *AUSS* 23 (1985) 29–35. **Riddle, D. W.** "Hebrews, First Clement, and the Persecution of Domitian." *JBL* 43 (1924) 329–48. **Riehm, E.** *Der Lehrbegriff des Hebräerbriefes.*[2] Basel: Balmer & Riehm, 1867. **Rienecker, F.** *A Linguistic Key to the Greek New Testament.* Grand Rapids: Zondervan, 1976. **Riggenbach, E.** "Der Begriff der ΔΙΑΘΗΚΗ im Hebräerbrief." In *Theologische Studien.* FS T. Zahn. Leipzig: Deichert, 1908. ———. "Der Begriff der ΤΕΛΕΙΩΣΙΣ im Hebräerbrief: Ein Beitrag zur Frage nach der Einwirkung der Mysterienreligion auf Sprache und Gedankenwelt des Neuen Testaments." *NKZ* 34 (1923) 184–95. ———. *Historische Studien zum Hebräerbrief.* Vol. 1: *Die ältesten lateinischen Kommentare zum Hebräerbrief.* FGNK 8/1. Leipzig: Deichert, 1907. **Rissi, M.** *Die Theologie des Hebräerbriefs.* WUNT 44. Tübingen: Mohr, 1987. **Ritschl, A.** "Über die Leser des Hebräerbriefs." *TSK* 39 (1866) 89–102. **Robertson, A. T.** *A Grammar of the Greek New Testament in the Light of Historical Research.* Nashville: Broadman, 1934. **Robertson, O. P.** "The People of the Wilderness: The Concept of the Church in Hebrews." Dissertation, Union Theological Seminary, Richmond, 1966. **Robinson, J. A. T.** *Redating the New Testament.* London: SCM, 1976. **Robinson, W.** *The Eschatology of the Epistle to the Hebrews.* Birmingham, AL: Overdale College, 1950. ———. "The Eschatology of the Epistle to the Hebrews: A Study in the Christian Doctrine of

Hope." *Enc* 22 (1961) 37–51. **Rogers, E. W.** *Him That Endured.* London: Pickering & Inglis, 1965. **Roloff, J.** "Der mitleidende Hohepriester: Zur Frage nach der Bedeutung des irdischen Jesus für die Christologie des Hebräerbriefes." In *Jesus Christus in Historie und Theologie.* FS H. Conzelmann. Ed. G. Strecker. Tübingen: Mohr, 1975. **Ross, A.** "The Message of the Epistle to the Hebrews for Today." *ExpTim* 51 (1942–43) 161–68. **Rowell, J. B.** "Our Great High Priest." *BSac* 118 (1961) 148–53. **Rusche, H.** "Glauben und Leben nach dem Hebräerbrief." *BibLeb* 12 (1971) 94–104. **Rylaarsdam, J. C.** "Jewish-Christian Relationships: The Two Covenants and the Dilemmas of Christology." In *Grace upon Grace.* FS L. J. Kuyper. Ed. J. I. Cook. Grand Rapids: Eerdmans, 1975. **Sabourin, L.** "Auctor Epistulae ad Hebraeos ut interpres Scripturae." *VD* 46 (1968) 275–85. ———. "Il sacrificio di Gèsu e le Realtà cultuali." *BeO* 10 (1968) 25–37. ———. *Priesthood: A Comparative Study.* Leiden: Brill, 1973. ———. "Sacrificium et liturgia in Epistula ad Hebreos." *VD* 46 (1968) 235–58. **Saito, T.** *Die Mosevorstellungen im Neuen Testament.* Bern/Frankfurt: Lang, 1977. **Salmon, G.** "The Keynote of the Epistle to the Hebrews." *Exp* 2nd ser. 3 (1882) 81–93. **Salom, A. P.** "*Ta Hagia* in the Epistle to the Hebrews." *AUSS* 5 (1967) 59–70. **Sandegren, C.** "The Addressees of the Epistle to the Hebrews." *EvQ* 27 (1955) 221–24. **Sanders, J. T.** *The New Testament Christological Hymns.* SNTSMS 15. Cambridge: Cambridge UP, 1971. **Sanford, C. J.** "The Addressees of Hebrews." Dissertation, Dallas Theological Seminary, 1962. **Saydon, P. P.** "The Master Idea of the Epistle to the Hebrews." *MelTheol* 13 (1961) 19–26. **Schaefer, J. R.** "The Relationship between Priestly and Servant Messianism in the Epistle to the Hebrews." *CBQ* 30 (1968) 359–85. **Schäfer, K. T.** *Untersuchungen zur Geschichte der lateinischen Übersetzungen des Hebräerbriefes.* Freiburg: Herder, 1929. **Scheller, E. J.** *Das Priestertum Christi im Anschluss an den hl. Thomas von Aquin.* Paderborn: Schöniagh, 1934. **Schenke, H. M.** "Erwägungen zum Rätsel des Hebräerbriefes." In *Neues Testament und christliche Existenz.* FS H. Braun. Tübingen: Mohr, 1973. **Schick, E.** *Im Glauben Kraft empfangen Betrachtungen zum Brief an die Hebräer.* Stuttgart: Katholisches Bibelwerk, 1978. **Schiele, F. M.** "Harnack's 'Probabilia' Concerning the Address and the Author of the Epistle to the Hebrews." *AJT* 9 (1905) 290–308. **Schierse, F. J.** *Verheissung und Heilsvollendung: Zur theologischen Grundfrage des Hebräerbriefes.* MTS 1/9. Munich: Zink, 1955. **Schildenberger, J.** "Psalm 109 (110): Christus, König und Priester." *BenM* 20 (1938) 361–74. **Schille, G.** "Die Basis des Hebräerbriefes." *ZNW* 48 (1957) 270–80. ———. "Erwägungen zur Hohenpriesterlehre des Hebräerbriefes." *ZNW* 46 (1955) 81–109. ———. *Frühchristliche Hymnen.* Berlin: Akademie, 1962. **Schillebeeckx, E.** "Die Welt der Zukunft und die grosse Gnade Gottes: Der Hebräerbrief." In *Christus und die Christen.* Freiburg: Herder, 1977. **Schlatter, A.** *Der Glaube im Neuen Testament.* 5th ed. Stuttgart: Calwer, 1963. **Schmidgall, P.** "The Influence of Jewish Apocalyptic Literature on the Book of Hebrews." Dissertation, Western Kentucky University, 1980. **Schmitz, O.** *Die Opferanschauung des späteren Judentums und die Opferaussagungen des Neuen Testaments: Eine Untersuchung ihres geschichtlichen Verhältnisses.* Tübingen: Mohr, 1910. **Schoonhoven, C. R.** "The 'Analogy of Faith' and the Intent of Hebrews." In *Scripture, Tradition, and Interpretation.* FS E. F. Harrison. Ed. W. W. Gasque and W. S. LaSor. Grand Rapids: Eerdmans, 1978. 92–110. **Schröger, F.** "Der Gottesdienst der Hebräerbriefgemeinde." *MTZ* 19 (1968) 161–81. ———. "Der Hebräerbrief—paulinisch?" In *Kontinuität und Einheit.* FS F. Mussner. Ed. P. G. Müller and W. Stenger. Freiburg/Basel/Vienna: Herder, 1981. 211–22. ———. "Das hermeneutische Instrumentarium des Hebräerbriefverfassers." *TGl* 60 (1970) 344–59. ———. *Der Verfasser des Hebräerbriefes als Schriftausleger.* Regensburg: Pustet, 1968. **Schubert, P.** "Der Verbindung von Königtum und Priestertum in der Vorgeschichte der Christusoffenbarung: Eine Voruntersuchung der Christologie des Hebräerbriefs." Dissertation, Leipzig, 1955. **Scott, E. F.** "The Epistle to the Hebrews and Roman Christianity." *HTR* 13 (1930) 205–19. ———. *The Epistle to the Hebrews: Its Doctrine and Significance.* Edinburgh: Clark, 1923. **Scott, W. M. F.** "Priesthood in the New Testament." *SJT* 10 (1957) 399–415. **Selph, B. K.** "The Christology of the Book of Hebrews." Dissertation, Southwestern Baptist Seminary, 1948. **Sen, F.** "La Carta a los Hebreos en el Canon y en el corpus paulino." *CB* 25 (1968) 35–40.

Shuster, I. "I destinatari dell' epistola agli Ebrei." *ScC* 66 (1938) 641–65. **Siegman, E. F.** "The Blood of the Covenant." *AER* 136 (1957) 167–74. **Silva, M.** *Biblical Words and Their Meanings: An Introduction to Lexical Semantics.* Grand Rapids: Zondervan, 1983. ———. "Perfection and Eschatology in Hebrews." *WTJ* 39 (1976) 60–71. **Simon, M.** *Hercule et le Christianisme.* Paris: Publications de la faculté de Strasbourg, 1955. **Simpson, E. K.** "The Vocabulary of the Epistle to the Hebrews." *EvQ* 18 (1946) 35–38, 187–90. **Slot, W.** *De Letterkundige Vorm van de Brief aan de Hebreeën.* Gröningen: Wolters, 1912. **Smalley, S. S.** "The Atonement in the Epistle to the Hebrews." *EvQ* 33 (1961) 36–43. **Smith, J.** *A Priest for Ever: A Study of Typology and Eschatology in Hebrews.* London/Sydney: Sheed and Ward, 1969. **Smith, L.** "Metaphor and Truth in Hebrews." *NBl* 57 (1976) 227–33. **Smith, R. B.** "Apostasy in the Book of Hebrews." Dissertation, Southern Baptist Theological Seminary, 1959. **Smith, R. W.** *The Art of Rhetoric in Alexandria: Its Theory and Practice in the Ancient World.* The Hague: Nijhoff, 1974. **Smits, C.** *Oud-testamentische Citaten in het Nieuw Testament.* Malmberg: Hertogenbosch, 1963. **Soden, H. von.** "Der Hebräerbrief." *JPTh* 10 (1884) 435–93, 627–56. **Solari, J. K.** "The Problem of *Metanoia* in the Epistle to the Hebrews." Dissertation, Catholic University of America, 1970. **Sowers, S. G.** *The Hermeneutics of Philo and Hebrews: A Comparison of the Interpretation of the Old Testament in Philo Judaeus and the Epistle to the Hebrews.* Richmond: Knox, 1965. **Spicq, C.** "Alexandrinismes dans l'Épître aux Hébreux." *RB* 58 (1951) 481–502. ———. "Contemplation, théologie et vie morale d'après l'Épître aux Hébreux." *RSR* 39 (1951) 289–300. ———. "L'Épître aux Hébreux, Apollos, Jean-Baptiste, les Hellénistes et Qumran." *RevQ* 1 (1958–59) 365–90. ———. "Hébreux (Épître aux)." DBSup 7: 226–79. ———. "L'Origine johannique de la conception du Christ-prêtre dans l'Épître aux Hébreux." In *Aux sources de la tradition chrétienne.* FS M. Goguel. Neuchâtel/Paris: Delachaux & Niestlé, 1956. ———. "La perfection chrétienne d'après l'Épître aux Hébreux." In *Bibliothèque de la faculté Catholique de Théologie de Lyon* 5. FS J. Chaine. Ed. G. Villepelet. Lyon: Facultés Catholiques, 1950. ———. "Le Philonisme de l'Épître aux Hébreux." *RB* 56 (1949) 542–72; 57 (1950) 212–42. ———. "La théologie des deux alliances dans l'Épître aux Hébreux." *RSPT* 33 (1949) 15–30. ———. *Vie chrétienne et pérégrination selon le Nouveau Testament.* LD 71. Paris: Cerf, 1972. **Stadelmann, A.** "Zur Christologie des Hebräerbriefes in der neueren Diskussion." In *Theologische Berichte.* Vol. 2. Ed. J. Pfammatter and F. Furger. Zürich: Zwingli, 1973. **Stagl, H.** "Pauline Authorship of the Epistle to the Hebrews according to Mt. Sinai Arabic Manuscript 151." *RefRev* 21 (1961) 14, 51–53. **Staples, A. F.** "The Book of Hebrews in Its Relationship to the Writings of Philo Judaeus." Dissertation, Southern Baptist Theological Seminary, 1951. **Stine, D. M.** "The Finality of the Christian Faith: A Study of the Unfolding Argument of the Epistle to the Hebrews, Chapters 1–7." Dissertation, Princeton Theological Seminary, 1964. **Stöger, A.** "Der Hohepriester Jesus Christus." *TPQ* 100 (1952) 309–19. **Stott, W.** "The Conception of 'Offering' in the Epistle to the Hebrews." *NTS* 11 (1962–63) 62–67. **Stuart, S. S.** "The Exodus Tradition in Late Jewish and Early Christian Literature: A General Survey of the Literature and a Particular Analysis of the Wisdom of Solomon, II Esdras and the Epistle to the Hebrews." Dissertation, Vanderbilt University, 1973. **Suárez, P. L.** "Cesárea, lugar de composición de la Epístola a los Hebreos?" *CB* 13 (1956) 226–31. ———. "Casárea y la Epístola 'ad Hebraeos.'" In *Studiorum Paulinorum Congressus Internationalis Catholici 1961.* AnBib 17–18. Rome: Pontifical Biblical Institute, 1963. **Swetnam, J.** "Form and Content in Hebrews 1–6." *Bib* 53 (1972) 368–85. ———. "Form and Content in Hebrews 7–13." *Bib* 55 (1974) 333–48. ———. *Jesus and Isaac: A Study of the Epistle to the Hebrews in the Light of the Aqedah.* AnBib 94. Rome: Biblical Institute Press, 1981. ———. "On the Literary Genre of the 'Epistle' to the Hebrews." *NovT* 13 (1969) 261–69. **Synge, F. C.** *Hebrews and the Scriptures.* London: SPCK, 1959. **Tabachovitz, D.** *Die Septuaginta und das Neue Testament.* Lund: Gleerup, 1956. **Tasker, R. V. G.** *The Gospel in the Epistle to the Hebrews.* London: Tyndale, 1956. ———. "The Text of the 'Corpus Paulinum.'" *NTS* 1 (1954–55) 180–91. **Taylor, C. D.** "A Comparative Study of the Concepts of Worship in Colossians and Hebrews." Dissertation, Southern Baptist Theological Seminary, 1957.

Tenney, M. C. "A New Approach to the Book of Hebrews." *BSac* 123 (1966) 230–36. **Teodorico, P.** "Alcuni aspetti dell' ecclesiologia della Lettera agli Ebrei." *Bib* 24 (1943) 125–61, 323–69. ———. *La Chiesa della Lettora agli Ebrie.* Torin/Rome: Marietti, 1945. ———. "Il sacerdozio celeste di cristo della lettera agli Ebrei." *Greg* 39 (1958) 319–34. **Terra, J. E. M.** "A Libertação Escatológica na Epístola aos Hebreus: O Povo de Deus a Caminho do Santúario." *RCB* 2 (1978) 325–43. **Thayer, J. H.** "Authorship and Canonicity of the Epistle to the Hebrews." *BSac* 24 (1867) 681–722. **Theissen, G.** *Untersuchungen zum Hebräerbrief.* SNT 2. Gütersloh: Mohn, 1969. **Thien, F.** "Analyse de l'Épître aux Hébreux." *RB* 11 (1902) 74–86. **Thiselton, A.** "Semantics and New Testament Interpretation." In *New Testament Interpretation: Essays on Principles and Methods.* Ed. I. H. Marshall. Grand Rapids: Eerdmans, 1977. 75–104. **Thomas, J.** "The Use of Voice, Moods and Tenses in the Epistle to the Hebrews." Dissertation, Western Kentucky University, 1980. **Thomas, K. J.** "The Old Testament Citations in Hebrews." *NTS* 11 (1964–65) 303–25. ———. "The Use of the Septuagint in the Epistle to the Hebrews." Dissertation, University of Manchester, 1959. **Thompson, J. W.** *The Beginnings of Christian Philosophy: The Epistle to the Hebrews.* CBQMS 13. Washington, DC: The Catholic Biblical Association of America, 1981. ———. *Strategy for Survival: A Plan for Church Renewal from Hebrews.* Austin, TX: Sweet, 1980. ———. "'That Which Abides': Some Metaphysical Assumptions in the Epistle to the Hebrews." Dissertation, Vanderbilt University, 1974. ———. "The Underlying Unity of Hebrews." *ResQ* 18 (1975) 129–36. **Thrall, M. E.** *Greek Particles in the New Testament.* Linguistic and Exegetical Studies. Grand Rapids: Eerdmans, 1962. **Thurston, R. W.** "Philo and the Epistle to the Hebrews." *EvQ* 58 (1986) 133–43. **Thüsing, W.** "Erhöhungsvorstellung und Parusieerwartung in der ältesten nach-österlichen Christologie." *BZ* 11 (1967) 95–108, 205–22; 12 (1968) 54–80. ———. "Das Opfer der Christen nach dem Neuen Testament." *BibLeb* 6 (1965) 37–50. **Thyen, H.** *Der Stil der jüdisch-hellenistischen Homilie.* FRLANT 47. Göttingen: Vandenhoeck & Ruprecht, 1955. **Tiede, D. L.** *The Charismatic Figure as Miracle Worker.* SBLDS 1. Missoula, MT: Scholars, 1972. **Torm, F.** "Om τελειοῦν. Hebraeerbrevet." *SEÅ* 5 (1940) 116–25. **Torrance, J. B.** "The Priesthood of Jesus." In *Essays in Christology for Karl Barth.* Ed. T. H. L. Parker. London: Lotterworth Press, 1956. 153–73. **Torrey, C. C.** "The Authorship and Character of the So-Called 'Epistle to the Hebrews.'" *JBL* 30 (1911) 137–56. **Toy, C. H.** *Quotations in the New Testament.* New York: Scribner's, 1884. **Trinidad, J.** "De sacrificio Christi in Epistola ad Hebraeos." *VD* 19 (1939) 180–86, 207–12. **Trites, A. A.** *The New Testament Concept of Witness.* SNTSMS 31. Cambridge: Cambridge UP, 1977. **Tucker, M. A. R.** "The Gospel according to Prisca." *NC* 73 (1913) 81–98. **Turner, G. A.** *The New and Living Way: A Fresh Exposition of the Epistle to the Hebrews.* Minneapolis: Bethany Fellowship, 1975. **Turner, N.** *A Grammar of New Testament Greek: III. Syntax.* Edinburgh: Clark, 1963. ———. *A Grammar of New Testament Greek: IV. Style.* Edinburgh: Clark, 1976. **Ubbrink, J. T.** "De Hoogepriester en zijn Offer in de Brief aan de Hebreeën." *NThS* 22 (1939) 172–84. **Ungeheuer, J.** *Der grosse Priester über dem Hause Gottes: Die Christologie des Hebräerbriefes.* Würzburg: Stürtz, 1939. **Vaccari, A.** "Las citas del Antiquo Testamento en la Epístola a los Hebreos." *CB* 13 (1956) 239–43. **Vaganay, L.** "Le Plan de l'Épître aux Hébreux." In *Mémorial Lagrange.* Paris: Gabalda, 1940. **Vandenbroucke, F.** *Les Psaumes et le Christ.* Louvain: Abbé Mont-César, 1955. **Vanhoye, A.** "Cristo Sumo Sacerdote." *RCB* 2 (1978) 313–23. ———. "De 'aspectu' oblationis Christi secundum Epistolam ad Hebraeos." *VD* 37 (1959) 32–38. ———. "Discussion sur la structure de l'Épître aux Hébreux." *Bib* 55 (1974) 349–80. ———. "De Sacerdotio Christi in Hebr." *VD* 47 (1969) 22–30. ———. "De sessione celesti in epistola ad Hebraeos." *VD* 44 (1966) 131–34. ———. *Epistolae ad Hebraeos: Textus de Sacerdotio Christo.* Rome: Pontifical Biblical Institute, 1968–69. ———. *Homilie für haltbedürftige Christen: Struktur und Botschaft des Hebräerbriefes.* Regensburg: Pustet, 1981. ———. "L'Épître aux Éphésiens et l'Épître aux Hébreux." *Bib* 59 (1978) 198–230. ———. "Le Dieu de la nouvelle alliance dans l'Épître aux Hébreux." In *Le notion biblique de Dieu.* BETL 41. Louvain: Louvain UP, 1976. 315–30. ———. "Les indices de la structure littéraire de l'Épître aux Hébreux." *SE* 2 (1964) 493–509. ———. "Literarische Struktur und theologische Botschaft des Hebräerbriefs." *SNTU* 4 (1979) 119–47; 5 (1980) 18–49. ———. *Le message de l'Épître aux Hébreux.* Paris: Cerf, 1977. ———. *Our Priest in God: The Doctrine of the Epistle to the Hebrews.* Rome: Biblical Institute Press, 1977. ———. *Prêtres anciens, prêtre nouveau selon le Nouveau Testament.* Paris: Cerf, 1980. ———. "Sacerdoce du Christ et culte chrétien selon l'Épître aux Hébreux." *Chr* 28 (1981) 216–30. ———. *Situation du Christ, Hébreux 1–2.* LD 58. Paris: Cerf, 1969. ———. *Structure and Message of the Epistle to the Hebrews.* Rome: Pontificio Instituto Biblico, 1989. ———. *A Structured Translation of the Epistle to the Hebrews.* Tr. J. Swetnam. Rome: Pontifical Biblical Institute, 1964. ———. "La structure centrale de l'Épître aux Hébreux (Héb 8/1–9/28)." *RSR* 47 (1959) 44–60. ———. *La structure littéraire de l'Épître aux Hébreux.* 2nd ed. StudNeot 1. Paris/Bruges: Desclée de Brouwer, 1976. **Vansant, A. C.** "The Humanity of Jesus in the Epistle to the Hebrews." Dissertation, Southern Baptist Theological Seminary, 1951. **Venard, L.** "L'utilisation des Psaumes dans l'Épître aux Hébreux." In *FS E. Podechard.* Lyons: Faculté Catholique, 1945. **Viard, A.** "Le salut par la foi dans l'Épître aux Hébreux." *Ang* 58 (1981) 115–36. **Vis, A.** *The Messianic Psalm Quotations in the New Testament.* Amsterdam: Hertberger, 1936. **Vitti, A. M.** "Le bellezze stilistiche nella Lettera agli Ebrei." *Bib* 7 (1936) 137–66. ———. "La lettera agli Ebrei." *RivB* 3 (1955) 289–310. ———. "Il sacerdozio di Gesù Cristo." In *Conferenze Bibliche.* Rome: Pontifical Biblical Institute, 1934. ———. "Ultimi studi sulla Lettera agli Ebrei." *Bib* 22 (1941) 412–32. **Vos, G.** "Hebrews—the Epistle of the *Diathēkē*." *PTR* 13 (1915) 587–632; 14 (1916) 1–61. ———. "The Priesthood of Christ in the Epistle to the Hebrews." *PTR* 4 (1907) 423–47, 579–604. ———. *The Teaching of the Epistle to the Hebrews.* Ed. and rev. J. Vos. Grand Rapids: Eerdmans, 1956. **Voulgaris, C. H.** *Η ΠΡΟΣ ΕΒΡΑΙΟΥΣ ΕΠΙΣΤΟΛΗ: ΠΕΡΙΣΤΑΤΙΚΑ, ΠΑΡΑΛΗΠΤΑΙ, ΣΥΓΓΡΑΦΕΥΣ, ΤΟΠΟΣ ΚΑΙ ΧΡΟΝΟΣ ΣΥΓΓΡΑΦΗΣ.* Athens: University of Athens, 1986. **Vuyst, J. de.** *"Oud en nieuw Verbond" in de Brief aan de Hebreeën.* Kampen: Kok, 1964. **Waal, C. van der.** "The 'People of God' in the Epistle to the Hebrews." *Neot* 5 (1971) 83–92. **Waddell, H. C.** "The Readers of the Epistle to the Hebrews." *Exp* 8th ser. 26 (1923) 88–105. **Walden, H. E.** "The Christology of the Epistle to the Hebrews." Dissertation, Southern Baptist Theological Seminary, 1944. **Warfield, B. B.** "Christ Our Sacrifice." In *The Person and Work of Christ.* Ed. S. G. Craig. Philadelphia: Presbyterian and Reformed, 1950. 391–426. **Watson, J. K.** "L'Épître aux Hébreux." *CCER* 15 (1968) 10–16. ———. "L'Épître aux Hébreux et l'historicité." *CCER* 20 (1972) 1–13. **Webster, J. H.** "The Epistle to the Hebrews." *BSac* 85 (1928) 347–60. **Wengst, K.** *Christologische Formeln und Lieder des Urchristentums.* SNT 7. Gütersloh: Bertelsmann, 1972. **Wenschkewitz, H.** "Die Spiritualisierung der Kultusbegriffe Tempel, Priester und Opfer im Neuen Testament." *Angelos* 4 (1932) 70–230. **Werner, E.** *The Sacred Bridge.* London: Dobson, 1959. **Wette, W. M. L. de.** "Über die symbolisch-typische Lehrart des Briefes an die Hebräer." *TZ* 3 (1822) 1–51. **Whitley, W. T.** "The Epistle to the Hebrews." *RevExp* 3 (1906) 214–29. **Wiefel, W.** "The Jewish Community in Ancient Rome and the Origins of Roman Christianity." In *The Romans Debate.* Ed. K. P. Dornfried. Minneapolis: Augsburg, 1977. **Wikgren, A.** "Patterns of Perfection in the Epistle to the Hebrews." *NTS* 6 (1959–60) 159–67. ———. "Some Greek Idioms in the Epistle to the Hebrews." In *The Teacher's Yoke.* FS H. Trantham. Ed. E. J. Vardaman and J. L. Garrett. Waco, TX: Baylor UP, 1964. **Williams, A. H.** "An Early Christology: A Systematic and Exegetical Investigation of the Traditions Contained in Hebrews." Dissertation, Mainz, 1971. **Williams, S. K.** *Jesus' Death as Saving Event: The Background and Origin of a Concept.* HDR 2. Missoula, MT: Scholars, 1975. **Williamson, R.** "The Background to the Epistle to the Hebrews." *ExpTim* 87 (1975–76) 232–37. ———. "The Eucharist and the Epistle to the Hebrews." *NTS* 21 (1974–75) 300–12. ———. "Hebrews and Doctrine." *ExpTim* 81 (1969–70) 371–76. ———. *Philo and the Epistle to the Hebrews.* ALGHJ 4. Leiden: Brill, 1970. ———. "Philo and New Testament Christology." In *Studia Biblica 1978* III. JSNTSup 3. Sheffield: JSOT Press, 1980. 439–45. ———. "Platonism and Hebrews." *SJT* 16 (1963) 415–24. **Willis, C. G.** "St. Augustine's Text of the Epistle to the Hebrews." *SP* 6 (1962) 543–47. **Wilson, R. McL.** "Coptisms in the Epistle to the Hebrews?" *NovT* 1 (1956) 322–24. **Winter, A.** "*ἅπαξ, ἐφάπαξ* im Hebräerbrief." Dissertation, Rome, 1960. **Worden, T.** "Before Reading the Epistle to the Hebrews." *Scr* 14 (1962) 48–57. **Worley, D. R.** "God's Faithfulness to Promise: The Hortatory Use of Commissive Language in Hebrews." Dissertation, Yale University, 1981. **Wrede, W.** *Das literarische Rätsel des Hebräerbriefs.* FRLANT 8. Göttingen: Vandenhoeck & Ruprecht, 1906. **Yadin, Y.** *The Art of Warfare in Biblical Lands in the Light of Archaeological Study.* 2 vols. Tr. M. Pearlman. New York: McGraw-Hill, 1963. ———. "The Dead Sea Scrolls and the Epistle to the Hebrews." *ScrHier* 4 (1958) 36–55. **Young, F. M.** "Christological Ideas in the Greek Commentaries on the Epistle to the Hebrews." *JTS* 20 (1969) 150–63. ———. *Sacrifice and the Death of Christ.* London: SPCK, 1975. ———. "The Use of Sacrificial Ideas in Greek Christian Writers from the New Testament to John Chrysostom." Dissertation, Cambridge University, 1967. **Young, J. A.** "The Significance of Sacrifice in the Epistle to the Hebrews." Dissertation, Southwestern Baptist Theological Seminary, 1963. **Zedda, S.** *Lettera agli Ebrei: Versione, introduzione, note.* Rome: Edizioni Paoline, 1967. **Zerwick, M.** *Biblical Greek, Illustrated by Examples.* Tr. J. Smith. Rome: Pontifical Biblical Institute, 1963. ——— and **Grosvenor, M.** *A Grammatical Analysis of the Greek New Testament.* Vol. 2: *Epistles-Apocalypse.* Rome: Pontifical Biblical Institute, 1979. **Zimmer, F.** *Exegetische Probleme des Hebräer- und Galaterbriefes.* Hildburghausen: Gradow, 1882. **Zimmermann, H.** *Das Bekenntnis der Hoffnung: Tradition und Redaktion im Hebräerbrief.* BBB 47. Cologne/Bonn: Hanstein, 1977. ———. *Die Hohepriester-Christologie des Hebräerbriefes.* Paderborn: F. Schöningh, 1964. ———. *Neutestamentliche Methodenlehre: Darstellung der historische-kritischen Methode.* 7th ed. Stuttgart: Katholisches Bibelwerk, 1982. **Zorn, R.** "Die Fürbitte und Interzession im Spätjudentum und im Neuen Testament." Dissertation, Göttingen, 1957. **Zuntz, G.** *The Text of the Epistles: A Disquisition upon the 'Corpus Paulinum.'* Schweich Lectures, 1946. London: The British Academy, 1953. **Zupez, J.** "Salvation in the Epistle to the Hebrews." *TBT* 37 (1968) 2590–95.

Introduction

Hebrews is a delight for the person who enjoys puzzles. Its form is unusual, its setting in life is uncertain, and its argument is unfamiliar. It invites engagement in the task of defining the undefined. Undefined are the identity of the writer, his conceptual background, the character and location of the community addressed, the circumstances and date of composition, the setting in life, the nature of the crisis to which the document is a response, the literary genre, and the purpose and plan of the work. Although these undefined issues continue to be addressed and debated vigorously, no real consensus has been reached.

As long as there are texts, there will be the challenge of reconstructing history from them, and historical methodology is the only rational means by which this can be done. Historical intuition is an essential element in the task of reconstruction. Nowhere is this more true than in the case of Hebrews. Hebrews is distinctive in form and complex in literary structure. The tradition concerning its authorship, purpose, and intended audience is conflicting and unreliable. The evidence provided by the text itself is open to divergent interpretations. These facts constitute a continual reminder that every statement about Hebrews is a personal synthesis, an interpretive statement. Interpretation calls for humility. Any critical reconstruction must be proposed as tentative and exploratory in nature.

The purpose of this Introduction is to address the undefined issues in the light of patient interaction with the text and with the discussion it has prompted over the course of the centuries, and more particularly during the last decades. The synthesis supported by the commentary is that Hebrews is a sermon rooted in actual life. It is addressed to a local gathering of men and women who discovered that they could be penetrated by adverse circumstances over which they exercised no control. It throbs with an awareness of the privilege and the cost of discipleship. It is a sensitive pastoral response to the sagging faith of older and tired individuals who were in danger of relinquishing their Christian commitment. It seeks to strengthen them in the face of a new crisis so that they may stand firm in their faith. It warns them of the judgment of God they would incur if they were to waver in their commitment. Exhortations to covenant fidelity and perseverance are grounded in a fresh understanding of the significance of Jesus and his sacrifice. As high priestly Son of God in solidarity with the human family, he is the supreme exemplar of faithfulness to God and endurance, whose sacrificial death secured for his people unlimited access to God and the assurance of the help that arrives at the right time.

The Writer

Bibliography

Albani, J. "Hebr. v,11–vi,8: Ein Wort zur Verfasserschaft des Apollos." *ZWT* 47 (1904) 88–93.
Anderson, C. P. "Hebrews among the Letters of Paul." *SR* 5 (1975–76) 258–66. ———.

"Who Wrote 'The Epistle From Laodicea'?" *JBL* 85 (1966) 436–40. **Appel, H.** *Der Hebräerbrief: Ein Schreiben des Apollos an Judenchristen der korinthischen Gemeinde.* Leipzig: Deichert, 1918. **Ayles, H. H. B.** *Destination, Date and Authorship of the Epistle to the Hebrews.* London: Clay, 1899. **Barnes, A. S.** "St. Barnabas and the Epistle to the Hebrews." *HibJ* 30 (1931–32) 103–17. **Bartlet, V.** "Barnabas and His Genuine Epistle." *Exp* 6th ser. 6 (1902) 28–30. ———. "The Epistle to the Hebrews as the Work of Barnabas." *Exp* 6th ser. 8 (1903) 381–86. **Bates, W. H.** "Authorship of the Epistle to the Hebrews Again." *BSac* 79 (1922) 93–96. **Batiffol, P.** "L'attribution de l'Épître aux Hébreux à S. Barnabé." *RB* 8 (1899) 278–83. **Biesenthal, J. H. R.** *Das Trostschreiben des Apostels Paulus an die Hebräer.* Leipzig: Fernau, 1878. **Bornhäuser, K. B.** *Empfänger und Verfasser des Briefes an die Hebräer.* BFCT 35/3. Gütersloh: Bertelsmann, 1932. **Bover, J. M.** "Inspiración divina del redactor de la Epistola a los Hebreos." *EE* 14 (1935) 433–66. **Brown, J. V.** "The Authorship and Circumstances of 'Hebrews'—Again!" *BSac* 80 (1923) 505–38. **Campos, J.** "A Carta aos Hebreus como Apolo ã superasão de 'Certa Religiosidade Popular.'" *RCB* 8 (1984) 122–24. **Chapman, J.** "Aristion, Author of the Epistle to the Hebrews." *RBén* 22 (1905) 50–64. **Collins, R. F.** *Letters that Paul Did Not Write: The Epistle to the Hebrews and the Pauline Pseudepigrapha.* Wilmington, DE: Glazier, 1988. **Dibelius, F.** *Der Verfasser des Hebräerbrief: Eine Untersuchung zur Geschichte des Urchristentums.* Strassburg: Heitz & Mundel, 1910. **Dubarle, A. M.** "Rédacteur et destinataires de l'Épître aux Hébreux." *RB* 48 (1939) 506–29. **Eagar, A. R.** "The Authorship of the Epistle to the Hebrews." *Exp* 6th ser. 10 (1904) 74–80, 110–23. **Ford, J. M.** "The Mother of Jesus and the Authorship of the Epistle to the Hebrews." *TBT* 82 (1976) 683–94. **Gardiner, F.** "The Language of the Epistle to the Hebrews as Bearing upon Its Authorship." *JBL* 7 (1887) 1–25. **Harnack, A.** "Probabilia über die Adresse und den Verfasser des Hebräerbriefs." *ZNW* 1 (1900) 16–41. **Harris, J. R.** "Side-Lights on the Authorship of the Epistle to the Hebrews." In *Side-Lights on New Testament Research.* London: Kingsgate, 1908. **Heigl, B.** *Verfasser und Adresse des Briefes an die Hebräer: Eine Studie zur neutestamentlichen Einleitung.* Freiburg i/B.: Wagner, 1905. **Herrmann, L.** "Apollos." *RSR* 50 (1976) 330–36. **Hoppin, R.** *Priscilla: Author of the Epistle to the Hebrews, and Other Essays.* New York: Exposition, 1969. **Hunter, A. M.** "Apollos the Alexandrian." In *Biblical Studies.* FS W. Barclay. Ed. J. R. McKay and J. F. Miller. Philadelphia: Westminster, 1976. 147–56. **Hurst, L. D.** "Apollos, Hebrews, and Corinth: Bishop Montefiore's Theory Examined." *SJT* 38 (1985) 505–13. **Kallenbach, W. D.** *The Message and Authorship of the Epistle "to the Hebrews."* St. Paul, MN: Northland, 1938. **Kirby, V. T.** "The Authorship of the Epistle to the Hebrews." *ExpTim* 35 (1923–24) 375–76. **Kuss, O.** "Der Verfasser des Hebräerbriefes als Seelsorger." *TTZ* 67 (1958) 1–12, 65–80. **Legg, J. D.** "Our Brother Timothy: A Suggested Solution to the Problem of the Authorship of the Epistle to the Hebrews." *EvQ* 40 (1968) 220–23. **Leonard, W.** *The Authorship of the Epistle to the Hebrews: Critical Problem and Use of the Old Testament.* London/Vatican: Polyglott, 1939. **Lo Bue, F.** "The Historical Background of the Epistle to the Hebrews." *JBL* 75 (1956) 52–57. **Maeso, D. G.** "Lengua original, autor y estilo de la epístola a los Hebreos." *CB* 13 (1956) 202–15. **Manson, T. W.** "The Problem of the Epistle to the Hebrews." *BJRL* 32 (1949) 1–17. **Méchineau, L.** *L'Epistola agli Ebrei secondo le risposte della Commissione Biblica.* Rome: Pontifical Biblical Commission, 1917. **Medico, M. dal.** *L'auteur de l'épître aux Hébreux.* Rome: Pontifical Biblical Institute, 1914. **Mora, G.** *La Carta a los Hebreos como Escrito Pastoral.* Barcelona: Herder, 1974. **Obiols, S.** *Epístoles de Sant Pau: Als Hebreus.* Montserrat: Monestir de Montserrat, 1930. **Perdelwitz, R.** "Das literarische Problem des Hebräerbriefs: 1. Der literarische Charakter des Schreiben. 2. Der Verfasser. 3. Die Addressaten." *ZNW* 11 (1910) 59–78, 105–23. **Peterson, D. G.** "The Ministry of Encouragement." In *God Who Is Rich in Mercy.* FS D. B. Knox. Ed. P. T. O'Brien and D. G. Peterson. Honebush West, NSW: Lancer, 1986. 235–53. **Plumptre, E. H.** "The Writings of Apollos." *Exp* n.s. 1 (1885) 329–48, 409–35. **Ramsay, W. M.** "The Date and Authorship of the Epistle to the Hebrews." *ExpTim* 5 (1899) 401–22. **Schiele, F. M.** "Harnack's 'Probabilia' Concerning the Address and the Author of the Epistle to the Hebrews." *AJT* 9 (1905) 290–308. **Schröger, F.** "Der Hebräerbrief—paulinisch?" in *Kontinuität und Einheit.* FS F. Mussner. Ed. P. G. Müller &

W. Stenger. Freiburg/Basel/Vienna: Herder, 1981. 211–22. **Spicq, C.** "L'Épître aux Hébreux, Apollos, Jean-Baptiste, les Hellénistes et Qumran." *RevQ* 1 (1959) 365–90. **Suarez, P. L.** "Cesarea y la Epistola 'ad Hebreos.'" In *Studiorum Paulinorum Congressus Internationalis Catholicus 1961.* AnBib 18. Rome: Pontifical Biblical Institute, 1963. 2:169–74. **Thayer, J. H.** "Authorship and Canonicity of the Epistle to the Hebrews." *BSac* 24 (1867) 681–722. **Torrey, C. C.** "The Authorship and Character of the So-Called 'Epistle to the Hebrews.'" *JBL* 30 (1911) 137–56. **Tucker, M. A. R.** "The Gospel according to Prisca." *NC* 73 (1913) 81–98.

The limits of historical knowledge preclude positive identification of the writer. No firm tradition concerning his identity exists from the earliest period. He was clearly known to the community to whom he wrote (13:19). The brief personal notes in chap. 13, however, are not sufficiently specific to establish his identity. While the use of the masculine pronoun in referring to the writer is advisable in the light of the formulation in 11:32, Hebrews is anonymous.

Although the writer is presumably within the Pauline circle and expects to travel with Timothy "our brother" (13:23), it is certain that he is not Paul, but one who numbered himself among those to whom the immediate hearers of the Lord had delivered the gospel (2:3–4). The language of Hebrews constitutes the finest Greek in the NT, far superior to the Pauline standard both in vocabulary and sentence-building (cf. N. Turner, "The Style of the Epistle to the Hebrews," in *Grammar*, 4:106–13; Wikgren, "Some Greek Idioms," 145–53). The writer's use of imagery is also distinctive: a ship missing the harbor (2:1), an anchor gripping the seabed (6:19), a double-edged sword that penetrates and divides the inmost faculties of the soul (4:12), a wrestler hopelessly exposed in a headlock (4:13), fields richly watered by rain and producing useful crops or worthless weeds (6:7–8). All of these images are foreign to Pauline usage. The writer moves confidently within the conceptual world of cultic concerns centering in priesthood and sacrifice. Many of the emphases of Hebrews are alien to those of Paul.

In antiquity, the names of Paul, Barnabas, Luke, and Clement of Rome were mentioned in certain church centers as the author of Hebrews. In current scholarship, Apollos, Silvanus, the deacon Philip, Priscilla and Aquila, Jude, Aristion, and others have found their proponents (for useful surveys of the older primary sources and the more recent proposals of scholars, see Attridge, 1–6; D. Guthrie, *New Testament Introduction*[4], 668–82). This divergence underscores the impossibility of establishing the writer's identity. All that can be said with certainty is that Hebrews was composed by a creative theologian who was well trained in the exposition of the Greek Scriptures. For the writer, "formative" Judaism was hellenistic Judaism. He was thoroughly familiar with the refined style, language, traditions, and theological conceptions of hellenistic Judaism, but he was also informed by the theology of the hellenistic Church. He was surely a hellenistic Jewish-Christian.

From the composition of Hebrews it is possible to draw a number of plausible inferences about the writer. He possessed an architectural mind; he affirms a thesis and then develops it by way of analysis. (On his exceptional reasoning power, cf. W. C. Linss, "Logical Terminology in the Epistle to the Hebrews," *CTM* 37 [1966] 365–69.) For example, in the opening period (Heb 1:1–4) the accent falls upon God who intervened in human history through his sovereign word. He is the God who speaks. The revelation granted through the prophets is summarized with reference to its variety and fullness (1:1). He uttered his ultimate and decisive word through the Son (1:2*a*). The majestic opening statement of Hebrews is programmatic for the entire discourse: God spoke! As the argument unfolds, it is alternatively God, the Son, the Holy Spirit who speaks. The several strands of the development are then taken up and reaffirmed in a final climactic warning: "Be careful that you do not disregard the one who is speaking" (12:25).

The manner in which the writer structures his material for maximum effect lends credence to the supposition that he was formally trained in rhetoric (see below, "Rhetorical Analysis"). He understood speech as a means and medium of power. He appreciated speech as agonistic and used it effectively in the service of the Jewish Christian mission. He was prepared to entrust the power of speech to the written text as a tool of advocacy. The voice of the text is uttered as a response to other voices distracting the community from its devotion to God and to the assembly.

The writer's rhetorical skill is universally recognized. C. Spicq has compiled an impressive list of stylistic features and rhetorical devices that are to be found in Hebrews (1:351–78). The author possessed a rich vocabulary and cultured diction. Of the total of 4,942 words in Hebrews, the writer uses 1,038 different words; of that number, 169 are found only in Hebrews in the NT (Morgenthaler, *Statistik,* 164).

The writer was evidently well educated by hellenistic standards. It is reasonable to assume a similar educational background to that enjoyed by Philo. He almost certainly had enjoyed the advantages of training in a gymnasium or a private rhetorical school (on primary and secondary levels of education in Alexandria, for example, where rhetorical training flourished in the Roman period, see R. W. Smith, *The Art of Rhetoric in Alexandria,* 110–54; cf. H. I. Marrou, *A History of Education in Antiquity* [London: Sheed & Ward, 1956] 232–42). It is, perhaps, natural to recall Luke's description of the Alexandrian, Apollos, as an ἀνὴρ λόγιος, "an eloquent man" (Acts 18:24), a designation clearly associated with rhetorical training (cf. E. Orth, *Logios* [Leipzig: Teubner, 1926] 46, who states that Luke's expression signifies a scholar with rhetorical ability). Philo uses the identical expression to refer to those with rhetorical training (e.g., *On the Posterity and Exile of Cain* 53; *On the Embassy to Gaius* 142, 237, 310; *Life of Moses* 1.2; on this and related terms with clear rhetorical connotations in Acts 18:24–28, see now B. W. Winter, "Philo and Paul among the Sophists," Dissertation, Macquarrie University, North Ryde, NSW, 1989, 183–85). The appropriateness of this description to the writer to the Hebrews explains the popularity of the suggestion that Hebrews was actually written by Apollos.

The writer may be characterized as an intensely religious man. For him Christianity is an expression of God's new cultic action. W. G. Johnsson has suggested that cultic categories were ingrained in the subconscious mind of the writer, so that he argues spontaneously from cultic presuppositions such as "blood" as a medium of purgation. He is steeped in the cultic language of the LXX. Moreover, he lived in a society where cults and cultic sacrifice were common and in which "structures" of thought such as those of defilement, blood, and purgation were the common property of devoutly religious persons. The sustained references to the Jewish cultus and the conspicuous absence of any reference to pagan sacrifices reflect his Jewish background (Johnsson, "Defilement," 443–44).

Hebrews proves to be a unique blend of christology and primitive Christian eschatology within a cultic frame of reference. With the writer's focus upon the realization of the promised eschatological blessings of the new covenant through the sacrificial accomplishment of Christ, the discourse he prepared becomes a vehicle for challenging exhortation.

The writer, finally, was a pastoral theologian who adapted early Christian traditions to fashion an urgent appeal to a community in crisis (cf. O. Kuss, *TTZ* 67 [1958] 1–12, 65–80; Mora, *La Carta*). He was a gifted preacher and interpreter of salvation history for his own community. Human insight disciplined by the Spirit of God, scriptural exegesis, and situational discernment all play a role in the crafting of a communication for concrete encouragement, admonition, and pastoral direction. The writer of Hebrews can be described, as in fact Irenaeus was described by fellow Christians in the churches of Lyon and Vienne in A.D. 177 in a letter of recommendation to Eleutherus, the bishop of Rome, as "zealous for the covenant of Christ" (ζηλωτὴν ὄντα τῆς διαθήκης Χριστοῦ; Eusebius, *Church History*, 5.4.2). He appears to have been a charismatic leader who led by force of mind and personality rather than by virtue of an office or title.

It is as a substitute for personal action that the writer prepared his discourse. In Hebrews we are in the presence of a writer who at best wrote reluctantly and whose preference was to speak directly with those to whom circumstances forced him to address his "word of exhortation" (13:22). In reading and reflecting upon Hebrews, it is necessary to recognize the sense in which the statement in the discourse is fragmentary with respect to its representation of the writer as he would have been known by his contemporaries.

Intended Audience

Bibliography

Aguirre, R. "La casa como estructura base del christianismo primitivo: las iglesias domésticas." *EE* 59 (1984) 27–51. **Anderson, C. P.** "Who Wrote 'The Epistle From Laodicea'?" *JBL* 85 (1966) 436–40. **Andriessen, P.** "La communauté des 'Hébreux': était-elle tombée dans le relâchment?" *NRT* 106 (1974) 1054–66. **Appel, H.** *Der Hebräerbrief: Ein Schreiben des Apollos an Judenchristen der korinthischen Gemeinde.* Leipzig: Deichert, 1918. **Attridge, H. W.** "Paraenesis in a Homily (λόγος παρακλήσεως): The Possible Location of, and Socialization in, the 'Epistle to the Hebrews.'" *Semeia* 50 (1990) 211–26. **Ayles, H. H. B.** *Destination, Date, and Authorship of the Epistle to the Hebrews.* London: Clay, 1899. ———. "The References to Persecution in the Epistle to the Hebrews." *Exp* 8th ser. 12 (1916) 69–74. **Badcock, F. J.** *The Pauline Epistles and the Epistle to the Hebrews in Their Historical Setting.* London: SPCK, 1937. **Banks, R.** *Paul's Idea of Community: The Early House Churches in Their Historical Setting.* Grand Rapids: Eerdmans, 1980. **Bornhäuser, K.** *Empfänger und Verfasser des Briefes an die Hebräer.* BFCT 35/3. Gütersloh: Bertelsmann, 1932. **Bornkamm, G.** *Early Christian Experience.* New York: Harper & Row, 1969, 123–93. **Brown, J. V.** "The Authorship and Circumstances of 'Hebrews'—Again!" *BSac* 80 (1923) 505–38. **Bruce, F. F.** "Paul and Roman Christianity." In *Paul: Apostle of the Heart Set Free.* Grand Rapids: Eerdmans, 1977. 379–92. ———. "'To the Hebrews': A Document of Roman Christianity?" *ANRW* 25.4 (1987) 3496–3521. **Bullock, M. R.** "The Recipients and Destination of Hebrews." Dissertation, Dallas Theological Seminary, 1977. **Dahms, J. V.** "The First Readers of Hebrews." *JETS* 20

(1977) 365–75. **Dibelius, M.** "Rom und die Christen im ersten Jahrhundert." In *Botschaft und Geschichte.* Ed. G. Bornkamm. Tübingen: Mohr, 1956. 2:177–228. **Dubarle, A. M.** "Rédacteur et destinataires de l'Épître aux Hébreux." *RB* 48 (1939) 506–29. **Elliott, J. H.** "Patronage and Clientism in Early Christian Society: A Short Reading Guide." *Forum* 3 (1987) 39–48. **Filson, F. V.** "The Significance of the Early House Church." *JBL* 58 (1939) 105–12. **Ford, J. M.** "The First Epistle to the Corinthians or the First Epistle to the Hebrews." *CBQ* 28 (1966) 402–16. **Frey, J. B.** "L'Ancien Judaïsme, specialement à Rome, d'après les inscriptions juives." In *Corpus Inscriptionum Judaicarum.* Rome: Pontificio Instituto di Archeologia Cristiana, 1936. liii–cxliii. ———. "Le Judaïsme à Rome aux premiers temps de l'Église." *Bib* 12 (1931) 129–56. **Goguel, M.** "La second géneration chrétienne." *RHR* 136 (1949) 31–57, 180–208. **Grass, K. K.** *1st der Brief an die Hebräer an Heidenchristen gerichtet?* St. Petersburg: Köhne, 1892. **Harnack, A.** "Probabilia über die Adresse und den Verfasser des Hebräerbriefs." *ZNW* 1 (1900) 16–41. **Heigl, B.** *Verfasser und Adresse des Briefes an die Hebräer. Eine Studie zur neutestamentlichen Einleitung.* Freiburg i/B.: Wagner, 1905. **Herrmann, L.** "L'épître aux (Laodicéens et l'apologie aux) Hébreux." *CCER* 15 (1968) 1–16. **Hurst, L. D.** "Apollos, Hebrews, and Corinth: Bishop Montefiore's Theory Examined." *SJT* 38 (1985) 505–13. **Judge, E. A.** *The Conversion of Rome: Ancient Sources of Modern Social Tensions.* North Ryde, NSW: Macquarrie Ancient History Association, 1980. ———. *The Social Pattern of Christian Groups in the First Century.* London: Tyndale, 1950. ——— and **Thomas, G. S. R.** "The Origin of the Church at Rome: A New Solution?" *RTR* 25 (1966) 81–94. **Klauck, H. J.** *Hausgemeinde und Hauskirche im frühen Christentum.* Stuttgart: Katholische Bibelwerk, 1981. **Knoch, O.** "Die frühe Kirche als Familie Gottes: Gedanken zur Erneuerung christliches Gemeinschaft." *GuL* 60 (1987) 375–79. **Kraabel, A. T.** "Jews in Imperial Rome: More Archaeological Evidence from an Oxford Collection." *JJS* 30 (1978–79) 41–58. **Kuss, O.** "Der Verfasser des Hebräerbriefes als Seelsorger." *TTZ* 67 (1958) 1–12, 65–80. **Lane, W. L.** "Hebrews: A Sermon in Search of a Setting." *SWJT* 28 (1985) 13–18. **Leon, H. J.** "The Jews of Rome in the First Centuries of Christianity." In *The Teacher's Yoke: Studies in Memory of Henry Trantham.* Ed. E. J. Vardaman and J. L. Garrett. Waco, TX: Baylor University Press, 1964. 154–63. **Lewis, T. W.** "'. . . And if he shrinks back' (Heb X.38*b*)." *NTS* 22 (1975–76) 88–94. ———. "The Theological Logic in Hebrews 10:19–12:29 and the Appropriation of the Old Testament." Dissertation, Drew University, 1965. **Lo Bue, F.** "The Historical Background of the Epistle to the Hebrews." *JBL* 75 (1956) 52–57. **Lorenzen, T.** "Das christliche Hauskirche." *TZ* 43 (1987) 332–52. **Malherbe, A. J.** *Social Aspects of Early Christianity*[2]. Philadelphia: Fortress, 1983. **Manson, T. W.** "The Problem of the Epistle to the Hebrews." *BJRL* 32 (1949) 1–17. **Milligan, G.** "The Roman Destination of the Epistle to the Hebrews." *Exp* 6th ser. 4 (1901) 437–48. **Monod, V.** *De titulo epistolae vulgo ad Hebraeos inscriptae.* Montalbani: Grané, 1910. **Mora, G.** *La Carta a los Hebreos como Escrito Pastoral.* Barcelona: Herder, 1974. 69–118. **Murphy-O'Conner, J.** *St. Paul's Corinth: Texts and Archaeology.* Wilmington, DE: Glazier, 1983. 153–61. **Murray, R.** "Jews, Hebrews and Christians: Some Needed Distinctions." *NovT* 24 (1982) 194–208. **Nauck, W.** "Freude im Leiden: Zum Problem der urchristlichen Verfolgungstradition." *ZNW* 46 (1955) 68–80. **Nestle, E.** "On the Address of the Epistle to the Hebrews." *ExpTim* 10 (1898–99) 422. **Penna, R.** "Les Juifs à Rome au temps de l'Apôtre Paul." *NTS* 28 (1982) 321–47. **Perdelwitz, R.** "Das literarische Problem des Hebräerbriefs: 1. Der literarische Charakter des Schreiben. 2. Der Verfasser. 3. Die Adressaten." *ZNW* 11 (1910) 59–78, 105–23. **Peterson, J. M.** "House-churches in Rome." *VC* 23 (1969) 264–72. ———. "Some Titular Churches at Rome with Traditional New Testament Connexions." *ExpTim* 84 (1973) 277–79. **Piana, G. la.** "Foreign Groups in Rome during the First Centuries of the Empire." *HTR* 20 (1927) 183–403. **Pitigliani, L.** "A Rare Look at Jewish Catacombs in Rome." *BAR* 6 (1980) 32–43. **Quentel, J.** "Les destinataires de l'Épître aux Hébreux." *RB* 9 (1912) 50–68. **Ritschl, A.** "Über die Leser des Hebräerbriefs." *TSK* 39 (1866) 89–102. **Robinson, J. A. T.** *Redating the New Testament.* London: SCM, 1976. 200–220. **Sampley, J. P.** *Pauline Partnership in Christ: Christian Community and Commitment in the Light of Roman Law.* Philadelphia: Fortress, 1981. 51–115. **Sandegren,**

C. "The Addressees of the Epistle to the Hebrews." *EvQ* 27 (1955) 221–24. **Sanford, C. J.** "The Addressees of Hebrews." Dissertation, Dallas Theological Seminary, 1962. **Schiele, F. M.** "Harnack's 'Probabilia' concerning the Address and the Author of the Epistle to the Hebrews." *AJT* 9 (1905) 290–308. **Scott, E. F.** "The Epistle to the Hebrews and Roman Christianity." *HTR* 13 (1930) 205–19. **Shuster, I.** "I destinatari dell' epistola agli Ebrei." *ScC* 66 (1938) 641–65. **Theobald, M.** "'Wir haben hier keine bleibende Stadt, sonder suchen die zukünftige' (Hebr 13:14): Die Stadt als Ort der frühen christliche Gemeinde." *TGl* 78 (1988) 16–40. **Vanhoye, A.** *Homilie für haltbedürftige Christen: Struktur und Botschaft des Hebräerbriefes.* Regensburg: Pustet, 1981. **Vogler, W.** "Die Bedeutung der urchristlichen Hausgemeinden für die Ausbreitung des Evangeliums." *TLZ* 107 (1982) 785–94. **Waddell, H. C.** "The Readers of the Epistle to the Hebrews." *Exp* 8th ser. 26 (1923) 88–105. **White, L. M.** "Domus Ecclesiae—Domus Dei: Adaptation and Development in the Setting for Early Christian Assembly." Dissertation, Yale University, 1982. **Wiefel, W.** "The Jewish Community in Ancient Rome and the Origins of Roman Christianity." In *The Romans Debate.* Ed. K. P. Donfried. Minneapolis: Augsburg, 1977. 100–119.

A reconstruction of the life situation that makes Hebrews intelligible must be advanced tentatively as a working proposal. The evidence to be gathered from the document itself is ambiguous and open to divergent interpretations. The concern to establish a social and historical context for an early Christian communication is, nevertheless, legitimate. It is my concern to situate the document within its context in life. Methodologically, the initial step toward establishing a social context for Hebrews must be the sketching of a profile of the audience addressed on the basis of the detail of the text itself.

PROFILE OF THE AUDIENCE

The communication in Hebrews was prepared for a specific local group, who are distinguished from their leaders and from others with whom they form a Christian presence in that social setting (13:17, 24). The assumption that they are located in an urban setting is supported by the insistence that "here we do not have a permanent city" (13:14) as well as by the range and focus of the parenetic concerns expressed in 13:1–6. The extension of hospitality to Christian travelers unknown to them (13:2), the identification with those in prison and with other Christians who have suffered from ill treatment (13:3), a concern for the sanctity of marriage and for sexual responsibility (13:4), and the caution against greed and subversion through crass materialism (13:5–6) are natural and appropriate to an urban setting.

The intended audience was almost certainly a house church, one of several scattered throughout the different districts and sections of the city. The early Christians met in ordinary rooms in private houses. They are undoubtedly a small group, consisting of the members of a household and some of their associates and close friends. They number, perhaps, no more than fifteen or twenty persons (cf. Banks, *Paul's Idea of Community*, 41–42; Murphy-O'Connor, *St. Paul's Corinth*, 153–61). Although they had experienced a sense of identity and intimacy through participation in the fellowship of a household group, their numbers had been depleted through defections (10:25). The description of the church as the "house" of God (3:6*b*; 10:21) in Hebrews may be intentional in its implied reference to the gathering of the house church.

The social and religious roots of this community are almost certainly to be traced to the Jewish quarters and to participation in the life of a hellenistic synagogue. Several lines of evidence tend to support this deduction. Their source of authority is the Bible in an old Greek version, especially where its textual tradition is distinguished from the Hebrew text. They have an easy familiarity with the stories of the Bible, to which the writer can refer without elaboration (cf. 12:17, "for you know . . . ," with reference to the story of Esau, who was deprived of Isaac's blessing). The writer is confident that he can win a hearing for what he wished to say by employing vocabulary sanctioned by the Greek Scriptures.

More substantially, the opening lines of Hebrews, where the writer establishes emotional contact with his audience, introduces the transcendent Son of God in the categories of divine Wisdom (cf. W. L. Lane, "Detecting Divine Wisdom in Hebrews 1:1–4," *NTStud* 5 [1982] 150–58). Within a conceptual frame established by allusions to the royal Son of Ps 2 (1:2b) and to the royal Priest of Ps 110 (1:3c), the Son's role in creation, revelation, and redemption is recited in creedal fashion. The writer's formulation is clearly informed by the hellenistic-Jewish wisdom tradition. The categories of divine Wisdom were apparently current and meaningful for the audience. The concentration of unusual and distinctive vocabulary in 1:3 suggests a group for whom the tradition now frozen in Wis 7:24–27 was normative, whether that tradition circulated orally or in written form. The roots of this Christian assembly are in a Diaspora Judaism that has been significantly influenced by the hellenistic synagogue both in theological conception and vocabulary.

Numerous other details tend to substantiate the view that the members of the house church had been nurtured spiritually and intellectually in the hellenistic synagogue. In Heb 2:2, for example, the writer alludes to the angels as the heavenly mediators of the old revelation. There is no indication in Exod 19 and 20 that angels were present at the giving of the law. In Deut 33:2, however, in a passage celebrating the theophany at Sinai, Moses declares that God came with "myriads of holy ones," and the LXX adds, "angels were with him at his right hand" (cf. Ps 68:17). Sometime prior to the first century, the conviction spread, especially among hellenistic Jews, that angels had played a mediatorial role in the transmission of the law (cf. Acts 7:38, 53; Gal 3:19; Jos., *Ant.* 15.136) The positive role assigned to angels in Heb 2:2 together with the appeal to the normative character of the Mosaic law in Heb 2:2; 9:13; 10:28; and 12:25 tend to suggest that the intended audience continued to maintain intellectual and emotional ties with the hellenistic-Jewish community.

This proposal is congruent with the centrality of Moses in the development of Hebrews (cf. P. R. Jones, *RevExp* 76 [1979] 95–107). It is difficult to exaggerate the significance of Moses in hellenistic Judaism and the veneration with which he was regarded. If reference is restricted to Jewish-hellenistic texts, it is necessary only to recall a passage from *The Exodus* by Ezekiel the Tragedian (preserved by Eusebius, *Preparation for the Gospel* 9.29). Moses is shown in a dream that God will install him on a heavenly throne and invest him with a crown and a scepter as the symbols of his unique authority.

Although Moses is designated a priest only once in the OT (Ps 99:6), his Levitical family background (Exod 2:1–10) and his ministry of the word of God and privileged vision of God (Exod 33:12–34:35; Num 12:7–8), as well as his service at the altar (Exod 24:4–8), associate him with distinctly priestly functions (cf. C. Hauret, "Moïse était-il prêtre?" *Bib* 40 [1959] 509–21). Philo does not hesitate to describe Moses as a high priest (e.g., *The Life of Moses* 2.66–186; *Who is the Heir?* 182; *On Rewards and Punishments* 53, 56). In the hellenistic-Jewish tradition, Moses is the supreme exemplar of perfection in the sense of immediacy and access to God. If such views were the common property of men and women who had been nourished within the hellenistic-Jewish community, this explains why Moses and Jesus are yoked and compared throughout the argument developed in Hebrews (see, for example, *Comment* on 3:1–6; 8:3–5; 12:18–29; 13:20).

The cumulative weight of the evidence points to men and women who participate in a small house fellowship, loosely related to other house churches in an urban setting, whose theological vocabulary and conceptions were informed by the rich legacy of hellenistic Judaism.

PAST STANCE AND PRESENT CRISIS

The writer knew his audience personally and expected to revisit them soon (13:19, 23). At several points he displays a rather intimate knowledge of their past experience (see *Comment* on 2:3–4; 5:11–14; 6:9–11; 10:32–34). He knows, for example, that they had not participated in the original events surrounding Jesus' ministry. They had come to faith in response to the preaching of others who had heard Jesus (2:3). The testimony of these itinerant Christians had been made effective through the contingent witness of God, who endorsed their preaching of salvation with outward, tangible evidence that corroborated its veracity and validity (2:4). The spoken word was complemented by the visible demonstration of the power of the gospel, foreshadowing the completion of redemption (see on 6:5), confirming that the Lord himself continued to speak and act through evangelistic proclamation. Like ancient Israel, the Christian assembly had been constituted by an act of revelation.

Those who first preached the gospel to the community remained with them as their first leaders (see *Comment* on 13:7). The activity of these now deceased leaders was concentrated upon the early period in the life of the house church. Their authority resided solely in the word of salvation which they proclaimed and which God had endorsed with validating evidence (see F. Laub, "Verkündigung und Gemeindeamt: Die Authorität der ἡγούμενοι Hebr 13,7.17.24," *SNTU* 6–7 [1981–82] 171–77).

It is precisely at the point of the community's current response to the word which the former leaders had preached that the writer addresses his audience in 2:1: "We must pay the closest attention, therefore, to what we have heard, so that we do not drift off course." The unit of exhortation in 2:1–4 is the first of a series of smaller or larger sections that address the audience in their present situation (cf. 3:7–4:13; 5:11–6:12; 10:19–39; 12:14–29). These sections, in which the writer pauses to address a warning or an urgent pastoral appeal to the audience, have significant bearing upon the reconstruction of the social and historical setting of Hebrews. They relate the thrust of the message to the audience in a direct way and convey a cumulative impression of the manner in which the writer envisaged the situation to which he responded with such passionate earnestness.

The formulation in 2:1–4, for example, implies that the community had grown lax in their commitment to the Christian message that had secured their initial commitment to the early Christian movement (see *Comment* on 2:1–4). As M. Barth observed from the close connection between the scriptural demonstration of the superiority of the Son to the angels in 1:5–14 and the solemn warning in 2:1–4, "Scripture exposition is for this man not an end in itself. It is a brotherly service to a congregation that is in actual temptation" ("The Old Testament in Hebrews," 57). The temptation was to disregard the claim of the word of God that had been preached to them and the seriousness of Christian commitment, with the consequence that some members of the community were in danger of "drifting off course" (2:1). The source of the distraction is not specified at this point. The intended audience is summoned to appreciate the solemn import of the message of salvation they had received and to reaffirm their positive response to it.

Throughout Hebrews the writer expresses apprehension that the community may falter in its response to the spoken word of God. Significantly, his pastoral concern extends to the individual members of the audience (see *Comment* on 3:12, 13; 4:1, 11; 6:11; 12:15). The suggestion lies close at hand that within the house church there were stronger and weaker members. Some individuals were more prone to the danger of turning away from God than others. The intended audience, apparently, was not monolithic in experience, disposition, or maturity (see *Comment* on 12:13, 15). The admonition to "encourage one another every day" (3:13) may actually presuppose a daily gathering of the household fellowship as the occasion for mutual encouragement (10:25; so Windisch, 31; Michel, 106).

New and significant information about the intended audience is supplied in 5:11–6:12. The importance of this parenetic unit for discerning the historical circumstances that motivated the writing of Hebrews has been generally appreciated. G. Mora, for example, who has investigated Hebrews as a document of pastoral care, describes 5:11–6:12 as "the key text for the interpretation of Hebrews" (*La Carta*, 18; Mora devotes pp. 11–48, 69–118 to this unit). The charge of having become spiritually lethargic in 5:11 resumes the stress on the importance of responsible listening in the previous hortatory sections (2:1; 3:7*b*–8*a*, 15, 4:1–2, 7*b*). It serves to bring those passages directly into the experience of the audience. Implied is a lack of responsiveness to the gospel and an unwillingness to probe the implications of Christian confession and to respond with faith and obedience. If this apathetic disposition was not decisively checked, it could only result in spiritual inertia and the erosion of faith and hope.

The key to the interpretation of 5:12–14 is the recognition of the presence of irony. The rebuke administered in 5:12 may reflect an inclination to withdraw from contact with those outside the group and the loss of certainty which this presupposes. Such a reading of the text is supported by the incidental remark that the audience ought to be the instructors of others, since they have been Christians for an extended period of time. The correlative statement that "you need someone to teach you the elementary truths of God's revelation" is normally taken to be the writer's considered judgment on the actual condition of the community. This understanding, however, is difficult to reconcile with his determination to respond to them as mature believers (see *Comment* on 6:1, 3). The writer's response, "You are at the stage of needing milk, and not solid food" (5:12*b*), is ironical. With biting irony the writer calls the audience to acknowledge their maturity, which has both ethical and theological ramifications for responsible life as Christians in urban society.

The interpretation of 5:13 is contingent upon a proper understanding of the phrase "inexperienced [or, unacquainted] with the teaching about righteousness," or better, "unskilled in the word of righteousness." The expression λόγος δικαιοσύνης, "word of righteousness," is unusually difficult and has evoked a variety of proposals. In this commentary it is argued that a key to the correct interpretation of the expression is provided by Polycarp in his *Letter to the Philippians* 9:1, where this precise phrasing is linked with a call to endurance, as it is in Hebrews. The "word of righteousness" is the paramount lesson in holiness: that Christians must be prepared for the cost of discipleship, even if that cost extends to martyrdom (see *Comment* on 5:13). The phrase "unskilled in the word of righteousness" in Heb 5:13 suggests that it is the threat of renewed humiliation and suffering, perhaps even the violence of martyrdom itself, that has shaped the behavior of the group and the writer's reference to the prospect of crucifying the Son of God again and exposing him to public contempt in 6:4–6.

If this is a correct reading of the text, it can be said that the social history of the audience can be read in terms of its response to humiliation and public abuse. From the beginning, sufferings had been a constituent part of the Christian experience of the house church. In fact, in 10:32–34 the writer is able to make their own past stance of firm commitment to Christ and to one another under the pressure of abuse the paradigm for an appropriate response to new perils in the present and in the immediate future (see below, "The Edict of Claudius"). Perhaps the indelible memory of past suffering, abuse, and loss accounts for the desertion of the community that is frankly acknowledged in 10:25 and for a general inclination to avoid contact with outsiders observed in 5:11–14. The intended audience was experiencing a crisis of faith and a failure of nerve.

T. W. Lewis has suggested that the audience found a scriptural basis for interpreting its lifestyle in terms of withdrawal and concealment in Isa 26:20: "Go, my people, into your rooms and shut the door behind you; hide yourselves for a little while until his wrath has passed" (*NTS* 22 [1975–76] 91–93). The allusion to this biblical quotation in Heb 10:37, where it is significantly qualified by the citation of Hab 2:3–4, together with an explicit reference to God's displeasure with those who withdraw in Heb 10:38–39, lends a measure of support to this attractive proposal.

In 10:32–35 the writer seeks to counter an unhealthy attitude on the part of the audience by setting forth the community's courageous stance of commitment under adverse circumstances in the past as a model for sustained boldness in the present. Drawing upon a primitive Christian tradition designed to strengthen believers in the crisis of persecution (cf. Nauck, *ZNW* 46 [1955] 68–80), the writer applied the tradition to the experience of his intended audience in order to encourage them to emulate their own former loyalty.

This probe for the social context of the intended audience may be given closure with reference to the celebration of the faithfulness of men and women who were exposed to persecution, humiliation, and execution, and who were not delivered through divine intervention (11:35*b*–38). The catalogue of the martyrs is crowned with the reference to Jesus, who endured a cross, disregarding the disgrace (12:2). Jesus' endurance of unwarranted hostility, shame, and painful death

(12:2–3) provided perspective on the sufferings actually endured by the community (cf. 12:4, "You have not yet resisted to the point of bloodshed while struggling against sin"). The agonistic vocabulary is deliberate, preparing the audience for the summons to leave the security of the sacred enclosure and to risk public identification with Jesus, bearing the disgrace he bore (see *Comment* on 13:12–13).

THE SOCIAL LOCATION OF THE INTENDED AUDIENCE

Proposals for the social location of the community have ranged from Jerusalem in the East to Spain in the West (cf. the review of divergent proposals in F. F. Bruce, *ANRW* 25.4 [1987] 1313–17; D. Guthrie, *New Testament Introduction*[4], 696–701). The critical judgment reflected in this commentary is that the intended audience is to be located in or near Rome. The ambiguity in the formulation "Those from Italy greet you" (13:24*b*) is well known (see below *Note* i on 13:24). The fact remains, nevertheless, that in the sole parallel to ἀπὸ τῆς Ἰταλίας provided by the NT the phrase clearly means "from Italy" in the sense of outside the Italian peninsula (Acts 18:2). The expression is used in reference to Aquila and Priscilla who were currently in Corinth. They had sailed "from Italy" when Claudius issued a decree expelling Jews from Rome (cf. Suetonius, *Claudius* 25.4, discussed below in "The Edict of Claudius"). In Acts 18:2 "Italy" denotes "Rome." This may be the most natural way of reading Heb 13:24*b* as well. In the closing lines of Hebrews, the writer conveys to the members of the house church in or near Rome the greetings of Italian Christians who are currently away from their homeland (so Harnack, *ZNW* 1 [1900] 16–41; Scott, *HTR* 13 [1930] 205–19; F. F. Bruce, *ANRW* 25.4 [1987] 3513–19; among others).

The following evidence may be cited in support of this critical judgment:

(1) The allusions to the generosity of the audience in supporting other Christians in Heb 6:10–11 and 10:33–34 agree with the history of Christianity in Rome as known from other sources (cf. Ign., *Rom.*, Salutation; Dionysius of Corinth [cited by Eusebius, *Church History* 4.23.10]).

(2) The description of the early sufferings endured by the audience in 10:32–34 is congruent with the experience of those who were subject to the Claudian edict of expulsion in A.D. 49 (see below, "The Edict of Claudius").

(3) The designation of the leadership of the community in 13:7, 17, 24 as ἡγούμενοι, "leaders," is found outside the NT in early Christian sources associated with Rome (e.g., *1 Clem.* 21:6; *Herm.*, *Vis.* 2.2.6; 3.9.7; see *Comment* on Heb 13:7).

(4) Hebrews was first known and used in Rome. Clement of Rome, in his pastoral letter to Corinth, provides indisputable evidence of the circulation of Hebrews among the churches of Rome. Not only are there striking parallels to the form and statement of Hebrews throughout *1 Clement*, but Clement is literarily dependent upon Hebrews in *1 Clem.* 36:1–6 (see below "The Edict of Claudius," "Stephen and the Hellenists").

There is, of course, a considerable risk in assigning so definite a social location to the community in the absence of firm evidence from the text or in early Christian tradition. This construction is one that can never be proven, yet it gives a concreteness to Hebrews that other hypotheses lack, and it affords a plausible framework for the document. What is gained in exchange for the risk is a sense of social context for the statement in Hebrews that may be tested exegetically in the course of a commentary. If the supporting detail is deemed sufficient for locating the house church in or near Rome, then what is known of the Jewish community and of the early house churches in Rome can be invoked in seeking to reconstruct some of the social dynamics that impinged upon the life of the audience (see the valuable summaries of current research in Leon, "The Jews of Rome," 154–63; Penna, *NTS* 28 [1982] 321–47; F. F. Bruce, "Paul and Roman Christianity," 379–92; Wiefel, "The Jewish Community in Ancient Rome," 100–119).

Roman Christianity was originally Jewish, and apparently Jewish in a sectarian sense (cf. Ambrosiaster, in the preface to his exposition of Romans [ed. H. J. Vogels in CSEL 81.1 (1961) 6]: "The Romans had embraced the faith of Christ, albeit according to the Jewish rite, although they saw no sign of mighty works nor any of the apostles"; Hippolytus, *Apostolic Tradition* 20.5 [where the purificatory bath prescribed on Maundy Thursday for candidates for baptism on Easter Sunday presents affinities with sectarian Jewish rites]). By the time Paul wrote Romans there had been a significant influx of Gentiles to Christianity, and the balance of power had shifted to Gentile leadership.

In Rom 16:3–15 Paul shows an awareness of the existence of several house churches in Rome, one of which was associated with the Jewish-Christian leaders Aquila and Priscilla, who are now back in the imperial capital after the lapsing of the decree of expulsion (Rom 16:3–5; for other household fellowships, see Rom 16:10*b*, 11*b*, 14, 15; it is possible that the entire list of greetings is structured in terms of households). Christians in Rome during this period appear to have met as groups in house churches. The oldest congregation of Jewish Christians in Rome was the household in which Aquila and Priscilla functioned as hosts and patrons (so Wiefel, "The Jewish Community in Ancient Rome," 113).

An impression of what such early house churches in Rome may have been like is conveyed by the remains of buildings of several stories that date to the second and third centuries, but which have been modified over the course of time. Incorporated into the walls or preserved below the floors of at least three of the existing titular churches in Rome are the remnants of large tenement houses (cf. Peterson, *ExpTim* 84 [1973] 277–79; id. *VC* 23 [1969] 264–72). The ground floors appear to have been occupied by shops, and the upper levels by prosperous families. The connection of these buildings with the social world of craftsmen and artisans is suggestive in the light of the reference to the church in the house of Aquila and Priscilla (Rom 16:5), whose property must have served as workshop, residence, and meeting place. As yet there has been no excavation of common housing from the days of the early empire in Rome, but J. E. Packer's work on the *insulae*, or apartment buildings, points to the existence of amorphous blocks of tenements, one building abutting another ("Housing and Population in Imperial Ostia and Rome," *JRS* 57 [1967] 80–95).

The impression conveyed by Paul's greetings in Rom 16:3–15 is of a number of small household fellowships not in close relationship with one another. One purpose of Paul's greeting may have been to reinforce a sense of unity at a time when the several house churches enjoyed little interrelationship with one another. Ignatius and *Hermas* provide evidence that even in the first decades of the second century Rome was not centrally organized under the administrative authority of a single bishop. In six of his seven letters, Ignatius insists on the importance of the office of bishop. His silence concerning this pastoral concern in the *Letter to the Romans* (c. A.D. 110) is explained best by the absence of a monarchical bishop in Rome. A short time later Hermas refers only to "the elders who preside over the church" (*Vis.* 2.4.3; 3.9.7). The early house churches must have drawn whatever organizational structure they had primarily from hellenistic synagogues and the extended family structures of the Greco-Roman households. They may also have borrowed practices from trade guilds or other voluntary associations formed by special interest groups (cf. Malherbe, *Social Aspects*[2], 88–91).

The multiplicity of house churches throughout Rome suggests why diversity, disunity, and a tendency toward independence were persistent problems in the early days of the Church. In Hebrews there is evidence of tension between the audience and those currently recognized as leaders (see *Comment* on 13:17–18). There is an evident pastoral concern on the part of the writer to bring the two groups together in a social context of shared cordiality (see *Comment* on 13:24a). He could not allow the members of the house church to regard themselves as an autonomous society or to isolate themselves from other household groups within the city. It is possible that a source of the tension between the audience and their current leaders was strained relationships between the householder, who as host and patron held prerogatives of social authority within the household and the house church, and those whom the writer recognizes as their current leaders. (For a suggestive approach, focused on Paul, see L. M. White, "Social Authority in the House Church Setting and Ephesians 4:1–16," *ResQ* 31 (1988) 209–28; cf. J. H. Elliott, "Patronage and Clientism in early Christian Society: A Short Reading Guide," *Forum* 3 [1987] 39–48). To counter an inclination toward isolation on the part of the audience the writer asks them to convey his greetings "to all the saints" throughout the city (13:24a).

Circumstances and Date of Composition

Bibliography

Ayles, H. H. B. *Destination, Date, and Authorship of the Epistle of the Hebrews.* London: Clay, 1899. ————. "The References to Persecution in the Epistle to the Hebrews." *Exp* 8th ser. 12 (1916) 69–74. **Bacon, B. W.** "The Doctrine of Faith in Hebrews, James and Clement of Rome." *JBL* 19 (1900) 12–21. **Barton, G. A.** "The Date of the Epistle to the Hebrews." *JBL* 57 (1938) 195–207. **Cockerill, G. L.** "Heb 1:1–14, *1 Clem.* 36:1–6 and the High Priest Title." *JBL* 97 (1978) 437–40. **Ellingworth, P.** "Hebrews and 1 Clement: Literary Dependence or Common Tradition?" *BZ* 23 (1979) 262–69. **Ellis, E. E.** "Dating the New Testament." *NTS* 26 (1979–80) 487–502. **Freytag, W.** "Das Problem der zweiten Generation in der jungen Kirche." *EvMZ* 1 (1940) 198–210. **Goguel, M.** "La second géneration chrétienne." *RHR* 136 (1949) 31–57, 180–208. **Goodspeed, E. J.** "First Clement Called Forth by Hebrews." *JBL* 30 (1911) 157–60. **Hagner, D. A.** *The Use of the Old and New Testaments in Clement of Rome.* NovTSup 34. Leiden: Brill, 1973. 179–95. **Holtz, T.** "Einführung in die Probleme des Hebräerbriefes." *ZZ* 23 (1969) 321–27. **Mees, M.** "Die Hohepriester-Theologie des Hebräerbriefes im Vergleich mit dem ersten Clemensbrief." *BZ* 22 (1978) 115–24. **Parker, H. M. Jr.** "Domitian and the Epistle to the Hebrews." *IlRev* 36 (1979) 31–43. **Ramsay,**

W. M. "The Date and Authorship of the Epistle to the Hebrews." *ExpTim* 5 (1899) 401–22.
Riddle, D. W. "Hebrews, First Clement, and the Persecution of Domitian." *JBL* 43 (1924)
329–48. **Robinson, J. A. T.** *Redating the New Testament.* London: SCM, 1976. 200–220.
Welborn, L. L. "On the Date of First Clement." *BR* 24 (1984) 35–54.

In addressing the circumstances and general date for the composition of Hebrews, it is necessary to be guided by two analytical principles that are fundamental to the historical-critical paradigm. (1) A literary text provides a primary witness to the circumstances in and for which it was composed. In this respect it provides documentary evidence for the time of writing. (2) It is essential to seek the earliest and best evidence for the events to which reference is made in the text.

CIRCUMSTANCES OF COMPOSITION

For the reconstruction of the circumstances surrounding the composition of Hebrews, there is only the text itself. It is difficult, if not impossible, to determine the precise relationship of the writer to his audience. In 13:17–19 he grouped himself among the "leaders" to whom the community owed obedience and submission. The purpose clause in 13:19*b* ("so that I might be restored to you sooner") clearly implies that the writer and those whom he addressed were known to each other. He was persuaded that his sphere of pastoral responsibility extended to the men and women to whom he dispatched his "word of exhortation" (13:22). His homily (1:1–13:21), together with the brief personal note appended at the end (13:22–25), was intended as a substitute for his presence until he could come in person (13:19, 23). (For the suggestion that the writer actually belonged to the house church he addressed, and that he wrote at the instigation of the other leaders, who appealed to him "as a sort of elder statesman who is well known and respected by everyone in the church," see B. Lindars, "The Rhetorical Structure of Hebrews," *NTS* 35 [1989] 384–86.)

The targeted audience was an assembly in crisis. There had been defections from their number (10:25). Among those who remained, there was loss of confidence in the viability of their convictions. They displayed lack of interest in the message of salvation they had embraced (2:1–4), which formerly had given them a sense of identity as the new covenant people of God. The writer implies that they were no longer listening to the voice of God in Scripture and preaching (2:1; 3:7*b*–4:13, 5:11; 12:25). They clearly had regressed from the stance of bold commitment they had exhibited shortly after identifying themselves with the Jesus movement, when they had endured public abuse, imprisonment, and loss of property (10:32–34). They are described as lethargic and disheartened (5:11; 6:12; 12:3, 12–13). They had become weary with the necessity of sustaining their confession in a social climate hostile to their presence (12:3–4).

One consideration that alarmed the writer was the group's attraction for traditions that he regarded as conflicting with the word of God preached by their former leaders (13:7–9). This attraction appears to have been the source of unresolved tension between the community and their current leadership (13:1, 17–18). It would also account for the group's proneness to isolation, which left them without any sense of accountability to a larger network of household fellowships (13:24). Volatile social and religious factors combined to undermine the stability of the house church, making them vulnerable to fluctuations in the socio-political and religious climate.

This brief sketch suggests that Hebrews is a composition addressed to second-generation concerns (cf. Freytag, *EvMZ* 1 [1940] 198–210; Goguel, *RHR* 136 [1949] 31–57, 180–208). Whether the root of the problem was the delay of the Parousia (10:25, 35–39), social ostracism and impending persecution (12:4; 13:13–14), or a general waning of enthusiasm and erosion of confidence (3:14; 10:35) is a matter for debate. Whatever the case may be, one of the symptoms of a community in crisis was the faltering of hope (3:6; 6:18–20; 10:23–25; 11:1). The writer sensed that some members of the group were in grave danger of apostasy, which he defined as a turning away from the living God (3:12) and the subjecting of Jesus Christ to public contempt (6:4–6; 10:26–31). Such behavior would be a violation of covenant fidelity and would entail exclusion from covenant fellowship (cf. V. P. Verbrugge, "Towards a New Interpretation of Hebrews 6:4–6," *CTS* 15 [1980] 61–73). The writer was deeply concerned that the weaker members of the assembly would reject the grace of God and forfeit participation in the new covenant community through personal carelessness (3:12–15; 4:1, 11; 6:4–8, 11; 10:26–31; 12:15–17, 25–29). This reading of the evidence for the compositional circumstances of Hebrews would appear to account for the pastoral strategies adopted by the writer as well as for the urgent tone in his appeal.

DATE OF COMPOSITION: GENERAL CONSIDERATIONS

The writer and those whom he addressed had come to faith in response to the preaching of those who had heard Jesus (2:3–4). These had subsequently played a leading role in the life of the community during its formative period (13:7). They were now deceased. Because they "spoke the word of God," their preaching belonged to the community's past. This fact, together with the remark that the members of the community had been adherents of the gospel for an extended period of time (5:12), makes it probable that at least three or four decades have elapsed since the beginning or the Christian movement. The earliest date that can be assigned to Hebrews would seem to be around A.D. 60.

An upper limit in the range for a date is established by the fact that Hebrews was already being appropriated without explicit quotation in *1 Clement* (see *1 Clem.* 17:1 for the use of Heb 11:37; *1 Clem.* 36:2–6 for direct literary dependence upon Heb 1:3–5, 7; *1 Clem.* 36:3 for the quotation of Ps 104[103 LXX]:4 in the precise wording of Heb 1:7 [in variation from the LXX]). Although it has been argued that the two documents simply share a common tradition (so, e.g., Theissen, *Untersuchungen*, 35–37), it is broadly recognized that Clement was, in fact, literarily dependent upon Hebrews (see, e.g., Renner, 31–37; Hagner, *The Use of the Old and New Testaments in Clement of Rome*, 179–95; Cockerill, *JBL* 97 [1978] 437–40; Ellingworth, *BZ* 23 [1979] 262–69; Braun, 3, 32; Attridge, 6–8, for a full discussion of the parallels between Hebrews and *1 Clement*; see below, "Recognition in the West").

A conventional date of A.D. 95–96 has been assigned to *1 Clement*, but on insufficient grounds (see especially Welborn, *BR* 24 [1984] 35–54). Internal evidence and external attestation indicate that *1 Clement* was composed at some point between A.D. 80 and 140. In light of the fact that Hegesippus was shown the letter in

Corinth *c.* A.D. 150 (Eusebius, *Church History* 3.16; 4.22) and that a few years later Dionysius, the Bishop of Corinth, noted that the letter continued to be read publicly in the assembly from time to time (Eusebius, *Church History* 4.12; cf. Irenaeus, *Against Heresies* 3.3.3; Clement of Alexandria, *Stromata* 1.38.5; 4.105.1; 5.80.1), the upper limits of that range are unlikely. But the fact remains that no firm inference concerning the date of Hebrews may be drawn from its use by Clement of Rome.

It has been claimed that an upper limit in assigning a date for Hebrews can be set confidently at A.D. 70, the year in which the temple of Jerusalem was destroyed by Rome (e.g., Barton, *JBL* 57 [1938] 205–7; F. F. Bruce, xiii; Vanhoye, *Situation du Christ*, 50; Renner, 137; Buchanan, 261; Strobel, 83; P. E. Hughes, 30–32; Robinson, *Redating*, 202). The basis for this confidence is that the writer of Hebrews refers to cultic activity in the present tense (e.g., 7:27–28; 8:3–5; 9:7–8, 25; 10:1–3, 8; 13:10–11), presumably reflecting contemporary cultic practice in Jerusalem. The argument, however, is untenable. The writer of Hebrews shows no interest in the temple in any of its forms nor in contemporary cultic practice. In 9:1–10, for example, he concentrates his attention upon the tabernacle of the Israelites in the wilderness rather than upon the temple. His reason for doing so is almost certainly to be traced to the prior use of Exod 25:40, instructing Moses to erect a sanctuary according to the pattern God showed to him on Mount Sinai (8:5). The matter of the sanctuary is to be considered in relation to the old and new covenants, and the contrast between the two. It was only natural, therefore, for the writer to refer to the tabernacle rather than to the temple, because of the association of the desert sanctuary with the establishment of the old covenant at Sinai. That the argument in Hebrews is developed in terms of the tabernacle indicates that the present tenses in the account should be taken as "timeless," rather than as reflections of a continuing temple liturgy in Jerusalem. (For similar use of such "timeless" presents in describing the Temple itself and its sacrifices after the Temple had been destroyed, see Jos., *Ant.* 4.224–57; *1 Clem.* 41:2; *Barn.* 7–8; *Diogn.* 3.) They have no bearing upon a determination of a date for the composition of Hebrews.

THE EDICT OF CLAUDIUS

Bibliography

Bacchiocchi, S. "Rome and Christianity until A.D. 62." *AUSS* 21 (1983) 3–25. **Benko, S.** "The Edict of Claudius of A.D. 49 and the Instigator Chrestus." *TZ* 25 (1969) 406–18. **Bruce, F. F.** "Christianity under Claudius." *BJRL* 44 (1961–62) 309–26. **Howard, G.** "The Beginning of Christianity in Rome: A Note on Suetonius, Life of Claudius XXV.4." *ResQ* 24 (1981) 175–77. **Janne, H.** "*Impulsore Chresto.*" In *Mélanges Bidez*. AIPHO 2. Brussels: Secrétariat de l'Institut, 1934. 531–53. **Lampe, P.** *Die stadtrömischen Christen in der ersten beiden Jahrhunderten.* WUNT 2/18. Tübingen: Mohr, 1987. **Leon, H. J.** *The Jews of Ancient Rome.* Philadelphia: Jewish Publication Society, 1960. 23–27. **Melton, D. V.** "The Imperial Government and Christianity During the Principate of Claudius." Dissertation, University of Oklahoma, 1984. **Momigliano, A.** *Claudius—The Emperor and His Achievement.* Rev. ed. Cambridge: Heffer and Sons, 1961. 31–32, 98–99. **Nock, A. D.** "Religious Developments from the Close of the Republic to the Death of Nero." In *The Cambridge Ancient History.* Vol. 10. Ed. S. A. Cook et al.

Cambridge: UP, 1934. 465–511. **Piana, G. la.** "Foreign Groups in Rome during the First Centuries of the Empire." *HTR* 20 (1927) 183–403. **Preuschen, E.** "Chresto Impulsore." *ZNW* 15 (1914) 96. **Roth, C.** *The History of the Jews in Italy.* Philadelphia: Jewish Publication Society, 1946. 7–11. **Scramuzza, V.** *The Emperor Claudius.* Cambridge: Harvard UP, 1940. 145–56, 283–91. **Seston, W.** "L'Empereur Claude et les chrétiens." *RHPR* 3 (1931) 275–304. **Smallwood, E. M.** *Documents Illustrating the Principates of Gaius, Claudius and Nero.* Cambridge: Cambridge UP, 1967. ———. *The Jews under Roman Rule.* Leiden: Brill, 1981. **Vogelstein, H.** *The History of the Jews in Rome.* Trans. M. Hadas. Philadelphia: Jewish Publication Society, 1940. **Winslow, D.** "Religion and the Early Roman Empire." In *The Catacombs and the Colosseum.* Ed. S. Benko and J. J. O'Rourke. Valley Forge, PA: Judson, 1971. 237–54.

In seeking to narrow the range for assigning a tentative date for the composition of Hebrews, I have been guided especially by the analytical principle that it is necessary to seek the earliest and best evidence for the events to which reference is made in the text. The most vivid reference to a specific event in the community's past is found in 10:32–34, where the writer recalls a real experience of suffering, abuse, imprisonment, and the loss of property. In the context, he is making the past experience of the group a paradigm for the present and the immediate future. He appeals to the audience to subject their present experience of hardship and alienation to a fresh examination in the light of their past stance of unwavering commitment to Christ. By drawing the community's attention to the past as well as to the future, the writer seeks to strengthen their resolve for the present.

If the evidence is deemed strong enough to support a Roman destination for Hebrews (see above, "The Social Location of the Intended Audience"), then 10:32–34 sheds light on the earlier history of the congregation addressed. On my reading of the evidence, these men and women had been Christians since the Claudian period. They had been exposed to public ridicule because they had been defenseless against the seizure of their property. It cannot be determined now whether their loss was because of the official judicial action of magistrates, who imposed heavy fines or confiscated property for suspected infractions (cf. Philo, *Against Flaccus* 10), or their houses had been looted after they had been imprisoned or expelled from the city (cf. Philo, *Against Flaccus* 56). Whatever the precise circumstances, the Christians had cheerfully accepted their losses (see *Comment* on 10:33–34).

The description of the suffering endured in 10:32–34 is appropriate to the hardships borne by the Jewish Christians who were expelled from Rome by the emperor Claudius in A.D 49. Among them were Aquila and Priscilla, who arrived in Corinth c. A.D. 49 or 50 "because Claudius had commanded all the Jews to leave Rome" (Acts 18:2). This edict of expulsion is known from Suetonius, who published his *Lives of the Caesars* in A.D. 120. Commenting on Claudius' acts with regard to certain foreign groups in Rome, he states without elaboration, *Iudaeos impulsore Chresto adsidue tumultuantes Roma expulit* (*Claudius* 25.4).

The statement is ambiguous and may be translated in either of two ways: "He expelled from Rome the Jews constantly making disturbances at the instigation of Chrestus," or "Since the Jews constantly made disturbances at the instigation of Chrestus, he expelled them from Rome." The first translation allows the interpretation that Claudius expelled only those responsible for the disturbances among the Jews. The second translation suggests that the entire Jewish community was affected by the edict because they had been engaged in frequent rioting. The reason for favoring the first translation is that in Rome the Jewish community was divided into a number of district synagogues (Smallwood, *The Jews under Roman Rule*, 138). In all probability the decree of expulsion was directed against the members of one or two specific synagogues, who would have been forced to leave the city until there was a guarantee of no further disturbances.

The notorious confusion displayed in the words *impulsore Chresto* ("at the instigation of Chrestus") suggests a contemporary police record. It is well known that Suetonius merely reproduced his sources without attempting to evaluate them carefully (cf. Janne, "*Impulsore Chresto*," 537–46). Although "Chrestus" (signifying "good" or "useful") was a very common name among Roman slaves, it was not a common Jewish name. H. Leon lists over 550 names used by Jews in Rome in the first century, but "Chrestus" is not among them (*The Jews of Ancient Rome*, 93–121). The garbled reference to "Chrestus" is almost certainly evidence of the presence of Christians within the Jewish community of Rome. The source of the disruptions in the Jewish quarters was the propagation of the Christian message by Jewish Christians and especially their insistence that the crucified Jesus was the Jewish Messiah. The Jewish community was thrown into violent debate that soon attracted the unfavorable attention of the imperial authorities. Claudius, it would appear, issued a decree of expulsion affecting those most directly involved.

The confusion between *Chrestus* and *Christus* ("the Messiah") is natural enough. In antiquity the distinction in spelling and pronunciation was negligible. In the manuscript tradition of the NT the confusion is reflected in the spelling of the name "Christian" in Acts 11:26; 26:28; and 1 Pet 4:16, where the important uncial codex Sinaiticus (ℵ) reads Χρηστιανός (i.e., *Chrestianos*). Even after the distinction was known, it was quite popular among those who were not Christians to interchange the two forms. The urge to identify the founder of the new "superstition" with a common slave name may have been difficult to resist. Several of the early apologists complain that pagans often confuse the two spellings, much to the dismay of the Christians (cf. Justin, *Apology* 1.4; Tertullian, *Apology* 3; Lactantius, *Divine Institutes* 4.7).

The date of the Claudian edict is contested. Suetonius' compositional style does not permit any conclusion regarding a date for the disturbances or for the edict of expulsion. The only firm datum is provided by the fifth-century historian Orosius (*History* 7.6.15–16), who introduces the terse statement from Suetonius with the statement, "Josephus refers to the expulsion of the Jews by Claudius in his ninth year" (i.e., A.D 49). Although the extant writings of Josephus do not contain such a statement, the dating of the edict of expulsion to the year A.D. 49 is plausible. It was precisely in the period A.D. 47–52 that Claudius engaged in a campaign to restore the old Roman rites and to check the growth of foreign cults.

The date of A.D. 49 is accepted by a number of responsible scholars (see Nock, "Religious Developments," 500; Scramuzza, *The Emperor Claudius*, 145–56, 286–87; F. F. Bruce, *BJRL* 44 [1961–62] 317; Melton, "The Imperial Government and Christianity," 54–63, among others). This date has been corroborated independently by the Gallio inscription from Delphi, which has made it possible to determine when Paul entered Corinth and made the acquaintance of Aquila and Priscilla, who had arrived "only recently" (Acts 18:1–2). (On the Gallio inscription see Smallwood, *Documents Illustrating the Principates of Gaius, Claudius and Nero*, 105; cf. J. Murphy-O'Connor, *St. Paul's Corinth* [Wilmington, DE: Glazier, 1983] 129–52, 173–76, for a different reading of the evidence.)

In short, when heated disputes deteriorated to riots, Claudius banished from the city synagogue and church leaders responsible for the disruption of civil peace. The Suetonian formulation suggests that it was "mainly Christian missionaries and converts who were expelled," i.e., those Jewish Christians labeled under the name *Chrestus* (see Smallwood, *The Jews under Roman Rule*, 216). Insult, public abuse, and especially the loss of property were normal under the conditions of an edict of expulsion. If this reading of the evidence is correct, the writer of Hebrews prepared his discourse for some of the Jewish Christians who had shared banishment from Rome with Aquila and Priscilla. The reference to this experience in 10:32–34 is to the year A.D. 49.

Hebrews, of course, addresses the community at a later point in time. A new crisis has emerged, confronting the members of a house church with a fresh experience of suffering. Reference to enslavement through the fear of death (2:15), to loss of heart (12:3), and to the fact that the audience had *not yet* contended to the point of bloodshed (12:4), climaxing a section summarizing the experience of men and women of faith who endured torture, flogging, banishment, chains, and execution (11:35–12:3), suggests that the situation now facing the community is more serious than the earlier one under Claudius. It is not unreasonable to think of the suffering endured by Christians in Rome under Nero (Tacitus, *Annals of Rome* 15.44). Some Christians experienced loss of life, and not simply of property. Hebrews appears to be addressed to the members of a house church that had not yet borne the brunt of the persecution, or, less probably, to Jewish Christians who returned to Rome after that terrifying event. It is reasonable to assign tentatively a date for the composition of Hebrews to the insecure interval between the aftermath of the great fire of Rome (A.D. 64) and Nero's suicide in June, A.D. 68. Incidental features of the text, like the writer's imminent expectation of the Parousia (10:25, 36–39) or the reference to Timothy's release from prison (13:23), are congruent with this relatively early dating.

Integrity

Bibliography

Burggaler, E. "Das literarische Problem des Hebräerbriefes." *ZNW* 9 (1908) 110–31. **Filson, F. V.** *"Yesterday": A Study of Hebrews in the Light of Chapter 13.* Naperville: Allenson, 1967. **Jones, E. D.** "The Authorship of Hebrews xiii." *ExpTim* 46 (1934–35) 562–67. **McCown, W. G.** "*Ο ΛΟΓΟΣ ΤΗΣ ΠΑΡΑΚΛΗΣΕΩΣ*: The Nature and Function of the Hortatory Sections in the Epistle to the Hebrews." Dissertation, Union Theological Seminary, Richmond, 1970. 120–38, 145–49. **Nitschke, H.** "Das Ethos des wandernden Gottesvolkes: Erwägung zu Hebr 13 und zu den Möglichkeiten evangelischer Ethik." *MPTh* 46 (1957) 179–83. **Perdelwitz, R.** "Das literarische Problem des Hebräerbriefs." *ZNW* 11 (1910) 59–78. **Simcox, G. A.** "Heb. xiii; 2 Tim. iv." *ExpTim* 10 (1898–99) 430–32. **Spicq, C.** "L'authenticité du chapitre XIII de l'Épître aux Hébreux." *ConNT* 11 (1947) 226–36. **Synge, F. C.** *Hebrews and the Scriptures.* London: S.P.C.K., 1959. **Tasker, R. V. G.** "The Integrity of the Epistle to the Hebrews."

ExpTim 47 (1935–36) 136–38. **Thompson, J. W.** "The Underlying Unity of Hebrews." *ResQ* 18 (1975) 129–36. **Thurén, J.** *Das Lobopfer der Hebräer: Studien zum Aufbau und Anliegen von Hebräerbrief 13.* Åbo: Åbo Akademi, 1973. 49–70. **Torrey, C. C.** "The Authorship and Character of the so-called 'Epistle to the Hebrews.'" *JBL* 30 (1911) 137–56. **Vanhoye, A.** "La Question littéraire de Hébreux xiii. 1–6," *NTS* 23 (1976–77) 121–39. **Williams, C. R.** "A Word-Study of Hebrews 13." *JBL* 30.2 (1911) 129–36. **Wrede, W.** *Das literarische Rätsel des Hebräerbriefs.* FRLANT 8. Göttingen: Vandenhoeck & Ruprecht, 1906. 3–5, 39–73.

In 1959 F. C. Synge (*Hebrews and the Scriptures*, 43–52) argued that Hebrews in its present form fuses two originally independent written sources, one didactic and expositional in character (the "Testimony Book"), the other a call for Jews to risk identification with the Jewish Christian movement (the "Hortation"). To the latter document he assigned Heb 2:1–4; 3:7–4:13; 5:11–6:12; 10:26–31; 12:18–29; and possibly the block of material in 10:32–13:25. These units of exhortation he regarded as later interpolations into the Testimony Book. For example, from the observation that the exposition in Heb 1:5–14 and 2:5–16 possesses an intrinsic unity and that the exhortation in 2:1–4 actually interrupts the flow of the argument, he concluded that 2:1–4 is secondary in its context. Linguistic and conceptual parallels between 2:1–4 and other units of exhortation further convinced him that all of the hortatory units in Hebrews possess the character of secondary intrusions.

This hypothesis is neither plausible nor necessary and is sufficiently refuted by literary and thematic considerations which demonstrate the compositional unity of Hebrews. In the case of Heb 2:1–4, for example, the same evidence of artistic prose found in the opening lines (Heb 1:1–4) is found in 2:2–4, i.e., the use of a skillfully balanced periodic sentence, parallelism of sound and sense, alliteration, and cadence. Such stylistic features furnish a literary signature which verifies that both units were composed by the same writer. The two units are united thematically by vocabulary and conception (see *Comment* on 2:1–4). The arbitrary detachment of 2:1–4 from the context in which it is embedded would falsify the writer's concern to call his audience to recognize the inextricable unity between confession and experience.

Although the integrity of Heb 1–12 has been almost universally recognized, there have been lingering doubts concerning the authenticity of chap. 13. The final chapter of Hebrews appears to begin abruptly, without the writer's normal care to link a new section to the preceding unit of exhortation (Heb 12:14–29). The abruptness is accentuated by a sharp change in tone and theme. Moreover, the form of chap. 13 is unparalleled in the earlier sections of the document. The careful development of exhortation is suddenly replaced by catechetical precepts that exhibit the character of the general parenesis of the early Church as known from the letters of Paul or Peter (e.g., 1 Thess 5:12–22; Rom 12:9–21; 13:8–10; 1 Pet 3:8–12). The final section is noticeably different from the climactic exhortation in 10:19–12:29. In addition, the content of chap. 13 distinguishes this section from the rest of the document (see *Form/Structure/Setting* on 13:1–25). In short, it has been asserted that considerations of coherence, form, and content call into question the integrity of Hebrews and the authenticity or appropriateness of chap. 13 (so Simcox, *ExpTim* 10 [1898–99] 430–32; Jones, *ExpTim* 46 [1934–35] 562–67; Nitschke, *MPTh* 46 [1957] 179; and most recently, Buchanan, 229–45, 267–68).

It is unnecessary, however, to question the authenticity of chap. 13 in the light of the very evident links between the material in this section and the preceding chapters, both in content and thrust. The character of the vocabulary, the customary appeal to quotations from the Pentateuch and the Psalms, the recurrence of key concepts, and considerations of structure all tend to exhibit the homogeneity of chap. 13 with the rest of the composition (cf. Williams, *JBL* 30.2 [1911] 129–36; Tasker, *ExpTim* 47 [1935–36] 136–38; Spicq, *ConNT* 11 [1947] 226–36; Filson, "*Yesterday*," 22–26, 28–29; McCown, "*Ο ΛΟΓΟΣ ΤΗΣ ΠΑΡΑΚΛΗΣΕΩΣ*," 120–38, 145–49; Michel, 478–80; Thurén, *Das Lobopfer der Hebräer*, 57–70; Vanhoye, *NTS* 23 [1976–77] 128–30). These observations constitute a strong, cumulative argument for the authenticity of chap. 13 and for the integrity of Hebrews.

The arguments for authenticity that have been advanced by others can be strengthened by an appeal to considerations of literary style that demonstrate that the writer responsible for chaps. 1–12 is also the composer of chap. 13. In the *Notes* and *Form/Structure/Setting* sections of the commentary to 13:1–25, attention is called to chiastic structure within a clause, a sentence, or a section (13:2, 4, 10, 14; 13:10–16), paronomasia (or play on words) (13:2, 18, 20, 22), unusual word order designed to arouse and sustain attention (13:8, 11, 20), elegant style (13:17), linguistic rhythm (13:3), assonance (13:4, 5, 9, 13, 14, 16), alliterative arrangement of lines (13:5, 19), the deliberate use of syntax to display emphasis (13:3, 4, 5, 9, 11, 12, 15, 18, 20), and the use of classical idioms (13:2, 5, 15, 17). In combination these stylistic elements constitute a distinct literary signature that serves to identify the writer as conclusively as would an unsmudged set of fingerprints. This is precisely the literary signature written across chaps. 1–12. Such expressions of conscious literary artistry furnish an argument for the authenticity of all of chap. 13, since they have been culled from each of its constituent parts. Heb 13 as a whole was drafted by the writer responsible for chaps. 1–12 and was unquestionably composed to accompany the preceding sections of the document.

Methodologically, an argument for the integrity of a composition is advanced most effectively by proceeding from an assumption of coherence and allowing that assumption to be tested as rigorously as possible. The argument will be vindicated when the text yields better sense in its constituent parts and as a whole than when a contested unit of material is regarded as intrusive, poorly integrated, or corrupt. It will be shown in the commentary that chap. 13 transmits an essential message that can scarcely be separated from the concerns and conceptual themes expressed in Heb 1–12.

Briefly, the connection of 13:1–21 to the preceding section, 12:14–29, is established through 12:28. The writer summons the community to thanksgiving and urges them through thanksgiving to serve God acceptably. In the context, authentic worship is defined as the response of gratitude to objective covenant blessings already experienced and to the certainty of the reception of an unshakable kingdom in the future. The concept of worship is almost certainly to be expanded to include a lifestyle that is pleasing to God. The members of the community addressed are to regard every aspect of their lives as an expression of devoted service to God. What this entails demanded the specification provided in 13:1–21 (see *Form/Structure/Setting* on 13:1–25).

Genre

Bibliography

Attridge, H. W. "New Covenant Christology in an Early Christian Homily." *QuartRev* 8 (1988) 89–108. ———. "Paraenesis in a Homily (λόγος παρακλήσεως): The Possible Location of, and Socialization in, the 'Epistle to the Hebrews.'" *Semeia* 50 (1990) 211–26. **Bickermann, E. J.** "En marge de l'Écriture: III. Le titre de l'Épître aux Hébreux." *RB* 88 (1981) 28–41. **Black, C. C. II.** "The Rhetorical Form of the Hellenistic Jewish and Early Christian Sermon: A Response to Lawrence Wills." *HTR* 81 (1988) 1–18. **Bristol, L. O.** "Primitive Christian Preaching and the Epistle to the Hebrews." *JBL* 68 (1949) 89–97. **Burggaller, E.** "Das literarische Problem des Hebräerbriefes." *ZNW* 9 (1908) 110–31. **Clemen, C.** "The Oldest Christian Sermon." *Exp* 5 (1896) 392–400. **Dickie, J.** "The Literary Riddle of the 'Epistle to the Hebrews.'" *Exp* 8th ser. 5 (1913) 371–78. **Doty, W. G.** *Letters in Primitive Christianity.* Philadelphia: Fortress, 1973. 21–47. **Feld, H.** "Der Hebräerbrief: Literarische Form, religionsgeschichtlicher Hintergrund, theologische Fragen." *ANRW* 2.25.4 (1987) 3522–3601. **Gammie, J. G.** "Paraenetic Literature: Toward the Morphology of a Secondary Genre." *Semeia* 50 (1990) 41–77. **Hutaff, M. D.** "The Epistle to the Hebrews: An Early Christian Sermon." *TBT* 99 (1978) 1816–24. **Kirkpatrick, E.** "Hebrews: Its Evangelistic Purpose and Literary Form." Dissertation, Southern Baptist Theological Seminary, 1941. **Lane, W. L.** "Hebrews: A Sermon in Search of a Setting." *SWJT* 28 (1985) 13–18. **Larsson, E.** "Om Hebréerbrevets syfte." *SEÅ* 37–38 (1972–73) 296–309. **McGehee, M.** "Hebrews: The Letter Which Is Not a Letter." *TBT* 24 (1986) 213–16. **Monod, V.** *De titulo epistolae vulgo ad Hebraeos inscriptae.* Montalbani: Granié, 1910. **Perdelwitz, R.** "Das literarische Problem des Hebräerbriefs." *ZNW* 11 (1910) 59–78. **Perdue, L. G.** "The Social Character of Paraenesis and Paraenetic Literature." *Semeia* 50 (1990) 5–39. **Peterson, D. G.** "The Ministry of Encouragement." In *God Who Is Rich in Mercy.* FS D. B. Knox. Ed. P. T. O'Brien and D. G. Peterson. Homebush West, NSW: Lancer, 1986. 235–53. **Slot, W.** *De letterkundige Vorm van de Brief aan de Hebreeën.* Groningen: Wolters, 1912. 94–103. **Stegner, W. R.** "The Ancient Jewish Synagogue Homily." In *Greco-Roman Literature and the New Testament.* Ed. D. E. Aune. SBL Sources for Biblical Studies 21. Atlanta: Scholars Press, 1988. 51–69. **Swetnam, J.** "On the Literary Genre of the 'Epistle' to the Hebrews." *NovT* 11 (1969) 261–69. **Thyen, H.** *Der Stil der jüdisch-hellenistischen Homilie.* FRLANT 47. Göttingen: Vandenhoeck & Ruprecht, 1955. **Torrey, C. C.** "The Authorship and Character of the So-Called 'Epistle to the Hebrews.'" *JBL* 30 (1911) 137–56. **Übelacker, W. G.** *Der Hebräerbrief als Appell: Untersuchungen zu exordium, narratio und postscriptum (Hebr 1–2 und 13, 22–25).* Stockholm: Almqvist & Wiksell, 1989. **Vanhoye, A.** *Homilie für haltbedürftige Christen: Struktur und Botschaft des Hebräerbriefes.* Regensburg: Pustet, 1981. **Wills, L.** "The Form of the Sermon in Hellenistic Judaism and Early Christianity." *HTR* 77 (1984) 277–99. **Wood, J.** "A New Testament Pattern for Preachers." *EvQ* 47 (1975) 214–18. **Wrede, W.** *Das literarische Rätsel des Hebräerbriefs.* FRLANT 8. Göttingen: Vandenhoeck & Ruprecht, 1906. 3–5, 39–73.

In the manuscript tradition of the NT Hebrews appears exclusively in association with the letters of Paul. The oldest copy of this document is found in a collection of Pauline letters, the Chester Beatty Papyrus (P^{46}), which is dated at the beginning of the third century. There it is identified as "To the Hebrews," in the same manner that a letter of Paul's is identified as "To the Romans" or "To the Corinthians." In this manuscript Hebrews is positioned after Romans and before 1 Corinthians. In several of the later uncial codices (א, B, A, C, H, I, K, and P), it is placed after the letters to the churches, i.e., after 2 Thessalonians and before 1 Timothy. The association of Hebrews with the epistolary order of the NT has encouraged readers to regard this document as a letter. It is conventional to refer to the "Letter to the Hebrews" or to the "Epistle to the Hebrews."

Nevertheless, Hebrews does not possess the form of an ancient letter. It lacks the conventional prescript of a letter and has none of the characteristic features of ordinary letters from this general time period. (For a helpful summary of recent research, see W. G. Doty, *Letters in Primitive Christianity*, especially 21–47.) In the opening lines the writer fails to identify himself or the group to whom he was writing. He offers no prayer for grace and peace and no expression of thanksgiving or blessing. The document begins with a stately periodic sentence acclaiming the dignity of the Son through whom God has spoken his final word (Heb 1:1–4). These opening lines are without doubt a real introduction, which would not tolerate any prescript preceding them. (For the suggestion that very early in the textural transmission of Hebrews the initial epistolary protocol of the letter ceased to be copied, see Renner, 94–119, who finds the "missing" protocol in Rom 16:25–27; Bickermann, *RB* 88 [1981] 28–30, 36–41; and in response, see Vanhoye, *Situation du Christ*, 14–15.) The opening periodic sentence commands attention and engages a reader or auditor immediately. Hebrews begins like a sermon.

THE HOMILY OR SERMON FORM

The accuracy of this first impression is confirmed by the writer himself. In brief personal remarks appended to the close of the document, he describes what he has sent as a "word of exhortation" (ὁ λόγος τῆς παρακλήσεως) (13:22). This descriptive phrase evokes the invitation extended to Barnabas and Paul by synagogue officials in Antioch of Pisidia after the public reading from the Law and the Prophets to deliver to the congregation "a word of exhortation" (Acts 13:15). Paul responded by addressing the assembly in a homily or edifying discourse (Acts 13:16–41). "Word of exhortation" appears to be an idiomatic, fixed expression for a sermon in Jewish-hellenistic and early Christian circles (see *Comment* on 13:22).

The classic study of the Jewish-hellenistic and early Christian homily form in the period close to the first century is the investigation of H. Thyen, *Der Stil des jüdisch-hellenistischen Homilie* (1955). Thyen proposed that a number of Jewish and Christian writings in Greek from this general period reflect the style and influence of a Jewish-hellenistic homily. He based his study on Philo's allegorical commentary on Genesis, *1 Clement*, 4 Maccabees, James, Hebrews, parts of 1 Maccabees and 3 Maccabees, Stephen's speech in Acts 7, *Didache* 1–6 and 16, *Barnabas*, the *Shepherd of Hermas*, parts of Tobit, the *Testaments of the Twelve Patriarchs*, and the Wisdom of Solomon. For each of these primary sources he sought to trace the influence of the Cynic-Stoic diatribe (a particular style of popular preaching in Hellenism), the use of the OT, and the variety of ways in which parenetic tradition was treated. The following were factors that led him to classify Hebrews as a parenetic homily in the Jewish-hellenistic synagogue tradition:

(1) Hebrews shares in common with the parenetic sections of Jewish-hellenistic synagogue homilies numerous characteristics, including the communal "we" (as

opposed to the general use of the third person), the use of ἀδελφοί, "brothers," to address the congregation, the employment of the inferential particles or phrases διό, "therefore," διὰ τοῦτο, "for this reason," or οὖν, "therefore," to effect a transition from exposition to exhortation, the use of the second-person plural to address the auditors directly (as well as the shift back and forth between "we" and "you"), a personal, warm tone, the use of *exempla*, and an apocalyptic background to the thoughts being addressed (Thyen, *Stil,* 7–39, 85–110).

(2) The characteristic source of the Jewish-hellenistic homilies is the LXX. The writer of Hebrews has a remarkable knowledge of the LXX and used it exclusively. Moreover, Jewish-hellenistic homilies draw heavily upon the Pentateuch and Psalms, as does the writer of Hebrews. The mode of citing the biblical text in Hebrews exhibits a pattern readily discerned in the Jewish-hellenistic homilies (Thyen, *Stil,* 17, 62, 67, 69–74).

(3) The writer of Hebrews displays a command of many different rhetorical devices familiar from the Cynic-Stoic diatribe that recur in Jewish-hellenistic synagogue preaching (Thyen, *Stil,* 43, 47, 50, 53, 58–59). Among them Hebrews shares in common with other Jewish-hellenistic homiletical literature the practice of introducing biblical quotations with a rhetorical question (Thyen, *Stil,* 73).

(4) The many contacts between Hebrews and Jewish-hellenistic writers, and in particular with Philo and the author of the Wisdom of Solomon, the use of Scripture, and the exegetical methods that the writer employed all demonstrate that he was a hellenistic Jewish-Christian (Thyen, *Stil,* 17).

(5) The typical Jewish-hellenistic homily concludes with parenetic instruction. Heb 10:19–13:21 conforms to this trait (Thyen, *Stil,* 87–96, 106–10). In the effective use made of parenesis throughout Hebrews, the document resembles Philo's allegorical commentary on Genesis (Thyen, *Stil,* 10).

Thyen concluded that with the exception of the postscript (13:22–25), which was appended when the homily was sent as a written communication, Hebrews is a skillfully crafted homily of the type delivered in a Diaspora synagogue (Thyen, *Stil,* 17). In fact, Hebrews is "the only example of a completely preserved homily" from this period (Thyen, *Stil,* 106).

Thyen's volume marked an important advance in establishing the genre of Hebrews (for a summary of Thyen's argument in English, and a mildly critical evaluation, see J. Swetnam, *NovT* 11 [1969] 261–69; for a more recent investigation of synagogue preaching in the Diaspora, see W. R. Stegner, "The Ancient Jewish Synagogue Homily," 51–69). That Jewish-hellenistic preaching was a primary influence on Hebrews is today common opinion, and in the judgment of E. Grässer has been "convincingly established" by Thyen (*TRu* 30 [1964] 153; cf. 160, where Grässer calls Hebrews "a sermon sent from one place to another"). In his magisterial commentary on Hebrews, published prior to the work of Thyen, C. Spicq had already described Hebrews as "an apologetic treatise" that has "the eloquence of a discourse and the form of a homily." Writing subsequently to the publication of Thyen's book, O. Michel, in the masterful sixth edition of his own commentary on Hebrews, wrote, "Hebrews is the first complete primitive Christian sermon, perhaps built up from several independent parts, which has come down to us" (24; cf. Braun, 1–2; Attridge, 13–14). Thyen's work appeared to have provided a firm foundation for further study of the genre or form of Hebrews.

DEFINING THE GENRE

In spite of the generally positive reception Thyen's volume has received, more recent scholars have reminded their colleagues of the paucity of the evidence for what Jewish and Christian preaching was like in the period prior to the middle of the second century of the Common Era. H. Koester, for example, finds the terms "sermon" and "homily" imprecise and vague. He calls into question the categorization of Hebrews as a sermon on the grounds that the genre has not been defined (*Introduction to the New Testament*, 2:273). K. P. Donfried rejects the form-critical designations of sermon and homily as hopelessly vague and speculative. With characteristic vigor he writes, "We know virtually nothing about the contours of such a genre in the first century A.D.," and argues that "the term 'homily' is so vague and ambiguous that it should be withdrawn until its literarily generic legitimacy has been demonstrated" (*The Setting of Second Clement in Early Christianity* [Leiden: Brill, 1974] 26).

By way of response, in 1984 L. Wills published his research on a common form of the hellenistic Jewish and early Christian oral sermon that can be reconstructed in a precise way (*HTR* 77 [1984] 277–99). Using Acts 13:16–41 as a paradigmatic homily, Wills discerned a firmly entrenched pattern of argumentation that appears to reflect the typical synagogue hortatory homily. He tentatively applied the label "word of exhortation" to this oral form on the basis of Acts 13:15. The pattern can be divided formally in three parts:

(1) authoritative *exempla*, i.e., evidence in the form of biblical quotations, examples from the past or present, or reasoned exposition adduced to commend the points that follow; (2) a conclusion inferred from the preceding examples, indicating their relevance for the audience; and (3) a final exhortation. This identifiable tripartite pattern can be found in many early Christian writings (Hebrews, *1 Clement*, other speeches in Acts, 2 Cor 6:14–7:1, 1 Cor 10:1–14, 1 and 2 Peter, the Letters of Ignatius, *Barnabas*) and in Jewish sources from the hellenistic period (e.g., the old LXX version of Susanna and the Elders, where the story of Susanna becomes the *exemplum*, to which there has been appended a homiletical conclusion [v 63*a*] and an exhortation [v 63*b*]; the Epistle of Jeremy, where the several instances of idolatry provide the *exempla*, followed by the conclusion and exhortation in v 68; cf. *T. Reub.* 5:1–5; *T. Levi* 2:6–4:1; *T. Naph.* 1:1–8:2; Aristobulus [in Eusebius, *Preparation for the Gospel* 13.12, 664*c*–666*d*]; 4 Macc 16:16–22; Jos., *J. W.* 5.362–415; 7.341–80).

From these documents, all of which reflect the "word of exhortation" form, Wills argued, "it can be reasonably hypothesized that it became the form of the sermon in Hellenistic synagogues" (Wills, *HTR* 77 [1984] 293; cf. 299, "When approached in this way, a large number of Hellenistic Jewish and early Christian writings come to light which can accurately be called sermons or sermon-influenced"). The progression from *exempla* to the conclusion to the final exhortation carried a cumulative force that was well suited to the oral sermon of the hellenistic synagogue and early house church.

From the numerous sources that betray the influence of the tripartite pattern identified by Wills, it is clear that the form is flexible and can be developed in a variety of ways. It can stand alone, as in Acts 13:16–41, or be extended in a cyclical fashion as the pattern is repeated in a longer sermon (e.g., Heb 1:5–4:16;

8:1–12:28; *1 Clem.* 4:1–13*a*; 37:2–40:1*b*; Ign., *Eph.* 3:1–4:2; 5:1–36; 7:2–10:1). The writer of Hebrews appears to have followed a modified form of the latter pattern, creating a very complex sermonic text. Although Wills recognized that it was not possible to fit every section of Hebrews into the "word of exhortation" pattern, he was able to demonstrate that the writer used the form but adapted it to a more sophisticated structure (*HTR* 77 [1984] 280–83, where Wills is able to trace the pattern of argumentation in Heb 1–4 and 8–12). The assumption that a sermonic form lies behind the text of Hebrews, Wills insisted, "becomes compelling" (299).

In a follow-up article published in 1988, C. C. Black II stressed the remarkable coherence of the sermonic form discerned by Wills with the conventions of classical rhetoric (*HTR* 81 [1988] 1–18). He argued that "once the form of the hellenistic Jewish and early Christian sermon is viewed in alignment with the canons of Greco-Roman rhetoric, a number of Will's perceptive intuitions receive primary verification, and residual problems associated with his proposal are dispelled" (Black, 4).

Black located the setting of the "word of exhortation" form in classical rhetoric (4–16; for Black's own analysis of the paradigmatic homily, Acts 13:16–41, see 8–10, which identifies Paul's speech as "an epideictic address, aimed at engendering belief" [10]). He argued that the mainstream of classical rhetoric was unquestionably a major contributor to the cultural milieu of hellenistic Jews and Christians. From this perspective he was able to address the issue of *why* the recurring pattern of argumentation based upon *exempla* would be regarded as convincing by a hellenistic audience, and to demonstrate the fundamental congruence of the "word of exhortation" with classical oratory (Black, 12–15). He asserted that "the structure of these hellenistic Jewish and early Christian sermons is perfectly understandable in terms of the rhetorical conventions outlined in such ancient handbooks as Aristotle's *Rhetoric,* Quintilian's *Institutio oratoria,* and Cornificius' *Rhetorica ad Herennium*" (Black, 11). It is characteristic of the documents to which Wills appealed, including Hebrews, that they were addressed not just to the eye but to the ear, and that they were written with the intent to persuade (cf. Aristotle, *Rhetoric* 1.2.1355B).

Black freely illustrated his argument with reference to Hebrews, which he regards as an early Christian sermon exhibiting highly nuanced and sophisticated forms of proof (e.g., *HTR* 81 [1988] 13). He pointed out that to the extent that the various hortatory cycles in Hebrews attempt to augment complementary ideas with multiple arguments, the writer is engaging in what the classical handbooks refer to as "amplification" or "refinement" (15). He was able to account for the lengthy interruption in the "word of exhortation" form in Heb 5:1–10:18, where the writer deviates from the established hortatory pattern to present an extended exposition. The apparent anomaly vanishes once it is remembered that the writer explicitly aims not only to exhort his audience but also to fortify them in their present convictions on the basis of an exposition of the surpassing, unrepeatable priestly sacrifice of Jesus for the sins of the many (15, n. 42). Black discerns in Hebrews an "epideictic attempt to stimulate belief in the present" (5).

An independent approach to the "word of exhortation" form was published in 1990 by H. W. Attridge (*Semeia* 50 [1990], 215–17, 223). On the basis of an inductive analysis of the formal features of Hebrews, he suggests that the "homily" or "word of exhortation" form is a sub-genre within the generic taxonomy of parenesis offered by J. G. Gammie (*Semeia* 50 [1990], 41–77). Attridge discerns a formal pattern that serves as a structuring device in important sections of Hebrews (3:1–4:16; 8:1–10:18; 12:1–13). The pattern consists of formal introduction (e.g., 3:1–6; 8:1–6; 12:1–3), scriptural citation (e.g., 3:7–11; 8:7–13; 12:4–6), exposition or thematic elaboration (e.g., 3:12–4:13; 9:1–10:18; 12:7–11), and application (4:14–16; 10:19–21; 12:12–13). This pattern of form and content is partially replicated in other portions of Hebrews as well (e.g., 7:1–28). Attridge suggests that in all of these sections of Hebrews the analogous formal pattern is a constitutive feature of what should be defined as a major sub-genre within the genre of parenetic literature for which it is appropriate to use the modern terms "homily" or "sermon." The technical literary designation for this sub-genre is "word of exhortation" (Heb 13:22; Acts 13:15) or "paraclesis."

Attridge's analysis suggests the hortatory function of Hebrews and its unity as an example of "paraclesis." He proposes that the setting for the emergence of this homiletical form was the synagogue in the social world of the hellenistic city. Paraclesis is "the newly minted rhetorical form that actualizes traditional Scripture for a community in a non-traditional environment" (Attridge, *Semeia* 50 [1990] 217). The writer of Hebrews adapts this form in order to confirm the values and commitments of a Christian group who were experiencing social ostracism and alienation in their own environment (Attridge, 219–23).

While it is necessary to concede the tension between the analysis of the form of Hebrews in the articles by L. Wills, C. C. Black II, and H. W. Attridge, their research has done much to vindicate and refine the definition of Hebrews as a sermon or homily.

REFLECTIONS OF THE GENRE

Recognizing the oral, sermonic character of Hebrews permits important features of the style and structure to receive the attention they deserve. The writer skillfully conveys the impression that he is present with the assembled group and is actually delivering the sermon he has prepared. Until the postscript (13:22–25), he studiously avoids any reference to actions like writing or reading that would tend to emphasize the distance that separates him from the group he is addressing. Instead he stresses the actions of speaking and listening, which are appropriate to persons in conversation, and identifies himself with his audience in a direct way:

> It is not to angels that he has subjected the world to come, about which we are speaking (2:5).

> We have much to say about this, but it is hard to explain intelligibly, since you have become hard of hearing (5:11).

> Even though we speak like this, dear friends, . . . (6:9).

> Now the crowning affirmation to what we are saying is this . . . (8:1).

But we cannot discuss these things in detail now (9:5).

And what more shall I say? I do not have time to tell about . . . (11:32).

The writer assumes a conversational tone in order to diminish the sense of geographical distance that separates him from his audience and makes writing necessary. He conceives of his work as speech. By referring to speaking and listening, he is able to establish a sense of presence with his audience.

The writer was clearly a gifted preacher. Hebrews is characterized by a skillful use of alliteration, of oratorical imperatives, of euphonic phrases, of unusual word order calculated to arouse the attention, and of literary devices designed to enhance rhetorical effectiveness. The alternation between exposition and exhortation characteristic of the literary structure of Hebrews provides an effective vehicle for oral impact. Hebrews was prepared for oral delivery to a specific community. (Andriessen, *En lisant,* 60, has made the important observation that the so-called *Epistle of Diognetus* is a writing of the same genre. It presupposes throughout a listener or listeners, never readers [*Diog.* 1; 2:1–10; 3:1; 6:1; 7:1], and the use of the first person is alternately singular and plural.)

The character of Hebrews as sermonic discourse invites an interpreter or reader to be sensitive to the abrupt shifts from orality to textuality to orality. There is an important difference between oral preaching and written discourse (cf. E. des Places, "Style parlé at style oral chez les écrivains grecs," in *Mélanges Bidez,* AIPHO 2 [Brussels: Secrétariat de l'Institut, 1934] 267–86). The dynamic between speaker and audience is distinct in each case. The writer expressly declares in 13:22 that his "word of exhortation" has been reduced to writing. As such, it has become "frozen" and available for study to a modern reader, with a life of its own quite independent of the audience for whom it was written. But it is clear that that was not its original intention. It is equally clear that the writer would have preferred to have spoken directly and immediately with those whom he addressed (13:19, 23). In the realm of oral speech the speaker and the auditors are sustained in relationship within a world of sound. Although forced by geographical distance and a sense of urgency to reduce his homily to writing, the writer never loses sight of the power of oral impact.

Hebrews is a sermon prepared to be read aloud to a group of auditors who will receive its message not primarily through reading and leisured reflection but orally. Reading the document aloud entails oral performance, providing oral clues to those who listen to the public reading of the sermon. This complex reality underscores the importance of rhetorical form and the subtleties of expression in this homily. Hebrews was crafted to communicate its point as much aurally as logically. In point of fact, aural considerations, in the event of communication, often prove to be the decisive ones.

RHETORICAL ANALYSIS

Bibliography

Attridge, H. W. "Paraenesis in a Homily (λόγος παρακλήσεως):The Possible Location of, and Socialization in, the 'Epistle to the Hebrews.'" *Semeia* 50 (1990) 211–26. **Black, C. C. II.** "The Rhetorical Form of the Hellenistic Jewish and Early Christian Sermon: A Response to Lawrence Wills." *HTR* 81 (1988) 1–18. **Clark, D. L.** *Rhetoric in Greco-Roman Education.* New York: Columbia University Press, 1957. **Clarke, M. L.** *Higher Education in the Ancient World.* Albuquerque: University of New Mexico Press, 1971. ————. *Rhetoric at Rome: A Historical Survey.* London: Cohen and West, 1966. **Cosby, M. R.** *The Rhetorical Composition and Function of Hebrews 11: In Light of Example Lists in Antiquity.* Macon, GA: Mercer UP, 1988. ————. "The Rhetorical Composition of Hebrews 11." *JBL* 107 (1988) 257–73. **Daube, D.** "Rabbinic Methods of Interpretation and Hellenistic Rhetoric." *HUCA* 22 (1949) 239–64. **Evans, C. F.** *The Theology of Rhetoric: The Epistle to the Hebrews.* London: Dr. Williams's Trust, 1988. **Haering, T.** "Gedankengang und Grundgedanken des Hebräerbriefs." *ZNW* 18 (1917–18) 145–64. **Hay, D. M.** "What is Proof?—Rhetorical Verification in Philo, Josephus, and Quintilian." SBLASP 2 (1979) 87–100. **Kennedy, G. A.** *The Art of Persuasion in Greece.* Princeton: Princeton UP, 1963. ————. *The Art of Rhetoric in the Roman World 300 B.C.—A.D. 300.* Princeton: Princeton UP, 1972. ————. *Classical Rhetoric and Its Christian and Secular Tradition from Ancient to Modern Times.* Chapel Hill: University of North Carolina Press, 1980. ————. *New Testament Interpretation through Rhetorical Criticism.* Chapel Hill/London: University of North Carolina Press, 1984. **Lausberg, H.** *Elemente der literarischen Rhetorik*³. Munich: Heuber, 1967. ————. *Handbuch der literarischen Rhetorik: Eine Grundlegung der Literaturwissenschaft*². 2 Vols. Munich: Heuber, 1973. **Lindars, B.** "The Rhetorical Structure of Hebrews." *NTS* 35 (1989) 382–406. **Mack, B. L.** *Rhetoric and the New Testament.* Minneapolis: Fortress, 1990. **Marrou, H. I.** *A History of Education in Antiquity.* London/New York: Sheed & Ward, 1956. 194–205, 233–42, 284–91. **McCall, M. H.** *Ancient Rhetorical Theories of Simile and Comparison.* Cambridge: Harvard UP, 1969. **Nissilä, K.** *Das Hohepriestermotiv im Hebräerbrief: Eine exegetische Untersuchung.* Helsinki: Oy Liiton Kirjapaino, 1979. **Parunak, H. V. D.** "Transitional Techniques in the Bible." *JBL* 102 (1983) 525–48. **Smith, R. W.** *The Art of Rhetoric in Alexandria: Its Theory and Practice in the Ancient World.* The Hague: Nijhoff, 1974. 73–154. **Smith, W. A.** *Ancient Education.* New York: Philosophical Library, 1955. **Übelacker, W. G.** *Der Hebräerbrief als Appell: Untersuchungen zu* exordium, narratio *und* postscriptum *(Hebr 1–2 und 13, 22–25).* Stockholm: Almqvist & Wiksell, 1989. **Vitti, A. M.** "Le bellezze stilistiche nella Lettera agli Ebrei." *Bib* 7 (1936) 137–66. **Walden, J. W.** *The Universities of Ancient Greece.* New York: C. Scribner's Sons, 1910. **Watson, D. F.** "The New Testament and Greco-Roman Rhetoric: A Bibliography." *JETS* 31 (1988) 465–72. **Wills, L.** "The Form of the Sermon in Hellenistic Judaism and Early Christianity." *HTR* 77 (1984) 277–99. **Winter, B. W.** "Philo and Paul among the Sophists: A Hellenistic Jewish and Christian Response." Dissertation, Macquarrie University, North Ryde, NSW, 1988.

In Hebrews the voice of the writer is the voice of the speaker. The writer understood that it was necessary to provide an audience with verbal clues in order to aid his listeners in determining where one unit of the discourse ended and another began. Such clues were essential, especially in written discourse. It is necessary to recall that in ancient documents there was an absence of any indication of where component parts of a composition began and ended. This was an accepted convention in the pervasively oral culture of the environment. For that reason alone, verbal clues needed to be provided to disclose the organization of the argument. Devices like repetition, anaphora, *inclusio, responsio,* parallelism, catchword association, oratorical imperatives, direct address to the listeners, rhetorical questions, "hook-words," and the like are present in Hebrews because of the need to provide oral assistance to the listeners. They also aided the one reading the discourse to the assembled group to give the content a coherent hearing. For all of these reasons the written text was not crafted for the eye but for the ear, to convey a sense of structure and development. The appeal is to the emotions as much as to the intellect. Forceful and artistic prose provides the vehicle for the tenor of the argument.

Hebrews abounds in rhetorical language (see the extensive catalogue in Spicq, 1:351–78, and for a helpful introduction to the importance of rhetorical features in one unit of Hebrews, Cosby, *JBL* 107 [1988] 257–73). It provides constant illustration of the power in the artistic implementation of language. As M. R. Cosby has observed, there is in Hebrews "a dimension of persuasiveness available only to the ears of one listening to the Greek text" (258). An attempt has been made in the *Form/Structure/Setting, Comment,* and *Explanation* sections of the commentary on each of the pericopes of Hebrews to recognize these dimensions and to be sensitive to the rhetorical strategies employed by the writer. Hebrews is a highly rhetorical discourse both in style and in patterns of argumentation. It lends itself to rhetorical analysis.

The suggestion that Hebrews was developed as a discourse on the basis of ancient rhetorical principles is not new. It can be found already in the sixteenth century in the work of the commentator Niels Hemmingsen (*Commentaria in omnes Epistulas Apostolorum, Pauli, Petri, Iudae, Ioannis, Iacobi, et in eam quae ad Hebraeos inscribitur* [Frankfurt: Corvinus, 1579] 831; cf. K. Hagen, *Hebrews Commenting from Erasmus to Beza 1516–1598,* 80–81). At the beginning of the twentieth century H. F. von Soden asserted that the development of Hebrews demonstrates that the writer was not only alert to classical rhetorical conventions as practiced in the first century, but that Hebrews had been constructed in accordance with the rules of the rhetorical schools (*Urchristliche Literaturgeschichte: Die Schriften des Neuen Testaments* [Berlin: Duncker, 1905] 127–28). He developed this idea in a commentary on Hebrews, analyzing the construction of the document along the highly conceptualized lines of classical forensic rhetoric (*Hebräerbrief,* 8–11):

προοίμιον with a presentation of the πρόθεσις	prologue	Heb 1:1–4
	thematic statement	Heb 1:5–4:16
διήγησις πρὸς πιθανότητα	statement of the plausibility of the case	Heb 5–6
ἀπόδειξις πρὸς πειθώ	demonstration of proof	Heb 7:1–10:18
ἐπίλογος	peroration	Heb 10:19–13:25

Although no one today would follow von Soden in identifying Hebrews with forensic rhetoric, this four-part scheme was adopted, with slight revisions, by T. Haering (*ZNW* 18 [1917–18] 153–63) and H. Windisch (8).

During the past quarter of a century rhetorical criticism has developed as a distinct discipline. Its concern is to inform an analysis of the documents of the NT from the conceptualizations of rhetoric by the Greeks and by its borrowed and modified Roman form. This development has been fostered by the fact that Greco-Roman rhetoric is clearly systematized and is set forth in extant handbooks from the NT era. The NT documents were written in the context of hellenistic culture, and the educational center of that culture was in the inculcation of rhetoric. (On primary and secondary schooling in Alexandria, for example, see R. W. Smith, *The Art of Rhetoric in Alexandria,* 110–54.) Even those writers of the NT who had not received formal training in the rhetorical schools would have been influenced by public speeches in the marketplace and elsewhere in urban centers. For these reasons, it may be anticipated that patterns of rhetorical argumentation, as discussed in the Greco-Roman handbooks, will be present in an aurally sensitive document like Hebrews. The concern to understand the dynamic of persuasion and its function in a given social context is intrinsic to rhetorical analysis and is certainly germane to Hebrews.

In a recent approach to Hebrews through rhetorical analysis, B. Lindars observed that it is necessary to determine the class of rhetoric to which Hebrews belongs, because that determination will have a bearing upon the interpretation of the text (*NTS* 35 [1989] 382–406). He suggests, without any formal analysis, that Hebrews should be classified as deliberative rhetoric since it consists of advising and dissuading (383, with a reference to Quintilian, *Institutio oratoria* 3.8.6, who says of deliberative rhetoric "its functions are twofold and consist in advising and dissuading"; Lindars interprets λόγος τῆς παρακλήσεως in Heb 13:22 as "an exhortation to appropriate action" [386]). The title of Lindars' article is misleading, for apart from incidental comments he does not concern himself with rhetorical structure. His primary concern is to evaluate the rhetorical effectiveness of Hebrews, rather than to delineate the actual structural framework. He reviews the composition, which he insists has the essential character of a letter (383, n. 2), from the perspective of rhetorical aims and methods embedded in the text in order to assess the intended impact of each section upon the auditors (390–402).

A more extensive and useful contribution to research on the rhetorical form of Hebrews was published in 1989 by W. G. Übelacker (*Der Hebräerbrief als Appell*). In his detailed approach to the text, Übelacker combines rhetorical analysis with discourse analysis (see below, "Discourse Analysis"). He identifies Hebrews as a deliberative discourse (214–29), with a rhetorical *prooemium* (prologue, 1:1–4), *narratio* (necessary background information, 1:5–2:18) with the *propositio* (a lucid thematic statement, or the statement of what is to be proved, 2:17–18), *argumentatio* with *probatio* and *refutatio* (argumentation with the presentation of proof and refutation, 3:1–12:29), *peroratio* (peroration, 13:1–21), and *postscriptum* (postscript, 13:22–25) which identifies the discourse in 1:1–13:21 as an exhortation or urgent appeal. Übelacker provides an extensive analysis of the exordium, Heb 1:1–4 (66–138), and a less extensive treatment of the *narratio*, Heb 1:5–2:18 (140–96). His proposals concerning the remainder of the homily are derived from his analysis of these two initial units of the text. Übelacker concludes that the writer used the rhetorical conventions of classical antiquity to persuade his audience to accept Jesus' unique sacrifice for sins as fully sufficient to provide access to fellowship with God.

Übelacker's rhetorical analysis of Hebrews was anticipated in the 1979 Finnish dissertation of K. Nissilä (*Das Hohepriestermotiv im Hebräerbrief*, 15–19, 74–78, 143–47, 239–44). Nissilä subjected nine textual units (Heb 2:14–18; 3:1–6; 4:14–16; 5:1–10; 7:26–28; 8:1–6; 9:11–15; 9:24–28; 10:11–14) to an analysis involving considerations of structure, style, context, range of ideas, the relationship of the motif of high priest to other prominent motifs in Hebrews, and the rhetorical use made of the motif of high priest. He concluded that the high priest motif is the key structural element in Hebrews, binding the whole discourse together. It serves functionally as a rhetorical element to teach, admonish, delight, and reprove the auditors. Nissilä divided Hebrews into the *exordium* (1:1–14), *narratio* (1:5–2:18), *argumentatio* (3:1–12:29), and *epilogus* (13:1–25). It is important to observe that both Nissilä and Übelacker have made an assessment of the rhetorical structure of Hebrews on the basis of an analysis of parts of the homily.

The classification of Hebrews as deliberative rhetoric by B. Lindars, K. Nissilä, and W. G. Übelacker, of course, stands in tension with the equally confident appeal to the conventions of epideictic rhetoric by C. C. Black II (*HTR* 81 [1988] 5; so also D. E. Aune, *The New Testament in Its Literary Environment* [Philadelphia: Westminster, 1987] 212: "Hebrews is *epideictic*"). H. W. Attridge, with some reluctance, also classifies Hebrews as an epideictic oration, with a few appropriate deliberative elements, because "it celebrates the significance of a person and certain events connected with him. The celebration functions to reinforce values and commitments associated with that person and those events. Yet in reinforcing those values and commitments, it issues admonitions and specific recommendations" (*Semeia* 50 [1990] 214).

The difficulty in classifying Hebrews as "deliberative" or "epideictic" is easy to understand. Deliberative rhetoric is concerned with persuading an audience to make a choice on the basis of some future benefit or to dissuade them from some inappropriate action. It seeks to influence the listeners to make the right decision for the future. (For the discussion of the three types of rhetoric, see Aristotle, *Rhetoric* 1.2.1358B; Cicero, *De inventione* 2.3.12–13; 2.51.155–58, 176; 2.58.176–77; Cornificius [?], *Rhetorica ad Herennium* 1.2.2; 3.2.2–3; 3.6.10–11; Quintilian, *Institutio oratoria* 3.4.12–16; 3.7.1–28; 3.8.1–6; 3.9.1.) This is certainly congruent with the earnestly pastoral character of much of the exhortation in Hebrews. The writer is focused on persuading the auditors to hold fast to their confession and to dissuade them from abandoning their stance of faith, incurring the sanction of covenant exclusion from the presence of God (cf. the oratorical imperatives in Heb 2:1; 3:1; 4:11, 14; 10:22; 12:1, 12). Epideictic rhetoric is concerned with reinforcing beliefs already accepted by the audience. The rhetor turns teacher and seeks to entrench a pattern already embraced. It is clear that this is an essential function of the exposition in Hebrews, and to a degree to the exhortation not to cast aside the confidence and hope once firmly held by the members of the group because the one who has promised is faithful (cf. Heb 3:6, 14; 10:23, 35–39; 11:11, among other texts). Hebrews cannot be forced into the mold of a classical speech.

What must be appreciated with reference to the writer of Hebrews is that responsible persons are not bound by rhetorical conventions. Rhetorical advice in the standard handbooks was given in terms of declamation. Disputation necessarily entails a declamatory element. But the writer of Hebrews has a serious pastoral purpose and consequently is not bound by rhetorical conventions. He was not obliged to adhere to rigidly fixed rules of form and content. The same observation has been made forcefully by D. Runia with reference to Philo ("Philo's *De aeternitate mundi*: The Problem of Its Interpretation," *VC* 35 [1981] 105–51). Runia demonstrates that Philo's treatise has as its formal basis the genre of the *thesis* as practiced in the rhetorical and philosophical schools in his day, but he freely adapts this rhetorical convention to suit his purposes (Runia, 118, 139, 144, nn. 43, 46, 49; for Runia's rhetorical analysis of the treatise, see 121–30).

Rhetorical devices are clearly discernible in Hebrews, but the presence of an identifiable rhetorical structure is less evident. It should be recognized that we do not understand thoroughly even the rhetorical devices of the NT era. The present state of research on Hebrews is such that no one has yet produced a structural analysis of the homily that conforms strictly to the types of rhetoric defined in the handbooks. Even if it were possible to do so, caution would have to be exercised in adopting the analysis. Neither Philo nor Paul conformed strictly to identifiable forms (see Winter, "Philo and Paul among the Sophists," 236–42, 248–51). H. D. Betz, for example, acknowledged bewilderment when he attempted to analyze the rhetorical structure of Gal 3 and 4 (*Galatians: A Commentary on Paul's Letter to the Churches of Galatia*, Hermeneia [Philadelphia: Fortress, 1979] 129). Betz failed to observe that there is a significant rhetorical shift at Gal 4:12 from forensic to deliberative rhetoric (see now G. W. Hansen, *Abraham in Galatians: Epistolary and Rhetorical Contexts*, JSNTSup 29 [Sheffield: JSOT, 1989] 43–71; for Hansen's analysis of the rhetorical techniques and forms of argument used in this section of the letter, see 73–93; I am indebted to B. W. Winter for calling my attention to the observations of D. Runia and G. W. Hansen).

Rhetorical analysis has heightened an appreciation of the substantial rhetorical skills of the writer in conveying a message that had to be grasped aurally and that depended for its impact upon the sound of the statements as much as upon the unfolding of a compelling argument. The writer was clearly indebted to Greek rhetoric; there is clear evidence of his use of rhetorical forms in Hebrews. The fact that he was never tied to the rhetorical forms that he used but molded them to suit his own purposes indicates that he was at home with them, and his written discourse confirms this.

Rhetorical analysis is able to advance the interpretation of Hebrews by inquiring from a classical frame of reference concerning the argumentative strategies the writer pursued. What modes of persuasion other than logical argument are evident in the homily? How do the diction and composition of the sermon contribute to its effectiveness? It is legitimate to inquire concerning the rhetorical situation to which Hebrews is an appropriate response. But it will also be necessary to inquire concerning modes of argumentation and persuasion that had their primary home in Jewish schools and synagogues in hellenistic urban centers (see below, "The Writer's Appropriation of the OT Text").

DISCOURSE ANALYSIS

Bibliography

Berger, K. *Exegese des Neuen Testaments: Neue Wege vom Text zur Auslegung*[2]. Heidelberg: Quelle & Meyer, 1984. 11–32. **Black, D. A.** "Hebrews 1:1–4: A Study in Discourse Analysis." *WTJ* 49 (1987) 175–99. ———. *Linguistics, Biblical Semantics, and Bible Translation: An Annotated Bibliography of Periodical Literature from 1961.* La Mirada, CA: Biola University, 1984. ———. *Linguistics for Students of New Testament Greek: A Survey of Basic Concepts and Applications.* Grand Rapids: Baker, 1988. **Cotterell, P.** and **Turner, M.** *Linguistics and Biblical Interpretation.* Downers Grove, IL: Inter-Varsity Press, 1989. **Dussaut, L.** *Synopse structurelle de l'Épître aux Hébreux: Approache d'analyse structurelle.* Paris: Desclée, 1981. **Guthrie, G. H.** "The Structure of Hebrews: A Text-linguistic Analysis." Dissertation, Southwestern Baptist Theological Seminary, 1991. **Longacre, R. E.** *An Anatomy of Speech Notions.* Lisse, Belgium: de Ridder, 1976. ———. "Some Fundamental Insights of Tagmemics." *Language* 41 (1965) 66–76. ———. *Tagmemics.* Waco, TX: Word, 1985. **Louw, J. P.** *The Semantics of New Testament Greek.* Philadelphia: Fortress, 1982. **Neely, L. L.** "A Discourse Analysis of Hebrews." *OPTT* 3–4 (1987) 1–146. **Nissilä, K.** *Das Hohepriestermotiv im Hebräerbrief: Eine exegetische Untersuchung.*

Helsinki: Oy Liiton Kirjapaino, 1979. **Schenk, W.** "Hebräerbrief 4, 14–16: Textlinguistic als Kommentierungsprinzip." *NTS* 26 (1980) 380–96. **Übelacker, W. G.** *Der Hebräerbrief als Appell: Untersuchungen zu* exordium, narratio *und* postscriptum (*Hebr 1–2 und 13:22–25*). Stockholm: Almqvist & Wiksell, 1989.

As a written communication, Hebrews lends itself to discourse, or text-linguistic, analysis. This relatively new form of analysis is only now emerging as an application of modern linguistic techniques to biblical criticism. Writing in 1989, P. Cotterell and M. Turner comment, "The fact is that at present there are no firm conclusions, no generally accepted formulae, no fixed methodology, not even an agreed terminology" (*Linguistics,* 233). Linguistics is simply the study of human language, and especially of the inner dynamics within a network of relationships that must come together harmoniously in order to effect the event of communication (e.g., speech sounds, word meanings, grammar, word grouping in phrases, sentences, and paragraphs; cf. Black, *Linguistics,* 4–5). The young discipline of discourse analysis is endeavoring to develop perspectives and tools of analysis that will prove useful in the interpretation of the biblical text.

The proper concerns of discourse analysis are semantic cohesion, the constituent relationships within a unit of discourse, and the identification of unit boundaries within discourse. The primary goal of discourse analysis is an understanding of the individual paragraphs that constitute the building blocks of a discourse since it is the paragraph, rather than individual semantic units like words or sentences, that provides the key to understanding the total (or main) discourse. The semantic content of the main discourse is more than the sum of the semantic content of each sentence. This is because a writer has grouped sentences together to form larger semantic units (i.e., paragraphs), which are assigned a variety of semantic functions in the development of the discourse (cf. Louw, *Semantics,* 97–98; Cotterell and Turner, *Linguistics,* 230–31).

The fundamental assumption of discourse analysis is that written texts have their origin in the writer's conceptualization of the theme he wished to communicate. This theme is given expression and development by linguistic choices (diction, grammar, style), which lend meaning and structure to paragraph-units. In order to comprehend the writer's development of his theme, it is necessary to examine the text on the lexical, syntactic, and rhetorical levels, as in the diagram provided by G. H. Guthrie in discussion with J. S. Duvall ("The Structure of Hebrews," 105; cf. Louw, *Semantics,* 94):

The Processes of Communication and Analysis

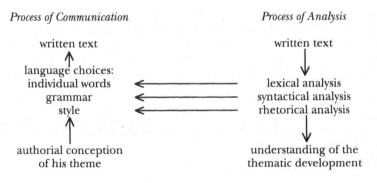

Process of Communication	*Process of Analysis*
written text	written text
↑	↓
language choices:	
individual words ←	lexical analysis
grammar ←	syntactical analysis
style ←	rhetorical analysis
↑	↓
authorial conception of his theme	understanding of the thematic development

The goal of lexical, syntactical, and rhetorical analysis is to understand the paragraphs, which are the fundamental units for understanding the meaning of the discourse as a whole (cf. Berger, *Exegese*, 111). An analysis of the dynamic relationships between the constituent paragraphs is ultimately necessary in order to understand the semantic program of the main discourse. Discourse analysis attempts to identify how a writer linguistically marked his paragraphs and embedded discourses (i.e., identifiable, distinct units of discourse, which have a beginning and an end) in the process of developing the main discourse.

The potential importance of discourse analysis as a tool for interpreting Hebrews has been demonstrated by L. L. Neeley (*OPTT* 3–4 [1987] 1–146). Her research was based upon the method of discourse analysis developed by the contemporary linguist R. E. Longacre (*Language* 41 [1965] 66–76; *An Anatomy of Speech Notions* [1976]; *Tagmemics* [1985]). Longacre identifies four major systems of organization that are used by a writer in developing a discourse: (1) the combining of sentences into larger units of discourse, namely paragraphs and embedded discourses; (2) constituent structure, reflecting the linguistic functions of units of discourse; (3) the discrimination between *backbone* (i.e., structural) and support information; and (4) semantic organization. Neeley endeavors to analyze Hebrews on the basis of these systems of organization (*OPTT* 3–4 [1987] 1).

Applying Longacre's discourse analysis to Hebrews, Neeley proposes four criteria for isolating units of discourse within the homily: (1) a change of genre (e.g., from exposition to exhortation); (2) transition introductions or conclusions (e.g., back-references like "hook-words," reiterations, and summaries); (3) the use of relatively rare linguistic devices (e.g., rhetorical questions, rare particles, vocatives); and (4) evidence of the lexical and semantic cohesion of the preceding embedded discourse (e.g., *inclusio*, which she refers to as "sandwich structures," *chiasmus*, and the tracking of characteristic words; *OPTT* 3–4 [1987] 6–18). Neeley also concerns herself with the functions of the various constituents that form each of the larger units of the discourse. She suggests that in most well-developed discourses (and embedded discourses) it is possible to identify an *introduction*, various *points* which develop the writer's argument, a *peak* (i.e., climax), and a *conclusion* (3–4, 23–25; she concedes that "a particular discourse or embedded discourse is not required to have all four types of constituents in order to be a well formed discourse" [3]). The identification of these constituents in a discourse can aid in confirming the structure of the discourse.

On the basis of these considerations, Neeley isolates larger units of discourse (22) and of embedded discourse (141) in Hebrews that disclose the *constituent structure* of the discourse as a whole. The constituents consist of a *thematic introduction* (Heb 1:1–4), *point 1* (embedded discourse 1, Heb 1:5–4:13), *point 2* (embedded discourse 2, Heb 4:14–10:18), *peak* (embedded discourse 3, Heb 10:19–13:19), *conclusion* (Heb 13:20–21), and *finis* (Heb 13:22–25; 41). According to Neeley's analysis, Hebrews comprises, therefore, three major embedded discourses (points 1, 2, and the peak) bracketed by an introduction and a conclusion. The formalized closing at the end of the homily is unrelated to the thematic development of the discourse.

I am indebted to G. H. Guthrie for introducing me to Neeley's use of discourse analysis with reference to Hebrews. He has extracted from her discussions of the units of discourse in Hebrews the following assessment of the linguistic structure of Hebrews ("The Structure of Hebrews," 65, figure 10, "Linda Neeley's discourse analysis of the structure of Hebrews," where "ED" signifies embedded discourse):

1:1–4 Thematic Introduction to the Book

Embedded Discourse 1 (1:1–4:13): God Has Spoken to Us in His Son.
    Introduction (1:1–4)
    ED 1a (1:1–2:18) The Divinity and Humanity of Christ
    ED 1a$_1$ (1:1–14) The Divinity
    ED 1a$_2$ (2:1–18) The Humanity
    ED 1b (3:1–4:13) Do Not Harden Your Hearts

Embedded Discourse 2 (4:14–10:18): [The Son] as Our High Priest Has Offered a
    Complete Sacrifice for Sins and by This Obtained Salvation for Us.
    ED 2a (4:14–6:20) Introduction
    ED 2b (7:1–28) Christ a Superior Priest
    ED 2c (8:1–10:18) Christ's Superior Ministry

Embedded Discourse 3 (10:19–13:21) Therefore Let Us Draw Near to God with a True
    Heart in Full Assurance of Faith . . . Let us Hold Fast Our Confession . . . and
    Let us Consider Each Other to Stir Up to Love and Good Works.
    ED 3a (10:19–39) Introduction
    ED 3b (11:1–40) By Faith Endure
    ED 3c (12:1–29) Run the Race
    ED 3d (13:1–21) Practical Exhortation

13:20–21 Conclusion

13:22–25 Finis (Formalized Closing)

Neeley's analysis represents a serious attempt to analyze the text of Hebrews as an act of coherent communication on the basis of identifiable principles of communication present in most languages of the world. It is a purely linguistic approach, which is interested only in the linguistic character of the main discourse. She takes into account literary devices, the use of various genres, the semantic cohesion of individual sections, the functional roles of "constituents" (or subsections of material), and the development of the discourse. As such, her approach incorporates important elements from literary analysis, rhetorical criticism, and conceptual (or thematic) analysis. She has no interest in social or historical considerations that may have influenced or determined the surface structures of the discourse in conscious or unconscious ways. The principles invoked by Neeley were identified through the study of *modern* languages.

In his attempt to refine the application of discourse analysis to Hebrews, G. H. Guthrie calls for a fully contextual approach to the discourse, which recognizes its character as *ancient* discourse. He has devised an eclectic approach that he labels "rhetorico-discourse analysis" ("The Structure of Hebrews," 103–25). He adds the prefix "rhetorico-" to the designation "discourse analysis" to emphasize the need to be sensitive to the oral and literary environment of the ancient world. His method seeks to integrate the strengths of a number of approaches. The dominant methodological influence, however, remains discourse analysis, or text linguistics, which incorporates concerns intrinsic to both rhetorical and literary analysis. For example, the analysis of patterns of argumentation in Hebrews, which is a primary concern of rhetorical analysis, is subsumed under "constituent analysis" in discourse analysis.

Guthrie's procedure entails an examination of the embedded discourse units in Hebrews. At this stage he concerns himself with the identification of unit boundaries, as well as with an analysis of the level of semantic cohesion in the unit, and of the constituents that compose the unit. He then examines, with the aid of the results he has gathered from the analysis of the embedded discourse units, the main discourse of Hebrews, employing cohesion analysis and constituent analysis ("The Structure of Hebrews," 112–25).

A major contribution of his research is attention to the dynamic known as *transition*. He recognizes that in a well-written discourse like Hebrews there is commonly both structural and semantic overlap between units of discourse. One of Guthrie's primary concerns has been to discern the indicators by which unit boundaries may be identified and defended (109–11; cf. Cotterell and Turner, *Linguistics*, 98–99). Appealing to genre change, *inclusio*, and particle usage to establish unit boundaries, he then employs cohesion analysis and constituent analysis to defend the distinctiveness and structural integrity of a given unit of discourse. He has discerned no fewer than nine specific types of transitional techniques by which the writer of Hebrews ties together the sequence of discourse units that together compose the main discourse (see below, "Addendum: The Text-Linguistic Approach of G. H. Guthrie").

Guthrie extends his analysis beyond the paragraph unit to include sentences and "cola." Linguistically, a "colon" is a unit of grammatical structure possessing overtly or covertly a central matrix consisting of a subject and a predicate, each of which has the potential for extended features. The importance of analyzing each colon separately is that the cola provide a means of detecting the propositions which are central to an argument (see Louw, *Semantics*, 67–158; for an application of this approach to a single unit of discourse in Hebrews, see Black, *WTJ* 49 [1987] 175–99; Schenk, *NTS* 26 [1980] 380–96). With his attention to the cola, sentences, paragraphs, and embedded discourses of Hebrews, Guthrie is able to provide a comprehensive linguistic analysis of Hebrews as discourse.

Literary Structure

Bibliography

Attridge, H. W. "The Uses of Antithesis in Hebrews 8–10." *HTR* 79 (1986) 1–9. **Black, D. A.** "The Problem of the Literary Structure of Hebrews: An Evaluation and a Proposal."

GTJ 7 (1986) 163–77. **Bligh, J.** *Chiastic Analysis of the Epistle to the Hebrews.* Heythrop: Athenaeum, 1966. ———. "The Structure of Hebrews." *HeyJ* 5 (1964) 170–77. **Bruce, F. F.** "The Structure and Argument of Hebrews." *SWJT* 28 (1985) 6–12. **F. Büchsel,** "Hebräerbrief." *RGG²* (1928) 2:1669–73. **Cladder, H.** "Hebr. 1,1–5,10." *ZKT* 29 (1905) 1–27. ———. "Hebr. 5,11–10,39." *ZKT* 29 (1905) 500–524. **Descamps, A.** "La structure de l'Épître aux Hébreux." *RDT* 9 (1954) 251–58, 333–38. **Dussaut, L.** *Synopse structurelle de l'Épître aux Hébreux: Approche d'analysis structurelle.* Paris: Cerf, 1981. **Gourgues, M.** "Remarques sur la 'structure centrale' de l'Épître aux Hébreux." *RB* 84 (1977) 26–37. **Guthrie, G. H.** "The Structure of Hebrews: A Text-linguistic Analysis." Dissertation, Southwestern Baptist Theological Seminary, 1991. 16–34, 55–60. **Gyllenberg, R.** "Die Komposition des Hebräerbriefs." *SEÅ* 22–23 (1957–58) 137–47. **Haering, T.** "Gedankengang und Grundgedanken des Hebräerbriefs." *ZNW* 18 (1917–18) 145–64. **Nauck, W.** "Zum Aufbau des Hebräerbriefes." In *Judentum, Urchristentum, Kirche.* Ed. W. Eltester. BZNW 26. Giessen: Töpelmann, 1960. 199–206. **Rice, G. E.** "Apostasy as a Motif and Its Effect on the Structure of Hebrews." *AUSS* 23 (1985) 29–35. ———. "The Chiastic Structure of the Central Section of the Epistle to the Hebrews." *AUSS* 19 (1981) 243–46. **Swetnam, J.** "Form and Content in Hebrews 1–6." *Bib* 53 (1972) 368–85. ———. "Form and Content in Hebrews 7–13." *Bib* 55 (1974) 333–48. **Thien, F.** "Analyse de l'Épître aux Hébreux." *RB* 11 (1902) 74–86. **Vaganay, L.** "Le Plan de l'Épître aux Hébreux." In *Mémorial Lagrange.* Paris: Gabalda, 1940. 269–77. **Vanhoye, A.** "De structura litteraria Epistulae ad Hebraeos." *VD* 40 (1962) 73–80. ———. "Discussion sur la structure de l'Épître aux Hébreux." *Bib* 55 (1974) 349–80. ———. "Les indices de la structure littéraire de l'Épître aux Hébreux." *SE* 2 (1964) 493–509. ———. "Literarische Struktur und theologische Botschaft des Hebräerbriefs." *SNTU* 4 (1979) 119–47; 5 (1980) 18–49. ———. "La structure centrale de l'Épître aux Hébreux (Heb. 8/1–9/28)." *RSR* 47 (1959) 44–60. ———. *Structure and Message of the Epistle to the Hebrews.* Rome: Pontificio Instituto Biblico, 1989. ———. *La structure littéraire de l'Épître aux Hébreux.*. 2nd ed. StudNeot 1. Paris/Bruges: Desclée de Brouwer, 1976. ———. "Structure littéraire et thèmes théologique de l'Épître aux Hébreux." In *Studiorum Paulinorum Congressus Internationalis Catholicus 1961.* AnBib 17–18. Rome: Pontifical Biblical Institute, 1963. 2:175–81.

The literary structure of Hebrews is uniquely complex and elusive. As recently as 1987, D. E. Aune stated categorically, "The structure of Hebrews remains an unsolved problem" (*The New Testament in Its Literary Environment,* 213). As D. A. Black has observed, if the writer had a carefully planned structure in mind for the development of the discourse, his arrangement is not easily perceived by those who have made Hebrews an object of intensive study (*GTJ* 7 [1986] 164).

EARLY SUGGESTIVE APPROACHES

Advances in the quest for the literary structure of Hebrews have been made through the combined efforts of several scholars, each approaching the discourse from a particular vantage point. F. Büchsel, for example, called attention to the importance of genre differentiation, as the writer alternates between exposition and exhortation (*RGG²*, 2:1669–73). His insight has been sharpened by R. Gyllenberg (*SEÅ* 22–23 [1957–58] 137–47) and remains a significant clue in the detection of the literary structure of Hebrews.

Significant verbal clues supplied by the writer have been observed by those who have employed literary analysis in their approach to the text of Hebrews.

Near the turn of the century F. Thien recognized that the writer announces his primary themes just prior to the introduction of the unit in which they are to be developed *in inverse order* (*RB* 11 [1902] 74–86). Accordingly, in Heb 2:17 Jesus is designated a "merciful and faithful high priest in the service of God." In 3:1–5:10 the writer directs attention to Jesus as "faithful" (3:1–4:13) and then to Jesus as "merciful" (4:14–5:10). This procedure is repeated in 7:1–10:39. In 5:9–10 Jesus is described as "the source of an eternal salvation" and as "a priest like Melchizedek." Following a hortatory introduction to the next major division (5:11–6:20), the writer develops the notion of Jesus as a priest like Melchizedek (7:1–28) before developing the theme of Jesus as the source of an eternal salvation (8:1–10:18). In 10:36–39 the writer announces the themes to be developed in 11:1–12:29, namely, endurance (10:36) and faith (10:38–39). Thien considered 1:1–14 the introduction to the discourse and 13:1–25 its conclusion.

Thien's proposals were taken up and developed in 1940 by L. Vaganay, whose significant article, "Le Plan de l'Épître aux Hébreux" (269–77), has been heralded as the beginning of the modern discussion of the literary structure of Hebrews (Michel, 29; H. Feld, 23–25; G. H. Guthrie, "The Structure of Hebrews," 21). Focusing on the problem of the distribution of the units of discourse in Hebrews, Vaganay advanced the discussion of the structure of the document with his recognition of "hook-words" *(mot-crochets)* throughout the composition. Hook-words were a rhetorical device developed in antiquity to tie together two blocks of material (cf. Michel, 29–31). The introduction of a key word at the end of one section and its repetition at the beginning of the next served to mark formally the transition between the two units. The process is sustained throughout Hebrews, tying each section of discourse to the one that follows (Vaganay, "Le Plan," 271–72).

Basing his analysis of structure on the writer's use of such rhetorical devices, Vaganay was able to offer an outline of Hebrews that was thematically symmetrical:

Introduction (1:1–4)
First Theme in Only One Section: Jesus Superior to the Angels (1:5–2:18)
Second Theme in Two Sections: Jesus, Compassionate and Faithful High Priest (3:1–5:10)
  §1: Jesus, faithful high priest (3:1–4:16)
  §2: Jesus, compassionate high priest (5:1–10)
Third Theme in Three Sections: Jesus, Source of Eternal Salvation, Perfected Priest, High Priest like Melchizedek (5:11–10:39)
  Exhortation (5:11–6:20)
  §1: Jesus, high priest like Melchizedek (7:1–28)
  §2: Jesus, perfected priest (8:1–9:28)
  §3: Jesus, source of an eternal salvation (10:1–39)
Fourth Theme in Two Sections: Perseverance in the Faith (11:1–12:13)
  §1: Faith (11:1–12:2)
  §2: Perseverance (12:3–13)
Fifth Theme in Only One Section: The Need to be Holy (12:14–13:21)
Conclusion: Final Recommendations (13:22–25)

Vaganay's article remains a milestone in the structural assessment of Hebrews.

A different approach to identifying the literary structure of Hebrews was proposed in 1954 by A. Descamps, who called attention to the writer's conscious use of "characteristic terms" (*RDT* 9 [1954] 251–58, 333–38). The expression "characteristic terms" refers to the concentration of key vocabulary or of cognate terms within a section of discourse that serves to articulate and develop a primary theme. Descamps observed, for example, that the writer introduced the term "angels" eleven times in 1:5 to 2:16, and only twice after that point in the remainder of the discourse. The density of the concentration of this "characteristic term" serves to identify the thematic limits of a block of material. It extends from 1:5 to 2:16, together with the thematic announcement of the subject of the following section in 2:17–18. The use of "characteristic words" is a literary device by which the writer builds semantic cohesion into the several sections of the discourse.

THE SYNTHETIC APPROACH OF A. VANHOYE

A. Vanhoye became the heir to all of these suggestive approaches to uncovering the literary structure of Hebrews. In a landmark monograph published in 1963 entitled *La structure littéraire de l'Épître aux Hébreux* (2nd rev. ed., 1976), Vanhoye synthesized the insights of F. Thien, R. Gyllenberg, A. Descamps, and especially L. Vaganay with his own meticulous research on the literary structure of Hebrews. He identified five literary devices employed by the writer to indicate formally the opening and closing of unified sections throughout the discourse: (1) the announcement of the subject; (2) transitional hook-words; (3) change of genre; (4) characteristic terms; and (5) *inclusio,* i.e., the bracketing of a unit of discourse by the repetition of a striking expression or key word at the beginning and close of a section. The presence of these literary devices provided an objective means for determining the beginning and end of a unit of discourse. Vanhoye also stressed the importance of symmetrical structures in the construction of the discourse as a whole and in the subsections of which it was composed.

In the lively debate that followed the publication of Vanhoye's monograph, he has proven to be an indefatigable conversation-partner. He has shown an openness to modify details of his proposal but remains convinced of its essential correctness (see especially *Bib* 55 [1974] 349–80, and *SNTU* 4 [1979] 133–41; for a useful summary of Vanhoye's approach to the structure of Hebrews in English, see Black, *GTJ* 7 [1986] 168–73, and for an appreciation for Vanhoye's rigorous research, 173–76).

Although Vanhoye's synthetic approach to the literary structure of Hebrews has not escaped criticism (see, e.g., T. C. G. Thorton's review of Vanhoye's monograph in *JTS* n.s. 15 [1964] 137–41; Bligh, *HeyJ* 5 [1964] 170–77; Swetnam, *Bib* 53 [1964] 368–85, and id., *Bib* 55 [1974] 333–48; Zimmermann, *Bekenntnis,* 20–22), it remains influential and significant (cf. Black, *GTJ* 7 [1986] 168–76; Attridge, 16–27). I am eager to acknowledge my own reliance upon the work of Vanhoye, even when the analysis of the literary structure that I propose differs from his own. The detail of Vanhoye's mature reflections on the literary structure of Hebrews is consistently reviewed in the *Introduction* to each of the five main divisions of the discourse (1:1–2:18; 3:1–5:10; 5:11–10:39; 11:1–12:13;

12:14–13:21) and in the *Form/Structure/Setting* section for each of the constituent units of the discourse.

THE TRIPARTITE SCHEME OF W. NAUCK

Those who have been less convinced of the value of Vanhoye's proposals have tended to align themselves with the modified tripartite scheme advanced in 1960 by W. Nauck ("Zum Aufbau des Hebräerbriefes," 199–206). Nauck dialogued with the current proposals concerning the structure of Hebrews advanced in the influential commentaries of C. Spicq and O. Michel (5th ed.). He found himself attracted to the tripartite scheme championed by Michel, who found points of division in Hebrews after 4:13 and 10:18. The strength of this approach was that it recognized the organization of Hebrews in terms of the primacy of parenesis (Nauck, "Zum Aufbau," 201–3). Nauck noted that hortatory blocks of material are assigned the dominant role in framing structurally the three major divisions of Hebrews. He proposed that 1:1–4:13 be seen as an integrated unit framed by the logos-hymn in 1:2*b*–3 at the opening and the sophia-hymn in 4:12–13 at the close of the division. He then modified Michel's proposal concerning the central division, extending it from 4:14–10:18 to 4:14–10:31. He contended that the writer of Hebrews marked the central division of the discourse with strikingly parallel formulations at the beginning (4:14–16) and at the end (10:19–23) and that this indicated that there could not be a divisional break at 10:18. The final division (10:32–13:17), he argued, begins and ends with a similar type of exhortation. On this reading, Hebrews is a discourse composed of three major divisions, each identifiable by the presence of parallel passages at the opening and closing of the divisions ("Zum Aufbau," 200–203). Nauck's proposal has been accepted by O. Michel (in the sixth and subsequent editions of his commentary, 29–35) and by others (e.g., W. G. Kümmel, *Introduction to the New Testament*, rev. ed. [Nashville: Abingdon, 1975] 390; Zimmermann, *Bekenntnis*, 18–24; on the importance of the parallelism between 4:14–16 and 10:19–23 observed by Nauck, see G. H. Guthrie, "The Structure of Hebrews," 59–60, 74).

THE ABSENCE OF A CONSENSUS

There is at the present time no consensus regarding the literary structure of Hebrews. The extent of the disparity in current proposals concerning the structure of Hebrews has been charted suggestively by G. H. Guthrie ("The Structure of Hebrews," 37; D. Guthrie's analysis is set forth in his *New Testament Introduction*[4], 728–33; the approaches of Spicq, Michel, Attridge, and F. F. Bruce, respectively, are based on their commentaries; this chart is reproduced by permission; see Fig. 1).

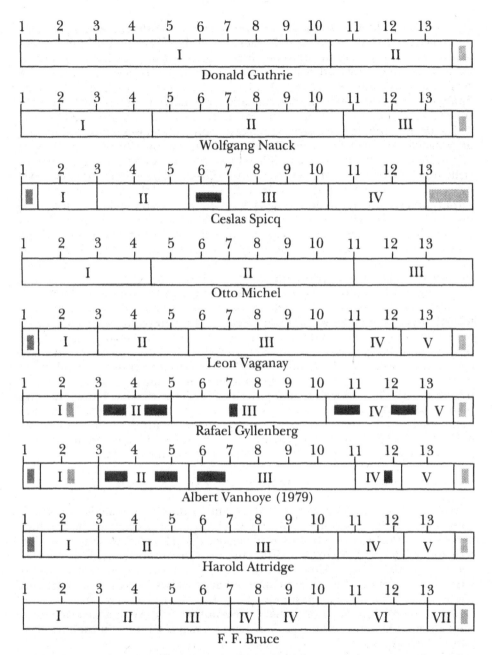

Fig. 1. Proposals regarding literary structure of Hebrews as charted by G. H. Guthrie.

Approaches to structural divisions of Hebrews: 1, 2, 3, etc. = chapter divisions; I, II, III, etc. = primary sections; ▓ = the introduction (when the introduction is emphasized in the outline; ▒ = the appendix or conclusion; ■ = hortatory material (when it is emphasized as a strategic factor in the outline).

There are multiple reasons for the absence of a consensus concerning the literary structure of Hebrews. Critical decisions concerning sectional boundary limits and the identification of the transitional devices employed consciously or subconsciously by the writer are rooted in methodology. My own wrestling with methodological issues will be reflected in this commentary in the *Form/Structure/Setting* sections, especially in the determination of boundary limits in 3:1–4:14; 4:15–5:10; 12:14–29; and 13:1–25, and in the *Introduction* to the final division, 12:14–13:25.

Factors inherent in the discourse make a confident decision concerning literary structure difficult to attain. The unusual alternation and intermingling of exposition and exhortation are problematical when seeking to assess the literary structure of Hebrews, as Michel recognized (26–28). The writer's "style of delivery," introducing a tantalizingly brief reference (e.g., 1:3, "After having made purification for sins"), but deferring its development to a much later point in the discourse (9:11–10:18), creates genuine difficulties for structural analysis. Topics are foreshadowed and repeated. An adequate approach to the structure of Hebrews must be able to assess the use of repetition of thought and reprises. It must be able to account for the weaving in and out of motifs and themes throughout the discourse like threads in an intricately woven tapestry.

The range of proposals concerning the structure of Hebrews attests the artistic and literary complexity of this discourse. In the quest for the demarcation of formal divisions in Hebrews, two considerations remain paramount. First, there were in antiquity literary and rhetorical conventions for the arrangement of material in an orderly fashion. It can be expected that the writer observed these conventions. Secondly, the reduction of the discourse to writing demanded the provision of verbal clues to assist the audience in following the unfolding of the argument. The explicit use of transitional devices to signal a defined turning point in an argument was essential to a discourse that would be heard and comprehended aurally. In spite of its elusiveness, the quest for the literary structure of Hebrews is legitimate. In the pursuit of that quest, in this commentary literary, rhetorical, conceptual, and semantic analyses have been employed.

ADDENDUM: THE TEXT-LINGUISTIC APPROACH OF G. H. GUTHRIE

With the aid of the relatively new discipline of discourse analysis or text linguistics (see above, "Discourse Analysis"), G. H. Guthrie has taken up the question of the structure of Hebrews from a fresh perspective in his 1991 dissertation, "The Structure of Hebrews: A Text-linguistic Analysis" (for Guthrie's method, see "Discourse Analysis" above). Although I did not enjoy access to his research until after the completion of the commentary, his approach is impressive and will certainly influence all subsequent studies of the structure of Hebrews. In particular, Guthrie's attention to the transitional devices utilized by the writer to tie together the different segments of his discourse marks a major advance in the investigation of the literary structure of Hebrews.

Guthrie recognized that an area of investigation that has tended to be neglected in discussions of the structure of Hebrews is the writer's method of executing smooth transitions from one segment of the discourse to another. Perhaps more than any other consideration, that fact accounts for the range of diversity in current attempts to outline Hebrews. Guthrie's concern has been to discern those elements in the discourse that are transitional in character and to determine the types of transitions generated by those elements. He has identified nine transitional techniques that he groups under two broad categories. "Constituent transitions" are those located in one or more of the constituents of the two blocks of material joined by the transition. The constituents will always be an introduction or a conclusion. "Intermediary transitions" are those effected by a unit of text positioned between two major sections of the discourse. In this case the transitional unit belongs exclusively neither to the unit of discourse that precedes nor to the one that follows, but contains elements of both.

1. *Constituent Transitions*

   a. Hook-words. The writer frequently generates a smooth transition between two units of discourse by the use of the same word at *the end* of one section and at *the beginning* of the next. Guthrie depicts the relationship in a simple diagram, where the symbol • represents a term in the text (see Fig. 2). Examples of the use of this transitional device to tie together two units of discourse may be found in 1:1–4/5–14, where the hook-word is τῶν ἀγγέλων, "the angels" (1:4/5), or in 2:10–18/3:1–6, where the hook-word is ἀρχιερεύς ("high priest," 2:17/3:1).

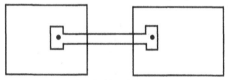

Fig. 2. Hook-words.

   b. Distant Hook-words. When an expository unit of discourse is followed by an exhortation, which is in turn followed by another expository unit, the writer uses at least *two* sets of hook-words to tie the three units together. The first simply joins the unit of exposition to the exhortation; the second joins the initial unit of exposition to the next unit of exposition in the discourse. This variation on the hook-word technique not only serves to effect a transition; it signals that in the units of exposition the writer is developing a step-by-step argument and that each unit of exposition builds on the preceding expository unit. The writer's use of exposition for thematic development made essential the tying together of the units of exposition, even when the flow of the argument was interrupted by an intervening unit of exhortation. Guthrie illustrates the use of distant hook-words as a transitional device in a diagram (see Fig. 3).

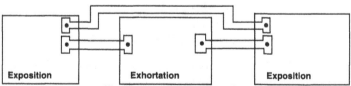

Fig. 3. Distant Hook-words.

An example is provided by the manner in which the writer ties together 1:5–14/2:1–4/2:5–9. 1:5–14 is joined to 2:1–4 by the hook-word σωτηρία, "salvation" (1:4/2:3). 2:1–4 is connected to 2:5–9 by the verbal hookword λαλεῖν, "to speak" (2:3/2:5) and the forms of μαρτυρεῖν, "to bear witness" (2:4/2:6). These transitions illustrate the normal use of simple hook-words. The exposition in 1:5–14, however, is joined to the next unit of exposition, 2:5–9, by forms of μέλλειν, "to come" (1:14/2:5), and of ἄγγελος, "angel" (1:13/2:5). The connection is important because in 2:5–9 the writer resumes the comparison of the Son to the angels that was developed in 1:5–14 but was interrupted in 2:1–4. Guthrie finds other examples of the use of distant hook-words to tie together separated units of exposition in 2:17–18/5:1 (τὰ πρὸς τὸν θεόν . . . τὰς ἁμαρτίας, "in the service of God . . . the sins"), producing a strong transition from 2:10–18 to 5:1–10:25, and in 5:10/7:1, where the reference to Melchizedek serves to join 5:1–10 to 7:1–28. The presence of distant hook-words indicates the writer's intention to tie together units of exposition separated by a unit of exhortation.

c. *Hooked Key Words.* This designation refers to *three* transitional devices that employ characteristic terms, i.e., words or their cognates used throughout a unit of discourse to give that unit lexical and semantic cohesion. A transition may be effected by (1) a characteristic term in the second unit that was actually introduced in the conclusion of the first unit; (2) the repetition of a characteristic term from the preceding unit in the introduction to the unit that follows, or (3) a combination of the two. Guthrie depicts the three patterns diagrammatically (see Figs. 4, 5, and 6).

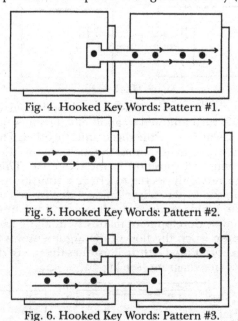

Fig. 4. Hooked Key Words: Pattern #1.

Fig. 5. Hooked Key Words: Pattern #2.

Fig. 6. Hooked Key Words: Pattern #3.

A clear example of the first pattern is evident in the manner in which the exordium, 1:1–4, is connected to the first major division, 1:5–2:18. The semantic content of 1:4 foreshadows the development in 1:5–2:18, i.e., the superiority of the transcendent Son of God to the angels. The term ἄγγελοι, "angels," in 1:4 introduces the characteristic term, or "key word," for 1:5–2:18, where it will recur ten times, and only twice more in the remainder of the discourse. Thus in the final assertion of the exordium the writer announces the theme of his first major division and introduces the key word that will become the characteristic term for that division, generating an effective transition between the two blocks of discourse.

The second pattern, in which a characteristic term from the preceding unit is repeated at the beginning of the unit that follows, may be illustrated from the manner in which 1:5–14 is joined to 2:1–4. The term ἄγγελοι, "angels," which is a key word for 1:5–14, is repeated in 2:2.

The third pattern can be seen in the manner in which a seam is established between 2:5–9 and 2:10–18. The transition is established when a characteristic term in 2:5–9, δόξη, "glory" (2:7, 9), is repeated at the beginning of 2:10–18 (εἰς δόξαν, "to glory," 2:10) and two characteristic terms from 2:10–18 are introduced at the close of 2:5–9. These terms are πάθημα, "suffering," and θάνατος, "death," in 2:9, which play a major role in communicating the argument in 2:10–18, i.e., that the Son became for a little while lower than the angels to establish solidarity with the human family in order to experience the suffering of death. Cognate forms of πάθημα occur in 2:10 and 18 to aid in the forming of an *inclusio*, and θάνατος is developed in 2:14–15.

d. Overlapping Constituents. The designation "overlapping constituents" refers to a unit of text that the writer uses simultaneously to conclude one segment of the discourse and to introduce the next unit. In Guthrie's diagram, the conclusion of section A is equally the introduction to section B (see Fig. 7). The two instances of overlapping constituents in Hebrews are located at 4:14–16 and 10:19–25, the two units of discourse that bracket the second major movement of the exposition in Guthrie's analysis. The initial unit, 4:14–16, furnishes the conclusion to 3:1–4:16. The terms "Jesus," "high priest," and "confession" in 4:14–15 form an *inclusio* with the formulation in 3:1. Moreover, 4:14–16 shares with 3:1–4:13 the genre of exhortation, admonishing the audience to a specific action. It is thus an integral element of a larger unit of discourse extending from 3:1 to 4:16. Simultaneously, 4:14–16 is integral to the exposition in 5:10–10:18 and provides the opening of a triple *inclusio*, which serves to mark out the boundaries of that great block of discourse. The reference to "Jesus" as the "high priest" who has passed "through the heavens" links 4:14–16 conceptually with the two main thematic movements of 5:10–10:18, i.e., the Son's appointment as high priest (5:1–7:28) and his unique, fully sufficient sacrificial offering in heaven (8:3–10:18). In this manner 4:14–16 furnishes an appropriate conclusion to 3:1–4:16 and an equally appropriate introduction to 4:14–10:18.

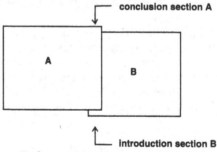

Fig.7. Overlapping Constituents.

The lower bracket of the *inclusio* introduced in 4:14–16 is supplied in 10:19–25, which also serves to introduce the block of exhortation that follows.

Conceptually 10:19–25 is linked with the great central division of the discourse, which concerns Christ's appointment as high priest, his sufficient offering in the heavenly sanctuary, and the decisive purgation from sin that he achieved. It provides closure to that extensive unit of exposition. It also furnishes an appropriate bridge to the remainder of the discourse, introducing the sustained exhortation of 10:19–13:19. Accordingly, 10:19–25 is conceptually the conclusion to 4:14–10:18 and the hortatory introduction to all that follows.

e. Parallel Introductions. The writer makes use of roughly parallel statements at the beginning of two successive units of discourse to effect the transition. In 5:1, for example, he states that "every high priest elected from among men is appointed to act on their behalf in the service of God to offer both gifts and sacrifices for the purging of sins." That statement is reiterated, with only slight variation, in 8:3. This repeated thematic statement sets forth the two topics developed in 4:14–10:25, i.e., the divine appointment of the Son to priesthood (5:1–7:28) and his superior sacrifice (8:3–10:18). In 5:1 the explicit reference to "appointment" ($\kappa\alpha\theta\acute{\iota}\sigma\tau\alpha\tau\alpha\iota$) precedes the statement concerning "gifts and sacrifices." In 8:3 the reference to the offering of gifts and sacrifices precedes the reference to the Son's appointment ($\kappa\alpha\theta\acute{\iota}\sigma\tau\alpha\tau\alpha\iota$). The parallel introductions serve to alert the auditors to the flow of the argument and its development. The use of parallel introductions in 5:1 and 8:3 as a transitional device is depicted by Guthrie in the following diagram, where 8:1–2 functions as still another type of transition (see Fig. 8).

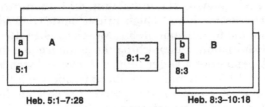

Fig. 8. Parallel Introductions.

This pattern generates the transition by means of substantial repetition.

2. *Intermediary Transitions.*

Intermediary transitions are those achieved by a unit of text that stands between two major segments of the discourse. The writer of Hebrews makes use of two variations on this technique.

a. The Direct Intermediary Transition. This designation denotes a unit of text that functions as a "hinge" joining together two larger units of discourse. The intermediary unit of text contains at its beginning a prominent element from the preceding segment of the discourse. It then introduces an element that will be developed in the segment of the discourse that follows. Guthrie illustrates the movement of the discourse in a diagram (see Fig. 9).

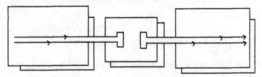

Fig. 9. The Direct Intermediary Transition.

The small textual unit 8:1–2, which stands between 5:1–7:28 and 8:3–10:18, illustrates the function of a direct intermediary discourse. The confessional statement in 8:1 looks back retrospectively on what has been demonstrated to this point in the discourse, i.e., that Jesus is God's Son who has been appointed as high priest on our behalf. He is now enthroned at God's right hand. The continuation of the statement, however, locates his enthronement "in the heavens" and introduces the new notion of the heavenly sanctuary, the true tabernacle that the Lord erected (8:1*c*–2). The continuation prepares for the ensuing discussion concerning the heavenly (and thus superior) offering of the appointed high priest. An allusion to "the sanctuary" (τῶν ἁγίων) and "the tabernacle" (τῆς σκηνῆς) is introduced for the first time in the discourse in 8:2, but each term figures prominently in the argument developed in 8:3–10:18. The function of 8:1–2 is to furnish a direct intermediary transition between 5:1–7:28 and 8:3–10:18, as illustrated in Guthrie's diagram (Fig. 9).

    b.   *The Woven Intermediary Transition.* In this variation on the intermediary transition, characteristic elements from the preceding unit of discourse and from the following unit of discourse are interwoven, as in Guthrie's diagram (see Fig. 10).

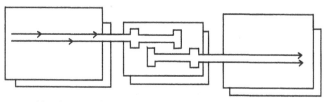

Fig. 10. The Woven Intermediary Transition.

An illustration of this transitional technique is furnished in 2:5–9, which provides an intermediary transition between the first main movement of the discourse, concerning the superiority of the Son to the angels (1:5–2:4), and the second main movement, concerning the necessity of the Son's abasement (2:10–18). In the intermediary transitional unit, 2:5–9, elements from the preceding unit of discourse and from the following unit are woven together. The semantic and conceptual elements in 2:5–9, which link that unit to 1:5–2:4, focus attention on the Son's status. They revolve around the forms of ὑποτάσσειν, "to subject" (2:5, 8), of στεφανοῦν, "to crown" (2:7, 9), and the statement "You have subjected everything under his feet" (2:8). The key clause that relates 2:5–9 to 2:10–18 is the statement "You made him for a little while lower than the angels" (2:7) and the repetition of that clause in 2:9, with the qualification "for the suffering of death."

In 2:5–9 the writer introduces Ps 8:4–6 to his audience, because that biblical quotation contains elements that reflect upon the superior status of the Son (the theme of 1:5–14) and upon his temporary abasement (the theme of 2:10–18). The common thread tying the three units together is the relationship of the Son to the angels. The appeal to the biblical quotation moves the argument from the first point (the Son's transcendent superiority) to the second (the Son's temporary abasement). As such, 2:5–9 does not belong exclusively either to 1:5–2:4 or to 2:10–18 but generates an effective transition between the two units of discourse.

Guthrie's demonstration that the writer of Hebrews used no fewer than nine identifiable devices for executing transitions in the discourse (i.e., hook-words, distant hook-words, three types of hooked key words, overlapping constituents, parallel introductions, direct intermediary transitions and woven intermediary transitions) does much to advance the quest for the elusive structure of Hebrews.

Another major contribution is Guthrie's appreciation of the distinct functions of exposition and exhortation in Hebrews. The function of the expository units is thematic development, step-by-step, each unit of exposition building upon the preceding unit. The function of the hortatory units of the discourse is to articulate the urgency for obeying the word of God and to define the consequences for failing to do so. It is Guthrie's contention that in an outline of Hebrews it is necessary to distinguish sharply between exposition and exhortation, since each genre is assigned a distinctive function. His outline reflects his understanding of the relationship between the alternating genres, based on a text-linguistic analysis.

OUTLINE OF THE BOOK OF HEBREWS

1:1–4	Introduction	
1:5–2:18	I. The Position of the Son in Relation to the Angels	
1:5–14	A. The Son Superior to the Angels	
2:1–4	$\longrightarrow$ (Implication)	ε. **Warning**: related to rejection of the Superior Lord's Words
2:5–9	ab. The Superior Son for a Time Became Positionally Lower than the Angels (intermediary transition)	
2:10–18	B. The Son Became Positionally Lower than the Angels (i.e., among men) to Suffer and Die	
3:1–6		ε. Exhortation on Faithfulness (1) Consider Jesus' faithfulness—greater than Moses
3:7–19		(2) Israel an Example of Unfaithfulness
4:1–11		(3) Exhortation to Enter God's Rest
4:12–13		(4) **Warning**: related to God's Word
4:14–10:25	II. The Position of the Son, Our High Priest, in Relation to the Earthly Sacrificial System	
4:14–16		(5) Final Exhortation: Hold fast and draw near
	(overlap)	
4:14–16	Introduction: We have a Sinless High Priest Who Has Gone into Heaven	
5:1–7:28	A. The Son Taken from among Men and Appointed High Priest	

A few explanatory comments may be helpful. According to Guthrie, the thematic exposition in Hebrews falls into two larger blocks of embedded discourse, the first showing the relationship of the Son to the angels and the second the position of the Son as high priest in relation to the earthly sacrificial system. Each of these large blocks is divided into two movements separated by an intermediary transition. The movement supported by the expositional units is both logical and spatial:

I.   A.   The Son higher (i.e., exalted)
I.   ab.   *Transition:* The superior Son becomes lower
I.   B.   The Son lower (i.e., in solidarity with the human family)
II. A.   The Son taken "from among men" (5:1), having been made perfect by his earthly sufferings (5:7–9), and appointed High Priest
II. ab.   *Transition:* the appointed High Priest a minister in the true tabernacle in Heaven
II. B.   The Heavenly High Priest offers a superior offering.

On Guthrie's analysis of the text, Part II. A. and II. B. are each divided into three corresponding subdivisions. A. 1 and B. 1 are both introductory; A. 2 and B. 2 deal with the superiority of Melchizedek and of the new covenant, respectively, on the basis of OT passages (Gen 14 and Jer 31); A. 3 and B. 3 relate that superiority to Jesus' superior ministry as the priest (A. 3) who offers the superior sacrifice (B. 3). Significantly, A. 3 and B. 3 are each introduced with $\mu \grave{\epsilon} \nu$ $o \tilde{\tilde{v}} \nu$ constructions ("Now therefore . . .").

All of the warning passages in the hortatory units of the discourse reflect the same basic admonition to be responsive to the word of God. The five divisions of the hortatory material introduced in 3:1–4:16 (#1–5) are balanced by corresponding elements in inverted order in 10:19–12:3 (#1–5).

At two points in the discourse, the writer makes use of an "overlap transition," i.e., in 4:14–16 and 10:19–25. Each of these units of text provides an important cluster of expressions that together produce the triple *inclusio* bracketing the central segment of the discourse, i.e., movement II. Each supplies both a conclusion and an introduction by blending the main theme of the central section with an exhortation to endure and to draw near to God. The point at which the hortatory and expository units overlap is not in thematic development but in the implementation of the writer's goal to encourage the community to consider the Son (3:1–3; 12:1–3) as a means of gaining the strength to hold fast to their confession (4:14–16; 10:19–25) and to endure without wavering in their Christian stance.

Guthrie's proposals merit serious consideration in the light of the detail of the text. I am pleased to be able to share them with a wider readership by means of this addendum.

Purpose and Plan

Bibliography

Attridge, H. W. "Paraenesis in a Homily ($\lambda \acute{o} \gamma o \varsigma$ $\pi a \rho a \kappa \lambda \acute{\eta} \sigma \epsilon \omega \varsigma$): The Possible Location of, and Socialization in, the 'Epistle to the Hebrews.'" *Semeia* 50 (1990) 211–26. **Black, D. A.**

"The Problem of the Literary Structure of Hebrews: An Evaluation and a Proposal." *GTJ* 7 (1986) 163–77. **Fenton, J. C.** "The Argument in Hebrews." *SE* 7 (1982) 175–81. **Filson, F. V.** *"Yesterday": A Study of Hebrews in the Light of Chapter 13.* SBT 2nd ser. 4. Naperville: Allenson, 1967. 21, 27–30. **Grässer, E.** "Der Hebräerbrief 1938–1963." *TRu* 30 (1964) 138–236. **Haering, T.** "Gedankengang und Grundgedanken des Hebräerbriefes." *ZNW* 18 (1917) 145–64. **Lindars, B.** "The Rhetorical Structure of Hebrews." *NTS* 35 (1989) 382–406. **Maxwell, K. L.** "Doctrine and Paraenesis in the Epistle to the Hebrews, with Special Reference to Pre-Christian Gnosticism." Dissertation, Yale University, 1952. **Nauck, W.** "Zum Aufbau des Hebräerbriefes." In *Judentum, Urchristentum, Kirche.* FS J. Jeremias. Ed. W. Eltester. BZNW 26. Giessen: Töpelmann, 1960. 199–206. **Purdy, A. C.** "The Purpose of the Epistle to the Hebrews." *Exp* 8th ser. 19 (1920) 123–39. ———. "The Purpose of the Epistle to the Hebrews in the Light of Recent Studies in Judaism." In *Amicitiae Corolla.* Ed. H. G. Wood. London: University of London, 1933. 253–64. **Rice, G. E.** "Apostasy as a Motif and Its Effect on the Structure of Hebrews." *AUSS* 23 (1985) 29–35. **Saydon, P. P.** "The Master-Idea of the Epistle to the Hebrews." *MelTheol* 13 (1961) 19–26. **Schoonhoven, C. R.** "The 'Analogy of Faith' and the Intent of Hebrews." In *Scripture, Tradition, and Interpretation.* FS E. F. Harrison. Ed. W. W. Gasque and W. S. Lasor. Grand Rapids: Eerdmans, 1978. 92–110. **Stine, D. M.** "The Finality of the Christian Faith: A Study of the Unfolding Argument of the Epistle to the Hebrews, Chapters 1–7." Dissertation, Princeton Theological Seminary, 1964. **Übelacker, W. G.** *Der Hebräerbrief als Appell: Untersuchungen zu* exordium, narratio *und* postscriptum *(Hebr 1–2 und 13, 22–25).* Stockholm: Almqvist & Wiksell, 1989. 17, 32–36, 150–62, 197–222.

Consideration of the purpose and plan of Hebrews is integrally related to an assessment of the literary structure of the document. At issue is the distinctive role assigned by the writer to the expository and hortatory sections of the homily. It has been necessary to inquire concerning the functions of each of the principal genres in the development of the discourse. How do the expository sections serve the writer's essential purpose? How is that purpose affirmed by the blocks of exhortation? What is the intended relationship between the indicative and the imperative, between thesis and parenesis, within the total discourse? What is demanded from the interpreter is a balanced assessment of the particularity and interrelatedness of exposition and exhortation in the composition of a homily prepared as a pastoral response to a community in crisis.

A differentiation between the genres and purposes of expository and hortatory units of a text is a basic tenet of NT exegesis and interpretation (cf. Berger, *Exegese,* 15, 36–58). In most of the letters of Paul, for example, each of these blocks of material plays a subsidiary but complementary role in advancing the purpose of the apostle's communication. But the unique literary structure of Hebrews, in which exhortation is interspersed with exposition, disallows such a facile analysis. The sustained alternation between thesis and parenesis inevitably raises the question of the essential relationship between these two distinct types of discourse. Are the blocks of exhortation interspersed throughout the homily merely an intrusive digression, disrupting the flow of the exposition of Christ's priesthood and unique sacrifice, or ancillary to the development of the main themes? Alternatively, is the exposition foundational to the writer's primary purpose, which is exhortation?

A variation in genre certainly signals some shift in the movement of the discourse. When the writer turns abruptly from exposition to admonition, addressing his auditors directly (e.g., 1:5–14/2:1–4), the unit of exhortation is distinguished by style and form (and in the case of 2:1–4, by diction) from the unit of exposition.

It is the presupposition of this commentary that in Hebrews parenesis takes precedence over thesis in expressing the writer's purpose. Argumentation serves exhortation. Hebrews is a pastorally oriented sermon whose goal is given expression in the parenetic sections of the discourse. In a striking descriptive phrase appended to the homily, the writer characterizes the whole discourse as parenesis or *paraclesis* (13:22, "my word of exhortation [*paraclesis*]"). Intrinsic to all the meanings of *paraclesis* is the notion of an earnest appeal. Hebrews is an expression of passionate and personal concern for the Christians addressed. The writer's characterization of the homily as *paraclesis* clearly suggests that biblical and theological exposition is subordinate to a parenetic purpose. Hebrews was written to arouse, urge, encourage, and exhort those addressed to maintain their Christian confession and to dissuade them from a course of action that the writer believed would be catastrophic. He calls them to fidelity and obedience and seeks to prepare them for suffering (cf. Michel, 26–27).

The primary function of exposition is thematic development. The primary function of exhortation is to motivate the community to appropriate action. The developed exposition demonstrates that it makes sense to continue to be responsive to the gospel in the light of the identity and accomplishment of Jesus. Exhortation confronts, with implications for obedience and disobedience. Exposition instructs, showing why obedience will be amply rewarded. In Hebrews, exposition provides an essential foundation for exhortation.

Biblical exposition and theological development ultimately serve a hortatory purpose. The expository units of the discourse do not stand on their own but rather furnish the presupposition for the parenesis. Concurrently, the persuasive force of the exhortation is derived from the convincing thematic development in the expository sections of the sermon. The basis for the exhortation in 2:1–4, for example, is provided in 1:1–14. These are distinct, but complementary, units in the discourse that demonstrate how thesis serves parenesis. An appreciation of this vital interrelationship between exposition and exhortation is crucial to an adequate understanding of the function of either component of the discourse (so correctly Attridge, *Semeia* 50 [1990] 215; cf. Nauck, "Zum Aufbau," 201–3; Michel, 29–35; Zimmermann, *Bekenntnis*, 17–24; Black, *GTJ* 7 [1986] 166–68; Lindars, *NTS* 35 [1989] 392).

The purpose of Hebrews is to strengthen, encourage, and exhort the tired and weary members of a house church to respond with courage and vitality to the prospect of renewed suffering in view of the gifts and resources God has lavished upon them. The writer's intention is to address the sagging faith of men and women within the group and to remind them of their responsibility to live actively in response to God's absolute claim upon their lives through the gospel. He urges his listeners to hold loyally to their confession of Jesus Christ as the sole mediator of salvation in a time of crisis and warns them of the judgment of God they would incur if they should renounce their Christian commitment.

The plan of the homily is appropriate to this intensely practical purpose. In moving language there is set forth the finality of God's revelation in his Son, whose transcendent dignity is superior both to the angels, who are ministering spirits (1:1–14), and to Moses, whose status was that of a servant in the household of faith

(3:1–6). Within this setting the writer warns his hearers against indifference to the gospel message they have heard (2:1–4) or blatant unbelief (3:7–4:13). The unique priesthood of Jesus is introduced in 2:17–3:1 and 4:14–5:10. It is treated at length in 7:1–10:18. Three contrasts that demonstrate the superior dignity of Jesus as priest and sacrifice are developed.

(1) The temporal, ephemeral character of the Aaronic priesthood is overshadowed by the eternal ministry of the priest like Melchizedek (5:1–10; 7:1–28).

(2) The priestly ministry in the tabernacle under the old covenant is superseded by the priestly ministry of Jesus in the heavenly sanctuary establishing the new covenant (8:1–9:28).

(3) The inadequacy of the sacrifices under the law is contrasted with the efficacy and finality of Christ's sacrifice (10:1–18).

The development of the thesis concerning Jesus' priesthood and unique sacrifice lends substance to the parenetic warnings concerning immaturity and the apostasy, which can be avoided only by faith, endurance, and hope (5:11–6:20; 10:19–39). The group is exhorted to steadfast endurance. They are to exercise eschatological faith, which appropriates the future and acts in the present in the light of the certainty of that future (11:1–12:3). The writer parades before his audience the heroes and heroines of the past, whose faith was attested by God (11:1–40), and then appeals to the supreme example of faith, Jesus himself (12:1–3), as an incentive to responsible conduct. In the theological and pastoral climax to the sermon (12:14–29), the writer again warns the congregation of their peril if they should refuse God's gracious word. A concluding exhortation calls them to demonstrate a lifestyle that reflects the worship of God and unqualified identification with the confessing community (13:1–25).

An analysis of the plan of Hebrews must reflect an intensive listening to the detail of the text. In the analysis presented here, an attempt has been made to distinguish between thesis and parenesis, and to indicate the primacy of parenesis in the discourse by italicizing the five warning passages that expose the peril to which the community was vulnerable (2:1–4; 3:7–19; 5:11–6:12; 10:19–39; 12:14–29). These warnings are integral to the writer's purpose and plan. The other passages listed in the right-hand column give a measure of visual expression of the extent to which Hebrews is organized around parenesis.

There is a degree of artificiality in the analysis. The division, for example, between 3:7–19 and 4:1–14 is simply one of convenience. It should not obscure the fact that in the flow of the argument 4:1–14 is integrally related to the warning not to replicate the experience of Israel at Kadesh, where the people hardened their hearts against God, as 4:2–3, 5–7, 11–13 make clear. Moreover, the large block of material in 11:1–40 is expositional in form, but its function is clearly hortatory, providing an elaborate foundation for the exhortation in 12:1–13. The recurrence of exhortation and the fact that it is interspersed in blocks throughout the homily indicate that parenesis holds the various sections of discourse together as a unified whole. The dominant motif in Hebrews is parenetic.

ANALYSIS OF HEBREWS

		Thesis	Parenesis
1:1–2:18	I.	The Revelation of God through His Son	
1:1–4	A.	God Has Spoken His Ultimate Word in His Son	
1:5–14	B.	The Transcendent Dignity of the Son	
2:1–4	C.		*The First Warning:* The Peril of Ignoring the Word Delivered by the Son
2:5–9	D.	The Humiliation and Glory of the Son	
2:10–18	E.	The Solidarity of the Son with the Human Family	
3:1–5:10	II.	The High Priestly Character of the Son	
3:1–6	A.		Consider that Jesus Was Faithful to God who Appointed Him
3:7–19	B.		*The Second Warning:* The Peril of Refusing to Believe God's Word
4:1–14	C.		Strive to Enter God's Rest, the Sabbath Celebration for the People of God
4:15–5:10	D.	A High Priest Worthy of Our Faith Because He Is the Son of God Who Is Compassionate	
5:11–10:39	III.	The High Priestly Office of the Son	
5:11–6:12	A.		*The Third Warning:* The Peril of Spiritual Immaturity
6:13–20	B.	A Basis for Confidence and Steadfastness	
7:1–10	C.	Melchizedek, the Royal Priest	
7:11–28	D.	Jesus, Eternal Priest like Melchizedek	
8:1–13	E.	Sanctuary and Covenant	
9:1–10	F.	The Necessity for New Cultic Action	
9:11–28	G.	Decisive Purgation through the Blood of Christ	

Conceptual Background

The question of the conceptual background of Hebrews concerns the identification of the cultural and intellectual milieu from which the ideas and themes of the discourse derive. The positing of a particular conceptual background is intended to clarify the distinctive features of the document. During the past century Hebrews has been identified with a variety of widely differing backgrounds. For the sake of clarity and convenience of reference, it will be useful to present the relevant bibliography under headings that identify the dominant influences that have been detected in Hebrews. It will also be practical to differentiate between proposals that locate the conceptual background in a non-Christian setting and those that have tended to identify Hebrews with the mainstream of the Christian tradition or with a particular school of thought within early Christianity. The works listed under each heading include both proponents of a proposal and those who have been critical of the proposal. In the preparation of this commentary, I have enjoyed access to the investigation of the several proposals for the conceptual background of Hebrews completed in 1981 by L. D. Hurst ("The Background and Introduction of the Epistle to the Hebrews," Dissertation, Oxford University, now published as *The Epistle to the Hebrews: Its Background of Thought*, SNTSMS 65 [Cambridge: Cambridge UP, 1990]; references are made to Hurst's dissertation, since I had access to his work only in this form).

PROPOSALS OF NON-CHRISTIAN BACKGROUNDS

Bibliography

Philo, Alexandria, and Platonism

Bietenhard, H. *Die himmlische Welt im Urchristentum und Spätjudentum.* WUNT 2. Tübingen: Mohr, 1951. **Braun, H.** "Das himmlische Vaterland bei Philo und im Hebräerbrief." In *Verborum Veritas.* FS G. Stälin. Ed. O. Böcher & K. Haacker. Wuppertal: Brockhaus, 1970. 319–27. **Burtness, J. H.** "Plato, Philo and the author of Hebrews." *LQ* 10 (1958) 54–64. **Cabantous, J.** *Philon et l'Épître aux Hébreux ou Essai sur les Rapports del la Christologie de l'Épître aux Hébreux avec la Philosophie Judéo-Alexandrine.* Montauban: Granié, 1895. **Cambier, J.** "Eschatologie ou héllenisme dans l'épître aux Hébreux: Une étude sur μένειν et l'exhortation finale de l'épître." *Sal* 11 (1949) 62–96. **Carlston, C.** "The Vocabulary of Perfection in Philo and Hebrews." In *Unity and Diversity in New Testament Theology.* FS G. E. Ladd. Ed. R. A. Guelich. Grand Rapids: Eerdmans, 1978. 133–60. **Cody, A.** *Heavenly Sanctuary and Liturgy in the Epistle to the Hebrews: The Achievement of Salvation in the Epistle's Perspective.* St. Meinrad, IN: Grail, 1960. **Dey, L. K. K.** *The Intermediary World and Patterns of Perfection in Philo and Hebrews.* SBLDS 25. Missoula, MT: Scholars, 1975. **Dibelius, M.** "Der himmlische Kultus nach dem Hebräerbrief." *TBl* 21 (1942) 1–11. **Eagar, A. R.** "Hellenistic Elements in the Epistle to the Hebrews." *Her* 11 (1901) 263–87. **Fairhurst, A. M.** "Hellenistic Influence in the Epistle to the Hebrews." *TynBul* 7–8 (1961) 17–27. **Gamble, J.** "Symbol and Reality in the Epistle to the Hebrews," *JBL* 45 (1926) 162–70. **Gilbert, G. H.** "The Greek Element in the Epistle to the Hebrews." *AJT* 14 (1910) 521–32. **Hanson, R. P. C.** *Allegory and Event.* London: SCM, 1959. **Héring, J.** "Eschatologie biblique et idéalisme platonicien." In *The Background to the New Testament and Its Eschatology.* Ed. W. D. Davies and D. Daube. Cambridge: Cambridge UP, 1954. 444–63. **Hurst, L. D.** "The Background and Interpretation of the Epistle to the Hebrews." Dissertation, University of Oxford, 1981. 5–68 (now published as *The Epistle to the Hebrews: Its Background of Thought,* SNTSMS 65 [Cambridge: Cambridge UP, 1990]). ————. "Eschatology and 'Platonism' in the Epistle to the Hebrews." SBLASP (1984) 41–74. **Luck, U.** "Himmlisches und irdisches Geschehen im Hebräerbrief: Ein Beitrag zum Problem des 'historischer Jesus' im Urchristentum." *NovT* 6 (1963) 192–215. **Maar, O.** "Philo und Hebräerbrief." Dissertation, University of Vienna, 1964. **Ménégoz, E.** *La théologie de l'Épître aux Hébreux.* Paris: Fischbacher, 1894. **Nash, R. H.** "The Notion of Mediator in Alexandrian Judaism and the Epistle to the Hebrews." *WTJ* 40 (1977) 89–115. **Nikiprowetsky, V.** "La spiritualisation des sacrifices et le cult sacrificial au temple de Jérusalem chez Philon d'Alexandrie." *Sem* 17 (1967) 98–114. **Nomoto, S.** "Die Hohenpriester-Typologie im Hebräerbrief: Ihre traditionsgeschichtliche Herkunft und ihr religionsgeschichtlicher Hintergrund." Dissertation, University of Hamburg, 1965. **Schmitz, O.** *Die Opferanschauung des späteren Judentums und die Opferaussagungen des Neuen Testaments: Eine Untersuchung ihres geschichtlichen Verhältnisses.* Tübingen: Mohr, 1910. **Sowers, S. G.** *The Hermeneutics of Philo and Hebrews: A Comparison of the Old Testament in Philo Judaeus and the Epistle to the Hebrews.* Richmond: Knox, 1965. **Spicq, C.** "Alexandrinismes dans l'Épître aux Hébreux." *RB* 58 (1951) 481–502. ————. "Le Philonisme de l'Épître aux Hébreux." *RB* 56 (1949) 542–72; 57 (1950) 212–42. **Staples, A. F.** "The Book of Hebrews in Its Relationship to the Writings of Philo Judaeus." Dissertation, Southern Baptist Theological Seminary, 1951. **Thurston, R. W.** "Philo and the Epistle to the Hebrews." *EvQ* 58 (1986) 133–43. **Wenschkewitz, H.** "Die Spiritualisierung der Kultusbegriffe Tempel, Priester und Opfer im Neuen Testament." *Angelos* 4 (1932) 70–230. **Wette, W. M. L. de.** "Über die symbolisch-typische Lehrart des Briefes an die Hebräer." *TZ* 3 (1822) 1–51.

Wikgren, A. "Patterns of Perfection in the Epistle to the Hebrews." *NTS* 6 (1959–60) 159–67. **Williamson, R.** *Philo and the Epistle to the Hebrews.* ALGHJ 4. Leiden: Brill, 1970. ———, "Philo and New Testament Christology." *ExpTim* 90 (1980) 361–65. ———. "Platonism and Hebrews." *SJT* 16 (1963) 415–24.

Qumran

Batdorf, I. W. "Hebrews and Qumran: Old Methods and New Directions." In *FS F. W. Gingrich.* Ed. E. H. Barth and R. E. Cocroft. Leiden: Brill, 1972. 16–35. **Betz, O.** "The Eschatological Interpretation of the Sinai-Tradition in Qumran and in the NT." *RevQ* 6 (1967) 89–108. **Braun, H.** "Qumran und das Neue Testament: Ein Bericht über 10 Jahr Forschung (1950–59): Hebräer." *TRu* 30 (1964) 1–38. **Bruce, F. F.** "'To the Hebrews' or 'To the Essenes'?" *NTS* 9 (1963) 217–32. **Buchanan, G. W.** "The Present State of Scholarship on Hebrews." In *Christianity, Judaism and Other Greco-Roman Cults.* FS M. Smith. Ed. J. Neusner. Leiden: Brill, 1975. 1:299–330. **Carmignac, J.** "Le document de Qumran sur Melkisédeq." *RevQ* 27 (1970) 348–78. **Coppens, J.** "Les Affinitiés Qumrâniennes de l'Épître aux Hébreux." *NRT* 84 (1962) 128–41, 257–82. **Delcor, M.** "Melchizedek from Genesis to the Qumran Texts and the Epistle to the Hebrews." *JSJ* 2 (1971) 115–35. **Fensham, F. C.** "Hebrews and Qumran." *Neot* 5 (1971) 9–21. **Fitzmyer, J. A.** "Further Light on Melchizedek from Qumran Cave 11." *JBL* 86 (1967) 25–41. ———. "Now this Melchizedek . . . (Heb. 7:1)." *CBQ* 25 (1963) 305–21. **Gemés, I.** "Alianca no Documento de Damasco e na Epístola aos Hebreus. Una contribuicão a questão: Qumran e as origens do Christianismo." *RCB* 6 (1969) 28–68. **Gnilka, J.** "Der Erwartung des messianisches Hohenpriesters in den Schriften von Qumran und im Neuen Testament." *RevQ* 2 (1960) 395–426. **Grothe, J. F.** "Was Jesus the Priestly Messiah? A Study of the New Testament's Teaching of Jesus' Priestly Office against the Background of Jewish Hopes for a Priestly Messiah." Dissertation, Concordia Seminary, St. Louis, 1981. **Higgins, A. J. B.** "The Priestly Messiah." *NTS* 13 (1967) 211–39. **Hurst, L. D.** "The Background and Interpretation of the Epistle to the Hebrews." Dissertation, University of Oxford, 1981. 69–114 (see under "Philo, Alexandria, and Platonism" above). **Jonge, M. de,** and **Woude, A. S. van der.** "11Q Melchizedek and the New Testament." *NTS* 12 (1965–66) 301–26. **Kosmala, H.** *Hebräer, Essener, Christen: Studien zur Vorgeschichte der frühchristlichen Verkündigung.* SPB 1. Leiden: Brill, 1959. **LaSor, W. S.** "The Epistle to the Hebrews and the Qumran Writings." In *The Dead Sea Scrolls and the New Testament.* Grand Rapids: Eerdmans, 1972. 179–90. **Spicq, C.** "L'Épître aux Hébreux, Apollos, Jean-Baptiste, les Hellénistes et Qumran." *RevQ* 1 (1958–59) 365–90. **Woude, A. S. van der.** "Melchisedek als himmlische Erlösergestalt in den neugefunden eschatologischen Midraschim aus Qumran Höhle XI." *OTS* 14 (1965) 354–73. **Yadin, Y.** "The Dead Sea Scrolls and the Epistle to the Hebrews." *ScrHier* 4 (1958) 36–55.

Apocalyptic Judaism

Barrett, C. K. "The Eschatology of the Epistle to the Hebrews." In *The Background of the New Testament and Its Eschatology.* Ed. W. D. Davies and D. Daube. Cambridge: Cambridge UP, 1954. 363–93. **Hofius, O.** *Katapausis: Die Vorstellung vom endzeitlichen Ruheort im Hebräerbrief.* WUNT 11. Tübingen: Mohr, 1970. **Lueken, W.** *Michael: Eine Darstellung und Vergleichung der jüdischen und der morgenländisch-christlichen Tradition vom Erzengel Michael.* Göttingen: Vandenhoeck & Ruprecht, 1898. **MacRae, G. W.** "Heavenly Temple and Eschatology in the Letter to the Hebrews." *Semeia* 12 (1978) 179–99. **McNicol, A. J.** "The Relationship of the Image of the Highest Angel to the High Priest Concept in Hebrews." Dissertation, Vanderbilt University, 1974. **McRay, J.** "Atonement and Apocalyptic in the Book of Hebrews." *ResQ* 23 (1980) 1–9. **Schmidgall, P.** "The Influence of Jewish Apocalyptic Literature on the Book of Hebrews." Dissertation, Western Kentucky University, 1980. **Zorn,**

R. "Die Fürbitte und Interzession im Spätjudentum und im Neuen Testament." Dissertation, University of Göttingen, 1957.

Merkabah Mysticism

Hurst, L. D. "The Background and Interpretation of the Epistle to the Hebrews." Dissertation, University of Oxford, 1981. 133–39 (see under "Philo, Alexandria, and Platonism" above). **Hofius, O.** *Der Christushymnus Philipper 2.6–11.* Tübingen: Mohr, 1976. 87–88.
———. *Der Vorhang vor dem Thron Gottes: Eine exegetisch-religionsgeschichtliche Untersuchung zu Hebräer 6, 19f. und 10, 19f.* WUNT 14. Tübingen: Mohr, 1972. **Schenke, H.-M.** "Erwägung zum Rätsel des Hebräerbriefes." In *Neues Testament und christliche Existenz.* FS H. Braun. Ed. H. D. Betz & L. Schrottroff. Tübingen: Mohr, 1973. 421–37. **Scholem, G.** *Major Trends in Jewish Mysticism.* New York: KTAV, 1954. **Williamson, R.** "The Background to the Epistle to the Hebrews." *ExpTim* 87 (1975–76) 232–37.

The Samaritans

Bowman, J. "Early Samaritan Eschatology." *JJS* 6 (1955) 63–72. **Cullmann, O.** "Samaria and the Origins of the Christian Mission." In *The Early Church.* Philadelphia: Westminster, 1956. **Hurst, L. D.** "The Background and Interpretation of the Epistle to the Hebrews." Dissertation, University of Oxford, 1981. 125–32 (see under "Philo, Alexandria, and Platonism" above). **Knox, E. A.** "The Samaritans and the Epistle to the Hebrews." *TCh* 22 (1927) 184–93. **MacDonald, J.** "The Samaritan Doctrine of Moses." *SJT* 13 (1960) 149–62. **Plummer, R.** "The Samaritan Pentateuch and the New Testament." *NTS* 22 (1976) 441–43. **Scobie, C. H. H.** "The Origins and Development of Samaritan Christianity." *NTS* 19 (1972–73) 390–414.

Pre-Christian Gnosticism

Bornkamm, G. "Das Bekenntnis im Hebräerbrief." *TBl* 21 (1942) 56–66. **Colpe, C.** "New Testament and Gnostic Christology." In *Religions in Antiquity.* FS E. R. Goodenough. Ed. J. Neusner. Leiden: Brill, 1968. 227–43. **Eccles, R. S.** "Hellenistic Mysticism in the Epistle to the Hebrews." Dissertation, Yale University, 1952. ———. "The Purpose of Hellenistic Patterns in the Epistle to the Hebrews." In *Religions in Antiquity.* FS E. R. Goodenough. Ed. J. Neusner. Leiden: Brill, 1968. 207–26. **Friedländer, M.** "La sect de Melchisédech et l'Épître aux Hébreux." *REJ* 5 (1882) 1–26, 188–98; 6 (1883) 187–99. **Giversen, S.** "Evangelium Veritatis and the Epistle to the Hebrews." *ST* 13 (1959) 87–96. **Grässer, E.** "Das wandernde Gottesvolk zum Basismotiv des Hebräerbriefes." *ZNW* 77 (1986) 160–79. ———. *Der Glaube im Hebräerbrief.* Marburg: Elwert, 1965. ———. "Zur Christologie des Hebräerbriefes: Eine Auseinandersetzung mit Herbert Braun." In *Neues Testament und christliche Existenz.* FS H. Braun. Ed. H. D. Betz & L. Schrottroff. Tübingen: Mohr, 1973. **Hurst, L. D.** "The Background and Interpretation of the Epistle to the Hebrews." Dissertation, University of Oxford, 1981. 116–25 (see under "Philo, Alexandria, and Platonism" above). **Käsemann, E.** *Das wandernde Gottesvolk: Eine Untersuchung zum Hebräerbrief* 4. FRLANT 55. 1939. Göttingen: Vandenhoeck & Ruprecht, 1961 [ET: *The Wandering People of God: An Investigation of the Letter to the Hebrews.* Tr. R. A. Harrisville and I. L. Sandberg. Minneapolis: Augsburg, 1984]. **Koester, W.** "Platonische Ideenwelt und Gnosis im Hebräerbrief." *Schol* 4 (1956) 545–55. **Maxwell, K. L.** "Doctrine and Parenesis in the Epistle to the Hebrews, with Special Reference to Pre-Christian Gnosticism." Dissertation, Yale University, 1952. **Pearson, B. A.** "The Figure of Melchizedek in the First Tractate of the Unpublished Coptic-Gnostic Codex IX from Nag Hammadi." In *Proceedings from the XIIth International Congress of the International Association for the History of Religions.* Ed. C. J. Bleeker, G. Widengren, and E. J. Sharpe.

Leiden: Brill, 1975. 200–208. **Theissen, G.** *Untersuchungen zum Hebräerbrief.* SNT 2. Gütersloh: Mohn, 1969. **Thompson, J. W.** *The Beginnings of Christian Philosophy: The Epistle to the Hebrews.* CBQMS 13. Washington, DC: The Catholic Biblical Association of America, 1981. ———. "The Conceptual Background and Purpose of the Midrash in Hebrews VII." *NovT* 19 (1977) 209–23. ———. "Heb. 9 and Hellenistic Concepts of Sacrifice." *JBL* 98 (1979) 567–78. ———. "'That Which Abides': Some Metaphysical Assumptions in the Epistle to the Hebrews." Dissertation, Vanderbilt University, 1974. ———. "That Which Cannot Be Shaken: Some Metaphysical Assumptions in Heb. 12:27." *JBL* 94 (1975) 580–87. **Waal, C. van der.** "The 'People of God' in the Epistle to the Hebrews." *Neot* 5 (1971) 83–92. **Wilson, R. McL.** *Gnosis and the New Testament.* Oxford: Blackwell, 1968.

Mystery Religions

Riggenbach, E. "Der Begriff der *ΤΕΛΕΙΩΣΙΣ* im Hebräerbrief: Ein Beitrag zur Frage nach der Einwirkung der Mysterienreligion auf Sprache und Gedankenwelt des Neuen Testaments." *NKZ* 34 (1923) 184–95.

Once the Pauline authorship of Hebrews was considered indefensible, it was necessary to inquire concerning the conceptual background that made Hebrews intelligible. The dominant proposal during the first half of the twentieth century was that Hebrews is clarified when read against the background of Philo, Alexandria, and Platonism. When C. Spicq lent the weight of his erudition to this proposal (*RB* 56 [1949] 542–72; 57 [1950] 212–42; *RB* 58 [1951] 481–502) and demonstrated its cogency in his massive two-volume commentary on Hebrews, it attained the status of a critical consensus. Some form of affinity with Alexandria, Platonism, and Philo provided the explanation for the distinctive features of Hebrews. (For a helpful summary of the arguments mounted in support of Philonic influence on Hebrews, see Hurst, "Background," 6–14.)

Two quite independent developments dismantled the consensus. First, the publication of the sectarian Jewish documents from Qumran was greeted with enthusiasm and diverted the attention of the academic community away from the dominant proposal in an insatiable quest to find a new key for unlocking old riddles. Even C. Spicq was sufficiently impressed by the new evidence to modify his own proposal that Hebrews was the work of a Philonist who had been converted to Christianity. He now argued that the author was Apollos, whose background in Alexandria clarified the contacts with Philo he had early demonstrated. But he was writing to a group of Jewish priests who had enjoyed contact with Qumran and who had recently fled from Jerusalem to Antioch (*RevQ* 1 [1958–59] 365–90).

The second development would prove to be more devastating. C. Spicq's arguments in support of Philonic influence on Hebrews began to be sifted by R. P. C. Hanson (*Allegory*, 83–86) and F. Schröger (*Verfasser*, 301–7). They showed that the purported similarities between Philo and Hebrews could be satisfactorily explained by reference to other forms of Judaism unrelated to Philo. The sharpest blow was delivered by R. Williamson in a meticulous study of the evidence that had appeared to be impeccable when presented by Spicq (*Philo and the Epistle to the Hebrews* [1970]). Williamson demonstrated that Spicq's research was flawed and that he had overstated his case. He concluded that the differences between Philo and the writer of Hebrews were so striking and fundamental, both in outlook and exegetical method, as to demonstrate that the two writers "belonged . . . to two entirely different schools of O.T. exegesis" (*Philo*, 576–79; for a review of the case against Philonic influence on Hebrews, see Hurst, "Background," 14–22).

Williamson's argument has now been strengthened by L. D. Hurst's extensive analysis of terms not treated by Williamson and by his fresh investigation of Jewish apocalyptic as the proper background against which to read elements in Hebrews that previously had been judged to be Platonic ("Background," 22–68). Hurst concludes that Philo and the writer of Hebrews shared a common conceptual background rooted in the Old Greek version of the Bible. Philo chose to develop certain OT themes Platonically. The writer of Hebrews, under the influences of Jewish apocalyptic and primitive Christian tradition, chose to develop them eschatologically. This conclusion is supported by the research underlying the present commentary (see *Comment* on 1:1–2a; 2:5; 6:5; 8:5; 9:8, 11, 23–24; 10:20; 11:10, 16; 12:22, 26–28; 13:14).

The publication of the scrolls from Qumran brought to light an expression of sectarian Judaism that has been identified with the Essenes. The first serious attempt to propose Qumran as the conceptual background of the intended audience in Hebrews, which clarifies distinctive features of the argument of Hebrews, was published in 1955 by Y. Yadin (*ScrHier* 4 [1958] 36–55). He suggested that those addressed in Hebrews had formerly been members of the Qumran community and that they continued to hold some of their prior beliefs (38). In support of this proposal, Yadin identified several points of contact between the argument in Hebrews and the sectarian beliefs at Qumran. Yadin's proposal was quickly followed by others who found in Qumran the conceptual basis for regarding believers as the community of the new covenant, for the conception of Jesus as a priestly Messiah, and for the distinctive interest in the person of Melchizedek in Hebrews. This construction of the conceptual background is the basis for the commentaries of G. W. Buchanan and P. E. Hughes. Hughes referred to Yadin's article as "the best theory yet advanced to explain the occasion and purpose of the Epistle to the Hebrews" (14).

Little consideration seemed to have been given to the striking linguistic and conceptual differences between the scrolls and Hebrews. The scrolls from Qumran were written in Hebrew and Aramaic and are Semitic in conception; Hebrews is written in exceptional Greek and is hellenistic Jewish in conception. Detailed consideration of the arguments offered by Yadin and others in support of their proposal have shown them to be capable of other, more plausible explanations (cf. F. F. Bruce, *NTS* 9 [1963] 217–32; Coppens, *NRT* 84 [1962] 128–41, 257–82; Hurst, "Background," 72–114). Moreover, the differences in the OT text to which an appeal is made and to the conception of the role of Melchizedek in 11QMelch and Hebrews are so fundamental as to preclude any influence of 11QMelch upon the argument developed in Hebrews (see *Comment* on Heb 7:1–25). There is no sound basis for affirming that Qumran provides the conceptual background for Hebrews. Similarities because of traditional exegesis of the OT are insufficient to offset the striking differences between Qumran and Hebrews.

The proposal that the conceptual background for Hebrews may be found in Jewish Merkabah mysticism was advanced in 1973 by H.-M. Schenke ("Erwägung zum Rätsel des Hebräerbriefes," 433–34). Jewish mysticism in this tradition displays a fascination with God's throne as the focus for emphasizing God's majesty, holiness, and transcendent glory. Hebrews, with its interest in the heavenly cultus, seemed to reflect these vital interests (e.g., Heb 1:3, 6; 2:10; 4:16; 8:1; 12:2, 10, 14). This suggestion was taken up and developed by R. Williamson in 1976 (*ExpTim* 87 [1975–76] 232–37). He marshalled ten arguments in support of this proposal and appealed to their cumulative weight. He recognized that the evidence to which he had to appeal for the reconstruction of Merkabah mysticism was late and openly acknowledged that the similarities he had shown between this form of piety and Hebrews could be explained on the basis of a common indebtedness to the OT.

An objection that tends to vitiate Williamson's proposal is the absence in Hebrews of any appeal to those passages in the OT that became central in later Merkabah mysticism (e.g., Dan 7; Isa 6; Ps 97; Ezek 1). In his own evaluation of the proposal, Hurst demonstrated that the purported parallels to which Williamson appealed were susceptible of other explanations and that the influences could have entered Hebrews from other expressions of Judaism, or even from Christian tradition reflected elsewhere in the NT ("Background," 136–37). Many of these parallels have their source in the Psalms and in apocalyptic Judaism.

More influential has been E. Käsemann's proposal that the conceptual background for Hebrews should be located in pre-Christian Gnosticism (*Das wandernde Gottesvolk* [ET: *The Wandering People of God*]). Käsemann detected behind Hebrews the gnostic motif of the heavenly pilgrimage of the self from the enslaving world of matter to the heavenly realm of the spirit. He provided a thorough exposition of Hebrews against this background and identified the motif of pilgrimage as central to the development of Hebrews. (For a review of his argument and evaluation, see Hurst, "Background," 116–25.) Käsemann's proposal has been supported and developed in the important work of E. Grässer (see especially his monograph *Der Glaube im Hebräerbrief*, and now *An die Hebräer: 1. Teilband: Hebr 1–6*, EKKNT 17/1 [Zürich: Benziger, 1990]), G. Theissen (*Untersuchungen zur Hebräerbrief*), and J. W. Thompson, who finds evidence for a gnostic-Platonic background for Hebrews (see especially *The Beginnings of Christian Philosophy*).

Despite the strength of the support for this proposal in the academic community, it is hampered by a number of crippling objections. Chief among them are the following. The sources to which Käsemann appealed (Mandaean, Manichaean, Rabbinic, Hermetic, the *Acts of Thomas*, *Pistis Sophia*, *3 Enoch*, the *Odes of Solomon*) are late; it cannot be demonstrated that they reflect traditions that antedate Hebrews. Moreover, there is no documentary support for the existence in the first century of a myth of the redeemed redeemer, who descends from heaven to lead those enslaved in the material realm on pilgrimage to the heavenly realm of light (see especially Colpe, "New Testament and Gnostic Christology," 227–43). The gratuitous assertion that Melchizedek was considered an incarnation of the primal Man in Jewish sources is without support. Finally, the existence of any first-century Gnosticism, or proto-Gnosticism, that could have supplied the conceptual background for Hebrews has not been established.

The components of the conceptual background that illumines Hebrews from a non-Christian background consist of influences from the interpretation of the OT in Greek, the traditions of hellenistic Judaism (which is not to say Philonic or Platonic), and of apocalyptic Judaism. It is obvious that all of these components could have been filtered through the mainstream of early Christianity to which the writer of Hebrews was exposed at the formative period in his experience as a Christian.

PROPOSALS OF CHRISTIAN BACKGROUNDS

Bibliography

Primitive Christian Tradition

Barrett, C. K. "The Eschatology of the Epistle to the Hebrews." In *The Background of the New Testament and Its Eschatology.* Ed. W. D. Davies and D. Daube. Cambridge: Cambridge UP, 1954. 363–93. **Dukes, J. G.** "Eschatology in the Epistle to the Hebrews." Dissertation, Southern Baptist Theological Seminary, 1956. **Feuillet, A.** "Les points de vue nouveaux dans l'eschatologie de l'Épître aux Hébreux." *SE* 2 (1964) 369–87. **Gordon, V. R.** "Studies in the Covenantal Theology of the Epistle to the Hebrews in Light of Its Setting." Dissertation, Fuller Theological Seminary, 1979. **Klappert, B.** *Die Eschatologie des Hebräerbriefs.* Munich: Kaiser, 1969. **Peterson, D. G.** *Hebrews and Perfection: An Examination of the Concept of Perfection in the "Epistle to the Hebrews."* SNTSMS 47. Cambridge: Cambridge UP, 1982. **Silva, M.** "Perfection and Eschatology in Hebrews." *WTJ* 39 (1976) 60–71. **Terra, J. E. M.** "A Libertação Escatológica na Epístola aos Hebreus: O Povo de Deus a Caminho do Santuário." *RCB* 2 (1978) 325–43.

Paul

Anderson, C. P. "Hebrews among the Letters of Paul." *SR* 5 (1975–76) 258–66. ———. "The Setting of the Epistle to the Hebrews." Dissertation, Columbia University, 1969. **Badcock, F. J.** *The Pauline Epistles and the Epistle to the Hebrews in Their Historical Setting.* London: SPCK, 1937. **Burch, V.** *The Epistle to the Hebrews: Its Sources and Message.* London: William & Norgate, 1936. **Hurst, L. D.** "The Background and Interpretation of the Epistle to the Hebrews." Dissertation, University of Oxford, 1981. 175–236 (now published as *The Epistle to the Hebrews: Its Background of Thought,* SNTSMS 65 [Cambridge: Cambridge UP, 1990]). **Schröger, F.** "Der Hebräerbrief—paulinisch?" In *Kontinuität und Einheit.* FS F. Mussner. Ed. P. G. Müller & W. Stenger. Freiburg/Basel/Vienna: Herder, 1981. 211–22. **Taylor, C. D.** "A Comparative Study of the Concepts of Worship in Colossians and Hebrews." Dissertation, Southern Baptist Theological Seminary, 1957. **Vanhoye, A.** "L'Épître aux Ephésiens et l'Épître aux Hébreux." *Bib* 59 (1978) 198–230.

John

Cothenet, E., LeFort, P., Prigent, P., and **Dussaut, L.** *Les écrits de Saint Jean et l'Épître aux Hébreux.* Paris: Desclée, 1984. **Henderson, M. W.** "The Priestly Ministry of Jesus in the Gospel of John and the Epistle to the Hebrews." Dissertation, Southern Baptist Theological Seminary, 1965. **Hickling, C. J. A.** "John and Hebrews: The Background of Hebrews 2:10–18." *NTS* 29 (1983) 112–16. **Spicq, C.** "L'Origine johannique de la conception du Christ-prêtre dans l'Épître aux Hébreux." In *Aux Sources de la Tradition Chrétienne.* FS M. Goguel. Neuchâtel/Paris: Delachaux & Niestlé, 1956. 258–69.

Other Influences

Ferris, T. E. S. "A Comparison of I Peter and Hebrews." *CQR* 3 (1930–31) 123–27. **Graham, A. A. K.** "Mark and Hebrews." *SE* 4 (1968) 411–16. **Jones, C. P. M.** "The Epistle to the Hebrews and the Lucan Writings." In *Studies in the Gospels*. FS R. H. Lightfoot. Ed. D. E. Nineham. Oxford: Oxford UP, 1957. 113–43.

Among the primary influences to which the writer was exposed as a Christian was the eschatological perspective of the early Christian movement. He shares with primitive Christianity the understanding that the ministry of Jesus introduced the final phase of history (Heb 1:2*a*). That insight had been validated by the experience of the powers of the age to come breaking into the structures of the present age (see *Comment* on 2:3–4; 6:5). The writer was convinced that the next event on God's agenda was the consummation, when Jesus would appear to bring the realization of salvation to all who were waiting for him (see *Comment* on 9:28; cf. 10:25, 35–39). He shared with others in the early Church in an earnest expectation of the apocalyptic manifestation of the city God has prepared for his people (11:10, 16; 12:22–24; 13:14). The conceptual background of Hebrews is richly informed by primitive Christian eschatology and by the perspectives of Jewish apocalyptic.

A second primary influence upon the writer is the tradition associated with Stephen and the early Christian Hellenists (see below, "Hebrews and the Theology of the Hellenistic Church," with bibliography). In his own assessment of this influence upon the conceptual background of Hebrews, L. D. Hurst has strengthened the case for Christian Hellenism as a formative influence upon the writer of Hebrews ("Background," 140–74).

A third influence may have been exerted through the writer's association with Paul or with one or more of his associates. The reference to Timothy in Heb 13:23 lends plausibility to the suggestion that the writer was a member of the Pauline circle. It is the merit of Hurst to have investigated this question from a fresh perspective ("Background," 175–236). Although there is no evidence in Hebrews of a literary dependence upon the letters of Paul, it is certainly possible that the apostolic tradition upon which the writer drew had been influenced at certain strategic points by Paul. It is this possibility that Hurst has explored by selecting five sample motifs that permit a comparison between the theology of Paul and that of Hebrews. For example, both Paul and the writer of Hebrews appear to interpret Ps 8:4–6 in terms of the promised human destiny rather than from an exclusively christological perspective (cf. 1 Cor. 15:22–28; Rom 8:20; Heb 2:6–9). For both writers, human destiny and vocation are realized in the man Jesus (Hurst, "Background," 181–89). Hurst posits some form of preliterary contact between Paul and the author of Hebrews.

Hurst pursues this line of inquiry in reference to Christ's glory and role in creation and in sustaining the cosmos, his humbling as man, his obedience and subsequent exaltation, the idea of faith, and the concept of union with Christ. In each instance he finds striking similarities and differences. The similarities are sufficient to establish some form of contact. Yet the differences are sufficiently numerous to preclude literary contact. Hurst suggests that the writer of Hebrews may have discussed his ideas with Paul or with one or more of Paul's associates who had been influenced by the Apostle. The development of the ideas is his own, but a formative influence upon the conceptual background of Hebrews is Paul. If this conclusion can be sustained, it will do much to locate Hebrews within the mainstream of Christian tradition.

The primary concern in this commentary has been to interpret the statement of Hebrews from the rich perspectives developed in Hebrews. The distinctiveness of the writer's own theological understanding to that of Paul's or others within the early Church has sometimes been stressed (see, for example, on the writer's use of "promise" in 4:1; 6:12, 13–20; 10:23, 35–36, or his use of "faith" in 4:2; 6:12; 10:22; 11:1). This should not obscure the fact that the conceptual background of the writer of Hebrews was indelibly informed by the early Christian tradition, particularly as this was transmitted in the hellenistic wing of the Church.

Importance and Appropriation of the Old Testament Text

Bibliography

Archer, G. L., and Chirichigne, G. *Old Testament Quotations in the New Testament.* Chicago: Moody, 1983. Barth, M. "The Old Testament in Hebrews: An Essay in Biblical Hermeneutics." In *Current Issues in New Testament Interpretation.* Ed. W. Klassen and G. F. Snyder. New York: Harper & Row, 1962. 53–78, 263–73. Betz, O. "The Eschatological Interpretation of the Sinai-Tradition in Qumran and in the New Testament." *RevQ* 21 (1967) 89–107. Black, M. "The Christological Use of the Old Testament in the New Testament." *NTS* 18 (1971–72) 1–14. Büchel, C. "Der Hebräerbrief und das Alte Testament." *TSK* 79 (1906) 508–91. Caird, G. B. "The Exegetical Method of the Epistle to the Hebrews." *CJT* 5 (1959) 44–51. Clements, R. E. "The Use of the Old Testament in Hebrews." *SWJT* 28 (1985) 36–45. Combrink, H. J. B. "Some Thoughts on the Old Testament Citations in the Epistle to the Hebrews." *Neot* 5 (1971) 22–36. Fabris, R. "La lettera agli Ebrei e l'Antico Testamento." *RivB* 32 (1984) 237–52. Gotaas, D. S. "The Old Testament in the Epistle to the Hebrews, the Epistle of James, and the Epistle of Peter." Dissertation, Northern Baptist Theological Seminary, 1958. Grogan, G. W. "The New Testament Interpretation of the Old Testament: A Comparative Study." *TynBul* 18 (1967) 59–68. Guthrie, G. H. "The Structure of Hebrews: A Text-linguistic Analysis." Dissertation, Southwestern Baptist Theological Seminary, 1991. 77–101. Hanson, A. T. "Christ in the Old Testament according to Hebrews." *SE* 2 (1964) 393–98. Kistemaker, S. *The Psalm Citations in the Epistle to the Hebrews.* Amsterdam: Van Soest, 1961. Lindars, B. *New Testament Apologetic: The Doctrinal Significance of the Old Testament Quotations.* London: SCM, 1961. Loane, M. L. "The Unity of the Old and New Testaments as Illustrated in the Epistle to the Hebrews." In *God Who Is Rich in Mercy.* FS D. B. Knox. Ed. P. T. O'Brien and D. G. Peterson. Homebush West, NSW: Lancer, 1986. 255–64. Longenecker, R. N. *Biblical Exegesis in the Apostolic Period.* Grand Rapids: Eerdmans, 1975. Metzger, B. M. "The Formulas Introducing Quotations of Scripture in the NT and the Mishnah." *JBL* 70 (1951) 297–307. Müller, P. G. "Die Funktion der Psalmzitate im Hebräerbrief." In *Freude an der Weisung des Herrn.* Ed. E. Haag & F. L. Hossfeld. Stuttgart: Katholisches Bibelwerk, 1986. 223–42. Oudersluys, R. C. "Exodus in the Letter to the Hebrews." In *Grace Upon Grace.* FS L. J. Kuyper. Ed. J. I. Cook. Grand Rapids: Eerdmans, 1975. 143–52. Padva, P. *Les citations de l'Ancien Testament dans l'Épître aux Hébreux.* Paris: Danzig, 1904. Pollard, E. B. "Notes on the Old Testament Citations in the Epistle to the Hebrews." *CrozQ* 1 (1924) 447–52. Smits, C. *Oud-testamentische Citaten in het Nieuw Testament.* Malmberg: Hertogenbosch, 1963. Stuart, S. S. "The Exodus Tradition in Late Jewish and Early Christian Literature: A General Survey of the Literature and a Particular Analysis of the Wisdom of Solomon, II Esdras and the Epistle to the Hebrews." Dissertation, Vanderbilt University, 1973. **Swetnam, J.** *Jesus and Isaac: A Study of the Epistle to the Hebrews in the Light of the Aqedah.* AnBib 94. Rome: Biblical Institute Press, 1981. **Synge, F. C.** *Hebrews and the Scriptures.* London: SPCK, 1959. **Toy, C. H.** *Quotations in the New Testament.* New York: Scribner's, 1884. **Vaccari, A.** "Las citas del Antiquo Testamento en la Epístola a los Hebreos." *CB* 13 (1956) 239–43. **Venard, L.** "L'utilisation des Psaumes dans l'Épître aux Hébreux." In *Mélanges E. Podechard.* Lyons: Faculté Catholique, 1945. 253–64. **Vis, A.** *The Messianic Psalm Quotations in the New Testament.* Amsterdam: Hertberger, 1936.

THE FUNCTION OF OT TEXTS IN THE STRUCTURE OF HEBREWS

As early as the eighteenth century, the biblical scholar J. A. Bengel called attention to the role of the OT, especially Pss 2, 8, and 110, in the development of the argument in Hebrews (*Gnomon Novi Testamenti* [Tübingen: Schramm, 1742] 2.2.333–505 [ET by C. T. Lewis and M. R. Vincent, *Gnomon of the New Testament* (Philadelphia: Perkinpine & Higgens, 1864)]). Bengel observed that the introduction of a citation from the OT provided a point of departure for the ensuing discussion. This was the case in Heb 2:5–18, for example, on which Bengel wrote, "Here we must observe the proposition and sum from Ps 8:5–9." It was also the case in 5:4–7:28, where he observed that "the sum [of Christ's priesthood] is set forth from Ps 2 and Ps 110." Commenting on the use of Ps 110:4 in Heb 7:1–28, Bengel wrote, "The fact itself is copiously explained. [Christ] is to us a great high priest such as Psalm 110 describes (1) according to the order of Melchizedek (7:1–19); (2) with an oath (7:20–22); (3) forever (7:23–24, 26–28)." On the basis of a careful exegetical approach to the text of Hebrews, Bengel demonstrated that quotations from the OT are functionally pivotal in the thematic development of the discourse.

This sound observation has not always received the attention it deserves in current studies of the structure and argument of Hebrews. G. B. Caird was exceptional in proposing that in Hebrews the writer's argument is actually arranged in sections around four OT texts, i.e., Ps 110:1–4, Ps 8:4–6, Ps 95:7–11, and Jer 31:31–34 (*CJT* 5 [1959] 44–51). In each section after the first, which is introduced by a chain of biblical quotations, the primary scriptural citation is positioned at the beginning of its respective section. Caird (47) further observed that the biblical texts chosen by the writer actually argue the case for the ineffectiveness of the institutions of the old covenant:

> [The] argument falls into four sections, each having as its core an Old Testament passage which declares the ineffectiveness and symbolic or provisional nature of the Old Testament religious institutions. All other scriptural references are ancillary to these four . . . which control the drift of the argument.

The observation that in Hebrews the argument is based on the witness of Scripture to the avowedly provisional character of the old covenant led Caird to regard Jer 31 as the fourth main text (rather than Ps 40). The attractiveness of his proposal was that he was able to uncover a rationale behind the writer's selection of the primary quotations and to show the relations among them in the thematic development of the unfolding argument.

Caird's analysis, however, was unable to account for the manner in which the parenesis in 10:19–13:21 was integrated into the structure and thematic arrangement of Hebrews. He had tended to focus upon the content of the document rather than its intent. In 1989 J. Walters returned to Caird's presentation of evidence that links the structure of Hebrews to the argument it advances ("The Rhetorical Arrangement of Hebrews," unpublished paper presented to the annual Christmas Conference of the John Wesley Fellows, meeting in Shakertown, KY). He recognized that the ultimate purpose of Hebrews is pastoral and that theological considerations are offered only to elicit an appropriate response from the group addressed. If in Hebrews theology and biblical exposition serve parenetic interests, Walters reasoned, the employment of primary biblical texts to apply the closing parenesis to the community should be expected. He proceeded to demonstrate the importance of the rhetorical use of OT texts in defining the arrangement and the argument in Hebrews as a whole.

Walters proposed that the writer arranged his argument as a series of *six* scriptural explications, each framed with exhortation. The writer introduces a key text from the OT, clarifies its eschatological significance, and draws the parenetic implications for the community. This rhetorical strategy accounts for the arrangement of the whole discourse from 2:5 to 13:19. The argument in Hebrews is directed to the eschatological appeal for unqualified faithfulness in light of the fact that Christ's high priestly ministry has now secured the promised "good things" (9:11). Once this is recognized, Walters argues, "the entire document falls readily into a structure organized according to scriptural quotations and directed toward exhortation, a structure eminently suitable for homiletical discourse and not simply doctrinal formulation. This structure is carried forward through the whole book" ("Rhetorical Arrangement," 16). In order to demonstrate this arrangement, Walters emends Caird's analysis slightly. In addition to the four primary quotations noted by Caird, he directs attention to two later citations that carry the argument to its parenetic conclusion, i.e., Hab 2:3–4 and Prov 3:11–12.

In proceeding to map out the arrangement and argument of the discourse, Walters shows that the parenetic passages are grouped fairly uniformly in proximity to the six primary scriptural quotations. The following table is taken from his paper ("Rhetorical Arrangement," 18–19).

Section	OT Text	Placement	Parenesis
Introduction			
1:1–2:4	Catena		2:1–4
First Point:	"You Crowned Him"		
2:5–18	Ps 8	2:6–8	
Second Point:	"Today"		
3:1–4:13	Ps 95	3:7–11	3:1–2, 12–14
			4:1, 11
Third Point:	"A Priest Forever"		
4:14–7:28	Ps 110	5:6	4:14–16
			5:11–6:12
Fourth Point:	"A New Covenant"		
8:1–10:31	Jer 31	8:8–12	10:19–29

Fifth Point:	"By Faith"		
10:32–12:2	Hab 2	10:37–38	10:32–36
			12:1–2
Sixth Point:	"Do Not Lose Heart"		
12:3–13:19	Prov 3	12:5–6	12:3–29
			13:1–19
Closing			
13:20–21			

Under Walters' proposal, the parenesis in 10:19–13:19 is shown to be consistent with the earlier sections of the discourse. It displays the same rhetorical arrangement. His insight concerning the importance of Hab 2:3–4 and Prov 3:11–12 as primary quotations allows the argument of the homily to move "directly to its crowning parenetic conclusion" (19).

In his 1991 dissertation, G. H. Guthrie has identified the failure to take into account the writer's use of the OT as one of the factors that has made a structural analysis of Hebrews especially difficult ("The Structure of Hebrews," 69, 77–101). He insists that an appreciation of the thematic development in the homily, the form of certain segments, and the transitions between sections will often be dependent upon an understanding of the functions of OT texts in defining the arrangement and argument in Hebrews. The research of Caird, Walters, and Guthrie underscores the importance of the writer's appropriation of the OT text.

THE EXTENT OF THE WRITER'S INDEBTEDNESS TO THE OT

Hebrews is impregnated with the OT. The writer makes vital use of the OT text in developing his parenetic sections as well as those that are more theologically oriented. Every chapter is marked by explicit or implicit references to the biblical text. The writer's use of Scripture expresses his conviction of the continuity between God's speaking and action under the old and new covenants, which has urgent implications for Israel and for the Church. He presupposes both an essential unity and a development between the old and new economies of redemption. A detailed knowledge of the OT is indispensable for understanding what the writer of Hebrews is endeavoring to say. He assumes on the part of his audience a deep familiarity with their contents.

Any consideration of the use of the OT in Hebrews must provide more than a tabulation of the quotations or allusions to specific biblical texts. M. Barth has rightly insisted that it is necessary to differentiate between explicit quotations (identified by a formula of introduction) and implicit quotations (those without an introductory formula), between allusions to the OT text (where the criterion for distinguishing between a quotation and an allusion is the relative degree of conformity to the exact wording of the biblical text), summaries of OT material (e.g., Heb 1:1; 10:1–4), and mere references to an OT name or topic without regard to a specific context ("The Old Testament in Hebrews," 54).

There is no common agreement even on the number of quotations from the OT text in Hebrews. The difficulty in determining the frequency with which the writer cites the biblical text has been pointed out by R. N. Longenecker (*Biblical Exegesis*, 164):

Nowhere in the New Testament is the listing of biblical quotations more difficult than in the Letter to the Hebrews. Not only are we faced with the usual problem of distinguishing between direct quotations, on the one hand, and what may be called allusions, employment of biblical phraseology, or reference to Old Testament history, on the other hand, but we are also confronted in Hebrews with certain passages that are formally quoted again and again in the same discussion (e.g., Ps 95:7–11; 110:1–4) and other passages that are so elusively introduced as to frustrate any confident enumeration.

Longenecker suggested that there are thirty-eight quotations in Hebrews. G. B. Caird found only twenty-nine (*CJT* 5 [1959] 47). C. Spicq identified thirty-six (1:331), but O. Michel only thirty-two (151). In this commentary it is proposed that there are thirty-one explicit quotations and four more implicit quotations, a minimum of thirty-seven allusions, nineteen instances where OT material is summarized, and thirteen more where a biblical name or topic is cited without reference to a specific context.

The extensive appeal to the detail of the OT text is an essential element in the writer's design and intention. It demonstrates how richly valuable the OT remains for the Christian community concerned with the fullness of God's revelation.

PRIMARY SOURCES FOR THE WRITER'S THEOLOGY

In common with other Jewish-hellenistic homilies, Hebrews draws most heavily upon the Pentateuch and Psalms (cf. Thyen, *Stil,* 67). The writer develops his discussion of redemption primarily on the basis of the Pentateuch. Twelve of his quotations are taken from "the Five Books," and ten of his allusions are to that section of the Jewish Scriptures. Even when the writer appears to depart from his customary approach, as in Heb 3:7–4:13, where the structuring text is Ps 95:7*b*–11, it becomes clear that he has been reading the Psalm from the vantage point of Num 13–14 (see *Comment* on Heb 3:16–19). In this instance the text of the Pentateuch has been approached through its interpretation in the Psalter. The writer pursues this tactic again in Heb 7:1–25, where the terse reference to Melchizedek in Gen 14:17–20 is approached through the acclamation of Melchizedek in Ps 110:4. With the single exception of the historical summary based on Josh 6, all of the "summary" material as well as the names and topics introduced without reference to a specific biblical context appear to be derived from the Pentateuch.

The primary sources for developing the writer's christology, however, are derived from the Psalms. (Cf. R. N. Longenecker, *Biblical Exegesis*, 167, who notes that with the exception of 2 Sam 7:14, Deut 32:43 LXX, and Isa 8:17, which are introduced as direct messianic prophecies, "all the biblical portions used to explicate the nature of the person of Christ are drawn entirely from the Psalms.") The christology of Hebrews is developed primarily through the exposition of the biblical text. The writer quotes from the Psalms seventeen times and alludes to texts from the Psalter sixteen more times. Repeated citation and appeal to Ps 110:1 and 4 throughout the homily indicate the extent of the writer's reliance upon the Psalms as a primary source for his christology.

MODE OF CITATION

Unlike Paul, who shows a preference for the introductory formula καθὼς γέγραπται, the writer of Hebrews never introduces a quotation from the OT with a form of the verb γράφειν, "to write." His preference is for the verb λέγειν, "to say," especially in the form of the present participle λέγων, "saying." The text of the OT is presented dynamically. The writer is persuaded that God continues to speak today in the biblical passages that are cited. What was said in the past continues to be said now as well (G. Hughes, *Hebrews and Hermeneutics*, 35). Although λέγειν is used in introductory formulae by other NT writers, it is usually combined with either the name of the prophetic speaker or with "Scripture" (e.g., Rom 4:3; 9:15, 17, 25; 10:16, 19, 20, 21; 11:9). In striking contrast, the writer of Hebrews usually introduces the words of the OT as the direct speaking of God, for which he prefers the present tense and the active voice (Barth, "The Old Testament in Hebrews," 58–59). Although the representation of a biblical quotation as the word that God is speaking to the audience *at that moment* can be documented from other Jewish-hellenistic homilies (see Thyen, *Stil*, 69–74), this manner of presenting the OT text is without parallel elsewhere in the NT.

The writer shows no concern to provide specific references for his quotations from the OT. With rare exception (Heb 4:7; 9:20) they are presented anonymously. The authority of the biblical text resides in its ultimate speaker, namely, God. In twenty of the thirty-five quotations in Hebrews, God is the grammatical subject in the context (1:5*a*, 5*b*, 6, 7, 8–9, 10–12, 13; 4:4; 5:5, 6; 6:14; 7:17, 21; 8:5, 8–12; 10:30*a*, 30*b*, 37–38; 12:26; 13:5). Four quotations are assigned to the Son (2:12, 13*a*, 13*b*; 10:5–7), and five others are attributed to the Holy Spirit (3:7*b*–11; presumably 4:3, 5, 7; 10:16–17). Such figures are, of course, "soft" rather than firm, because the writer can assign the same quotation to God or to the Holy Spirit (e.g., 8:8–12; 10:15–17; it is difficult to decide whether the writer attributed the quotations in 4:3–5, 7 to God or to the Holy Spirit; the initial citation of Ps 95:7*b*–11 is assigned to the Holy Spirit [Heb 3:7*a*]).

The mode of citation in Heb 4:4 deserves special mention. The writer uses the introductory verbal form εἴρηκεν, "he has spoken," with God as the grammatical subject from the context, to introduce the narrator's comment in Gen 2:2, "And God rested on the seventh day from all his works." The implication that God made this statement about himself reflects the writer's conviction that the ultimate source of the biblical text is God. Since the words of the quotation originated from God, they are appropriately represented as the word that God "has spoken."

THE WRITER'S PREFERRED TEXT

Bibliography

Ahlborn, E. "Die Septuaginta-Vorlage des Hebräerbriefes." Dissertation, Göttingen University, 1966. **Harder, G.** "Die Septuagintazitate des Hebräerbriefs: Ein Beitrag zum Problem der Auslegung des Alten Testaments." In *Theologia Viatorum*. Ed. M. Albertz. Munich: Kaiser, 1939. 33–52. **Howard, G.** "Hebrews and Old Testament Quotations." *NovT* 10 (1968)

208–16. **Katz, P.** "The Quotations from Deuteronomy in Hebrews." *ZNW* 49 (1958) 213–23. **McCullough, J. C.** "Hebrews and the Old Testament." Dissertation, Queen's University, Belfast, 1971. ———. "The Old Testament Quotations in Hebrews." *NTS* 26 (1979–80) 363–79. **Thomas, K. J.** "The Old Testament Citations in Hebrews." *NTS* 11 (1964–65) 303–25. ———. "The Use of the Septuagint in the Epistle to the Hebrews." Dissertation, University of Manchester, 1959.

A virtual consensus has been reached that the writer read his Bible in Greek (cf. E. Grässer, *TRu* 30 [1964] 156–59; J. C. McCullough, "Some Recent Developments in Research on the Epistle to the Hebrews: II," *IBS* 3 [1981] 28–31). The character of the text that he had before him, however, continues to be debated. The importance of the debate was signaled over 150 years ago when F. Bleek argued in his commentary that Paul could not have written Hebrews because he used a Greek text similar to Codex Vaticanus (B), while the writer of Hebrews seems to have had access to a Greek text similar to Codex Alexandrinus (A) (3:234). Although many of Bleek's statements about Alexandrinus have been shown to be unreliable (see Katz, *ZNW* 49 [1958] 217), his observation determined the course of subsequent research on the text of the quotations and allusions to the OT text in Hebrews.

Discussions of the writer's text tend to concern themselves with the relationship of the detail of his text to one, or both, of these major codices. The problem is that the quotations in Hebrews show characteristics of both Alexandrinus and Vaticanus. In seeking to evaluate the evidence, we must be aware of the complexity of the textual situation with respect to the Old Greek versions. A wide variety of readings was available to writers during the NT period. The writer of Hebrews used a form of the Greek text to which he enjoyed access. Presumably it was the local form of the text used by the community of which he was a part. It is necessary to allow for major differences between the first-century text to which he had access and the text of the "Old Greek Version" as known from the fourth-century manuscripts B and A. Reference in the commentary to "the Old Greek Version" and to the writer's use of "the LXX" are convenient forms of reference, but they lack precision. (See now L. Greenspoon, "The Use and Abuse of the Term 'LXX' and Related Terminology in Recent Scholarship," *BIOSCS* 20 [1987] 21–29.)

One approach in research on the writer's preferred text has sought to explain divergences in the quotations found in Hebrews from the Old Greek text as known from Codex Alexandrinus (LXX[A]) or Codex Vaticanus (LXX[B]). (K. J. Thomas summarized his 1959 University of Manchester dissertation, "The Use of the Septuagint in the Epistle to the Hebrews," which pursued this line of research, in *NTS* 11 [1964–65] 303–25.) Subsequent research has cautioned that there cannot be uncritical reliance on the older LXX[A] and LXX[B] traditions in seeking the source of the quotations in Hebrews (so correctly, Howard, *NovT* 10 [1968] 208–16, who demonstrated how complex the problem of the source of the quotations in Hebrews actually is; see further McCullough, *NTS* 26 [1979–80] 363–79). Interaction with the current discussion concerning the form of the Greek text used by the writer in quotations and allusions to the OT text will be found throughout the commentary.

THE WRITER'S APPROPRIATION OF THE OT TEXT

Bibliography

Barth M. "The Old Testament in Hebrews: An Essay in Biblical Hermeneutics." In *Current Issues in New Testament Interpretation.* Ed. W. Klassen and G. F. Snyder. New York: Harper & Row, 1962. 53–78, 263–73. **Cohn-Sherbok, D.** "Paul and Rabbinic Exegesis." *SJT* 35 (1982) 117–32. **Daube, D.** "Rabbinic Methods of Interpretation and Hellenistic Rhetoric." *HUCA* 22 (1949) 239–64. **Davidson, R. M.** *Typology in Scripture: A Study of Hermeneutical τύπος Structures.* Andrews University Seminary Doctoral Dissertation Series. Berrien Springs, MI: Andrews UP, 1981. **Edgar, S. L.** "Respect for Context in Quotations from the Old Testament." *NTS* 9 (1962–63) 55–62. **Ellingworth, P.** "The Old Testament in Hebrews: Exegesis, Method and Hermeneutics." Dissertation, University of Aberdeen, 1977. **Fitzmyer, J. A.** "The Use of Explicit Old Testament Quotations in Qumran Literature and in the New Testament." *NTS* 7 (1960/61) 297–333. **Hughes, G.** *Hebrews and Hermeneutics: The Epistle to the Hebrews as a New Testament Example of Biblical Interpretation.* SNTSMS 36. Cambridge: Cambridge UP, 1979. **Lampe, G. W. H.,** and **Woollcombe, K. J.** *Essays on Typology.* SBT 22. London: SCM Press, 1957. ———. "Hermeneutics and Typology." *LQHR* 190 (1965) 17–25. ———. "Typological Exegesis." *Th* 56 (1953) 201–8. **Leschert, D.** "Hermeneutical Foundations of the Epistle to the Hebrews: A Study in the Validity of Its Interpretation of Some Core Citations from the Psalms." Dissertation, Fuller Theological Seminary, 1991. **Lewis, T. W.** "The Theological Logic in Hebrews 10:19–12:29 and the Appropriation of the Old Testament." Dissertation, Drew University, 1965. **Luther, J. H.** "The Use of the Old Testament by the Author of Hebrews." Dissertation, Bob Jones University, 1977. **McGaughey, D. H.** "The Hermeneutical Method of the Epistle to the Hebrews." Dissertation, Boston University, 1963. **Mickelsen, A. B.** "Methods of Interpretaton in the Epistle to the Hebrews." Dissertation, University of Chicago, 1950. **Ploeg, J. van der.** "L'exégèse de l'Ancien Testament dans l'Épître aux Hébreux." *RB* 54 (1947) 187–228. **Reid, R.** "The Use of the Old Testament in the Epistle to the Hebrews." Dissertation, Union Theological Seminary, New York, 1964. **Rendall, R.** "The Method of the Writer to the Hebrews in Using Old Testament Quotations." *EvQ* 27 (1955) 214–20. **Sabourin, L.** "Auctor Epistulae ad Hebraeos ut interpres Scripturae." *VD* 46 (1968) 275–85. **Schröger, F.** "Das hermeneutische Instrumentarium des Hebräerbriefverfasser." *TGl* 60 (1970) 344–59. ———. *Der Verfasser des Hebräerbriefes als Schriftausleger.* Regensburg: Pustet, 1968. **Sowers, S. G.** *The Hermeneutics of Philo and Hebrews: A Comparison of the Interpretation of the Old Testament in Philo Judaeus and the Epistle to the Hebrews.* Richmond: Knox, 1965.

It is valid to inquire concerning the writer's manner of using the biblical text in the light of practice of his contemporaries in schools and synagogues throughout the Diaspora. A convenient survey of contemporary rabbinical practice in treating the biblical text has been provided by D. Cohn-Sherbok (*SJT* 35 [1982] 117–32), which can assist the student of Hebrews to identify some of the principles guiding the writer in his approach to the OT text. (The following discussion is indebted to G. H. Guthrie, "The Structure of Hebrews," 88–90, 94–99.)

1. Dispelling Confusion. It was common practice among the rabbis to clarify a verse of Scripture about which there was potential confusion (for the rabbinical treatment of Ps 50:1, see Cohn-Sherbok, *SJT* 35 [1982] 119). An example of dispelling confusion in Hebrews may be found in 2:8–9, where the writer is commenting on Ps 8:4–6. Having asserted God's subjugation of "everything" to "man" in an absolute way (2:8*b*), he comments, "But in fact we do not yet see everything subject to his control. But we see Jesus . . . crowned with glory and splendor" (Heb 2:8c–9). The writer's concern is to dispel any confusion regarding the intention of the biblical quotation from Ps 8:4–6. Although the extravagance of the writer's statement in Heb 2:8b is mocked by the common human experience, the perception of reality is not to contradict the reality asserted in the biblical quotation. The temporal expression "not yet" in the writer's concession that "we do not yet see everything subject to his control" is crucial. It indicates that he found in the Psalm text a prophetic announcement that eventually will be realized. The biblical text possesses the character of a legal decree that cannot be set aside. In point of fact, the current unrealized state of affairs shows that the promised subjugation of everything finally has reference not to "man" in general, but to Jesus (Heb 2:9), in whom the human vocation finds its true expression.

2. *Reinforcement.* By "reinforcement" Cohn-Sherbok refers to the common rabbinical practice of strengthening an exhortation by citing a supporting biblical statement (*SJT* 35 [1982] 119). An illustration of this principle is provided in Heb 10:19–39, where the writer is admonishing his audience to remain true to their baptismal confession. Near the conclusion of an extended exhortation, he introduces a conflated quotation that brings together a phrase from Isa 26:20 and from Hab 2:3–4. His primary interest is in the scriptural warning, "And if he shrinks back I will not be pleased with him" (see *Comment* on Heb 10:39). The exhortation to faithfulness is reinforced with the quotation of the biblical text.

3. *Implications.* During the course of preaching, it was common for a rabbi to draw out the implications of the biblical text (Cohn-Sherbok, *SJT* 35 [1982] 121). This practice is illustrated by the writer's treatment of Jer 31:31–34 in Heb 8:8–13. After citing the text in full (8:8–12), he draws out its implications by focusing the attention of his audience upon the key word "new": "In that he says 'new,' he treats the first covenant as obsolete, and what is obsolete and outdated will soon disappear" (8:13). Other examples of this concern with the implications of Scripture will be found in Heb 2:8a; 3:16–19; 4:6–10; 7:11–12; 10:8–9; 12:7–10; and notably in 12:26–29.

4. *The Literal Sense of a Word or Phrase.* A rabbi would often appeal to the literal sense of a particular word or phrase in the biblical text (Cohn-Sherbok, *SJT* 35 [1982] 125). This type of appeal is common in Hebrews. It is essential to the extended exhortation in 3:7–4:13, where the writer seizes on the literal meaning of the word "today" in Ps 95:7b (Heb 3:13, 15; 4:7–8). It stands behind the argumentation in Heb 7:11, where the writer is pressing home the significance of the phrase, "like Melchizedek," or 7:20–22, where he insists that Jesus was confirmed in his priestly office with an oath, or 7:23–25, where he explores the significance of the biblical expression "forever" in Ps 110:4. It is also the key to the writer's interpretation of Jer 31:31–34 in Heb 8:8–13, and to the exposition of Hag 2:6–7 in Heb 12:26–29. The literal sense of the text was very important to the writer of Hebrews.

5. *Other Early Rabbinical Principles of Interpretation.* The *Tosepta* associates seven ancient guidelines for the appropriation of Scripture with the practice of Hillel (*t. Sanh.* 7.11), who antedates the inception of the early Christian movement by a generation or so. The *so-called* "seven *middôt*" (hermeneutical principles) appear to be a codification of contemporary practices, or possibly limitations imposed

upon current practice (so D. Moo, *The Old Testament in the Gospel Passion Narratives* [Sheffield: Almond, 1983] 28). The writer of Hebrews adopts two of the seven *middôt*: *qal wāḥômer* (what applies in a less important case will certainly be applicable to a more important case) and *gĕzêrâ šāwâ* (the presence of the same words [or cognates] in two passages of Scripture is designed to call attention to their mutual relationship). The first principle is simply the appeal from the lesser to the greater, which is found in ancient literature throughout the Mediterranean world (*a fortiori*). The second is the principle of verbal analogy, which allows one verse to explain another.

The writer of Hebrews appeals to his audience on the basis of *qal wāḥômer* in 2:2–4; 9:13–14; 10:28–29; and 12:25. In 2:2–4 he argues that, if disregard for the Mosaic law was appropriately punished, unconcern for the gospel must be catastrophic. Since the message delivered through angels demanded accountability, *how much more* is this true of the message of salvation announced by the Lord? The fundamental assumption of the argument is that the dignity of the messenger provides the test of the importance and finality of the message delivered. The transcendent dignity of the Son (1:2–14) demonstrates that the message of salvation that had reached the community through attested witnesses merited the strictest attention. The appeal to this argument is heard sharply again in 10:28–29 and 12:25. In 9:13–14 the writer concedes that the blood of goats and bulls and the ashes of a red heifer provided purgation from external defilement. He argues "how much more" will the blood of Christ make clean the people of God and qualify them for the worship of God. Standing behind the argument in each case is the conviction that Jesus, as the mediator of God's final word, is greater than Moses and that the Christian message is greater than the revelation given to Moses. Consequently, Christians are faced with greater responsibility and greater peril than those who stood before God under the old covenant.

Illustrations of *gĕzêrâ šāwâ* may be found in Heb 4:1–11 and 5:5–6. The new development in 4:1–11 is the enrichment of the interpretation of Ps 95:7*b*–11 by the use of Gen 2:2 to clarify the character of the rest from which the desert generation was excluded. The argument turns on the verb used to state that God "took rest" (κατέπαυσεν) in Gen 2:2 LXX being cognate to the term for "rest" in Ps 95[LXX 94]:11 (κατάπαυσις). Use of the cognate terms permitted the inference that "my rest" in Ps 95:11 is properly interpreted in terms of God's primordial rest following the works of creation according to Gen 2:1–3. The inference is drawn on the basis of the analogy of words. That the writer and those whom he addressed read the biblical text in Greek was crucial in this instance, since the MT used different Hebrew roots to describe God's rest in the two biblical passages.

In 5:5–6 the writer joins together two of the most important biblical quotations for the development of his discourse, Ps 2:7 and Ps 110:4. They are joined on the basis of the emphatic pronoun of address σύ, "you." The writer correctly interpreted Ps 2:7 and Ps 110:4 as declarations of appointment. Both texts declare the decrees in accordance with which Jesus was installed in his office and invested with power. In this instance *gĕzêrâ šāwâ* is used effectively to mark the transition from the presentation of Jesus as Son to the discussion of Jesus as Priest. A conscious concern to associate the titles "Son" and "Priest," the primary models for the writer's christology, is apparent in the conjunction of the Psalm quotations in 5:5–6.

6. *Chain Quotations.* The rabbis occasionally would string together a chain of biblical quotations on the basis of recurring expressions that functioned as catchwords. As in the case of gĕzêrâ šāwâ, they were appealing to the analogy of Scripture. In this instance, however, there was no engagement in a detailed interpretation of the analogous texts. Such chain quotations, or ḥāraz, "to string pearls," were introduced to indicate the strength of the scriptural support for a given theme. The usual rabbinical practice was to cite a passage from the Pentateuch and then join to the quotation, often by gĕzêrâ šāwâ, similar statements from the Prophets and the Writings (cf. Barth, "The Old Testament in Hebrews," 64; G. H. Guthrie, "The Structure of Hebrews," 97).

An example of ḥāraz occurs in Heb 1:5–13, where the writer joins together with minimal comment three pairs of passages and a concluding quotation. In this case, the quotations are taken primarily from the Psalms and Odes that were sung in the liturgy of the synagogue. The first pair of quotations concerns sonship: Ps 2:7 and 2 Sam 7:14 are joined together on the basis of the term υἱός, "son." The second pair documents the subservient role of the angels in reference to the Son: Deut 32:43 (in the form of the biblical Odes appended to the Greek Psalter [Ode 2:43]) and Ps 104:4 are joined on the basis of the plural terms "angels." The third pair of quotations announces the eternal character of the Son's reign: Ps 45:6–7 and Ps 102:25–27 appear to be linked not only by conceptual parallelism (the enduring nature of the Son) but by the common use of the personal pronoun σου, "your." The concluding quotation introduces the significant royal enthronement text, which will be cited and to which there will be allusions throughout the homily, Ps 110:1. (Cf. J. W. Thompson, "The Structure and Purpose of the Catena in Heb 1:5–13," *CBQ* 38 [1976] 352–63; R. Koops, "Chains of Contrast in Hebrews 1," *BT* 34 [1983] 220–25; J. P. Meier, "Structure and Theology in Hebrews 1, 1–14," *Bib* 66 [1985] 168–89.)

7 *Example Lists.* In classical antiquity, lists of examples were frequently employed to motivate an audience or readers to strive for virtue. When Judaism took its place in hellenistic society, it was influenced by Hellenism to adopt and adapt this practice for its own purposes (cf. W. S. Towner, *The Rabbinical "Enumeration of Examples"* [Leiden: Brill, 1973] 100–116; M. R. Cosby, "The Rhetorical Composition and Function of Hebrews 11 in the Light of the Example-lists in Antiquity," Dissertation, Emory University, 1985, 114–37). Primary source evidence for this is provided by documents emanating from the Jewish wisdom tradition (e.g., Wis 10:1–11:1; Sir 44:1–49:16). Recourse to lists of OT personages attested an interest in redemptive history that was new to the Jewish wisdom tradition (so J. Fichtner, "Zum Problem Glaube und Geschichte in der israelitisch-jüdischen Weisheitliteratur," *TLZ* 76 [1952] 141–50). The impact of this development can be traced both in the liturgy and in the preaching of the hellenistic synagogues (cf. W. S. Towner, *The Rabbinical "Enumeration of Examples,"* 95–117, 214–30). Such lists constitute a distinctive preaching form, the testimony list. They served defined apologetic and parenetic purposes and were used effectively in the missionary propaganda in which Judaism was engaged (cf. Thyen, *Stil,* 115–16; Cosby, "The Rhetorical Composition and Function of Hebrews 11," 114–61, 186–90, 260–63).

In Hebrews 11 the writer displays his skill in appropriating this preaching form, drawing up a list of attested examples from the biblical record. What is distinctive in his use of the form is that he shows less interest in the positive exemplary function of his models of faithfulness than in the fact that their actions, responses, and death are informative of the content of *Christian* faith (for the detail, see the *Comment* sections on Heb 11). In this way the list of those who are attested by God as faithful has been transformed into a list of witnesses whose faith testifies to the writer's generation concerning the reality of the blessings for which *Christians* hope.

8. *Typology.* Typological interpretation plays a key role in the developing argument in Hebrews. In 3:12–19, for example, a typological interpretation of Ps 95:7*b*–11 suggested to the writer that Israel at Kadesh stood in relationship to the Christian community as type to antitype. The theology of rest developed in 4:1–11 takes account of the pattern of archetype (God's primal rest, 4:4), type (the settlement of Canaan under Joshua, 4:8), and antitype (the Sabbath celebration of the consummation, 4:9).

Prior to 1950, typology tended to be defined as the recognition of divinely intended and predictive *prefigurations* in Scripture. More recently the dominant tendency has been to identify typology with "historical *correspondences* retrospectively recognized within the consistent redemptive activity of God" (Davidson, *Typology in Scripture*, 94). For the writer of Hebrews, the history of Israel is redemptive history, and the significance of an OT type resides in its particular relationship to the divine plan of salvation. His typological interpretation of the OT depends on the historical correspondences between the old and new orders of redemption.

The central section of Hebrews, extending from 8:1 to 10:18, provides abundant illustration of the manner in which the writer employs typology. The contrast between the earthly and the heavenly sanctuaries in 8:1–5 is not an expression of Alexandrian metaphysics but the writer's way of presenting the typological relation between the old and new covenants. The relationship between the two sanctuaries is essentially a *temporal* one. The old covenant was a necessary, but provisional, episode in the accomplishing of redemptive history. The writer considers the relative merits of the old and new covenants in terms of their respective provisions for worship (9:1, 9, 14). The heavenly liturgy is eschatological reality, which the cultic provisions of the Sinai covenant only foreshadowed. The writer employs typology to demonstrate that the possibility of access to God through a Levitical arrangement no longer exists because it was intrinsically inadequate. Access to God is possible only through the ministering priest who serves in the heavenly sanctuary.

The tabernacle and its ritual provided the writer with a vocabulary and grammar with which to express the insights disclosed to him by the Holy Spirit (Heb 9:8). Although the division of the tabernacle into two parts, the front and rear compartments, was essentially spatial, in the writer's typological exposition it possesses temporal significance (9:8–10). The writer's concern is the elaboration of a theology of salvation that recognizes the eschatological newness of the period of redemptive history that was introduced by God's act of speaking decisively and definitively through the Son (1:1–2*a*). Typological appeal to the cultic appointments and actions in the tabernacle (9:1–7) is intended to demonstrate the ultimate inadequacy of the Levitical arrangement and the necessity for the new cultic action of Christ (9:8–10).

In this mode of approaching the biblical text, the writer found in the ritual of the Day of Atonement a point of comparison with which to describe the significance of the sacrificial death of Christ and his subsequent exaltation (9:11–10:18). The saving event by which Christ secured salvation is described graphically under the symbolism of a liturgical action, namely, Christ's single and fully adequate priestly offering and entrance into the heavenly sanctuary. The manner in which the writer has shaded his use of typology in Hebrews has been a sustained concern in the community.

9. *Homiletical Midrash.* Homiletical midrash refers to the interpretation of the biblical text in the event of preaching. Its function was to bring the text into the experience of the congregation. It involved making the Scriptures contemporary so that they could no longer be regarded as a record of past events and sayings but a living word through which God addressed the audience directly. Hebrews provides a series of illustrations of this dynamic approach to Scripture (see on 2:5–9; 3:7–4:13; 6:13–20; 7:11–25; 8:7–13; 10:5–10, 15–18, 35–39; 12:5–13, 25–29). So important is this approach to the OT text in Hebrews that it is given extended treatment in the following section, discussing Hebrews and Judaism.

At this point it is sufficient to remark on one aspect of the writer's appropriation of Scripture that is evident in the midrashic use he makes of Ps 110:4. He introduces the quotation of the text to his audience in 5:6 and alludes to it again in 5:10–11 and 6:20. But in characteristic fashion, he defers his development of the quotation until 7:11–25. The practice of introducing a biblical passage but offering its explanation only later in the homily appears to be a deliberate device to arouse and sustain the interest of the audience.

Conclusion. The survey of the manner in which the writer of Hebrews makes use of the OT text indicates that he stands in the mainstream of Judaism and early Jewish Christianity. The determining factor for the distinctiveness of his interpretation of Scripture is not the methodology he employed in appropriating the OT text but his Christian theology of the interrelationships among history, eschatology, and revelation (cf. G. Hughes, *Hebrews and Hermeneutics,* 36). His approach to the text is certainly colored by his convictions concerning Jesus. But the principles by which he was guided in his approach to the OT text and the forms of exposition he adopts were those with which he had become familiar from a life enriched by synagogue preaching. It may be assumed that his audience was thoroughly familiar with the approaches to the text of the OT that are characteristic of this homily from their own exposure to the liturgy and preaching in synagogues throughout the Diaspora.

Hebrews demonstrates that the OT remains a valid and significant witness to God's redemptive word and deed. Christians must grasp this witness in the light of God's decisive act of speaking through the Son (1:1–2a). The words of the OT are quoted not for their significance in the past but rather for their significance in the present. All of Scripture remains a revelation of God's unalterable plan of salvation for the human family. Its relevance to the members of a house church in crisis is driven home forcefully by the writer's appropriation of the OT text.

Hebrews and Judaism: Faith, Polemic, and Pastoral Strategy

Bibliography

Beck, N. A. *Mature Christianity: The Recognition and Repudiation of the Anti-Jewish Polemic of the New Testament.* Knoxville: Susquehanna UP, 1985. **Bloch, R.** "Midrash." In *Approaches to Ancient Judaism: Theory and Practice.* Ed. W. S. Green. Callaway, MT: Scholars Press, 1978. 29–50. **D'Angelo, M. R.** *Moses in the Letter to the Hebrews.* SBLDS 42. Missoula, MT: Scholars Press, 1979. 95–131. **Déaut, R. le.** "Apropos a Definition of Midrash." *Int* 25 (1971) 259–82. **Eckert, W. P., Levinson, N. P. and Stör, M.,** eds. *Antijudaismus im Neuen Testament? Exegetische und systematische Beiträge.* Munich: Kaiser, 1967. **Ellis, E. E.** "Midrash, Targum and New Testament Quotations." In *Neotestamentica et Semitica.* FS M. Black. Ed. E. E. Ellis and M. Wilcox. Edinburgh: Clark, 1969. 61–69. **Fischer, J.** "Covenant, Fulfilment and Judaism in Hebrews." *ERT* 13 (1989) 175–87. **Harrisville, R. A.** *The Concept of Newness in the New Testament.* Minneapolis: Augsburg, 1960. 48–53. **Hunt, B. P. W. S.** "The 'Epistle to the Hebrews': An Anti-judaic treatise?" In *SE* 2 (1964) 408–10. **Johnson, L. T.** "The New Testament's Anti-Jewish Slander and the Conventions of Ancient Polemic." *JBL* 108 (1989) 419–44. **Jones, P. R.** "The Figure of Moses as a Heuristic Device for Understanding the Pastoral Intent of Hebrews." *RevExp* 76 (1979) 95–107. **Klassen, W.** "To the Hebrews or against the Hebrews? Anti-Judaism and the Epistle to the Hebrews." In *Anti-Judaism in Early Christianity.* Vol. 2: *Separation and Polemic.* Ed. S. G. Wilson. Waterloo, Ont.: Wilfred Laurier University, 1986. 1–16. **Kuss, O.** "Der Verfasser des Hebräerbriefes als Seelsorger." *TTZ* 67 (1958) 1–12, 65–80. **Langmuir, G. I.** *History, Religion, and Antisemitism.* Berkeley: University of California, 1990. 275–305. **McNamara, M.** "Some Issues and Recent Writings on Judaism and the New Testament." *IBS* 9 (1987) 136–49. **Miller, M. P.** "Targum, Midrash and the Use of the Old Testament in the New Testament." *JSJ* 2 (1971) 29–82. **Mora, G.** *La Carta a los Hebreos como Escrito Pastoral.* Barcelona: Herder, 1974. **Neusner, J.** *What is Midrash?* Philadelphia: Fortress, 1987. **Peterson, D. G.** "The Prophecy of the New Covenant in the Argument of Hebrews." *RTR* 38 (1979) 74–81. **Pinto, L. di.** *Volontà di Dio e legge antica nell' Epistola agli Ebrei.* Naples: Pontificia Universitate Gregoriana, 1976. 23–33, 49–52. **Porton, G. G.** "Defining Midrash." In *The Study of Ancient Judaism.* Ed. J. Neusner. New York: KTAV, 1981. 1:55–95. **Rylaarsdam, J. C.** "Jewish-Christian Relationships: The Two Covenants and the Dilemmas of Christology." In *Grace upon Grace.* FS L. J. Kuyper. Ed. J. I. Cook. Grand Rapids: Eerdmans, 1975. 70–84. **Sandmel, S.** *Anti-Semitism in the New Testament?* Philadelphia: Fortress, 1978. **Sanger, D.** "Neues Testament und Antijudaismus: Versuch einer exegetischen und hermeneutischen Vergewisserung im innerchristlichen Gespräch." *KD* 34 (1988) 210–31. **Synge, F. C.** *Hebrews and the Scriptures.* London: SPCK, 1959. **Vuyst, J. de.** *'Oud en Nieuw Verbond' in de Brief aan de Hebreeën.* Kampen: Kok, 1964. **Wright, A. G.** *Midrash: The Literary Genre.* Staten Island, NY: Alba House, 1968. 52–59, 64–67. **Young, F. M.** "Temple Cult and Law in Early Christianity." *NTS* 19 (1972–73) 325–38. **Zeitlin, S.** "Midrash: A Historical Study." *JQR* 44 (1953) 21–36.

Appeal to the history of the interpretation of Hebrews immediately focuses the importance of the issue of faith, polemic, and pastoral strategy. The argument of Hebrews has been used and misused for polemic against antecedent forms of Judaism. The writer's sustained use of *syncrisis* (comparison) to demonstrate the superiority of Jesus to the angels, to Moses, to Joshua, and to other mediators of the word and grace of God to Israel has been cited by Christian interpreters to denigrate Judaism. Employment of the vocabulary of shadow and type in reference to the tabernacle and the provisions for worship under the old covenant has been invoked to discount the sacrificial arrangement and the Levitical priest-hood. These developments underscore the difficulty of interpreting Hebrews in light of its past use to discredit Judaism.

The importance of referring to the history of interpretation lies in the prob-lematic nature of the term "anti-Judaism" when it is used to characterize NT texts and themes that are pejorative in reference to Jews and to Judaism. The prob-lematic nature of the term becomes evident as soon as one realizes that early Christians considered themselves to a large extent part of Judaism. For that rea-son NT statements critical of Judaism have to be interpreted within the context of intramural conflicts among Jews in the first century. These conflicts were rooted in divergent attitudes toward the Torah and halakhah, with Christians formulat-ing their positions in the light of their convictions about Jesus. It is appropriate to talk about Christian anti-Judaism only at a later period when statements from the NT were detached from their context and were misinterpreted as anti-Judaic. (See especially Sanger, *KD* 34 [1988] 210–31.) This is precisely what is shown by the history of the interpretation of Hebrews.

The superscription "to the Hebrews" was not a part of the original document. It was almost certainly added during the course of the canonizing process to lo-cate Hebrews within the Jewish mission of the early Church. The character of the Jewish Christianity represented by Hebrews must be assessed on the basis of the text itself. A close reading of the text suggests that both the writer and his audience had been nurtured through Scripture and the traditions of hellenistic Judaism prior to their response to the preaching of those who had heard Jesus (Heb 2:3–4; 13:7). Hellenistic Judaism in the first century was by no means monolithic, but it is convenient to use this designation to connote the varieties of Jewish piety and praxis that emerged in urban centers throughout the Greek-speaking Roman world.

There is in Hebrews a constant appeal to the normative character of the Scrip-tures, and more particularly of the Torah (2:2; 9:13; 10:28–29; 12:25–26). The writer readily concedes, for example, that "what was once spoken by God through the angels proved to be legally valid, and every infringement and disobedience received the appropriate punishment" (2:2). The accumulation of juridical ex-pressions ("proved legally valid," "every infringement and disobedience," "received appropriate punishment") confirms that "the message delivered by angels" signi-fies the law delivered to Moses at Sinai. The positive role assigned to the angels and the appeal to the normative character of the Torah tend to suggest that both the writer and the community addressed continued to maintain emotional and intellectual ties with the larger Jewish community.

Throughout Hebrews, the argument is developed exegetically on the basis of the wording in current Greek translations of the biblical text. This is espe-cially evident at points where older Greek versions differ from the Hebrew text (e.g., 3:7*b*–11, citing Ps 95:7*b*–11; 10:5–7, citing Ps 40:6–8). The writer read his Bible in Greek, as did those whom he addressed. He was able to presuppose their general familiarity with Scripture (e.g., 12:17, "for you know that . . . ," with reference to Gen 27:30–40) and with Jewish tradition. The form of his own homily reflects the influence of hellenistic-Jewish synagogue preaching. (See above, "The Homily or Sermon Form" and "Defining the Genre.") Hebrews is a Jewish-Christian writing that retains a distinctly Jewish ethos shaped by hellenistic

Judaism. Moreover, the writer's constant reflection on Scripture presupposes continuity with "old Israel."

Interpreters who see Hebrews addressed to Jewish Christians have often assumed that the document was composed to warn the audience not to retreat into Judaism and that the writer accomplished this by means of an anti-Judaic polemic. (Cf. Hunt, *SE* 2 [1964] 408–11; Synge, *Hebrews and the Scriptures*, 44, who argue that the superscription πρὸς Ἐβραίους means "against the Jews," in spite of the implausibility of this proposal.) This assumption needs to be tested in light of the observation that in its literary structure Hebrews intersperses exposition and exhortation, thesis and parenesis. In the parenesis there is no differentiation or separation from Judaism; the distinctively Christian perspective of the writer is expressed rather in the thesis. This generalization is an important observation, since in Hebrews parenesis takes precedence over thesis (see above, "Purpose and Plan"). All of the assertions made by the writer in the thesis sections of Hebrews serve to support the parenesis, where there is no differentiation from Judaism.

THE CENTRAL THEME OF HEBREWS

The central theme of Hebrews is the importance of listening to the voice of God in Scripture and in the act of Christian preaching. The opening lines of the homily focus attention upon the God who speaks. The characterization of God as the one who intervened in Israel's history through the spoken word serves to introduce the characterization of the Son as the one through whom God has spoken the ultimate word (1:1–2a). That theme is sustained with variations throughout the homily (2:1–4; 3:7b–4:13; 5:11; 10:23, 35–39; 11:11). It is recapitulated in a climactic warning, "Be careful that you do not disregard the one who is speaking" (12:25a). The redemptive accomplishment and transcendent dignity of the Son through whom God has spoken the final word demonstrates that it will be catastrophic to ignore the word of salvation delivered through the Son (2:1–4).

The writer elaborated upon this thesis through the interpretation of Scripture and by an appeal to the reality of Christian experience. The development in Hebrews conforms to the Judaic tradition of homiletical midrash, in which key phrases of an extended quotation from Scripture are taken up and expounded for the congregation (e.g., 2:5–9; 3:7b–4:11; 8:6–13; 10:5–10, 15–18; 12:26–29). This approach to Scripture, which was developed in the homiletical tradition of the synagogue, served to bring the text into the experience of an audience through preaching. (See Zeitlin, *JQR* 44 [1953] 21–36; Ellis, "Midrash, Targum and New Testament Quotations," 61–69; Wright, *Midrash: The Literary Genre*, 52–59, 64–67; le Déaut, *Int* 25 [1971] 259–82; M. P. Miller, *JSJ* 2 [1971] 29–82; Bloch, "Midrash," 29–50; Porton, "Defining Midrash," 55–95; McNamara, *IBS* 9 [1987] 136–49.)

Both the writer and his audience were thoroughly familiar with homiletical midrash by virtue of their participation in the life of hellenistic synagogues. When the writer employs homiletical midrash, he does so in continuity with his peers in hellenistic Judaism. The act of reflecting on Scripture and of interpreting Scripture presupposes certain shared assumptions about how the voice of God is recovered. It presupposes that Scripture announces a promise of things to come. This is a thoroughly Jewish understanding of Scripture. The apology developed in Hebrews will necessarily focus upon the continuity and discontinuity of the new covenant community with the traditions, understanding, and supports of the larger Jewish community in which the writer and his audience had been nurtured. By examining this aspect of Hebrews, the issues of faith, polemic, and pastoral strategy will remain sharply in focus.

THE TREATMENT OF MOSES IN HEBREWS

In considering whether Hebrews contains any obvious polemic against Judaism, we may observe that it is instructive to consider initially the writer's treatment of Moses. The figure of Moses, as the mediator of Israel's covenant and cult, is of central importance in Hebrews. The writer contrasts the Mosaic era, the Mosaic covenant, and the Mosaic cult with the new situation introduced by God through Jesus. This is intimated in the opening lines of the homily, in the contrast between the word spoken to the fathers through the prophets and the word spoken through the Son (1:1–2a). It is confirmed in 2:1–4, when the Mosaic law mediated by the angels throws into bold relief the ultimacy of the salvation proclaimed by the Lord and by those who heard him.

This approach is sustained throughout Hebrews. The extended comparison of the old and new cult (4:15–10:31; 12:18–24) focuses upon access to God in the Mosaic era and in Christian worship respectively. It develops the parallel between Moses as the mediator of the old cult and Jesus as the mediator of the new. By creative reference to Moses and the wilderness generation, the writer presents Christ as the mediator of the new covenant and clarifies the dynamic character of Christian existence. Moses is not simply one figure among several who is compared to Jesus. Instead, Moses and Jesus are yoked throughout the homily (see especially Jones, *RevExp* 76 [1979] 95–107).

The authority claimed for the Son as the mediator of God's final word in 1:1–2:18 inevitably invited comparison with the unique authority of Moses as the man with whom God spoke more intimately and directly than with an ordinary prophet (Num 12:5–8). The allusion to Num. 12:7 in Heb. 3:2, 5 suggests that the demonstration of Jesus' superiority to Moses in Heb. 3:1–6 is already anticipated in the opening sentence of the homily. In some strands of the Jewish tradition, the testimony to Moses in Num 12:7 was used to prove that Moses had been granted a higher rank and privilege than the ministering angels (see D'Angelo, *Moses in the Letter to the Hebrews*, 95–131, who calls attention to *Sipre Zuta* to Num 12:6–8 [ed. H. S. Horowitz, 275–76] and *Sipre Num.* 103 [ed. H. S. Horowitz, 101–2]). If this interpretation may be presupposed among Greek-speaking Jewish communities of the Diaspora, it clarifies the structure of Hebrews, where the Son is compared first to the angels (1:4–2:16) and then to Moses, their superior (3:1–6). Although Jesus had been shown on the basis of Scripture to be superior to the angels, it was by no means superfluous to continue with a demonstration of his superiority to Moses.

The comparison of Jesus and Moses in 3:1–6 has been placed strategically within the structure of the homily. There it is clearly asserted that Moses should be honored, for he was faithful in all of God's house (3:2, 5). Although the writer is concerned to demonstrate that Jesus is worthy of greater honor than Moses, there is no denigration of Moses in Hebrews.

THE WRITER'S USE OF COMPARISON

The use of comparison as a rhetorical strategy is employed throughout Hebrews. The comparative adjective κρείσσων/κρείττων and the comparative adverb κρεῖττον, in the sense of "superior" or "better," are characteristic speech-forms for the writer, occurring twelve times in Hebrews, and are fundamental to his argument. Commenting on the prominence of these terms, W. Klassen observes that "The sense 'to be superior' or 'to be better than,' the comparative form of the adjective, appears only in the epistle to the Hebrews with reference to the relation between Christianity and Judaism" ("To the Hebrews or against the Hebrews?" 6). The writer describes the possession of the community as a "better hope through which we draw near to God" (7:19). Reflecting on Ps 110:4, he exclaims "how far superior must the covenant also be of which Jesus is the guarantor!" (7:22). Comparing the ministry of Jesus to that of the Levitical priests he argues, "In fact the ministry which he has attained is as superior to theirs as the covenant of which he is the mediator is superior to the old one, seeing that this covenant has been drawn up on the basis of better promises, for if that first covenant had been irreproachable, there would have been no occasion sought for a second" (8:6–7). The theological and pastoral climax of the homily in 12:18–29 is an elaborate comparison between the experience of Israel at Sinai and that of the audience. They have come to "Mount Zion" and stand before "Jesus, the mediator of a new covenant, whose sprinkled blood speaks of better things than the blood of Abel" (12:24).

Even when comparative terms are absent, the argument assumes the form of a comparison (e.g., 2:2–4; 3:3–6*a*; 5:4–10; 10:27–28; 12:25). Moreover, the comparisons drawn by the writer do not concern peripheral matters. They have to do with matters "at the center: covenant, hope, promises, law, approach to God" (Klassen, "To the Hebrews or against the Hebrews?" 7). The detailed comparisons developed in the text necessarily pose the question whether this is an indication of the polemical anti-Judaic character of Hebrews.

What makes this question insistent is that the writer does not restrict himself to commenting upon the preeminence of Jesus, his priestly ministry, and the covenant he has mediated. He goes beyond this pastoral strategy to make deprecatory statements about the resources and supports of those who rely upon the provisions of the first covenant for access to God, i.e., those who continue to identify themselves with the traditional perspectives and structures of Judaism. Among the pejorative statements of Hebrews are the following:

Now there was the annulment of a former commandment, because of its weakness and uselessness (for the law perfected nothing), but the introduction of the better hope through which we are drawing near to God (7:18–19).

For if the first covenant had been irreproachable, there would have been no occasion sought for a second (8:7).

In that [God] says "new," [God] treated the first covenant as obsolete, and what is obsolete and outdated will soon disappear (8:13).

The holy Spirit was showing by this that the way into the real sanctuary had not yet been disclosed while the first compartment had cultic status. This is an illustration pointing to the present time, according to which the gifts and sacrifices being offered are unable to bring decisive purgation to the worshiper so far as the conscience is concerned, [but] only on the basis of food and drink and various ceremonial washings, regulations pertaining to the human order which were imposed until the time of correction (9:8–10).

For since the law possesses only a foreshadowing of the good things which are to come, and not the actual form of those realities, it can never decisively purge those who draw near by the same sacrifices which are offered continuously year after year. (Otherwise would not these sacrifices have ceased to be offered, since the worshipers, once cleansed, would have no consciousness of sins any longer? In these sacrifices there is really a reminder of sins year after year.) For it is impossible for the blood of bulls and goats to take away sins (10:1–4).

[God] does away with the first arrangement in order to confirm the validity of the second (10:9).

Are such statements anti-Judaic?

In order to answer this question responsibly, it is necessary to restore these pejorative statements to their literary context within the homily. In each instance the writer's negative comments are a response to Scripture. His assessment of the old and new covenants and of the ministries of their respective mediators derives from *midrash*, the interpretation of the biblical text. The writer finds in Scripture announcements that God intended to do something radically new. In each instance he interprets God's new action in terms of his convictions about Jesus. Without attempting to be exhaustive, this critical observation can be illustrated and tested with reference to the writer's reading of Ps 110:4, Jer 31:31–34, and Ps 40:6–8, which address the crucial matters of priesthood, covenant, and sacrifice respectively.

NEW PRIESTHOOD

In 7:1–28 the writer explains for the first time why he has described Jesus as a high priest "like Melchizedek" (5:6, 10; 6:20). Melchizedek is, of course, a historical figure who is remembered in Scripture because of a single episode in the life of the patriarch Abraham. Melchizedek met Abraham, refreshed him, and then receded into the shadows of history (Gen. 14:17–20). There is no mention of him in the subsequent history or literature of Israel until the unexplained reference to Melchizedek in Ps 110:4: "The Lord has sworn, he will not change his mind, 'You are a priest forever, just like Melchizedek.'" This oracular statement was made at a time when the divinely established Levitical priesthood had been a highly visible presence in the life of Israel for about 350 years. Suddenly God declares something new: God will install in the priestly office an individual who will be a priest *like Melchizedek*. "Like Melchizedek," the new priest will owe his priesthood to the appointment of God. In addition, God swears he will be "a priest forever." The fulfillment of this promise is guaranteed by an oath, which serves to emphasize the unchangeable character of the divine purpose.

As the writer of Hebrews reflected upon the biblical oracle, he recognized a fundamental difference between Melchizedek and the Levitical priests. The appointment of the Levitical high priest was regulated by the Torah. According to the Mosaic law, the high priest had to be able to trace a line of physical descent back to Aaron on his father's side. His mother had to be a pure Israelite woman. Melchizedek, however, was a priest solely through the appointment of God. The silence of Scripture concerning his parents and family line throws into bold relief the uniqueness of his priesthood. Since the new priest is characterized as a priest "like Melchizedek," and not "like Aaron," the writer deduced that God was announcing a change in the law (7:11–12).

There was a second fundamental difference between Melchizedek and the Levitical priests. There was an established line of succession to the Levitical high priesthood. But this is not true of Melchizedek in Scripture. For the writer of Hebrews, engaged in the interpretation of Scripture, this was a crucial consideration. Scripture does not refer to any predecessor, and it is silent concerning any successor. Consequently, there were no Scriptural limitations to Melchizedek's life and work. He did not require priestly ancestry nor priestly succession to authorize his unique and unending priesthood. Consequently, whenever one thinks of Melchizedek in terms of Scripture, it is necessary to think of him as possessing a permanent priesthood. The new priesthood announced in the prophetic oracle will be qualitatively different from the old priesthood.

Two considerations, then, appear to have explained to the writer why God spoke of a new kind of priesthood in Ps 110:4 when he promised the coming of one who is a priest "like Melchizedek." (1) He will be a priest who owes his appointment to God rather than to the law of physical descent. (2) He will enjoy a permanent priesthood, acknowledged in the formula "You are a priest forever." Both of these considerations possessed significance for the writer of Hebrews. They become crucial when he speaks of the priesthood of Jesus, for they demonstrated to him that Jesus is a priest "like Melchizedek." They clarify why the writer read the prophetic oracle in Ps 110:4 as a solemn decree of appointment spoken by God to the Son!

The detail of the writer's argument by which he demonstrates that Jesus is the promised new priest is at this point less important than that the development in Hebrews proceeds step by step from the interpretation of Scripture. The pejorative statements that there has been a change in the law (Heb 7:12) and that the law that regulated the priesthood has been annulled (Heb 7:18) are not intentionally polemical. They occur as reflections on a prophetic oracle announcing a startling departure from Israel's priestly tradition. They are put forth not as anti-Judaic polemic but as deductions from the biblical text, which draw their support from the formulation of the oracle. The basis of the development in Hebrews is the interpretation and appropriation of the text of Scripture in the Judaic tradition of homiletical midrash. This conclusion has direct bearing on the issue of faith, polemic, and pastoral strategy. It is confirmed by the writer's use of Jer 31:31–34 [38:31–34 LXX] and Ps 40:6–8 [39:7–9 LXX] in Heb 8:6–13 and 10:5–10.

NEW COVENANT

In Heb 8:6–13 the ministry of the new heavenly high priest, enthroned at God's right hand, is associated with the new covenant. The measure of the superiority of Jesus' priestly ministry is expressed with a comparison: Jesus, unlike the Levitical high priest, entered the heavenly sanctuary as the mediator of the new covenant.

The writer presupposes that the new covenant required a new mediator. By means of his death on the cross as a covenant sacrifice, Jesus inaugurated the new covenant of Jer 31:31–34. His entrance into the heavenly sanctuary guarantees God's acceptance of his sacrifice and the actualization of the provisions of the superior covenant he mediated.

The prophetic oracle in which God promised to establish a covenant with his people that was qualitatively new (Jer 31:31–34) is cited in full in Heb 8:8–12. The appeal to Jer 31:31–34 is remarkable. (C. Wolff has shown that no use is made of Jer 31:31–34 in Jewish sources until after A.D. 70 and the destruction of the Temple. Even sources which refer to "the new covenant" [e.g., CD 6:18–19; 8:21] make no allusion to Jer 31:31–34. See *Jeremia im Frühjudentum und Urchristentum*, TU 118 [Berlin: Akademie, 1976].) The writer's use of the present tense of the verb ("he says") to introduce the quotation served to make the text contemporary with the audience. He examines the prophetic word of censure and promise from the perspective of Jeremiah's time, when the promise was first announced.

The introductory and concluding verses to the extensive citation (Heb 8:7–8a, 13) stress the imperfect and provisional character of "that first" covenant concluded at Sinai. The writer directs the audience's attention to the blame contained within the oracle itself (see vv 8–9). At this point in Hebrews, the citation of Jer 31:31–34 serves the fundamentally negative function of exposing the defective character of the old covenant. The type of reasoning displayed is similar to the argument concerning the ineffectiveness of the Levitical arrangement in Heb 7:11–19.

The treatment of the two covenants in Heb 8:7–8a exposes the eschatological outlook of the writer. The supersession of the old covenant occurred not simply because of the unfaithfulness of Israel to the stipulations of the covenant. It occurred because a new unfolding of God's redemptive purpose had taken place that called for new covenantal action on the part of God. The writer regards God's taking the initiative in announcing the divine intention to establish a new covenant with Israel (8:8a) as a hint that God fully intended the first covenant to be provisional.

In spite of the censure implied in the quotation, the writer's citation and use of Jer 31:31–34 are not simply polemical. Like Jeremiah, he saw the relation between the old and new covenants in dialectical terms. Although the old covenant is to be superseded and invalidated, it receives recognition as shadow and example. God will do something new, which implies discontinuity, but between the old and the new there will also be genuine continuity.

The central affirmation of the new covenant is the pledge of the presence of the law in the hearts of believers as the gift of God (Heb 8:10). The mention of such a gift occurs nowhere else in the old biblical text. (The closest parallel is Jer 24:7: God will give his people a new heart capable of knowing him.) The quality of newness intrinsic to the new covenant consists in the manner of presenting Torah, not in newness of content. The people of God will be inwardly established in the law and knowledge of the Lord. The emphasis falls on the interior quality of the human response to God through the new covenant, not on the replacement of the Torah. The new covenant thus brings to realization the relationship between God and his people, which is at the heart of all covenantal disclosure.

The writer was convinced that redemptive grace had reached its zenith in the priestly ministry of Jesus. The entrance of the eschatological high priest into the heavenly sanctuary (8:6) indicates that the provisions of the new covenant are now in force. But the writer's appeal in Jer 31:31–34 implies for the Christian community continuity as well as discontinuity with those who continued to regulate their lives by reference to the Mosaic covenant.

This needs to be emphasized because it provides perspective on the pejorative statement in Heb 8:13, where the accent falls on discontinuity. The argument that by designating the covenant "new" God declared the covenant concluded at Sinai to be unserviceable and obsolete carried for the writer the corollary that God himself had canceled its validity. Consequently, the old arrangement is on the point of disappearing. The principle that a new act of God makes the old obsolete (cf. Heb 7:11–12) reflects a Jewish-Christian perspective. The perception that the Mosaic and Levitical institutions have been fulfilled and superseded by the priestly mediation of Christ is the hallmark of the Jewish Christianity of Hebrews.

Two observations are appropriate. First, the argument developed in Hebrews on the basis of Jer 31:31–34 exhibits the writer's ability to recognize a significant announcement in Scripture that was overlooked by contemporary writers. His procedure in drawing from the biblical text the theological implications for his audience illustrates the character and practice of homiletical midrash as it was employed in the Jewish homiletical tradition. Secondly, the comparison of the old and new covenants, not only here but elsewhere in the homily (e.g., 12:18–29), is not an indication of the polemical anti-Judaic character of Hebrews. For the writer this represents simply an application of a hermeneutical method by which he sought to make clear to his audience the irrevocable guarantee of the divine promise that had been subjected to questioning. It is an expression of pastoral strategy.

NEW SACRIFICE

The writer's apology is carried a step further in Heb 10:5–10 when he argues that the ineffective sacrifices of the old covenant have been superseded by the sufficient sacrifice of Jesus. The cultic arrangements of the Levitical law, with its annual provision for a Day of Atonement, have been set aside. The basis for the consecration of the new covenant community to the service of God is the unrepeatable offering of the body of Jesus. In developing this point, the writer of Hebrews again makes effective use of homiletical midrash, citing a portion of the biblical text and commenting upon it. He appeals to Ps 40:6–8 (39:7–9 LXX) to demonstrate that it had been prophesied in Scripture that God would accord superior status to a human body as the instrument for accomplishing the divine will over the sacrificial offerings prescribed in the law. The text of the oracle, the writer deduced, implied the discontinuance of the old cultus because of the arrival of the new.

The words of Ps 40:6–8 are heard as those of the Son addressed to God. The statement "See, I have come" furnished the textual basis for attributing these verses of the Psalm to the divine Son at the moment when he entered the world. The detail that God had prepared a body for the speaker, who entered the world to do God's will, accounts for the writer's selection of this quotation. It indicated to him that the incarnation and active obedience of the divine Son had been prophesied in Scripture; it also provided the exegetical support for the thesis that the "offering of the body of Jesus Christ" was qualitatively superior to the offerings prescribed by the law (10:8–10).

On the writer's reading of the text, what has been annulled are the repeated sacrifices and the law that prescribed them. Confirmed as valid are the structural link between the will of God and the effective sacrifice of Christ. The lines quoted from the Psalm and the event of Jesus Christ confirmed to the writer that the old religious order had been abolished definitively. In the design of God, the two redemptive arrangements are irreconcilable; the one excludes the other. The suppression of the first occurs in order that the validity of the new order of relationship may be confirmed. This is essentially the same argument that was developed on the basis of Jer 31:31–34 in Heb 8:7–13. For the writer, Jesus Christ and the detail of Scripture are agents of epochal change, which introduced a radically new situation for the community of God's people (cf. di Pinto, *Volontà di Dio*, 23–33, 49–52).

From the perspective of the psalm, the writer looks to Jesus and to the value of his death on the cross. In the sacrifice of his body on the cross, Jesus freely and fully made the will of God his own. Consequently, his sacrifice embodied the totality of obedience and eradicated the disparity between sacrifice and obedience presupposed in Ps 40:6–8. Jesus' self-sacrifice fulfilled the human vocation enunciated in the psalm. Because Jesus embraced the will of God in solidarity with the human family, the writer of Hebrews deduced, the new people of God have been consecrated to the service of God.

CONCLUSION

These three examples of how the writer read his Bible and used the detail of the biblical text to minister pastorally to a community that was wavering in its convictions and in danger of abandoning its confession provide a sufficient basis for answering the question whether Hebrews is in fact anti-Judaic. The statements in Hebrews that may be identified as pejorative occur in a literary context in which the writer brings the witness of the biblical text to bear upon considerations that were crucial to the self-understanding of the community. They concern priesthood, covenant, and sacrifice. In each case the writer proves to be creative in his selection of texts to be brought before the community. No other writer in the NT cited Ps 110:4, Jer 31:31–34, or Ps 40:6–8. These biblical texts, nevertheless, establish a context for appreciating the validity of the Christian message. From the writer's pastoral perspective, the issue of adherence to the confession of Jesus the community had made was of critical importance because it would determine salvation or absolute loss (cf. 3:12–15; 6:4–8; 10:26–31, 35–39; 12:14–17, 25–29). His concern was not that members of the community would simply return to the synagogue but that they would turn away from the living God altogether (3:12–13)!

The writer was persuaded that this matter must be decided on the basis of the word God had spoken in Scripture and through the Son. For that reason, he brought before the community biblical texts demonstrating that God had announced a new arrangement to provide decisive purgation for a defiled people and unrestricted access to the divine presence. Those announcements pointed to the unique priestly ministry of Jesus and his sacrifice by which the new covenant had been inaugurated. It is on this basis that the writer calls the new covenant community to the worship of God (4:15–16; 7:24–25; 9:11–28; 10:19–25; 12:14, 18–29; 13:15–16). This represents a different perspective from that of Paul or of any other writer in the NT. Nevertheless, what the writer of Hebrews was doing was profoundly Judaic. He shares fully Judaism's understanding of the role of Scripture in the life of the faith community.

The pastoral strategies adopted in Hebrews were all designed to stir the members of a Jewish-Christian assembly to recognize that they could not turn back the hands of the clock and deny their Christian understanding and experience. They must hold firmly to their Christian confession.

The premise that Hebrews engages in any form of anti-Judaic polemic, however, is untenable. Certainly the writer appreciated the historical and theological lines of differentiation between Jewish Christianity and Judaism. He clearly believed that God had acted decisively in Jesus to accomplish salvation and to create the people of the new covenant. Only from such an eschatological perspective could he speak of God's final word, or of the coming of the new, which made the old obsolete, or of the incarnation of the Son of God. But this is not anti-Judaism; it is the reflection of a distinctive reading of Scripture in the light of the writer's convictions about Jesus.

The writer fully recognized that God was at work in the old covenant. God's decisive action in Jesus occurred within the context of divine intervention in the life of Israel. The word that God spoke in the past was invested with authority, even when it was fragmentary and partial. It remained normative for the writer and for those whom he addressed. The writer of Hebrews traced a line of continuity from the event of God's speaking at Sinai to the event of God's speaking at that moment. God's character remained unchanged. Like Israel at Sinai, for the writer of Hebrews the Christian community stands before the God who is a consuming fire (12:25–29). Greater covenant privilege simply entails greater covenant responsibility. The writer of Hebrews calls the community to a costly identification with Jesus (13:12–14), whose sacrificial ministry was the culmination of God's promise to Israel. He does not set aside Jewish identity and tradition, nor the authority of the biblical text for the community of faith.

Christology as Pastoral Response

Bibliography

Alfaro, J. "Christo glorioso, revelador del Padre." *Greg* 39 (1958) 220–70. **Baignent, J. W.** "Jesus as Priest: An Examination of the Claim that the Concept of Jesus as Priest May Be Found Outside of the Epistle to the Hebrews." *VoxEv* 12 (1981) 33–44. **Bolewski, H.** "*Christos Archiereus:* Über die Entstehung der hohenpriesterlichen Wurdenamens Christi." Dissertation, University of Halle, 1939. **Bonsirven, J.** "La sacerdoce et le sacrifice de Jésus-Christ après l'Épître aux Hébreux." *NRT* 71 (1939) 641–60, 769–86. **Brown, R.** *Christ above All: The*

Message of Hebrews. Downers Grove, IL: Inter-Varsity Press, 1982. **Büchsel, F.** *Die Christologie des Hebräerbriefs.* BFCT 27/2. Gütersloh: Bertelsmann, 1922. **Burch, V.** "Factors in the Christology of the Letter to the Hebrews." *Exp* 47 (1921) 68–79. **Clarkson, M. E.** "The Antecedents of the High Priest Theme in Hebrews." *ATR* 29 (1947) 89–95. **Cox, W. L. P.** *The Heavenly Priesthood of Our Lord.* Oxford: Blackwell, 1929. **Descamps, A.** "La Sacerdoce du Christ d'après l'Épître aux Hébreux." *RDT* 9 (1954) 529–34. **Dunbar, D. G.** "The Relation of Christ's Sonship and Priesthood in the Epistle to the Hebrews." Dissertation, Westminster Theological Seminary, 1974. **Feuillet, A.** *The Priesthood of Christ and His Ministers.* Garden City: Doubleday, 1975. **Fransen, I.** "Jésus Pontife parfait du parfait sanctuaire (Épître aux Hébreux)." *BVC* 20 (1957) 262–81. **Gayford, S. C.** *Sacrifice and Priesthood²*. London: Methuen, 1953. **Grässer, E.** "Zur Christologie des Hebräerbriefes: Eine Auseinandersetzung mit Herbert Braun." In *Neues Testament und christliche Existenz.* FS H. Braun. Tübingen: Mohr, 1973. ———. "Der historische Jesus im Hebräerbrief." *ZNW* 56 (1965) 63–91. **Griffin, H.** "The Origin of the High Priestly Christology of the Epistle to the Hebrews." Dissertation, University of Aberdeen, 1978. **Grothe, J. F.** "Was Jesus the Priestly Messiah? A Study of the New Testament's Teaching of Jesus' Priestly Office against the Background of Jewish Hopes for a Priestly Messiah." Dissertation, Concordia Seminary, 1981. **Gyllenberg, R.** "Die Christologie des Hebräerbriefes." *ZST* 11 (1934) 662–90. **Hamerton-Kelly, R. G.** *Pre-Existence, Wisdom, and the Son of Man: A Study of the Idea of Pre-Existence in the New Testament.* SNTSMS 21. Cambridge: Cambridge UP, 1973. **Harrison, M. P.** "Psalm 110 in the Epistle to the Hebrews." Dissertation, Southern Baptist Theological Seminary, 1950. **Hay, D. M.** *Glory at the Right Hand: Psalm 110 in Early Christianity.* SBLMS 18. Nashville: Abingdon, 1973. **Henderson, M. W.** "The Priestly Ministry of Jesus in the Gospel of John and the Epistle to the Hebrews." Dissertation, Southern Baptist Theological Seminary, 1965. **Hillmann, W.** "Der Höhenpriester der künftigen Güter: Einführung in die Grundgedanken des Hebräerbriefes (4:14–10:31)." *BibLeb* 1 (1960) 157–78. **Hughes, P. E.** "The Christology of Hebrews." *SWJT* 28 (1985) 19–27. **Humphrey, J. F.** "The Christology of the Epistle to the Hebrews." *LQHR* 14 (1945) 425–32. **Immer, K.** "Jesus Christus und die Versuchten: Ein Beitrag zur Christologie des Hebräerbriefes." Dissertation, University of Halle, 1943. **Jansen, A.** "Schwäche und Vollkommenheit der Hohepriesters Christus: Ein Beitrag zur Christologie des Hebräerbriefes." Dissertation, Gregorian Pontifical University, Rome, 1957. **Jeffrey, P. J.** "Priesthood of Christ in the Epistle to the Hebrews." Dissertation, University of Melbourne, 1974. **Kitchens, J. A.** "The Death of Jesus in the Epistle to the Hebrews." Dissertation, New Orleans Baptist Theological Seminary, 1964. **Knox, W. L.** "The Divine Hero Christology of the New Testament." *HTR* 41 (1948) 229–49. **Kuss, O.** "Der theologische Grundgedanke des Hebräerbriefes: Zur Deutung des Tod Jesu im Neuen Testament." *MTZ* 7 (1956) 233–71. ———. "Der Tod Jesu im Hebräerbrief." *MTZ* 7 (1956) 1–22. **Laub, F.** *Bekenntnis und Auslegung: Die paränetische Funktion der Christologie im Hebräerbrief.* BU 15. Regensburg: Pustet, 1980, **Leivestad, R.** *Christ the Conqueror: Ideas of Conflict and Victory in the New Testament.* New York: Macmillan, 1954. **Linton, O.** "Hebreerbrevet och 'den historiske Jesus.'" *STK* 26 (1950) 335–45. **Loader, W. R. G.** *Sohn und Hoherpriester: Eine traditions-geschichtliche Untersuchung zur Christologie des Hebräerbriefes.* WMANT 53. Neukirchen/Vluyn: Neukirchener Verlag, 1981. **Lussier, E.** *Christ's Priesthood according to the Epistle to the Hebrews.* Collegeville, MN: Liturgical, 1975. **MacNeil, H. L.** *The Christology of the Epistle to the Hebrews.* Chicago: University of Chicago, 1914. **Manson, T. W.** *Ministry and Priesthood: Christ's and Ours.* Richmond: John Knox, 1958. **McNicol, A. J.** "The Relationship of the Image of the Highest Angel to the High Priest Concept in Hebrews." Dissertation, Vanderbilt University, 1974. **Meeter, H. H.** *The Heavenly High Priesthood of Christ.* Grand Rapids: Eerdmans-Sevensma, 1916. **Merle, G.** *La christologie de l'Épître aux Hébreux.* Montauban: Granié, 1877. **Moffatt, J.** "The Christology of the Epistle to the Hebrews." *ExpTim* 28 (1916–17) 505–8, 563–66; 29 (1917–18) 26–30. ———. *Jesus Christ the Same.* The Shaffer Lectures for 1940 in Yale University

Divinity School. New York: Abingdon-Cokesbury, 1940. **Moule, C. F. D.** "The Influence of Circumstances on the Use of Christological Terms." *JTS* n.s. 10 (1959) 247–63. ———. *The Sacrifice of Christ*. Greenwich: Seabury Press, 1957. **Müller, P. G.** *XPIΣTOΣ APXHΓOΣ: Der religionsgeschichtliche und theologische Hintergrund einer neutestamentlichen Christusprädikation*. Frankfurt a/M: Lang, 1973. **Nakagawa, H.** "Christology in the Epistle to the Hebrews." Dissertation, Yale University, 1955. **Nissilä, K.** *Das Hohepriestmotiv in Hebräerbrief: Eine exegetische Untersuchung*. Helsinki: Oy Liiton Kirjapaino, 1979. **Nomoto, S.** "Die Hohenpriester-Typologie im Hebräerbrief: Ihre traditionsgeschichtliche Herkunft und ihr religionsgeschichtlicher Hintergrund." Dissertation, University of Hamburg, 1965. **Padolski, M. V.** *L'idée du sacrifice de la croix dans l'Épître aux Hébreux*. Paris: Gabalda, 1935. **Pittard, C. R.** "The Person and Work of Christ in the Epistle to the Hebrews." Dissertation, Southern Baptist Theological Seminary, 1926. **Rábanos, R.** "Sacerdocio de Melquisedec, sacerdocio de Aarón, Sacerdocio de Cristo." *CB* 13 (1956) 264–75. **Roloff, J.** "Der mitleidende Hohepriester: Zur Frage nach der Bedeutung des irdischen Jesus für die Christologie des Hebräerbriefes." In *Jesus Christus in Historie und Theologie*. FS H. Conzelmann. Ed. G. Strecker. Tübingen: Mohr, 1975. **Sabourin. L.** *Priesthood: A Comparative Study*. Leiden: Brill, 1973. **Schaefer, J. R.** "The Relationship between Priestly and Servant Messianism in the Epistle to the Hebrews." *CBQ* 30 (1968) 359–85. **Schille, G.** "Erwägungen zur Hohenpriesterlehre des Hebräerbriefes." *ZNW* 46 (1955) 81–109. **Schubert, P.** "Der Verbindung von Königtum und Priestertum in der Vorgeschichte der Christusoffenbarung: Eine Voruntersuchung der Christologie des Hebräerbriefs." Dissertation, University of Leipzig, 1955. **Selph, B. K.** "The Christology of the Book of Hebrews." Dissertation, Southwestern Baptist Theological Seminary, 1948. **Stadelmann, A.** "Zur Christologie des Hebräerbriefes in der neueren Diskussion." In *Theologische Berichte* 2. Ed. J. Pfammatter & F. Furger. Zürich: Zwingli, 1973. **Teodorico, P.** "Il sacerdozio celeste di cristi della lettera agli Ebrei." *Greg* 39 (1958) 319–34. **Torrance, J. B.** "The Priesthood of Jesus." In *Essays in Christology for Karl Barth*. Ed. T. H. L. Parker. London: Letterworth Press, 1956. 153–73. **Trinidad, J.** "De sacrificio Christi in Epistola ad Hebreos." *VD* 19 (1939) 180–86, 207–12. **Ubbrink, J. T.** "De Hoogepriester en zijn Offer in de Brief aan de Hebreeën." *NThS* 22 (1939) 172–84. **Ungeheuer, J.** *Der grosse Priester über dem Hause Gottes: Die Christologie des Hebräerbriefes*. Würzburg: Stürtz, 1939. **Vanhoye, A.** *Our Priest in God: The Doctrine of the Epistle to the Hebrews*. Rome: Biblical Institute, 1977. ———. "Sacerdoce du Christ et culte chrétien selon l'Épître aux Hébreux." *Chr* 28 (1981) 216–30. ———. *Situation du Christ: Hébreux 1–2*. LD 58. Paris: Cerf, 1969. **Vansant, A. C.** "The Humanity of Jesus in the Epistle to the Hebrews." Dissertation, Southern Baptist Theological Seminary, 1951. **Vos, G.** "The Priesthood of Christ in the Epistle to the Hebrews." *PTR* 5 (1907) 423–47, 579–604. **Walden, H. E.** "The Christology of the Epistle to the Hebrews." Dissertation, Southern Baptist Theological Seminary, 1944. **Warfield, B. B.** "Christ Our Sacrifice." In *The Person and Work of Christ*. Ed. S. G. Craig. Philadelphia: Presbyterian and Reformed, 1950. 391–426. **Wengst, K.** *Christologische Formeln und Lieder des Urchristentum*. SNT 7. Gütersloh: Bertelsmann, 1972. **Williams, A. H.** "An Early Christology: A Systematic and Exegetical Investigation of the Traditions Contained in Hebrews." Dissertation, University of Mainz, 1971. **Young, F. M.** *Sacrifice and the Death of Christ*. London: SPCK, 1975. **Zimmermann, H.** *Die Hohepriester-Christologie des Hebräerbriefes*. Paderborn: Bonifacius, 1964. **Zorn, R.** "Die Fürbitte und Interzession im Spätjudentum und im Neuen Testament." Dissertation, University of Göttingen, 1957.

The writer of Hebrews held a high christology. A high christology is one that acknowledges that God's self-disclosure found its ultimate expression in Jesus of Nazareth, who was the Son of God incarnate. Although God's revelation had possessed a clearly defined character prior to Jesus, it had been fragmentary and incomplete (Heb 1:1). The divine word of promise called for fulfillment. The presence of Scripture in the community of faith nurtured an expectation of something more. The events that clustered about Jesus in the course of his ministry prompted the insistent question, "Who is this man?" It was his death on the cross and his resurrection on the third day, however, that created the demand for sustained and profound reflection upon that question. It is safe to say that if it had not been for his resurrection, Jesus of Nazareth would have been reduced to a line in Josephus' *Antiquities of the Jews*, as were other prophets and revolutionaries of the period. He might have been remembered as a popular teacher or as a disturbing presence in Galilee or Jerusalem, but there would have been no enduring significance to his life and death. Many persons had been crucified. Through reflection on the Easter-event, it was recognized that God had spoken his definitive word and had acted with decisive finality for the redemption of the human family through Jesus.

In the light of Easter and the subsequent gift of the Holy Spirit at Pentecost, it became evident that previous answers to the question of Jesus' identity were inadequate. The documents of the NT bear witness to a Church in ferment as it sought to clarify more adequately the significance of the person and mission of Jesus. There was an earnest quest for fresh vocabulary and formulations. The variety of the conceptual models employed to describe Jesus convey an impression of a sustained concern to grasp his reality more adequately in response to particular concerns in the churches and in a society as well. The writer of Hebrews participated fully in this ferment.

From the perspective of christology, Hebrews is an unusually important document because of the distinctiveness and clarity of its witness to Jesus Christ. The key to that witness is the recognition that christology in Hebrews is pastoral response to crisis. The failure of nerve on the part of the community addressed, evidenced by the parenetic warning sections, occurred because of an inadequate christology, an inadequacy the writer is endeavoring to address in the expositional sections of the discourse. The laxity against which the writer is striving in the series of exhortations he directs to his audience results at least partly from a deficiency he attempts to remedy in the development of his theology. To be more precise, the readers' lethargy derives from their failure to grasp the full significance of Christ. They were prepared to abandon their confession because they had lost the realization of its significance.

Social alienation and persecution encourage one to doubt the willingness or the power of God to act in the present. The community appears to have doubted the ability of God to help them in their circumstances. Doubt in the ability of God to act would appear to be closely associated with doubt that he had acted definitively in Christ. The writer's pastoral task was to help the community realize the reality of God's decisive action in Christ and of Christ's present ability to intervene on their behalf. Stated in another way, he had to motivate them to grasp anew the meaning and significance of their confession of Jesus. They needed a new vision of the necessity of holding to their confession and of the provision God had made to enable them to hold on. His strongest encouragement was to remind the members of the house church of the character, the accomplishment, and the exalted status of their Lord. What follows can only be suggestive. The detail is set forth fully in the pages of the commentary.

AN ORCHESTRATED CHRISTOLOGY

Christology in Hebrews is richly orchestrated. Individual motifs and constructs are readily recognizable, but they flow into one another so adroitly that the consideration of a dominant motif invariably involves simultaneously the consideration of secondary and tertiary themes that are introduced in concert with the dominant motif.

The metaphor of composition and orchestration suggests itself already in the majestic period with which the writer opens his sermon (1:1–4). The dominant motif is that of Jesus as the Son of God. The richness of the writer's conception is evident as one perspective follows another in rapid succession. He contemplates Jesus as the eternal, essential Son who bore in his person the light of God's own glory and who is the exact representation of God's own being, through whom God created the universe (1:2*c*–3*a*). He envisions Jesus as the incarnate Son through whom God spoke his definitive word (1:2*a*), who made cleansing for sins (1:3*c*). He bows before Jesus as the transcendent Son who sat down in the position of honor at God's right hand, who has been exalted far above the angels (1:3*d*–4). Like the changing configurations of a kaleidoscope as it is turned, the writer sees the eternal Son, the incarnate Son, the exalted Son.

Although the dominant motif is that of Jesus as the Son of God, the introduction of subdominant motifs is quickly detected. The conception of the Son as the one through whom God created the universe and who now sustains everything by his powerful word (1:2*c*, 3*b*) is expressed with phrases elsewhere associated with a different construct, that of divine Wisdom. The writer selects rare, evocative vocabulary and striking formulations that occur elsewhere only in the praise of divine Wisdom: the Son is the effulgence of God's glory, the exact representation of his being (cf. Wis 7:21–27). The writer speaks of the Son, but his conception is informed by the biblical and hellenistic-Jewish tradition that God related to his creation through Wisdom (Prov 8:22–30; Wis 7:21–27). Moreover, the functions of Wisdom are in Hebrews assigned to the Son: the task of creation and of sustaining the creation, of revelation, and of the making of friends for God among the human family. The writer does not declare that Jesus was divine Wisdom. He does not speak of the personal Word who was with God from the beginning, as does John (John 1:1–3). He simply clothes the Son in the garb of Wisdom. Jesus as the divine Wisdom is a secondary theme in the description of the Son.

There is also a tertiary theme. It was after Jesus had made cleansing for sins that he sat down at God's right hand (1:3*c, d*). The source of this solitary allusion to the earthly life of Jesus in the exordium is not the Wisdom tradition. It is reflection on the incarnation and the cross. The ministry of Jesus is described from the first in distinctly cultic categories. This terse, unadorned reference to Jesus' accomplishment is slanted in the direction of the later full discussion of priesthood and sacrifice. The effect of Christ's death is cleansing from sins. The defilement of sin erects a barrier to the approach to God, which must be removed. Sin and worship exclude one another. Purification from the defilement of sin is a distinctly priestly action. That the writer intends to draw upon this conceptual framework for interpreting the death of Jesus is confirmed by chaps. 9 and 10, where the categories of defilement and purgation are essential to the argument. The brief statement in 1:3 that Jesus made cleansing for sins anticipates the elaboration of the argument that he is our great high priest who secured atonement for the people because he himself was the unblemished sacrifice offered to God (cf. 7:26; 9:13–14).

At this point the writer does not say that Jesus is a priest. This tertiary theme is simply a subdominant motif that is introduced in articulating the dominant motif of the glory of God's unique Son. The motifs of sonship, wisdom, and priesthood are so skillfully integrated that they can be isolated and examined individually only at the risk of decomposing a brilliantly orchestrated statement.

JESUS AS THE HUMILIATED AND EXALTED SON

The dominant expression of christology in Heb 1:1–4:14 is the description of Jesus as the humiliated and exalted Son. The primary reason for this is made apparent when the writer designates Jesus as "the Son of God" in the course of exhorting the community to continue to adhere to their confession (4:14). In this context, the designation of Jesus as the Son of God is almost certainly a reflection of the confession acknowledged by members of the house church at their baptism: Jesus is the Son of God. The appeal for adherence to the confession was intended to promote the faithfulness of the community at a time when they were displaying a lack of concern for spiritual integrity and steadfastness. By concentrating on the sonship of Jesus, the writer was able to explore with his audience the significance of their confession.

Other motifs are introduced in these early sections of the homily. Jesus is the protagonist who came to the defense of those who were being enslaved through the fear of death. He secured their deliverance by wrestling with the devil and wresting from him the power of death, ironically, through his own death (see *Comment* on 2:10–16). Jesus is the merciful and faithful high priest who has made atonement for sins. He is able to exercise a ministry of assistance to those who are being sorely tested because he has known experientially the nature of testing through the suffering of death (see *Comment* on 2:17–18). The description of Jesus as the champion of his people, or as high priest, does not have its source in the confession of the community. Each is a subdominant motif that serves to interpret the confession and to clarify its significance for the oppressed community. In the flow of the statement of the discourse, these reflective constructs are integrated with the exposition of Jesus as the humiliated and exalted Son of God.

SONSHIP INTERPRETED IN TERMS OF PRIESTHOOD

One of the striking features of the christology of Hebrews is that Jesus is designated as high priest *before* there has been any theological explanation of the concept by the writer (2:17; 3:1; 4:14). This fact suggested to W. Manson that the office of Jesus as high priest belonged to the foundational truths of the received Christian faith (*The Epistle to the Hebrews*, 54, 108–9). Other scholars have detected an early Christian "hymn of the high priest" behind the writer's formulation in 5:7–10. They draw the conclusion that the conception of Jesus as high priest was not the distinctive teaching of the writer of Hebrews but a strand of the tradition that was firmly embedded in the faith and liturgy of the primitive church (cf. M. Rissi, "Die Menschlichkeit Jesu nach Hebr. 5,7–8," *TZ* 11 [1955] 28–45; Schille,

ZNW 64 [1955] 81–109; G. Friedrich, "Das Leid vom Hohenpriester im Zusammenhang vom Hebr. 4,14–5,10," *TZ* 18 [1962] 95–115; T. Lescow, "Jesus in Gethsemane bei Lukas und im Hebräerbrief," *ZNW* 58 [1967] 224–39; E. Brandenburger, "Text und Vorlagen von Hebr. V 7–10: Eine Beitrag zur Christologie des Hebräerbriefs," *NovT* 11 [1969] 190–224). This contention is part of a larger argument. The lyrical quality of the writer's statement concerning Jesus in 1:1–4, 5:7–10, and 7:26–28 has encouraged a series of proposals that the sources for the writer's christological conceptions are to be traced in the reconstructed fragments of hymns and creeds.

The writer may have used liturgical materials in the composition of his sermon. The contention that the conception of Jesus as high priest was the common property of the early hellenistic Church, however, cannot be verified on the basis of source-reconstruction. That point becomes abundantly clear when a comparison is made among the widely diverse proposals for reconstructing the primitive sources purportedly borrowed from the tradition. Each of the passages where a hymnic fragment has been detected is a Greek period, i.e., an extended, carefully balanced example of artistic prose. The writer of Hebrews is a master of the intricate, disciplined, and yet lucid periodic sentence. My own investigation of the several hymn-hypotheses has led me to conclude that in each case the writer is himself responsible for the tight, continuous flow of his statement and for the conceptual freight it bears.

In the case of 5:7–10 it is possible to be more precise. In 5:6 the writer cites Ps 110:4 for the first time to show that God, who addressed Christ as the Son in Ps 2:7, also addressed him as priest in Ps 110:4. He then goes on in 5:7–9 to describe the humiliation of the Son by means of a correspondingly significant word from the Psalter, in this instance an allusion to Ps 116. The unit is then rounded off in 5:10 with the statement that the Son was designated by God to be a high priest like Melchizedek, a clear allusion to Ps 110:4.

The evidence of 5:5–10 indicates that the writer formulated the conception of Jesus as high priest on the basis of a messianic interpretation of Pss 2, 110, and 116 (see *Comment* on 5:5–7). Ps 2:7 ("You are my Son; today I have become your father") and Ps 110:4 ("You are a priest forever, just like Melchizedek") are understood as parallel declarations of appointment. Both texts declare the decrees in accordance with which Jesus was installed in his office and invested with power. A deliberate concern to associate the titles "Son" and "Priest" is apparent in the conjunction of the Psalm quotations in 5:5–6. The correlation between Christ's sonship and priesthood that was implied in the opening sentence of the sermon is here asserted explicitly. "Son" and "priest" are the primary models for the writer's christology. In 1:1–4:14 the description of Jesus as God's Son predominates; in 4:15–10:22 the primary focus is upon the titles "priest" and "high priest," and sonship is interpreted in terms of priesthood.

The introduction into the discussion of Ps 110:4 as a testimony about Jesus is the singular contribution of the writer. No other Christian writer of this period draws attention to this passage, but in Hebrews there are more references to Ps 110:4 than to any other biblical text. In addition to three quotations of the passage (5:6; 7:17, 21), there are eight allusions to it in chaps. 5, 6, and 7, and each of the allusions is distinctive in form and function. The primary reason for the emphasis on Ps 110:4 in Hebrews is that it supplied a scriptural basis for the writer's priestly christology. The text is brought before the audience repeatedly to substantiate the argument that Jesus is a heavenly high priest. It can be safely assumed that the original readers were unfamiliar with the concept that Jesus was a priest like Melchizedek, a christological theme found nowhere else in the NT.

The primary exposition of Ps 110:4 occurs in chap. 7. A proper appreciation of the conceptions embodied in the radically new priesthood of Christ implicit in Ps 110:4 depends upon a correct understanding of the excellence of Melchizedek and his priesthood. The writer is persuaded that an understanding of Christ's eternal priesthood will be gained from a consideration of selected features of the perpetual priesthood of Melchizedek. He treats Melchizedek not as a type to be fulfilled but as a witness to the higher priesthood he finds foreshadowed in the OT. Melchizedek serves as a precedent for a superior priesthood based on character apart from line of descent and ordained by God apart from law. He represents an exception to the common interpretation of priesthood in the OT, which anticipates the ultimate displacement of the Levitical priesthood. The symbolic significance of Melchizedek lies in the timeless nature of his office as priest without successor (see above, "New Priesthood").

The use that is made of Melchizedek in 7:1–10 is thoroughly christological. He has no independent significance; he is introduced only for the sake of clarifying the character of the Son. His function is prophetic. He is illustrative of those prophecies of the OT that pointed to the insufficiency of the old order and to the superiority and sufficiency of the new. It is this persuasion that explains why the writer understands Melchizedek from the perspective of Ps 110:4. It is only in the perspective of the eternal Son that the "eternal" character of Melchizedek and his priesthood becomes evident.

In 7:11–25 the writer turns directly to Ps 110:4 and its designation of a new eternal priest. That oracle becomes the basis for a series of intricate comparisons between the new priesthood based on God's solemn oath and the old Levitical priesthood based on law. From the detail of Ps 110:4, the writer deduces that the old priesthood, sacrifice, and covenant have been replaced by the new priest, by his sacrifice, and by the new covenant that he inaugurated. The old arrangement had been unable to achieve its goal. It suffered from a shortness of spiritual breath. It has been replaced by the priesthood of Jesus, which is endowed with a life impervious to death. The new priesthood is qualitatively different from the old because it is fully effective.

By interpreting sonship in terms of priesthood, the writer is able to show the members of the community how the Son can help them in their present adverse circumstances and in any future circumstances they may experience. By contrasting the Son to the Levitical priesthood, he is able to show the ability of the Son to save them finally and completely. The main purpose of the Melchizedek christology of 7:1–25 is to prove the effectiveness of the Son's eternal priesthood, to show that the Son can save the community in the present and to the end. It is the writer's attempt to give them a fresh grasp of the meaning of their confession that Jesus is the Son of God.

The Melchizedek christology is clearly a pastoral response to the situation of the community. But it is not, and it could not be, the sole basis for the development of the priestly christology in Hebrews. Melchizedek has nothing to do with sacrifice. For that reason, in the closing paragraph of chap. 7 the writer moves beyond the warrant of Ps 110:4 in order to speak of the sinless character, the sacrificial death, and the exalted status of the Son (vv 26–28). These verses touch upon themes that are fully explored only in the exposition that follows in 8:1–10:18. They affirm that the high priest who is precisely appropriate to the community is the one whose unique offering of himself put an end to the whole system of Levitical sacrifices. He was able to make a definitive sacrifice because he was the sinless high priest. The sufficiency of his sacrifice was the consequence of the spiritual and moral perfection of his life (4:15; 7:26). The description of the kind of high priest who fits the circumstances of the community proceeds not from a testimony text but from the cross. His subsequent exaltation obtained for him unhindered access to the presence of God (9:11–28; 10:11–14, 19–21). This is the fundamental qualification for the exercise of a fully effective, perpetual priesthood. The contemplation of that ministry as an accomplished fact was of singular importance to the stability of the community addressed.

CONCLUDING OBSERVATIONS

This brief review of some of the christological emphases of Hebrews must provide a basis for a few concluding observations.

(1) Christology in Hebrews is culturally sensitive. It draws upon the cultural heritage of the community. It is not, however, primarily a response to culture. Culturally sensitive expression merely provides a vehicle for effective communication. The content of christology is determined not by culture but by the early Church tradition, which remains normative.

(2) A particular christological emphasis in Hebrews offers a pastoral response to the life-situation of the community addressed. There is clear evidence for an intimate relationship between *the form* of the writer's presentation of Jesus and the current experience of his audience. Each of the major christological emphases reflects the writer's desire to provide an interpretation of Jesus that will address the community directly in terms of the realities of their lives, offering them a basis for encouragement and strength necessary to sustain them in a period marked by stress. Christology in Hebrews is fully contextualized.

(3) The point at which a particular christological emphasis is introduced and developed in Hebrews has important bearing on the statement made. In the course of interpreting the confession that Jesus is the Son of God, the writer speaks of Jesus as the defender and champion of the people and as priest. The introduction of a champion motif occurs early and late in the sermon (2:10–16; 12:1–4). The center of the homily is reserved for the development of the high priestly construct (7:1–10:18). If the champion motif had been introduced at the center, the notion of rescue would have been dominant, and christology would have encouraged an attitude of triumphalism. By assigning the center to the exposition of Jesus as exalted priest, the dominant notion is that of sustained care, and christology encourages an attitude of confident trust.

(4) The use of figures and constructs for expressing christology in Hebrews is highly selective. The primary concern was to present Jesus as the one who identified himself with his people and who effectively represents them in a ministry of advocacy. Identification and representation were key considerations in calling the community to renewed commitment and fidelity. The images and constructs

introduced in Hebrews to describe Christ cluster around these emphases. The champion identified himself with those enslaved through the fear of death and represented them in combat with the devil (2:10–16). The high priest identifies himself with his people and represents them even now in the heavenly sanctuary (2:17–18; 4:15; 5:7–10; 7:23–25; 8:1–2).

(5) Christology in Hebrews is a richly integrated synthesis. For the writer, the integrating factor was the confession that Jesus is the Son of God. In his expression of christology he made rich use of analogical figures and reflective constructs to interpret the significance of the confession. The hallmark of his christology is the dynamic way in which motifs merge and flow together in his presentation of Jesus as the incarnate Son of God.

Hebrews and the Theology of the Hellenistic Church

Bibliography

Bacon, B. W. "The Doctrine of Faith in Hebrews, James and Clement of Rome." *JBL* 19 (1900) 12–21. ———. "St. Stephen's Speech: Its Argument and Doctrinal Relationships." In *Biblical and Semantic Studies*. New York: Scribner's Sons, 1902. 213–76. **Ballarini, T.** "Il peccato nell' epistola agli Ebrei." *ScC* 106 (1978) 358–71. **Barrett, C. K.** "The Eschatology of the Epistle to the Hebrews." In *The Background of the New Testament and Its Eschatology*. Ed. W. D. Davies and D. Daube. Cambridge: Cambridge UP, 1954. 363–93. **Bihler, J.** *Die Stephanusgeschichte*. Munich: Heuber, 1963. **Bover, J. M.** "La esperanza en la Epístola a los Hebreos." *Greg* 19 (1938) 110–20. **Brown, R.** "Pilgrimage in Faith: The Christian Life in Hebrews." *SWJT* 28 (1985) 28–35. **Cambier, J.** "Eschatologie ou héllenisme dans l'Épître aux Hébreux: Une étude sur μένειν et l'exhortation finale de l'épître." *Sal* 11 (1949) 62–96. **Dautzenberg, G.** "Der Glaube in Hebräerbrief." *BZ* 17 (1963) 163–77. **Eagar, A. R.** "The Hellenistic Elements in the Epistle to the Hebrews." *Her* 11 (1901) 263–87. **Eccles, R. S.** "The Purpose of the Hellenistic Patterns in the Epistle to the Hebrews." In *Religions in Antiquity*. FS E. R. Goodenough. Ed. J. Neusner. Leiden: Brill, 1968. 207–26. **Fairhurst, A. M.** "Hellenistic Influence in the Epistle to the Hebrews." *TynBul* 7–8 (1961) 17–21. **Fiorenza, E. Schüssler** "Der Anführer und Vollender unseres Glaubens: Zum theologischen Verständnis des Hebräerbriefes." In *Gestalt und Anspruch des Neuen Testaments*. Ed. J. Schreiner. Würzburg: Echter, 1969. 262–81. **Fitzer, G.** "Auch der Hebräerbrief legitimiert nicht eine Opfertodchristologie: Zur Frage der Intention des Hebräerbriefes und seiner Bedeutung für die Theologie." *KD* 15 (1969) 294–319. **Foerster, W.** "Stephanus und die Urgemeinde." In *Dienst unter dem Wort*. FS D. H. Schreiner. Gütersloh: Bertelsmann, 1953. 9–30. **Grässer, E.** *Der Glaube im Hebräerbrief*. Marburg: Elwert, 1965. ———. "Das wandernde Gottesvolk zum Basismotiv des Hebräerbriefes." *ZNW* 77 (1986) 160–79. **Harrison, E. F.** "The Theology of the Epistle to the Hebrews." *BSac* 121 (1964) 333–40. **Harrop, C. K.** "The Influence of the Thought of Stephen upon the Epistle to the Hebrews." Dissertation, Southern Baptist Theological Seminary, 1955. **Hengel, M.** "Zwischen Jesus und Paulus: Die Hellenisten, die 'Sieben' und Stephanus (Apg 6:1–15; 7:54–8:3)." *ZTK* 72 (1975) 151–206 (ET: *Between Jesus and Paul: Studies in the Earliest History of Christianity*, tr. J. Bowden [Philadelphia: Fortress, 1983] 1–29). **Hillmann, W.** "Glaube und Verheissung: Einführung in die Grundgedanken des Hebräerbriefes (10,32–13,25)." *BibLeb* 1 (1960) 237–52. **Hillmer, M. R.** "Priesthood and Pilgrimage: Hebrews in Recent Research." *ThBullMDC* 5 (1969) 66–89. **Hurst, L. D.** "The Stephen Tradition." In "The

Background and Interpretation of the Epistle to the Hebrews." Dissertation, University of Oxford, 1981. 140–74. **Huxhold, H. N.** "Faith in the Epistle to the Hebrews." *CTM* 38 (1967) 657–61. **Johnsson, W. G.** "The Pilgrimage Motif in the Book of Hebrews." *JBL* 97 (1978) 239–51. **Käsemann, E.** *Das wandernde Gottesvolk: Eine Untersuchung zum Hebräerbrief* [4]. FRLANT 55. Göttingen: Vandenhoeck & Ruprecht, 1961 (ET: *The Wandering People of God*, tr. R. A. Harrisville and I. L. Sandberg [Minneapolis: Augsburg, 1984). **Lane, W. L.** "Stephen and the Mission of the Hellenists." In G. W. Barker, W. L. Lane, and J. R. Michaels. *The New Testament Speaks*. New York: Harper & Row, 1969. 134–42. **Loew, W.** *Der Glaubensweg des Neuen Bundes: Eine Einführung in den Brief an die Hebräer.* UCB. Berlin: Akademie, 1941. **Lohmann, T.** "Zur Heilsgeschichte des Hebräerbriefes." *OLZ* 79 (1984) 117–25. **Manson, W.** *The Epistle to the Hebrews: An Historical Theological Reconsideration.* London: Hodder & Stoughton, 1951. 25–46. **McCown, W. G.** "Holiness in Hebrews." *WesThJ* 16 (1981) 58–78. **Menchini, L. M.** *Il discorso di S. Stephano Protomartire nella Letteratura e Predicazione Cristiana Primitiva.* Rome: Pontifical Biblical Institute, 1951. **Ménégoz, E.** *Le théologie de l'Épître aux Hébreux.* Paris: Fischbacher, 1894. **Milligan, G.** *The Theology of the Epistle to the Hebrews with a Critical Introduction.* Edinburgh: Clark, 1899. **Moule, C. F. D.** "Once More, Who Were the Hellenists?" *ExpTim* 70 (1959) 100–102. **Moxnes, H.** *Theology in Conflict.* NovTSup 53. Leiden: Brill, 1980. **Olson, S. N.** "Wandering but Not Lost." *WW* 5 (1985) 426–33. **Oudersluys, R. C.** "Exodus in the Letter to the Hebrews." In *Grace upon Grace.* FS L. J. Kuyper. Ed. J. I. Cook. Grand Rapids: Eerdmans, 1975. 143–52. **Perkins, D. W.** "A Call to Pilgrimage: The Challenge of Hebrews." *ThEduc* 32 (1985) 69–81. **Pesch, R.** "'Hellenisten' und 'Hebräer': Zu Apg 9:29 und 6:1." *BZ* 23 (1979) 87–92. **Peterson, D. G.** "Towards a New Testament Theology of Worship." *RTR* 43 (1984) 65–73. **Pretorius, E. A. C.** "Christusbeeld en Kerkmodel in die Hebräerbrief." *ThEv* 15 (1982) 3–18. **Rendall, F.** *Theology of the Hebrew Christians.* London: Macmillan, 1886. **Riehm, E.** *Der Lehrbegriff des Hebräerbriefes* [2]. Basel: Balmer & Riehm, 1867. **Rissi, M.** *Die Theologie des Hebräerbriefs.* WUNT 44. Tübingen: Mohr, 1987. **Robinson, W.** "The Eschatology of the Epistle to the Hebrews: A Study in the Christian Doctrine of Hope." *Enc* 22 (1961) 37–51. **Rusche, H.** "Glauben und Leben nach dem Hebräerbrief." *BibLeb* 12 (1971) 94–104. **Scharlemann, M. H.** *Stephen: A Singular Saint.* Rome: Pontifical Biblical Institute, 1968. **Schick, E. A.** *Im Glauben Kraft empfangen: Betrachtungen zum Brief an die Hebräer.* Stuttgart: Katholisches Bibelwerk, 1978. **Schierse, F. J.** *Verheissung und Heilsvollendung: Zur theologischen Grundfrage des Hebräerbriefes.* MTS 1/9. Munich: Zink, 1955. **Schlatter, A.** *Der Glaube im Neuen Testament* [5]. Stuttgart: Calwer, 1963. **Scott, J. J.** "The Church of Jerusalem: An Investigation of the Growth of Internal Factions and the Extension of Its Influence in the Larger Church." Dissertation, University of Manchester, 1969. 98–133, 242–56. **Scroggs, R.** "The Earliest Hellenistic Christianity." In *Religions in Antiquity.* FS E. R. Goodenough. Ed. J. Neusner. Leiden: Brill, 1968. 176–206. **Simon, M.** *St. Stephen and the Hellenists in the Primitive Church.* London: Longmans, Green & Co., 1958. **Spicq, C.** "Contemplation, théologie et vie morale d'après l'Épître aux Hébreux." *RSR* 39 (1951) 289–300. ———. "La théologie des deux Alliances dans l'Épître aux Hébreux." *RSPT* 33 (1949) 15–30. ———. *Vie chrétienne et pérégrination selon le Nouveau Testament.* LD 71. Paris: Cerf, 1972. **Teodorico, P.** "Alcuni aspette dell' ecclesiologia della Lettera agli Ebrei." *Bib* 24 (1943) 125–61, 323–69. ———. *La Chiesa della Lettera agli Ebrie.* Torin/Rome: Marietta, 1945. **Theissen, G.** *Untersuchungen zum Hebäerbrief.* SNT 2. Gütersloh: Mohn, 1969. **Thompson, J. W.** *Strategy for Survival: A Plan for Church Renewal from Hebrews.* Austin, TX: Sweet, 1980. **Vanhoye, A.** *Homilie für haltbedürftige Christen: Struktur und Botschaft des Hebräerbriefes.* Regensburg: Pustet, 1981. ———. *Our Priest in God: The Doctrine of the Epistle to the Hebrews.* Rome: Biblical Institute, 1977. **Viard, A.** "Le Salut par la foi dans l'Épître aux Hébreux." *Ang* 58 (1981) 115–36. **Williamson, R.** "Hebrews and Doctrine." *ExpTim* 81 (1969–70) 371–76. **Worley, D. R.** "God's Faithfulness to Promise: The Hortatory Use of Commissive Language in Hebrews." Dissertation, Yale University, 1981.

STEPHEN AND THE HELLENISTS

The importance of the Hellenists as a cultural bridge between the Aramaic-speaking ministry of Jesus and the early Jerusalem Church and Paul's urban ministry to Greek-speaking Gentile centers is universally recognized (cf. Moule, *ExpTim* 70 [1959] 100–102; Hengel, *ZTK* 72 [1975] 151–206; Pesch, *BZ* 23 [1979] 87–92). M. Hengel, for example, has remarked on the importance of the Hellenists in orienting the early Christian mission toward cities, where there were large population centers (*ZTK* 72 [1975] 200). Being forced by their expulsion from Jerusalem to reaffirm in new categories the primitive messianic faith of the Jerusalem Church for cosmopolitan hellenistic centers, the Hellenists gave shape to much of the theology that is expressed in the NT. Christianity in its canonical form is less the direct achievement of Galileans than of these cultivated representatives of international Jewry who became its principal sponsors. The adoption of Greek as the language of discourse for the new movement, the establishment of major church centers in Caesarea, Antioch, Alexandria, Ephesus, and Rome, the nurture and development of a distinctive mission theology, all these were the enduring contributions of the Hellenists. Theologically, the road from Jerusalem to Rome runs through Antioch, the formative center of Christian Hellenism.

In a series of seminal lectures delivered in 1950, W. Manson sought to ground the theology of Hebrews in the theology of the early Hellenists, represented by Stephen, Philip, and the other leaders among "the seven" (*The Epistle to the Hebrews*, 25–46). He posited that Stephen developed and articulated a theology fostering world mission, and that the writer to the Hebrews was heir to this rich legacy. Manson's development of this thesis drew its primary support from the narrative concerning the mission activity of those Hellenists who were driven out of Jerusalem following Stephen's execution rather than on Stephen's actual speech before the Sanhedrin (Acts 7:2–53). He reasoned that engagement in mission presupposes prior theological reflection on the biblical supports for world mission. It is worthwhile to reexamine Manson's proposal in the light of some of the detail of Stephen's speech.

Briefly, Stephen's apology may be viewed as a radical reinterpretation of Israel's redemptive history. In this revisionist interpretation, the accent falls on obedience and disobedience. Stephen insists that God has not confined his presence or revelation to any one place (Acts 7:2, 4–7, 22–25, 48). He intended that his word be known and obeyed everywhere. His most significant disclosures actually occurred outside the promised land of Israel. The call of God is to be a pilgrim people as the response of obedience to his word. But Israel resisted pilgrimage and constantly failed to recognize the reiteration of the sustaining promise of God.

Stephen's reinterpretation extended to the role of Moses as well. Approximately half of the recorded speech is centered upon Moses: Moses in Egypt, Moses in Midian, Moses at Sinai (but only to hear the voice of the Lord mediated by an angel in the flame of a thornbush), Moses back in Egypt to deliver the Hebrews, who rebel against Moses (and God). Conspicuously absent is any reference to Moses as the mediator of the old covenant. There is a single, terse allusion to the law mediated by an angel (Acts 7:38), withheld until the conclusion of the speech: "You who received the law as delivered by angels but did not keep it" (Acts 7:53).

By the effective rhetorical technique of conspicuous underplay, Moses' crucial importance to Israel is defined not in reference to the law but as an exemplar of unwavering obedience to God and as a prophet who announced to Israel the coming of his prophetic successor (Acts 7:37).

Equally striking is the reinterpretation of the significance of Aaron, Moses' brother and the first Levitical high priest. He is presented as the one who created the golden calf at the request of the "fathers" (Acts 7:39–43). Israel then became idolatrous, on a par with the most debased peoples among the nations. In the sphere of worship and devotion to God, the people of Israel proved to be indistinguishable from those who had no knowledge of God.

Stephen's speech indicates that among the Hellenists there were serious differences with the traditional Jewish understanding of Israel's history and of the significance of the law and Temple cultus. In all stages of its history, Israel had refused to obey the commandments of God, rejecting both the living oracles delivered by Moses and the deliverers raised up by God (Acts 7:9–10, 27–28, 35–36, 39, 51–52). For Stephen, the most meaningful time in Israel's past was the pilgrimage in the wilderness, typified by the portability and the transitory nature of the tabernacle (Acts 7:44–50).

The hellenistic movement may actually have begun prior to the commitment of Stephen and others to Jesus of Nazareth. It was rooted in disillusionment with the conventional tradition of Israel's proud redemptive history. The displacement from the promised land that accounted for the existence of international Jewry was frequently interpreted in Scripture as God's judgment on Israel's disobedience. It underscored that Israel's "sacred history" was in fact a history of rebellion and disobedience. Stephen does not rebuke the members of the court for having a sacred history but for their consistent and perverse failure to live up to the covenant obligations that God's redemptive and revelatory activity imposed upon Israel. For Stephen, the key to understanding the history of the people of God is obedience and disobedience. The recognition of Jesus as Lord served to weave the strands of insight expressed by Stephen and other Hellenists into a recognizable pattern that may be designated the distinctive theology of the "hellenistic Church."

LOCATING HEBREWS IN THE HELLENISTIC TRADITION

The writer of Hebrews was a profound theologian who appears to have received his theological and spiritual formation within the hellenistic wing of the Church. His thought displays both originality and complexity as he reflects upon early Christian tradition. Yet several of his primary emphases can be recognized as developments of theological motifs that were already articulated by Stephen in his address to the Sanhedrin.

It was essential to Stephen's reinterpretation of Israel's history that from its inception God's intervention in human history had an end in view toward which all of his promises pointed (Acts 7:5–7, 17, 37–38, 52). In developing this thought Stephen made much of the motif of pilgrimage and promise, finding primary examples in Abraham, who was called to be a nomad (Acts 7:2–5a), in Joseph, who was carried off to an alien land (Acts 7:9), and in the events of the Exodus, when Israel became the wandering people of God (Acts 7:36–38, 44).

The theme of pilgrimage and promise is one of the most distinctive notes in Hebrews, as the writer develops the conception of Christian life as pilgrimage to the city of God. It constitutes the substance of Heb 3:7–4:13, when attention is focused upon the wilderness experience of Israel, who failed to enter God's promised rest because of unbelief and disobedience. The certainty that the community of faith lives in terms of the promise of God (4:1–2, 6–7, 9–11) throws into bold relief their peril if they replicate the disobedience that characterized Israel at Kadesh.

In Heb 11:8–16 the pilgrimage of the patriarchs who were attested by God as faithful is recited as the model for obedience. The writer states plainly that in this life Christians have no enduring city; they seek intently the city that is to come (13:14). Only from this perspective do they emulate faithful men and women of God like Abraham and his family who lived in tents, seeking a city or home (11:10, 14, 16). Pilgrimage is characteristic of the obedient people of God under both the old and the new covenants, and it cannot be in vain, since God has prepared for them a city (11:10, 16). The new people of God must remain a pilgrim generation, continually open to the call of God upon their lives.

The concept of the Christian life as pilgrimage is derived not merely from the OT tradition, which recounts actual experiences of pilgrimage, but from a fresh theological and pastoral understanding of the circumstances in which it is necessary to respond to the call of God. Pilgrim ecclesiology is a survival ecclesiology; it implies separation—from a place—and it entails hardship (cf. Johnsson, *JBL* 97 [1978] 239–51; Barrett, "The Eschatology of the Epistle to the Hebrews," 373–83). This understanding is implicit in Stephen's speech, and it informs the theology of the hellenistic Church.

In Hebrews this understanding comes to sharp expression in the profound theological insight that Christians on earth possess the realities of which God has spoken only in the form of promise. The writer clearly regards the faith community as heirs to the promises of God (cf. 1:14; 6:12, 17; 9:15). In Hebrews the familiar pattern of promise and fulfillment (i.e., what God has promised to the fathers he has fulfilled in sending Jesus), which is characteristic of the other documents of the NT, is modified. The stress falls on the fact that what God promised to the fathers he has repeated with assurance to the people of the new covenant. They are to find in the priestly office of Jesus the guarantee of the ultimate fulfillment of the promise (see *Comment* on 4:1; 8:6; 10:23, 36; 11:11, 39–40). The pattern in Hebrews is promise, reaffirmed with intensity, and fulfillment yet in the future. The fact that the revelation of God is possessed on earth only as promise explains why the one form of existence appropriate to the community of faith is pilgrimage. Christians must pursue the promise and lay hold of it for themselves. Reference to the wandering of Abraham, or of Israel through the wilderness, becomes a useful vehicle for calling the Christian community to the life of faith and obedience shaped and sustained by the promise of God.

In the course of developing homiletically and theologically the motif of pilgrimage and promise, the writer clarifies his distinctive understanding of faith. For Paul, faith is essentially firm commitment to God's accomplished redemptive action through Jesus; it entails a retrospective turn especially to the cross and resurrection. The theological perspective of Hebrews is profoundly different. Faith is both an openness to the future, which is given expression in obedient trust in the God who has promised, and a present grasp upon truth now invisible but certain because it is grounded in the word of promise (see *Comment* on 4:1; 6:12; 11:1–2, 13, 39; 12:2).

It was this kind of faith in the power of God that made it possible for Abraham to offer to God his son Isaac, whose life was essential to the fulfillment of God's word of promise (11:17–19). It was this aspect of faith that enabled Moses to defy Pharaoh's wrath and to lead Israel from slavery. Under pressure he stood firm because through faith "he kept the one who is invisible before his eyes, as it were" (11:26–27). The faith the writer commends to his audience is a confident reliance upon the future, which makes possible responsible action in the present in the light of that confidence. This distinctly eschatological understanding of faith is the corollary of the motif of pilgrimage.

Like Stephen before him, the writer of Hebrews develops the consequences of Israel's history as a record of rebellion and resistance to the purposes of God (3:7–4:13). His emphasis, however, is different from that of Stephen, who carried the record of Israel's disobedience to its culmination in the betrayal and murder of Jesus (Acts 7:51–53). The writer of Hebrews is concerned rather with the Jewish-Christian members of the house church who were in danger of repeating in their experience the disobedience of Israel. His concern reflects a primary tenet of the hellenistic Church that there is no necessary continuity between the people who receive the promises and those who participate in their realization. The distinguishing marks of the true people of God are obedience and faith in the promise (see *Comment* on 5:11–6:12).

The writer calls the community back to this fundamental insight as he directs their attention to Jesus, who placed his trust in God and proved to be faithful to the one who appointed him to his mission (2:13; 3:1–2; 12:2). He learned obedience experientially through the suffering of death (5:7–8). After having been qualified to come before God in priestly action, he has become the source of an eternal salvation to all who obey him (5:9). The community can hold firmly to their confidence and their baptismal confession as they consider "Jesus, the apostle and high priest" to whom they pledge their allegiance in the recital of the confession (3:1, 6, 14; 4:14).

The community must not emulate Israel in its disobedience to God but take full advantage of the new access to God provided by the personal, sufficient sacrifice of Jesus (10:19–22). To fail to do so, to shrink back, to sin deliberately after having received the knowledge of the truth, is to incur in a heightened form the rejection and death experienced by Israel in the wilderness (10:26–31, 35–39). It is to know experientially "a fearful prospect of judgment, and a fury of fire which will consume the adversaries" (10:27), when one encounters face to face the God who has said, "Vengeance is mine, I will repay" (10:30). In dwelling upon the motif of the judgment and its decisive consequences (cf. 9:27; 10:31; 12:25–27), the writer carries the argument of Stephen to its logical conclusion, applying it to the new covenant community in danger of forgetting the awesome character of God who has spoken his final word through the Son.

The parallels between Stephen's speech and Hebrews indicate that the writer of Hebrews is to be identified with the theological perspective that was first articulated by the early Hellenists. The differences in emphasis indicate that Hebrews provides a developed and mature expression of the distinctive theology of the hellenistic Church. The writer deserves to be recognized as a major theologian within the early Church. He possessed a first-rate mind and a gift for keen theological insight disciplined to the service of the Church.

A question that continues to be debated concerns the source of the conception of Jesus as an eternal priest like Melchizedek. Was this conception an insight first grasped by the writer, or did he receive it as an integral part of the theological legacy of the early Hellenists? The fact that the writer can refer to Christ as high priest *before* he has given any theological elaboration of this conception (2:17–18; 3:1–2; 4:14–16) suggested to W. Manson that it was the common property of the hellenistic movement (*The Epistle to the Hebrews*, 54). That is possible. But there is little doubt that the development of this theme in 5:1–10:18 bears the marks of original and creative reflection by a charismatically gifted teacher who had thought long and meaningfully on the Christian traditions treasured by the Hellenists. (For a more considered judgment on this issue, see above, "Sonship Interpreted in Terms of Priesthood.") One of the enduring values of Hebrews is its continuity with the theological tradition of the Hellenists, preserving and developing insights that continue to enrich the theology, liturgy, piety, and praxis of the Christian Church.

Recognition

Bibliography

Aland, K. *The Problem of the New Testament Canon.* London: Mowbray, 1962. **Anderson, C. P.** "The Epistle to the Hebrews and the Pauline Letter Collection." *HTR* 59 (1966) 429–38. ———. "Hebrews among the Letters of Paul." *SR* 5 (1975–76) 258–66. **Farmer, W. R.,** and **Farkasfalvey, D. M.** *The Formation of the New Testament Canon: An Ecumenical Approach.* New York/Ramsey/Toronto: Paulist, 1983. **Ferguson, E.** "Canon Muratori: Date and Provenance." In *Studia Patristica: Eighth International Congress on Patristic Studies.* Ed. E. A. Livingstone. Oxford/New York: Pergamon, 1982. 677–83. **Gamble, H. Y.** *The New Testament Canon: Its Making and Meaning.* Philadelphia: Fortress, 1985. **Grant, R. M.** "Literary Criticism and the NT Canon." *JSNT* 16 (1982) 22–44. **Gwilliam, G. H.** "The Epistle to the Hebrews in the Syrian Church." *ExpTim* 8 (1896–97) 154–56. **Hatch, W. H. P.** "The Position of Hebrews in the Canon of the New Testament." *HTR* 29 (1936) 133–51. **Käsemann, E.,** ed. *Das Neue Testament als Kanon: Dokumentation und kritischen Analyze zur gegenwärtige Diskussion.* Göttingen: Vandenhoeck & Ruprecht, 1970. **Meade, D. G.** *Pseudonymity and Canon: An Investigation into the Relationship of Authorship and Authority in Jewish and Earliest Christian Tradition.* Grand Rapids: Eerdmans, 1986. **Metzger, B. M.** *The Canon of the New Testament: Its Origin, Development, and Significance.* Oxford: Clarendon, 1987. **Nellessen, E.** "Lateinische Summarien zum Hebräerbrief." *BZ* 14 (1970) 240–51. **Ohlig, K. H.** *Die theologische Begründung des neutestamentlichen Kanons in der alten Kirche: Kommentare und Beiträge zum Alten und Neuen Testament.* Düsseldorf: Patmos, 1972. **Pérez, G.** "Autenticidad y canonicidad de la carta a los Hebreos." *CB* 13 (1956) 216–26. **Riggenbach, E.** *Historische Studien zum Hebräerbrief: 1. Teil: Die ältesten lateinischen Kommentare zum Hebräerbrief.* FGNK 8/1. Leipzig: Deichert, 1907. **Sanders, J. A.** *Canon and Community: A Guide to Canonical Criticism.* Philadelphia: Fortress, 1984. **Sen, F.** "La carta a los Hebreos en el Canon y en el corpus paulino." *CB* 25 (1968) 35–40. **Sundberg, A. C.** "Canon Muratori: A Fourth-Century List." *HTR* 66 (1973) 1–41. **Thayer, J. H.** "Authorship and Canonicity of the Epistle to the Hebrews." *BSac* 24 (1867) 681–722.

Hebrews may be described as the "loose end" of the NT when we seek to rationalize its canonicity. It clearly asserted an intrinsic authority in the Church both in the West and in the East. In spite of that fact, there was a reluctance to acknowledge it as integral to the Church's rule of faith and practice.

RECOGNITION IN THE WEST

Evidence of the impact of Hebrews upon the life of the Christian community in Rome is provided by *1 Clement,* a pastoral letter sent by the church in Rome to the church in Corinth, which was experiencing disruptions. Although the letter is anonymous, an unbroken tradition ascribes it to Clement, a senior pastor of the church in Rome during the closing decades of the first century or relatively early in the second century (see above, "Date of Composition: General Considerations"). Clement provides indisputable evidence that Hebrews exercised a formative influence upon the form and statement of his pastoral letter. (Passages that reflect literary acquaintance with Hebrews are *1 Clem.* 9:3–4 [cf. Heb 11:5–7]; 12:1–3 [cf. Heb 11:31]; 17:1 [cf. Heb 11:37]; 19:2 [cf. Heb 12:1]; 21:9 [cf. Heb 4:12]; 27:2 [cf. Heb 6:18]; 36:1–6 [cf. Heb 1:3–13; 2:17–18; 4:15–16]; 43:1 [cf. Heb 3:2–5].)

The extent of Clement's knowledge of Hebrews is reflected particularly in *1 Clem.* 36:1–6.

> This is the way, beloved, in which we found our salvation, Jesus Christ, the high priest of our offerings, the defender and helper of our weaknesses . . . "who being the radiance of his Majesty is so much greater than the angels as he had inherited a more excellent name." For it is written, "who makes his angels spirits, and his ministers a flame of fire." But of the Son the Master said, "You are my son. Today I have become your father. Ask me, and I will give you the nations for your inheritance, and the ends of the earth for your possession." And again he says to him, "Sit at my right hand until I make your enemies a stool for your feet."

The designation of Jesus as "high priest" and as "defender of our weaknesses" (cf. Heb 2:17–18; 4:15–16) occurs in a paragraph that has the appearance of a patchwork of phrases culled from Heb 1:3–13. The descriptive clause, "who being the radiance of his Majesty is so much greater than the angels as he has inherited a more excellent name" is virtually a quotation, conflating Heb 1:3–4. Moreover, when Clement quotes Ps 110:1 as a direct word of address by God to the Son, as in Heb 1:13, he betrays his literary dependence upon the formula of introduction employed by the writer in Heb 1:13. This manner of introducing quotations is typical of Hebrews (1:5–13; 5:5–6; 7:17, 21) but occurs only here in *1 Clement* (cf. G. L. Cockerill, "Heb 1:1–14, *1 Clem.* 36:1–6 and the High Priest Title," *JBL* 97 [1978] 437–40; P. Ellingworth, "Hebrews and 1 Clement: Literary Dependence or Common Tradition?" *BZ* n.s. 23 [1979] 262–69).

It is striking that the chain of quotations brought together by Clement would invite a writer to designate Jesus as the Son, not as "high priest." It is the presentation of the Son as high priest in Hebrews that encouraged Clement to link his paraphrase of Heb 1 with Jesus' high priestly ministry and further to qualify Jesus as "the defender and helper of our weaknesses." Clement clearly knew the detail of the text of Hebrews and drew upon its distinctive presentation of Jesus as Son and high priest. The manner in which he made use of Hebrews shows that he recognized its authority.

Recognition in Rome by way of response is attested by the *Shepherd of Hermas*, an apocalyptic prophecy written in Rome between A.D. 120 and 140. This document is reflective of questions that had been raised in the church of Rome concerning an appropriate practice of repentance. The considerations advanced in *Hermas* begin with the recognition that repentance was a singular, saving possibility granted by God. The writer refers to this in a scene in which he inquires about some teaching he had received of the angel who had appeared to him:

> "I have heard, sir, . . . from some teachers that there is no second repentance beyond the one given when we went down to the water and received remission for our former sins." He said to me, "You have heard correctly, for this is so. For the one who has received remission of sins ought never to sin again, but to live in purity" (*Mand.* 4.3.1–2).

The writer of Hebrews is the only teacher in the period prior to *Hermas* who is known to have expressed exactly the eschatological singularity of baptismal repentance and of forgiveness in this way. Since Hebrews was definitely circulating within the Roman Christian community, the writer may have been the source from which *Hermas* received the teaching about the singularity of repentance. *Hermas* developed its prophetic message of a second repentance in formal recognition of the teaching of Hebrews but in substantial contrast to Hebrews (*Vis.* 2.2.4–5). (Cf. K. Rahner, "Die Busslehre des Hirten des Hermas," *ZKT* 77 [1955] 385–431; B. Poschmann, *Paenitentia secunda, die kirchliche Busse im ältesten Christentum bis Cyprian und Origenes* [Bonn: Hanstein, 1940] 38–52.) In that dispute, the Church in the West ultimately sided with *Hermas* rather than with Hebrews. (Other passages in *Hermas* that appear to reflect an acquaintance with Hebrews are *Vis.* 2.2.7 [cf. Heb 11:33]; *Vis.* 2.3.2 [cf. Heb 3:13]; *Vis.* 3.7.2 [cf. Heb 3:13]; *Vis.* 4.2.4; *Sim.* 9.13.7 [cf. Heb 11:33]; *Sim.* 9.2.2 [cf. Heb 10:19–20].)

Justin clearly knew Hebrews (*Apology* 12.9 [cf. Heb 3:1]; *Dialogue* 13:1 [cf. Heb 9:13–14]; 19.3 [cf. Heb 11:5]; 19.4 [cf. Heb 5:6; 6:20; 7:1–2]; 46.3; 56:1 [cf. Heb 3:5]; 67:9 [cf. Heb 12:21]; 96:1 [cf. Heb 7:17, 24]; 113.5 [cf. Heb 5:6, 10]; 121.2 [cf. Heb 4:12–13]). Hebrews was known and used by Irenaeus (Eusebius, *Church History* 5.26.3), by the presbyter Gaius of Rome (c. A.D. 200; Eusebius, *Church History* 6.20.3), and by Hippolytus (*Refutation of All Heresies* 6.30.9), all three of whom recognized that it was not Pauline in origin.

The absence of Hebrews from Marcion's *Apostolicon* (Tertullian, *Against Marcion*, 5) is sufficiently explained by its strong reliance upon the OT and upon Jewish thought-forms. The Muratonian Canon, which appears to date from the last quarter of the second century (cf. E. Ferguson, "Canon Muratori: Date and Provenance," 677–83) and provides a list of the documents acknowledged as authoritative in the church in Rome, makes no mention of Hebrews. It was seldom quoted in the third century and in the first half of the fourth century.

Vital impact followed by an extended period of neglect appears to have been characteristic of Hebrews in the West. It may well be that the rigor with which the writer argued for the impossibility of repentance after apostasy accounts for its relative neglect in the second and third centuries in the West, and for the reluctance of the Western Church to acknowledge its authority under pressure from the East in the fourth century. A remark made by Tertullian (c. A.D. 200–220) is instructive in this regard. In his early Montanist period he opposed the teaching concerning the possibility of post-baptismal repentance that had been introduced with *Hermas* and that had been adopted by the Western Church. In support of his position, Tertullian cited Heb 6:4–8:

> I wish, however, redundantly to add the testimony likewise of one particular companion of the apostles. . . . For there exists [a document] to the Hebrews [with the] superscription of Barnabas, a man with adequate authority from God. . . . And, of course, the Epistle of Barnabas is more generally received among the churches than that apocryphal "Shepherd of Adulterers" (*On Modesty* 20.3).

The sarcastic reference to the "Shepherd of Adulterers" is, of course, an allusion to the *Shepherd of Hermas,* whose teaching concerning a second, post-baptismal repentance had been extended to those who had committed adultery in Tertullian's day.

Some church leaders in the West undoubtedly questioned the authority of Hebrews. Confusion over the distinction between authorship and authority was widespread. Divergent points of view over the authorship of Hebrews may have prevented the Church from listening to its witness. By the end of the second century and the beginning of the third, Roman opinion had crystallized in excluding Hebrews from the Pauline letter canon. For all intents and purposes, the voice of Hebrews was muted for the Church in the West. Even when its authority was fully recognized in the fourth century and it was acknowledged to belong to the canon of Scripture, there is little evidence that it exercised any considerable influence upon the thought, life, and liturgy of the Western Church.

RECOGNITION IN THE EAST

The early Alexandrian fathers, and the eastern half of the Church in general, appear to have attributed Hebrews to Paul and to have recognized its intrinsic authority. It is probable that it was in the East that the title $\pi\rho\grave{o}s$ Ἑβραίους, "to the Hebrews," was first added to the manuscripts of the document, locating Hebrews within the Jewish mission of earliest Christianity. It was known already to Pantaenus (c. A.D. 180) and to his pupil Clement of Alexandria (c. A.D. 200) (Eusebius, *Church History* 6.14.1–4). It is also attested in the earliest extant manuscript of the letters of Paul, the Chester Beatty Papyrus II (P[46]), which has been assigned a date in the early third century, perhaps as early as A.D 200. It was, of course, known in North Africa as well by Tertullian in the early third century.

What is striking about the references to Hebrews by Pantaenus, Clement, and Origen (Eusebius, *Church History* 6.14.1–4; 6.25.11–14) is that they acknowledge the presence of Hebrews among a collection of Paul's letters and feel the necessity of justifying that association (cf. Anderson, *HTR* 59 [1966] 129–38). The arguments advanced by Clement and Origen to defend the legitimacy of this situation are of less interest than the witness they bear to the recognition of the intrinsic authority of Hebrews in the East by the end of the second century.

Of particular interest is Origen's comment that "the men of old times [ἀρχαῖοι ἄνδρες] passed it [i.e., Hebrews] down as Paul's" (Eusebius, *Church History* 6.25.13).

Although Hebrews is certainly not a composition of Paul's, the early tradition is a recognition of the conceptual continuity of Hebrews with the genuine, earlier writings of a figure like Paul. The name "Paul" has to do with the authority of Paul to address the post-Pauline community. It was this conceptual continuity that was acknowledged by these earlier church leaders when they recognized the authority of Hebrews. The attribution of Hebrews to Paul was an open acknowledgment of the intrinsic importance of Hebrews.

Eusebius was fully aware of the questions posed in the West concerning the Pauline authorship of Hebrews but included the document in his own fourteen-letter corpus of Paul's writings (*Church History* 3.5; 6.20.3). Athanasius also listed Hebrews among the fourteen letters of Paul (*Festal Letter* 39.5). In the NT manuscript tradition, Hebrews was transmitted exclusively in association with the letters of Paul, although it occupies three different positions in the tradition (see Hatch, *HTR* 29 [1936] 133–51).

Late in the fourth century, under the influence of Western fathers who had spent time in the East, an agreement was reached between East and West that Hebrews was a fourteenth letter of Paul's. Hiliary of Poitiers, for example, had spent a period of exile in Asia Minor, during which time he came to regard Hebrews as written by Paul and authoritative. In A.D. 367 he became the first church leader in the West to lend his support to the Pauline authorship of Hebrews (*On the Trinity* 4.11). The decisive influence upon Western opinion, however, was exerted by Jerome and Augustine. Jerome was alert to the diversity of opinion regarding Hebrews in the East and the West. He exercised caution in his citations of Hebrews but implicitly treated it as he would a Pauline letter. He had no doubt concerning its intrinsic authority and its right to be included in the NT (*On Illustrious Men* 5; *Epistles* 53.8; 129.3). Augustine was equally alert to the controversy surrounding the authorship of Hebrews. He fully recognized its authority and listed Hebrews among the letters of Paul (*Christian Doctrine* 2.8; *City of God* 16.22).

The measure of the influence exerted by these two men can be gauged by considering the action of the church leaders who gathered in Carthage in A.D. 397, and again in 419. The council of Carthage in 397 officially recognized the authority of Hebrews, but differentiated between Hebrews and the thirteen letters of Paul by appending Hebrews to the end of the Pauline letter collection. This is the position occupied by Hebrews in the Old Latin manuscripts *d*, *e*, and *f* and in the Latin Vulgate. Those who assembled at Carthage in A.D. 419 describe the Pauline letter collection as consisting of fourteen letters, a shift in opinion reflective of the influence of Jerome and Augustine.

CONCLUDING OBSERVATIONS

Ultimately it is the performance of the text that determines the authority of the text. If Hebrews had not been a "performative" text, it would not have been preserved and recognized as authoritative. Hebrews was preserved and transmitted because Christian leaders kept picking it up and positive results followed. In the use of Hebrews in the early centuries of the Church, its authority was recognized. This is attested by Clement's use of Hebrews for encouragement, liturgy, and prayer, or by *Hermas*' concern to respond to Hebrews in terms of the pastoral problem of repentance. Both cases illustrate the recognition of Hebrews through the appeal to Hebrews. The concern of the early church was with praxis, with piety, with an experienced, vital faith, with spiritual utility, and Hebrews demanded that its voice be heard.

The authority asserted by Hebrews very early in the life of the Church is an important reminder that it is more than a sensitive pastoral response relevant only to a specific occasion in the past. Certainly the situation that threatened to subvert the members of a Jewish-Christian house church was catalytic. It evoked creative and prayerful thinking that is reflected upon every page of the discourse. Hebrews, however, is more than a response to that local situation. It is a response to revelation. It conveys a word from God addressed to the Church in response to the sometimes harsh reality of life encountered by Christians in a fallen and insecure world. As an integral part of the NT canon, Hebrews adds its essential witness to the decisive eschatological character of God's action through Jesus Christ and to the urgency of unwavering commitment to him.

Canonical status both reflects and confers normative status. It is a confession of the usefulness and of the normative value of Hebrews. Canon universalizes a text; i.e., it takes a very particular text and endows it with a life of its own so that it may address a variety of situations not identical with the original life situation. Canonical recognition is a confessional acknowledgment that the community of believers was able to make meaning of this particular text for spiritual and theological formation in new situations. The authority of Hebrews to function as a rule of faith shaping the life of the Church and the churches in continuity with Jesus and the apostles was recognized when it was used by the community of faith for teaching, correcting, equipping, and leading the community into the reality of the holiness that is indispensable to the enjoyment of the vision of God (Heb 12:14).

Text

Bibliography

Aland, K., ed. *Die alten Übersetzungen des Neuen Testaments, die kirchenvaterzitate und Lektionare.* Berlin: de Gruyter, 1972. ———. *Kurzegefasste Liste der griechischen Handscriften des Neuen Testaments: Vol. 1. Gesamtübersicht.* Berlin: de Gruyter, 1963. ———. "Neue Neutestamentliche Papyri." *NTS* 3 (1956–57) 261–86. ———. "Neue Neutestamentliche Papyri II." *NTS* 9 (1962–63) 303–16. ———. "Neue Neutestamentliche Papyri III." *NTS* 22 (1975–76) 375–96. ———. *Studien zur Überlieferung des Neuen Testaments und seines Textes.* Berlin: de Gruyter, 1967. 91–136. ——— and **Aland, B.** *The Text of the New Testament: An Introduction to the Critical Editions and to the Theory and Practice of Modern Textual Criticism.* Tr. E. F. Rhodes. Grand Rapids: Eerdmans, 1987. **Beare, F. W.** "The Text of the Epistle to the Hebrews." *JBL* 63 (1944) 379–96. **Bensley, R. L.** *The Harklean Version of the Epistle to the Hebrews XI. 28–XIII. 25.* Cambridge: Cambridge UP, 1889. **Elliott, J. K.** "Keeping Up with Recent Studies: XV. New Testament Textual Criticism." *ExpTim* 99 (1987) 40–45. **Harnack, A. V.** "Studien zur Vulgata des Hebräerbriefes." SPAW (1920) 179–201. [Reprinted in *Studien zur Geschichte des Neuen Testaments und der alten Kirche.* Berlin: de Gruyter, 1931. 191–234.] **Hoskier, H. C.** *A Commentary on the Various Readings in the Text of the Epistle to the Hebrews in the Chester Beatty Papyrus P[46].* London: Quaritch, 1938. **Kim, Y. K.** "Palaeographical Dating of P[46] to the Later First Century." *Bib* 69 (1988) 248–57. **Metzger, B. M.** *The Text of the New Testament: Its Transmission, Corruption, and Restoration[2].* New York/Oxford: Oxford UP, 1968. 247–56.

————. *A Textual Commentary of the Greek New Testament: A Companion Volume to the United Bible Societies' Greek New Testament (Third Edition)*. London/New York: United Bible Societies, 1971. 661–78. **Sanders, H. A.**, ed. *A Third-Century Papyrus Codex of the Epistles of Paul.* Ann Arbor: University of Michigan Press, 1935. **Schäfer, K. T.** *Üntersuchungen zur Geschichte der lateinischen Ubersetzung des Hebräerbriefes.* Freiburg im Breisgau: Herder, 1929. **Schofield, E. M.** "The Papyrus Fragments of the Greek New Testament." Dissertation, Southern Baptist Theological Seminary, 1936. **Tasker, R. V. G.** "The Text of the 'Corpus Paulinum.'" *NTS* 1 (1954–55) 180–91. **Treu, K.** "Neue neutestamentliche Fragmente der Berlin Papyrussammlung." *Archiv für Papyrusforschung* 18 (1960) 37–48. **Willis, C. G.** "St. Augustine's Text of the Epistle to the Hebrews." *SE* 6 (1962) 543–47. **Zuntz, G.** *The Text of the Epistles: A Disquisition upon the Corpus Paulinum.* Schweich Lectures, 1946. London: The British Academy, 1953.

The text of Hebrews has been well preserved, due undoubtedly to the fact that it was transmitted almost exclusively as an integral part of the Pauline corpus. The major witnesses, with the portions of the text preserved, are the following:

PAPYRI

P^{12}	P. Amherst 3b (3rd cent.): 1:1
P^{13}	P. Oxyrhyncus 657 (3rd/4th cent.): 2:14–5:5; 10:8–12; 10:29–11:13; 11:28–12:17
P^{17}	P. Oxyrhyncus 1078 (4th cent.): 9:12–19
P^{46}	P. Chester Beatty II (c. A.D. 200): 1:1–9:16; 9:18–10:20, 22–30; 10:32–13:25
P^{79}	Berlin Staatliche Museen Inv. 6774 (7th cent.): 10:10–12, 28–30.

UNCIAL CODICES

ℵ	(01)	Codex Sinaiticus (4th cent.): complete
A	(02)	Codex Alexandrinus (5th cent.): complete
B	(03)	Codex Vaticanus (4th cent.): 1:1–9:13
C	(04)	Codex Ephraemi Syri Rescriptus (5th cent.): 2:4–7:26; 9:15–10:24; 12:16–13:25
D	(06)	Codex Claromontanus (6th cent.): 1:1–13:20, a bilingual Greek and Latin MS
E	(06^abs)	Codex Sangermanesis (9th cent.): a copy of Codex Claromontanus
H	(015)	Codex Euthalianus (6th cent.): 1:3–8; 2:11–16; 3:13–18; 4:12–15; 10:1–7, 32–38; 12:10–15; 13:24–25.
I	(016)	Codex Freerianus (5th cent.): 1:1–3, 9–12; 2:4–7, 12–14; 3:4–6, 14–16; 4:3–6, 12–14; 5:5–7; 6:1–3, 10–13; 6:20–7:2; 7:7–11, 18–20; 7:27–8:1; 8:7–9; 9:1–4, 9–11, 16–19, 25–27; 10:5–8, 16–18, 26–29, 35–38; 11:6–7, 12–15, 22–24, 31–33; 11:38–12:1; 12:7–9, 16–18, 25–27; 13:7–9, 16–18, 23–25
K	(018)	Codex Mosquensis (9th cent.): complete
L	(020)	Codex Angelicus (9th cent.): 1:1–13:9
P	(025)	Codex Porphyrianus (9th cent.): complete
Ψ	(044)	Codex Athous Laurae (8th/9th cent.): 1:1–8:10; 9:20–13:25

048	(5th cent.):	11:32–38; 12:3–13:4

0121b   (10th cent.):   1:1–4:3; 12:20–13:25
0122   (9th cent.):   5:8–6:10
0227   (5th cent.):   11:18–19, 29
0228   (4th cent.):   12:19–21, 23–25
0252   (5th cent.):   6:2–4, 6–7

IMPORTANT MINUSCULES

33   (9th cent.)   1739   (10th cent.)
81   (A.D. 1044)   1881   (14th cent.)
104   (A.D. 1087)   2464   (10th cent.)
326   (12th cent.)

VERSIONS

The Old Latin (OL) is represented by *d*, the Latin column in Codex Claromontanus (D), by *r*, the 6th-cent. Freising fragments (Munich Bayer. Staatsbibliothek Clm. 6436) containing 6:6–7:5; 7:8–18; 7:20–8:1; 9:27–10:9; 10:11–11:7, and by *z* (9th cent.), containing 10:1–13:25. The uncial manuscript F (010) Codex Augiensis (9th cent.) contains the Pauline letters in double columns of Greek and Latin, but Hebrews is preserved only in Latin.

The Coptic version (co) is represented by both Sahidic (sa) and Bohairic (bo) witnesses.

The Syriac version (sy) is represented in both the Peshitta (p) and the Harclean (h) translations. There are important marginal notes in the Harclean version (hmg).

The type of text represented by the principal witnesses is predominently Alexandrian, although very early manuscripts and fragments preserve a mixed text. A Byzantine text is transmitted in C K L and many minuscules. A Western text has been identified in D, the Latin column of Hebrews in F, and the Old Latin.

Textual variations in the manuscript tradition and conjectural emendations proposed when the preserved reading is suspected of being corrupt must be considered on a case-by-case basis in the attempt to reconstruct the original text. Nevertheless, the extent of the agreement among the editors of the text is far greater than has been recognized. A comparison of the critical editions of Tischendorf, von Soden, Vogels, Merk, and Bover with the text adopted in the Nestle-Aland[25] shows that 234 of the 303 verses of Hebrews are variant-free, representing 77.2 percent of the text (see K. Aland and B. Aland, *The Text of the New Testament*, 29–30). The total number of variants adopted by one or more of the editors is 71 (roughly 2.9 per page). The basis of the translation in this commentary is the Nestle-Aland 26th edition (Eberhard Nestle and Erwin Nestle, eds., *Novum Testamentum Graece*, 26th ed., rev. K. Aland, M. Black, C. M. Martini, B. M. Metzger, and A. Wikgren [Stuttgart: Deutsche Bibelstiftung, 1979]) but with reliance on other critical judgments as well.

Textual questions are normally addressed in the commentary in the *Notes* sections to the *Translations*. Important readings affecting translation and interpretation are discussed in the *Notes* to 1:3, 8, 12; 2:6, 9; 3:2, 6, 18; 4:2; 5:6, 7; 6:2, 18; 8:8, 11; 9:1, 11, 14, 19; 10:1, 11, 34, 38; 11:4, 11, 13, 17, 23, 37, 39; 12:1, 3, 4, 7, 15, 18, 24, 25, 27, 28; 13:6, 12, 15, 21, 25.

I. The Revelation of God through His Son (1:1–2:18)

Bibliography

Black, D. A. "The Problem of the Literary Structure of Hebrews: An Evaluation and a Proposal." *GTJ* 7 (1986) 163–77. **Bligh, J.** *Chiastic Analysis of the Epistle to the Hebrews.* Oxford: Heythrop College, 1966. ————. "The Structure of Hebrews." *HeyJ* 5 (1964) 170–77. **Cladder, H.** "Hebr 1,1–5,10." *ZKT* 29 (1905) 1–27. **Descamps, A.** "La structure de l'Épître aux Hébreux." *RDT* 9 (1954) 251–58, 333–38. **Dussaut, L.** *Synopse structurelle de l'Épître aux Hébreux.* 5–32. **Gyllenberg, R.** "Die Komposition des Hebräerbriefs." *SEÅ* 22–23 (1957–58) 137–47. **Haering, T.** "Gedankengang und Grundgedanken des Hebräerbriefs." *ZNW* 18 (1917–18) 145–64. **Nauck, W.** "Zum Aufbau des Hebräerbriefes." In *Judentum, Urchristentum, Kirche.* FS Joachim Jeremias. Ed. W. Eltester. BZNW 26. Giessen: Töpelmann, 1960. 199–206. **Rice, G. E.** "Apostasy as a Motif and Its Effect on the Structure of Hebrews." *AUSS* 23 (1985) 29–35. **Smothers, T. G.** "A Superior Model: Hebrews 1:1–4:13." *RevExp* 82 (1985) 333–43. **Swetnam, J.** "Form and Content in Hebrews 1–6." *Bib* 53 (1972) 368–85. **Thien, F.** "Analyse de l'Épître aux Hébreux." *RB* 11 (1902) 74–86. **Vaganay, L.** "Le plan de l'Épître aux Hébreux." In *Mémorial Lagrange.* Paris: Gabalda, 1940. 269–77. **Vanhoye, A.** "Discussions sur la structure de l'Épître aux Hébreux." *Bib* 55 (1974) 349–80. ————. "Les indices de la structure littéraire de l'Épître aux Hébreux." *SE* 2 (1964) 493–509. ————. *La structure littéraire de l'Épître aux Hébreux.* StudNeot 1. Paris/Bruges: Desclée de Brouwer, 1963. ————. "Structure littéraire et thèmes théologiques de l'Épître aux Hébreux." In *Studiorum Paulinorum Congressus Internationalis Catholicus 1961.* Vol. 2. AnBib 18. Rome: Biblical Institute, 1963. 175–81. ————. *A Structured Translation of the Epistle to the Hebrews.* Tr. J. Swetnam. Rome: Pontifical Biblical Institute, 1964. ————. "Thema sacerdotii praeparatur in Heb. 1, 1–2, 18." *VD* 47 (1969) 284–97.

Introduction

Although an impression of careful composition according to a well-ordered plan is conveyed on every page of Hebrews, there has been no common agreement concerning the literary structure of the document. The broad range of critical opinion has been conveniently reviewed by A. Vanhoye (*La structure,* 11–32), who found in the lack of consensus a mandate for a fresh investigation of the question. His detailed studies have demonstrated the importance of both conceptual and literary considerations for discovering the plan of the work.

The writer's intention is direct address. He classifies Hebrews as a sermon reduced to writing (13:22). That explains why he expresses himself in the categories of speaking and hearing (cf. 2:5; 5:11; 8:1; 9:5; 11:32). The writer's rhetorical style is more characteristic of the spoken word than of formal composition. Convinced that what he has to say must be understood, he provided his readers with formal literary indications of the course of his thought. He knew that these would be readily recognized by his intended audience. They had become familiar with such rhetorical procedures through repeated exposure to preaching in the synagogue and the church (ibid., 34–49; id., *SE* 2 [1964] 493–509). Recognition of these fixed techniques of style assists the modern interpreter to recover the literary structure of Hebrews.

The most important of these procedures is *the announcement of the subject.* The writer customarily introduces a brief formulation that presents the theme of each of the major divisions of his discourse. The subject of the first unit, which extends from 1:5–2:18, is announced at the end of the exordium, or introduction (1:1–4), when the writer affirms that the Son is superior to the angels (v 4). In 1:5–14 the superiority of Jesus to the angels who mediated the message of the Law (2:2) is documented by repeated reference to biblical statements. This section serves to prepare the readers for an earnest admonition to respect the authority of the redemptive word delivered through the Son (2:1–4). The comparison between Jesus and the angels is sustained in 2:5–16, where it is demonstrated that Jesus' condescension to be made "lower than the angels" (2:9) does not call into question his transcendent dignity. His incarnation (2:5–9) and solidarity with the human family (2:10–18) were necessary for the achievement of redemption. With the statement of 2:16 ("for surely it is not angels he helps"), angels are mentioned for the last time, apart from two incidental references near the end of the discourse (12:22; 13:2). The writer is prepared to lead his readers in a new direction, and in 2:17–18 he announces the subject to be developed in the next major unit of the presentation (Vanhoye, *SE* 2 [1964] 496–97).

Within the framework established by the formal announcement of the subject, the writer provides other literary indications that disclose the structure of his thinking. He makes use of the literary device of an *inclusio*, the introduction of the same expression or phrase at the opening and at the close of a paragraph of integrated thought. In the initial segment of his address two examples of this rhetorical procedure may be observed. The first serves to identify 1:5–14 as a unified paragraph:

> 1:5   "To which of the angels did God ever say . . . ?"
> 1:13   "To which of the angels has God ever said . . . ?"

The second *inclusio* establishes the limits of the development in 2:5–16:

> 2:5   "For it is not to angels that he has subjected the world to come."
> 2:16   "For surely it is not angels that he helps."

Since the function of 2:17–18 is to announce the subject of the next major division, these verses stand outside the *inclusio*. Nevertheless, on the basis of the writer's rhetorical procedure, 1:5–14, 2:1–4, and 2:5–18 may be identified as separate but related paragraphs within the first major division of the address.

Relationship between the several paragraphs may be established by *catchword association.* At the beginning of a new paragraph, a word or expression may be repeated from the close of the preceding paragraph (Vaganay, "Le plan," 269–77). The initial presentation of the writer's argument (1:5–14), for example, is tied to the exordium (1:1–4) by reference to *the angels:*

> 1:4   "So he became so much superior to *the angels* [τῶν ἀγγέλων]."
> 1:5   "For to which of *the angels* [τῶν ἀγγέλων] did God ever say . . . ?"

The two paragraphs are linked together by the repetition of the expression. As a result, the transition from assertion to demonstration is achieved smoothly.

Another literary device that serves to identify the limits of a larger unit of thought is *the repetition of characteristic terms.* This technique gives to a section a recognizable character that is altered only when the writer is prepared to introduce another section of his argument. In the opening segment of the discourse the characteristic term is *angels;* ten of the twelve occurrences of this term are concentrated in 1:1–2:18. The introduction of other characteristic terms after 2:16 serves to alert the readers that another line of thought is being introduced in 2:17–18.

These literary procedures are not incidental to the conceptual development in Hebrews. They were conventional techniques of composition upon which the writer could rely for identifying the course of his argument. They are used consistently throughout the document and furnish an invaluable support to the exegetical study of the text.

Other stylistic devices are employed to emphasize the writer's pastoral concern for his readers. Attention is arrested and interest is sustained by the alternation between two types of discourse: exposition and admonition (see especially Gyllenberg, *SEÅ* 22–23 [1957–58] 137–47). The initial segment of this address consists of two paragraphs of exposition (1:5–14 and 2:5–18) that are separated from each other by a paragraph of solemn exhortation (2:1–4).

On the basis of these formal rhetorical procedures, the theme of the first major division of Hebrews can be identified as the revelation of God through his Son. The writer first demonstrates the relationship of the divine Son to the God who speaks. The characterization of God as the one who has intervened in human history with his spoken word is the prelude to the characterization of the divine Son as the one through whom God has spoken his ultimate word (1:1–4) exposes the peril of ignoring the word of redemption delivered by the Son (2:1–4). The recital of the Scriptures that confirm the transcendent dignity of the Son (1:5–14). The writer then exhibits the solidarity of the Son with those who have been addressed by God (2:5–18). He considers the humiliation and glory of the Son (2:5–9) and affirms the appropriateness of his identification with suffering humanity oppressed by the fear of death (2:10–18). The first major division thus serves as a foundational statement for the body of the sermon that follows, which reaches its climax in the pointed appeal, "See that you do not refuse the one who is speaking" (12:25).

A. God Has Spoken His Ultimate Word in His Son (1:1–4)

Bibliography

Attridge, H. W. "New Covenant Christology in an Early Christian Homily." *QuartRev* 8 (1988) 89–108. **Black, D. A.** "Hebrews 1:1–4: A Study in Discourse Analysis." *WTJ* 49 (1987) 175–99. **Bornkamm, G.** "Das Bekenntnis im Hebräerbrief." In *Studien zu Antike und*

Urchristentum: Gesammelte Aufsätze. Vol. 2 Munich: C. Kaiser, 1963. 188–203. [Reprinted from *ThBl* 21 (1942) 56–66.] **Bovon, F.** "Le Christ, la foi, et la sagesse dans l'Épître aux Hébreux (Hébreux 11 et 1)." *RTP* 18 (1968) 129–44. **Charles, J. D.** "The Angels, Sonship and Birthright in the Letter to the Hebrews." *JETS* 33 (1990) 171–78. **Cockerill, G. L.** "Heb 1:1–14, *1 Clem.* 36:1–6 and the High Priest Title." *JBL* 97 (1978) 437–40. **Dey, L. K. K.** *The Intermediary World and Patterns of Perfection in Philo and Hebrews.* SBLDS 25. Missoula, MT: Scholars, 1975. **Ellingworth, P.** "Paul, Hebrews and 1 Clement: Literary Dependence or Common Tradition?" *BZ* n.s. 23 (1979) 262–69. ———. "Jesus and the Universe in Hebrews." *EvQ* 58 (1986) 337–50. **Frankowski, J.** "Early Christian Hymns Recorded in the New Testament: A Reconsideration of the Question in the Light of Heb 1,3." *BZ* 27 (1983) 183–94. **Garuti, P.** "Il prologo della lettera agli Ebrei (Eb 1,1–4)." *SacDoc* 34 (1989) 533–56. **Gayford, S. C.** "The Aorist Participles in Heb 1:3; 7:27; 10:12." *Th* 7 (1923) 282. **Grässer, E.** "Hebräer 1, 1–4: Ein exegetischer Versuch." In *Text und Situation: Gesammelte Aufsätze zum Neuen Testament.* Gütersloh: Mohn, 1973. 182–228. **Gray, W.** "Wisdom Christology in the New Testament: Its Scope and Relevance." *Th* 89 (1986) 448–59. **Hamerton-Kelly, R. G.** *Pre-Existence, Wisdom, and the Son of Man.* SNTSMS 21. Cambridge: Cambridge UP, 1973. 243–58. **Hay, D. M.** *Glory at the Right Hand: Psalm 110 in Early Christianity.* SBLMS 18. Nashville: Abingdon, 1973. **Helyer, L. R.** "Arius Revisited: The Firstborn Over All Creation (Col 1:15)." *JETS* 31 (1988) 59–67. **Hurst, L. D.** "The Christology of Hebrews 1 and 2." In *The Glory of Christ in the New Testament.* FS G. B. Caird. Ed. L. D. Hurst and N. T. Wright. Oxford: Clarendon Press, 1987, 151–64. **Koops, R.** "Chains of Contrasts in Hebrews 1." *BT* 34 (1983) 220–25. **Körte, A.** "XAPAKTHP." *Hermes* 64 (1929) 69–86. **Lane, W. L.** "Detecting Divine Wisdom Christology in Hebrews 1:1–4." *NTStud* 5 (1982) 150–58. **Laub, F.** *Bekenntnis und Auslegung.* 14–27. **Loader, W. R. G.** "Christ at the Right Hand—Ps. CX.1 in the New Testament." *NTS* 24 (1977–78) 199–217. **McNicol, A. J.** "The Relationship of the Image of the Highest Angel to the High Priest Concept in Hebrews." Dissertation, Vanderbilt University, 1974. 1–38, 204–8, 212–17. **Meier, J. P.** "Structure and Theology in Hebrews 1,1–14." *Bib* 66 (1985) 168–89. **Normandy, R.** "Hebrews 1:1–2 and the Parable of the Wicked Husbandmen." *ExpTim* 100 (1989) 371–75. **Parsons, M. C.** "Son and High Priest: A Study in the Christology of Hebrews." *EvQ* 60 (1988) 195–215. **Pillai, C. A. J.** "In Many and Various Ways." *TBT* 21 (1965) 1385–89. **Robinson, D. W. B.** "The Literary Structure of Hebrews 1:1–4." *AJBA* 2 (1972) 178–86. **Sahlin, H.** "Adam-Christologie im Neuen Testament." *ST* 41 (1987) 11–32. **Sanders, J. T.** *The New Testament Christological Hymns.* SNTSMS 15. Cambridge: Cambridge UP, 1971. **Tetley, J.** "The Priesthood of Christ in Hebrews." *Anvil* 5 (1988) 195–206. **Übelacker, W. G.** *Der Hebräerbrief als Appell: Untersuchungen zu exordium, narratio und postscriptum (Hebr 1–2 und 13,22–25).* Stockholm: Almqvist & Wiksell, 1989. 66–138. **Ulrichsen, J.** "Διαφορώτερον ὄνομα in Hebr. 1,4. Christus als Träger des Gottesnamens." *ST* 38 (1984) 65–75. **Vanhoye, A.** "Christologia a qua initium sumit epistula ad Hebraeos (Hebr 1, 2b, 3, 4)." *VD* 43 (1965) 3–14, 49–61, 113–23. ———. *Exegesis Epistulae ad Hebraeos Cap. I-II.* Rome: Pontifical Biblical Institute, 1968. 7–14, 25–76. ———. *Situation du Christ: Hébreux 1–2.* Paris: Cerf, 1969. 9–17, 51–117. **Vitti, A. M.** "'Quem constituit heredem universorum, per quem fecit et saecula' (Hebr. 1,2)." *VD* 21 (1941) 40–48. **Welander, D. C. S. V.** "Hebrews 1:1–3." *ExpTim* 65 (1954) 315. **Williamson, R.** "The Incarnation of the Logos in Hebrews." *ExpTim* 95 (1983–84) 4–8. ———. *Philo and the Epistle to the Hebrews.* Leiden: Brill, 1970.

Translation

[1] *In the past God spoke to the fathers at various times and in many ways through the prophets,* [2] *but in this final age* [a] *he has spoken to us by his Son,* [b] *whom he appointed heir of everything, and who yet* [c] *is the one through whom he created the world.* [d] [3] *This Son,* [e]

although the radiance of God's glory and the exact representation of his nature, and although sustaining the universe by his powerful word, yet made purification[f] for sins and then sat down at the right hand of the divine Majesty on high, [4]*having been exalted as far above the angels as the name[g] which he has inherited is superior to theirs.*

Notes

[a] The expression ἐπ' ἐσχάτου τῶν ἡμερῶν is a common Septuagintal idiom, where ἐπ' ἐσχάτου is equivalent to the simple dative, "in these final days." This idiom is the first indication that the writer's expression is profoundly colored by the language of the LXX. Cf. Turner, *Grammar*, 4: 109–10.

[b] The noun is anarthrous (ἐν υἱῷ), drawing attention to the essential character of the one who is Son, in contrast to *the prophets* (τοῖς προφήταις).

[c] Giving καί its adversative effect (with D. W. B. Robinson, *AJBA* 2 [1972] 183, 185).

[d] Following the Heb. pattern of the LXX, the pl αἰῶνας is used in the sense of "world." Cf. BDF §§4(2), 141(1).

[e] The subj of vv 1–2 is *God* (ὁ θεὸς . . . ἐλάλησεν), but the subj of vv 3–4 is *the Son*, represented by the relative pronoun (ὅς . . . ἐκάθισεν). Although the second half of the exordium is syntactically dependent upon the first, since it is introduced with a relative, it is appropriate to express the change in subj in the translation. The three terms descriptive of the Son in v 3 are attached to present ptcps (ὢν . . . φέρων τε), which are to be understood as adv ptcps of concession. They refer to facts that are unfavorable to the occurrence of the event denoted by the main assertion, expressed with an aor ind (ἐκάθισεν, "sat down") and a contingent aor ptcp (καθαρισμὸν . . . ποιησάμενος, "having made purification"). See Burton, *Moods*, 170; Moule, *Idiom-Book*, 102; and D. W. B. Robinson, *AJBA* 2 (1972) 183–84.

[f] Zuntz (*Text*, 43–45, 285), appealing to textual, theological, and stylistic considerations, argued strongly for the originality of the reading δι' ἑαυτοῦ καθαρισμόν (p[46] D[gr*] 236 263 1739). He translated "through himself he has effected the purification of sins," and found in the assertion an anticipation of the major argument that the Son made himself the purifying sacrifice. It seems probable, however, that δι' αὐτοῦ or δι' ἑαυτοῦ was added to the text to clarify the meaning of the ambiguous middle voice in ποιησάμενος. The phrase is omitted in good representatives of the Alexandrian text (ℵ A B 33 81) as well as in Western witnesses (it vg). Cf. Metzger, *Textual Commentary*, 662.

[g] By placing ἀγγέλων and ὄνομα in an emphatic position, the contrast between the angels and the Son is emphasized (BDF § 473[2]). ὄνομα was placed in the final position in the Gk. text because it forms a link with the following clause (in v 5).

Form/Structure/Setting

Hebrews has a rhetorical and literary flavor that distinguishes it from any other document in the NT canon. The composition of its words and sentences serves to identify the work as artistic prose (BDF §§464, 486–87). Its distinctive character is evident already in the opening statement, which is a long and contrived period (BDF §464, for a grammatical analysis of 1:1–4). The periodic sentence demanded the organization of a number of clauses and phrases into awell-balanced unity and is characteristic of artistically developed prose (cf. Aristotle, *Rhetoric* 3.9, 1409a). Such stylistic elegance is rare in the NT but appears in Hebrews with relative frequency (e.g., 1:1–4; 2:2–4, 14–15; 3:12–15; 4:12–13; 5:1–3, 7–10; et al.). The opening four verses exhibit the style of a scholar whose expression is polished. His education is reflected in his observance of the canons of rhetorical prose recommended by Isocrates (cf. Moffatt, lvi–lix; Turner, *Grammar*, 4:106–8). These include a developed sense of rhythm, the variation of meter, and the cultivation of those elements of a literary style that command the attention of the ear when read aloud:

> Alliteration (five words beginning with the letter π (p) in v 1: πολυμερῶς, πολυτρόπως, πάλαι, πατράσιν, προφήταις);
> variation of word order (the insertion of material between the adjective and noun in v 4: κρείττων γενόμενος τῶν ἀγγέλων... διαφορώτερον παρ' αὐτοὺς κεκληρονόμηκεν ὄνομα);
> parallelism of sound (v 3: τῆς ὑποστάσεως αὐτοῦ... τῆς δυνάμεως αὐτοῦ);
> parallelism of sense (v 1: πάλαι ὁ θεὸς λαλήσας τοῖς πατράσιν ἐν τοῖς προφήταις to which corresponds ἐπ' ἐσχάτου τῶν ἡμερῶν τούτων ἐλάλησεν ἡμῖν ἐν υἱῷ).

The writer has cultivated the instincts of an orator, which are now brought into the service of preaching.

The literary structure of the exordium exhibits a concentric symmetry (A B C C' B'A'): the conceptual correspondence of vv 1 and 4 serves to frame the several statements concerning the Son in vv 2 and 3 (see the diagram following). The period begins and ends by asserting the ultimate significance of the revelation through the Son. The completion of the prophetic revelation with the word spoken through the Son and the superiority of his name to the rank and titles of the angels are parallel concepts. The revelation of God in the OT may be described by referring to the human messengers (the prophets) or the divine messengers (the angels) who delivered God's word. Consequently, the reference to the angels in the comparison developed in v 4 is not as abrupt as it might appear to someone unfamiliar with the prominent role assigned to angelic intermediaries in early Jewish and Christian conceptions of revelation (cf. Michl, "Engel," *RAC* 5 [1960] 59–110). The allusion to revelation through the prophets in v 1 is appropriately balanced by the reference to the angels in v 4.

The central core of the paragraph is developed within this conceptual frame. It consists of a series of skillfully arranged affirmations concerning the Son. The series begins with a predication based upon Ps 2 ("whom he appointed heir of everything"; cf. Ps 2:8) and concludes with one derived from Ps 110 ("he sat down at the right hand . . . "; cf. Ps 110:1). In each instance the source of the declaration concerning the Son is a coronation psalm celebrating the enthronement of a royal figure. The intervening affirmations consist of predications familiar from Jewish wisdom literature, which exalts divine Wisdom as the agent of creation, revelation, and reconciliation (e.g., Wis 7:21–27; 9:2). The first of these statements (v 2c, "through whom he made the world") is separated from those which follow by the change of subject in v 3. D. W. B. Robinson (*AJBA* 2 [1972] 182–84) has shown that this arrangement serves to establish two striking equations: (1) the royal Son of Ps 2 is identified as divine Wisdom, the agent of creation (v 2b–c); (2) divine Wisdom, the representative of God in the world and sustainer of creation, is identified as the royal Priest of Ps 110 (v 3a–b–c).

The chiastic pattern of thought within the central core (B C C' B') may be set within the framing reference to the old dispensation (A A') to exhibit the concentric symmetry of the period:

A   ὁ θεὸς λαλήσας... ἐν τοῖς προφήταις... ἐλάλησεν... ἐν υἱῷ   (1–2a)
     "God spoke to the fathers . . . through the prophets . . . he has spoken . . . by his Son"

B   ὃν ἔθηκεν κληρονόμον πάντων   (2b)
     "Whom he appointed heir of everything"
  C   δι' οὗ καὶ ἐποίησεν τοὺς αἰῶνας   (2c)
      "and who yet is the one through whom he created the world"
  C' ὃς ὢν ἀπαύγασμα ... καὶ χαρακτὴρ ... φέρων τε τὰ πάντα   (3a–b)
      "This Son, although the radiance ... and exact representation
      ... and although sustaining the universe"
  B' καθαρισμὸν ... ποιησάμενος ἐκάθισεν ἐν δεξιᾳ   (3c)
      "yet made purification for sins and then sat down at the
      right hand"
A' τοσούτῳ κρείττων γενόμενος τῶν ἀγγέλων ὅσῳ διαφορώτερον
    παρ' αὐτοὺς κεκληρονόμηκεν ὄνομα.   (4)
    "having been exalted as far above the angels as the name
    which he has inherited is superior to theirs."

The framing statements (A A') enunciate emphatically the theme of supreme
revelation through the Son. The core of the exordium (B C C' B') describes
Jesus in an arresting way as the royal Son, divine Wisdom, and the royal Priest.
    On the basis of earlier suggestions by Lohmeyer and Käsemann, Bornkamm
("Bekenntnis," 197–200) proposed that the source of v 3 was an early Christian
confessional hymn. This critical judgment has been adopted by many subsequent
interpreters (e.g., Schille, *Frühchristliche Hymnen*, 42; Deichgräber, *Gotteshymnus*,
137–38; Sanders, *NT Christological Hymns*, 19–20; Wengst, *Christologische Formeln*,
179, 208). The indebtedness of the formulation to a liturgical form is suggested
by the abrupt change in subject in the middle of the sentence (from *God*, vv 1–2,
to *the Son*, v 3), the preference for an opening relative clause (ὅς), the presence
of participial predications employing substantive participles without the article,
the concentration of rare vocabulary in the first line, the rhythmical style, the
formal parallelism, and the presentation of the Son of God in language that is
exalted and creedal in character. Comparison with other passages, where similar
criteria lead one to expect hymnic material (Phil 2:6–11; Col 1:15–20; 1 Tim
3:16; 1 Pet 3:18–22), suggested to Sanders (19) that the initial ὅς of v 3 signaled
the introduction of the hymn, which was tied originally to a preceding thanksgiving. Bornkamm further suggested that v 4 may in fact rely on a following part
of the confessional hymn, but found in v 2 "no more than an isolated Christ
predication" (198–99).
    In the absence of any collection of early Christian creeds or hymns, the for-
mal criteria proposed for recognizing liturgical fragments are necessarily
inconclusive (see especially the cautions urged by E. Schüssler Fiorenza, "Wisdom
Mythology and the Christological Hymns," in *Aspects of Wisdom in Judaism and Christianity*, ed. R. Wilken [Notre Dame: UP, 1975] 19–20). One detail that Bornkamm
neglected, however, tends to lend a measure of support to his proposal. When
the writer quotes Ps 110:1 in v 13, he follows the Old Greek version in reading the
genitive ἐκ δεξιῶν, but when he alludes to this passage in v 3 he writes the dative ἐν
δεξιᾳ. Moreover, all the other allusions to the session at God's right hand in
Hebrews (8:1; 10:12; 12:2) agree with v 3 in using the dative ἐν δεξιᾳ rather than
the genitive ἐκ δεξιῶν. A probable explanation for this variation is that the allusions
are based on a liturgical confession rather than the text of the psalm (Hay,
Glory, 35, 41).

Nevertheless, only qualified approval can be given to the proposal that the exordium preserves a fragment of a liturgical source. From a literary standpoint, v 3 is not as distinctive in its context as Bornkamm and others have suggested. A disjunction between v 2*b* and v 3 cannot be maintained. The relative pronoun that supposedly indicates the beginning of the hymn in v 3 is actually the third relative in succession that depends upon the antecedent "Son": ὃν ἔθηκεν . . . δι᾽ οὗ καὶ ἐποίησεν . . . ὅς . . . ἐκάθισεν, "whom he appointed . . . through whom he made . . . he who . . . sat down" (vv 2*b*–3). Although it is only in the third relative clause that the Son becomes the subject, and the relative pronoun is cast in the nominative case, the presence of the personal pronoun in the expression χαρακτὴρ τῆς ὑποστάσεως αὐτοῦ, "exact representation of *his* nature," ties v 3 to the antecedent supplied by the opening line of the period, i. e., *God*. Stylistic criteria are insufficient to excise v 2*b* from v 3, and the allusions to Ps 2 and Ps 110 firmly sandwich this unit together (D. W. B. Robinson, *AJBA* 2 [1972] 180, 186; Hay, *Glory*, 41–43). If the source of the description of the Son is a liturgical confession, it must begin with v 2*b*. The fact that the predications concerning the Son have been thoroughly integrated into the structure of the paragraph as a whole, however, tends to make the hypothesis of a source behind vv 2*b*–3 less attractive.

An important clue to the historical setting of Hebrews has sometimes been found in the reference to the angels in v 4, which introduces the developed contrast between Christ and the angels in 1:5–2:16. It has been argued that the writer found it necessary to combat a heretical form of christology that confused Christ with the highest angel in Judaism. An alternative proposal is that the readers were engaged in the erroneous practice of worshiping angels. In either instance it has been held that the intention of v 4, and of Hebrews as a whole, is polemical (see especially McNicol, "Image of the Highest Angel," 1–38).

W. Lueken gave classical expression to the first of these proposals (*Michael* [1898] 30–31, 143–49). He argued that at the time Hebrews was written there was in Judaism a widespread belief that the archangel Michael functioned as a heavenly high priest. The presentation of the exalted Christ on the model of a high priestly angelic figure blurred the contours of his distinctive character and role in the community to which Hebrews was addressed. The writer's intention was to prevent Jesus from being confused with an angelic figure to whom similar functions had been ascribed. A. Bakker carried the discussion further, in the persuasion that the community addressed in Hebrews actually regarded Jesus as an angel ("Was Christ an Angel? A Study of Early Christian Docetism," *ZNW* 32 [1933] 255–65). More recently, Y. Yadin found in the advanced angelology at Qumran additional support for proposing that Hebrews was a polemic directed against Michael speculation (*ScrHier* 4 [1958] 36–55, esp. 39–47; cf. Hamerton-Kelly, *Pre-Existence*, 244–47).

The alternative proposal that v 4 anticipates a polemic against a cult that stressed the worship of angels (W. Lueken, 134–39; Windisch, 17; T. W. Manson, "The Problem," 253–54; Jewett, 5–7, 20–27) draws its strength from purported parallels between Hebrews and Colossians. In fact, Manson suggested that Heb 1–10 was composed as a refutation of the Colossian "heresy."

These approaches to the historical setting of Hebrews are discredited by the document itself. They fail to relate the statements concerning Christ's superiority to the angels to the positive role assigned to the angels in 2:2, and they are refuted by the absence of any polemical statement directed against the angels in Hebrews as a whole. The proper frame of reference for interpreting v 4 is provided by the structural analysis of 1:1–4 and by the reference to the angels as the mediators of the law in 2:1–4.

Comment

The initial paragraph functions as an exordium to the written address that follows. It introduces the theme of the superiority of God's Son to all other previous modes of revelation. This theme receives emphatic expression in the first and last verses, where the revelation delivered by the Son is contrasted with that delivered through men and angels. The writer's perspective is distinctly theocentric; he confronts his readers immediately with the God who intervened in human history with his sovereign word addressed to humankind. His ultimate word, however, was spoken through one who is distinguished from others by reason of the unique relationship he sustains to God. The core of the paragraph, which consists of seven predicates, explores the character of the divine Son in terms of expectations prompted by reflection upon Ps 2 and Ps 110 as well as by contemporary currents of Jewish wisdom theology. The Son unites in his person the attributes and privileges of the royal Son, the Wisdom of God, and the royal Priest. Consequently, he is uniquely qualified to be the one through whom God spoke his final word.

Vanhoye (*La structure*, 65–68) has shown that the effect of the change of subject from *God* to *Son* in the middle of the sentence is to arrange the several clauses of the period into two units, vv 1–2 and vv 3–4. Grammatically, the second unit depends upon the first because it begins with a relative clause. By virtue of its pregnant expression, however, the second unit assumes the dominant position and tends to reduce the initial lines to the role of a preamble. Both units are composed around a central statement, to which the remaining clauses are attached. The center of the first unit is the assertion that "at the end of these days, he has spoken to us in the Son" (v 2a). This proposition is preceded by the solemn and stately beginning of the period, with its focus on the revelation through the prophets (v 1), and is followed by two relative clauses that succinctly qualify the status and character of the Son (v 2b-c). At the center of vv 3–4 stands the proposition, "having made purification for sins, he sat down at the right hand of the divine majesty on high" (v 3c). This declaration summarizes the redemptive accomplishment of the Son and his subsequent exaltation at its completion. It is harmoniously balanced by two coordinating phrases introduced by present participles ($\overset{\,\,\circ}{\omega}\nu$ . . . $\phi\acute{\epsilon}\rho\omega\nu$ $\tau\epsilon$) that effectively suggest the transcendent dignity of the Son on one side and by two correlative members of a comparison which assert his excellence on the other side. The two units of the period have been artistically unified so that the first concludes with the word $\upsilon\grave{\iota}\widehat{\omega}$, "Son," which in turn prepares for the second unit, which concludes with the corresponding noun $\overset{\,\,{\prime}}{o}\nu o\mu a$, "name."

1a πολυμερῶς καὶ πολυτρόπως, "at various times and in many ways." Although the use of alliterative combinations of πολυ- words in rhetorical openings was a common practice in this period (Moffatt, 2), the initial adverbial phrase in Hebrews is more than a literary convention. These πολυ- compounds express in an emphatic way the writer's conviction concerning the extent of the OT revelation. He surveys the revelation granted through the prophets in its variety and fullness but implies that until the coming of the Son the revelation of God remained incomplete.

Both compounds occur only here in the NT, and it has been asserted that they betray an indebtedness to Philo (e.g., Spicq, 1:46). Although Philo does have a fondness for πολυ- compounds and for alliteration involving πολυ- words, the particular combination found in 1:1 never occurs in his writings. There is, in fact, nothing in the Philonic corpus corresponding to this sonorous description of the OT revelation as manifold and varied. No evidence exists that the writer to the Hebrews was influenced in his choice of expression or its application by anything he found in Philo (Williamson, *Philo*, 70–74, 133–34).

1b–2a The contrast implied by the temporal references to past time (πάλαι) and to the present marked by the utterance of God's decisive and climactic word (ἐπ' ἐσχάτου τῶν ἡμερῶν τούτων, "this final age") expresses the classic Jewish and primitive Christian conception of the succession of two ages in the course of redemptive history. The characterization of the present time as "this final age" is qualitative and indicative of the dominant eschatological orientation of the writer's thought. He is persuaded that certain decisive events have already taken place marking the fulfillment of the promise and foreshadowing of the OT Scriptures, and that certain other decisive and final events will yet occur. Apocalyptic eschatology provided him the categories with which to interpret the entire history of God's redemptive action (Klappert, *Eschatologie*, 11–61; on the fundamental difference between Philo and Hebrews on the subjects of time and history, see Williamson, *Philo*, 142–59). The distinctly Christian perspective reflected in the opening lines of Hebrews is thrown into bold relief when the writer's statement is compared with the temporal contrast developed by a contemporary, who viewed the destruction of Jerusalem in A.D. 70 from a Jewish apocalyptic point of view: "In former times, even in the generations of old, our fathers had helpers, righteous men and holy prophets . . . . But now the righteous have been gathered, and the prophets have fallen asleep. We also have gone forth from the land, and Zion has been taken from us, and we have nothing now except the Mighty One and his law" (*2 Apoc. Bar.* 81:1, 3).

ἐπ' ἐσχάτου τῶν ἡμερῶν is a Septuagintal expression that translates a Semitic temporal idiom for the future as distinct from the past (Num 24:14; Jer 23:20; 25:19; 49:39; Dan 10:14). The meaning of ἔσχατος in hellenistic-Jewish literature, however, especially in eschatological contexts, so colored the expression that it came to possess technical significance (G. W. Buchanan, "Eschatology and the 'End of Days,'" *JNES* 20 [1961] 188–93). The interpretation of the expression in Hebrews is determined by the reference to God's utterance through the prophets in v 1. During the hellenistic-Roman period the conviction became widespread that the prophetic message to Israel was concerned with eschatology. This conception can now be attested for the pre-Christian period in a collection of biblical texts from Qumran (4QFlor 1:15, "as it is written in the book of Isaiah the prophet concerning the latter days," followed by a citation of Isa 8:11; cf. Sir 48:24–25). The force of the expression in Hebrews is to characterize the Son as the one through whom God spoke his final and decisive word.

The temporal idioms qualify the central affirmation that God has spoken. The conviction that God cares for people and relates himself to them through his spoken word is developed as a major motif by the writer. In the opening lines he concentrates his hearers' attention on the authority of the God who speaks. The locus of God's spoken word for him was the Scriptures. He customarily introduces passages from the OT as God's direct speech (e.g., 1:5–13; 5:5–6; 7:17, 21). The persuasion that God's word is living and active in human experience (4:12) undergirds the appeal to the authority of the Scriptures throughout Hebrews and prepares the hearers for the solemn exhortation not to refuse the God who is speaking (12:25) at the conclusion of the sermon. Although the instrumental dative ἐν υἱῷ ("God spoke . . . by his Son") would encourage the interpretation of the phrase ἐν τοῖς προφήταις in an instrumental sense ("through the prophets"), it is possible that the phrase may actually refer to the OT Scriptures (as in Luke 24:25; John 6:45; so BAGD, 723).

God's continuing disclosure of himself found its ultimate expression in the revelation through the Son. The complementary phrases "God spoke" ἐν τοῖς προφήταις . . . ἐν υἱῷ, "through the prophets . . . by the Son," establish that the revelation of God in Jesus Christ can be understood only within the context of God's revelation to Israel. The OT witness actually foreshadowed the utterance of God's decisive and climactic word. The fragmentary and varied character of God's self-disclosure under the old covenant awakened within the fathers an expectation that he would continue to speak to his people. Those who are the sons of the fathers understand that the word spoken through the Son constituted an extension of a specific history marked by divine revelation. The ministry of the prophets marked the preparatory phase of that history.

The form of the statement in vv 1b–2a implies both continuity and discontinuity in the divine self-disclosure. The element of continuity is asserted in the clauses expressing the event of God's speaking (ὁ θεὸς λαλήσας τοῖς πατράσιν. . . ἐλάλησεν ἡμῖν, "God having spoken to the fathers . . . he spoke to us"); discontinuity is expressed in the contrast between revelation *through the prophets* and revelation *through the Son.* The anarthrous ἐν υἱῷ is qualitative. The eternal, essential quality of Jesus' sonship qualified him to be the one through whom God uttered his final word. The antithesis in the two phases of revelation lies in the distinction between the prophets who were men and the Son who enjoys a unique relationship to God. In 7:28 a similar distinction is made between high priests who were men and the one who is the Son.

What God said through the Son clarified the intention of the word spoken to the fathers. From this perspective, the recent revelation in the Son is viewed as fulfillment (although the distinctive vocabulary of fulfillment, πληρόω/πλήρωμα, never occurs in the address).

2b The reference to the Son introduces the core of the paragraph, which extends to the end of v 3. At this point the writer may have introduced a fragment of an early liturgical tradition. If this actually is the case, the tradition celebrating Christ's dignity as mediator and heir has been thoroughly integrated into the structure of the paragraph as a whole. Within a frame established by allusions to the royal Son of Ps 2 (v 2*b*) and to the royal Priest of Ps 110 (v 3*c*), the Son's role in creation, revelation, and redemption is recited in creedal fashion.

ὃν ἔθηκεν κληρονόμον πάντων, "whom he appointed heir of everything." The Son has been installed as heir. The clause contains a clear allusion to Ps 2:8, where the royal Son is assured that in response to his petition the sovereign Lord will give him the nations (ἔθνη) as his inheritance (τὴν κληρονομίαν). H. Langkammer ("'Den er zum Erben von allem *eingesetz* hat' [Hebr 1, 2]," *BZ* 10 [1966] 273–80) observed the literary similarity between the statement in Hebrews and Gen 17:5, where the investiture of Abraham as heir marks the beginning of redemptive history. On that occasion Abram received a new name (cf. Heb 1:4) and the solemn assurance "I have appointed [τέθεικα] you the father of many nations [ἐθνῶν]." In Hebrews the Son is invested as the universal heir of all creation (not merely of all the nations, as in Gen 17:5 and Ps 2:8). The formal similarity between these passages suggests that the writer, or the liturgical tradition upon which he drew, made use of the OT motif of the investiture of the heir in order to connect the beginning of redemptive history with its accomplishment in the Son.

δι' οὗ καὶ ἐποίησεν τοὺς αἰῶνας, "who yet is the one through whom he created the world." The force of the καί is to link this second relative clause to the first, possibly in an adversative sense: the Son was appointed heir, and yet he was the one through whom God created the world. This clause and those which immediately follow belong to a class of statements descriptive of divine Wisdom in the theology of Alexandrian Judaism (cf. Mack, *Logos*, 1973). As a hellenistic Jew, the writer was thoroughly familiar with the teaching concerning the Wisdom of God now preserved in the OT and in such later documents as the Wisdom of Solomon. The antecedents of his christology are recoverable in the wisdom writings of Judaism. Reflection on the Wisdom of God in Alexandrian theology provided him with categories and vocabulary with which to intrepret the person and work of Christ. Although Jesus is introduced as the divine Son (v 2*a*), the functions attributed to him are those of the Wisdom of God: he is the mediator of revelation, the agent and sustainer of creation, and the reconciler of others to God. Each of these christological affirmations echoes declarations concerning the role of divine Wisdom in the Wisdom of Solomon (cf. Wis 7:21–27). Once the categories of divine Wisdom were applied to Jesus, his association with the creative activity of God was strengthened (cf. Prov 8:22–31; Wis 7:22; 9:2, 9). The conviction that Jesus was the pre-existent Son of God encouraged the identification of him as the one through whom God created the world. Conversely, since Jesus was the one through whom God created the world, he must be the pre-existent Son of God.

The second unit of the period (vv 3–4) develops the three predications introduced at the end of the first unit, i.e., revelation through the Son (v 2*a*), his status as heir (v 2*b*), and his role in the creation (v 2*c*). The order in which these elements are taken up is the logical one of Son (v 3*a*), creation (v 3*b*), and inheritance (v 4).

3a ὃς ὢν ἀπαύγασμα . . . καὶ χαρακτήρ, "the one who is the radiance . . . and the exact representation." The subject of the statements that follow in vv 3–4 is "the Son." This is indicated by the relative pronoun in the nominative case. In the first declaration the arrangement of the two members of the first clause in synonymous parallelism is intentional. They are meant to say the same thing. Wilckens has observed that "as δόξα and ὑπόστασις are synonymous to the degree that God's glory is his nature, so the same function of the Son is expressed by ἀπαύγασμα and χαρακτήρ" (*TDNT* 9:421). The concentration of rare and distinctive vocabulary to describe the relationship of the Son to God has been one factor that has encouraged many interpreters to find in v 3 a hymn-fragment. ἀπαύγασμα is found nowhere else in the NT and is relatively rare elsewhere. It occurs only once in the LXX, in the context of celebrating the praise of divine Wisdom: Wisdom is "the radiance [ἀπαύγασμα] from everlasting light . . . and the image [εἰκών] of God's goodness" (Wis 7:26). The writer appears to have borrowed a word employed in the LXX to describe the relationship between Wisdom and the eternal, divine light. He used it in v 3 because it seemed an appropriate term to express the relationship he believed existed between God and the Son. The Son is "the radiance of God's glory."

The term χαρακτήρ occurs only here in the NT. It is found three times in the LXX, but in a nontechnical sense (Lev 13:28; 2 Macc 4:10; 4 Macc 15:4; cf. *T. Sim.* 5:5). Philo shows a strong preference for this term, which occurs fifty-one times in his works with a variety of associated meanings. He applies it frequently to man, whose soul bears the imprint (χαρακτήρ) of God (*Allegorical Interpretation* 3.95; *On the Virtues* 52; *The Worse Attacks the Better* 83). But if the soul may be compared to the image of the invisible God bearing the engraving of the divine seal, the stamp of that seal is the eternal Logos (ἧς ὁ χαρακτήρ ἐστιν ὁ ἀΐδιος λόγος; *On Noah's Work as a Planter* 18). It is imperative, however, not to exaggerate the importance of such alleged "parallels" to the expression in v 3. In his work *On the Unchangeableness of God* (55), Philo states that God's being is "simple" (ψιλὴν τὴν ὕπαρξιν), "without other definite characteristic" (ἄνευ χαρακτῆρος). This means that God's nature is such that nothing, and presumably no one, can be said to be *an exact representation of his nature* (χαρακτὴρ τῆς ὑποστάσεως αὐτοῦ). Yet this is precisely what the writer to the Hebrews declares concerning the Son.

The writer may have become familiar with the terms like ἀπαύγασμα and χαρακτήρ from an Alexandrian education, but he has brought this distinctive vocabulary into the service of Christian confession. In v 3*a* he used the word χαρακτήρ to convey as emphatically as he could his conviction that in Jesus Christ there had been provided a perfect, visible expression of the reality of God. If the formulation of v 3*a* owes something to the vocabulary and concepts of Alexandrian Judaism, it has been thoroughly assimilated and refashioned by a distinctly Christian thinker (cf. Williamson, *Philo,* 74–80).

The description of Jesus as ἀπαύγασμα is repeated in *1 Clement* in a paragraph that looks like a patchwork of phrases culled from Heb 1. The remarkable fact is that the entire statement has been made subservient to Jesus' divine priesthood:

This is the way, beloved, in which we found our salvation, Jesus Christ, the high priest [ἀρχιερεύς] of our offerings, the defender and helper of our weaknesses . . . who being the radiance of his majesty [ὃς ὢν ἀπαύγασμα τῆς μεγαλωσύνης αὐτοῦ] is so much greater than the angels as he has inherited a more excellent name. For it is written . . .

[Ps 104:4]. But of his Son the Master said . . . [Ps 2:7]. And again he says to him . . .
[Ps 110:1] (*1 Clem.* 36.1–6).

On the basis of this passage Theissen (*Untersuchung*, 33–38) has argued that Heb
1:1–14 and *1 Clem.* 36.1–6 reflect independent drawings upon a common liturgical tradition that already designated Jesus as high priest. He sought to prove that
the primitive form of the liturgy is reproduced more faithfully in *1 Clement*, which
retains the ἀρχιερεύς, "high priest," title in 36.1.

Cockerill (*JBL* 97 [1978] 437–40) has shown, however, that this thesis cannot
be sustained. When Clement quotes Ps 110:1 as a direct address of God to the
Son (as in Heb 1:13), he betrays his dependence upon Hebrews for his formula
of introduction. This manner of introducing OT quotations is typical of Hebrews
(1:5–13; 5:5–6; 7:17, 21) but occurs only here in *1 Clement*. Moreover, the designation "Son," not "high priest," is more appropriate to the chain of OT citations
found in *1 Clem.* 36.3–5 and in Heb 1:5–13. Finally, the sustained concern of the
writer to the Hebrews to demonstrate that the divine Son is also high priest is
difficult to understand if this connection had already been established in the
tradition. It seems far more logical to assume that the tradition referred to Jesus
as the pre-existent Son, and that on the basis of the presentation of the Son as
high priest in Hebrews the author of *1 Clement* was able to associate his paraphrase of Heb 1 with the ἀρχιερεύς title (cf. M. Mees, "Die Hohepriester-
Theologie des Hebräerbriefes im Vergleich mit dem ersten Clemensbrief," *BZ*
22 [1978] 115–24). Clement's description of Jesus as "the radiance of the divine
majesty" (36.2) simply compresses into a pregnant statement the substance of
Heb 1:3 (ὃς ὢν ἀπαύγασμα . . . ἐκάθισεν ἐν δεξιᾷ τῆς μεγαλωσύνης, "[he],
although the radiance, . . . sat down at the right hand of the divine Majesty").

3b φέρων τε τὰ πάντα τῷ ῥήματι τῆς δυνάμεως αὐτοῦ, "although sustaining the universe by his powerful word." The description of the Son in his
pre-existence is followed logically by a clause descriptive of his relationship to the
creation. The new clause ascribes to the Son the providential government of
all created existence, which is the function of God himself. As the pre-creational
Wisdom of God, the Son not only embodies God's glory but also reveals this to
the universe as he sustains all things and bears them to their appointed end by
his omnipotent word. The ascription of cosmic dimensions to the work of the
Son was prompted by the total estimate which the writer had formed of his
transcendent dignity. One who revealed God as fully and ultimately as did the
Son must share in the divine government of the world (cf. Williamson, *Philo*, 95–
103). Like the previous phrase, the formulation in v 3*b* may be derived from
Wis 7, where v 27 states that although Wisdom "is but one, she has power to do all
things, and while remaining in herself, she renews all things." Wis 8:1 adds:
"She reaches mightily from one end of the earth to the other, and she orders all
things well." The transcendent dignity of the Son is confessed in Heb 1:3 in
language similar to that used in the praise of divine Wisdom in Alexandrian
theology.

3c καθαρισμὸν τῶν ἁμαρτιῶν ποιησάμενος, "yet made purification for sins."
The confession in v 3 surveys Christ's person and worth in his pre-existence, incarnation, and exaltation. Although his pre-existence has been described in
categories borrowed from the wisdom tradition, that tradition is sharply modi-

fied by the introduction of this participial clause. The reconciling activity of divine Wisdom was fundamentally educative (Wis 7:27; 9:9). There is no association of divine Wisdom with sacrifice in order to procure cleansing from sins (cf. Bovon, *RTP* 18 [1968] 143). The source of this solitary reference to the accomplishment of Jesus' earthly life in the exordium is thus not the wisdom tradition but reflection on the incarnation and the cross.

It is significant that the Son's ministry is described from the first in distinctly cultic categories. This brief, unadorned reference to Jesus' achievement is slanted in the direction of the later discussion of his priesthood and sacrifice. The effect of Christ's death is cleansing ($\kappa\alpha\theta\alpha\rho\iota\sigma\mu\acute{o}\nu$) from sins. Here sin is viewed as defilement which must be purged. This understanding has its roots in the LXX, where $\kappa\alpha\theta\alpha\rho\acute{\iota}\zeta\epsilon\iota\nu$ and its cognates relate to the removal of the defilement of sin, either in association with the altar (cf. Exod 29:37; 30:10; Lev 16:19) or the people (Lev 16:30). The uncleanness of the people of Israel was acknowledged before the Lord at the altar, and it was from this defilement that they had to be cleansed by the sprinkling of the blood of the sacrificial animal. The blood covered and obliterated the sins upon the altar (cf. Exod 30:10: $\kappa\alpha\theta\alpha\rho\iota\sigma\mu\acute{o}s$). The purification of the people was similarly achieved by blood in an act of expiation (cf. Lev 16:30). Purity is the essential condition for participation in the cultic life. The defilement of sin erects a barrier to the approach to God which must be removed (cf. Meeter, *Heavenly High Priesthood*, 155–57). That the writer to the Hebrews draws upon this conceptual framework for interpreting the death of Christ is confirmed by chaps. 9 and 10, where the categories of defilement and purgation are foundational to the argumentation. It is significant that the other six occurrences of $\kappa\alpha\theta\alpha\rho\acute{\iota}\zeta\epsilon\iota\nu$ and its cognates appear in these chapters (9:13, 14, 22, 23; 10:2, 22).

In the Old Greek version of Job 7:21, the patriarch objects, "Why do you not forget my offense and make cleansing for my sin?" ($\dot{\epsilon}\pi o\iota\acute{\eta}\sigma\omega \ldots \kappa\alpha\theta\alpha\rho\iota\sigma\mu\grave{o}\nu \ \tau\hat{\eta}s \ \dot{\alpha}\mu\alpha\rho\tau\acute{\iota}\alpha s \ \mu o\upsilon$). Perhaps with this formulation in mind, the writer states succinctly $\kappa\alpha\theta\alpha\rho\iota\sigma\mu\grave{o}\nu \ \tau\hat{\omega}\nu \ \dot{\alpha}\mu\alpha\rho\tau\iota\hat{\omega}\nu \ \pi o\iota\eta\sigma\acute{\alpha}\mu\epsilon\nu os$, "having made cleansing for sins." The aorist participle designates the purification as a definite act performed once for all. The middle voice indicates that the Son made purification for sins *in himself*, clearly relating the act of purification to his sacrifice. By that one action, the defilement of sins was removed forever. The genitive $\tau\hat{\omega}\nu \ \dot{\alpha}\mu\alpha\rho\tau\iota\hat{\omega}\nu \ \pi o\iota\eta\sigma\acute{\alpha}\mu\epsilon\nu os$ must accordingly be construed as objective, implying that the sins were purged away by the death of the Son. Heb 1:3 does not designate Jesus as "priest." But in this pregnant clause the writer strongly implies that God's unique Son is also a priest.

$\dot{\epsilon}\kappa\acute{\alpha}\theta\iota\sigma\epsilon\nu \ \dot{\epsilon}\nu \ \delta\epsilon\xi\iota\hat{q} \ \tau\hat{\eta}s \ \mu\epsilon\gamma\alpha\lambda\omega\sigma\acute{\upsilon}\nu\eta s \ \dot{\epsilon}\nu \ \dot{\upsilon}\psi\eta\lambda o\hat{\iota}s$, "he sat down at the right hand of the divine Majesty on high." Syntactically, each of the participial clauses of v 3 is dependent upon the finite $\dot{\epsilon}\kappa\acute{\alpha}\theta\iota\sigma\epsilon\nu$, which grammatically provides the main assertion of vv 3–4. This is particularly significant in the case of the preceding clause, for it establishes that the acts of purifying and sitting were temporally sequential ("after he had made purification for sins he sat down"). These two clauses announce the major themes of the writer's christology, i.e., sacrifice and exaltation. None of the other declarations in the opening paragraph will receive comparable elucidation in the body of the discourse.

The declaration that the Son has been exalted to a position at God's right hand bears an unmistakable allusion to Ps 110:1, for this is the only biblical text that speaks of someone enthroned beside God. In later Jewish literature the psalm was interpreted as addressed to an individual who enjoyed extraordinary favor with God (cf. Hay, *Glory*, 21–33, 54–56). The one clear allusion to Ps 110:1 in a pre-Christian literary source occurs in a hellenistic-Jewish document from the first century, the *Testament of Job* (33:3). When Elihu asks the humiliated patriarch eleven times, "Where now is the glory of your throne?" Job responds, "My throne is in the heavenly world and its glory and splendor are at God's right hand" (ἐκ δεξιῶν τοῦ θεοῦ). Elsewhere, divine Wisdom is depicted as sitting beside God's throne (Wis 9:4), and the Logos, who attacks Egypt in the night of the final plague, leaps down "from heaven, from the royal throne" (Wis 18:15).

The concept of enthronement at God's right hand would convey to contemporaries an impression of the Son's royal power and unparalleled glory. In antiquity generally the right side symbolized supreme authority and highest honor (e.g., 1 Kgs 2:19, "So Bathsheba went to King Solomon . . . . And the king rose to meet her, and bowed down to her; then he sat on his throne, and had a seat brought for the king's mother; and she sat on his right"; cf. Hay, *Glory*, 52–58; Gornatowski, *Rechts und Links;* O. Nussbaum, "Die Bewertung von Rechts und Links in der römische Liturgie," *JAC* 5 [1962] 158–71.) Christians were familiar with the notion of the Son's session at God's right hand from creedal confessions and hymns. They would recognize immediately that the reference was to Christ's exaltation after his resurrection. This may explain why there is so little direct appeal to the fact of Jesus' resurrection in Hebrews (cf. 13:20). In v 3, and elsewhere, an allusion to the position at God's right hand apparently served as an inclusive reference to Jesus' resurrection, ascension, and continuing exaltation (Hay, 43–45, 90).

The choice of μεγαλωσύνη, "majesty," as a circumlocution for God here (and in 8:1; cf. *T. Levi* 3:9) sharpens the impression of the Son's incomparable glory. Concurrently it affirms the eternal majesty of God. Enthronement at "the right hand of the divine Majesty" asserted the supreme exaltation of the Son without compromising the rank and rule of God the Father (cf. Hay, 91, 159). The addition of ἐν ὑψηλοῖς, "on high" (cf. Ps 92[93]:4; 112[113]:5), emphasizes the heavenly sphere of Christ's exaltation and intensifies the spatial aspect of the image (cf. ἐν τοῖς οὐρανοῖς, "in heaven," in 8:1).

Although the Son can be described as the radiance of the divine glory from eternity (v 3a), there is a profound sense in which it can be maintained that he entered into a perfect state of glory only after his humiliation and sacrificial death (cf. 2:9, "crowned with glory and honor"). The Son's exaltation is thus described as a heavenly enthronement (v 3), validated by the proclamation of his name (v 4) and rank (v 5), the call for angelic recognition of his supreme dignity (v 6), and the fresh enunciation of his exaltation (vv 8–13). This same pattern is recognizable in other confessional passages in the NT (e.g., Phil 2:9–11; 1 Tim 3:16; Rev 5:6–14; cf. Käsemann, *Das wandernde Gottesvolk*, 58–71). That the Son has been exalted to God's right hand means that he lives and rules with the authority and power of God himself.

4 The concluding clause flows naturally from the central affirmation of the exaltation of the Son and states its significance. The transcendent dignity of the Son is confirmed by the proclamation of his enthronement name and the announcement of his superiority to the angels. The motif of the acquisition of a new name and exaltation above the angels is found elsewhere in confessional material (cf. Phil 2:9; Eph 1:20; 1 Pet 3:22) and appears to be a common element in early tradition (cf. Deichgräber, *Gotteshymnus*, 138). In v 4 the superior name is almost certainly the acclamation "my son" of Ps 2:7 quoted in v 5 (so also Michel, 105; Hay, *Glory*, 109–10; et al.).

Hebrews shows a marked preference for the term κρείττων, "better," "superior," for the expression of value judgments (nineteen times in the NT, thirteen times in Hebrews). This descriptive term is complemented by the rare comparative διαφορώτερος, "more excellent," which is used again in 8:6 to describe the superiority of Christ's ministry in contrast to the Levitical priesthood (cf. Weiss, *TDNT* 9:64). These terms express a qualitative judgment; they declare that the status and name the Son has acquired in the heavenly world are superior to and more exalted than those enjoyed by the angels.

The expression τοσούτῳ . . . ὅσῳ, "as far above . . . as," is excellent Greek but is used elsewhere in the NT in this precise form only in Heb 10:25. It is a very common formula in classical authors and can be found in writers plying a good literary Greek in the hellenistic period as well (*Ep. Arist.* 13, 182, 290; Sir 3:18; 4 Macc 15:5; Philo, discussed by Williamson, *Philo*, 93–95).

The comparison between Christ and the angels is not prompted by the problem of an angelomorphic christology (i.e., confusion over the nature of Jesus and that of the angels), or by the erroneous practice of venerating angels (see above, *Form/Structure/Setting*). It provides a parallel to vv 1–2*a*, where revelation through the prophets is contrasted with the ultimate word spoken through the Son. The angels in v 4 are the counterpart to the prophets in v 1. In the OT angels were ascribed a broad role in revelation and redemption (e.g., Exod 3:2; Isa 63:9). It was commonly understood that the law had been mediated to Moses, the greatest of the prophets, through angels (cf. *Jub.* 1:29; Acts 7:38–39, 53; Gal 3:19; Jos., *Ant.* 15.5.3; *Mek.* on Exod 20:18; *Sipre* 102 on Num 12:5; *Pesiq. R.* 21). This conception was shared by the writer and his readers (2:2). The description of the Jewish law as "the message declared by angels" in 2:2 is determinative for the interpretation of the reference to the angels in v 4. The assertion of Christ's exaltation over the angels prepares for the demonstration of that superiority (1:5–14). That demonstration is foundational to the thought that Christ's revelation is far superior to that mediated by the angels (2:1–4) (cf. Spicq, 2:52–55).

The opening paragraph is thus framed by a twofold reference to the superiority of the Son as the bearer of the supreme revelation of God both to the prophets and to angels. V 4 terminates the exordium by returning to the theme announced in the initial lines. The shift from *the prophets* to *the angels* is deliberate, for it is the writer's intention to announce as the subject of his first major section (1:5–2:18) the superiority of the Son to the angels.

Explanation

The majestic opening statement is programmatic for the entire discourse. It focuses upon the event of revelation as a means of exhibiting the transcendent

dignity of the Son of God. The many and various episodes of revelation mentioned in the opening verse were crowned by the supreme revelation entrusted
to him. Within this conceptual framework the writer celebrates the character and
worth of the divine Son in a tightly organized confessional statement framed by
references to the enthronement of the royal Son (of Ps 2) and the royal Priest
(of Ps 110). Sandwiched between these more traditional declarations is the presentation of the Son in the categories of the Wisdom of God. The source of
a widespread theological tendency to refer to divine Wisdom when speaking of
creation, providence, revelation, and redemption was the development of the wisdom tradition in the hellenistic synagogues of diaspora Judaism. The mediatorial
role assigned to Wisdom in that tradition is in Hebrews ascribed to the divine
Son.

The presentation of the Son in the categories of divine Wisdom in the opening lines of Hebrews is initially surprising. It is clear that the writer's primary
intention is to develop the tenet that Jesus is the high priest like Melchizedek,
the heir to the promise in Ps 110:4. He defers the full treatment of this theme to the
body of the homily, although it is anticipated in the affirmation that the Son sat
down at the right hand of God "after he had made purification for sins"
(v 3). On reflection, however, reasons may be proposed for the distinctive presentation of Jesus in the exordium.

The writer's decision to present Jesus as God's Son who performs the functions assigned to Wisdom may have been motivated by a pastoral concern to
achieve a hearing for what he had to say. The categories of divine Wisdom were
apparently current and meaningful for his readers. The concentration of unusual
and distinctive vocabulary in v 3 suggests a congregation for whom the tradition
preserved in Wis 7:24–27 was normative. This Christian assembly has been significantly influenced by the hellenistic synagogue in terms of theological
conception and vocabulary.

A second concern may have dictated the choice of language in the exordium.
The writer was aware of certain perils that threatened the group he addressed.
His intention was to provide a word of encouragement and exhortation appropriate to their situation (13:22). The presentation of Jesus as the one who
sustains everything by his powerful word demonstrated that he was able to sustain the people of God in periods marked by stress, when the court of an
imperial magistrate or the arena could become an occasion for Christian confession.

One further suggestion may be ventured concerning the presentation of Jesus
in the garb of Wisdom. It may have been the writer's deliberate intention to
take up wisdom motifs familiar to his readers from synagogue and church liturgy and to relate them to the priestly motifs he was concerned to develop.
Support for this proposal is provided by *1 Clem.* 36.1–4, where Clement cites a
portion of Heb 1:3 but interprets the declaration in terms of the high priestly
christology of Heb 2:17–3:1. An understanding that the mediatorial functions
of divine Wisdom were priestly in character may have been widespread in the
hellenistic church. If such a theological conception had been popularized
through the hellenistic synagogues, the raw materials for a divine Wisdom
christology subservient to a high priestly christology were already at hand when the
writer to the Hebrews made use of liturgical tradition to introduce his statement

concerning the dignity of Jesus as royal Son and Priest. Divine Wisdom christology is one aspect of high priestly christology.

In 1:1–4 the writer gave christological precision to a cluster of ideas derived from hellenistic Judaism. He boldly applied the categories of Wisdom to a historical figure, Jesus. The writer to the Hebrews was a creative theologian who brought together wisdom motifs and priestly motifs in a tightly formulated statement concerning the dignity and achievement of the Son of God. The opening paragraph establishes a firm christological foundation for all that the writer has to say concerning the character and demands of the revelation mediated by the Son. The joining together of wisdom and priestly notes in the carefully orchestrated presentation of the Son provides the readers with the assurance of Jesus' sustained concern for them and his ability to strengthen and vindicate the people of God when they become objects of contempt in a hostile world.

B. The Transcendent Dignity of the Son (1:5–14)

Bibliography

Allen, C. L. "Psalm 45:7–8 (6–7) in Old and New Testament Settings." In *Christ the Lord*. FS D. Guthrie. Ed. H. H. Rowden. Downers Grove, IL: Inter-Varsity Press, 1982. 220–42. **Allis, O. T.** "'Thy Throne, O God, Is for Ever and Ever.'" *PTR* 21 (1923) 236–66. **Andriessen, P.** "La teneur judéo-chrétienne de Hé I 6 et II 14B-III 2." *NovT* 18 (1976) 293–313. **Bakker, A.** "Was Christ an Angel?" *ZNW* 32 (1933) 255–65. **Barth, M.** "The Old Testament in Hebrews: An Essay in Biblical Hermeneutics." In *Current Issues in New Testament Interpretation*. Ed. W. Klassen and G. F. Snyder. New York: Harper & Row, 1962. 53–78, 263–73. **Bishop, E. F. F.** "Angelology in Judaism, Islam and Christianity." *ATR* 46 (1964) 142–54. **Brady, C.** "The World to Come in the Epistle to the Hebrews." *Wor* 39 (1965) 329–39. **Brown, R. E.** "Does the N.T. Call Jesus God?" *TS* 26 (1965) 545–73. **Büchel, C.** "Der Hebräerbrief und das Alte Testament." *TSK* 79 (1906) 508–91. **Caird, G. B.** "Son by Appointment." In *The New Testament Age*. FS B. Reicke. Ed. W. C. Weinrich. Macon, GA: Mercer UP, 1984. 1:73–81. **Carr, G. L.** "The Old Testament Love Songs and Their Use in the New Testament." *JETS* 24 (1981) 97–105. **Cernuda, A. V.** "La introducción del Primogénito, segun Hebr. 1, 6." *EstBib* 39 (1981) 107–53. **Charles, J. D.** "The Angels, Sonship and Birthright in the Letter to the Hebrews." *JETS* 33 (1990) 171–78. **Combrink, H. J. B.** "Some Thoughts on the Old Testament Citations in the Epistle to the Hebrews." *Neot* 5 (1971) 22–36. **Couroyer, B.** "Dieu ou Roi? Le vocatif dans le Psaume 45 (vv 1–9)." *RB* 78 (1971) 233–41. **Dupont, J.** "'Filius meus es tu': L'interprétation du Ps 2,7 dans le N. T." *RSR* 35 (1948) 522–43. **Dussaut, L.** *Synopse structurelle de l'Épître aux Hébreux*. 19–24. **Dyck, T. L.** "Jesus Our Pioneer." 60–76. **Fabris, R.** "La lettera agli Ebrei e l'Antico Testamento." *RivB* 32 (1984) 237–52. **Fitzmyer, J. A.** "The Use of Explicit Old Testament Quotations in Qumran Literature and in the New Testament." *NTS* 7 (1960–61) 297–333. **Galot, J.** "Existence personnelle et mission des anges." *EV* 99 (1989) 257–63. **Glasson, T. F.** "'Plurality of Divine Persons' and the Quotations in Hebrews 1:6ff." *NTS* 12 (1965–66) 270–72. **Harris, M. J.** "The Translation and Significance of ὁ θεός in Hebrews 1:8–9." *TynBul* 36 (1985) 129–62. ———. "The Translation of *Elohim* in Psalm 45:7–8." *TynBul* 35 (1984) 65–89. **Helyer, L. R.** "The *Prōtotokos* Title in Hebrews." *StudBibTh* 6 (1976)

3–28. Howard, G. "Hebrews and Old Testament Quotations." *NovT* 10 (1968) 208–16.
Hurst, L. D. "The Christology of Hebrews 1 and 2." In *The Glory of Christ in the New Testament.* FS G. B. Caird. Ed. L. D. Hurst and N. T. Wright. Oxford: Clarendon Press, 1987.
151–64. **Katz, P.** "The Quotations from Deuteronomy in Hebrews." *ZNW* 49 (1958) 213–
23. **Kistemaker, S.** *The Psalm Citations in the Epistle to the Hebrews.* Amsterdam: G. van Soest,
1961. **Koops, R.** "Chains of Contrast in Hebrews 1." *BT* 34 (1983) 220–25. **Laub, F.**
Bekenntnis und Auslegung. 20–22, 52–61. **Lewis, W. M.** "Bringing the First-Begotten into
the World." *BW* 12 (1898) 104–12. **Meier, J. P.** "Structure and Theology in Heb 1:1–14."
Bib 66 (1985) 168–89. ———. "Symmetry and Theology in the Old Testament Citations
in Heb. 1:5–14." *Bib* 66 (1985) 504–33. **Oberholtzer, T. K.** "The Eschatological Salvation
of Hebrews 1:5–2:5." *BSac* 148 (1988) 83–97. **Old, H. O.** "The Psalms of Praise in the
Worship of the New Testament Church." *Int* 39 (1985) 20–33. **Padva, P.** *Les citations de
l'Ancien Testament dans l'Épître aux Hébreux.* Paris: Danzig, 1904. **Parsons, M. C.** "Son and
High Priest: A Study in the Christology of Hebrews." *EvQ* 60 (1988) 195–215. **Pérez, A.**
"Procedimientos derásicos del Sal 2, 7*b* en el Nuevo Testamento: 'Tu eres mi hijo, yo te
he engendrado hoy.'" *EstBib* 42 (1984) 391–414. **Ploeg, J. van der** "L'exégèse de l'Ancien
Testament de l'Épître aux Hébreux." *RB* 54 (1947) 187–228. **Pollard, E. B.** "Notes on the
Old Testament Citations in the Epistle to the Hebrews." *CrozQ* 1 (1924) 447–52. **Rendall,
R.** "The Method of the Writer to the Hebrews in Using Old Testament Quotations." *EvQ*
27 (1955) 214–20. **Robson, E. A.** "A Biblical-Theological Exposition of Psalm 2:7 Considering the Sonship of the Messiah." Dissertation, Westminster Theological Seminary,
1963. **Sahlin, H.** "Adam-Christologie im Neuen Testament." *ST* 41 (1987) 11–32. **Schröger,
F.** *Der Verfasser des Hebräerbriefes als Schriftausleger.* Regensburg: Pustet, 1968. **Smith, W. R.**
"Christ and the Angels." *Exp* 2nd ser. 1 (1881) 25–33, 138–47; 2 (1881) 18–27; 3 (1882) 63–
70, 128–39. **Sowers, S.** *The Hermeneutics of Philo and Hebrews.* Richmond: Knox, 1965. **Synge, F.
C.** *Hebrews and the Scriptures.* London: SPCK, 1959. **Taylor, V.** "Does the New Testament Call Jesus
God?" *ExpTim* 73 (1961–62) 116–18. **Tetley, J.** "The Priesthood of Christ in Hebrews." *Anvil* 5
(1988) 195–206. **Thomas, K. J.** "The Old Testament Citations in Hebrews." *NTS* 11 (1964–65)
303–25. **Thompson, J. W.** "The Structure and Purpose of the Catena in Heb 1:5–13." *CBQ* 38
(1976) 352–63. **Tournay, R.** "Les affinitiés du Ps 45 avec le Cantique et leur interprétation
messianique." In *Congress Volume: Bonn, 1962.* VTSup 9. Leiden: Brill, 1963. 168–212. ———. "Le
Psaume 110." *RB* 67 (1960) 5–14. **Übelacker, W. G.** *Der Hebräerbrief als Appell: Untersuchungen zu
exordium, narratio und postscriptum (Heb 1–2 und 13, 22–25).* Stockholm: Almqvist & Wiksell,
1989. **Vanhoye, A.** *Exegesis Epistulae ad Hebraeos Cap. I–II.* Rome: Pontifical Biblical Institute, 1968.
81–136. ———. *Situation de Christ: Hébreux 1–2.* Paris: Cerf, 1969. 119–226. **Venard, L.** "L'utilisation
des Psaumes dans l'épître aux Hébreux." In *Mélanges E. Podechard.* Lyon: Facultés Catholiques,
1945. 253–64. **Vitti, A.** "Et cum iterum introducit primogenitum in orbem terrae (Hebr 1,6)."
VD 14 (1934) 306–16, 368–74; 15 (1935) 15–21. **Warfield, B. B.** "The Divine Messiah in the Old
Testament." *PTR* 14 (1916) 379–416. **Williamson, R.** "The Incarnation of the Logos in Hebrews." *ExpTim* 95 (1983–84) 4–8.

Translation

5 *For to which of the angels did God*[a] *ever say,*
  "*You are my Son;*
  today I have become your Father"?
And furthermore,
  "*I will be his Father,*[b]
  and he will be my Son"?
6 *And again,*[c] *when God brings his firstborn Son into the [heavenly] world, he says,*
  "*Let all God's angels worship him.*"

[7] *In reference to the angels he says,*
 "He makes his angels winds,
 his servants flames of fire."
[8] *But referring to the Son he says,*
 "Your throne, O God,[d] *will endure for ever and ever,*
 and righteousness[e] *will be the scepter of your*[f] *kingdom.*
[9] *You have loved righteousness and hated lawlessness;*
 therefore God, your God, has exalted you above your companions[g]
 by anointing you with the oil of joy."
[10] *He also says,*
 "Lord, in the beginning you laid the foundation of the earth,
 and your hands made the heavens.
[11] *They will perish, but you remain;*
 they will all wear out like clothing.
[12] *You will roll them up like a cloak;*
 like a garment[h] *they will be changed.*
 But you remain the same;
 you will never grow old."[i]
[13] *But to which of the angels has God ever said,*
 "Sit at my right hand
 until I make your foes your footstool"?
[14] *Are not all angels serving spirits commissioned to render service to those who are to inherit salvation?*

Notes

[a] Although θεός does not appear in the text, the context clearly indicates that God is the subj, as often in Hebrews: 1:5, 6, 7, 13; 3:15; 4:3, 4, 7; 5:5, 6; 6:14; 8:8; 10:15, 30.

[b] εἰς with the acc is used in place of a predicate nominative. Cf. Moulton and Howard, *Grammar*, 2:463.

[c] The πάλιν may be construed with λέγει or with the subjunctive εἰσαγάγῃ. Considerations of context (v 5) and preference in Hebrews (2:13a, b; 4:5; 10:30) support the decision to take πάλιν as a formula of introduction for the quotation that follows rather than a reference to the parousia (cf. 9:28). (Cf. Windisch, 15: "Again, however, he said . . ."; Helyer, *StudBibTh* 6 [1976] 7–8.)

[d] In Koine Gk., the voc is being supplanted by the nom (cf. Moule, *Idiom-Book*, 32), and the nom of θεός usually does duty for the voc. In support of reading ὁ θεός as voc here, see Turner, *Grammar*, 4:15, and A. W. Wainwright, "The Confession 'Jesus is God' in the New Testament," *SJT* 10 (1959) 286–87; Schröger, *Verfasser*, 262–63.

[e] The gen in the expression ἡ ῥάβδος τῆς εὐθύτητος is qualitative, signifying "a righteous scepter," or simply "righteousness."

[f] Although the variant αὐτοῦ enjoys early and good support (p[46] א B) and may seem to be preferable because it differs from the OT passage being quoted, Ps 45:7 (=44:7 LXX), two considerations favor the adoption of the reading σου: (1) the weight and variety of the external evidence supporting σου (A D K P Ψ 33 81 1739 *pc* it vg sy[ph] cop arm Tert, Chr, Cyr, Euthalius) and (2) the internal difficulty of construing αὐτοῦ with the immediate context (cf. Metzger, *Textual Commentary*, 662–63). The fact that in v 9 the second personal pronoun is retained tends to confirm the integrity of σου in v 8. αὐτοῦ is apparently a transcriptional error.

[g] The prep παρά could be taken alternatively as signifying "God has anointed you, *rather than* your companions, with the oil of joy."

[h] The words ὡς ἱμάτιον are strongly attested (p[46] א A B [D*] 1739 it[d e] arm eth). The writer apparently inserted them in his quotation of Ps 102:26 to emphasize that the metaphor of the garment

is sustained. The absence of the words from the majority of witnesses is the result of assimilation of the text to the LXX (so Metzger, *Textual Commentary*, 663).

ⁱ Lit., "your years will never end" (as in RSV, JB, NIV).

Form/Structure/Setting

The internal structure of the first major segment of the address (1:5–2:18) exhibits the writer's customary style of alternating between two types of literary genre, exposition and exhortation. The chain of OT passages demonstrating the superiority of the Son to the angels (1:5–13) is expository in character and lays the foundation for the solemn appeal in 2:1–4. This exhortation is then followed by further exposition, which clarifies the relationship of the Son to the angels. The change from one literary genre to another in the course of the development permits the recognition of the limits of three paragraphs: 1:5–14 (exposition), 2:1–4 (exhortation), and 2:5–18 (exposition) (cf. Vanhoye, *La structure*, 69).

The several citations from the OT were selected to undergird the declarations concerning the Son in the core of the exordium (vv 2*b*–3*c*). A synthetic parallelism exists between the opening confession of the Son and the string of quotations which follows:

	1:1–4		1:5–13
A	Appointment as royal heir (v 2*b*)	A'	Appointment as royal Son and heir (vv 5–9)
B	Mediator of the creation (v 2*c*)	B'	Mediator of the creation (v 10)
C	Eternal nature and pre-existent glory (v 3*a, b*)	C'	Unchanging, eternal nature (vv 11–12)
D	Exaltation to God's right hand (v 3*c*)	D'	Exaltation to God's right hand (v 13)

The development in 1:5–14 thus documents the superiority of the Son to the angels in a manner that reinforces the church's confession of his transcendent dignity.

Considerations of structure are evident in the arrangement of the collection. By repeating a formula of introduction directing attention to the angels, the writer subdivides the paragraph into three units, each of which draws an antithetical comparison between the Son and the angels:

v 5　"To which of the angels did God ever say . . . ?"
v 7　"In reference to the angels he says . . . ."
v 13　"But to which of the angels has God ever said . . . ?"

The first comparison brings together two citations addressed to the Son, and concludes with a third concerning the angels. The tension between the dignity of the Son and that of the angels is sufficiently expressed by the adversative (δέ) in v 6. The formulas of recognition cited in v 5 validate the Son's right to enthronement and account for the command for the angels to recognize his dignity in v 6.

By repeating the catchword *angels* (found in v 6), the second comparison is linked to the first. The antithetical character of the comparison is accentuated by the particles μέν . . . δέ:

v 7   καὶ πρὸς μὲν τοὺς ἀγγέλους λέγει . . .
       "In reference to the angels he says . . ."
v 8   πρὸς δὲ τὸν υἱόν . . .
       "But referring to the Son . . ."

The order in which the two parties were addressed in vv 5–6 was first the Son, then the angels. Now the order is inverted, and the word to the angels precedes the words addressed to the Son. In contrast to the brevity of the first and third comparison, the second comparison provides an extended testimony to the abiding, eternal character of the Son (vv 7–12).

The third antithetical comparison (vv 13–14) follows without a transition. It is tied to the previous subdivision, however, by details of expression. The quotation of Ps 110:1*b* is appropriate to the mention of the established throne in v 8, while the description of the angels as *serving spirits* echoes the vocabulary of v 7, "who makes his angels *spirits*, his *servants* a flame of fire." It is striking that the first and last comparisons are introduced with a rhetorical question followed by the citation of one of the coronation psalms (v 5, citing Ps 2:7; v 13, citing Ps 110:1). The bracketing of the biblical proof of the Son's transcendent dignity with quotations from Ps 2 and Ps 110 furnishes an appropriate counterpart to the allusions to these same psalms that frame the confession in the exordium (vv 2*b*–3*c*).

The formal literary resemblance of vv 5–6 and vv 13–14 indicates the limits of the paragraph. But the structural function of vv 13–14 goes beyond a termination of the mosaic of OT citations. The reference to those who are to be the heirs of salvation (v 14) anticipates the solemn appeal not to neglect the message of salvation in 2:3. Similarly, the phrase "your footstool" from the quotation of Ps 110:1 (v 13) prepares for the development of this traditional image in 2:5–8. The third and final contrast between Christ and the angels thus concludes the series of three antithetical comparisons and provides an effective transition to the paragraphs that follow (Vanhoye, *La structure*, 69–74; cf. J. W. Thompson, *CBQ* 38 [1976] 352–63).

Several scholars have argued that the source of the quotations in 1:5–14 is a scriptural florilegium, derived from the tradition (Käsemann, *Das wandernde Gottesvolk*, 107–8; Synge, *Hebrews*, 3–6; 53–54; Theissen, *Untersuchungen*, 34–37; Hay, *Glory*, 38–39). They noted that much of the content in 1:5–14 is not closely related to the rest of the letter and reasoned that the length and partial irrelevance of the passage is understandable if the writer had availed himself of a traditional testimony collection. The obvious similarities between Heb 1:5–14 and *1 Clem.* 36.1–6 provided the primary support for this proposal. In *1 Clement* a set of affirmations with close verbal resemblances to Heb 1:3–4 is followed by a chain of quotations consisting of Pss 104:4; 2:7–8; and 110:1. The same texts are cited in Heb 1:5, 7, and 13, although the order in which the first two are cited is reversed. The christological concepts and language of the two passages are sufficiently alike that some literary relationship must be posited. These scholars proposed that both Hebrews and Clement drew their quotations from a common source, a collection of biblical texts bearing witness to the dignity of God's Son. On the basis of the language of *1 Clement*, G. Schille suggested baptism as an occasion for the citing of this source ("Die Basis des Hebräerbriefes," *ZNW* 48 [1957] 274–76).

One consideration, however, would appear to deny the plausibility of this otherwise attractive proposal. Clement's third citation is introduced as the direct address of God to the Son. This manner of introducing OT quotations is characteristic of Heb 1 but is not found elsewhere in *1 Clement.* Although the formulation καὶ πάλιν λέγει πρὸς αὐτόν, "and again he says to him" (*1 Clem.* 36.5*a*), does not correspond precisely to any of the introductory phrases in Hebrews, all its components are present in Heb 1:5–13. It seems better, therefore, to conclude that at this point Clement has borrowed from Hebrews, perhaps from memory, paraphrasing the substance of chap. 1. The influence of Hebrews is reflected in the retention of an introductory formula for the last quotation, which is typical for Hebrews but not in harmony with Clement's own manner of introducing the OT text (G. L. Cockerill, "Heb 1:1–14, *1 Clem.* 36:1–6 and the High Priest Title," *JBL* 97 [1978] 438–39; Renner, *An die Hebräer,* 35). The writer to the Hebrews may have derived his quotations from a traditional testimony collection, but no support for this proposal can be drawn from *1 Clem.* 36.

Comment

The string of quotations in 1:5–14 elaborates the assertion of v 4 that as a result of his exaltation the status of the Son has been declared superior to that of the angels, the heavenly mediators of the old revelation. Each of the texts cited is given a christological reference. The writer draws them together in order to expound and confirm what has already been confessed concerning the exalted Son in the exordium (see above, *Form/Structure/Setting*).

The seven citations have been arranged in three groups. The first group (vv 5–6) consists of three citations, of which the first two provide evidence for Jesus' divine sonship (Ps 2:7; 2 Sam 7:14), and the third (Deut 32:43 [Odes]) asserts his superiority in rank to the angels. With the second group (vv 7–12) the writer moves from assertion to argument. He brings together one citation concerning the angels (Ps 104:4) and two that refer to the Son (Pss 45:6–7; 102:25–27) to substantiate the conclusion that the Son is superior by documenting his eternal, unchangeable nature and his role in creation. The final group consists of the citation of Ps 110:1, the text that initially prompted the writer's reflections on the exaltation of the Son (v 3), and a concluding exegetical comment on the inferior rank and status of the angels (cf. Spicq, 2:15; Vanhoye, *Situation,* 121–23).

5 τίνι γὰρ εἶπέν ποτε τῶν ἀγγέλων, "for to which of the angels did [God] ever say?" V 5 is tied to the introductory paragraph by the connecting γάρ as well as by the repetition of τῶν ἀγγέλων from v 4. By prefacing the texts that concern the Son with a formulation that speaks of the angels, a smooth transition to the new unit of thought is assured. The question posed is rhetorical, and calls for a negative response. The words of Ps 2 are fully verified only in the Son who entered into his glory by way of sacrifice; nothing similar can be or ever will be affirmed of the angels. The form of the question thus furnishes an arresting introduction to the quotations that follow, which are viewed as the words of God addressed directly to the Son. The use of a similar rhetorical question to introduce the concluding quotation in v 13 establishes an *inclusio* that ties together all seven biblical texts into a harmonious unit.

Having declared in v 4 that the exalted Son received a more excellent name than the angels, the writer now identifies that name as υἱός μου, "my Son." He cites two passages from the Old Greek version of the Bible, Ps 2:7 and 2 Sam 7:14. Both were familiar messianic texts (cf. Dupont, *RSR* 35 [1948] 522–43; D. Goldsmith, "Acts 13:33–37, a Pesher on II Samuel 7," *JBL* 87 [1968] 321-23) that had already been brought together in early Jewish tradition (4QFlor 10:11, 18–19). The occurrence of a key word in a messianic text could function like a magnet drawing to it other OT texts that contained the same word (cf. R. W. Thurston, "Midrash and 'Magnet' Words in the New Testament," *EvQ* 51 [1979] 22–39; Kistemaker, *Psalm Citations*, 61–64, 78). In this instance the key word that served to attract 2 Sam 7:14 to Ps 2:7 was υἱός, the term that was of primary interest to the writer. The two quotations, joined by the common introductory formula καὶ πάλιν (2:13a, b; 4:5; 10:30; John 19:37; Rom 15:10–12; 1 Cor 3:20), have been artistically arranged so as to form a chiasm (A B B' A'). The first and last lines concern sonship and frame the second and third lines, which speak of paternity:

A   You are my Son;
  B   today I have become your Father.
  B'   I will be his Father,
A'   and he will be my Son.

In both passages sonship is the result of divine decree and favor. As M. Barth remarks, "God's own witness . . . is the decisive factor and act of the Son's enthronement and kingship" ("The OT in Hebrews," 63).

The confession of the transcendent dignity of the Son in the exordium is framed by allusions to Ps 2 and Ps 110. The same confessional pattern is evident in the string of citations in 1:5–14. Corresponding to the allusion to Ps 2:8 in v 2b, the initial quotation is drawn from Ps 2. Ps 2:7 confirms that the one addressed enjoys the status of Son and heir. The solemn pronouncement of 2 Sam 7:14 strengthens the impression of the unique relationship to God the Father enjoyed by the Son. In a narrow sense the oracle of Nathan (2 Sam 7:14–1 Chr 17:13) had reference to Solomon, but in the LXX a messianic interpretation had been encouraged by a phrase in v 12 that precedes the promise of sonship, ἀναστήσω τὸ σπέρμα, "I will raise up seed." The divine promise pointed to a successor, who would be raised up by God subsequent to David's generation, who would be the legitimate heir to the promised eternal kingdom (cf. Harder, *ThViat* 1 [1939] 33; Schröger, *Verfasser*, 262). That the passage was interpreted in a distinctively messianic sense in the first century is certain not only from the evidence from Qumran (4QFlor 10:11) but from the clear allusion to 2 Sam 7:12 in John 7:42: "Does not the Scripture say that the Messiah will come from David's *seed?*" By joining Ps 2:7 and 2 Sam 7:14 the writer to the Hebrews provides strong biblical support for the assertion that the position of the angels is subordinate to the status of the Son. He alone enjoys the unique relationship with the Father that finds expression in the designation "my Son."

There is a certain degree of unresolved tension in the writer's designation of Jesus as Son, since the title can be applied to the pre-existent Son (v 3a–b), to the incarnate Son (v 2a, where the use may be proleptic), and to the exalted Son. It was apparently the writer's conviction that although Jesus was the pre-existent Son of God (cf. 5:8, καίπερ ὢν υἱός, "although he was the Son"), he entered into a new dimension in the experience of sonship by virtue of his incarnation, his sacrificial death, and his subsequent exaltation. This new dimension finds expression in the legal formula of recognition, "You are *my Son*." The connection of v 5 with vv 3*c* and 4 establishes that the enthronement at the Father's right hand was the occasion when the name υἱός was conferred upon Jesus. Although the angels are sometimes designated as "sons of God" in the pages of the OT (e.g., Pss 29:1; 89:7; Job 1:6), Jesus alone is recognized by God as his unique Son (cf. Michel, 111).

6 That the Son is superior to the angels finds fresh support in a contrasting quotation concerning the angels. The introductory formula to the citation is fuller, but demands from an interpreter several exegetical decisions. The resolution of ambiguities depends upon the significance assigned to πάλιν, upon the force of the aorist subjunctive in the phrase ὅταν . . . εἰσαγάγῃ, and upon the determination of the reference in the term οἰκουμένη, "world."

A number of interpreters (e.g., Nairne [1917], 33; Michel, 113; Andriessen, *NovT* 18 [1976] 296–97, 299–300) connect πάλιν, "again," with the verb εἰσαγάγῃ, "he brings," so that it refers to "another" or "second" entrance into the οἰκουμένη. They point out that in every other place in Hebrews where πάλιν is followed by a verb it is construed with that verb (4:7; 5:12; 6:1, 6). A more decisive factor, however, weighs heavily in favor of regarding πάλιν as a connective. The author is fond of stringing quotations together and displays a decided preference for πάλιν in introductory formulas (1:5; 2:13*a*, *b*; 4:5; 10:30). It seems preferable, therefore, to construe πάλιν as a connective, following the interpretive tradition of the Old Latin *(deinde iterum cum inducit)* and the Syriac versions (Helyer, *StudBibTh* 6 [1976] 7–8). Its force is continuative ("and again he says") or mildly adversative ("but he says").

The significance of the aorist subjunctive in εἰσαγάγῃ, "he brings," cannot be resolved solely on grammatical and syntactical grounds. It is clear that the introduction of the firstborn Son into the οἰκουμένη, "world," occurs prior to the solemn command that he receive the homage of the angels. The time reference, however, remains ambiguous; the aorist subjunctive may imply an event in the future or in the present. Although the decision to read πάλιν with λέγει, "he says," in v 6*a* implies that the temporal aspect of εἰσαγάγῃ refers to the present, considerations of context alone can shed light on the time element involved (cf. Helyer, *StudBibTh* 6 [1976] 7–9). The key expressions for the determination are πρωτότοκος and οἰκουμένη.

πρωτότοκος, which signifies "the firstborn Son," appears to have been suggested by the twofold reference to υἱός in the previous verse. It resumes the thought of Christ's appointment as heir in the exordium (v 2*b*). The author may have intended an allusion to Ps 89:27, where God says of David, "And I will appoint him firstborn [κἀγὼ πρωτότοκον θήσομαι αὐτόν], higher than the kings of the earth" (Ps 88:28 LXX). In this context "firstborn" is a title of honor expressing priority in rank. The reference to covenantal appointment (Ps 89:27–28) and to the establishment of a throne that will endure as long as the heavens (v 29) served to bring Ps 89 into close association with Ps 2 and 2 Sam 7, already cited in v 5.

Andriessen (*NovT* 18 [1976] 295–97), however, has urged that it is unnecessary to find an allusion to Ps 89:27 in v 6. He calls attention to the formal verbal similarity between v 6 and Deut 6:10; 11:29, which speaks of the entrance of Israel into the promised land:

Hebrews: ὅταν δὲ πάλιν εἰσαγάγῃ τὸν πρωτότοκον εἰς τὴν οἰκουμένην
Deuteronomy: ὅταν εἰσαγάγῃ σε . . . εἰς τὴν γῆν

He proposes that the replacement of σε ("you" [Deut]) by πρωτότοκον ("firstborn" [Heb]) simply reflects the tradition that Israel is Yahweh's firstborn son (Exod 4:22, υἱὸς πρωτότοκός μου Ἰσραήλ, "Israel is my firstborn son"; cf. Num 11:12; Hos 2:1; 11:1, 3–4; Jer 31:9; Sir 17:17–18 in MSS 70, 248: "He appointed a ruler for every nation, but Israel is the Lord's own portion, his firstborn [πρωτόγονος] whom he nourishes with discipline"). If the introductory formula of v 6 is read against this background, the component parts are all derived from Deuteronomy. The writer wishes to suggest that just as God brought Israel into the promised land of Canaan, so he has brought his firstborn Son into the οἰκουμένη. On either understanding, the title πρωτότοκος is appropriate to a context developing the motif of Son and heir. It was well suited to express Jesus' supremacy over the angels.

The meaning of οἰκουμένη is also disputed. In the Greek Bible, οἰκουμένη customarily signifies habitable land, in contrast to the arid, uninhabitable desert (e.g., Exod 16:35, εἰς τὴν οἰκουμένην). In a derivative sense it comes to mean the world inhabited by men. Consequently, the majority of interpreters have identified the entrance of the Son into the οἰκουμένη with his incarnation (Spicq, 2:17) or the parousia (Michel, 113; Käsemann, *Das wandernde Gottesvolk*, 68–74). The context, however, points in another direction. It speaks of the sacrificial death of the Son followed by his exaltation (vv 3*b*–4). οἰκουμένη, then, concerns neither the incarnation nor the parousia but the entrance of Christ into the heavenly world following his sacrifical death. Christ's entrance into the world (εἰς τὸν κόσμον, 10:5) in his incarnation entailed the humiliation of being made "lower than the angels" (2:7, 9), but his entrance into the οἰκουμένην (v 6) signified his enthronement and exaltation above the angels (vv 3–6) (cf. G. Johnston, "οἰκουμένη and κόσμος in the New Testament," *NTS* 10 [1964] 352–54). The context requires that οἰκουμένη be understood as the heavenly world of eschatological salvation into which the Son entered at his ascension (cf. Schierse, *Verheissung*, 96; A. Vanhoye, "L'οἰκουμένη dans l'Épître aux Hébreux," *Bib* 45 [1964] 248–53; Andriessen, *NovT* 18 [1976] 293–304; Helyer, *StudBibTh* 6 [1976] 10–12).

This interpretation is confirmed in 2:5, when οἰκουμένη is qualified as "the world to come" (οἰκουμένην τὴν μέλλουσαν). The propriety of interpreting οἰκουμένη in v 6 in the light of the fuller expression in 2:5 follows from both passages being concerned with the subjection of the angels to the Son. Moreover, in 2:5 the appended phrase περὶ ἧς λαλοῦμεν, "about which we have been speaking," serves to tie the two passages together. The introductory formula in v 6 thus serves to identify the occasion when the angels were commanded to render homage to the Son with the exaltation. A later witness to this understanding of the text, but one which is particularly explicit, is furnished by an apocalyptic work that may have originated in the second century A.D., the *Ascension of Isaiah* (10:7–15; 11:23–32). When the divine Son descended into the world for the incarnation, he was unrecognized by the angels; but when he ascended to the right hand of the Father, he displayed his glory and received angelic homage (cited by Vanhoye, *Bib* 45 [1964] 253, n. 2).

The quotation is taken from the "Hymn of Moses," found originally in Deut 32. This well-known passage was subsequently removed from its context in Deuteronomy and adopted for liturgical use in the Temple, synagogue, and Church (cf. Elbogen, *Gottesdienst*, 169; H. Schneider, "Die biblischen Oden im christlichen Altertum," *Bib* 30 [1949] 28–65). Its popularity among Greek-speaking Jews is attested by its inclusion among the Odes appended to the Greek Psalter as well as by specific reference to it in writers from the first century A.D. (4 Macc 18:6, 9, 18, 19; Philo, *The Worse Attacks the Better* 114; *Allegorical Interpretation* 3.105; *On Noah's Work as a Planter* 59). The reference to the singing of the Hymn of Moses in heaven in Rev 15:3 may reflect its early adoption for liturgical use in the Church. At a later time, it was sung as part of the Easter vigil (Schneider, *Bib* 30 [1949] 35). The quotation in Hebrews corresponds exactly to Deut 32:43 in the translation provided in the Odes: καὶ προσκυνησάτωσαν αὐτῷ πάντες οἱ ἄγγελοι θεοῦ, "and let all the angels of God worship him" (Ode 2:43). It may be assumed that this form of the text, attested by Codex A, 55, and Justin (*Dialogue* 130), was familiar from a liturgical tradition (cf. Schröger, *Verfasser*, 49). In the older Greek version of Deut 32:43 (LXX$^{A/B}$), the subject of the command is not οἱ ἄγγελοι but υἱοὶ θεοῦ, "sons of God." The writer to the Hebrews appears to have purposefully selected the reading found in the Odes because it was immediately applicable as an indication of the subordination of the angels to the Son (Kistemaker, *Psalm Citations*, 20–23; Combrink, *Neot* 5 [1971] 27; Helyer, *StudBibTh* 6 [1976] 6–7, 20; cf. Katz, *ZNW* 49 [1958] 217–19). In its original context the summons has reference to the worship or homage due to God. But the writer to the Hebrews understands the text as a prophetic oracle concerning the Son at his exaltation. It is because of the surpassing superiority of the Son that the angels were commanded to worship him.

7   The new formula of introduction introduces the second set of contrasting statements concerning the angels and the Son, which is developed by means of a μὲν … δέ construction: καὶ πρὸς μὲν τοὺς ἀγγέλους λεγει … πρὸς δὲ τὸν υἱόν …, "In reference to the angels he says … But referring to the Son …" (vv 7, 8). It is distinguished from the first contrast by its extent (vv 7–12) and by the fullness of the quotations referring to the Son. The two lines of quotation that describe the status of the angels are followed by thirteen lines descriptive of the eternal Son. The writer is careful to provide the basis for his assertion that the Son is superior to the angels. The introduction of a quotation concerning the mutability of the angels serves primarily to emphasize the unchangeable, eternal character of the Son.

The quotation reflects the LXX version of Ps 104:4, with only minor variations. It offers a striking example of the writer's dependence upon the Greek Bible, for the text was useful to him only in this form (cf. Schröger, *Verfasser*, 262; Kistemaker, *Psalm Citations*, 23–24, 27–28). The MT speaks only of wind and fire as instruments of God's sovereign will: "who makes the winds his messengers, flames of fire his servants." Frequently in the OT wind and fire are the divine instruments for theophany. In this form the text was cited in the rabbinic tradition as evidence of the transcendence of God who executes his will through the angels (cf. *Exod. Rab.* 25.86*a:* "they sit and stand at his will, and appear in the form of a man or a woman, or even as wind and fire") or as a commentary on the superior powers of the angels (cf. *Tg.* Ps 104:4: "who makes his angels as swift as the wind, his servants as mighty as flaming fire"). In the LXX, however, the angels are not exalted. The objects in the text were reversed, with the result that it now speaks of the unstable nature of the angels who receive from God their respective form, rank, and task: "who makes his angels wind, his servants flames of fire." As those who belong to the created order, angels are subject to God's creative activity and may be transformed into the elemental forces of wind and fire. The writer to the Hebrews draws upon this interpretative tradition. The ephemeral, mutable form of the angels underscores their inferiority to the Son, who stands above the created order and is not subject to change and decay (cf. Kuss, 37; Michel, 117; Thompson, *CBQ* 38 [1976] 357).

8–9 The contrast implied in v 7 is borne out by the following two quotations from the Psalms, which establish that the Son does not belong to the created order, as do the angels. The adversative δέ in the introduction to the first citation indicates the writer intends to contrast the Son, whose throne endures forever, with the angels, whose existence is ephemeral. The quotation differs from the LXX version of Ps 45:6–7 in only minor details (cf. Kistemaker, *Psalm Citations,* 24–25). The motif of an eternal kingdom brings Ps 45 within the orbit of 2 Sam 7, where the establishment of an eternal throne is promised: "I will establish the throne of his kingdom forever" (v 13); "Your throne shall be established forever" (v 16). The verbal parallelism with the initial statement of Ps 45:6 may indicate why this extended passage was added to the collection of messianic testimonies that include 2 Sam 7:14 (v 5) (so Kistemaker, *Psalm Citations,* 78). On the other hand, the imagery of the session at God's right hand in the exordium (v 3*c*) would also be sufficient to call to mind the statement concerning the throne in Ps 45.

The application of Ps 45:6–7 to the Son is consistent with the indication that he is to receive the homage of the angels in v 6. The writer does not hesitate to apply to Jesus, as the legitimate object of worship, a passage in which he is addressed as God. The citation, however, remains an isolated confession, which receives no elaboration at any point in the address. It is probable that the quotation had been applied to Jesus in the liturgy of the early Church. The writer's primary interest in the quotation is not the predication of deity but of the eternal nature of the dominion exercised by the Son. The implication that the Son shares the quality of deity only intensifies the reference to his eternal rule and sharpens the contrast between the unchangeable Son and the mutable angels. In this context the phrase εἰς τὸν αἰῶνα τοῦ αἰῶνος, "for ever and ever," suggests the quality of immutability (cf. Thompson, *CBQ* 38 [1976] 358). The writer's emphasis upon the eternal nature of the Son is the first indication that eternity is for him a christological category that will assume increasing importance in the center of the address (cf. 5:5; 6:20; 7:3, 17, 21, 24, 28).

It is more difficult to see why the writer extended the quotation of Ps 45:6 to include v 7. The two verses may have been joined as a single quotation in an early testimony collection, for they are cited as a unit by Justin (*Dialogue* 56; but cf. 63 [Ps 45:6–11]; 86 [Ps 45:7]) and Irenaeus (*Against Heresies* 3.6.1; 4.33.11; *Demonstration* 47). The point of interest for the writer to the Hebrews in v 7 appears to have been the concluding words of the quotation, παρὰ τοὺς μετόχους σου, "above your companions." The preposition παρά, taken in the comparative sense ("more than," "beyond"), reinforces the contrast being drawn between Christ and the angels. Although angels participate in the implementation of God's will (cf. vv 7, 14), and in this sense are μέτοχοι of the Son, God has assigned *to him* a superior office. Their function is to serve; his is to rule. They are subject to constant change; he does not change, and his rule reflects a commitment to righteousness, which explains why God has crowned him with joy (cf. 12:2). Both verses of the extended quotation express the fundamental contrast between the divine Son of God and the angels.

10–12 The joining of the second extended quotation to the first by conjunctive καί conveys an impression of the mere stringing together of OT texts. The quotations, however, have been purposefully arranged so that they begin and end on the note of the Son's eternal nature.

> v 8   "Your throne, O God, endures forever and ever."
> v 12 "But you remain the same; you will never grow old."

The attribute of permanence in the Creator corresponds to the durability of his throne and serves to reinforce the contrast between the mutability of the angels and the stable, abiding character of the Son.

Up to this point (vv 5–9) the biblical quotations have undergirded the Church's confession that Jesus is the Son of God who has been appointed heir of all things (v 2*b*). Now Ps 102:25–27 is introduced to specify the relationship of the exalted Son to the creation. The quotation develops the affirmation of vv 2*c* and 3*b* that the Son is the mediator and sustainer of the creation. The quotation assigns to the divine Son responsibility both for the foundation and dissolution of the world. Jewish theology assigned a prominent role to the angels as those who were present at the moment of the creation and who assisted God in the government of the universe (cf. Job 38:7; Rev 7:1; 14:18; 16:5). The writer affirms it is the Son alone through whom God created the universe; it is the Son, not the angels, who upholds it through his sovereign word (cf. Williamson, *Philo*, 188).

In its original context Ps 102:25–27 refers to the immutable character of God. The psalmist contrasts the ability of Yahweh to stand above the change and decay of the created order with his own experience of affliction and exposure to death. In the LXX, however, a mistranslation of the unpointed Hebrew text opened the door for the christological appropriation of the passage. The radicals ענה/ʿ-*n-h* in v 24 (EV v 23), "he afflicted," were translated "he answered" (ἀπεκρίθη, Vg *respondit*), with the result that vv 23–28 become the response of Yahweh. Consequently, Ps 102:25–27 must refer to the creative activity of divine Wisdom or of the Messiah, not of God (cf. B. W. Bacon, "Heb 1, 10–12 and the Septuagint Rendering of Ps 102, 23," *ZNW* 3 [1902] 280–85).

Several variations from the LXX text may be observed in the quotation. σύ, "you," is placed before κατ᾽ ἀρχάς, "in the beginning" (v 10), for the sake of emphasis; it serves to bring the new quotation into immediate association with the previous one which concluded on the word σου, with reference to the Son. The alteration of the future form διαμενεῖς, "you will remain," to the present διαμένεις, "you remain" (v 11), provides a more adequate expression of the timeless quality of the Son's nature. The change from ἀλλάσσειν, "to change," to ἑλίσσειν, "to roll up" (v 12), which suggests the action of the rolling up of a cloak, provides the writer with a vivid image of change. The addition of ὡς ἱμάτιον, "like a garment," which is repeated from v 11, before καὶ ἀλλαγήσονται, "and they will be changed" (v 12*b*), keeps the imagery of clothing prominently in view and serves to stress the frequency and casualness with which the created order is altered. Each of the textual variations serves the writer's own interpretation (Schröger, *Verfasser,* 263; Kistemaker, *Psalm Citations,* 26–27, 79–80).

Ps 102:25–27 has been introduced into the argument because it supports the radical distinction between the transitoriness of the created order and the eternal, unchangeable nature of the Son (cf. Schröger, 69). Heaven and earth, the realm of the angels, both belong to the created order, which will change and decay. The quotation introduces several significant notes that will be picked up and developed at later points in the exposition. The concept of abiding permanence finds expression in the contrast between the perishability of the cosmos and the "remaining" of the Son: αὐτοὶ ἀπολοῦνται, σὺ δὲ διαμένεις, "they will perish, but you remain." Thompson (*CBQ* 38 [1976] 260–61) has suggested that the presence of διαμένεις in the quotation accounts for its inclusion in the catena of 1:5–13. Near the end of the address the writer regularly uses forms of μένειν in theologically significant contexts to describe the heavenly "abiding" reality that constitutes the Christian heritage in contrast with what does not "remain" in the structures of the world (cf. 10:34; 12:25–27; 13:14). The word παλαιοῦν, "to grow old" or "become obsolete," in the expression ὡς ἱμάτιον παλαιωθήσονται, "like clothing they will wear out," is also theologically significant for the writer. In 8:13, for example, the term is introduced to convey the temporary character of the Levitical cultus, which lacks ultimate validity. Finally, the expression σὺ δὲ ὁ αὐτός, "but you remain the same" (v 12), which furnishes a parallel to the statement σὺ δὲ διαμένεις, "but you remain" (v 11), anticipates the confession with which the address is brought to a climax near its conclusion, that Jesus Christ is ὁ αὐτός, "the same," yesterday and today and forever (13:8). The vocabulary and expression of Ps 102:25–27 clearly provided the writer with important categories with which to express the superior quality of Christian existence.

In this context, however, the accent falls upon the mutability of the created order, including the angels, in contrast to the Son who is exalted above that order. The quotation turns on common images of changeableness: clothes grow old and wear out; a cloak is rolled up and put away. But the Son "remains." The argument in vv 10–12 is thus parallel to that in vv 7–8, where the mutability of the angels is contrasted with the eternal, unchangeable character of the Son.

13 In the third group (vv 13–14), the writer returns to the literary device that introduced the series of quotations. A text that speaks of the Son is prefaced by a rhetorical question concerning the angels. The introduction to the quotations in vv 5 and 13 establishes an *inclusio,* which ties the paragraph together. As the introductory and concluding citations in the series, Ps 2:7 and

Ps 110:1 are bonded together as the framework both of the Church's confession and of the writer's exposition of that confession. The brevity of the third unit, which consists of a single quotation and an exegetical comment, reflects the author's sensitivity to balance in literary arrangement. He has skillfully flanked the long, central portion (vv 7–12) with briefer units of text and exposition (vv 5–6, 13–14).

The δέ of v 13 correlates this third unit to the preceding argument. The citation of Ps 110:1 marks a return to the text, which appears to have prompted the extended reflections concerning the Son and the angels (cf. v 3c). As the concluding and climactic quotation in the series, the text receives particular emphasis. It serves to recapitulate all that has been argued in the previous verses: angels are inferior to the exalted Son and can never share his position or glory. The writer cites Ps 110:1 as part of the colloquy between God and the Son that the Church on earth, as it were, overhears (cf. Barth, "The OT in Hebrews," 62). In v 3 it implied that the divine Son seated himself at God's right hand (cf. 8:1; 10:12–13; 12:2), but the quotation in v 13 explains that his enthronement was accomplished at the invitation of God (cf. Hay, *Glory*, 86).

14 The concluding rhetorical question is actually an exegetical comment on Ps 104:4, quoted in v 7. The designation of the angels as λειτουργικὰ πνεύματα, "serving spirits," echoes the key words in the quotation, πνεύματα and λειτουργούς. The assertion that the angels are sent forth on a mission of service (εἰς διακονίαν) to the heirs of the salvation is a logical inference from the biblical text. Angels clearly have their place in the economy of redemption, but it is not at the Father's right hand. They are ordained to ministry in the world of humanity (cf. Strathmann, *TDNT* 4: 231). The readers are, in fact, οἱ μέλλοντες κληρονομεῖν σωτηρίαν, "those who are to inherit salvation." This formulation conveys the further implication that entrance into the inheritance of salvation is the central theme of the new revelation (cf. 2:3–4; 9:15).

The rhetorical question in v 14 is designed to call the hearers to decision. It demands an affirmative answer. They are to recognize that in contrast to the Son, who is invited to share the divine presence and splendor, angels are sent forth on a mission of assistance to those who find themselves oppressed and confused in a hostile world.

Explanation

The catena of OT quotations in 1:5–13 elaborates the assertion in v 4 that by virtue of his exaltation the Son acquired a status superior to the angels. The biblical text is employed to exhibit the transcendent dignity of the Son. The seven quotations are presented as a succession of words spoken by God to the Son, which the Church on earth is permitted to overhear. They establish that God's own witness is the decisive factor in the enthronement of the Son. By implication, the hearers are invited to acknowledge the transcendent worth of the Son by displaying their confidence in him (cf. 1:1–4; 3:1, 14).

It may be assumed that the biblical passages cited were already familiar to the hearers from the liturgical tradition. All but one of the quotations are taken from the Greek Psalter, which provided the hymnbook for synagogue and Church. The one exception is a quotation from the Hymn of Moses, which had entered the worship of the hellenistic synagogues as an Ode appended to the Psalter. Although in vv 5 and 13 the supporting quotations are introduced with a rhetorical question, the writer's concern is not to set forth a formal proof in any strict sense of the word. The absence of logical argument, together with the observable fact that much of the content of 1:5–14 is not closely related to the further development of the address, provides evidence that the quotations serve another purpose. They simply summarize the biblical testimony to Jesus' sonship and rank, and establish his superiority to the heavenly mediators of the old revelation. The quotations thus reinforce the Church's confession (1:2*b*–4) and prepare for the solemn warning to respect the word of salvation proclaimed by the Lord (2:1–4).

C. The First Warning: The Peril of Ignoring the Word Delivered by the Son (2:1–4)

Bibliography

Auffret, P. "Note sur la structure littéraire d'Hb II. 1–4." *NTS* 25 (1978–79) 166–79. **Bachmann, M.** "'. . . gesprochen durch den Herrn' (Hebr 2, 3): Erwägungen zum Reden Gottes und Jesu im Hebräerbrief." *Bib* 71 (1990) 365–94. **Bandstra, A. J.** "The Law and Angels: *Antiquities* 15.136 and Galatians 3:19." *CTJ* 24 (1989) 223–40. **Bieder, W.** "Pneumatologische Aspekte im Hebräerbrief." In *Neues Testament und Geschichte.* FS O. Cullmann. Ed. H. Baltensweiler and B. Reicke. Tübingen: Mohr, 1972. 251–59. **Bishop, E. F. F.** "Angelology in Judaism, Islam, and Christianity." *ATR* 46 (1964) 142–54. **Exum, J. C.,** ed. *Signs and Wonders: Biblical Texts in Literary Focus.* Atlanta: Scholars Press, 1989. **Feuillet, A.** "Le 'commencement' de l'économie Chrétienne d'après Hé II. 3–4; Mc I. 1 et Ac I. 1–2." *NTS* 24 (1977–78) 163–74. **Galot, J.** "Existence personnelle et mission des anges." *EV* 99 (1989) 257–63. **Grässer, E.** "Das Heil als Wort: Exegetische Erwägungen zu Hebr 2, 1–4." In *Neues Testament und Geschichte.* FS O. Cullmann. Ed. H. Baltensweiler and B. Reicke. Tübingen: Mohr, 1972. 261–74. **Malan, F. S.** "Salvation in the New Testament: Emphases of the Different Writers." *ThViat* 17 (1989) 1–20. **Moule, C. F. D.** "The Vocabulary of Miracle." In *Miracles: Cambridge Studies in Their Philosophy and History.* Ed. C. F. D. Moule. London: Mowbray, 1965. 235–38. **Mugridge, A.** "Warnings in the Epistle to the Hebrews: An Exegetical and Theological Study." *RTR* 46 (1987) 74–82. **Oberholtzer, T. K.** "The Eschatological Salvation of Hebrews 1:5–2:5." *BSac* 145 (1988) 83–97. **Rice, G. E.** "Apostasy as a Motif and Its Effect on the Structure of Hebrews." *AUSS* 23 (1985) 29–35. **Selby, G. S.** "The Meaning and Function of *Suneidēsis* in Hebrews 9 and 10." *RestQ* 28 (1985–86) 145–54. **Silbermann, L. H.** "Prophets/Angels: LXX and Qumran Psalm 151 and the Epistle to the Hebrews." In *Standing before God.* FS J. M. Oesterreicher. New York: Ktav, 1981. 91–101. **Syzoulka, P. E.** "The Contribution of Hebrews 2:3–4 to the Problem of Apostolic Miracles." Dissertation, Dallas Theological Seminary, 1967. **Teodrico, P.** "Metafore nautiche in *Ebr.* 2, 1 e 6, 19." *RevistB* 6 (1958) 33–49. **Toussaint, S. D.** "The Eschatology of the Warning Passages in the Book of Hebrews." *GTJ* 3 (1982) 67–80. **Trites, A. A.** *The New Testament*

Concept of Witness. SNTSMS 31. Cambridge: Cambridge UP, 1977. **Übelacker, W. G.** *Der Hebräerbrief als Appell: Untersuchungen zu* exordium, narratio *und* postscriptum *(Hebr 1– 2 und 13,22–25).* Stockholm: Almqvist & Wiksell, 1989. 150–62, 189–90. **Vanhoye, A.** *Exegesis Epistulae ad Hebraeos Cap. I–II.* Rome: Pontifical Biblical Institute, 1968. 137– 46. ———. *Situation du Christ: Hébreux 1–2.* Paris: Cerf, 1969. 228–54. **Whitaker, M.** "'Signs and Wonders': The Pagan Background." *SE* 5 (1968) 155–58.

Translation

[1] *We must pay the closest* [a] *attention, therefore, to what we have heard, so that we do not drift off course.* [2] *For since* [b] *what was once spoken by God* [c] *through the angels proved to be valid, and every infringement and disobedience received the appropriate punishment,* [3] *how shall we escape if we disregard* [d] *a salvation as great as this?* [e] *First announced by God through the Lord himself, it was guaranteed to us by those who heard him,* [4] *while God, according to his own will,* [f] *plainly endorsed their witness* [g] *by signs and wonders and many kinds of miracles and by distribution of the gifts* [h] *of the Holy Spirit.*

Notes

[a] In Koine Gk. there was a decline in the use of the superlative form, and the comparative was pressed into service to take its place (cf. BDF §§60[1], 244). The comparative adv περισσοτέρως illustrates this tendency and probably carries an elative force not only here but whenever it occurs in the NT. Cf. Phillips: "We ought, therefore, to pay the greatest attention."

[b] The translation reflects the first class conditional clause (εἰ plus an ind in any tense in the protasis), which assumes the truth of the statement.

[c] The pass voice is employed frequently in the NT to avoid the use of the divine name (BDF § 130[1]). The pass λαληθείς (v 2) and λαλεῖσθαι (v 3) carry the implication that it is God who spoke, first through the angels and then through the Son. The same verb in the act voice with God as the subj occurs in 1:1–2: ὁ θεὸς λαλήσας . . . ἐλάλησεν.

[d] The adv ptcp ἀμελήσαντες is used in a conditional sense, "if we disregard" (cf. Burton, *Moods*, 436).

[e] Vv 2–4 constitute a long and involved periodic sentence. It has been broken up in the translation out of consideration for Eng. style.

[f] The translation reflects the exegetical decision that the concluding phrase, κατὰ τὴν αὐτοῦ θέλησιν, qualifies the entire statement and not simply the distribution of the gifts of the Spirit.

[g] The term συνεπιμαρτυρέω is common in nonbiblical Gk. (Aristotle, Polybius, Plutarch) but does not occur in the LXX and is found in the NT only here. It means "to bear witness at the same time" (cf. H. Strathmann, *TDNT* 4:510; Trites, *Witness*, 77).

[h] Lit., "distributions [μερισμοί] of the Holy Spirit," but with clear reference to the various gifts proceeding from the Holy Spirit.

Form/Structure/Setting

As the writer turns from exposition to exhortation, his gifts as an orator are displayed in the richness of his rhetorical style and vocabulary. The use of an oratorical imperative (v 1, "we must pay the closest attention") followed by a rhetorical question (v 3, "how shall we escape . . . ?") are characteristic features of the diatribe (cf. Turner, *Grammar,* 4:107). The carefully constructed period (vv 2–4) makes use of a rhetorical figure (*syncrisis*), which in Hebrews takes the form of "how much more" (cf. 2:3; 8:6; 9:14; 10:28–31). Alliteration, a standard device in oratory, particularly with the letter π, occurs in v 2, where the phrase πᾶσα παράβασις καὶ παρακοή, "every infringement and disobedience," provides a sonorous formulation. The effective use of the genitive absolute in v 4 is complemented by the rhymes of -σιν, which punctuate the final clause of the period: "by signs and wonders [τέρασιν] and many kinds of miracles [δυνάμεσιν] and by distribution of the gifts of the Holy Spirit, according to his will [θελήσιν]" (cf. Auffret, *NTS* 25 [1978–79] 174, n. 1, for other phonetic effects in the paragraph).

The most striking feature of the vocabulary is the turning away from language sanctioned by the LXX toward an idiomatic hellenistic diction. προσέχειν (v 1) is a nautical technical term, meaning to hold (a ship) toward port (LSJ, 1512), and appears to have called for its opposite παραρρεῖν, "to drift away from one's course" (cf. Teodorico, *RevistB* 6 [1958] 33–49, who suggests that προσέχειν indicates the fastening of the anchors to the sea bed to keep the ship from drifting; the nautical metaphor of the anchor occurs in 6:19). The concentration of juridical terminology in vv 2–4 offers other examples. In the vernacular βέβαιος, "valid," is often found with reference to λόγος; it signifies a "word" that is firm, sure, or legally valid. In the papyri, it is virtually a technical term implying legal security. But βέβαιος is rare in the LXX, and the expression βεβαιοῦν τὸν λόγον, "to validate the word," does not occur (A. Deissmann, *Bible Studies* [Edinburgh: Clark, 1903] 104–9; Schlier, *TDNT* 1:600–601). ἔνδικος, "appropriate," "just," is found in juridical contexts from the classical period on but is absent from the LXX and is found in the NT only here and in Rom 3:8. μισθαποδοσία, "punishment," appears to be a word coined by the writer on the basis of the rather common hellenistic expression ἀποδιδόναι τὸν μισθόν, "to award," "to pay." It occurs only in Hebrews and in later ecclesiastical literature (BAGD, 523). The phrase ἀρχὴν λαβοῦσα λαλεῖσθαι, "first announced," looks cumbersome but corresponds to classical Greek. The word συνεπιμαρτυροῦντος, "testify at the same time," "endorse," is well known from nonbiblical Greek (Aristotle, Polybius, Plutarch) but does not occur in the LXX and is found in the NT only here (Strathmann, *TDNT* 4:510). The number of unusual words and idioms and the avoidance of the vocabulary of the LXX suggest that in this paragraph it was the writer's intention to confront the thought and life of his readers in a more arresting way than reliance upon familiar words and phrases would foster.

Structurally, the paragraph consists of a direct statement (v 1) followed by an explanatory periodic sentence expressing a condition (vv 2–4). Within the condition, a protasis that concerns the message delivered by the angels is precisely matched by an apodosis concerning the message of salvation delivered by the Lord (cf. Vanhoye, *La structure*, 74–77). Vanhoye observed a further correspondence in thought between the opening statement (v 1) and the rhetorical question that introduces the apodosis (v 3a). The appeal to pay the closest attention to what has been heard anticipates the peril of ignoring the message of salvation proclaimed by the Lord. Similarly, the warning about drifting off course has in view the catastrophe envisioned in the question "How shall we escape?" (*La structure*, 265; for a more complex analysis, cf. Auffret, *NTS* 25 [1978–79] 166–79.)

The writer describes his work as a practical homily, a word of exhortation, which he asks his hearers to receive (13:22). This paragraph is the first in a series of smaller or larger sections that validate this description of Hebrews as a whole (cf. 3:12–4:13; 5:11–6:12; 10:19–39; 12:14–29). These passages, in which the writer pauses to address a warning or an appeal to the hearers, have significant bearing on the historical setting of Hebrews. They relate the thrust of the homily to the community in a direct way and convey a cumulative impression of how the writer envisaged the situation to which he responded with such passionate earnestness.

The close connection between 1:5–14 and the solemn warning in 2:1–4 demonstrates that "Scripture exposition is for this man not an end in itself. It is a brotherly service to a congregation that is in actual temptation" (Barth, "The Old Testament in Hebrews," 57). The temptation was to disregard the seriousness of Christian commitment, with the result that some were in danger of "drifting off course." Their interest in the Christian message had significantly slackened. Although the source of distraction is not specified at this point, the positive role assigned to angels and the appeal to the normative character of the Mosaic law in v 2 tend to suggest that the Christians addressed continued to maintain emotional and intellectual ties with the Jewish community. They needed to appreciate the solemn import of the message of salvation that they had received and to firm up their response to it.

The writer identifies himself explicitly with his hearers; he includes himself within the scope of the exhortation and warning addressed to them. Although the use of the personal pronouns "we" and "us" lends a tone of warmth to the admonition, the earnestness of the appeal indicates the existence of a situation that severely threatened the stability and life of the community.

F. C. Synge (*Hebrews*, 44–52) proposed that 2:1–4 be regarded as an interpolation. He assigned it to the source that contributed all of the hortatory passages to Hebrews. From the observation that the exposition in 1:1–14 and 2:5–16 possesses an internal unity and that the exhortation actually interrupts the course of the argument, he concluded that 2:2–4 is secondary to the context. Linguistic and conceptual parallels between this unit and other units of exhortation further convinced him that Hebrews in its present form fuses two written sources, one didactic and expositional in nature, the other a call to conversion. This hypothesis, however, is neither necessary nor plausible and is sufficiently refuted by literary and thematic considerations, which demonstrate the compositional unity of the document. The same evidence of artistic prose found in the exordium (1:1–4) recurs in 2:2–4: the employment of a skillfully balanced periodic sentence, parallelism of sound and sense, alliteration, and rhythm. Such stylistic features constitute a literary signature, which verifies that both paragraphs were composed by one writer. The reference to the God who has spoken in the exordium (1:1–2*a*) prepares for the solemn appeal to pay the closest attention to what has been heard in 2:1–4. Thematically, the two paragraphs are united by vocabulary and conception (cf. Vanhoye, *Situation*, 252–54). The arbitrary detachment of 2:1–4 from its context would falsify the writer's concern to call his hearers to perceive the inextricable unity between faith and experience.

Comment

1   The sequential connection between the preceding theological statement and the pointed appeal in 2:1–4 indicates that the confession of the incomparable superiority of the Son to the angels is presupposed. διὰ τοῦτο δεῖ, "it is

necessary, therefore," expresses a logical imperative: from the fact that Christ is greater than the angels it follows logically that the revelation delivered through the Son must be regarded with the utmost seriousness. The writer insists that adherence to the Christian tradition is the one thing that is necessary. In this context περισσοτέρως προσέχειν, "pay the closest attention," is analogous to the cognate κατέχειν in 3:6, 14; 10:23, where the hearers are urged to *hold fast to* their confession of faith, without which the goal of salvation cannot be reached (cf. Grässer, "Das Heil als Wort," 271). The language implies that the community had grown lax in their commitment to Christ and were neglecting the Christian message.

In his reference to the tradition, the writer does not use the familiar term εὐαγγέλιον, "gospel." The designation of the kerygma as "what has been heard" (τοῖς ἀκουσθεῖσιν) corresponds appropriately to the presentation of revelation in the exordium as the spoken utterance of God. Revelation is a word to be heard. The thematic connection between 1:1–4 and 2:1–4 needs to be appreciated. If God, in the final period of history, has spoken *to us* (ἡμῖν) his ultimate word in the Son (1:2*a*), then *we* (ἡμᾶς) must pay the closest attention to what has been heard (2:1). The reference is inclusive, signifying the words spoken to the Son, in the Son, and about the Son, as chap. 1 indicates.

The peril against which the community is asked to guard is that of drifting off course (μήποτε παραρυῶμεν). If it is proper to recognize (with Teodorico, *RevistB* 6 [1958] 33–39) a nautical overtone in προσέχειν, "to hold a ship toward port, or to fasten the anchors to the sea bed," the image of a drifting ship, carried by the current beyond a fixed point, furnished a vivid metaphor for the failure to keep a firm grip on the truth through carelessness and lack of concern. In Prov 3:21 (LXX) παραρρεῖν signifies to lose sight of advice and wisdom. The writer warns his readers that they are in danger of losing sight of the reality of Christian salvation.

2 The following three verses develop a comparison designed to reinforce the necessity of adhering to the Christian tradition. If disregard for the Mosaic law was appropriately punished, unconcern for the gospel must inevitably be catastrophic. The most striking feature of v 2 is the accumulation of juridicial expressions ("proved legally valid," "every infringement and disobedience," "received appropriate punishment"), which confirms that "the message declared by the angels" signifies the law delivered at Sinai.

There is no indication that angels were present at the giving of the law in Exod 19 and 20. In Deut 33:2, however, in a passage celebrating the theophany on Sinai, Moses declares that God came "with myriads of holy ones," and the LXX adds, "angels were with him at his right hand" (ἐκ δεξιῶν αὐτοῦ ἄγγελοι μετ' αὐτοῦ; cf. Ps 68:17). Sometime prior to the first century, the conviction spread that angels had played a mediatorial role in the transmission of the law. It finds expression as early as the Maccabean period in the *Book of Jubilees* (1:27; 2:1, 26–27; et al.) when the content of the Torah is dictated to Moses by "the Angel of the Presence." Stephen similarly speaks of the angel who spoke to Moses on Mount Sinai (Acts 7:38; cf. v 53), while Paul describes the law as "ordained by angels through an intermediary" (Gal 3:19; cf. John 7:19). Near the end of the first century Josephus wrote, "And for ourselves, we have learned from God the most excellent of our teachings, and the most holy part of our law by angels [δι' ἀγγέλων] or ambassadors" (*Ant.* 15.36). Similar statements occur in early collections of rabbinical tradition (*Mek.* on Exod 20:18; *Sipre* 102 on Num 12:5; *Pesiq. R.* 21). In Hebrews "the message delivered by angels" is an alternate expression for the word that God spoke through the prophets (1:1*b*). That message proved to be legally valid (ἐγένετο βέβαιος) precisely because it was a word spoken by God (λαληθείς, where the passive voice implies that it was God who had spoken).

Both παράβασις, "infringement," and παρακοή, "disobedience," involve a deliberate rejection of the divine will. The thought expressed is that under the old covenant every infringement of the Mosaic ordinances and each rejection of the will of God expressed in the law received appropriate redress. The noun παρακοή does not occur in the LXX but implies an unwillingness to listen to the voice of God (cf. Kittel, *TDNT* 1:233; Schneider, *TDNT* 5:740). The appearance of this disposition within the community needed to be checked before it incurred the judgment of God. The choice of the term παρακοή was dictated by the formulation of v 1 ("to pay the closest attention to what we have heard" [ἀκουσθεῖσιν]). By coining the term μισθαποδοσία, "punishment as reward," the writer arrests the attention of his hearers and reminds them that carelessness and contempt for God's revelation under the old covenant brought in its wake just and appropriate punishment (cf. Priesker, *TDNT* 4:702).

3-4 The urgent appeal to pay the closest attention to what has been heard (v 1) anticipated the warning that the message of salvation can be ignored, with catastrophic consequences. A lack of concern (ἀμελήσαντες) for God's word invites ἔνδικον μισθαποδοσίαν, "an appropriate punishment" (v 2*b*). The experience of Israel in this regard (cf. 3:7–4:11) provided a sobering model for those who were prone to become apathetic and unresponsive to God's revelation in the Son. Already under the old covenant carelessness toward the revealed will of God incurred appropriate punishment. No less can be anticipated by the people of God now that he has declared his ultimate word through the Son. In this sense the distinction between the old and the new people of God was only relative; both were the privileged heirs to revelation. The greater degree of privilege enjoyed by the new people of God, which finds ample expression in the phrase τηλικαύτης . . . σωτηρίας, "a salvation as great as this," simply means that they are faced with greater responsibility and greater peril. The writer returns to this model for the understanding of Christian responsibility twice more, and on each occasion he poses the issue sharply for his reader (10:28–31; 12:25; cf. especially Auffret, *NTS* 25 [1978–79] 177–79). Consequently, the rhetorical question in v 3 (πῶς ἡμεῖς ἐκφευξόμεθα, "how shall we escape . . . ?") calls for the reply that no escape is possible.

The character of the message of salvation received by the congregation is defined by the fact that God addresses people no longer through the agency of the angels, but through the Lord, who is his unique Son. λαλεῖσθαι διὰ τοῦ κυρίου, "announced through the Lord," resumes the affirmation of the exordium that in this last period of history God has spoken ἐν υἱῷ, "through the Son" (1:2*a*). The structural parallelism between ὁ δι' ἀγγέλων λαληθείς λόγος, "the word spoken through the angels" (v 2), and σωτηρίας ἥτις . . . λαλεῖσθαι διὰ τοῦ κυρίου, "salvation which was announced through the Lord" (v 3), presupposes the demonstration that the Son is incomparably superior to the angels (1:5–14). Since the message delivered through the angels demanded accountability, how much more is this true of the message of salvation announced by the Lord? The clauses in vv 3*b*–4 qualify σωτηρίας and serve to augment the impression of the exceptional character of the salvation that is in view.

The author of Hebrews is vitally interested in the activity of preaching. He is aware of the passage of time, which separates the period of Jesus' ministry from his own day; he had not participated in the events that marked the inauguration of salvation. But he insists upon the continuity of the present with that pristine past by sketching the character of the tradition through which he and his readers came to faith.

ἀρχὴν λαβοῦσα λαλεῖσθαι διὰ τοῦ κυρίου, "first announced [by God] through the Lord himself." The foundation of the Christian economy is traced to the ministry of the Lord. The text contains a profound concept of the Church as rooted in the activity of the Lord (cf. Feuillet, *NTS* 24 [1977–78] 163–66). The message of salvation began to be declared through him. Basic to the designation of Jesus as Lord (κύριος), however, is the writer's conception of the unity of word and deed in Jesus' ministry. Jesus' word is not simply information about salvation, for salvation concerns καθαρισμὸς τῶν ἁμαρτιῶν, "purification for sins" (1:3; cf. 9:14; 10:10). He embodied the word of God and accomplished it. The Son is the eschatological event of salvation (cf. 1:2). In this comprehensive sense his ministry, which passed through the successive stages of proclamation, sacrificial death, and exaltation, marked the ἀρχή, "beginning," of the message of salvation (cf. Grässer, "Das Heil als Wort," 263–66).

ὑπὸ τῶν ἀκουσάντων εἰς ἡμᾶς ἐβεβαιώθη, "guaranteed to us by those who heard him." The ministry of the Lord marked the first phase of God's final revelation. It was succeeded by a second, which consisted of accrediting the word (ἐβεβαιώθη), in the sense of guaranteeing its accuracy. The message of salvation was proclaimed to those who did not have the privilege of hearing the Lord by those who had been witnesses to his word and deed. In reference to these witnesses, it is not necessary to think of the apostolic company. It is significant that in Hebrews the office of apostle is reserved for Jesus alone (3:1). The highest office the writer acknowledges within the larger Christian community is that of a "hearer," i.e., one who could testify concerning the truth that Jesus had declared because he had heard the Lord. By speaking of "the hearers" (τῶν ἀκουσάντων), all interest is concentrated on the message, not the office, of those who had brought the word of redemption to the community (cf. Grässer, "Das Heil als Wort," 267–68).

συνεπιμαρτυροῦντος τοῦ θεοῦ, "while God endorsed their witness." The result of the act of speaking (λαλεῖσθαι) and hearing (τῶν ἀκουσάντων) was tradition. But the tradition was made effective only through the accompanying witness of God, who endorsed the preaching of salvation with evidence that corroborated its veracity (v 4). The present participle (rendered "while God endorsed") implies that the corroborative evidence was not confined to the initial act of preaching, but continued to be displayed within the life of the community. The accent in v 4, however, where the vocabulary denotes significant manifestations of power, falls upon outward, tangible evidence, which served to validate the message delivered to the community. The spoken word was complemented by the visible demonstration of the gospel, which foreshadowed the completion of salvation (cf. 6:5) and confirmed that the Lord continued to speak and act through the missionaries (cf. Trites, *Witness*, 77, 150, 217).

σημεῖα καὶ τέρατα, "signs and wonders," is to be taken as a fixed expression, in which the original distinction between the terms has not been maintained (cf. Hofius, *NIDNTT* 2:627). The originally pagan word τέρας, "wonder," which denoted something unnatural and monstrous (cf. Whitaker, *SE* 5[1968] 155–58), was brought within the scope of God's redemptive activity on behalf of Israel in the LXX, so that τέρατα, "wonders," became a vehicle for revelation. The term was frequently joined with σημεῖον, "sign," so that σημεῖα καὶ τέρατα became a standard phrase for the events of the Exodus, which served to identify God's relationship to his people and his purposes (Exod 7:3; Deut 4:34; 6:22; 7:19; 29:2; cf. Moule, "The Vocabulary of Miracle," 235–38). These passages provide the biblical background to the expression in v 4, while Mark 16:20 (in the Longer Ending) provides the earliest interpretation of the text (for a detailed analysis of the similarity between Heb. 2:3–4 and Mark 16:20 see J. P. van Casteren, "L'epilogue canonique du second évangile [Mc 16, 9–20]," *RB* 10 [1902] 240–43).

The reference to ποικίλαις δυνάμεσιν, "many kinds of miracles," similarly expresses God's concern for the community as he breaks into their affairs with power. Through the Holy Spirit, God is present with the witnesses as the dispenser of power (cf. C. H. Powell, *Power*, 107–16, 130–42). The bestowal of the charismatic gifts (μερισμοῖς) of the Holy Spirit also served to attest the message proclaimed. It is presumably the perpetuation of the charisma in the life of the community (cf. 6:4–5) that provides indisputable evidence of God's seal upon the word received by the congregation. The supporting evidence of signs and wonders, of various miracles and spiritual gifts, is anchored in the will of God (κατὰ τὴν αὐτοῦ θέλησιν). The writer's final phrase qualifies the entire series, and not simply the last member of the series (so also Rengstorf, *TDNT* 7:260).

Since the purpose of this evidence is the validation that God has spoken definitively in Christ, unbelief and carelessness can only be regarded as the expression of an utterly incomprehensible hardness of heart (cf. 3:7–8, 12, 15; 4:7).

Explanation

In 2:1–4, which momentarily interrupts the flow of the exposition, the writer turns from proclamation to application. In pastoral concern he pauses to relate the significance of the initial segment of the homily to the immediate situation of his readers. The purpose of the confessional recital of Jesus' superiority to the angels, the heavenly mediators of the law, was to emphasize the ultimate significance of the new word of revelation delivered by the Son. The fundamental assumption of the argument is that the character of the messenger provides the test of the importance and finality of his message. The transcendent dignity of the Son demonstrates that the message of salvation that had reached the community through witnesses who had been attested by God merits the strictest attention.

The Christian tradition confronted the congregation with God's word and deed. Like Israel, the Christian community was constituted by an act of revelation. The experience of Israel demonstrated that a reckless disregard for the tradition and the commitment to which it summoned the community of faith could only expose the people of God to divine judgment. It is this peril that the writer seeks to address. By stressing that the preaching of the gospel was itself a juridical activity, he calls for a response from his hearers that is consistent with the transcendent character of the message of salvation.

D. The Humiliation and Glory of the Son (2:5–9)

Bibliography

Attridge, H. W. "New Covenant Christology in an Early Christian Homily." *QuartRev* 8 (1988) 89–108. **Brady, C.** "The World to Come in the Epistle to the Hebrews." *Wor* 39 (1965) 329–39. **Brock, S. P.** "Hebrews 2:9b in Syriac Tradition." *NovT* 27 (1985) 236–44. **Brown, D.** "Hebrews 2:5–9." *ExpTim* 7 (1895/96) 133–34. **Childs, B.** "Psalm 8 in the Context of the Christian Canon." *Int* 18 (1969) 20–31. **Coppens, J.** "Le Fils de l'homme dans le dossier paulinien." *ETL* 52 (1976) 309–30. **Dukes, J.** "The Humanity of Jesus in Hebrews." *ThEduc* 32 (1985) 38–45. **Dyck, T. L.** "Jesus our Pioneer." 39–50. **Ellingworth, P.** "Jesus and the Universe in Hebrews." *EvQ* 58 (1986) 337–50. **Elliott, J. K.** "When Jesus Was Apart from God: An Examination of Hebrews 2:9." *ExpTim* 83 (1971–72) 339–41. **Ellis, E. E.** "Midrash, Targum and New Testament Quotations," In *Neotestamentica et Semitica*. FS M. Black. Ed. E. E. Ellis and M. Wilcox. Edinburgh: Clark, 1969. 61–69. **Fabris, R.** "La lettera agli Ebrei e l'Antico Testamento." *RivB* 32 (1984) 237–52. **Feld, H.** "Der Humanistenstreit um Hebräer 2, 7 (Psalm 8, 6)." *ARG* 61 (1970) 5–35. **Frede, H. J.** "Der Text des Hebräerbriefs bei Liudprand von Cremona." *RBén* 96 (1986) 94–99. **Garnet, P.** "Hebrews 2:9: χάριτι or χωρίς?" *SP* 18 (1983/85) 321–25. **Giles, P.** "The Son of Man in the Epistle to the Hebrews." *ExpTim* 86 (1974–75) 328–32. **Glenn, D. R.** "Psalm 8 and Hebrews 2: A Case Study in Biblical Hermeneutics and Biblical Theology." In *Walvoord: A Tribute*. Ed. D. K. Campbell. Chicago: Moody Press, 1982. 39–51. **Grässer, E.** "Beobachtungen zum Menschensohn in Hebr. 2, 6." In *Jesus und der Menschensohn*. FS A. Vogtle. Ed. R. Pesch and R. Schnackenburg. Freiburg/Basel/Vienna: Herder, 1975. 404–14. **Grogan, G. W.** "Christ and His People: An Exegetical and Theological Study of Hebrews 2:5–18." *VoxEv* 6 (1969) 54–71. **Harnack, A. von.** "Zwei alte dogmatische Korrekturen im Hebräerbrief." SPAW (1929) 63–73. **Henderson, A.** "Hebrews 2:9." *ExpTim* 7 (1895–96) 332–34. **Hickling, C. J. A.** "John and Hebrews: The Background of Hebrews 2.10–18." *NTS* 29 (1983) 112–16. **Hurst, L. D.** "The Background and Interpretation of the Epistle to the Hebrews." Dissertation, Oxford University, 1981. 181–89. ———. "The Christology of Hebrews 1 and 2." In *The Glory of Christ in the New Testament*. FS G. B. Caird. Ed. L. D. Hurst and N. T. Wright. Oxford: Clarendon Press, 1987. 151–64. **Kistemaker, S.** *The Psalm Citations in the Epistle to the Hebrews*. Amsterdam: G. van Soest, 1961. **Kögel, J.** *Der Sohn und die Söhne: Eine exegetische Studie zu Hebräer 2:5–18*. Gütersloh: Bertelsmann, 1904. **Kouto, J. K. M.** "Humanité et autorité du Christ-Prêtre: Une approche exégético-théologique de Hé. 2, 5–18; 3, 1–6 et 4, 15–5, 10." Dissertation, Pont. Univ. Urbaniana, Rome, 1985. **Laub, F.** *Bekenntnis und Auslegung*. 61–66. **Linton, O.** "Le Parallelismus Membrorum dans le Nouveau Testament: Simple remarques." In *Mélanges Bibliques*. FS B. Rigaux. Ed. A. Descamps and A. de Halleux. Gembloux: Duculot, 1970.

488–507. **Louis, C. J.** *The Theology of Psalm 8: A Study of the Traditions of the Text and the Theological Import.* Washington, DC: Catholic University of America, 1946. **Melbourne, B. L.** "An Examination of the Historical-Jesus Motif in the Epistle to the Hebrews." *AUSS* 26 (1988) 281–97. **Miller, D. G.** "Why God Became Man: From Text to Sermon on Heb. 2:5–18." *Int* 23 (1960) 3–19. **Minear, P. S.** *New Testament Apocalyptic.* 126–34. **Oberholtzer, T. K.** "The Eschatological Salvation of Hebrews 1:5–2:5." *BSac* 145 (1988) 83–97. **Oberholzer, J. P.** "What Is Man . . . ?" In *De Fructu Oris Sui.* FS A. Van Selms. Ed. I. H. Eybers, F. C. Fensham, et al. Leiden: Brill, 1971. 141–51. **O'Neill, J. C.** "Hebrews II.9." *JTS* n.s. 17 (1966) 79–82. **Parsons, M. C.** "Son and High Priest: A Study in the Christology of Hebrews." *EvQ* 60 (1988) 195–215. **Pryor, J. W.** "Hebrews and Incarnational Christology." *RTR* 40 (1981) 44–50. **Ringgren, H.** "Psalm 8 och Kristologin." *SEÅ* 37–38 (1972–73) 16–20. **Sahlin, H.** "Adam-Christologie im Neuen Testament." *ST* 41 (1987) 11–32. **Schröger, F.** *Der Verfasser des Hebräerbriefs als Schriftlausleger.* Regensburg: Pustet, 1968. 79–87. **Seeberg, A.** "Zur Auslegung von Hebr. 2:5–18." *NJDT* 3 (1894) 435–61. **Übelacker, W. G.** *Der Hebräerbrief als Appell: Untersuchungen zu* exordium, narratio *und* postscriptum *(Hebr 1–2 und 13,22–25).* Stockholm: Almqvist & Wiksell, 1989. 163–82. **Vanhoye, A.** *Exegesis Epistulae ad Hebraeos Cap. I–II.* Rome: Pontifical Biblical Institute, 1968. 147–87. ———. "L'οἰκουμένη dans l'Épître aux Hébreux." *Bib* 45 (1964) 248–53. ———. *Situation de Christ: Hébreux 1–2.* Paris: Cerf, 1969. 255–305. **Wallis, W. B.** "The Use of Psalms 8 and 110 in I Corinthians 15:25–27 and Hebrews 1 and 2." *JETS* 15 (1972) 25–29.

Translation

   [5]Now[a] *it is not to angels that he has subjected the heavenly world to come, about which we are speaking.* [6]*Somewhere someone has testified, saying,*
      "What[b] is man that[c] you take thought for him,
      or the son of man that you should care for him?
   [7]   *You made him for a little while[d] lower than the angels;*
      you crowned him with glory and splendor;[e]
   [8]   *you put everything in subjection under his feet."*
Now in putting everything in subjection to him, he left nothing out of his control. But in fact[f] we do not yet see everything subject to his control. [9]*But we see Jesus, who for a little while was made lower than the angels so that by the grace of God[g] he might taste death for everyone,[h] because of the suffering of death crowned with glory and splendor.[i]*

Notes

   [a] For the idiomatic translation of γάρ in the sense of "now," which is appropriate to the beginning of a new paragraph, see Moffatt, 21.

   [b] p[46] and a few less important authorities (C* P 104 917 1288 1319 1891 2127 d vg[tol] bo) read τίς ("who?") in place of τί ("what?"), and the originality of this reading has been defended by Zuntz (*Text*, 48–49). He argued that the writer deliberately altered the text in order to draw attention to its support for a Son of Man christology. He translated v 6, "Who is the man [ἄνθρωπος with rough breathing, by putative crasis for ὁ ἄνθρωπος] whom thou mindest? Truly [the classical ἦ with circumflex accent in place of ἤ, "or," as in the LXX] the Son of Man, for thou visitest him." The presence of τί in the majority of MSS he explained as assimilation to the LXX text. But see the critique of Tasker, *NTS* 1 (1954–55) 185.

   [c] Both occurrences of ὅτι in v 6 have a consecutive sense ("so that"), corresponding to the use of the Heb. conj, which is consec in the quotation (cf. F. M. Abel, *Grammaire du grec biblique* [Paris: Gabalda, 1927] 79 [353]; Moulton, *Grammar*, 3:318).

   [d] The expression βραχύ τι may be qualitative ("a little lower than") or temporal ("for a little while"). In Ps 8 it is almost certainly qualitative, and this has influenced the translation of this verse in the NIV

("You made him a little lower than the angels"). The understanding of the writer to the Hebrews, however, is made clear when this portion of the quotation is taken up in v 9 and the expression βραχύ τι is placed first for emphasis: Jesus was "for a short while" made lower than the angels. This has been the dominant understanding of the expression ever since the Humanist Controversy between Erasmus and the Parisian humanist Jacobius Faber Stapulensis (see Feld, *ARG* 61 [1970] 5–35). So RSV, NEB, NASB, JB, TEV, et al.

ᵉ The writer omitted from his quotation the clause "and set him over the works of your hands" (following the shorter reading supported by P⁴⁶ B Dᶜ K L al). The considerable support for the inclusion of these words (ℵ A C D* P Ψ 33 1739 it vg sy ᵖ·ʰ ᵂⁱᵗʰ * co arm aeth al) is almost certainly due to scribal assimilation of the text to the LXX of Ps 8:7 (cf. Metzger, *Textual Commentary*, 663–64).

ᶠ For the adversative force of δέ in v 8 see BDF §447(1).

ᵍ The textual support for the reading χάριτι θεοῦ ("by the grace of God") is very strong (P⁴⁶ ℵ A B C D 33 81 330 614 it vg co al) and seems decisive. Nevertheless, there is impressive patristic evidence that both in the East and in the West the reading χωρὶς θεοῦ (NEBᵐᵍ: "apart from God") was strongly attested as early as the third century. Although it is found now only in MS 1739, from which it entered into 0121 b and 424**, and in MS G of the Vulgate as well as in three copies of the Peshitta, it was present in MSS known to Origen, Ambrose, and Jerome, and it was adopted as the correct reading by a number of the church fathers. It has been defended as primitive by Harnack (SPAW [1929] 63–73: χάριτι θεοῦ is a "dogmatic" correction of the text by later scribes), Zuntz (*Text*, 34–35: χωρὶς θεοῦ, "separated from God," agrees with the writer's concept of the passion [cf. 5:7f.; 11:26; 12:2; 13:12–13]; moreover, χωρὶς is a favorite word with the writer and always is followed by an anarthrous noun in Hebrews), O'Neill (*JTS* n.s. 17 [1966] 79–82: χωρὶς θεοῦ, "far from God," expresses the spatial distance from God represented by the position lower than the angels), and J. K. Elliott (*ExpTim* 83 [1971–72] 339–41: χωρὶς θεοῦ means that Christ in his death was separated from God because he entered the realm of Satan, which is death). These writers appeal to the intrinsic improbability that χάριτι could be misread as χωρὶς or could be deliberately altered to χωρὶς, whereas the difficulty of construing the precise sense of χωρὶς θεοῦ would encourage the alteration of this reading to the more acceptable χάριτι θεοῦ. It is probable, however, that the reading χωρὶς θεοῦ originated as a marginal gloss (suggested by 1 Cor 15:27) to explain that "everything" (τὰ πάντα) does not include God. This gloss was erroneously regarded by a later transcriber as a correction of χάριτι θεοῦ and was introduced into the text of v 9 (so Metzger, *Textual Commentary*, 664; Tasker, *NTS* 1 [1954–55] 184; Vanhoye, *Situation*, 295–99; P. E. Hughes, "Note on the Variant Reading χωρὶς θεοῦ ['Apart from God'; 2:9]," in *Commentary*, 94–97; et al.). χάριτι θεοῦ fits in well with ἔπρεπεν . . . αὐτῷ [θεῷ], which follows in v 10.

ʰ The translation seeks to reflect the sense intended by the writer rather than the order of the clauses in v 9. It is imperative to recognize that in the Gk. text the clauses have been arranged in a chiastic fashion so that the first clause ("who for a little while was made lower than the angels") is complemented by the fourth ("so that by the grace of God he might taste death for everyone"). This literary arrangement served to bring together the two inner clauses ("because of the suffering of death" and "crowned with glory and splendor"). Only by rearranging the order of the clauses in the translation can the intended sense be expressed. This has been properly recognized by TEV and by P. E. Hughes, 90–91.

ⁱ The translation reflects the exegetical decision that Jesus was crowned with glory and splendor precisely because he suffered death. The two clauses, which stand in an emphatic position in the middle of the sentence in the Gk. text, express the same sequential pattern of humiliation and exaltation found in Heb 1:3c, "made purification for sins and then sat down at the right hand of the divine Majesty on high" (cf. F. F. Bruce, 38).

Form/Structure/Setting

The comparison between the Son and the angels is sustained in vv 5–9, as the point is made that Jesus' condescension to be made "lower than the angels" (v 9) does not call into question his transcendent dignity. The introduction of a new paragraph is indicated by a change of genre; the writer turns from admonition (2:1–4) to exposition (2:5–9). The exposition assumes the form of homiletical midrash, in which key phrases of an extended quotation are taken up and expounded for the hearers (cf. Ellis, "Midrash, Targum," 61–69 [with bibliography]).

The paragraph is so dominated by the citation and explanation of Ps 8 that it could be overlooked that the writer introduces a second string of OT passages (vv 6–8, 12–13), which serves to complement the quotations in 1:5–13.

An *inclusio* established by the form of the statement in v 5 and v 16 indicates the limits of the new unit:

> v 5   οὐ γὰρ ἀγγέλοις ὑπέταξεν
> "Now it is not to angels that he has subjected"
> v 16   οὐ γὰρ δήπου ἀγγέλων ἐπιλαμβάνεται
> "For of course it is not angels that he takes hold to help"

The reference to the angels in v 5 resumes the comparison developed in 1:5–14 and anticipates the exegetical interaction with Ps 8:5–7 (LXX) that follows. But after v 9 the exposition takes a different turn. The writer focuses not on the angels but on the solidarity of the Son with the people of God (vv 10–18). The reference to the angels in v 16 is solely literary; it serves to balance the parallel statement with which the unit was introduced (v 5) (cf. Vanhoye, *La structure*, 78–81). By framing the section in this manner the writer rounds off the comparison between the Son and the angels that was introduced in 1:5. The next unit of thought to be developed in the homily is announced by fresh vocabulary in vv 17–18, which brings to a conclusion the first major division of the address. The segment established by the *inclusio* falls naturally into two paragraphs exploring (1) the humiliation and glory of the Son (vv 5–9) and (2) his solidarity with the human family (vv 10–18).

The development in the initial paragraph is tied together by the wordplay on ὑποτάσσειν, "to subject," "subordinate," and its derivatives. The declaration that it was not to angels that God subjected (ὑπέταξεν) the world to come (v 5) anticipates the use of the same verbal form in the climactic refrain of Ps 8:7 ("you subjected [ὑπέταξας] all things under his feet" [v 8a]). This in turn provides the writer with the key to the interpretation of the entire quotation:

> Now in putting everything in subjection [ἐν τῷ γὰρ ὑποτάξαι] to him, he left nothing out of his control [ἀνυπότακτον]. But in fact we do not see everything subject to his control [ὑποτεταγμένα].

The repetition with variation in form is rhetorically effective. It introduces an element of suspense, which is not relieved until the emphatic and deferred statement of v 9, "but . . . we see Jesus" (τὸν δὲ . . . βλέπομεν Ἰησοῦν).

The manner in which the second half of the quotation is taken up and incorporated into the midrashic commentary in vv 8–9 adds another expression of stylistic variation. The writer regarded the declarations of Ps 8:6–7 as independent statements descriptive of three stages in the experience of Jesus: (A) incarnation and humiliation ("you made him for a little while lower than the angels" [v 7a]); (B) exaltation ("you crowned him with glory and splendor" [v 7b]); and (C) final triumph ("you put everything in subjection under his feet" [v 8a]). By commenting upon these statements in the order C (v 8 b–c), A (v 9a), B (v 9b), he made the entire exposition subservient to the perspective of the exaltation glory into which Jesus has entered as a result of the death he suffered on behalf of others (cf. Vanhoye, *La structure*, 78–79; Grogan, *VoxEv* 6 [1969] 56).

Comment

5 The explanatory clause περὶ ἧς λαλοῦμεν, "about which we are speaking," underscores the continuity in thought between 1:5–14 and the resumption of the exposition at this point. A string of OT quotations had exhibited the transcendent dignity of the Son, particularly in his exaltation. The writer intends now to examine other OT passages that also bear upon the character and dignity of Jesus. The thought that Ps 110:1 could be applied to the angels was advanced rhetorically in 1:13, only to be rejected (1:14). The invitation to be enthroned at God's right hand was addressed to the Son alone. The unexpounded citation of Ps 110:1, with its reference to the subduing of enemies, accounts for both the mention of the subjection of the world to come in 2:5 and the appeal to Ps 8:5–7 (LXX), where the writer finds an illustration of what he has been saying.

Οὐ γὰρ ἀγγέλοις ὑπέταξεν, "Now it is not to angels that he has subjected." The reference to the angels resumes the argument advanced rhetorically in 1:13–14. Although God has entrusted the administration of the terrestrial world to the angels, their prerogatives did not extend to the heavenly world to come. The formulation reflects an allusion to Deut 32:8, which speaks of the angelic government of the world (cf. Andriessen, *NovT* 18 [1976] 295, n. 3). In the Old Greek version the text reads:

> When the Most High gave the nations their inheritance,
> when he separated the sons of Adam,
> he established boundaries for the nations
> according to the number of the angels of God.

The establishment of boundaries for the nations "according to the number of the angels of God" implied that the nations of the world had been subjected (ὑπέταξεν) to the angels. The heritage of the new people of God, however, lies not in the present world but in the new creation inaugurated by the enthronement of the Son. The function of γάρ is thus to link this fresh affirmation to the theme of the supremacy of the Son that has been developed up to this point. It signifies "not to the angels" but to the Son (cf. Grogan, *VoxEv* 6 [1969] 56).

τὴν οἰκουμένην τὴν μέλλουσαν, "the heavenly world to come." The writer had already identified the entrance of the Son into τὴν οἰκουμένην, the heavenly world of reality, at his exaltation as the occasion when the angels of God were commanded to worship him (see *Comment* on 1:6). He now takes up the thought again by designating the new creation inaugurated by the Son's enthronement as τὴν οἰκουμένην τὴν μέλλουσαν. This distinctive designation, which finds equivalent expression in μέλλοντας αἰῶνος, "the age to come" (6:5), or πόλιν . . . τὴν μέλλουσαν, "the city to come" (13:14), reflects a class of statements in the Psalter that proclaim the establishment of the eschatological kingdom of God.

> The Lord has inaugurated his reign [ἐβασίλευσεν, ingressive aorist] . . . indeed, he has established the world [τὴν οἰκουμένην] that shall not be shaken.
> (Ps 92[MT 93]:1)

Say to the nations, the Lord has inaugurated his reign;
he has erected the world [τὴν οἰκουμένην] that shall not be shaken.
(Ps 95[MT 96]:10)

The explicit allusion to "a kingdom that cannot be shaken" in Heb 12:28 indicates that these passages were not far from the writer's mind when he penned v 5. They amply justified the full phrase, "the heavenly world to come," as a designation of the eschatological realm of salvation. The community had already begun to experience the impact of this reality (2:4; 6:4–5; cf. Vanhoye, *Bib* 45 [1964] 249–53). The expression anticipates the consummation when every relationship will reflect the sovereignty of God's Son (cf. v 8).

The function of v 5 is to link two chains of OT citations. The first (1:5–13) develops the superiority of Jesus in his exaltation to the angels. The second (2:6–16) refutes the objections that could be mustered against that superiority on the ground that the Son assumed a condition inferior to that of the angels and submitted to death (v 9). The reminder that God did not entrust the administration of the heavenly world to come to the angels but to the exalted Son puts in a proper perspective the exposition of Jesus' solidarity with the human condition that follows (cf. Coppens, *ETL* 52 [1976] 326).

6–8a διεμαρτύρατο δέ πού τις λέγων, "somewhere someone has testified, saying." The vagueness of the formula of quotation is consistent with the strong emphasis throughout Hebrews on the oracular character of Scripture. Precisely because it is God who speaks in the OT, the identity of the person through whom he uttered his word is relatively unimportant. A vague allusion is sufficient. It is the substantial authority of what is said, not its source, which is of primary importance to the argument (cf. 4:4). The formula emphasizes the witness-character of Scripture (διεμαρτύρατο). In the quotation from Ps 8:5–7 LXX (MT 8:4–6), the writer finds confirmation for what he has been saying.

Ps 8 is an expression of astonishment reflecting upon humankind's creatureliness before God. Remembered and cared for by the Lord, created a little less than a heavenly being, crowned with glory and honor, human beings had been given the status of creature-sovereign with responsibility for the ordering of the creation for God (Oberholzer, "What Is Man . . . ?" 147). The description corresponds to the divine intention expressed in Gen 1:26–28. Created in God's image, humans were entrusted with the cultural mandate to subdue the earth and to put everything in subjection to themselves. That goal had been frustrated by sin and death, but the sense of wonder expressed by the psalmist indicates that it had not been forgotten. The recital and celebration of the divine intention awakened the expectation that all that had been placed under human dominion at the time of the creation would yet be subject to humanity in the world to come (cf. Kistemaker, *Psalm Citations,* 103–4).

In the NT Ps 8 is almost invariably cited in association with Ps 110:1 (1 Cor 15:25–27; Eph 1:20–22; cf. Phil 3:21; 1 Pet 3:22). The tandem arrangement of the two OT texts that speak of subjecting everything beneath the feet (Ps 110:1 and Ps 8:7) provides evidence for a common exegetical tradition upon which Christian writers drew. In Hebrews the quotation of Ps 8:5–7 is preceded by the quotation of Ps 110:1 (1:13), with no intervening citation (cf. Lindars, *New Testament Apologetic,* 50–51, 168–69; Loader, *NTS* 24 [1977–78] 209–13). The quotation conforms to the Old Greek version, but the clause "you made him ruler over the works of your hands" (Ps 8:7a[MT 6a]) has been omitted.

It is commonly held that the writer found in the second line of the quotation a reference to Jesus as the Son of Man or the Second Adam. It was, in fact, this detail of the text that encouraged him to treat Ps 8 in an explicitly christological sense (cf. Cullmann, *Christology*, 188; F. F. Bruce, 35–36; Buchanan, 38–51; Giles, *ExpTim* 86 [1974–75] 328–32; et al.). In the Gospels, however, the title by which Jesus designated himself is uniformly the articular expression ὁ υἱὸς τοῦ ἀνθρώπου, "the Son of Man." The sole exception is John 5:27, where the absence of the article results apparently from the allusion to Dan 7:13 (LXX). The fact that υἱὸς ἀνθρώπου is anarthrous in Ps 8 supports the presumption that the writer to the Hebrews did not find a christological title in the designation. He cites Ps 8:5 because he wishes to emphasize that Jesus in a representative sense fulfilled the vocation intended for humankind. He understood that the parallel expressions ἄνθρωπος, "man," "humankind," and υἱὸς ἀνθρώπου, "son of man," "mortal," were perfectly synonymous and were to be interpreted in terms of that fact. When he supplies his own commentary upon the text, he shows no interest in the initial lines of the quotation but confines himself exclusively to Ps 8:6–7. The quotation of Ps 8 may readily be applied to Jesus without finding in the vocabulary an implied reference to the Son of Man christology of the Gospels (so also F. H. Borsch, *The Son of Man in Myth and History* [Philadelphia: Westminster Press, 1967] 237–38; Grässer, "Beobachtungen," 409–14; Coppens, *ETL* 52 [1976] 324–29).

The meaning of the Hebrew text of Ps 8:5 (=Ps 8:6 LXX) is ambiguous; the radicals in the Hebrew phrase could signify "little lower than God" (RSV) or "little lower than the heavenly beings" (NIV). The Greek translators resolved the ambiguity by referring explicitly to the angels (παρ' ἀγγέλους), and this interpretation is found in the *Targum* as well. This element of the text required explanation if the incomparable superiority of the divine Son to the angels was to be maintained.

8b–9 The writer's explanation of the text indicates precisely the point of his interest. It lies in the projection of an imperial destiny for humanity in the refrain, "You put everything in subjection under his feet" (v 8a). He takes up this theme only to underscore the absoluteness of the language by resorting to a double use of the negative: God, in determining to put everything (τὰ πάντα) in subjection, left nothing (οὐδέν) that was not under his control (ἀνυπότακτον, v 8b). The force of supplementing the negative substantive οὐδέν with the negative verbal adjective ἀνυπότακτον is to emphasize the collective expression "everything," which is inclusive of all that belongs to the realm of creation (Kistemaker, *Psalm Citations*, 103–4). The prior use of ὑπέταξεν, "he subjected," in v 5 has prepared for the expressions ἐν τῷ γὰρ ὑποτάξαι, "now in putting in subjection," and ἀνυπότακτον, "not made subject," in v 8b, which resume the thought that v 5 began. The subjection of "everything" has ultimately to do with "the world to come."

The extravagance of the statement in v 8b is mocked, of course, by human experience, and the writer immediately adds, "we do not yet [οὔπω] see everything subject to his control." The temporal expression οὔπω is crucial, for it indicates that the writer found in the quotation a prophecy that will eventually be fulfilled. He regards Ps 8:7b as a legal decree, the realization of which is yet deferred (cf.

Michel, 71; Kistemaker, *Psalm Citations*, 104–5). The recognition of the present unfilled state of affairs prepares him to see that the promised subjection has reference not to humankind in general (v 8) but to Jesus (v 9), whom God has appointed "heir of everything," κληρονόμον πάντων (1:2).

This understanding is made explicit in v 9, where it is evident that the writer interpreted the two lines of Ps 8:6 without reference to the synonymous parallelism of the Hebrew text. From the perspective of the psalmist, to be made "little lower" than a heavenly being is to be "crowned with glory and honor." But for the writer the two members of the parallelism expressed two phases in the life of the Lord. He explains that the first line concerns Jesus' temporary abasement, while the second speaks of his subsequent exaltation and glorification. This christological reading of the text also accounts for the omission of the first member of the following parallelism (Ps 8:7a). The three lines reproduced by the writer combine to form a confession of faith that celebrates the three successive moments in the drama of redemption, i.e., the incarnation, the exaltation, and the final victory of Jesus, the first pertaining to the past, the second to the present, and the third to the future. The departure from the original Semitic parallelism produces a distinctly confessional understanding of the quotation (Linton, "*Le Parallelismus Membrorum*," 495–96; cf. Delling, *TDNT* 8:42). What light does this shed on v 9? The following answers may be suggested:

(1) In Jesus we see exhibited humanity's true vocation. In an extraordinary way he fulfills God's design for all creation and displays what had always been intended for all humankind, according to Ps 8. He is the one in whom primal glory and sovereignty are restored. His experience of humiliation and exaltation guarantees that the absolute subjection of everything envisioned in Ps 8:7 and promised in Ps 110:1 will yet be achieved.

(2) An objection to Jesus' superiority on the ground of his abasement "lower than the angels" cannot be sustained. The humiliation to which he submitted was only temporary; it lasted "for a brief while" and has already been exchanged for exaltation glory. In this regard, it is important to observe that when the line from Ps 8:6a is repeated in v 9 the word order is changed to bring forward the expression βραχύ τι, "for a little while," into the emphatic position:

v 7   ἠλάττωσας αὐτὸν βραχύ τι παρ᾽ ἀγγέλους
      "You made him *a little while* lower than the angels."
v 9   βραχύ τι παρ᾽ ἀγγέλους ἠλαττωμένον
      "For *a little while* [he] was made lower than the angels."

By this change the stress falls upon the momentary character of the humiliation that was necessary to the accomplishment of redemption (cf. Kistemaker, *Psalm Citations*, 105–6).

(3) When the writer introduces the proper name *Jesus* for the first time in the address as appropriate to the focus upon his humanity and death, he assigns it a deferred position in apposition to the clause (τὸν δὲ . . . βλέπομεν Ἰησοῦν). The unusual word order is calculated to arouse attention; it conveys an element of surprise as well as emphasis (i.e., we see the one who for a little while was made lower than the angels—Jesus—dealing triumphantly with death on our behalf!). On seven other occasions the writer will introduce the proper name, and in

each instance it is given a position of great emphasis by its position at the end of the sentence (3:1; 6:20; 7:22; 10:19; 12:2, 24; 13:20). There is nothing corresponding to this in any other NT writer (Westcott, 33; Grässer, "Beobachtungen," 409).

(4) The purpose of Jesus' abasement to the human condition is expressed by the ὅπως- clause, i.e., that he might taste death ὑπὲρ παντός, "for everyone" (v 9d). The four clauses of v 9 express a chiasm in thought, so that clause 1 ("made lower than the angels") finds its complement in clause 4. Jesus' submission to solidarity with the human family in his humanity and exposure to death was necessary to the work of redemption. The expression "to taste death" is a Semitism. Although it is not found in the OT, it occurs occasionally in rabbinic literature (e.g., *Gen. Rab.* to 1:31; 3:22; *b. Yoma* 78b). In Codex Neofiti I, the complete recension of the Palestinian Pentateuch Targum, there are two examples of the full Semitic expression "to taste the cup of death" (on Deut 32:1; cf. R. le Déaut, "Goûter le calice de la mort," *Bib* 43 [1962] 82–86). The writer uses the Semitism to allude to the harsh reality of the violent death on the cross that Jesus endured for the benefit of others. That this occured χάριτι θεοῦ, "by the grace of God," has in view the gracious disposition of God who addresses man's failure to achieve his destiny by the provision of a redeemer through whose death many will be led to the experience of sonship and glory (v 10; cf. 12:15).

(5) The two clauses that stand in an emphatic position in the middle of the Greek sentence also express a sequence in thought: because he suffered death, Jesus was crowned with glory and splendor. Whenever the writer speaks of the death of Jesus he uses the verb πάσχειν, "to suffer," and its derivatives. In the clause διὰ τὸ πάθημα τοῦ θανάτου, the reference is to the suffering that consists in death, as the equivalent expression γεύσηται θανάτου, "he might taste death," indicates. This is the first explicit reference to the death of Jesus in the address, and the force of the tautology (since in Hebrews πάσχειν receives the meaning "to die") is to give it special stress (cf. Michaelis, *TDNT* 5:917, 934–35). The crowning with glory and splendor was the direct result of the death Jesus suffered (12:2). This understanding results from the distinctive manner in which the writer read the affirmations of Ps 8:6. The expression δόξῃ καὶ τιμῇ, "with glory and splendor," recalls the investiture of Aaron to the high priesthood, when God bestowed upon him "glory and splendor" (Exod 28:2, 40 LXX). It may be proper to find in the statement that Jesus was crowned with glory and splendor another anticipation (cf. 1:3) of his high priesthood, which is not formally introduced until 2:17–18 (cf. Michel, 71, n. 3; Strathmann, 84).

Explanation

In resuming the exposition the writer leads his readers to contemplate Jesus in his solidarity with humankind. The transcendent Son of God made the human condition, and especially its liability to death, his own in order to achieve for them the glorious destiny designed by God. That design informs Ps 8, which speaks of the creatureliness and subordination of human beings, and yet also of the glory, splendor, and universal authority for which they have been created. Unfortunately, the promise implied by the divine intention has plainly not been fulfilled in humanity's limited dominion over nature. It actually appears to be mocked and frustrated by the presence of sin and death in the world. Nevertheless, it has been secured by Jesus, who took upon himself humanity's full estate in order that by means of his own redemptive accomplishment he might bring the vision of the psalmist to its realization.

There is a profound note of anticipation in the OT teaching about humanity. The words of the psalmist look forward into the future, and that future is inextricably bound up with the person and work of Jesus. His condescension to be made for a brief while "lower than the angels" set in motion a sequence of events in which abasement and humiliation were the necessary prelude to exaltation. His coronation and investiture with priestly glory and splendor provide assurance that the power of sin and death has been nullified and that humanity will yet be led to the full realization of their intended glory. In Jesus the hearers are to find the pledge of their own entrance into the imperial destiny intended by God for them.

E. The Solidarity of the Son with the Human Family (2:10–18)

Bibliography

Andriessen, P. "La teneur judéo-chrétienne de Hé I 6 et II 14b–III 2." *NovT* 18 (1976) 293–313. **Attridge, H. W.** "New Covenant Christology in an Early Christian Homily." *QuartRev* 8 (1988) 89–108. **Ballarini, T.** "ARCHEGOS (*Atti* 3,15; 5,31; *Ebr.* 2, 10; 12, 2): autore o condottiero?" *SacDoc* 16 (1971) 535–51. **Bonus, A.** "Heb. II.16 in the Peshitta Syriac Version." *ExpTim* 33 (1921–22) 234–36. **Carlston, C. E.** "The Vocabulary of Perfection in Philo and Hebrews." In *Unity and Diversity in New Testament Theology.* FS G. E. Ladd. Ed. R. A. Guelich. Grand Rapids: Eerdmans, 1978. 133–60. **Clarkson, M. E.** "The Antecedents of the High-Priest Theme in Hebrews." *ATR* 29 (1947) 89–95. **Dhôtel, J. C.** "La 'sanctification' du Christ d'après Hébreux II, 11." *RSR* 47 (1959) 515–43; 48 (1960) 420–52. **Doormann, E.** "'Deinen Namen will ich meinen Brüdern verkünden' (Hebr 2, 11–13)." *BibLeb* 14 (1973) 245–52. **Dukes, J.** "The Humanity of Jesus in Hebrews." *ThEduc* 32 (1985) 38–45. **Dunkel, F.** "Expiation et Jour des expiations dans l'Épître aux Hébreux." *RevRéf* 33 (1982) 63–71. **Dussaut, L.** *Synopse structurelle de l'Épître aux Hébreux.* 26–32. **Dyck, T. L.** "Jesus Our Pioneer." 3–59. **Frede, H. J.** "Der Text des Hebräerbriefs bei Liudprand von Cremona." *RBén* 96 (1986) 94–99. **Grogan, G. W.** "Christ and His People: An Exegetical and Theological Study of Hebrews 2:5–18." *VoxEv* 6 (1969) 54–71. **Hickling, C. J. A.** "John and Hebrews: The Background of Hebrews 2:10–18." *NTS* 29 (1983) 112–16. **Horbury, W.** "The Aaronic Priesthood in the Epistle to the Hebrews." *JSNT* 19 (1983) 43–71. **Hurst, L. D.** "The Christology of Hebrews 1 and 2." In *The Glory of Christ in the New Testament.* FS G. B. Caird. Ed. L. D. Hurst and N. T. Wright. Oxford: Clarendon Press, 1987. 151–64. **Knauer, P.** "Erbsünde als Todesverfallenheit: Eine Deutung von Rom 5,12 aus dem Vergleich mit Hebr 2,14f." *TGl* 58 (1968) 153–58. **Knox, W. L.** "The Divine Hero Christology of the New Testament." *HTR* 41 (1948) 229–49. **Kögel, J.** *Der Sohn und die Söhne: Eine exegetische Studie zu*

Hebräer 2:5–18. Gütersloh: Bertelsmann, 1904. **Kouto, J. K. M.** "Humanité et autorité du Christ-Prêtre: Une approche exégético-théologique de Hé. 2, 5–18; 3, 1–6 et 4, 15–5, 10." Dissertation, Pont. Univ. Urbaniana, Rome, 1985. **Laub, F.** *Bekenntnis und Auslegung.* 66–104. **Longman, T.** "The Divine Warrior: The New Testament Use of an Old Testament Motif." *WTJ* 44 (1982) 290–307. **McPheeters, W. M.** "The Testing of Jesus." *BibRev* 4 (1919) 517–36. **Miller, D. G.** "Why God Became Man: From Text to Sermon on Hebrews 2:5–18." *Int* 23 (1960) 3–19. **Minear, P. S.** *New Testament Apocalyptic.* 126–34. **Müller, P. G.** *ΧΡΙΣΤΟΣ ΑΡΧΗΓΟΣ: Der religionsgeschichtliche und theologische Hintergrund einer neutestamentlichen Christusprädikation.* Bern: Lang, 1973. **Parsons, M. C.** "Son and High Priest: A Study in the Christology of Hebrews." *EvQ* 60 (1988) 195–215. **Plessis, P. J. du.** *ΤΕΛΕΙΟΣ: The Idea of Perfection in the New Testament.* Kampen: Kok, 1959. **Roloff, J.** "Der mitleidende Hohepriester: Zur Frage nach der Bedeutung des irdischen Jesus für die Christologie des Hebräerbriefes." In *Jesus Christus in Historie und Theologie.* FS H. Conzelmann. Ed. G. Strecker. Tübingen: Mohr, 1975. 143–66. **Scott, J. J.** "*Archēgos* in the Salvation History of the Epistle to the Hebrews." *JETS* 29 (1986) 47–54. **Seeberg, A.** "Zur Auslegung von Hebr. 2:5–18." *NJDT* 3 (1894) 435–61. **Silva, M.** "Perfection and Eschatology in Hebrews." *WTJ* 39 (1976) 60–71. **Simpson, E. K.** "The Vocabulary of the Epistle to the Hebrews. I." *EvQ* 18 (1946) 35–38. **Tascon, V.** "Jesucristo, sacerdote misericordioso y fiel." *CTom* 100 (1973) 139–90. **Tetley, J.** "The Priesthood of Christ in Hebrews." *Anvil* 5 (1988) 195–206. **Übelacker, W. G.** *Der Hebräerbrief als Appell: Untersuchungen zu* exordium, narratio *und* postscriptum *(Hebr 1–2 und 13,22–25).* Stockholm: Almqvist & Wiksell, 1989. 163–85, 190–96. **Vanhoye, A.** "Le Christ, grand-prêtre selon Héb. 2, 17–18." *NRT* 91 (1969) 449–74. ———. *Exegesis Epistulae ad Hebraeos Cap. I–II.* Rome: Pontifical Biblical Institute, 1968. 174–217. ———. *Situation du Christ: Hébreux 1–2.* Paris: Cerf, 1969. 305–87. **Vernet, J. M.** "Cristo, él que abre el camino." *Sal* 47 (1985) 419–31. **Wikgren, A.** "Patterns of Perfection in the Epistle to the Hebrews." *NTS* 6 (1960) 159–67. **Woschitz, K. M.** "Das Priestertum Jesu Christi nach dem Hebräerbrief." *BLit* 54 (1981) 139–50.

Translation

[10] *In bringing*[a] *many sons to glory, it was appropriate that God, for whom and through whom*[b] *everything exists, should make the champion who secured their salvation*[c] *perfect through suffering.* [11]*For the one who consecrates human beings and those whom he consecrates are all of one origin. That is why Jesus does not blush to call them his brothers,* [12]*when he says,*

"*I will declare your name to my brothers;*
in the presence of the congregation I will praise you."

[13]*He also says,*

"*I will trust him*";

and furthermore,

"*Here am I and the children whom God has given me.*"

[14]*Since the children share a mortal human nature,*[d] *he too shared in their humanity so that by his death he might break the power of the one who holds the power of death (that is, the devil)* [15]*and liberate those who all their lives were held in slavery by their fear of death.* [16]*(For of course*[e] *it is not angels that he takes hold to help,*[f] *but Abraham's descendants.)* [17]*This means that it was essential*[g] *for him to be made like these brothers of his in every respect, in order that he might become a merciful and faithful high priest in the service of God,*[h] *to make propitiation with regard to the sins of the people.*[i] [18]*Because*[j] *he himself suffered death, having been put to the test,*[k] *he is able to help those who are being tested.*

Notes

ᵃ On the agreement of the ptcp ἀγαγόντα with the unexpressed subj of the inf τελειῶσαι (i.e., God who makes perfect) and the interpretation of the tense as a proleptic aor "which envisages the work of Christ and its consequences for mankind as a unity," see P. E. Hughes, "Note on the Significance of the Participle ἀγαγόντα (2:10)," *Commentary*, 101–2.

ᵇ The idea of cause (δι' ὅν) and agency (δι' οὗ) are distinguished entirely by means of the cases. Cf. TEV: "God, who creates and preserves all things."

ᶜ The basis of the translation is set forth in the *Comment* on v 10.

ᵈ The phrase σάρξ καὶ αἷμα is "an established Jewish (though not OT) term for man, whether as individual or species, in his creatureliness and distinction from God" (Behm, *TDNT* 1:172). The context justifies the translation "mortal human nature" (cf. BAGD 22, 743–44). The inversion of the phrase (αἵματος καὶ σαρκός) is attested elsewhere (Philo, *Who Is the Heir of Divine Things* 57; in the NT, Eph 6:12; Justin, *Apology* 66.2; *Dialogue* 135.6).

ᵉ The classical particle δήπου, which occurs only here in the NT, marks an appeal to information shared by the hearers (BDF §441[3]). The entire statement is parenthetical in nature.

ᶠ The meaning of ἐπιλαμβάνεται continues to be disputed. In the LXX the verb is used of God who grasps the hand of his people to help them (Jer 38 [MT 31]:32, "on the day when I took their hand [ἐπιλαβομένου μου τῆς χειρὸς αὐτῶν] to lead them from the land of Egypt," cited in Heb 8:9), while the thought of taking hold to help is clear in Sir 4:11, "Wisdom exalts her sons and gives help (ἐπιλαμβάνεται) to those who seek her." The repetition of ἐπιλαμβάνεται in v 16 has the effect of heightening the antithetic parallelism (BDF §491). It would be cumbersome, however, to reflect the antistrophe in translation.

ᵍ The impf verb ὤφειλεν is used to express a past obligation (cf. Moulton, *Grammar*, 3:90–91).

ʰ The phrase τὰ πρὸς τὸν θεόν provides an example of the accusative of respect that was frequent in classical usage but was almost entirely displaced in the Koine by the dative (cf. BDF §160; Moule, *Idiom-Book*, 33).

ⁱ εἰς τό with the inf is used to express purpose (cf. Burton, *Moods*, 409). On the translation of ἱλάσκεσθαι as "make propitiation" and the understanding of τὰς ἁμαρτίας as an accusative of respect, see Morris, *Apostolic Preaching*, 174–77).

ʲ The force of ἐν ᾧ is causal (cf. Zerwick, *Biblical Greek*, 119; BAGD 261 [IV.6d]).

ᵏ The relationship of the suffering to the testing is problematic. Burton, for example, argued that πειρασθείς is used as an adv ptcp of means and is translated "he himself has suffered by being tempted" (*Moods*, 433). It seems necessary, however, to take into consideration the context (which speaks of the fear of death, v 15), the special meaning of πάσχω in Hebrews in the sense "to suffer death" (see *Comment* on 2:9), and the close connection between the suffering of death and testing. Cf. Michaelis, *TDNT* 5:917: "In 2:18 πέπονθεν πειρασθείς refers exclusively to the death of Jesus."

Form/Structure/Setting

With this paragraph the writer concludes the first major segment of his address and prepares for the new unit of thought to be developed in 3:1–5:10. The connection with 2:5–9 is firmly established by a series of correspondences between v 9 and v 10. Instead of repeating the θεός, "God," of v 9 as a connecting word, the writer replaces it by an extended circumlocution in v 10. ἔπρεπεν γὰρ αὐτῷ δι' ὅν τὰ πάντα καὶ δι' οὗ τὰ πάντα, "for it was appropriate to him for whom and through whom everything exists," corresponds to the phrase χάριτι θεοῦ, "by the grace of God," in the previous verse. The generalized παντός, "everyone," of v 9 is now made more precise in the phrase πολλοὺς υἱούς, "many sons." The expression "to lead many sons to glory" (εἰς δόξαν) was undoubtedly suggested by the reference to δόξα, "glory," in Ps 8:6b. Finally, the phrases τὸ πάθημα τοῦ θανάτου, "the suffering of death," and γεύσηται θανάτου, "he might taste death," in v 9 are repeated under another form in the expression διὰ παθημάτων τελειῶσαι, "to make perfect through suffering," in v 10. These linguistic and conceptual correspondences alert the hearers that in the following paragraph the writer intends to take up and extend the comments he has just made on the basis of Ps 8 (cf. Vanhoye, *La structure*, 79).

As in the previous paragraph, 2:10–18 assumes the form of homiletical midrash. The exposition turns on the citation and development of three biblical quotations. The statement that Jesus calls others his brothers (ἀδελφούς, v 11) is derived from the first quotation, which contains the crucial expression "my brothers" (τοῖς ἀδελφοῖς μου, v 12). The quotation also prepares for the statement in v 17 that it was essential that Jesus be made like "the brothers" (τοῖς ἀδελφοῖς). The note of trust introduced in the second quotation (ἐγὼ ἔσομαι πεποιθὼς ἐπ᾽ αὐτῷ, "I will trust him" [v 13a]) prepares for the description of Jesus as trustworthy (πιστός) in v 17, where the context establishes that he was trustworthy in response to the call of God (cf. 3:1–6). The key term in the third quotation is "the children" (τὰ παιδία, v 13b) which is taken up immediately in the pregnant statement of vv 14–15 ("Since, therefore, τὰ παιδία share a common mortal nature"). The pattern of quotation and explanation is characteristic of homiletical midrash and here serves to emphasize Jesus' solidarity with the human family.

The structure of the unit is sufficiently indicated by a rich use of particles. The connection with the previous paragraph is established by the coordinating conjunction γάρ in v 10, which introduces a statement implying the solidarity between the Son of God and the sons who are being led by God to their heritage (cf. τὸν ἀρχηγὸν τῆς σωτηρίας αὐτῶν, "the champion who secured *their* salvation"). What is implied in v 10 is made explicit in v 11: the Son who consecrates human beings to God and the children who are being consecrated have one origin (ἐξ ἑνὸς πάντες). The unity between the Son and those who are sons finds illustration in the quotations of vv 12 and 13, while the implications of this solidarity are expounded in vv 14–18. The exposition is strung together by the particles ἐπεὶ οὖν, "since therefore" (v 14), γὰρ δήπου, "for of course" (v 16), the inferential ὅθεν, "for this reason" (v 17), and the concluding causal ἐν ᾧ γάρ, "because" (v 18), which sums up the relevance of the development for the hearers.

Within this setting the periodic sentence in vv 14–15 provides an example of artistic prose, for in a single sentence the writer makes effective use of both parallel and concentric symmetry.

A   Since the children
  B   shared a common human nature
A' he too likewise
  B' shared the same humanity } Parallel symmetry

C   in order that by death
  D   he might break the power
  D' of the one who held the power
C' of death } Concentric symmetry

The regularity of the rhythm is broken momentarily by the parenthetical comment "that is, the devil," but it is then resumed immediately:

E   and that he might liberate those ⎫
  F   who from fear of death   ⎬   Concentric symmetry
  F'   throughout their lives   ⎪
E'   were held in a state of bondage. ⎭

The parallel symmetry emphasizes the resemblance of the Son to those who are "the children," while the concentric symmetry develops a contrast, first between the Son and the devil, and then between liberation and enslavement (Vanhoye, *La structure*, 80). The concern for symmetry reflects the rhetorical situation of striving for the effectiveness of the spoken word when circumstances demand dependence upon the written word. This is evident in v 16 as well, when the writer assumes a conversational stance, and repeats a phrase for the benefit of his hearers:

> for of course it is not angels he takes hold to help [ἐπιλαμβάνεται]
> but rather the descendants of Abraham he takes hold to help [ἐπιλαμβάνεται].

By casting the statement in the form of an antithetic parallelism, and then heightening the parallelism by the identity of the last words (i.e., antistrophe), he could be assured of arresting the attention of his hearers (cf. Turner, *Grammar,* 4:107).

The subject announced in 1:4, the incomparable superiority of the Son to the angels, is developed in 1:5–2:16. The function of 2:17–18 is more complex. It is clear from the inferential ὅθεν, "for this reason," that these verses serve to bring the first major unit of thought to a conclusion. They reduce to a pregnant formulation the point the writer wished to make from the beginning. But they also announce the subject to be developed in 3:1–5:10. The purpose of the Son's solidarity with the human family was that he might become "a merciful and faithful high priest in the service of God" (v 17). In characteristic fashion these qualities are taken up in inverse order in the next unit of the address. The writer draws attention to Jesus' fidelity to God and its implications for the hearers in 3:1–4:14, while his compassion as a high priest in the service of God is developed in 4:15–5:10 (cf. Vanhoye, *La structure*, 39–42, 81–83). The remaining clauses in 2:17–18 actually anticipate the full thrust of the address in speaking of the achievement of propitiation for the sins of the people (cf. 9:1–10:18) and the extension of help to those who are being severely tested (cf. 10:19–13:6; cf. Kistemaker, *Psalm Citations*, 101).

In the hortatory section 2:1–4 it was apparent that the hearers had shown a tendency to drift from their moorings and even to display a reckless lack of concern for the Christian message they had received. There was no indication at that point, however, why they were being distracted from their commitment. Now for the first time there is a strong suggestion that allegiance to Jesus is costly. It exposed the hearers to testing (v 18). The community found itself in circumstances that were sufficiently serious to induce the fear of death (v 14). The details that warranted such language remain unspecified, but as the address unfolds there will be more pointed allusions to the situation that precipitated a crisis of faith within the congregation. The presentation of Jesus as ἀρχηγός, "champion" (v 10), and ἀρχιερεύς, "high priest" (v 17), is highly significant, for it may be assumed that christological titles reflect a sensitivity to the situation addressed. It is imperative that these titles be interpreted from the perspectives offered within the immediate context. It can be anticipated that they too will shed a measure of light on the situation of the readers and the historical setting for the address.

Comment

10 ἔπρεπεν γὰρ αὐτῷ, "for it was appropriate to him." The writer's intention is to provide a commentary on the last clause of v 9 and more particularly on the expression "by the grace of God." The introductory phrase ἔπρεπεν γὰρ αὐτῷ qualifies the declaration that Jesus tasted death for others χάριτι θεοῦ, "by the grace of God." Although the formula πρέπει θεῷ, "it is appropriate to God," does not occur in the LXX nor elsewhere in the NT, it is found in Philo (*Allegorical Interpretation* 1.48; *On the Eternity of the World* 41; *On the Confusion of Tongues* 175) and Josephus (*Ag. Ap.* 168), as well as in secular writers (cf. M. Pohlenz, "τὸ πρέπον," *NGWG* [1933] 53–92; Williamson, 88–93). It reflects an educational and religious background where questions of theodicy called for the response ἔπρεπεν θεῷ, "it was appropriate to God." Here it affirms that what has taken place in the experience of Jesus was consistent with God's known character and purpose. The divine intention to lead human beings to the goal for which they had been created appeared to be mocked by human experience. It was entirely congruous with the primal intention celebrated in Ps 8 that God should graciously decree that his Son identify himself with the human condition and rescue humanity through his own humiliation and death. The sufferings of Jesus were appropriate (ἔπρεπεν) to the goal to be attained and were experienced in accordance with God's fixed purpose.

The circumlocution for God as the one δι' ὃν τὰ πάντα καὶ δι' οὗ τὰ πάντα, "for whom and through whom everything exists," is not found elsewhere in the Greek Bible but is entirely appropriate to the context, which concerns the fulfillment of the divine intention for humanity at creation. God who creates and preserves all things is precisely the one who is able to act in such a way that his design for humankind will be achieved. The use of circumlocution occurs elsewhere in Hebrews (cf. 1:3; 8:1; μεγαλωσύνη, "the divine Majesty"). It is not a rhetorical embellishment but a complement to the divine appointment of the Son to his redemptive mission (cf. du Plessis, ΤΕΛΕΙΟΣ, 217–18).

πολλοὺς υἱοὺς εἰς δόξαν ἀγαγόντα, "in bringing many sons to glory." God's fixed purpose is to lead many children to glory. The use of πολλοί, "many," in the expression "many sons" is inclusive; the adjective embraces all those to whom the saving work of Jesus applies (cf. Jeremias, *TDNT* 6:536–42). The writer envisions the great host of those for whom Jesus secured the fulfillment of the divine intention and whose "sonship" is established by virtue of his relationship to them (cf. Kögel, *Sohn*, 52–53). The expression determines the scope of ὑπὲρ παντός, "for everyone," in v 9. The future glorification of the "many sons" is secured in the present glorification enjoyed by Jesus in his exaltation. Because the participle ἀγαγόντα, "bringing," matches the contiguous noun τὸν ἀρχηγόν, "the champion," in case, gender, and number, there are those who assign to Christ the action of "leading many sons to glory" (e.g., du Plessis, ΤΕΛΕΙΟΣ, 219; Grogan, *VoxEv* 6 [1969] 61–62). He is "the leader" (τὸν ἀρχηγόν). A variation of this interpretation was urged by Dibelius. He held that the vocabulary of v 10 stands under the influence of the mystery cults. The presentation of Jesus as the forerunner who has himself been completely initiated, who leads many sons to glory, recalls the activity of a hellenistic mystagogue ("Der himmlische Kultus," 170–72; cf. Käsemann, *Das wandernde Gottesvolk*, 82–90).

The participle, however, agrees with the unexpressed subject of the infinitive τελειῶσαι, "to make perfect," i.e., God. If ἀγαγόντα had been intended to qualify ἀρχηγόν, the adjective πολλούς would have been preceded by the article τόν (Moffatt, 31; du Plessis, *ΤΕΛΕΙΟΣ*, 214). The motif of God's leading of many sons is familiar from the OT, particularly in connection with the Exodus from Egypt, where the divine initiative is frequently stressed (e.g., Exod 3:8, 17; 6:6–7; 7:4–5, passim; cf. J. Schreiner, "Führung—Thema der Heilsgeschichte im Alten Testament," *BZ* 5 [1961] 2–18; Müller, *ΧΡΙΣΤΟΣ ΑΡΧΗΓΟΣ*, 114–48). The writer understands the goal of God's leadership to be entrance into the glory (δόξαν) envisioned in the statement from Ps 8:6b (LXX), which he has cited in v 7, "crowned with glory [δόξῃ] and splendor." The redemptive associations of the term *glory* are apparent in the subsequent phrase "their salvation" (τῆς σωτηρίας αὐτῶν). The reference is to the heritage reserved for the redeemed in the world to come (cf. v 5).

The designation of Jesus as τὸν ἀρχηγὸν τῆς σωτηρίας αὐτῶν, "the champion who secures their salvation," is intriguing (cf. 12:2; Acts 3:15; 5:31). The Greek term ἀρχηγός is a vehicle for a broad range of nuances, both in Jewish and in secular sources (cf. Delling, *TDNT* 1:487–88; Ballarini, *SacDoc* 16 [1971] 535–51; Müller, *ΧΡΙΣΤΟΣ ΑΡΧΗΓΟΣ*, 18–42, 68–102). Its meaning in any given context can be determined only on the basis of cultural as well as literary considerations. W. L. Knox has properly stressed that "hellenistic Judaism was always receiving from its surroundings a coloring of popular religious language, and contributing to the general amalgam from the Septuagint and the prayers of the hellenistic synagogue." Consequently, "all that we have is the use of a common stock of ideas, ultimately religious, but adopted by rhetoric and popular philosophy and carried over into the liturgical and homiletical language of the hellenistic world, including that of the Church" (*HTR* 41 [1948] 239, 242).

On the basis of this sound observation he suggested that the language of Heb 2:10, 18 displays a close affinity with the descriptions and panegyrics of some of the most popular cult figures of the hellenistic world, the "divine hero" who descends from heaven to earth in order to rescue humankind. Although Jesus is of divine origin, he accepts a human nature, in which he can serve humanity, experience testing, and ultimately suffer death. Through his death and resurrection he attains to his perfection, wins his exaltation to heaven, and receives a new name or title to mark his achievement in the sphere of redemption. This description, Knox observed, represented Jesus in much the same light as the divine hero figures of the pagan world, of whom Hercules was the most prominent. He concluded that it was the hellenistic conception of the redeemer who earns his exaltation by the services rendered to humankind that made it possible for the writer to the Hebrews to insist on the absolute humanity of Jesus and his experience of every trial that comes to humanity. His exaltation to the right hand of God was won by a life of service and the suffering of death (Knox, *HTR* 41 [1948] 234–35, 245–47).

This suggestive proposal finds a strong measure of support in the development of the paragraph. Hearers familiar with the common stock of ideas in the hellenistic world knew that the legendary hero Hercules was designated ἀρχηγός, "champion," and σωτήρ, "savior." (For useful collections of literary sources, inscriptions, and coins, cf. Simon, *Hercule et le Christianisme;* Galinsky, *The Herakles Theme;* Tiede, *Charismatic Figure,* 71–100.) They would almost certainly interpret the term ἀρχηγός in v 10 in the light of the allusion to Jesus as the protagonist who came to the aid of the oppressed people of God in vv 14–16. Locked in mortal combat with the one who held the power of death, he overthrew him in order to release all those who had been enslaved by this evil tyrant. This representation of the achievement of Jesus was calculated to recall one of the more famous labors of Hercules, his wrestling with Death, "the dark-robed lord of the dead" (Euripides, *Alcestis,* ll. 843, 844; see below on vv 14–15). The designation of Jesus as ἀρχηγός in a context depicting him as protagonist suggests that the writer intended to present Jesus to his hearers in language that drew freely upon the Hercules tradition in popular Hellenism (cf. W. Manson, *The Epistle to the Hebrews,* 103–4; see *Comment* on 12:2).

A translation of ἀρχηγός sensitive to the cultural nuances of the term in Hellenism and appropriate to the literary context of v 10 is "champion." This translation is to be preferred to others which have been proposed ("leader": NEB, JB, cf. Müller, *ΧΡΙΣΤΟΣ ΑΡΧΗΓΟΣ,* 111–13, 279–92, 300–1; "guide": cf. Ballarini, *SacDoc* 16 [1971] 535–41, "pioneer": RSV; cf. Käsemann, *Das wandernde Gottesvolk,* 81–82; "author": NIV), because it does not restrict the interpretation of ἀρχηγός to the perspectives of v 10 alone but takes into account the distinctive color of the paragraph as a whole. Jesus is "the champion" who secured the salvation of his people through the sufferings he endured in his identification with them, and more particularly through his death.

διὰ παθημάτων τελειῶσαι, "to make perfect through suffering." The statement that Jesus was "perfected through suffering" draws upon a special nuance of the verb τελειοῦν in the LXX. In ceremonial texts of the Pentateuch the verb is used to signify the act of consecrating a priest to his office (Exod 29:9, 29, 33, 35; Lev 4:5; 8:33; 16:32; 21:10; Num 3:3). The normal idiom is "to fill the hands" (τελειοῦν τὰς χείρας), and in Exod 29:33 this expression is elucidated by the verb ἁγιάζειν, "to consecrate, to qualify someone for priestly service." That the Semitic idiom could be translated by τελειοῦν itself is demonstrated by Lev 21:10, which speaks of "the priest . . . who had been consecrated to wear the garments" (ὁ ἱερεὺς . . . τετελειωμένου ἐνδύσασθαι τὰ ἱμάτια). This cultic sense of the verb clarifies the meaning of τελειῶσαι in v 10 (cf. du Plessis, *ΤΕΛΕΙΟΣ,* 94–103, 121, 213–15; Delling, *TDNT* 8:82–84) and explains the close association of the ideas of perfection and consecration in vv 10–11 (cf. the translation of v 11 in NEB: "for a *consecrating priest* and those whom he consecrates are all of one stock").

Silva has properly observed that the key to the concept of the perfection of Jesus in Hebrews is provided by the eschatological character of the discourse. Although the cultic note provides the background for the use of τελειῶσαι, the eschatological exaltation of Jesus as the fulfillment of the promises of God constitutes its specific designation (*WTJ* 39 [1976] 62–68; cf. Klappert, *Eschatologie,* 54–57). The pattern of suffering and exaltation found in v 9 finds its equivalent in the reference to suffering and perfection in v 10 (cf. Silva, 66).

The "perfection" of Jesus in this context (cf. 5:8–9; 7:28) has functional implications. The emphasis falls on the notion that he was fully equipped for his office.

God qualified Jesus to come before him in priestly action. He perfected him as a priest of his people through his sufferings, which permitted him to accomplish his redemptive mission (cf. Grogan, *VoxEv* 6 [1969] 60–61, 67). The expression "perfected through suffering" thus anticipates the full development of the paragraph, which moves from the champion motif of vv 10–16 to the presentation of Jesus as high priest in vv 17–18.

11 ὅ τε γὰρ ἁγιάζων καὶ οἱ ἁγιαζόμενοι, "for the one who consecrates human beings and those whom he consecrates." The cultic character of τελειῶσαι in v 10 is confirmed by the reference to consecration in v 11. The vocabulary appears to be used in its OT significance, in which the people of Israel were sanctified or consecrated to God and his service in order to be admitted into his presence (cf. Procksch, *TDNT* 1:89–97). The designation ὁ ἁγιάζων, "he who consecrates," seems to reflect the concept of God in the Pentateuch, where he identifies himself with the formula "I am the Lord who consecrates you" (ἐγὼ κύριος ὁ ἁγιάζων ὑμᾶς; Exod 31:13; Lev 20:8; 21:15; 22:9, 16, 32; cf. Ezek 20:12; 37:28). The reference here, however, is clearly to Jesus, who is named explicitly in 13:12 as the one who consecrates his people to the service of God through his own blood, even as 10:14 describes Christians as those who are being consecrated (τοὺς ἁγιαζομένους) by his one sacrifice. Cleansing from defilement is the necessary corollary to the concept of sanctification as consecration, and in Hebrews references to sanctification are regularly coupled to a statement about the offering of the blood of Jesus (cf. 9:13; 10:10, 14, 29; 13:12). Only one who is himself fully consecrated to the service of God (cf. 10:5–10) may exercise the power of making others holy (Procksch, *TDNT* 1:103). Although the writer's intention in v 11 is to speak of solidarity, the description of Jesus as "the one who consecrates" and of Christians as those who need consecration sufficiently defines the radical difference between the transcendent Son of God and those who are "sons."

ἐξ ἑνὸς πάντες, "all of one origin." Despite the qualitative difference between Jesus and the people of God, they share a unity based upon their common origin. The πάντες, "all," is clearly inclusive of both parties mentioned in v 11, the one who consecrates and those who are being consecrated. The precise source of unity, however, is ambiguous. The pronoun "one" in the phrase ἐξ ἑνός may be either masculine or neuter in gender. Those who understand the expression as neuter find in the text a reference to the fact that Christ and his people share a common human nature (Phillips, "share a common humanity"; JB, "are of the same stock"; NEB, "are all of one stock"; cf. P. E. Hughes, 105–6). Others, who prefer to accept the pronoun as masculine ("from one man"), find an allusion to Adam or Abraham (cf. Héring, 19). The contextual references to God in v 10 and to the family relationship in v 11, however, tend to support the contention that ἑνός is masculine and has reference to God (TEV, "all have the same Father"; NIV, "are of the same family"). Both the Son and those who are sons share a common familial relationship that is rooted in the gracious determination of God to bring his children to their destiny through the redemptive mission of the Son (cf. Kögel, *Sohn*, 59–62; Spicq, 2:41; Michel, 80; et al.).

The function of the explanatory clause that follows is to introduce the scriptural support for the solidarity affirmed between the Son and those who are sons. In spite of the qualitative difference in the sonship shared and the position of Jesus as sanctifier as opposed to theirs as those who need sanctification, he does not hesitate to declare that they are his brothers. The formulation "he is not ashamed [οὐκ ἐπαισχύνεται] to call them brothers" may contain an allusion to Jesus' warning that the disciple who seeks to evade the cost of discipleship by denying his relationship to Jesus will find that the exalted Son of Man is ashamed of him ("whoever is ashamed [ἐπαισχυνθῇ] of me and my words . . . of him will the Son of Man be ashamed [ἐπαισχυνθήσεται] when he comes in the glory of his Father with the holy angels," Mark 8:38; Luke 9:26). Jesus' own commitment to his disciples is expressed in the positive declaration that he is "not ashamed" to call them brothers. This affirmation provides the encouragement needed by the hearers and prepares for the subsequent declaration that "God is not ashamed [οὐκ ἐπαισχύνεται] to be called their God" in 11:16, where the context is distinctly covenantal. The image of the family is appropriate in this context. Because the divine Son identifies himself with the covenantal family, he is able to achieve in others that perfect consecration to God that he himself embodies. The connection with v 10 further suggests that the occasion when Jesus is not ashamed to call others his brothers is the parousia when God will lead many sons to glory (cf. Doormann, *BibLeb* 14 [1973] 249). The declaration anticipates the eschatological entrance of the redeemed community into the world to come (cf. v 5).

12–13 The quotations in vv 12 and 13 illustrate that Jesus does not blush to identify himself with the people of God. The three biblical passages have been brought together because they share the common perspective of personal affirmation ("I will proclaim . . . I will sing hymns to you," "I will place my trust," "Here am I and the children whom God has given to me"). The first quotation is taken from Ps 22:22 (21:23 LXX). Apart from the translation variant ἀπαγγελῶ for διηγήσομαι (both of which mean "I will proclaim"), the form of the text is identical with the LXX. The quotation is tied to v 11b by the key word "brothers." The exalted Lord, who is not ashamed to call those consecrated to God "brothers" (ἀδελφούς), affirms, "I will proclaim your name to my brothers" (τοῖς ἀδελφοῖς μου). The statement is taken from that part of the psalm where lament is exchanged for an expression of joyful thanksgiving. It is appropriate to an experience of vindication and exaltation after suffering and affliction. The writer to the Hebrews locates here a reference to the exalted Lord who finds in the gathering of the people of God at the parousia an occasion for the proclamation of God's name and who as the singing priest leads the redeemed community (ἐν μέσῳ ἐκκλησίας) in songs of praise (cf. Rom 15:7–12; Doormann, *BibLeb* 14 [1973] 247–50).

The two citations in v 13 are closely associated with the passage from the Psalter by the intorductory formula καὶ πάλιν, "and furthermore." The second of the two quotations was clearly drawn from Isa 8:18, and the source of the first is probably Isa 8:17 (cf. Isa 12:2). The separation of the two declarations by καὶ πάλιν does not argue against this proposal, for in 10:30 contiguous quotations from Deut 32:35–36 are separated by the same formula. The citation, however, is very brief, and it is possible that it was taken from the hymn of David recorded in 2 Sam 22 (v 3). This hymn was apparently sung by the early Christians. It is found in a list of biblical odes adopted for liturgical use recorded by Origen (cf. H. Schneider, "Die biblischen Öden in christlichen Altertum," *Bib* 30 [1949] 51–52, citing Origen, GCS 7:501–2; 8:27–28, 80–83). In either case the word order was altered by the addition of the emphatic personal pronoun ἐγώ, "I," which had the effect of attracting the main verb ἔσομαι to itself (Kistemaker, *Psalm Citations*, 33). The addition, which brought the citation into sharper parallelism with the next quotation (which begins ἰδοὺ ἐγώ, "Here am I"), served to stress that Jesus identifies himself with the community of faith in his absolute trust and dependence upon God. The citation had immediate relevance for the hearers. The fact that Jesus' confidence was fully vindicated after he had experienced suffering and affliction assured them that they could also trust God in difficult circumstances (cf. Doormann, *BibLeb* 14 [1973] 250–51).

The third citation, taken from Isa 8:18, locates the solidarity between Jesus and those associated with him in the action of God (cf. v 10). The form of the text agrees with the LXX. In its original context, the passage describes the prophet Isaiah, his children, and his disciples, who constituted a faithful remnant in that day. There was a distinct parallel between the experience of Isaiah and of Jesus that made the quotation appropriate at this point. The prophet was persecuted and rejected by the people, but he became a rallying point for faith (cf. Grogan, *VoxEv* 6 [1969] 61–62). Jesus is now the representative head of a new humanity which is being led to glory through suffering (Doormann, *BibLeb* 14 [1973] 251). Although the concept of the people of God as τὰ παιδία, "the children," of the exalted Son is not found elsewhere in the NT, the image of the family suggests an intimacy of relationship and a tenderness that broadens the concept of solidarity.

14–15 The implications of the solidarity affirmed in vv 11–13 are developed in the balanced clauses of a periodic sentence. The exposition is related organically to its biblical support by the repetition of the expression τὰ παιδία, "the children," contributed by the previous quotation (cf. Kögel, *Sohn,* 72). Since "the children" share a common human nature (αἵματος καὶ σαρκός, lit., "blood and flesh"), it was necessary for the one who identified himself with them (v 13b) to assume the same full humanity (μετέσχεν τῶν αὐτῶν). This assertion grounds the bond of unity between Christ and his people in the reality of the incarnation. In the incarnation the transcendent Son accepted the mode of existence common to all humanity.

The synonymous parallelism in the statements of v 14a indicates that any semantic difference between the verbs that refer to "the children" and to the Son respectively ought not to be pressed here. The meaning of the two roots is virtually synonymous; both describe a full participation in a shared reality (cf. J. Y. Campbell, "κοινωνία and its Cognates in the New Testament," *JBL* 51 [1932] 353, 355, 363). The distinction lies in the variation of the verbal tenses. The perfect tense of κεκοινώνηκεν, "share," marks the "original and natural" state of humanity, while the aorist tense of μετέσχεν, "shared," emphasizes that the Son assumed human nature "at a fixed point in time, by his own choice" (F. F. Bruce, 41, n. 55). By means of this distinction the transcendent character of the incarnate Son is maintained precisely in a context in which the accent falls upon his full participation in the human condition. The addition of the adverb παραπλησίως, "in just the same way," which signifies total likeness, underscores the extent of the identity of the Son's involvement in the conditions of human experience common to other persons (cf. Williamson, 82). It anticipates the inferential statement of v 17, that "obligation was upon him to be made like his brothers *in every respect*" (κατὰ πάντα).

The purpose for which the transcendent Son of God entered human life is indicated by an expanded purpose clause (ἵνα . . . καταργήσῃ καὶ . . . ἀπαλλάξῃ). He assumed a mortal human nature "in order that he might nullify" the power of an evil tyrant who possessed the power of death and "that he might rescue" those who had been enslaved. The identification of the tyrant as the devil exposes the depth of the human plight. The devil did not possess control over death inherently but gained his power when he seduced humankind to rebel against God. The representation of death as a henchman in the devil's service and the threat of death as an instrument with which he bludgeons humanity into submission (cf. Michaelis, *TDNT* 3:907) depend on the interpretation of Gen 3 in the tradition of the hellenistic synagogue: "God created man for incorruption, and made him in the image of his own eternity, but through the devil's envy death entered the world, and those who belong to his party experience it" (Wis 2:23–24). It is ironical that human beings, destined to rule over the creation (Ps 8:5–7 LXX, cited in vv 6–8), should find themselves in the posture of a slave, paralyzed through the fear of death (Kögel, *Sohn*, 80). Hopeless subjection to death characterizes earthly existence apart from the intervention of God (cf. Knauer, *TGl* 58 [1968] 155–57). Moreover, the presence of death makes itself felt in the experience of anxiety (cf. Sir 40:1–5a). The definition of the state of mind that reduced humankind to enslavement as the "fear of death" (φόβῳ θανάτου), however, almost certainly has a specific reference. It refers to a disposition within the hearers and is a first indication of the serious situation addressed in this pastoral homily. The crisis they faced was demonic in character.

ἵνα διὰ τοῦ θανάτου καταργήσῃ . . . καὶ ἀπαλλάξῃ, "that by his death he might break the power . . . and liberate." The primary goal of the incarnation was the Son's participation in death, through which he nullified the devil's ability to enslave the children of God through the fear of death. Jesus' death was the logical consequence of his determination to identify himself so completely with his brothers and sisters that there would be no aspect of human experience which he did not share. But in this instance death was not the consequence of rebellion. It was an expression of consecration to do the will of God (10:5–7), with the result that Satan's ability to wield the power of death was rendered ineffective in relationship to the Christian (cf. Delling, *TDNT* 1:453, who calls attention to 2 Tim 1:10: "the appearing of our Savior, Christ Jesus, who has broken the power of Death"). The incarnation was thus the appropriate and necessary means of delivering the people of God from the devil's tyranny and the fear of death.

The depiction of Jesus as the champion (ὁ ἀρχηγός) who crushed the tyrant who possessed the power of death in order to rescue those whom he had enslaved calls to mind the legendary exploits of Hercules. The oldest tradition that has been preserved of Hercules associates him with the conquest of Death (Homer, *Iliad* 5.394–400; cf. Pindar, *Olympian Odes* 9.33). This brief account provided the core of the classical legend of Hercules' rescue of Alcestis by wrestling with Death (Apollodorus Mythographus, *Bibliotheca* 1.106). In Euripides' dramatization of this incident, Death (ὁ θάνατος) is personified as a warrior, "the dark-robed lord of the dead" armed with a sword (*Alcestis*, ll. 76, 843–44). In a still later period, the theme was elaborated in popular accounts of the Herculean labors, particularly in the assignment to descend to the underworld and to steal Cerberus, the infernal watchdog (Virgil, *Aeneid* 6, ll. 417–23; 8, ll. 293–300). If it was the writer's intention to portray the divine Son in language that would evoke the exploits of Hercules, there was a rich stock of popular notions upon which he could draw.

There was another strand of tradition, however, with which the writer and his hearers were thoroughly familiar because it was based upon the OT. The prophets at times described God as the divine warrior, who armed himself in order to defend his people from humiliation and enslavement (cf. P. D. Miller, *The Divine Warrior*). The motif draws upon the older practice of conducting warfare as a contest of champions, as an alternative to the costly commitment of armies in standard combat (cf. R. de Vaux, "Les combats singuliers dans l'Ancien Testament," *Bib* 40 [1959] 459–508; H. A. Hoffner, "A Hittite Analogue to the David and Goliath Contest of Champions?" *CBQ* 30 [1969] 220–25). Opposing commanders would agree in advance to settle the military issue in accordance with the outcome of a contest between two or more champions representing the two armies. Although this practice did not extend beyond the Bronze Age (cf. Yadin, *Art of Warfare*, 2:265–67, 362), the tradition provided the prophets with the basis for developing the significant theological motif of God as the champion of Israel. Isaiah, for example, announces the intervention of God in stirring words:

> Yahweh advances as a champion
>   as a man accustomed to battle he will stir up his zeal;
> with a shout he will raise the cry of battle
>   and will triumph over his enemies.
>   (Isa 42:13; cf. 49:24–26; 59:15*b*–20)

The portrayal of God as a champion engaged in individual combat on behalf of his people appears as one strand of the apocalyptic tradition in the documents of the intertestamental period. For example, in a passage of uncertain date and provenance in some manuscripts of *T. Zeb.* 9:8. (b d g), the seer announces, "And after that your God himself shall shine forth as the light of righteousness, and salvation and mercy shall be in his wings. He will liberate all the prisoners of Beliar, and every spirit of error shall be scattered" (cf. *T. Levi* 18:10–12). A similar prophecy appears in the *Assumption of Moses* (10:1–10; cf. 11QMelch 2:13).

Within the gospel tradition Jesus resorts to the metaphor of a contest between champions in response to certain scribes who accused him of collusion with Beelzebul, the prince of demons:

> When a strong man, fully armed, guards his own palace, his possessions are safe; but when someone stronger attacks him and overpowers him, he takes away the armor in which the man trusted, and divides up the spoils (Luke 11:21–22).

In the context of the Beelzebul controversy, the strong man is the demonic prince. The stronger one who vanquishes him is Jesus, who defeats his adversary by the finger of God and releases those who had been enslaved through demonic possession (Luke 11:18–20). Jesus' ministry of exorcism entails an engagement with Satan, the adversary of humankind. This brief logion, however, offers the only explicit appeal to a champion motif in the tradition of Jesus' words.

The writer to the Hebrews develops this strand of the gospel tradition into a significant pastoral response to the crisis facing his hearers. Although God intended that his people should participate in his glory, they experienced bondage through the fear of death. They became the captives of an evil tyrant who possessed the power to intimidate them. The writer to the Hebrews affirms that the

Son of God assumed humanity in order to become their champion and to secure their release. Through his death, he crushed the antagonist who had the power of death and so brought deliverance to the captives.

The unusual formulation in vv 14–15 is consonant with Jesus' statement about disarming the strong man and dividing his spoils. It appears to draw upon the older prophetic tradition of God as the champion of his people as set forth in Isa 49:24–26:

> Can plunder be taken from a champion,
> or captives rescued from a tyrant?
> This is what the Lord says:
> "Yes, captives will be taken from the champion
> and plunder retrieved from the tyrants;
> I will contend with those who contend with you,
> and your children will I rescue . . . .
> Then all humankind will know that I, the Lord, am your Savior,
> your Redeemer, the champion of Jacob."

The christological perspective developed in Heb 2:10–16 has its clearest anticipation in this passage from Isaiah. A continuity in tradition may be traced from the prophetic depiction of God as the champion who rescues the captives of an evil tyrant to Jesus' word concerning the stronger combatant who retrieves the plunder of a champion to the distinctive formulation of the writer to the Hebrews. The writer affirms that what God had pledged to do as Israel's redeemer, Jesus has accomplished. Jesus is the protagonist who broke the devil's power and so secured deliverance for the people of God. This fruitful approach to the incarnation and death of Jesus was designed to strengthen the hearers by reminding them of their liberated status. They are no longer to be paralyzed by the fear of death, even when they experience imperial opposition.

16 The parenthetical character of the statement introduced by γάρ, "for," and the sudden intrusion of the present tense (ἐπιλαμβάνεται, "he takes hold to help") indicate the writer's intention. He assumes a conversational posture in order to engage his hearers in the argument he is developing. He appeals to a statement of fact, reinforced by the particle δήπου, "surely," "of course," that his conversation-partners will readily acknowledge.

The verb ἐπιλαμβάνεται is indefinite. Bonus (*ExpTim* 33 [1921–22] 235–36) called attention to the fact that in the manuscript tradition of the Peshitta Syriac version the subject of the sentence is "death": "for death does not take hold of angels, but it takes hold of Abraham's descendants." The point made is that angels experience neither death nor the fear of death, but the descendants of Abraham do, and so the incarnate Son died to deliver them from bondage to the fear of death. Since, however, the subject both of the clause preceding v 16 and of the clause following it is the incarnate Son, it is likely that he is the subject in v 16 as well. The reference to the angels is essentially rhetorical; it marks the limits of the exposition introduced by v 5. All of the interest is concentrated on the statement that the incarnate Son takes hold of Abraham's descendants to draw them into the fellowship of their own destiny (cf. Delling, *TDNT* 4:9).

The description of the community of faith as σπέρματος 'Αβραάμ, "Abraham's descendants," conveys an allusion to Isa 41:8–10, where the faithful remnant is

the object of God's comfort: "But you, . . . Abraham's descendants, upon whom
I took hold . . . do not fear, for I am with you . . . and I have helped you" (σπέρμα
'Αβραάμ . . . οὗ ἀντελαβόμην . . . μὴ φοβοῦ μετὰ σοῦ γάρ εἰμι . . . καὶ ἐβοήθησά
σοι). The passage from Isaiah was appropriate to the situation of the hearers.
The summons not to fear (μὴ φοβοῦ), supported by the solemn pledge of God's
presence, is the divine response to the "fear of death" mentioned in v 15. The
assurance of divine help (ἐβοήθησα) prepares for the climactic assertion in v 18 that
Jesus is able to help (βοηθῆσαι) those who are being tested. The substitution
of ἐπιλαμβάνεται in Hebrews for the cognate ἀντιλαμβάνεται found in Isa 41:9
may reflect the formulation of Jer 31 (LXX 38):31–32, where the Exodus is described in terms of God's taking Israel by the hand (ἐπιλαβομένου) in order to lead
them from bondage. This text is cited in 8:9, and the exodus motif which the
two OT passages share would tend to bring them together in the writer's thought
(so Andriessen, *NovT* 18 [1976] 308–9). An implied reference to deliverance from
bondage would follow naturally from the thought expressed in vv 14–15. That
the incarnate Son comes to the aid of oppressed men and women whom he
takes by the hand in order to lead them to safety corresponded to the experience of the congregation addressed. What they needed to appreciate once more
was that the harsh authority formerly wielded by the devil has been replaced by
the gentle authority of the exalted Son who continues to identify himself with
them.

17 ὅθεν ὤφειλεν κατὰ πάντα τοῖς ἀδελφοῖς ὁμοιωθῆναι, "this means that it
was essential for him to be made like these brothers of his in every respect." The
inferential particle ὅθεν, "for this reason," looks back upon the argument developed in vv 10–16. Before proceeding to announce the subject to be treated in
3:1–5:10, the writer summarizes his argument in a single compact clause (v 17a).
The reference to the "brothers" (τοῖς ἀδελφοῖς) picks up the keynote of vv 11b
and 12, where Jesus' solidarity with the community of faith was first affirmed in
terms of a relationship among brothers. In the statement that obligation was laid
upon the incarnate Son to become altogether like his brothers, however, the accent falls upon the qualifying phrase κατὰ πάντα, "in every respect," which has
been placed in the emphatic position in the clause. In context, the phrase refers
primarily to the humiliation of testing and the suffering of death (v 18), but it
also extends to every quality that demonstrated that Jesus shared a full and true
human existence (cf. v 14a). At a later point the writer will guard his statement
from possible misunderstanding by insisting upon the sinless character of Jesus,
which sets him apart from other men and women (4:15; 7:26). Here, however, he
wants to stress the total identification of the incarnate Son with the human situation of his audience (cf. Grogan, *VoxEv* 6 [1969] 64–67). Jesus had to resemble
the brothers in reality, as one brother resembles another.

ἵνα ἐλεήμων γένηται καὶ πιστὸς ἀρχιερεὺς τὰ πρὸς τὸν θεόν, "that he might
become a merciful and faithful high priest in the service of God." The element
of moral obligation contemplated in the term ὤφειλεν, "it was essential," is clarified by the two purpose clauses, which follow in sequence. Only by standing with
others in human solidarity could the transcendent Son of God be qualified to
participate in the life of the people as a merciful and faithful high priest. What
this entailed is explained in the exposition that follows, as the writer addresses
himself first to the quality of faithfulness (3:1–4:14), and then to the quality of

compassion (4:15–5:10). The formulation of v 17 reflects the influence of the Septuagint where the expression τὰ πρὸς τὸν θεόν is a standard phrase in the Pentateuch meaning "with regard to God" (e.g., Exod. 4:16; 18:19).

This is the first application of the title ἀρχιερεύς, "high priest," to Jesus in the address. That his ministry was priestly in character was implied as early as 1:3, and the introduction of cultic terminology in 2:9–11 tended to confirm that impression. But with the description of Jesus as high priest, what had only been implied becomes explicit. There is no general agreement on the sources of the high priestly christology that colors the homily so profoundly after this point (see *Introduction*, "Sonship Interpreted . . . "; "Locating Hebrews"). The fact that the writer can refer to Jesus as high priest before he has provided any theological exposition of this conception (cf. 3:1; 4:14–16) strongly suggests that it was the common property of the hellenistic wing of the Church. One of the significant values of Hebrews is its preservation and development of the insights of the Hellenists. The treatment of the high priestly theme in 5:1–10:18 bears the marks of original and creative reflection on the part of a teacher who brought to the tradition a penetrating grasp of its value for the enrichment of the theology and life of the Christian community.

What is distinctive about 2:10–18 is that the portrayal of Jesus as champion or protagonist (vv 10–16) leads directly into the body of the address, with its interpretation of Jesus in priestly categories. Although the Greek *Testament of Levi* poses a number of critical questions that have not yet been resolved (cf. J. H. Charlesworth, *The Pseudepigrapha and Modern Research* [Chico, CA: Scholars Press, 1981] 211–15), one passage is of special interest because it establishes a link between priestly and champion motifs:

> Then shall the Lord raise up a new priest . . . .
> And he shall execute a righteous judgment upon the earth.
> And he shall open the gates of paradise
>   and shall remove the threatening sword against Adam.
> And Beliar shall be bound by him,
>   and he shall give power to his children to tread upon evil spirits.
> (*T. Levi* 18:10–12)

This text, like others that represent God as the champion of Israel, preserves an apocalyptic point of view. It offers a hellenistic-Jewish paradigm for the christological perspectives developed in Heb 2:10–18. The element of representation that is common to the offices of champion and of high priest may account for the fact that in Hebrews champion perspectives flow smoothly into the presentation of a high priestly christology.

The description of Jesus as a "faithful high priest in the service of God" constitutes an allusion to 1 Sam 2:35, where God announces, "I will raise up for myself a faithful priest, who shall act according to what is in my heart and in my mind; and I will build him a sure house." The recognition of the allusion prepares for the transition to 3:1–6, where the writer calls attention to Jesus as the high priest who "was faithful to the one who appointed him . . . as a Son over God's house" (3:2, 6).

εἰς τὸ ἱλάσκεσθαι τὰς ἁμαρτίας τοῦ λαοῦ, "to make propitiation with regard to the sins of the people." The second purpose clause is a natural extension of the first; it describes the activity of the incarnate Son in distinctly priestly categories. The proper translation of ἱλάσκεσθαι has been a matter of academic debate. In a full and balanced treatment of the subject Morris has demonstrated that "to make propitiation" is to be preferred rather than "to make expiation," because this is the usual meaning of the verb and its cognates not only in secular usage but in the LXX (*Apostolic Preaching*, 125–60). Moreover, the accusative of respect in the expression ἱλάσκεσθαι τὰς ἁμαρτίας, "to make propitiation with respect to sin," is an unusual Greek construction, but in the few examples where it is preserved it "seems generally to imply the thought of propitiation" (175–76). The making of propitiation for sins exhibits the primary concern of the high priestly office with the reconciliation of the people to God. The concept implies sacrifice, and in this context the propitiatory work of the Son consisted in the laying down of his life for others (cf. vv 10, 14, 18).

The description of those on whose behalf the high priest functions as "the people" (τοῦ λαοῦ) has its background in the Greek Bible, where ὁ λαός [τοῦ θεοῦ] is a technical term for Israel in its character as the nation chosen by God and separated from the other nations by covenant relationship (cf. Strathmann, *TDNT* 4:29–57, esp. 54–55). The writer does not hesitate to transfer this title of honor to the Christian community, for all of the OT is for him a parable of God's provision for the Church. Although the expression draws upon the rich associations that cluster about the term in the OT (cf. Deut 7:6–8; 14:2; 21:8), its ultimate application is to the new people of God who are the beneficiaries of the high priestly ministry of Jesus. "The people" corresponds to "Abraham's descendants" in v 16, but now the general statement that Jesus came to the aid of God's people finds a greater measure of precision in the reference to the high priestly action of making propitiation for their sins.

18 The final statement points to the relevance of the development in vv 10–17 for the community. It is designed to strengthen them in their temptations and conflicts. The writer touches upon both the faithfulness (he is πιστός) and compassion (he is ἐλεήμων) of Jesus in his representative capacity as high priest (v 17). The incarnation exposed the Son to the conflicts and tensions of human life, which were climaxed by the suffering of death in a final act of obedience to the will of God (cf. 4:15; 5:2, 7–8). It was at this point that his fidelity to God was put to the extreme test, and he proved to be a faithful high priest. Because he did not divorce himself from the human experience of conflict in the world and was tested in this specific sense, he is able to help those who are now exposed to the ordeal of trial. He thus proves to be a compassionate high priest as well. Williamson comments that his encounter with sin and the suffering of death "equipped him, as nothing else could have done, to help ordinary, sinful, suffering men and women" (90). The first major section of the address is thus brought to a conclusion on the note of pastoral encouragement.

Explanation

The larger context of 2:10–18 is a meditation on Ps 8, which serves to direct attention to the man Jesus in his humiliation and exaltation. Although for a brief while he had been made "lower than the angels," he is now "crowned with glory and splendor because he suffered death, so that by the grace of God he might taste death for everyone" (v 9). The reference to Jesus' death prompts the writer's reflection upon the appropriateness of the incarnation and death of the Son of God. The pre-existent Son entered the human race and assumed its conditions, especially its liability to death, in order to redeem humankind. The paragraph thus brings into focus the full and authentic reality of the humanity of Jesus and its significance for the redeemed community.

The dominant concept of the entire passage is that of the solidarity of the Son with his people. That solidarity is affirmed in the statement that the one who makes people holy and those who are made holy are of the same family (v 11) and in the list of citations from Psalms and Isaiah (vv 12–13). The "brothers" of the psalmist are "the congregation of the faithful" with whom Jesus lifts his voice in singing the praises of God. They are those who trust the Lord, the spiritual remnant concerning whom Isaiah had so much to say, and who were represented in the writer's day by Jesus and all those who responded to his call.

The divine Son became one with his people in order to die for them. This was affirmed very generally in v 9, where the declaration "that he might taste death for everyone" indicated that his death was for the benefit of others. The nature of the benefit derived from his death, however, remained unspecified. The following verses clarify that the death of Jesus opened the way for others to participate in the glory of God as a result of deliverance from enslavement to the devil and the removal of their fear of death (vv 10–16). Jesus' acceptance of the mode of existence common to all persons and his identification with the community of faith constituted a pledge of the glorification of the human family in the people of God.

Within this setting Jesus is presented as champion and high priest. Drawing upon the motif of individual, representative combat, the portrayal of Jesus as the protagonist of an oppressed people addressed a word of comfort and encouragement to Christians in crisis. The depiction of Jesus as champion pointed beyond the immediate crisis of the community to the triumph that already has been secured for the people of God. The element of triumphalism in the metaphor complemented the theology of glory expressed in v 10. Champion christology provided a fresh interpretation of the incarnation from the perspective of the tradition that God or Jesus is the champion who rescues those enslaved by the prince of death (cf. Isa 49:24–26; Luke 11:21–22). The sober reminder that the champion overcame his adversary through death (vv 14–15) exhibited the costly character of the grace of God extended to the community through the Son (v 9).

This fruitful approach to the incarnation and death of the Son is not sustained, however, beyond v 16. With vv 17–18 the writer prepares to lead his hearers directly into the body of the discourse devoted to the exposition of Jesus as priest and sacrifice. Common to the concepts both of champion and of high priest are the elements of representation and solidarity with a particular people. The presentation of Jesus in 2:10–18 provided assurance that the exalted Son continues to identify himself with the oppressed people of God exposed to humiliation and testing in a hostile world.

II. The High Priestly Character of
the Son (3:1–5:10)

Bibliography

Black, D. A. "The Problem of the Literary Structure of Hebrews: An Evaluation and a Proposal." *GTJ* 7 (1986) 163–77. **Bligh, J.** *Chiastic Analysis of the Epistle to the Hebrews.* 4–8. ———. "The Structure of Hebrews." *HeyJ* 5 (1964) 170–77. **Cladder, H.** "Hebr. 1,1–5, 10." *ZKT* 29 (1905) 1–27. **Descamps, A.** "La structure de l'Épître aux Hébreux." *RDT* 9 (1954) 251–58. **Dussaut, L.** *Synopse structurelle de l'Épître aux Hébreux.* 33–53. **Gyllenberg, R.** "Die Komposition des Hebräerbriefs." *SEÅ* 22–23 (1957–58) 137–47. **Hillmann, W.** "Lebend und wirksam ist Gottes Wort: Einführung in die Grundgedanken des Hebräerbriefes (1,5–4,13)." *BibLeb* 1 (1960) 87–99. **Nauck, W.** "Zum Aufbau des Hebräerbriefes." In *Judentum, Urchristentum, Kirche.* FS J. Jeremias. Ed. W. Eltester. BZNW 26. Berlin: Töpelmann, 1960. 199–206. **Rice, G. E.** "Apostasy as a Motif and Its Effect on the Structure of Hebrews." *AUSS* 23 (1985) 29–35. **Smothers, T. G.** "A Superior Model: Hebrews 1:1–4:13." *RevExp* 82 (1985) 333–43. **Songer, H. S.** "A Superior Priesthood: Hebrews 4:14–7:28." *RevExp* 82 (1985) 345–59. **Swetnam, J.** "Form and Content in Hebrews 1–6." *Bib* 53 (1972) 368–85. **Vanhoye, A.** "Discussions sur la structure de l'Épître aux Hébreux." *Bib* 55 (1974) 349–80. ———. "Les indices de la structure littéraire de l'Épître aux Hébreux." *SE* 2 (1964) 493–509. ———. "Literarische Struktur und theologische Botschaft des Hebräerbriefs." *SNTU* 4 (1979) 119–47; 5 (1980) 18–49. ———. *La structure littéraire.* 38–42, 86–114. ———. "Structure littéraire et thèmes théologiques de l'Épître aux Hébreux." In *Studiorum Paulinorum Congressus Internationalis Catholicus 1961.* AnBib 18. Rome: Biblical Institute, 1963. 175–81.

Introduction

The second major division of Hebrews extends from 3:1–5:10. The writer's specific concern is the development of the priestly character of the divine Son. This subject was formally announced in 2:17, where Jesus is described as a "merciful and faithful high priest in the service of God." In characteristic fashion the key terms *merciful* and *faithful* are taken up in this segment of the sermon in inverted order. The writer addresses himself first to the faithfulness of Jesus (3:1–6) and to the urgent need for the hearers to prove faithful as well (3:6b–4:14). He then provides encouragement by calling attention to Jesus' compassion as a merciful high priest in the service of God (4:15–5:10).

Most commentators and all English translations prefer to find in 4:14 the beginning of a new paragraph rather than the conclusion to a larger unit of integrated exposition and exhortation. This consensus, however, is challenged by formal literary and thematic considerations. The writer has already employed the literary device of *inclusio* to bracket the exposition in 1:5–14 and 2:5–16. He follows this procedure in 3:1–4:14 as well:

3:1–2a Therefore, holy brothers, . . . observe that the apostle and high priest of whom our confession speaks, Jesus, was faithful . . . .

4:14 Therefore, since we have a great high priest who has gone into heaven, Jesus the Son of God, let us hold firmly the confession.

The repetition of the significant terms *Jesus*, *high priest*, and *confession*, and the correspondence in thought, indicates that the development begun in 3:1 extends to 4:14 (Descamps, *RDT* 9 [1954] 256; Vanhoye, *La structure*, 38–39). The hearers are urged to find in the faithfulness of Jesus an incentive for their own fidelity as Christians.

The correctness of this analysis finds a degree of confirmation in the unitary character of the vocabulary distributed throughout this first section. The significant terms relate to the vital issue of faith and faithfulness: *faithful* (πιστός, 3:2, 5), *faith* (πίστις, 4:2), *believe* (πιστεύειν, 4:3), *unbelief* (ἀπιστία, 3:12, 19), *disobey*, in the sense of "disbelieve" (ἀπειθεῖν, 3:18), and *disobedience*, in the sense of "disbelief" (ἀπείθεια, 4:6, 11). The concentration of this vocabulary accounts for the unified character of the section.

Although Jesus is designated *high priest* in 3:1 and 4:14, there is no explicit exposition of his high priestly office in the initial section. It is only in the second section (4:15–5:10) that the significance of describing Jesus as a *great high priest* (4:14) is considered. The writer achieves a smooth transition to this new unit of thought by repeating, with only slight variation, the same initial expression in two consecutive statements:

4:14   ἔχοντες οὖν ἀρχιερέα μέγαν
        "Therefore, since we have a great high priest who"
4:15   οὐ γὰρ ἔχομεν ἀρχιερέα
        "For we do not have a high priest who"

The repetition marks the transition from exhortation to exposition and signals the introduction of a new paragraph demonstrating that Jesus is also "a merciful high priest in the service of God" (2:17). The ground of his compassion is his own experience of testing (2:18). Consequently, he is able to extend mercy (ἔλεος) to the community exposed to the ordeal of testing (4:15–16). The recurring references to Jesus' submission to testing and suffering (4:15; 5:7–8) resume the statement made in 2:18 and provide it with specific content. The second section is rounded off in 5:9–10 with the announcement of the subjects to be considered in the great central portion of the sermon, 7:1–10:18, namely, the high priesthood like Melchizedek's (7:1–28), the perfection of Jesus (8:1–9:28), and Jesus as the source of eternal salvation (10:1–18).

Although the new division begins with an oratorical imperative ("observe that . . . ," 3:1), the initial paragraph (3:1–6) consists of exposition. A sudden shift in genre, from exposition to exhortation, serves to subdivide the first section and introduces a lengthy appeal to the hearers to remain faithful (3:7–4:14). The second section is indicated by a return to exposition (4:15–5:10). The care with which this sermon has been constructed is evident in the balance achieved through the alternation of exposition and exhortation. In the first major division (1:5–2:18) a brief unit of exhortation (2:1–4) separates two larger units of exposition (1:5–14; 2:5–18). In the second major division two briefer paragraphs of exposition (3:1–6; 4:15–5:10) serve to bracket an extended exhortation. It is evident that the writer intended both to instruct and to engage his hearers by skillfully combining exposition with exhortation.

A. A High Priest Worthy of Our Faith Because He Is the Son of God Who Was Faithful (3:1–6)

Bibliography

Aalen, S. "'Reign' and 'House' in the Kingdom of God; Supplement: 'Kingdom' and 'House' in Pre-Christian Judaism." *NTS* 8 (1961) 215–40. **Allen, E. L.** "Jesus and Moses in the New Testament." *ExpTim* 67 (1955–56) 104–6. **Andriessen, P.** "La teneur judéo-chrétienne de Hé I 6 et II 14B-III 2." *NovT* 18 (1976) 293–313. **Auffret, P.** "Essai sur la structure littéraire et l'interprétation d'Hébreux 3, 1-6." *NTS* 26 (1979–80) 380–96. **Bartelink, G. J.** *Quelques observations sur Παρρησία dans la littérature paléo-chrétienne.* Supplementa. Nijmegen: Dekker & Van de Vegt, 1970. **Berger, K.** "Zum traditionsgeschichtlichen Hintergrund christologischer Hoheitstitel." *NTS* 17 (1970–71) 413–22. **Bornkamm, G.** "Das Bekenntnis im Hebräerbrief." In *Studien zu Antike und Urchristentum: Gesammelte Aufsätze II.* Munich: Kaiser, 1963. 188–203. [Reprinted from *TBl* 21 (1942) 56–66.] **Castelvecchi, I.** *La homologia en la carta a los Hebreos.* Montevideo: Pellegrini, 1964. **Chavasse, C.** "Jesus: Christ and Moses." *Theol* 54 (1951) 244–50. **D'Angelo, M. R.** *Moses in the Letter to the Hebrews.* 65–199. **Dey, L. K. K.** *The Intermediary World and Patterns of Perfection.* 155–83, 227–33. **Grässer, E.** "Mose und Jesus: Zur Auslegung von Hebr 3:1–6." *ZNW* 75 (1984) 2–23. **Hamm, D.** "Faith in the Epistle to the Hebrews: The Jesus Factor." *CBQ* 52 (1990) 270–91. **Hanson, A. T.** "Christ in the Old Testament according to Hebrews." *SE* 2 (1964) 393–98. **Hay, D. M.** "Moses through New Testament Spectacles." *Int* 44 (1990) 240–52. **Horbury, W.** "The Aaronic Priesthood in the Epistle to the Hebrews." *JSNT* 19 (1983) 43–71. **Jones, P. R.** "The Figure of Moses as a Heuristic Device for Understanding the Pastoral Intent of Hebrews." *RevExp* 76 (1979) 95–107. **Kouto, J. K. M.** "Humanité et autorité du Christ-Prêtre: Une approche exégético-théologique de Hé. 2,5–18; 3,1–6 et 4,15–5,10." Dissertation, Pont. Univ. Urbaniana, Rome, 1985. **Laub, F.** *Bekenntnis und Auslegung.* 27–30. **Marrow, S. B.** "Παρρησία and the New Testament." *CBQ* 44 (1982) 431–46. **Melbourne, B. L.** "An Examination of the Historical-Jesus Motif in the Epistle to the Hebrews." *AUSS* 26 (1988) 281–97. **Neufeld, V. H.** *The Earliest Christian Confessions.* 133–37. **Oberholtzer, T. K.** "The Kingdom Rest in Hebrews 3:1–4:13." *BSac* 145 (1988) 185–96. **Otto, C. W.** *Der Apostel und Hohepriester unseres Bekenntnisses: Eine exegetische Studie über Hebr. 3,1–6.* Leipzig: Deichert, 1861. **Parsons, M. C.** "Son and High Priest: A Study in the Christology of Hebrews." *EvQ* 60 (1988) 195–215. **Plooij, D.** "The Apostle and Faithful High Priest, Jesus." In *Studies in the Testimony Book.* Amsterdam: Noord-Hollandische Uitgevers-Maatschappij, 1932. 31–48. **Robertson, O. P.** "The People of the Wilderness." 71–82. **Saito, T.** *Die Mosevorstellungen.* 95–108, 136–49. **Schröger, F.** *Der Verfasser des Hebräerbriefes.* 95–101. **Swetnam, J.** "Form and Content in Hebrews 1–6." *Bib* 53 (1972) 369–78. **Tascon, V.** "Jesucristo, sacerdote misericordioso y fiel." *CTom* 100 (1973) 139–90. **Vanhoye, A.** "Jesus 'fidelis ei qui fecit eum' (Hebr 3, 2)." *VD* 45 (1967) 291–305. **Williamson, R.** *Philo and the Epistle to the Hebrews.* 109–14, 449–69.

Translation

[1] *For this reason, holy brothers, sharing in a heavenly calling, observe that*[a] *the apostle and high priest of whom our confession speaks, Jesus,*[b] [2] *was faithful to the one who appointed him in his house*[c] *(as was Moses also).*[d] [3] *For*[e] *Jesus*[f] *has been considered worthy of greater glory than Moses, in the same measure as the builder of a house has greater honor than the house itself.* [4] *For every house is built by someone, but God is the builder of all things.* [5] *Now Moses was faithful in all God's household as a servant to bear witness*[g]

to those things which were to be spoken by God in the future,[h] [6]*but Christ is faithful*[i] *as the Son*[j] *presiding over God's household. We are God's household,*[k] *supposing that*[l] *we continue to hold firmly to our confidence and the hope of which we boast.*[m]

Notes

[a] Almost all translators treat "the apostle . . . Jesus" as the direct obj of the verb κατανοήσατε, "observe," taking the participial phrase in v 2, πιστὸν ὄντα, "being faithful," as attributive, rendering it by a relative clause (KJV, RV, NEB) or a new sentence (RSV, JB, NIV). The use of a ptcp in the predicate after certain verbs of knowing or perceiving to express indirect discourse elsewhere in Hebrews (2:8, 9; 10:25; 13:23) predisposes one to recognize the construction here (cf. Turner, *Grammar*, 3:161; Wikgren, "Greek Idioms," 149).

[b] As elsewhere in Hebrews (2:9; 6:20; 7:22; 10:19; 12:2, 24; 13:20), the name "Jesus" is assigned a deferred position in apposition to the main clause (see *Comment* on 2:9). The effect of the unusual word order is to throw great emphasis upon the name.

[c] The translation is based on the reading ἐν τῷ οἴκῳ αὐτοῦ, attested by P[13] P[46] B co Ambr Cyr. The variant text ἐν ὅλῳ οἴκῳ αὐτοῦ, "in his whole household," is supported by ℵ A C D lat vg sy arm aeth Chry, but the adjective ὅλῳ stands under suspicion of having been added to v 2 under the influence of the allusion to Num 12:7 in v 5. (See further, Metzger, *Textual Commentary*, 664.) The allusion to Num 12:7 establishes that "his house" signifies the household of God.

[d] The reference to Moses is parenthetical. It previews the allusion to Num 12:7 in v 5.

[e] The conj γάρ connects the statement with the appeal expressed in vv 1–2. The reason the readers are urged to observe that Jesus was faithful is that he has been considered worthy of greater glory than Moses.

[f] The translation of the demonstrative pronoun οὗτος, "this one," by "Jesus" draws upon the antecedent in v 1.

[g] For the use of the prep εἰς to indicate the goal or vocation announced in μαρτύριον, "witness," see BAG 228 (4d).

[h] The translation reflects the fut tense and the pass mood of τῶν λαληθησομένων. This is the only example of the fut pass ptcp in the NT. Cf. BDF §351(2).

[i] The rendering "is faithful" is implied by the explicit reference to Moses' faithfulness in v 5. It is justified by the presence of the μέν . . . δέ construction in vv 5–6, which calls for a degree of parallelism in the two statements.

[j] The noun is anarthrous (ὡς υἱός), as often in Hebrews, but clearly has reference to Jesus' status as the divine Son. (See *Notes* on 1:2a.)

[k] The reading ὅς, supported by P[46] and predominantly Western witnesses (D* 0121b 88 424[c] 1739 it vg Lcf Ambr), would appear to be correct (see Zuntz, *Text*, 92–93, 117, 287; Tasker, *NTS* [1954–55] 186). For a dissenting opinion, see Metzger, *Textual Commentary*, 664–65. Within the structure of the clause, ἐσμὲν ἡμεῖς, "we are [his household]," is emphatic.

[l] The translation reflects the textual variant ἐάνπερ, "if indeed, if only, supposing that," supported by P[46] ℵ A C D[2] Ψ and the majority text, with reference to another conditional fact (see BDF §454[2]). The same construction is found in 3:14. The use of a third class condition (ἐάνπερ with κατάσχωμεν) implies that the outcome is contingent upon the response of the hearers.

[m] The qualification μέχρι τέλους βεβαίαν, "until the end," which is found in ℵ A C D K P Ψ 0121b and the majority text, appears to be an interpolation from 3:14. Metzger (*Textual Commentary*, 665) remarks that the gender one would have expected the writer to use, qualifying the nearest noun τὸ καύχημα, is not βεβαίαν but βέβαιον (neuter). The qualifying phrase is absent from P[13] P[46] B sa.

Form/Structure/Setting

Heb 3:1–6 is a tightly constructed unit of exposition, which finds its point of departure in Jesus' faithfulness as a high priest in the service of God (2:17). The beginning of a new unit is signaled by a change in literary style. In 2:5–18 the style is appropriate to homiletical midrash. The biblical text is cited and its implications are established through interpretation. But in 3:1–2a the writer employs direct address and an oratorical imperative to focus the attention of his readers upon his theme: "For this reason, holy brothers, . . . observe that . . . Jesus was faithful to the one who appointed him." The biblical witness continues to be important, but the text is implied through allusion rather than direct citation. Appeal is made to the oracles to Eli (1 Sam 2:35) and to Nathan (1 Chr 7:14) as well as to Num 12:7 LXX. These texts share in common the thematic words "faithful" and "house." The writer seizes upon the term *house* (οἶκος) and makes it the vehicle for demonstrating that Jesus is superior to Moses. The paragraph is knit together by this characteristic term, which occurs six times in 3:2–6.

A consideration of the structure of the paragraph must face the question of the coherence of vv 3–6. It is clear that vv 1–2a belong together syntactically and that v 2b is a parenthesis, which anticipates the testimony to Moses in v 5. Vv 5–6a are united by a μὲν . . . δέ . . . construction ("on the one hand . . . but on the other hand"). V 6b functions as a hinge-passage. By pointing up the relevance of the exposition for the readers, it marks the conclusion of the paragraph and provides a transition to the exhortation that follows. What must be determined is the precise relationship of v 3 to the statements made in v 4.

A number of commentators conclude that vv 3–6 consist of three independent statements:

v 3   a first comparison between Moses and Jesus;
v 4   a parenthesis;
vv 5–6   a second comparison between Moses and Jesus.

They argue that the logic of v 3 demands the equation of Jesus (v 3a) and "the house-builder" (v 3b) (cf. Hanson, *SE* 2 [1964] 394–96; Williamson, *Philo*, 461). But on this understanding v 4 cannot be integrated with the development, since there the action of building is assigned to God, and not to Jesus. The unresolved tension in the logic of vv 3 and 4 indicates that v 4 must be a parenthetical statement, which separates the first comparison (v 3) from the second (vv 5–6) (so Windisch, 29; Moffatt, 40–43; Spicq, 2:66–68; Buchanan, 57–58).

The weakness of this analysis is that it ignores the writer's practice of using particles and conjunctions to indicate the progression of his argument. In 3:1–6 the internal structure of the paragraph is exhibited by the conjunctions γάρ and καί. The third verse is integrated with the opening statement by the presence of γάρ. The absence of a copula between vv 3 and 4 suggests that these two verses form a unit; the function of v 4 is to clarify the preceding statement. The repetition of γάρ at the beginning of v 4 indicates that it cannot be an independent unit. Finally, the γάρ of v 4 is prolonged by the καί at the beginning of v 5, so that the explanation provided in v 4 extends to vv 5–6 as well (Vanhoye, *La structure*, 88–89; Bonsirven, 232; Dey, *Intermediary World*, 166–68, 172–73, 181–82). Observing the grammatical markers supplied by the writer, we submit that the development of the author's thought reflects the following scheme:

vv 1–2   introduction of the comparison between Jesus and Moses;
v 3   assertion of Jesus' superiority to Moses;
vv 4–6a   explanation for this assertion;
v 6b   relevance for the congregation.

If v 4 is not parenthetical, but marks the point of transition from assertion to explanation, the exposition is developed coherently. (For a more detailed analysis of the internal structure of the paragraph, see Vanhoye, *La structure*, 86–92; Auffret, *NTS* 26 [1979] 380–96.)

The figure of Moses as the mediator of Israel's covenant and cult is of critical importance in Hebrews. The writer contrasts the Mosaic era, the Mosaic covenant, and the Mosaic cult with the new situation introduced by God through Jesus. This is intimated in the opening lines of the homily, in the contrast of the word spoken to the fathers through the prophets with the word spoken through the divine Son. It is confirmed in 2:1–4, when the Mosaic dispensation mediated by the angels throws into bold relief the ultimacy of the salvation proclaimed by the Lord and by those who heard him. This approach is sustained throughout Hebrews. The extended comparison of the old and new cult (4:15–10:31; 12:18–24), with its focus upon access to God in the Mosaic era and in Christian worship, develops the parallel between Moses as the mediator of the old cult and Jesus as the mediator of the new. By creative reference to Moses and the wilderness generation, the writer presents Christ as the mediator of the new covenant and clarifies the dynamic character of Christian existence. Moses is not simply one figure among several who is compared unfavorably to Jesus. Instead, Moses and Jesus are joined together throughout the homily (P. R. Jones, *RevExp* 76 [1979] 95–97).

Several writers have proposed that the writer prepared for 3:1–6 in 2:14–18, or even 2:10–18, finding in the language of those verses a Moses typology (E. L. Allen, *ExpTim* 67 [1955–56] 104; Andriessen, *NovT* 18 [1976] 304–13; Thurston, *EvQ* 51 [1979] 33; Grogan, *VoxEv* 6 [1969] 56–57). It seems preferable to recognize a larger context for 3:1–6. The inferential particle ὅθεν, "for this reason," in 3:1 looks back upon all that the writer has said in 1:1–2:18 about the transcendent dignity of the Son, the mediator of God's final word. The authority claimed for the Son inevitably invited comparison with the unique authority of Moses as the man with whom God spoke more intimately and directly than with an ordinary prophet, according to Num 12:6–8. The allusion to Num 12:7 in Heb 3:2, 5 suggests that the demonstration of Jesus' superiority to Moses in 3:1–6 is already anticipated in the opening sentence of the homily (P. R. Jones, *RevExp* 76 [1979] 97–98; cf. Saito, *Mosevorstellungen*, 95). In some strands of the Jewish tradition the testimony to Moses in Num 12:7 was used to prove that Moses had been granted a higher rank and privilege than the ministering angels (D'Angelo, *Moses*, 95–131, calls attention to *Sipre Zuta* attached to Num 12:6–8 [ed. H. S. Horowitz, 275–76] and *Sipre Num.* 103 [ed. H. S. Horowitz, 101–2]). If this interpretation may be presupposed among Jewish communities of the Diaspora as well, it clarifies the structure of Hebrews, where the Son is compared first to the angels (1:1–2:16) and then to Moses, their superior (3:1–6). It would indicate that it was by no means superfluous when Jesus had been proven superior to the angels to continue with a demonstration of his superiority to Moses.

Auffret (*NTS* 26 [1979] 385–86) associates 3:1–6 with 1:1–2:18 on the basis of thematic and literary considerations:

1:1–4	the Son	[a brief unit]
1:5–14	his superiority to the angels	[a longer unit]
2:1–4	the word spoken through the angels,	
	to which corresponds the word of salvation spoken through the Son	

2:5–18   Jesus   [a longer unit]
3:1–6   his superiority to Moses   [a brief unit]

This analysis establishes the context of 3:1–6 and recognizes its significance. It indicates that the comparison of Jesus and Moses has been placed strategically within the structure of the homily.

Comment

It is difficult to exaggerate the importance of Moses in Judaism, and the veneration with which he was regarded. If reference is restricted to Jewish-hellenistic texts, it is necessary only to recall a passage from *The Exodus* by Ezekiel the Tragedian, cited by Eusebius. Moses is shown in a dream that God will place him on a heavenly throne and invest him with a crown and a scepter, the symbols of his unique authority (Eusebius, *Preparation for the Gospel* 9.29 [ed. E. H. Gifford, 440]). Although Moses is designated a priest only once in the OT (Ps 99:6), his levitical background (Exod 2:1–10), his ministry of the word and privileged vision of God (Exod 33:12–34:35; Num 12:7–8), and his service at the altar (Exod 24:4–8) associate him with priestly functions (cf. C. Hauret, "Moïse était-il prêtre?" *Bib* 40 [1959] 509–21). Philo does not hesitate to describe Moses as high priest (e.g., *The Life of Moses* 2.66–186; *Who Is the Heir?* 182; *On Rewards and Punishments* 53, 56). In this tradition Moses is the supreme example of perfection in the sense of immediacy and access to God (cf. Williamson, *Philo*, 449; Dey, *Intermediary World*, 63–68, 157). If such views were the common property of men and women in dialogue with the hellenistic Jewish community, they have bearing on the comparison of Jesus and Moses developed in 3:1–6. The writer demonstrates that both Jesus and Moses are "faithful," but that Jesus has a superior rank as Son in contrast to Moses' status as servant.

1–2a   The writer does not identify himself with his audience at this point, as he had done in 2:1–4. For the first time he addresses them directly. The connection with what precedes is established not only by the inferential particle ὅθεν, "for this reason," but by the designation ἀδελφοὶ ἅγιοι, "holy brothers," as well. The group description has its basis in the weighted vocabulary of 2:11, 12, 17. The "brothers" are "holy" because they have been consecrated to the service of God by Jesus in his priestly role as the consecrator of the people of God (2:11). The additional qualification, κλήσεως ἐπουρανίου μέτοχοι, "sharers in a heavenly calling," occurs nowhere else in the NT (unless Phil 3:14 provides a parallel expression). The plural form μέτοχοι occurs in 3:14 ("sharers in Christ") and in 6:4 ("sharers in the Holy Spirit") as a technical term for those who have responded to God's call to salvation (cf. Schmidt, *TDNT* 3:487–93). In 3:1 the writer describes the community as those called into the presence of God where they enjoy privileged access to him. The unusual designation corresponds to the description of the Church in 2:10 as those who are being led to enjoy the glory of God's presence (cf. 11:16; 12:22). They owe their privileged status not to Moses or to Aaron but to Jesus as their high priest who has entered heaven (9:24) (cf. Dey, *Intermediary World*, 161–64). The compelling force of the oratorical imperative κατανοήσατε . . . Ἰησοῦν πιστὸν ὄντα, "observe that . . . Jesus was faithful," demands the hearers' immediate attention and sharply focuses that attention upon Jesus.

τὸν ἀπόστολον καὶ ἀρχιερέα τῆς ὁμολογίας ἡμῶν, "the apostle and high priest of whom our confession speaks." With this phrase the writer gathers up what he has said about Jesus as the divine Son and relates it to the commitment expressed by his hearers. The term ὁμολογία, "confession," denotes a binding expression of obligation and commitment, the response of faith to the action of God. It connotes the essential core of Christian conviction that the writer shared with his audience ("our confession"). In the community addressed, the core was the acknowledgment of Jesus as the Son of God (4:14) (cf. Neufeld, *Earliest Christian Confessions*, 133–37). It has been argued that the appeal was to a traditional liturgical form of confession associated with baptism (Bornkamm, "Das Bekenntnis," 188–93), or to a liturgy of praise based on the titles of Jesus (Käsemann, *Das wandernde Gottesvolk*, 105–10). In this context, however, the reference to the confession prepares for the presentation of Jesus as the exalted Son who presides over God's household in v 6 (Williamson, *Philo*, 457–58).

There is no evidence that the titles "apostle" and "high priest" derive from a fixed confession of faith. They simply sum up the presentation of Jesus in 1:1–2:18 as the one through whom God proclaimed the definitive word of salvation and made propitiation for the sins of the people. The omission of the article before ἀρχιερέα, "high priest," suggests that the titles are parallel designations, which view the accomplishment of Jesus in terms of the divine authorization for his word and work (cf. K. H. Rengstorf, *TDNT* 1:423–24).

Although the conception of Jesus as "the one sent" by the Father is familiar from the Fourth Gospel, he is never called ὁ ἀπόστολος, "the apostle/the sent one." That term is applied to Jesus only here in the NT. The quest for the source and significance of the term as a christological title has invited numerous conjectures (cf. Michel, 171–75). Three proposals are attractive, and may be listed as follows:

(1) Whenever "high priest" occurs in Hebrews, the Day of Atonement stands in the background. Jewish sources indicate that the high priest was regarded as the fully accredited representative (שליח) of God before the people on that solemn day (*b. Qidd.* 23b; *Ned.* 35b; *Yoma* 19a-b). The translation of שליח into Greek would be ἀπόστολος. The coordinated phrase "the apostle and high priest" in Heb 3:1 reflects this traditional understanding (Str-B 3:4; W. Manson, *The Epistle to the Hebrews*, 53–54).

(2) In his *First Apology* Justin identifies Jesus as "Son of God and Apostle" (12:9) and as "Angel/Messenger [ἄγγελος] and Apostle" (63:5, 10, 14). Justin derived the designation "Angel/Messenger" from Exod 23:20 LXX: "Behold, I send my angel [ἄγγελος] before you" (cf. Justin, *Dialogue* 75). The LXX agrees with the MT and the Targums in speaking of an "angel" or "messenger." But a striking variant reading is preserved in the *Sam. Tg.* Exod 23:20, 23. Instead of מלאך, "angel," the text reads שליחי, "my apostle." The same variant tradition is found in the *Sam. Tg.* Exod 32:34 ("Behold, my apostle shall go before you") and to Exod 33:2 ("And I will send an apostle"). In all other passages the *Sam. Tg.* agrees with the MT in reading מלאך ("angel"). If the reading of the *Sam. Tg.* is not simply a local text, the source for the christological title "Apostle" was a variant textual tradition attested by the *Sam. Tg.* The citation of Exod 23:20 in the collection of texts used by Justin combined the original reading מלאך/ἄγγελος with the variant שלח/ἀπόστολος. Heb 3:1 provides a witness to the currency of this variant tradition in early Christian circles (Plooij, "The Apostle," 45–47).

(3) The title ὁ ἀπόστολος derives from the figure of Moses, who is described as an apostle in Exod 3:10 LXX (καὶ νῦν δεῦρο ἀποστείλω σε πρὸς Φαραὼ βασιλέα Ἀιγύπτου, "And come now, I will send you to Pharoah, king of Egypt"). Although Moses is never designated ὁ ἀπόστολος, the conception of him as one called, appointed, and sent by God stands behind the term. The designations "apostle and high priest" in Heb 3:1 anticipate the comparison to be developed between Jesus and Moses in their office as commissioned representatives of God (P. R. Jones, *RevExp* 76 [1979] 98).

The coordination of the phrase "apostle and high priest" indicates that the writer is concerned to emphasize the indivisibility of the two offices. The revelation accomplished in Jesus is characterized neither by the word alone nor by the priestly office alone, but by both in conjunction.

The hearers were summoned to "observe that . . . Jesus was faithful to the one who appointed him in his house . . . ." The reference to the faithfulness of Jesus repeats the note sounded first in 2:17, but provides no additional detail. That Jesus is a faithful high priest has already been demonstrated in 2:5–18. The repetition of that theme here prepares for the comparison between Jesus and Moses, since both were faithful to God, who appointed them to their respective missions.

It is common to recognize in v 2 an allusion to Num 12:7. The primary allusion, however, is to 1 Chr 17:14 LXX, πιστώσω αὐτὸν ἐν οἴκῳ μου, "I will make him faithful in my house," where the verb πιστοῦν in the active voice means "to make πιστός (faithful, reliable)" or "to appoint." The double meaning "appointed/faithful" is reflected in the form of the allusion in 2*a*, "faithful to the one who appointed him in his house" (D'Angelo, *Moses*, 74–75, 78, 91–92). (For ποιεῖν in the sense of "appoint," cf. 1 Sam 12:6 LXX, κύριος ὁ ποιήσας τὸν Μωϋσῆν καὶ τὸν Ἀαρων, "the Lord who appointed Moses and Aaron"; Mark 3:14, καὶ ἐποίησεν δώδεκα, "and he appointed twelve.")

The allusion to 1 Chr 17:14 introduces a reference to the oracle delivered by Nathan to David. The writer made use of the oracle already in 1:5*b*, when he quoted the formulation "I will be his father and he shall be my son" (1 Chr 17:13 LXX) as a testimony to the unique status of the Son of God. The form of the allusion in v 2*a* reflects a modification of the Nathan oracle under the influence of the oracle to Eli in 1 Sam 2:35. The interpenetration of the two oracles can be traced in the tradition:

1 Sam 2:35 MT	"I will raise up for myself a *faithful* priest . . . and I will build him a *faithful* house"
1 Chr 17:14 MT	"I will maintain him in my house"
Tg. 1 Chr 17:14	"I will maintain him *faithful* among my people, in my holy house"
1 Chr 17:14 LXX	"I will make him *faithful* in my house"

As modified, the Nathan oracle became a testimony for a royal messianic figure, providing a parallel to the oracle to Eli and its testimony to a faithful priest. The writer to the Hebrews appears to have regarded the two oracles as amplifications of a single oracular witness to a royal priest, which provided him with the major model for his christology (cf. Aalen, *NTS* 8 [1961] 233–37; D'Angelo, *Moses*, 71–90). The oracle provided a testimony to Jesus as the faithful high priest whom God raised up in fulfillment of his ancient promise. It is introduced in v 2*a* to structure the comparison between Jesus and Moses.

2b ὡς καὶ Μωϋσῆς, "as was Moses also." When the reference to Moses is treated as a parenthesis, the emphasis in v 2 shifts appropriately to the statement that Jesus "was faithful to the one who appointed him in his house." The christological oracle provides the structural basis of the exposition, and the testimony to Moses is set within it. An allusion to Num 12:7 is implied but is held in abeyance until v 5. The writer's intention is to juxtapose two texts that are nearly identical in wording: the oracle cited on the basis of 1 Chr 7:14/1 Sam 2:35, with its testimony to Jesus, and the testimony to Moses in Num 12:7. This permits him to begin the comparison from the likeness between Jesus and Moses, rather than from the difference between them. Both were faithful to God who appointed them. This point is misconstrued by those who find in the term "faithful" the basis of the demonstration that Jesus is superior to Moses (cf. Spicq, 2:62–63; Williamson, *Philo*, 457; et al.).

3–4 Having stressed the continuity between Jesus and Moses on the point of faithfulness, the writer asserts discontinuity and the superiority of Jesus to Moses. The basis of the comparison is glory. Although Moses was faithful, Jesus is superior to him because he was considered worthy of greater glory (v 3a). The glory (δόξα) of Moses is the tribute he received from God in Num 12:7; the glory of Jesus is the christological oracle concerning the faithful priest, which finds its fulfillment in the one who was crowned with glory and honor (δόξα καὶ τιμή) at his exaltation (see *Comment* on 2:9).

The claim of the ultimacy of Jesus, which may have been unclear to the troubled believers addressed in Hebrews, is pressed overtly in vv 3–6a with ad hominem arguments. Vv 3 and 4 assume the form of a comparative argument based on analogy. Such an argument does not entail a one-to-one equivalence but establishes a relation of proportion by means of analogous comparison (cf. Dey, *Intermediary World*, 167–68, 72–73, 81–82). The initial basis of the analogy is the general principle that a house-builder receives more honor than the house he has built (v 3b). The analogy was suggested by the reference to "his house" in v 2, but the statement in v 3b has no theological significance. Like the correlative statement in v 4a ("for every house is built by someone"), it simply enunciates a truism. The theological statement is provided in v 4b, where God is identified as the builder of all things. The substitution of πάντα, "all things," for οἶκος, "house," and the employment of the verb κατασκευάζειν, "to make, create" (cf. Isa 40:28; 45:7 LXX; Wis 7:27; 9:2; 11:24; 13:4), indicate that it is God in his role as creator who is in view. The function of v 4 is to clarify the comparison asserted in v 3a. It explains the other side of the analogy (v 3b) by correlating it first with another general principle (v 4a) and then with the theological principle that God is the creator of everything. The structure of the argument proceeds chiastically:

A   Jesus is worthy of more glory than Moses
  B as the house-builder receives more honor than the house
  B' for every house is built by someone
A'   but God is the builder of everything

Jesus is worthy of more glory than Moses in the same measure as God has more honor than the universe he created. So, far from being parenthetical, v 4 is the center of the argument set forth in 3:1–6 (Dey, *Intermediary World*, 173; Auffret, *NTS* 26 [1979–80] 388–90).

5–6a The function of these verses is to extend the assertion of the superiority of Jesus to Moses in v 3a and to explain it on the basis of the biblical text. Moses fulfilled the office of a servant within the household of God; Jesus was the Son appointed to preside over the household. The argument turns on the distinction between θεράπων, "servant," and υἱός, "son," and between the prepositions ἐν ("*in* the house") and ἐπί ("*over* the house").

The allusion to Num 12:7 LXX in v 5 provides a clear testimony to the unique character of Moses' prophetic authority. The formulation is remarkable for its verbal similarity to the oracle of the royal priest cited in v 2. Not only are the thematic words "faithful" and "house" repeated, but the significance of these terms appears to be similar. The key word πιστός appears to carry the double meaning "appointed/faithful." Moses was appointed to, and was faithful in, his office as prophet par excellence in the household of God. Moreover, the term *house* in Num 12:7 appears to have reference to the people of God; in the *Tg. Ps.-J.* and *Tg. Onq.* this is made explicit (cf. D'Angelo, *Moses*, 91–92, 97–104). The official title θεράπων, "servant," which occurs only here in the NT, is derived from the LXX, where the word is used of Moses not only in Num 12:7 but elsewhere (Exod 4:10; 14:31; Num 11:11; Deut 3:24; Josh 1:2, 8:31, 33; 1 Chr 16:40; Wis 10:16; 18:21). In context it carries overtones of dignity and honor and describes a relationship of intimacy and trust between Moses and Yahweh (cf. C. Spicq, "Le vocabulaire de l'esclavage dans le Nouveau Testament," *RB* 85 [1978] 214–16). Moses stands among the covenant people and the whole retinue of God as "honored servant" (cf. the marginal reading to *Tg. Neof.* Num 12:7, "my servant Moses in my whole court is trusted"). The basis of his dignity was his relationship to God, in which he proved trustworthy.

But having affirmed Moses' faithfulness on the basis of Scripture, the writer immediately gives precision to the degree of authority conceded to Moses and its goal by stating that his service was directed toward testifying about revelations still to come (v 5b). This qualification reflects the point of view of primitive Christian eschatology. Moses' prophecy was a corroboration of the new salvation, which began to find expression in the preaching of Jesus (2:3). The future passive participle τῶν λαληθησομένων, "things which were to be spoken in the future," recalls the use of the verb λαλεῖν, "to speak," in 1:1–2a; 2:2–3. On the occasion when God vindicated Moses as his faithful servant, he said στόμα κατὰ στόμα λαλήσω [future!] αὐτῷ, "I *will speak* to him mouth to mouth" (Num 12:8 LXX). By defining Moses' service in this way, the writer indicates that Moses' status as servant corresponds to that of the angels, who are servants to the heirs of salvation (see *Comment* on 1:14).

The superior status of Jesus is indicated by the designation υἱός, "Son," and by his appointment to exercise his rule over (ἐπί) the house of God. What the writer understands by "Son" has been demonstrated in 1:3–6, where he refers to the exaltation and dignity of the Son in terms of enthronement, acclamation, and the worship of the angels. Here the same exalted status is affirmed in the contrast between a servant within the household and the Son who presides over its administration. The assertion of Jesus' dignity in v 6a anticipates the acclamation in 10:21, "we have a great priest over the house of God." The reference is to the heavenly tabernacle where Jesus exercises his priestly role at the right hand of God (cf. 7:26; 8:1–2; 9:11, 24; 10:19–21). The hearers are no longer to consider

Moses as the supreme example of perfection in his service to God and in the encomium he received from God but Jesus, as the exalted Son whose glory surpasses that of Moses (cf. Dey, *Intermediary World*, 174–75).

6b According to 1 Sam 2:35 God promised not only that he would raise up a faithful priest but that he would build a faithful house. This latter promise is taken up in v 6b. The emphatic position of ἐσμὲν ἡμεῖς, "we are," serves to emphasize the corporate conception of the church as the "house of God." The correlation between Jesus and the house is the relationship between the faithful priest and the faithful house (Aalen, *NTS* 8 [1961] 236). The priestly service of the community is their adherence to their confession (v 1), through which they have expressed their confidence and hope based on Jesus' faithfulness as high priest in the service of God. The hearers became the house of God through Christian faith and hope. Now they must maintain their stance of commitment (cf. 10:23, "let us hold unswervingly to the confession of our hope," in the context of 10:19–22).

The emphasis in the writer's appeal falls upon παρρησία, "confidence," and ἐλπίς, "hope," as the hallmarks of the members of God's household. In secular Greek, παρρησία described the open and frank relationship of citizens within the state, but within hellenistic Judaism the significance of the term was extended to connote the boldness of the person of faith before God (Philo, *Who Is the Heir?* 5–7; Jos., *Ant.* 2.52; 5.38). It is this cultic nuance that is expressed in v 6b to denote the conviction of the eschatological community that they enjoy free access to God through Christ. Because Jesus is a faithful high priest in the service of God, Christians have the right to approach God (cf. 4:15–16) and can openly acknowledge their faith, which is the basis of an unshakeable hope (cf. W. C. van Unnik, "The Christian's Freedom of Speech in the New Testament," *BJRL* 41 [1961–62] 484–86; W. S. Vorster, "The Meaning of ΠΑΡΡΗΣΙΑ in the Epistle to the Hebrews," *Neot* 5 [1971] 51–59).

Explanation

Heb 3:1–6 is a paragraph of unusual importance within the structure of the homily. The writer's christology controls the development of the argument and the portrait of Moses. The paragraph is structured by reference to a complex oracle concerning the royal priest, which reflects the interpenetration of 1 Chr 17:14 and 1 Sam 2:35. The testimony to Moses' unique authority in Num 12:7 is related to that oracle. The writer compares the respective status of Moses and Jesus. Each was faithful to God in fulfilling his office, but the former as servant, the latter as exalted Son. At his exaltation Jesus was invested with greater glory and authority than God entrusted to Moses, according to the biblical witness. The recognition that the oracle of the royal priest stands behind 3:1–6 indicates that the theme of Jesus' priesthood is not held in abeyance in 3:1–4:14 but is taken up immediately following its announcement in 2:17–18. Through the process of interpretation the writer is able to articulate his conviction that Jesus is the royal priest whose status as the Son of God assures his precedence over Moses.

The comparison between Jesus and Moses was not simply a literary exercise that enabled the writer to speak of the excellence of Jesus or to exhibit his own exegetical skill. If that were the case, he could have stressed that Moses was not faithful (cf. Num 20:12). He chose to acknowledge the faithfulness of Moses because this appears to have been a significant consideration to the men and women whom he addressed. They may have shared a high regard for Moses as the one uniquely qualified to speak for God because of his extraordinary vision of God. In the tradition of hellenistic Judaism attested by Philo, Moses is venerated as the high priest who enjoyed the immediacy of God's presence. The issues posed for the hearers were real. They are addressed as those who have been summoned to the highest reaches of the heavens, where they enjoy open access to God through their high priest. The writer initiates the comparison between Jesus and Moses out of necessity, as a point of argument intended to affirm the ultimacy of Jesus. The exegetical and theological demonstration that faithful sonship is superior to faithful servanthood is an apologetic and pastoral response to the confusion of a dispirited congregation. It is the beginning of a sustained effort to persuade the hearers to remain loyal to Christ in the presence of pressures that would encourage them to abandon their confession. Consequently, Heb 3:1–6 provides a significant clue to one of the major purposes of Hebrews.

B. The Second Warning: The Peril of Refusing to Believe God's Word   (3:7–19)

Bibliography

Abels, P. S. "The Rest of God." Dissertation, Dallas Theological Seminary, 1977. **Arowele, P. J.** "The Pilgrim People of God (An African's Reflections on the Motif of Sojourn in the Epistle to the Hebrews)." *AsiaJT* 4 (1990) 438–55. **Barrett, C. K.** "The Eschatology of the Epistle to the Hebrews." 363–73. **Bater, R. B.** "The Church in the Wilderness: A Study in Biblical Theology." Dissertation, Union Theological Seminary, New York, 1962. **Betz, O.** "The Eschatological Interpretation of the Sinai-Tradition in Qumran and in the New Testament." *RevQ* 21 (1967) 89–107. **Bonnard, P.** "La significàtion du désert selon le Nouveau Testament." In *Hommage et Reconnaissance.* FS K. Barth. Ed. J. J. von Allmen. Paris: Delachaux & Niestle, 1946. 9–18. **Clendenen, E. R.** "Yahweh's 'Rest' in Psalm 95." Dissertation, Dallas Theological Seminary, 1975. **Coats, G. W.** *Rebellion in the Wilderness.* Nashville: Abingdon, 1968. **Davies, G. H.** "Psalm 95." *ZAW* 85 (1973) 183–95. **Dey, L. K. K.** *The Intermediary World and Patterns of Perfection.* 227–33. **Dussaut, L.** *Synopse structurelle de l'Épître aux Hébreux.* 33–39. **Fabris, R.** "La lettera agli Ebrei e l'Antico Testamento." *RivB* 32 (1984) 237–52. **Fischer, F. L.** "The New and Greater Exodus: The Exodus Pattern in the New Testament." *SWJT* 20 (1977) 69–79. **Fontecha, J. F.** "La Vida christiana como Peregrinación según la Epistola a los Hebreos." In *Studium Legionense.* Leon, 1961. 2:251–306. **Frankowski, J.** "Requies, Bonum promissum populi Dei in VT et Judaismo (Hbr 3,7–4,11)." *VD* 43 (1965) 124–49, 225–40. **Guillet, J.** "Thème de la marche au Désert dans l'Ancien et le Nouveau Testament." *RSR* 36 (1949) 161–81. **Hofius, O.** *Katapausis.* 51–58, 117–43. **Johnsson, W. G.** "The Pilgrimage Motif in the Book of Hebrews." *JBL* 97 (1978) 239–51. **Kaiser, W. C.** "The Promise Theme and the Theology of Rest." *BSac* 130 (1973) 135–50. **Käsemann, E.** *Das wandernde Gottesvolk.* 5–45. **Kistemaker, S.** *The Psalm Citations in the Epistle to the Hebrews.* 35–36, 85–86, 108–16, 141–42. **Laub, F.** *Bekenntnis und Auslegung.* 246–53. **Losada, D. A.**

"La Reconciliación como 'Reposo.'" *RevistB* 36 (1974) 113-28. **Machado, J. B.** "A redenção, caminho do santuário." *RCB* 3 (1966) 31–49. **Marshall, I. H.** "The Problem of Apostasy in New Testament Theology." *PRS* 14 (1987) 65–80. **Miller, M. P.** "Targum, Midrash and the Use of the Old Testament in the New Testament." *JSJ* 2 (1971) 29–82. **Mugridge, A.** "Warnings in the Epistle to the Hebrews: An Exegetical and Theological Study." *RTR* 46 (1987) 74–82. **Nestle, E.** "Hebrews 3:8, 15." *ExpTim* 21 (1909–10) 94. **Nixon, R. E.** *The Exodus in the New Testament.* London: Tyndale, 1963. **Oberholtzer, T. K.** "The Kingdom Rest in Hebrews 3:1–4:13." *BSac* 145 (1988) 185–96. **Obermüller, R.** "Una mística del camino: El tema de la peregrinación en la carta a los Hebreos." *RevistB* 33 (1971) 55–66. **Ouderslys, R. C.** "Exodus in the Letter to the Hebrews." In *Grace upon Grace.* FS L. J. Kuyper. Ed. J. I. Cook. Grand Rapids, MI: Eerdmans, 1975. 143–52. **Peter, N. E.** "Bible Study— Practical Exhortation: Hebrews 3:7–15." *AsiaJT* 3 (1989) 576–81. **Rice, G. E.** "Apostasy as a Motif and Its Effect on the Structure of Hebrews." *AUSS* 23 (1985) 29–35. **Robertson, O. P.** "The People of the Wilderness: The Concept of the Church in Hebrews." 107–28. **Schröger, F.** *Der Verfasser des Hebräerbriefes als Schriftausleger.* 101–15. **Solari, S. K.** "The Problem of *Metanoia* in the Epistle to the Hebrews." Dissertation, Catholic University of America, 1970. 135–42. **Spicq, C.** *Vie chrétienne et pérégrination.* 77–111. **Stuart, S. S.** "The Exodus Tradition in Late Jewish and Early Christian Literature." 55–63, 98–103, 145–48. **Toussaint, S. D.** "The Eschatology of the Warning Passages in the Book of Hebrews." *GTJ* 3 (1982) 67–80. **Vanhoye, A.** "Longue marche ou accès tout proche? Le contexte biblique de Hébreux 3,7–4,11." *Bib* 49 (1968) 9–26.

Translation

[7]*So then, as the Holy Spirit is saying,*
 "Today, if you hear his voice,
[8] *do not harden your hearts as you did in the rebellion,*
 on the day of testing in the wilderness,
[9] *where your fathers put me*[a] *to the test through their distrust,*[b]
 even though[c] *they saw my judgments*[d] *for* [10]*forty years.*
 For that reason I was angry with this generation,
 and said, 'Their hearts are always going astray.'
 But they have not known my ways.
[11] *So*[e] *I declared by an oath in my anger,*
 'They shall certainly not[f] *enter my rest.'"*

[12g] *Be careful, brothers, that no one*[h] *among you has an evil, unbelieving*[i] *heart that turns away*[j] *from the living God.*[k] [13]*But encourage one another every day, so long as it is still*[l] *called*[m] *"Today," so that no one among you allows himself to be hardened*[n] *by the delusive attractiveness*[o] *of sin.* [14]*For we have become*[p] *partners with Christ, supposing that we hold firmly to the end the basic position*[q] *we had at the beginning.* [15]*As has just been said:*

 "Today, if you hear his voice,
 do not harden your hearts as you did in the rebellion."

[16]*For who were they who heard*[r] *and rebelled? Were they not really*[s] *all those Moses led out of Egypt?* [17]*And with whom was he angry for forty years? Was it not with those who sinned, whose bodies fell in the desert?* [18]*And to whom did he declare by an oath that they would not enter his rest, if not to those who had refused to obey?*[t] [19]*So*[u] *then we see that they were unable to enter because of unbelief.*

Notes

[a] Although the word $\mu\epsilon$, "me," should be omitted from the text with P^{13} P^{46} ℵ A B C D* 33 sa Cl Lcf, its inclusion in the translation brings out the implied sense.

[b] The phrase ἐν δοκιμασίᾳ is difficult. The noun δοκιμασία occurs only once in the LXX (Sir 6:12) and only here in the NT. The phrase in Heb 3:9 is ambiguous, since it can be taken in both an active ("in their mistrust of me") and a passive sense ("in their time of testing"). The translation reflects the active sense and accepts the proposal of Hofius (*Katapausis,* 213, n. 797) that δοκιμασία describes the attitude that is the opposite of radical faith, which can be displayed in response to the word of God. While faith trusts the promises of God, even in spite of all appearances (cf. Heb 11:1, 7, 27), unbelief responds with distrust and doubt that demands proof and certainty before it will entrust itself to the promise of God.

[c] The conj καί is used in an adversative sense (cf. Hofius, *Katapausis,* 129).

[d] The text reads τὰ ἔργα μου, "my works," but the reference is clearly to acts of judgment. That explains why God was angry with this generation (so Schröger, *Verfasser,* 103).

[e] The particle ὡς (which commonly expresses comparison) is used in a consecutive sense (BAGD 898).

[f] The construction εἰ with the future ind corresponds to a familiar Heb. construction where the particle אם (which commonly means "if") followed by a verb expresses emphatic denial. See Moule, *Idiom-Book,* 179; BDF §372(4).

[g] Heb 3:12–15 is a long and contrived periodic sentence, approaching the style of classical Gk. It has been broken up in the translation out of deference to English style. See *Comment* on 1:1–4; 2:2–4, 14–15.

[h] In cautious assertions the negative particles μή/μήποτε are often equivalent to the English "perhaps." If that nuance is present in the caution βλέπετε . . . μήποτε, the translation would be "Take heed! Perhaps there will be someone among you who . . . ." Cf. Moulton, *Grammar,* 1:192–93.

[i] The gen (ἀπιστίας) is a gen of quality, further defining the character of the heart (BDF §165).

[j] The construction ἐν τῷ with the inf is epexegetical or explanatory. It indicates the content or expression of "an evil heart." See Turner, *Grammar,* 3:166; cf. BDF §404(3): "in the form of an (accomplished) apostasy."

[k] The omission of the article in the phrase ἀπὸ θεοῦ ζῶντος serves to focus the attention upon the character of God as distinguished from his person. See Moule, *Idiom-Book,* 114. The expression occurs again in 9:14; 10:31; 12:22, and in each instance the reference to God is anarthrous.

[l] For a discussion of the idiom ἄχρις οὗ in the light of classical and hellenistic usage, see W. L. Lorimer, "Romans xiii.3, Hebrews iii.13," *NTS* 12 (1965–66) 390–91.

[m] It is virtually impossible to reflect in translation the striking play on words in the similarity in appearance and sound between παρακαλεῖτε, "encourage," and καλεῖται, "is called."

[n] The pass in the form σκληρυνθῇ has been understood as a pass of permission (cf. BDF §314).

[o] The translation seeks to bring out the double nuance of deceitfulness and of pleasantness that comes to expression in the word ἀπάτη (cf. BAGD 82 [2]).

[p] The connotation of the pf tense in γεγόναμεν seems to be intensive: "we have become (and consequently still are) partners."

[q] A determination of the nuance in the word ὑπόστασις is difficult. Köster (*TDNT* 8:585–88) argues on the basis of the word in Heb 1:3 that the term denotes the reality of God, which lies hidden beneath the transitory and shadowy appearances of the present world (so also Swetnam, *Bib* 53 [1972] 378–82). H. Dörrie, ("Ὑπόστασις: Wort und Bedeutungsgeschichte," NAWG 3 [1955] 39) interprets the term in 3:14 as "frame of mind," with reference to the frame of mind described in 3:6. The sense "confidence," "assurance," must be eliminated, since examples of the word with this nuance cannot be found in early sources (cf. Schlatter, *Glaube,* 614–17). For the rendering "original conviction," see BAG 854; BAGD 111.

For the correct understanding of the nuance of the word, it is imperative to observe that ὑπόστασις in v 14 presents the antithesis to ἀποστῆναι, "to turn away, to fall away," in v 12 (so Schlatter, *Glaube,* 617; Grässer, *Glaube,* 18, 46–48; Hofius, *Katapausis,* 133). Cf. Bornkamm (*TBl* 21 [1942] 191, n. 8): ἀρχὴ τῆς ὑποστάσεως signifies the beginning of the Christian stand of the believers, when they placed themselves under the obligation of giving the confession that Jesus is the Son of God.

[r] The aor ptcp ἀκούσαντες expresses action antecedent to the verb παραπικράνειν, "to rebel." If the ptcp is also concessive, translate, "For who were they who rebelled, although they had heard?"

[s] The use of ἀλλά (usually rendered "but") as an adv particle rather than an adversative conj is well attested in literary Gk. The usage occurs after both assertions and rhetorical questions, where

the idea of assent is found. Another example is probably to be recognized in the assertion of Heb 10:3. See Wikgren, "Greek Idioms," 150–51.

ᵗ P⁴⁶ is alone in reading ἀπιστήσασιν, "they refused to believe," for ἀπειθήσασιν, "they refused to obey." This seems to express an editorial preference in this MS, which consistently substitutes cognates expressing unbelief where Hebrews speaks of disobedience (cf. 4:6, ἀπιστίαν [where P⁴⁶ is joined by א and bo]; 4:11, ἀπιστίας [P⁴⁶ alone]; 11:31, ἀπιστήσασιν [P⁴⁶ alone]). See Hoskier, *Text*, 36, 54; Beare, *JBL* 63 [1944] 386.

ᵘ The conj καί is used in a consecutive sense, "and so we see." Cf. BDF §442(2).

Form/Structure/Setting

A change in style, form, and genre announces the introduction of the next unit of thought in the homily prepared for the community. In 3:1–6 the writer had simply alluded to the biblical texts that served as the basis for his exposition of Jesus' superiority to Moses. In 3:7–11 he cites the OT text directly and at length. So important is the statement of the text to his purpose that he introduces it again in 3:15; 4:3, 5, and 7. The appeal to an explicit quotation, which is then explained, repeated, and applied to the hearers in their situation, signals a return to homiletical midrash (see *Form/Structure/Setting* on 2:5–9). The entire unit assumes the form of a commentary on Ps 95 (LXX 94):7*b*–11, in which the writer presupposes a correspondence between the successive generations of the people of God and consistency in the conduct of God.

In the laminated construction of the sermon layers of exposition and exhortation alternate. By making the final statement in 3:1–6 contingent upon the response of his hearers ("we are God's house, supposing that we hold firmly to our confidence" [v 6*b*]), the writer assures a smooth transition to the exhortation that follows. His concern is that the community should maintain its integrity and continue to live in terms of the divine promises. The memory of Israel's failure in this regard, as set forth in Ps 95, provides the basis for the sober warning that a refusal to listen to God's voice and to respond in obedience would entail the tragic loss of their promised inheritance.

The parenetic section introduced by the quotation in 3:7–11 extends to 4:14. It is proper, however, to consider 3:7–19 as a discrete literary unit, consisting of the primary text (vv 7–11) and the initial commentary upon it (vv 12–19). The first section of the commentary is framed by the repetition of the verb βλέπειν and the noun ἀπιστία in vv 12 and 19:

v 12   "*See to it* [βλέπετε], brothers, that no one among you has an evil heart of *unbelief* [ἀπιστίας]."

v 19   "So *we see* [βλέπομεν] that they were unable to enter because of *unbelief* [ἀπιστίαν]."

The choice of ἀπιστία, which occurs only here in Hebrews, indicates that the writer intended to use the literary technique of *inclusio* to mark off the limits of the unit. Theologically, he stresses that the response to the word of God can be unbelief (cf. Vanhoye, *La structure*, 94–95; Losada, *RevistB* 36 [1974] 123). The warning against unbelief in vv 12 and 19 provides a literary and theological frame for the admonition to maintain the basic position of faith, which is centrally placed in v 14.

The writer's formal training in rhetoric is evident in the composition of vv 12–19. The commentary is introduced with an oratorical imperative (βλέπετε, "Be careful" [v 12]). It is advanced by striking plays on words which depend for their effectiveness on oral delivery (ἀπιστίας ἐν τῷ ἀποστῆναι ἀπό, "unbelief in turning away from" [v 12]; παρακαλεῖτε . . . καλεῖται, "encourage . . . called" [v 13]). A concentration of words beginning with the Greek letter *alpha* (*a*) describes Israel's disposition and the danger facing the community (ἀπιστίας ["unbelief"], ἀποστῆναι ["turn away"], v 12; ἀπάτη τῆς ἁμαρτίας ["the deceitfulness of sin"], v 13; τοῖς ἁμαρτήσασιν ["those who sinned"], v 17; τοῖς ἀπειθήσασιν ["those who disobeyed"], v 18; ἀπιστίαν ["unbelief"], v 19). The periodic sentence in vv 12–15, which is an expression of artistic prose, is followed by a series of rhetorical questions in vv 16–18. The formulation of questions, with the answers supplied in an interrogative form, was a recognized rhetorical method designated *subiectio.* It consisted of a fixed dialogue form, in which the speaker sought to make the movement of his ideas more lively by means of a series of rapid questions and answers. This rhetorical form is displayed in the preaching of the Cynic Teles, who lived in the third century B.C., and became a standard feature of the diatribe style (cf. H. Lausberg, *Handbuch der literarische Rhetorik* [Munich: Beck, 1960] 381–83). In Heb 3:16–18 the use of *subiectio* is oratorical and serves to engage the readers in the sober reality of Israel's failure. The use of the present tense in v 19 (καὶ βλέπομεν, "So we see"), after the series of aorists in vv 16–18, is stylistically effective and brings the auditors before the unavoidable conclusion that unbelief is catastrophic.

Comment

In 3:7–19 the quotation from Ps 95 furnishes the basis for the exhortation to remain sensitive to the promise of eschatological salvation. In his own remarks the writer introduces salient words and thoughts from the text and relates them to the situation of his readers. His interpretation of the text was heavily influenced by Num 14. According to Num 13–14 Israel was camped at Kadesh in the Desert of Paran, on the verge of entering Canaan. Entrance into the land was the goal of the Exodus and was necessary for the fulfillment of the promise. When those who had been sent into Canaan to explore the land brought back a bad report, however, the Israelites refused to enter. They rejected the promise through unbelief. Ps 95 recalls that their disposition incurred the wrath of God; Israel was refused entry into God's promised rest because of their rebellion. The Christian community finds itself in the comparable situation of standing immediately before the fulfillment of God's promise. The solemn review of the divine response to the Exodus generation served to warn the community not to emulate the unbelief of Israel at Kadesh.

7a The writer establishes an intrinsic connection between 3:6 and the exhortation from Ps 95. The particle διό, "so then," carries forward the thought expressed conditionally in v 6b and relates it to the admonition "do not harden your hearts" in v 8. An alternative proposal to connect διό with the imperative βλέπετε, "be careful," in v 12 and to regard vv 7b–11 as a parenthetical thought (so Kistemaker, *Psalm Citations,* 85) is to be rejected. The proposal blunts the force of the admonition and obscures the central importance of the quotation to the entire section.

The formula of introduction (καθὼς λέγει τὸ πνεῦμα τὸ ἅγιον, "as the Holy Spirit is saying") is one found elsewhere in Jewish sources (cf. *m. Soṭa* 9:6, "The Holy Spirit proclaims to them," followed by a quotation from Scripture). It is characteristic of the writer's high conception of Scripture. In 9:8 details of cultic procedure are cited as the means by which "the Holy Spirit indicates"; in 10:15 a quotation from Jer 31 is introduced with the formula, "The Holy Spirit also bears witness to us." The writer never names the person through whom Scripture was recorded but relates it to the gracious activity of God (cf. Schröger, *Verfasser,* 101, n. 3). The present tense of the verb λέγει is important; through the quotation of Scripture the Holy Spirit *is speaking* now. Consequently, the witness of the Scripture is brought from the past into the present, contemporary with the experience of the readers. What was spoken or written concerning the desert generation centuries before has immediate relevance to the community addressed (P. E. Hughes, 141).

7b–11 The quotation is taken from Ps 95(LXX 94):7b–11, following the OG version. The liturgical use of Ps 95 as a preamble to synagogue services on Friday evening and Sabbath morning is well established (Elbogen, *Der jüdische Gottesdienst,* 82, 108, 113). It is probable, therefore, that the community addressed in Hebrews was familiar with the details of the psalm. In the first half of the psalm Israel is summoned to praise and worship (vv 2, 6), but the second half conveyed the warning that the hardness of heart displayed by the desert generation must not be emulated.

According to the MT the psalmist spoke of Massah and Meribah (v 8; cf. Exod 17:1–7; Num 20:2–13), where the Israelites quarreled with Moses over the shortage of water (cf. S. Lehming, "Massa und Meriba," *ZAW* 71 [1961] 71–77). But he also referred to the incident at Kadesh where God declared on oath that the rebellious desert fathers would not enter Canaan (v 11; cf. Num 14:20–23, 28–35). In the LXX the specific reference to Massah and Meribah was obscured by the interpretive rendering of the place names as ὁ παραπικρασμός, "the rebellion," and ὁ πειρασμός, "the testing." The alteration indicates the translator's intention to interpret Ps 95:7b–11 in the light of Num 14, where Israel incurred God's wrath by the refusal to enter the promised land. It is that event which is aptly described as the "rebellion on the day when your fathers put me to the test." The memory of that catastrophic defiance left an indelible mark in a broad spectrum of sources (cf. Num 32:7–13; Deut 1:19–35; 9:33; Neh 9:15–17; Ps 106:24–26; CD 3:6–9; Ps-Philo, *Bib. Ant.* 15; *Sipre Num.* 82 to 10:33; 4 Ezra 7:106; 1 Cor 10:5–10; and for discussion of these sources, see Hofius, *Katapausis,* 44–45, 52, 118–27). Kadesh became the symbol of Israel's disobedience, the place where God's past redemption was forgotten and where the divine promise no longer impelled the people to obedience. The LXX presents Ps 95:7b–11 as a meditation on Num 14, and this perspective is basic to the interpretation in Hebrews (cf. Vanhoye, *Bib* 49 [1968] 10–21; Hofius, *Katapausis,* 127–31; Schröger, *Verfasser,* 103–4).

The influence of Num 14 on the quotation is pervasive (see especially the analysis of Hofius, *Katapausis,* 118–31). The opening line, "Today, if you hear his voice" (v 7), is a response to the charge lodged by God in Num 14:22, "They did not listen to my voice," an accusation that is echoed in subsequent references to the episode at Kadesh (Deut 9:23b; Ps 106 [LXX 105]:25b; CD 3:7–8; Ps-Philo, *Bib. Ant.* 15.5). The rare term παραπικρασμός, "rebellion," in v 8, which occurs nowhere else in the LXX (but cf. 1 Kgs 15:23 Aq.; Prov 17:11 Theod.) and was apparently coined on the basis of the cognate verb παραπικράνειν, "to rebel," at the time the psalm was translated, was well chosen to convey the concept of rebellion in Num 14:35. The "day of testing in the desert" has clear reference to Num 14:11b, 21–22, when the Israelites defied God in a particularly offensive manner, in spite of the fact that they had experienced the miraculous intervention of God in Egypt and the desert. The complaint, "Their hearts are always going astray" (v 10*b*), corresponds to Num 14:22*b*, "They have already tested me ten times." It indicates that God's anger (cf. Num 14:11, 23, 43*b*) was not aroused by a single incident but by a persistent tendency to refuse his direction. Finally, the quotation of God's solemn oath resumes Num 14:21–23, 28–30. The formulation of v 11 corresponds to the words in Num 14:30, "You will certainly not enter the land!" The finality of God's oath and the judgment it sealed must be seen as a just and adequate recompense for Israel's tragic defiance (Hofius, *Katapausis*, 126).

Apart from insignificant variations involving spelling, verbal forms, and stylistic changes that may reflect prior liturgical usage, the writer provides an interpretation of the passage within the text. The insertion of the particle διό before προσώχθισα in v 10 ("for that reason I was angry") has the effect of altering the punctuation, so that the reference to "forty years" (v 10) becomes attached to the preceding statement. In the MT and the LXX the forty years are years of God's wrath. The association of the forty years with grace and blessing that God bestowed through his judgments is the most distinctive element in the interpretation of the LXX text by the writer (cf. Schröger, *Verfasser*, 102–3; Kistemaker, *Psalm Citations*, 35–36, 85; McCullough, *NTS* 26 [1979–80] 369–72). The rearrangement of the quotation serves to bring the admonition directly before the community in its situation.

12–13 The application of Ps 95 to the community exhibits a method of exegesis that has been designated midrash *pesher* (cf. Schröger, *Verfasser*, 113–15; Kistemaker, *Psalm Citations*, 111). The writer has selected certain words and thoughts from the quotation that he considers appropriate to his readers and works them into his pastoral instruction. The reference to an "evil heart" that "turns away" from God (v 12), the description of the present period as "Today," and the warning not to allow themselves "to be hardened" by sin (v 13) are interpretive links with the citation. They serve to draw the text into the experience of the hearers.

The imperative βλέπετε, "Be careful," followed by the negative particle and the verb in the indicative mood, introduces a sharp warning. The writer is apprehensive that the community may falter in its response to the promise of God. Recognizing that it is individuals who are exposed to the peril of apostasy, his pastoral concern extends to every member of the congregation (τινὶ ὑμῶν, "[even] one among you," v 12; cf. 3:13; 4:1, 11; 6:12; 12:15). The reference to "an evil unbelieving heart" interprets the expression in v 10, "their hearts are always going astray," which in OT terms is described as "turning away from the living God."

Particular importance must be attached to the term ἀπιστία, "unbelief," because it is introduced at the opening and close of the writer's commentary (vv 12, 19). That element was not contributed by Ps 95. The reproach of unbelief is narrowly related to the tradition concerning Israel at Kadesh in the Pentateuch (Num 14:11, "How long will they refuse to believe me?"; cf. Deut 1:32; 9:32; Ps 106:24). The description of the heart as πονηρά, "evil," also reflects the influence of Num 14, where the term occurs twice in the expression "this *evil* congregation" (Num 14:27, 35) but nowhere else in the Pentateuch (Vanhoye, *Bib* 49 [1968] 19). The allusions to Num 14 are significant because they indicate that unbelief is not a lack of faith or trust. It is the refusal to believe God. It leads inevitably to a turning away from God in a deliberate act of rejection. The play on words ἀπιστίας ἐν τῷ ἀποστῆναι, "unbelief in turning away," reinforces the fact that falling away and unbelief reflect the same disposition (cf. Hofius, *Katapausis*, 124, 131–32). The pastoral injunction in v 12 takes up the plea of Joshua and Caleb in Num 14:9, "Do not turn away from the Lord" (cf. Deut 1:28, "Your brothers turned away your heart"). It recognizes that the Christian community is not immune from the recalcitrant spirit expressed by the generation in the desert.

The avoidance of apostasy demands not simply individual vigilance but the constant care of each member of the community for one another (v 13). The admonition "encourage one another every day" may actually presuppose a daily gathering of the house church, which would provide the occasion for mutual encouragement (cf. Windisch, 31; Michel, 106). The verb παρακαλεῖν covers warning and reproof as well as encouragement, with the implication that reproof should be given in a brotherly and loving way (Forkman, *Religious Community*, 47–50). The reflexive pronoun ἑαυτούς, "one another," which is used here instead of the reciprocal pronoun ἀλλήλους, "each other," emphasizes the mutual responsibility that each member of the community should feel for the others.

The urgency for encouragement and reproof is that the community of faith experiences an unresolved tension between peril and promise. The danger of deception by sin and apostasy persists so long as the moment of demand and opportunity, which is called "Today," is valid. The initial word in the quotation from Ps 95:7*b*, σήμερον, "Today," provided the writer with a catchword for bringing the biblical statement before his hearers sharply. "Today" is no longer the today of the past, surveyed by the psalmist in his situation, but the today of the present, which continues to be conditioned by the voice of God that speaks day after day through the Scriptures and in the gospel tradition. Moreover, its perspective extends from the present to the approaching parousia and judgment ("as long as 'Today' lasts"; cf. 9:27–28; 10:37–39). The quality of the day is that it is a day of promise (cf. 4:1). But it forces upon the community the same alternatives of faith and obedience or unbelief and disobedience which confronted Israel at Kadesh (Num 14:34*b*). The prospect of "being hardened by the delusive attractiveness of sin" is possible only in response to the revelation of God. The passive voice of σκληρυνθῇ, "be hardened," is important because it indicates that sin is conceived as an agent that deceives and leads an individual to an irretrievably hopeless position. In this context ἁμαρτία, "sin," has a specific connotation. It is the sin of refusing to obey God and to act upon his promise (Num 14:19, 34 LXX; cf. Käsemann, *Das wandernde Gottesvolk*, 25).

14 In the periodic sentence that extends from v 12 to v 15, the assurance that the community enjoys a firm relationship with Christ is of crucial importance. It is one of the central assertions in the homily, which provides strong encouragement even as it summons the readers to display genuine and persevering faith (cf. 3:6; 4:14). Hofius (*Katapausis* 133, 215, n. 820) has argued that μέτοχοι is an eschatological technical term, designating the companions of the heavenly hosts or of the Lord (cf. *1 Enoch* 104:6 [Greek fragment]; *Epistle of the Apostles* 19). It seems preferable to recognize that the term μέτοχοι commonly carries the nuance of "partner" in the papyri. The word βεβαίαν, "firm guarantee," also reflects business terminology (MM 107, 406; Wikgren, "Greek Idioms," 147). These words are used here metaphorically. The relationship between Christ and the community is conceived in the binding terms of a business partnership. The community can rely on the faithfulness of Christ (cf. 3:1–2), but they too must display "good faith." They have been placed under obligation.

The conditional clause introduced by ἐάνπερ, "supposing that," resumes the ἐάνπερ of 3:6 and stresses the provisional character of the relationship. The appeal to hold firmly to the basic position held at the beginning in v 14 presents the antithesis to the ἀποστῆναι, "turning away," in v 12 (Hofius, *Katapausis*, 133). It draws its emotional force from the disposition of Israel at Kadesh, where the people determined to elect new leadership and return to Egypt (Num 14:3–4) rather than to maintain their position and to act on the promise of God (cf. Vanhoye, *Bib* 49 [1968] 21). The readers are reminded that perseverance until the time of the actual realization of the promise and entrance into the eschatological rest prepared for the people of God is required of those who are "partners with Christ." The community is called to expectant waiting.

15 The fresh quotation of the opening lines of the psalm (95[LXX 94]: 7*b*–8*a*) does not mark a new stage in the argument (as argued by Hofius, *Katapausis*, 133–37) but summarizes the argument presented to that point. The recognition of the periodic sentence in vv 12–15 makes that clear. The writer desired to show the Christians addressed that what is written in the psalm has direct bearing upon their lives. The quotation draws together the key words and concepts interpreted in vv 12–13 and serves to bring the exhortation before the community in a form that had immediate relevance for them. The response of the desert generation at Kadesh can momentarily be forgotten as the community hears the Holy Spirit warning them not to respond to God's voice with stubborn rebelliousness.

16–18 The fact of rebellion and its catastrophic results is pressed in the formulation of a series of rhetorical questions. Three parallel questions are posed, and the response to them in the first two cases is cast in an interrogative form, and in the third in the form of a clause incorporated within the question itself. The terms of Ps 95 are taken up in vv 16*a*, 17*a*, and 18*a*, while the responses are formulated on the basis of the familiar account of Israel at Kadesh in Num 14. The course of the argument can be set forth in a table:

v 16*a*	(Ps 95:7–8)	v 16*b*	(Num 14:13, 19, 22)
v 17*a*	(Ps 95:10)	v 17*b*	(Num 14:10, 29, 32)
v 18*a*	(Ps 95:11)	v 18*b*	(Num 14:30, 33, 43)

The response of Israel is underscored in a manner that exhibits the climate of defiant unbelief: they rebelled against God (v 16); they sinned against God (v 17); they refused to obey God (v 18). The anger of God was the just response to this rebellious disposition (cf. Losada, *RevistB* 36 [1974] 123–24).

In v 16*a* the verb παραπικράνειν, "to rebel," carries forward the thought of rebellion expressed by the cognate noun παραπικρασμός, "rebellion," in v 15. It could conceivably refer to a number of provocations, when Israel complained against the hardships of the pilgrimage through the desert. The context, however, supports an allusion to the rebellion at Kadesh. The response in v 16*b* associates Moses, whose faithfulness was praised in 3:2, 5, with his leadership of those who participated in the Exodus. The stress falls on the fact that "all" who left Egypt had heard God's voice and "all" had rebelled, even though they witnessed the redemptive power of God.

The formulation of v 17*a* reflects the punctuation of Ps 95:10 in the MT and the LXX but stands in tension with the quotation in vv 9–10. In the quotation, the "forty years" are associated with the grace and blessing of God displayed in his judgments; in 17*a*, the "forty years" are years of wrath. An attractive proposal is that the writer is thinking of two different time periods that were separated by the oath of God (Losada, *RevistB* 36 [1974] 122). The differentiation between the two periods is encouraged by the OT itself. Certain texts (e.g., Exod 16:35; Deut 2:7; Neh 9:21) speak of forty years during which Israel experienced God's gracious provision. On the other hand, texts like Num 14:33–34; 32:13 clearly speak of forty years of wrath. The writer incorporates both strands of the tradition in his interpretation of Ps 95. In v 9 he considers the forty years as a time of salvation, while in v 17 he speaks of a time of perdition. This shift in perspective serves to bring the psalm into the experience of the community. The forty years of the goodness and mercy of God intensifies the culpability of those who then turned away from him. It puts into proper perspective the wrath of God and his oath of rejection (v 17*b*). The consequence of refusing to acknowledge the presence and promise of God was the radical discipline of death in the desert. The Christian community had also experienced the redemptive grace of God. They must not perpetuate the sin of Israel (cf. Hofius, *Katapausis*, 129–30).

The final rhetorical question (v 18) associates the oath of rejection with the sin of disobedience. The formulation in v 18*b* ("those who had refused to obey" [τοῖς ἀπειθήσασιν]) reflects Num 14:43 LXX, where Moses says, "you turned away from the Lord in disobedience" (ἀπεστράφητε ἀπειθοῦντες κυρίῳ). Earlier in the passage the desert generation is described as those "who disobeyed me and tested me ten times" (Num 14:22, with reference to Exod 5:21; 14:11; 15:24; 16:2; 17:2, 3; 32:1; Num 11:1, 4; 12:1; 14:2, according to Kistemaker, *Psalm Citations*, 115, n. 1). The culmination of unbelief was the open defiance of God, and it was this that barred entrance into the promised rest of God.

19 The conclusion that the consequence of unbelief was exclusion from God's promised rest flows inexorably from the argument. Although there is no reference to unbelief in Ps 95:7*b*–11, the term ἀπιστία finds ample support in Num 14:11 and complements the reference to ἀπιστία in v 12. The new element in v 19 is the allusion to the sequel of the tragic decision to defy God at Kadesh. When the Israelites realized their folly, they sought to repent. In their presumption they decided they would enter Canaan after all, in spite of the divine oath. Their mission was abortive and they were soundly defeated (Num 14:39–45; cf. Deut 1:41–44). The oath of God was final. It is this epilogue to the transactions at Kadesh that is involved with the statement, "they were unable to enter because of unbelief" (Vanhoye, *Bib* 49 [1968] 22–23). The conclusion thus introduces the motif of the impossibility of a second repentance after apostasy, in anticipation of a fuller treatment later in the sermon (6:4–8; 10:26–31; 12:16–17; cf. Hofius, *Katapausis*, 137). The hearers are left with the overwhelming impression that unbelief would expose them to the same precarious situation as Israel at Kadesh.

Explanation

A major theme in Hebrews is that Christians are the people of God who, like the generation in the desert, experience the tensions of an interim existence between redemption and rest, between promise and fulfillment. The tragic failure of that generation to attain the goal of their redemption calls attention to a pattern of response to God's voice that must not be emulated. That fact had already been recognized in Ps 95:7*b*–11 and was reiterated whenever the psalm was used liturgically in the synagogue and church to summon the congregation to worship. The plea, "Today, if you hear his voice, do not harden your hearts as in the rebellion," was intended to bring the memory of Israel at Kadesh before the people as a sober reminder that each generation has the awesome responsibility of standing before the claim of God expressed in his word. "Today" signals a fresh moment of biography and history, which is always conditioned by the response of obedience or disobedience, of faith or unbelief.

The writer quotes Ps 95 to extend to his hearers a serious call to persevering discipleship. It is imperative that their partnership with Christ be affirmed by unfaltering adherence to the basic position acknowledged in their baptismal confession. The demand for fidelity and endurance is supported by the promise of rest. But the writer urges the mutual care and concern of every member of the community for one another to ensure that no one should respond to the voice of God inappropriately. The psalmist had posed the issue of response to God for his own generation in terms of the response of the desert generation at Kadesh. This understanding controls the interpretation of Ps 95 in Hebrews. The writer does not compare Christian existence to a long period of wandering in the desert but to the situation of a people whose pilgrimage was almost over and who were on the verge of attaining what God had promised. The eschatological conviction of the writer is that Christians stand in a comparable situation with respect to entrance into God's rest. The basis of the comparison between Israel at Kadesh and the Christian community addressed is the unresolved tension of standing before the promise of God in a moment conditioned by trials and peril.

It would appear that the writer had the Book of Numbers opened before him when he composed this section of the sermon. In 3:1–6 he seized on Num 12:7 and found in the testimony to Moses' faithfulness an occasion for comparing Jesus and Moses. In Num 13:1–25 he read of Israel's encampment at Kadesh, the gateway to Canaan, and of the sending of scouts to explore the promised land. In response to their report (Num 13:26–33), Israel determined to defy the Lord and return to Egypt, in spite of the assurances of Joshua and Caleb. Their rebellion called forth the solemn oath of God that barred their entrance into the land (Num 14:1–35).

The writer regarded the first phase of Israel's trek through the wilderness as normative in the life of the people of God because it was a period of spiritual formation. In the isolation and desolateness of the desert Israel met God; but they also discovered their own unwillingness to be a people engaged in pilgrimage, yielding obedience to the voice of God. The costly decision to resist God at Kadesh was the culmination of a series of episodes in which Israel provoked the Lord through bitter complaint, disobedience, and unbelief.

The fundamental failure of the desert generation was their refusal to believe that God was actually present among them, directing them through his word. Refusing to acknowledge his presence and voice, they forfeited the possibility of entrance into God's rest. In calling attention to their fate, the writer warns the community not to lose faith in the presence of God with them that is celebrated whenever the word of God is read or the gospel tradition is proclaimed.

The comparison of the generation encamped at Kadesh with the Christian house church in its own distinctive situation reflects the writer's understanding of typology and of the legitimacy of typological exegesis. Typology acknowledges the factuality of the past event and presupposes a genuine correspondence between the saving and judging activity of God in the past and the present. It is based not on superficial resemblances but on the consistency of the divine action within the frame of reference established by revelation. In Heb 3:7–19 typological exegesis entails the use of historical memory to nurture and formulate eschatological faith. The contrary alternatives of blessing and curse that confronted Israel at Kadesh were conditioned upon faith or unbelief in response to the promise of God. The refusal to believe God excluded Israel from the realization of the promise. In 3:7–19 the community is summoned to recognize the peril of refusing to believe God. The condition for the fulfillment of the divine promise remains active faith, expressed through obedience and adherence to the Christian confession.

C. Rest as Sabbath Celebration for the People of God (4:1–14)

Bibliography

Abels, P. S. "The Rest of God." Dissertation, Dallas Theological Seminary, 1977. **Arowele, P. J.** "The Pilgrim People of God (An African's Reflections on the Motif of Sojourn in the Epistle to the Hebrews)." *AsiaJT* 4 (1990) 438–55. **Attridge, H. W.** "'Let Us Strive to Enter that Rest': The Logic of Hebrews 4:1–11." *HTR* 73 (1980) 279–88. ———. "New Covenant Christology in an Early Christian Homily." *QuartRev* 8 (1988) 89–108. **Baba, K.** "A Great High Priest (Heb. 4:14)." *ExpTim* 34 (1922–23) 476–77. **Bourgin, C.** "La Passion du Christ et la nôtre: Hé 4:14–16; 5:7–9." *AsSeign* 21 (1969) 15–20. **Clavier, H.** "*Ο ΛΟΓΟΣ ΤΟΥ ΘΕΟΥ* dans l'Épître aux Hébreux." In *New Testament Essays.* FS T. W. Manson. Ed. A. J. B. Higgins. Manchester: University of Manchester, 1959. 81–93. **Clendenen, E. R.** "Yahweh's 'Rest' in Psalm 95." Dissertation, Dallas Theological Seminary, 1975. **Coats, G. W.** *Rebellion in the Wilderness.* Nashville: Abingdon, 1968. **Dussaut, L.** *Synopse structurelle de l'Épître aux Hébreux.* 36–41. **Ellingworth, P.** "Jesus and the Universe in Hebrews." *EvQ* 58 (1986) 337–50. **Fabris, R.** "La lettera agli Ebrei e l'Antico Testamento." *RivB* 32 (1984) 237–52. **Fontecha, J. F.** "La Vida cristiana como Peregrinación según la Epistola a los Hebreos." In *Studium Legionense.* Leon, 1961. 2:251–306. **Frankowski, J.** "Requies, Bonum Promissum populi Dei in VT et in Judaismo (Hebr 3,7–4,11)." *VD* 43 (1965) 124–49, 225–40. **Gaffin, R. B.** "A Sabbath Rest Still Awaits the People of God." In *Pressing Toward the Mark.* Ed. C. G. Dennison and R. C. Gamble. Philadelphia: The Orthodox Presbyterian Church, 1986. 33–51. **Galling, K.** "Durch die Himmel hindurch-geschritten (Hb. 4,14)." *ZNW* 43 (1950–51) 263–64. **Graham, R.** "A Note on Hebrews 4:4–9." In *The Sabbath in Scripture and History.* Ed. K. Strand. Washington, DC: Review and Herald, 1982. **Hamm, D.** "Faith in the Epistle to the Hebrews: The Jesus Factor." *CBQ* 52 (1990) 270–91. **Hofius, O.** *Katapausis.* 22–115, 137–43. **Hutton, W. R.** "Hebrews iv.11." *ExpTim* 52 (1940–41) 316–17. **Kaiser, W. C.** "The Promise Theme and the Theology of Rest." *BSac* 130 (1973) 135–50. **Kistemaker, S.** *The Psalm Citations in the Epistle to the Hebrews.* 36–37, 108–16. **Kuist, H. T.** "Hebrews 4:11–13." *BibRev* 16 (1931) 579–81. **Laub, F.** *Bekenntnis und Auslegung.* 104–7, 246–53. **Lauterbach, J. Z.** "The Sabbath in Jewish Ritual and Folklore." In *Rabbinic Essays.* Cincinnati: Hebrew Union College, 1951. 437–70. **Lincoln, A. T.** "Sabbath, Rest, and Eschatology in the New Testament." In *From Sabbath to Lord's Day: A Biblical, Historical,* *and Theological Investigation.* Ed. D. A. Carson. Grand Rapids: Zondervan, 1982. 177–201. **Lombard, H. A.** *"Katápausis* in the Letter to the Hebrews." *Neot* 5 (1971) 60–71. **Losada, D. A.** "La Reconciliatión como 'Reposo.'" *RevistB* 36 (1974) 113–28. **Marshall, I. H.** "The Problem of Apostasy in New Testament Theology." *PRS* 14 (1987) 65–80. **Martin, A. D.** *"Σαββατισμός."* *ExpTim* 26 (1914–15) 563–65. **Miller, M. P.** "Targum, Midrash and the Use of the Old Testament in the New Testament." *JSJ* 2 (1971) 29–82. **Mugridge, A.** "Warnings in the Epistle to the Hebrews: An Exegetical and Theological Study." *RTR* 46 (1987) 74–82. **Oberholtzer, T. K.** "The Kingdom Rest in Hebrews 3:1–4:13." *BSac* 145 (1988) 185–96. **Proulx, B.**, and **Schökel, L. A.** "Heb 4, 12–13: componentes y estructura." *Bib* 54 (1973) 331–39. **Rad, G. von.** "There Remains Still a Rest for the People of God: An Investigation of a Biblical Conception." In *The Problem of the Hexateuch and Other Essays.* Tr. E. W. T. Dicken. London: Oliver & Boyd, 1966. 94–102. **Rice, G. E.** "Apostasy as a Motif and Its Effect on the Structure of Hebrews." *AUSS* 23 (1985) 29–35. **Riesenfeld, H.** "Sabbat et Jour du Seigneur dans le Judaïsme, la prédication de Jésus et le christianisme primitif." *ASNS* 18 (1959) 52–70. **Robertson, O. P.** "The People of the Wilderness." 107–28, 167–71. **Rordorf, W.** *Der Sonntag.* Zurich: Zwingli, 1962. 88–111. **Rose, C.** "Verheissung und Erfüllung: Zum Verständnis von *ἐπαγγελία* im Hebräerbrief." *BZ* 33 (1989) 60–80. **Schaefer, K. T.** *"κρατεῖν τῆς ὁμολογίας* (Hebr 4,14)." In *Die Kirche im Wandel der Zeit.* FS J. Höffner. Cologne: Hanstein, 1971. 59–70. **Schrenk, W.** "Hebräerbrief 4, 14–16: Textlinguistik als Kommentierungsprinzip." *NTS* 26 (1980) 242–52. **Schröger, F.** *Der Verfasser des Hebräerbriefes als Schriftausleger.* 106–15. **Sherman, C. P.** "'A Great High Priest' (Hebrews iv.14)." *ExpTim* 34 (1922–23) 235–36. **Swetnam, J.** "Jesus as *Λόγος* in Hebrews 4, 12–13." *Bib* 62 (1981) 214–24. **Tetley, J.** "The Priesthood of Christ in Hebrews." *Anvil* 5 (1988) 195–206. **Toussaint, S. D.** "The Eschatology of the Warning Passages in the Book of Hebrews." *GTJ* 3 (1982) 67–80. **Trompf, G.** "The Conception of God in Hebrews 4:12–13." *ST* 25 (1971) 123–32. **Vanhoye, A.** "Longue marche ou accès tout proche? Le contexte biblique de Hébreux 3, 7–4, 11." *Bib* 49 (1968) 9–26. ———. "La parole qui juge: Hé 4, 12–13." *AsSeign* 59 (1974) 36–42. **Williamson, R.** "The Incarnation of the Logos in Hebrews." *ExpTim* 95 (1983–84) 4–8. ———. *Philo and the Epistle to the Hebrews.* 130–32, 241–44, 386–409, 544–57. **Wood, C. M.** "On Being Known." *TToday* 44 (1987) 197–206.

Translation

¹ *Therefore, while a promise of entering*[a] *his rest remains open, let us begin to fear*[b] *that*[c] *even one among you would seem*[d] *to be excluded from it.*[e] ²*For we also have had good news preached*[f] *to us, just as they did; but the word which they heard*[g] *did not benefit them, because they did not share the faith of those who listened.*[h] ³*For we*[i] *who have believed do enter*[j] *that rest, just as God has said,*

> *"So I declared by an oath in my anger,*
> *'They shall certainly not*[k] *enter my rest,'"*

and yet[l] *his work has been completed since*[m] *the foundation of the world.* ⁴*For somewhere he has spoken about the seventh day in this manner,*

> *"And on the seventh day God took rest*[n] *from all his works,"*

⁵ *and furthermore, in this context*[o] *he has said,*

> *"'They shall certainly not enter my rest.'"*

⁶ *Therefore, since the fact remains that some are to enter rest, and those who formerly*[p] *had good news proclaimed to them did not enter because of their disobedience,* ⁷*God again appointed a certain day, saying in the Psalter,*[q] *so much later, "Today," in the text already quoted:*

> *"Today, if you hear his voice,*
> *do not harden your hearts."*

⁸ *For if Joshua had given them rest,*^r *God would not have spoken of another time later on.* ⁹*Consequently,*^s *there remains a Sabbath celebration*^t *for the people of God.* ¹⁰*For whoever enters God's rest has also rested*^u *from his own work, as God did from his.* ¹¹*Let us, therefore, make every effort*^v *to enter that rest; otherwise,*^w *one of you might perish*^x *through*^y *the same example of disobedience.*^z ^{12aa}*For the word of God is living*^{bb} *and effective.*^{cc} *Sharper than any double-edged sword, it penetrates so as to separate soul and spirit, both joints and marrow,*^{dd} *and is able to judge the thoughts and deliberations of the heart.* ¹³*Nothing in creation is hidden from God's sight, but* ^{ee} *everything is uncovered and exposed*^{ff} *to the eyes of the one to whom we must give account.*^{gg} ¹⁴*Therefore, since we have a great high priest who has gone into*^{hh} *heaven, Jesus the Son of God, let us continue to hold fast*ⁱⁱ *to our confession.*

Notes

^a The aor inf εἰσελθεῖν is epexegetical, or explanatory, of the promise.

^b The position of the verb φοβηθῶμεν is emphatic in the structure of the sentence. An aor subjunctive is often used to imply a contrast between a previous way of life and a new one. In such cases, the verb is ingressive, as here. Cf. BDF §337(1).

^c The use of μήποτε to introduce an object clause after the verb φοβηθῶμεν is a feature of literary, rather than popular, style. See Turner, *Grammar*, 3:99; BDF §370(1).

^d For the suggestion that δοκῇ has a forensic idea, "to be found," cf. Rienecker, *Linguistic Key*, 328.

^e An alternative interpretation, based on the papyri (cf. MM 661), recognizes in ὑστερηκέναι the idea of coming too late (so Zerwick and Grosvenor, *Grammatical Analysis*, 660; cf. JB: "and none of you must think that he has come too late for it"). For the translation adopted, see BAGD, 849.

^f The pf tense of the ptcp emphasizes the completeness of the act of preaching, and thus leaves no room for any excuse to the effect that the proclamation had been inadequate or deficient (so Rienecker, *Linguistic Key*, 329).

^g The adjectival gen τῆς ἀκοῆς is used descriptively to qualify "the word." See Moule, *Idiom-Book*, 175.

^h The MSS preserve a bewildering variety of readings, and several critics suspect primitive corruption in the text. The translation accepts the text adopted for the UBSGNT. The accusative pl. form συγκεκερασμένους enjoys early and diverse support from both Alexandrian and Western types of text (p¹³ p⁴⁶ A B C D* ψ 69 81 88 1739 2127 vg^w sy^h bo sa^{3 mss} Chr Theodore of Mopsuestia Aug). Cf. JB: "because they did not share the faith of those who listened" (with reference to Joshua and Caleb). Understood in this light, the reference to the believing minority clarifies the source of the good news heard by Israel at Kadesh and anticipates v 8. The easier nom sg reading συγκεκερασμένος is less strongly attested (ℵ 57 [102] it vg^{s,cl} sy^p sa^{2 mss} Ephr Lcf) but has been preferred by many of the better commentaries and modern translations (RSV, NEB, TEV, NIV). The sense would be that the word that was heard did not meet with a believing response. For a discussion of the textual issue, see Metzger, *Textual Commentary*, 665; and for a different point of view, with translation of the different combinations of variant readings, see P. E. Hughes, 157–58, n. 62.

ⁱ The first person is known from the finite verb εἰσερχόμεθα (cf. Zerwick and Grosvenor, *Grammatical Analysis*, 661).

^j εἰσερχόμεθα is placed first in the structure of the sentence for emphasis. The present tense could express the idea "we are already in the process of entering" (so Rienecker, *Linguistic Key*, 329).

^k The construction εἰ with the fut ind has the force of an emphatic negative assertion here and in v 5, where the statement is repeated. See BDF §372(4); 454(5).

^l The introductory particle καίτοι, which is common in classical and later literary Gk., is used to clarify or strengthen the concessive idea in the ptcp. See BDF §425(1).

^m The prep ἀπό (which frequently means "from") is used here in a temporal sense (cf. Moule, *Idiom-Book*, 73).

ⁿ For κατέπαυσεν in the sense "took rest," see Turner, *Grammar*, 3:52.

^o The expression ἐν τούτῳ means "here," or "in this place," and consequently "in this context."

^p The word πρότερον, which is here used adverbially, has reference to the first of two actions. The reference is to the invitation to enter Canaan. Contrast the πάλιν, "again," in v 7. Cf. BDF §62.

[q] The versatile prep ἐν here has a local sense, "in David," where "David" clearly has reference to the Book of Psalms (BDF §219[1]). Cf. the paraphrase by J. W. C. Wand, "the old invitation in the Psalms" (*The New Testament Letters* [London: Cambridge UP, 1944] 179).

[r] The use of a second class conditional clause (εἰ in the protasis with a past tense in the ind mood; a past tense of the verb in the ind mood with ἄν in the apodosis) expresses an unfulfilled condition (see BDF §360[4]; Zerwick, *Biblical Greek* §313). The fact is that Joshua did not give them rest.

[s] The particle ἄρα draws a conclusion from the preceding argument: cf. Thrall, *Greek Particles*, 36–39.

[t] The rare noun σαββατισμός was apparently coined from the cognate verb σαββατίζειν, "to observe or celebrate the Sabbath" (cf. Exod 16:30; Lev 23:32; 26:34–35; 2 Chr 36:21 LXX). See Moulton and Howard, *Grammar*, 2:409. It has in view the festivity and praise of a Sabbath celebration. For a helpful discussion, see especially Hofius, *Katapausis*, 106–10.

[u] The aor tense in κατέπαυσεν is proleptic; what is enunciated as a consequence of the condition ("whoever enters God's rest") is expressed as if it had already come to pass, the condition being regarded as fulfilled (see Zerwick, *Biblical Greek* §257).

[v] The aor tense in the hortatory subjunctive σπουδάσωμεν is probably ingressive, "let us become zealous," "let us do our utmost."

[w] The translation reflects the decision to treat ἵνα μή as final, introducing a result clause rather than a purpose clause.

[x] That the verb πίπτειν (which ordinarily means "to fall") carries the nuance of "perish" here has been recognized by Zerwick and Grosvenor, *Grammatical Analysis*, 661. Cf. the use of the same verb in 3:17, where the nuance clearly comes to expression.

[y] The prep ἐν after πίπτειν has the resultant meaning "lest any one fall after" or "by" (so Turner, *Grammar*, 3:257).

[z] In their note, BAGD (844) argue that ὑπόδειγμα, "example," does not refer to an example of disobedience but to an example of falling into destruction as a result of disobedience. This paraphrastic approach to the text would appear to be unnecessary if the nuance of "perish" is recognized in the verb πίπτειν.

[aa] Vv 12–13 provide yet another example of a periodic sentence (see above on 1:1–4; 2:2–4, 14–15; 3:12–15). The sentence has been violated in translation out of deference to English style.

[bb] The initial position of ζῶν in the structure of the sentence is emphatic, i.e., "living is the word of God."

[cc] The variant reading preserved by B, and in part by Jerome, ἐναργής (as opposed to ἐνεργής), describes the word as "clear" or "evident." The variant, which has no claim to serious consideration, is nevertheless interesting in that it may represent an error in hearing as the text was transcribed.

[dd] The writer used a τε . . . καί construction, with the intention of distinguishing as well as connecting the two components, i.e., "of *both* joints *and* marrow."

[ee] After the preceding negative clause, the mildly adversative δέ gains the stronger adversative force of ἀλλά (so Turner, *Grammar*, 3:331).

[ff] There is considerable difference of opinion concerning the source of the metaphor expressed by the pf ptcp τετραχηλισμένα. The use of the verb τραχηλίζειν, "to grip in a neck-hold," as a term appropriate to wrestling finds vivid illustration in Philo. See, for example, *On Dreams* 2.34: evil men think it right to overthrow the good "by using ingenious and complicated tricks to seize their neck and get their head gripped in a neck-hold [ἐκτραχηλίζειν] and then by sweeping their legs from under them to hurl them to the ground"; *On Rewards and Punishments* 29: "here to admit defeat, like an athlete with his head gripped in a neck-hold [ἐκτραχηλιζόμενος] by a stronger rival." In v 13 the pf ptcp coupled with γυμνά, "uncovered," "naked," can only express a state of exposure to God's scrutiny. Cf. Simpson, *EvQ* 18 (1946) 38.

[gg] For the use of the prep πρός to denote a hostile or friendly relationship, see BDF §239(5); Moule, *Idiom-Book*, 52–54. For λόγος in the sense of "account," cf. Heb 13:17. Zerwick and Grosvenor (*Grammatical Analysis*, 662) render "the reckoning with whom is (up) to us" or "is our responsibility." Trompf (*ST* 25 [1971] 125, n. 9) draws attention to numerous instances in the Oxyrhynchus papyri where λόγος in this sense belongs to the world of business.

[hh] The central idea of διεληλυθότα is "passed through." As the high priest passes through the holy place into the most holy place to stand before the divine presence on the Day of Atonement, Jesus has passed through the heavens to the divine presence. Unfortunately, "passed through the heavens" does not convey this idea in English.

[ii] The translation of the hortatory subjunctive κρατῶμεν attempts to express the durative quality of the present tense.

Form/Structure/Setting

The parenetic unit introduced by 3:7–19 is brought to completion in 4:1–14. The writer continues to use the form of homiletical midrash, citing and interpreting the detail of Ps 95:7*b*–11 in order to apply the quotation to the situation of his readers. The new development in 4:1–11 is the enrichment of the interpretation of Ps 95 by the use of Gen 2:2 to clarify the character of the rest from which the generation in the desert was excluded. The argument turns on the fact that in Gen 2:2 LXX the verb used to state that God "took rest" (κατέπαυσεν) is cognate to the term for "rest" in Ps 95(LXX 94):11 (κατάπαυσις). The use of cognate terms permitted the inference that "my rest" in Ps 95:11 is properly interpreted in terms of God's primordial rest following the works of creation in Gen 2:1–3. The drawing of an inference based on the analogy of words, which is common in rabbinical interpretation, is designated *gĕzērâ šāwâ* in Hebrew (cf. Hofius, *Katapausis*, 55). The fact that the writer and those whom he addressed read the biblical text in Greek was crucial in this instance, since the MT used different Hebrew roots to describe God's rest in the two passages.

The structure of 4:1–14 is sufficiently indicated by parallel constructions and conjunctions. The first literary unit is established by the *inclusio* formed by the use of hortatory subjunctives and the phrase "to enter that rest" in vv 1 and 11.

> v 1   φοβηθῶμεν οὖν . . . εἰσελθεῖν εἰς τὴν κατάπαυσιν αὐτοῦ
> "Let us begin to fear, therefore, while . . . entering his rest"
> v 11   σπουδάσωμεν οὖν εἰσελθεῖν εἰς ἐκείνην τὴν κατάπαυσιν
> "Let us, therefore, make every effort to enter that rest"

Beyond that, the unit is tied together by the repeated thought of entering into God's rest:

> v 1   "a promise of entering his rest"
> v 3*a*   "we . . . do enter that rest"
> v 3*b*   "They shall certainly not enter my rest"
> v 5   "They shall certainly not enter my rest"
> v 6   "some are to enter that rest"
> v 10   "whoever enters God's rest"
> v 11   "to enter that rest"

It is clear that εἰσέρχεσθαι κατάπαυσιν, "to enter rest," is the characteristic expression in this paragraph, and that in each instance the basis of the expression is its use in Ps 95 (LXX 94):11 (cf. Attridge, *HTR* 73 [1980] 281; Losada, *RevistB* 36 [1974] 125).

Within 4:1–11 it is possible to discern two paragraphs on the basis of an *inclusio* between v 1 and v 5 and between v 6 and v 11:

> v 1   εἰσελθεῖν εἰς τὴν κατάπαυσιν αὐτοῦ
> "entering his rest"
> v 5   εἰσελεύσονται εἰς τὴν κατάπαυσίν μου
> "shall enter my rest"
> v 6   οὐκ εἰσῆλθον δι᾿ ἀπείθειαν
> "[they] did not enter because of their disobedience"

v 11   εἰσελθεῖν . . . τις ὑποδείγματι πέσῃ τῆς ἀπειθείας
        "To enter . . . otherwise, one of you might perish through the same
        example of disobedience "

The presence of the substantive ἀπείθεια, "disobedience," is particularly striking
because it is found in vv 6 and 11, and nowhere else in Hebrews. Its literary
function is to mark off the limits of a paragraph, precisely as the writer used the
related term ἀπιστία, "unbelief," in 3:12 and 19 (cf. Vanhoye, *La structure*, 96–97).

The two paragraphs have been so arranged that at the center of each stands a
citation from Ps 95 (v 3 = Ps 95:11; v 7 = Ps 95:7*b*–8*a*). By careful structural arrangement the writer keeps the detail of the biblical quotation before his readers
and engages them in his own reflections upon the text. The first paragraph stresses
the idea of entering God's rest and clarifies the distinctive character of that
rest; the second paragraph interprets the significance of the term "Today" and
relates it to the opportunity and peril of the congregation addressed. (For a
minute analysis of the concentric symmetry in each of the two paragraphs, see
Vanhoye, *La structure*, 98–99.)

The statement concerning the word of God in vv 12–13 is linked to the preceding
unit by the conjunction γάρ, "for." It provides the supporting reason for the diligence
to enter God's rest enjoined in v 11. Any attempt to separate vv 12–13 from the
preceding context and to treat them as a transition or preface to the consideration of Jesus in his office as high priest in 4:14–5:10 is misdirected (Kuist, *BibRev*
16 [1931] 579–81; Trompf, *ST* 25 [1971] 127). The function of these verses in
the consideration of Ps 95 becomes clear when they are viewed within the structure
of 3:7–4:13. The unit begins with the quotation of Ps 95:7*b*–11 in 3:7–11. The
homiletical midrash upon the text extends from 3:12 to 4:11. The writer provides
a pointed conclusion to the interpretation by the appeal for diligence in 4:11
and the corresponding reason for it in 4:12–13. Within the structure of 3:7–4:13 the
position of 4:12–13 balances the placement of the biblical quotation in 3:7–11.
The citation of the word of God in 3:7–11 is complemented by the warning concerning the trenchant character of the word of God in 4:12–13. The initial and
concluding units thus provide the literary frame for the interpretation of Ps 95
in 3:12–4:11 (Vanhoye, *La structure*, 101–3).

Several commentators contend that in vv 12–13 the writer included a poem
(Michel, 197–98) or a hymn (Kuss, 67; Nauck, "Zum Aufbau des Hebräerbriefes,"
205: "a Logos-hymn"; Spicq, 1:51: "a hymn to the Word"). This proposal is not
convincing. The periodic sentence is certainly a highly polished piece of prose
which employs rhythmical patterns (cf. Proulx and Schökel, *Bib* 54 [1973] 331–33,
for an analysis of the rhetorical features of the unit). Only v 12, however, speaks
of "the word of God"; the repeated αὐτοῦ, "before him"/"his eyes," in v 13 refers
to God himself. It is better to recognize in vv 12–13 a careful formulation for
which the writer himself is responsible, which provides the substantiation for the
exhortation in v 11 (so also Riggenbach, 115; Hofius, *Katapausis*, 138–39). The
statement in vv 12–13 crowns the sermonic development of Ps 95, which began
with the quotation of the text in 3:7.

The function of v 14 is more complex. It is attached to the hortatory section
3:7–4:13 by the conjunction οὖν, "therefore." The writer reflects upon the meditation he has developed on the basis of Ps 95 and sums up in a final admonition
the parenesis of 3:7–4:11: "let us hold fast our confession." From this perspective

v 14 marks the conclusion to the larger unit under consideration. The reference to "the confession," as well as to Jesus as high priest, however, marks a return to the distinctive vocabulary of 3:1. From this perspective v 14 establishes an *inclusio* that brackets 3:1–4:14 as an integral unit based on Jesus' faithfulness as high priest (see *Comment* on 3:1–2*a*). The appeal for fidelity in v 14 was already implied in 3:1–6, and especially in 3:6*b*. Accordingly, v 14 marks the conclusion of the larger unit 3:1–4:14, as well as the close of the section 4:1–14.

Comment

In 4:1–11 the writer advances the interpretation of Ps 95 to a new stage. The focus of 3:12–19 was upon the exclusion of the desert generation from God's rest because of blatant unbelief and rebellion. The tragic aftermath of death in the desert as the result of failing to believe God constituted the basis of warning for the hearers. In 4:1–11 the accent falls upon the Christian community as heir to the promise of entrance into God's rest. The writer's task in this section is to pose in sharp terms the alternatives of rest and peril that now confront the new people of God. In the course of the hortatory argument he defines more precisely the character of the rest envisioned and the concomitant responsibility of a community constituted by the voice of God in Scripture.

1   The use of a hortatory subjunctive is common when a writer intends to call his hearers from one mode of life or disposition to another (BDF §337 [1]). The emphatic position of φοβηθῶμεν, "let us begin to fear," at the beginning of the paragraph implies that the attitude toward the word of God in Scripture within the community has not been acceptable. The appeal for a more sensitive attitude was motivated by earnest pastoral concern for every individual within the house-church ("that even one among you would seem to be excluded"; cf. 3:12, 13; 4:11). The fact that a promise of entering God's rest remains open explains the urgency expressed in the exhortation.

The word ἐπαγγελία, "promise," is a significant term in the writer's vocabulary and occurs here for the first time. It is the distinctive understanding of the writer that Christians on earth possess the realities of which God has spoken in the form of promise. He regards the believing community as heirs to the divine promises (cf. 1:14; 6:12, 17; 9:15). In Hebrews the pattern of promise and fulfillment (i.e., what God promised to the fathers he has fulfilled in Christ), which is characteristic of the other documents of the NT, is modified. The stress falls on the fact that what God promised to the fathers he has repeated with assurance to the people of the new covenant; they are to find in the priestly office of Jesus the guarantee of the ultimate fulfillment of the promise (cf. 8:6; 10:23, 36; 11:39–40).

That the promise of entering God's rest remains valid was a logical deduction from the opening words of the quotation, "Today, if you hear his voice do not harden your hearts" (Ps 95:7*b*–8*a*). In the context of God's oath barring the rebellious fathers in the desert from his rest (Ps 95:11), they implied the permanent availability of that rest for those who remained responsive to the word of promise. The Kadesh narrative in Num 14, which heavily influenced the interpretation of Ps 95:7*b*–11 in 3:12–19, furnished the writer with firm support for the conviction that the promise had not been revoked. The formulation of v 1 takes account of Num 14:31, where the rejected promise is extended to the children of the desert generation. God will give them entrance and enjoyment in the land (Vanhoye, *Bib* 49 [1968] 23). The account of Israel at Kadesh in Num 14 provided a biblical foundation for the pattern of promise, and promise renewed.

The concept of κατάπαυσις, "rest," in the context of the promise to the Exodus generation had the local connotation of entrance into Canaan, where Israel would experience relief from turmoil and security from their enemies (cf. Deut 12:9–10). But over the course of time a distinctly eschatological concept of rest developed, presumably through synagogue preaching and school debate. Jewish teachers of the early second century debated, on the basis of Num 14:35 and Ps 95:11, whether the oath of God excluding the desert fathers from entrance into his rest implied their exclusion from participation in the age to come at the consummation of redemption (*t. Sanh.* 13:10 [Zuck. 435]; *b. Sanh.* 110*b* [Baraitha]; *y. Sanh.* 10.29*c* [Baraitha]; *ʾAbot R. Nat.* 36; cf. Hofius, *Katapausis*, 44–47, 52). An eschatological understanding of "my rest" in Ps 95:11 is presupposed in v 1 and is fundamental to the exhortation to diligence to enter God's rest in 4:1–11. It is possible that the hearers were already familiar with this concept through their past association with the hellenistic Jewish synagogue. The principle that unbelief invited exclusion from God's rest (3:19) remains valid in the present and assumes profound significance when rest is understood in this eschatological sense.

2 V 2*a* is linked to the preceding exhortation by the conjunction γάρ, "for." The peril of exclusion from God's rest exists precisely because of the privileged position of standing before the word of promise. The assertion καὶ γὰρ ἐσμεν εὐηγγελισμένοι, "for we also have had good news preached to us," reflects the formulation of 2:3–4; there the writer associated himself with his hearers as those who had come to faith through the preaching of witnesses who had heard the Lord and whose message had been confirmed by charismatic endowment. The message of good news heard by the Exodus generation was the announcement of Caleb and Joshua concerning the goodness of the land and its possession (Num 13:30; 14:7–9, cf. Vanhoye, *Bib* 49 [1968] 22). The allusion to Caleb and Joshua prepares for the contrast developed in v 2*b* between the negative response of despair and unbelief (cf. Num 13:26–29, 31–14:4, 10) and the positive response of faith at Kadesh.

The past generation received the promise in vain because they refused to believe the word they heard (Num 14:11; cf. 3:12, 19). They did not share the faith of Joshua and Caleb who listened to the promise of God and regarded it as certain. Already in its first occurrence in Hebrews πίστις, "faith," is clearly confident expectation for the future (cf. 6:12; 10:38–39; 11:1). It is a quality of response that appropriates the divine promise and recognizes the reliability of God. In v 2*b* faith is a relationship to ὁ λόγος τῆς ἀκοῆς, "the word which they heard," an expression that anticipates the use of ὁ λόγος in v 12 as the revealed word of God. The generation in the desert did not trust the unproved word they had heard and so were disqualified from enjoying what had been promised. For the men and women addressed, who were called to faith on the basis of God's final word spoken through the Lord (1:1–2*a*; 2:3), πίστις is clearly eschatological faith, a present grasp upon future reality (cf. Grässer, *Glaube*, 13–16). Hearing a message of good news does not guarantee that what has been promised will be received. Only faith as confident expectation for the future can secure the promised reality.

3–5 The demonstration that God's rest still remains open is achieved exegetically. The writer carefully defines the term κατάπαυσις in the expression "my rest" (Ps 95:11) in a manner that supports his essential contention. The failure of the Exodus generation to enter the promised rest does not abrogate the reality and presence of that rest. The argument employs the rabbinic principle and interpretation that the presence of cognate vocabulary in two passages of Scripture is designated to call attention to their mutual relationship (see above, on *gĕzērâ šāwâ, Form/Structure/Setting* on 4:1–14). The presence of the cognate verb κατέπαυσεν in Gen 2:2 allows the inference to be drawn that God's rest in Ps 95:11 had reference to the primal Sabbath rest of God, which marked the completion of the works of creation. Gen 2:2 indicates that God's promised rest has been prepared and available since that time (cf. Attridge, *HTR* 73 [1980] 281–83).

Although the writer continues to interpret Ps 95 and to apply its statement to the situation of his hearers, his approach reflects a tactical shift. Warning is no longer in the foreground; instead, the detail of the statement provides a basis for hope and encouragment. Unbelief excluded the Exodus generation from God's rest; in response to faith there will be, and there is, entrance into God's rest. The assertion in v 3*a* provides an antithesis to v 2: what was lost to those who refused to believe the promise becomes the possession of those who believe God (cf. Num 14:24 [of Caleb]). The description of the community as οἱ πιστεύσαντες, "[we] who have believed," reflects what was stated about πίστις, "faith," and the λόγος τῆς ἀκοῆς, "the word which was heard," in v 2. They are those who have responded to the message with conviction and who live in the present in the light of the promise extended for the future (cf. Grässer, *Glaube*, 13–17). Faith brings into the present the reality of that which is future, unseen, or heavenly. For that reason, those who have believed can be said to enter God's rest already (Lincoln, "Sabbath, Rest, and Eschatology," 191).

Consequently, the bold assertion εἰσερχόμεθα γὰρ εἰς τὴν κατάπαυσιν, "for we do enter that rest," implies more than proleptic enjoyment of what God has promised. The present tense of the verb is to be regarded as a true present and not simply viewed as future in reference. God's promise is predicated upon reality, and believers are already to enjoy the rest referred to in the quotation of Ps 95:11 (cf. Kistemaker, *Psalm Citations*, 109; H. Montefiore, 83).

The final clause of v 3 is concessive in character and prepares for the citation of Gen 2:2 in v 4. The generation in the wilderness was excluded from God's rest, and yet (καίτοι) that rest had been available since God completed the works of creation. The notion of an eschatological resting place as one of the realities prepared from the foundation of the world has abundant parallels in apocalyptic and rabbinic literature (cf. Hofius, *Katapausis*, 53–54, 91–97). But this notion should not be introduced in the interpretation of v 3*c*. It would be appropriate only if God's rest had been one of the works of creation. As a matter of fact, the writer carefully follows Gen 2:1–3 in distinguishing God's rest from his works. God's rest consists in the completion of his works, and consequently his rest has been in existence since the foundation of the world. The force of the final clause is to emphasize that the promised rest does not refer in the first instance to some future reality prepared for humanity, but has primary reference to God's own repose, which precedes and stands outside human history. A proper understanding of the relationship between the works of creation and the promised rest prepares for the parallel drawn between God and the believing community in v 10 (so Attridge, *HTR* 73 [1980] 282, n. 8; 283, n. 14).

The appeal to the rest of τῆς ἑβδόμης, "the seventh day," in v 4 follows naturally from the reference to the completion of God's works in v 3c. Although the formula of introduction for the quotation of Gen 2:2 is indefinite (εἴρηκεν γάρ που "for somewhere he has spoken"; cf. 2:6), the subject of the verb is clearly God (Schröger, *Verfasser*, 109). Such expressions occur infrequently in the Mishnah (*m. Nazir* 9:5; *Soṭa* 6:3) and in Philo (*On Drunkenness* 14; *On the Unchangeableness of God* 16; *On the Preliminary Studies* 31) but are more common in *1 Clement* (15:2; 21:2; 26:2; 28:2; 42:5). Gen 2:2 is quoted with only minor variation from the LXX (cf. Kistemaker, *Psalm Citations*, 37).

In the synagogue liturgy for the beginning of the Sabbath, the recital of Ps 95:1–11 was followed by Gen 2:1–3 (Elbogen, *Der jüdische Gottesdienst*, 110, 115). The association and order of the two texts in the Friday evening service of prayer, which in the Diaspora would presumably be conducted in Greek, may have suggested the hermeneutical step taken in v 4. The writer interprets the personalized expression κατάπαυσίν μου, "my rest," in Ps 95:11 (vv 3, 5) from the vantage point of Gen 2:2, which contained the cognate verb κατέπαυσεν, God "took rest." The analogous use of terminology permitted the inference that the primordial rest of God reported in Gen 2:2 is the archetype of all later experiences of rest, and thus typifies the rest intended for the people of God (cf. Padva, *Les citations de l'Ancien Testament*, 63; Harder, *ThViat* 1 [1939], 35–36, 40). The repetition of Ps 95:11b in v 5 links the rest following creation with the promise of rest that was the goal of redemption (cf. Schröger, *Verfasser*, 109–10, 114). The writer's intention is to define the character of the promise extended for the encouragment of the community. For that reason, perhaps, the reference to God's anger in Ps 95:11a is suppressed when Ps 95:11 is quoted for the second time.

6–8   The preceding argument is summarized in v 6, and an exegetical inference is drawn from it. The divine promise of rest indicates that God provided rest not only for himself but also for his people. The oath of exclusion was uttered against only some of those who camped at Kadesh. That implies that some others (τινάς) will enter God's rest. The identification of the first group as the Exodus generation contemplated in Ps 95:8–11 (cf. Num 13:26–14:9), who were excluded from God's rest on the ground of disobedience (v 6b; cf. Num 14:11–12, 21–23), recapitulates the argument developed in 3:16–18 and 4:2. God's promise nevertheless remains valid and directs attention to another group who will enter his rest. That group is contemplated in Ps 95:7b–8a; it consists of all those who heed the warning uttered by the Holy Spirit (Heb 3:7a) and who respond to God's voice with faith and obedience.

The shift in focus from Ps 95:11, which was cited in vv 3 and 5, to Ps 95:7b–8a in vv 6–8 introduces another factor to be considered by the readers. The writer seizes upon the term σήμερον, "today," as having fundamental significance for a deeper understanding of the concept of rest. The introductory admonition to the solemn review of Israel's rebellion in Ps 95:7b–8a was a prophetic announcement that God was determining a future date for making his rest available. Approximately four centuries after the exclusion of the desert generation from his rest, God announced prophetically through the psalmist a new day of opportunity, "today," in which his voice would be heard and the promise of entrance into his rest would be actualized. The announcement implied that until the time of the psalmist no one had entered God's complete rest. If they had done so, the matter would not have been reviewed so many centuries after Israel entered Canaan under the leadership of Joshua and Caleb. It is Ps 95 that calls for an eschatological understanding of κατάπαυσις, "rest." The admonition in Ps 95:7*b*–8*a* is both an urgent call to the people of God and an announcement of the eschatological time of salvation. That time has come. It is the final period of redemptive history, which has begun with the speaking of God through his Son (1:1–2*a*). It is the present time of salvation for the Christian community, for whom the issue of entrance into God's rest remains alive (cf. Hofius, *Katapausis*, 56–57, 106–7; Lombard, *Neot* 5 [1971] 66).

In the Hexateuch the content of the promise was associated with the settlement of Canaan (cf. Deut 3:20; 12:9; 25:19; Josh 1:13). After the conquest the promise of rest is said to have been fulfilled (Josh 21:44; 22:4; cf. Frankowski, *VD* 43 [1965] 125–41). In v 8 the writer addresses the intramural tension between that tradition and the different perspective expressed in Ps 95. The settlement of Canaan did not mark the fulfillment of the divine promise but pointed to another, more fundamental reality. If in fact Joshua had achieved the promised rest, there would have been no need for the renewal of the promise in Ps 95. Accordingly, the experience of rest in Canaan was only a type or symbol of the complete rest that God intended for his people, which was prefigured in the Sabbath rest of God, according to Gen 2:2 (cf. Frankowski, *VD* 43 [1965] 141–46; Attridge, *HTR* 73 [1980] 286).

9–10 The preceding lines of argument are summed up in the conclusion drawn in v 9. The statement is structurally parallel in form to v 6*a*:

v 6*a*: ἀπολείπεται τινὰς εἰσελθεῖν εἰς αὐτήν [= τὴν κατάπαυσιν]
  "The fact remains that some are to enter it [= the rest]."
v 9: ἀπολείπεται σαββατισμὸς τῷ λαῷ τοῦ θεοῦ
  "There remains a Sabbath celebration for the people of God."

In v 9 the writer repeats the conclusion of v 6*a*, but the term σαββατισμός is substituted for the characteristic term κατάπαυσις. The formal parallelism suggests that the substitution is meant to define more precisely the character of the future rest promised to the people of God (Hofius, *Katapausis*, 106). If it had been the writer's intention to say only "there remains a Sabbath rest for the people of God" (cf. RSV, NEB, NIV), he could have retained the word κατάπαυσις. In v 4 he had associated κατάπαυσις with God's rest on the seventh day, and he undoubtedly knew that the word was used for the Sabbath rest in the LXX (Exod 35:2; 2 Macc 15:1). The deliberate choice of σαββατισμός, which finds its earliest occurrence in extant Greek literature here, must have been dictated by the fact that it conveyed a nuance not found in κατάπαυσις.

The term σαββατισμός appears to have been coined from the cognate verb σαββατίζειν, "to observe/to celebrate the Sabbath." In its only occurrence in non-Christian literature (Plutarch, *Concerning Superstition* 3 [Moralia 166 A]), the term signifies Sabbath observance. In four other documents from the patristic period that are independent of Heb 4:9, the term denotes the celebration or festivity of the Sabbath (Justin, *Dialogue with Trypho* 23.3; Epiphanius, *Against All Heresies*

30.2.2; *The Martyrdom of Peter and Paul,* chap. 1; *Apost. Const.* 2.36.2; discussed by Hofius, *Katapausis,* 103–6). The term received its particular nuance from the Sabbath instruction that developed in Judaism on the basis of Exod 20:8–10, where it was emphasized that rest and praise belong together (cf. 2 Macc 8:27; *Jub.* 50:8; Ps-Philo, *Bib. Ant.* 11.8). The term σαββατισμός stresses the special aspect of festivity and joy, expressed in the adoration and praise of God (cf. Hofius, *Katapausis,* 106–10; Losada, *RevistB* 36 [1974] 127). In v 9 this nuance defines the character of the promised rest awaiting the people of God in the consummation.

The assertion in v 10 stands in a causal relationship to v 9 and clarifies why in the eschatologial rest a σαββατισμός will be possible. Whoever has entered the consummation-rest will experience the completion of his work, as did God after the creation (vv 3c–4), and will enjoy the rest that is necessary for the festivity and praise of a Sabbath celebration. In conjunction, vv 9–10 anticipate the festival of the priestly people of God in the heavenly sanctuary, celebrating in the presence of God the eternal Sabbath with unceasing praise and adoration (Hofius, *Katapausis,* 109–10).

11   The Sabbath observance now demanded of the community is diligence to enter God's rest through the exercise of faith in the word of promise and the response of obedience to the voice of God in Scripture (cf. Lincoln, "Sabbath, Rest, and Eschatology," 193–94). The exhortation to make every effort to enter God's rest presupposes what was said in v 3, that God's rest is entered by believing. It also takes account of Israel's failure to attain God's rest through unbelief and disobedience (vv 2, 6). The consummation-rest, in which everything that God intended for humanity by his own Sabbath rest will be realized, remains future. It can be forfeited through a careless and hardened disposition. The stern warning in v 11 b recapitulates what was said about the generation of those who died in the desert as the consequence of their disobedience (3:17–18; 4:6). The focus upon the threat posed to even one member of the congregation (ἵνα μή . . . τις . . . πέσῃ, "otherwise one of you might perish") is parallel to the formulation in v 1 and is motivated by the earnest concern the writer felt for every member of the community.

12–13   The parenetic unit begun in 3:7 is brought to a brief and vigorous conclusion in vv 12–13, where the writer provides the supporting reason for the diligence enjoined in v 11 (see *Comment* above). God's word, whose sanctions were imposed so effectively upon the Exodus generation, is performative today and confronts the Christian community with the same alternatives of rest and wrath (cf. Trompf, *ST* 25 [1971] 123). Those who remain insensitive to the voice of God in Scripture may discover that God's word is also a lethal weapon. When the past generation sought to contravene the oath of God and to enter Canaan, they were driven back and fell by the sword (μάχαιρα) of the Amalekites and the Canaanites (Num 14:43–45). The word of God poses a judgment that is more threatening and sharper than any double-edged sword (μάχαιρα, v 12) because it exposes the intentions of the heart and renders one defenseless before God's scrutinizing gaze (cf. Hofius, *Katapausis,* 139; Lincoln, "Sabbath, Rest, and Eschatology," 187).

The clear allusion to the folly of Israel at Kadesh in disregard of God's oath and the warning of Moses (Num 14:43) indicates that the expression ὁ λόγος τοῦ θεοῦ, "the word of God," must have specific reference to the text of Scripture cited so extensively in 3:7–4:11, and especially to Ps 95:7*b*–11. This needs to be affirmed in the presence of a persistent desire to find in v 12 a personal reference to Jesus as the Logos (Clavier, "O ΛΟΓΟΣ ΤΟΥ ΘΕΟΥ," 81–93; Williamson, *Philo*, 390, 398; Swetnam, *Bib* 62 [1981] 214–24). There is no hypostatization of the Logos in v 12 (rightly insisted on by Trompf, *ST* 25 [1971] 123–27). The reference is to Ps 95:7*b*–11 in which the living, piercing word of God addresses this generation in a critical fashion and poses as the only alternative to faithfulness the option of death (3:17; 4:11).

This dynamic conception of the word of God is a proper corollary to the introduction of the quotation of Ps 95:7*b*–11 as the words of the Holy Spirit (3:7*a*). The description of God's word as ζῶν . . . καὶ ἐνεργής, "living and effective," signifies that it is performative; it possesses the power to effect its own utterance. Performatives, by definition, commit the speaker to stand by his words. That is demonstrated with reference to Ps 95:7*b*–11 in 3:7–11 (cf. Caird, *Language and Imagery of the Bible*, 20–25) and had immediate relevance for a community that had become careless in its attitude toward the word of promise expressed in Scripture.

The predicates ascribed to the word of God in v 12*b* (διϊκνούμενος . . . κριτικός, "penetrating . . . capable of judging") introduce figurative and popular language that effectively conveys the notion of an extreme power of penetration. The word of God is able to reach into the deepest recesses of the human personality (Ps 95:10*b;* cf. Wis 1:6). The discrimination of the heart's thoughts and intentions entails a sifting process that exhibits the penetrative and unmasking potency of the word (cf. Simpson, *EvQ* 18 [1946] 37–38).

An impression of total exposure and utter defenselessness in the presence of God is sharpened in v 13. That nothing in creation is hidden from God's sight was a Jewish commonplace (e.g., *Tg. Neof.* Gen 3:9, "And the Lord God called the man and said to him: Look, the whole world which I created is manifest before me; darkness and light are manifest before me; and do you think that the place where you are standing is not manifest before me?" Cf. *Tg. Neof.* Gen 4:14; *Tg. Ps.-J.* Gen 3:9; 24:62; Deut 1:17; 29:8; 32:34; and often). The surveillance predicated of God is exhaustive; nothing escapes his scrutiny. The images of nakedness (γυμνά) and helpless exposure (τετραχηλισμένα, see above, *Note* ff) express vividly the plight of anyone who believes he can deceive his creator and judge. In context, the force of v 13 is to assert that exposure to the word of Scripture entails exposure to God himself.

14 The fearful prospect of judgment that is held out to the community in vv 11–13 is balanced by the reminder of the high priestly ministry of Jesus in the heavenly sanctuary. In the description of Jesus as ἀρχιερέα μέγαν, "a great high priest," the term μέγαν is a qualification of excellence (cf. 1 Macc 13:42, "Simon the great high priest [ἀρχιερέως μεγάλου] and commander and leader of the Jews"; Philo, *On Dreams* 1.219). His greatness is expressed in the language of transcendence. He has passed through the heavens (διεληλυθότα τοὺς οὐρανούς) to the presence of God (cf. 9:24). The implied reference to the heavenly sanctuary provides yet another dimension to the discussion of the place of rest in 4:1–11. Jesus' high priestly ministry is the guarantee that God's people will celebrate the Sabbath in his presence.

The encouragement of Jesus' high priestly ministry underscores the reasonableness of the exhortation to continue to hold fast to the confession (v 14*b*). The use of the verb κρατεῖν, "hold fast/cling to," supports the conclusion that ὁμολογία, "confession," has reference to a specific formulation of faith that had once been accepted and openly acknowledged by the members of the community. In this context the designation of Jesus as τὸν υἱὸν τοῦ θεοῦ, "the Son of God," is almost certainly an echo of that confession (so Bornkamm, *TBl* 21 [1942] 190, 192–94, 201–2; Neufeld, *Earliest Christian Confessions*, 135–37). The description of Jesus as "high priest" is not itself taken from the confession but serves to interpret it (see on 3:1). The appeal for adherence to the confession has the function of promoting the faithfulness of the community at a time they were displaying a lack of concern for spiritual integrity and steadfastness (cf. 2:1; 3:6*b*; 10:23). It appropriately concludes the unit introduced in 3:1, in which the faithfulness of Jesus as high priest establishes the context for calling the members of the congregation to faithfulness (see *Comment* on 3:1).

Explanation

The purpose of introducing Ps 95:7*b*–11 in 3:7–19 was to exhibit the severe consequences of unbelief and rebellion. Israel at Kadesh, at the point of attaining the goal of the Exodus and pilgrimage through the wilderness, rebelled against God and refused to trust the word of promise. Their subsequent forfeiture of the promise and death in the desert is brought forcefully before the hearers to warn them of the danger of a calloused disposition and apostasy. The generation in the desert provided the writer with a warning paradigm.

In 4:1–13 the note of warning is sustained by specific reference to Israel's unbelief and disobedience at Kadesh (vv 2, 6, 11) and by a pattern of exhortation that exposes the peril of an indifferent community (vv 1, 11–13). But the warning is tempered by the encouragement that the promise of entering God's rest has not been revoked. The failure of the Exodus generation to enter the promised rest did not abrogate the reality and accessibility of that rest. The issue of entering God's rest must be faced by each generation. The continuation of the interpretation of Ps 95:7*b*–11 in 4:1–11 permits the writer to develop a theology of rest.

The notion of rest within the Scriptures is one of expanding horizons. For Israel at Kadesh, and in the Hexateuch generally, the promise of rest connoted entrance into Canaan. But the review of Israel's failure to enter God's rest in Ps 95, long after the conquest and settlement of the land under Joshua, indicated that those events did not exhaust the divine intention. They represented only a type of the rest promised to the people of God.

Already in 3:12–19 a typological interpretation of Ps 95:7*b*–11 had suggested that Israel at Kadesh stood in relation to the Christian community as type to antitype. The argument developed in 4:1–11 is more complex. The expression "my rest" in Ps 95:11 called to mind God's primordial rest announced in Gen 2:2. The state of completion and harmony experienced by God after his creative labor is the archetype and goal of all subsequent experiences of rest. The rest intended for the people of God was prefigured in the Sabbath rest of God. The theology of rest developed in 4:1–11 takes account of the pattern of archetype (God's primal rest, v 4), type (the settlement of the land under Joshua, v 8), and antitype (the Sabbath celebration of the consummation, v 9). The prophetic announcement of another day in which the promise of entering God's rest would be renewed in

Ps 95:7*b*–8*a* addressed the community in their situation and supported an eschatological understanding of God's rest. It anticipated the consummation when the completion of work and the experience of rest would provide the setting for a Sabbath celebration marked by festivity and the praise of God (v 9). The task of the community is to enter that rest through faith in God's word of promise and obedient response to the voice of God in Scripture (vv 11–13).

The reference to Jesus in his office as high priest in v 14 is not an afterthought, but the intended conclusion of the entire argument. The crucial issue for the community is whether they will maintain their Christian stance. The issue was posed conditionally in 3:6*b*, and more pointedly in 3:14. It was raised again forcefully in v 14 in the exhortation to hold fast to the confession that identified Christians as those who had responded to the message they had heard with faith (cf. v 2). The ministry of Jesus in the heavenly sanctuary as a faithful high priest in the service of God gives certainty to the promise that God's people will celebrate the Sabbath in his presence if they hold fast their initial confidence.

D. A High Priest Worthy of Our Faith Because He Is the Son of God Who Is Compassionate (4:15–5:10)

Bibliography

Allen, W. "The Translation of ἀπὸ τῆς εὐλαβείας at Hebrews 5.7." *BIRBS* 1 (1989) 9–10. **Andriessen, P.** "Angiosse de la mort dans l'Épître aux Hébreux." *NRT* 96 (1974) 282–92. ——— and **Lenglet, A.** "Quelques passages difficiles de l'Épître aux Hébreux (5, 7, 11; 10:20; 12,2)." *Bib* 51 (1970) 207–20. **Attridge, H. W.** "'Heard Because of His Reverence' (Heb 5:7)." *JBL* 98 (1979) 90–93. ———. "New Covenant Christology in an Early Christian Homily." *QuartRev* 8 (1988) 89–108. **Bachmann, M.** "Hohepriesterliches Leiden: Beobachtungen zu Hebr 5:1–10." *ZNW* 78 (1987) 244–66. **Bertetto, D.** "La natura del sacerdozio secondo Heb 5,1–4, e le sue realizzazioni nel N.T." *Sal* 26 (1964) 395–440. **Biser, E.** "Die älteste Passionsgeschichte." *GL* 56 (1983) 111–18. **Boman, T.** "Das Gebetskampf Jesu." *NTS* 10 (1963–64) 261–73. **Bornhäuser, K.** "Die Versuchungen Jesu nach dem Hebräerbrief." In *Theologische Studien*. FS M. Kähler. Leipzig: Deichert, 1905. 69–86. **Bourgin, C.** "La Passion du Christ et la nôtre: Hé 4, 14–16; 5:7–9." *AsSeign* 21 (1969) 15–20. **Brandenburger, E.** "Text und Vorlagen von Hebr. V 7–10: Ein Beitrag zur Christologie des Hebräerbriefs." *NovT* 11 (1969) 190–224. **Braumann, G.** "Hebr 5, 7–10." *ZNW* 51 (1960) 278–80. **Caird, G. B.** "Son by Appointment." In *The New Testament Age*. FS B. Reicke. Ed. W. C. Weinrich. Macon, GA: Mercer University Press, 1984. 1:73–81. **Coste, J.** "Notion greque et notion biblique de la 'souffrance éducatrice' (A propos d'Hébreux, v,8)." *RSR* 43 (1955) 481–523. **Dibelius, M.** "Der himmlische Kultus nach dem Hebräerbrief." *TBl* 21 (1942) 1–11. **Dörrie, H.** *Leid und Erfahrung: Die Wort- und Sinn-Verbindung* παθεῖν—μαθεῖν *im griechischen Denken*. Wiesbaden: Steiner, 1956. **Dukes, J.** "The Humanity of Jesus in Hebrews." *ThEduc* 32 (1985) 38–45. **Dunbar, D.** "The Relationship of Christ's Sonship and Priesthood." 26–39, 50–72, 83–106. **Dyck, T. L.** "Jesus Our Pioneer." 85–95. **Ellingworth, P.** "Just Like Melchizedek." *BT* 28 (1977) 236–39. **Eminyan, M.** "A Note on Christian Affectivity." *MelTheol* 37 (1986) 1–12. **Estrada, C. Z.** *Hebreos 5, 7–8: Estudio histórico-exegético*. Rome: Pont. Inst. Biblico, 1990.———. **Feuillet, A.** "L'evocation

de l'agonie de Gethsémani dans l'Épître aux Hébreux (5:7–8)." *EV* 86 (1976) 49–53.
————. "Une triple préparation du sacerdoce du Christ dans l'Ancien Testament (Melchisédec, le Messie du Ps 110, le Serviteur d'Is 53): Introduction a la doctrine sacerdotale de l'Épître aux Hébreux." *Div* 28 (1984) 103–36. **Friedrich, G.** "Das Leid vom Hohenpriester im Zusammenhang von Hebr. 4,14–5,10." *TZ* 18 (1962) 95–115. **Galot, J.** "Le sacerdoce catholique: III. Le sacerdoce du Christ selon l'Épître aux Hébreux." *EV* 91 (1981) 689–96. **Gambiza, F. K. M.** *"Teleiosis* and *Paideia* as Interpretation of Sufferings: The Perfection of Jesus and the Disciplining of Christians in the Letter to the Hebrews." Dissertation, Christ Seminary-Seminex, 1981. **Grässer, E.** "Der historische Jesus in Hebräerbrief." *ZNW* 56 (1965) 63–91. **Hamm, D.** "Faith in the Epistle to the Hebrews: The Jesus Factor." *CBQ* 52 (1990) 270–91. **Harnack, A.** "Zwei alte dogmatische Korrekturen im Hebräerbrief." SPAW (1929) 69–73. **Harris, J. R.** "The Sinless High Priest." *ExpTim* 33 (1921–22) 217–18. **Horbury, W.** "The Aaronic Priesthood in the Epistle to the Hebrews." *JSNT* 19 (1983) 43–71. **Javierre, A. M.** "Réalité et transcendance du sacerdoce du Christ: Hé 5, 1–6." *AsSeign* 61 (1972) 36–43. **Jeremias, J.** "Hbr 5,7–10." *ZNW* 44 (1952–53) 107–11. **Käsemann, E.** "Hebräer 4,14–16." In *Exegetische Versuche und Besinnungen.* Göttingen: Vandenhoeck & Ruprecht, 1970. 1:303–7. **Kouto, J. K. M.** "Humanité et autorité du Christ-Prêtre: Une approche exégético-théologique de Hé. 2, 5–18; 3, 1–6 et 4, 15–5, 10." Dissertation, Pont. Univ. Urbaniana, Rome, 1985. **Laub, F.** *Bekenntnis und Auslegung.* 104–43. **Lescow, T.** "Jesus in Gethsemane bei Lukas und im Hebräerbrief." *ZNW* 58 (1967) 215–39. **Lightfoot, N.** "The Saving of the Savior: Hebrews 5:7ff." *RestQ* 16 (1973) 166–73. **Lightner, R. P.** "The Savior's Sufferings in Life." *BSac* 127 (1970) 26–37. **Longenecker, R. N.** "The Obedience of Christ in the Theology of the Early Church." In *Reconciliation and Hope.* FS L. L. Morris. Ed. R. Banks. Grand Rapids: Eerdmans, 1974. 141–52. **Luck, U.** "Himmlisches und Irdisches im Hebräerbrief." *NovT* 6 (1963) 192–215. **MacKay, C.** "The Order of Melchizedek, Heb. v.6." *CQR* 138 (1944) 175–91. **Marrow, S. B.** *"Παρρησία* and the New Testament." *CBQ* 44 (1982) 431–46. **Maurer, C.** "'Erhört wegen der Gottesfurcht' Hebr 5,7." In *Neues Testament und Geschichte.* FS O. Cullmann. Ed. H. Baltensweiler and B. Reicke. Tübingen: Mohr, 1972. 275–84. **McPheeters, W. M.** "The Testing of Jesus." *BibRev* 4 (1919) 517–36. **Melbourne, B. L.** "An Examination of the Historical-Jesus Motif in the Epistle to the Hebrews." *AUSS* 26 (1988) 281–97. **Olson, S. N.** "Wandering but Not Lost." *WW* 5 (1985) 426–33. **Omark, R. E.** "The Saving of the Savior: Exegesis and Christology in Hebrews 5:7–10." *Int* 12 (1958) 39–51. **Parsons, M. C.** "Son and High Priest: A Study in the Christology of Hebrews." *EvQ* 60 (1988) 195–215. **Pérez, A.** "Procedimientos derásicos de Sal 2,7b en el Nuevo Testamento: 'Tu eres mi hijo, yo te he engendrado hoy,'" *EstBib* 42 (1984) 391–414. **Peterson, D. G.** "An Examination of the Concept of 'Perfection' in the 'Epistle to the Hebrews.'" 124–72, 326–31. **Rasco, E.** "La oración sacerdotal de Cristo en la tierra según Hebr. 5,7." *Greg* 43 (1962) 723–55. **Reid, J. K. S.** "Tempted, Yet without Sin." *EvQ* 21 (1949) 161–67. **Rinaldi, G.** "L'uomo del Getsemani (Ebr. 5, 7–10)." *BibOr* 24 (1982) 15–17. **Rissi, M.** "Die Menschlichkeit Jesu nach Hebr. 5, 7–8." *TZ* 11 (1955) 28–45. **Roloff, J.** "Der mitleidende Hohepriester: Zur Frage nach der Bedeutung des irdischen Jesus für die Christologie des Hebräerbriefes." In *Jesus Christus in Historie und Theologie.* FS H. Conzelmann. Ed. G. Strecker. Tübingen: Mohr, 1975. 143–66. **Schenk, W.** "Hebräerbrief 4, 14–16: Textlinguistik als Kommentierungsprinzip." *NTS* 26 (1979–80) 242–52. **Schille, G.** "Erwägungen zur Hohepriesterlehre des Hebräerbriefs." *ZNW* 64 (1955) 81–109. **Schmidt, A.** *Hebr. IV, 14 bis V, 10 Ein exegetische Studie.* Duberan: Rehse, 1898. **Schröger, F.** *Der Verfasser des Hebräerbriefes als Schriftausleger.* 115–27. **Serra, A. M.** "Passione e preghiera di Cristo secondo Ebrei 5, 7–10." *Serv* 4 (1970) 441–48. **Songer, H. S.** "A Superior Priesthood: Hebrews 4:14–7:28." *RevExp* 82 (1985) 345–59. **Stewart, R. A.** "The Sinless High-Priest." *NTS* 14 (1967–68) 126–35. **Strobel, A.** "Die Psalmengrundlage der Gethsemane-Parallele Hbr 5, 7ff." *ZNW* 45 (1954) 252–66. **Swetnam, J.** *Jesus and Isaac.* 178–84. **Tascon, V.** "Jesu Cristo, sacerdote misericordioso y fiel." *CTom* 100 (1973) 139–90.

Teodorico, P. "Il sacerdozio celeste di Cristo nella lettera agli Ebrei." *Greg* 39 (1958) 319–34. **Tetley, J.** "The Priesthood of Christ in Hebrews." *Anvil* 5 (1988) 195–206. **Thúren, J.** "Gebet und Gehorsam des Erniedrigten (Hebr. v 7–10 noch einmal)." *NovT* 13 (1971) 136–46. **Vanhoye, A.** "Situation et signification de Hébreux V.1–10." *NTS* 23 (1976–77) 445–56. **Vos, G.** "The Priesthood of Christ in the Epistle to the Hebrews." *PTR* 5 (1907) 423–47, 579–604. **Williamson, R.** "Hebrews 4:15 and the Sinlessness of Jesus." *ExpTim* 86 (1974–75) 4–8.
———. *Philo and the Epistle to the Hebrews.* 25–30, 51–64, 84–88. **Woschitz, K. M.** "'Erlösende Tränen': Gendanken zu Hebr 5,7." *BLit* 56 (1983) 196–201. ———. "Das Priestertum Jesu Christi nach dem Hebräerbrief." *BLit* 54 (1981) 139–50. **Wrege, H. T.** "Jesusgeschichte und Jüngergeschick nach Joh. 12, 20–23 und Hebr. 5, 7–10." In *Der Ruf Jesu und die Antwort der Gemeinde.* FS J. Jeremias. Ed. E. Lohse. Göttingen: Vandenhoeck & Ruprecht, 1970. 259–88. **Yarnold, E. J.** "*Metriopathein apud* Heb 5, 2." *VD* 38 (1960) 149–55. **Zimmermann, H.** *Das Bekenntnis der Hoffnung.* 60–79, 153–54, 176–80.

Translation

[15] For[a] we do not have a high priest who is unable to feel our weaknesses[b] with us,[c] but one who has been tested[d] in every respect, in quite the same way as we are, only without the result of sin.[e] [16] Therefore, let us draw near[f] to the throne of grace[g] with a bold frankness, so that we may receive mercy and obtain grace at the right time when we are in need of help.

[5:1] For every high priest selected from among men is appointed to act on their behalf in the service of God,[h] to offer[i] both gifts and sacrifices[j] for the purging of sins. [2] He is able to deal gently[k] with those who sin through ignorance and are going astray,[l] since he too is subject to weakness. [3] That is why he is under obligation[m] to offer sacrifices for[n] his own sins, just as he does for the sins of the people. [4] And no one takes this office[o] of his own accord, but he receives it[p] when called by God, just as Aaron also was.

[5] In the same way, the Christ did not take for himself the honor of becoming[q] high priest, but he was called by God, who said to him,

"You are my Son;
    Today I have become your Father,"
[6] even as he says in another place,

"You are a priest[r] forever,
    just like[s] Melchizedek."

[7] During his life on earth[t] Jesus, having offered both prayers and earnest entreaties with fervent cries and tears to God, who was able to save him from death, and having been heard[u] because of his godly fear,[v] [8] although he was the Son,[w] he learned obedience from what he suffered,[x] [9] and once made perfect,[y] he became the source of eternal salvation for all who obey him, [10] being designated[z] by God a high priest just like Melchizedek.

Notes

[a] The conj γάρ is intended to guard against the mistaken inference that the exalted nature and position of the heavenly high priest will detract in any way from his ability to identify with the weariness and defenselessness of the church in a hostile world (so Vos, *PTR* 5 [1907] 582–83; Zerwick and Grosvenor, *Grammatical Analysis*, 662).

[b] The dative ταῖς ἀσθενείαις is used with an associative idea, "with our weaknesses" (A. T. Robertson, *Grammar*, 530). The reference is to weaknesses inherent in human nature that may render a person susceptible to temptation and sin.

c The complementary inf συμπαθῆσαι means to share the experience of someone. It is not to be understood in a psychological sense ("sympathize with") but in an existential sense; the exalted high priest suffers together with the weakness of the one who is tested and brings active help (cf. Schenk, *NTS* 26 [1979–80] 247, who calls attention to the synonym βοήθεια, "help," which stands in the emphatic final position in v 16; W. Burkert, "Zum altgriechischen Mitleidsbegriff" [Dissertation, Erlangen, 1955] 63–66).

d The pf tense of the pass ptcp πεπειρασμένον emphasizes the completed state and continuing result of Jesus' status. Having triumphantly sustained the test, Jesus is forever tried and tested (Zerwick and Grosvenor, *Grammatical Analysis*, 662).

e B. F. C. Atkinson translated the prep χωρίς, "apart from," and argued that when this prep follows the distributive adj πᾶς, "all, every," the natural meaning is "with the exception of." He translated the phrase "tempted in all points like as we are with the exception of sin," and drew the theological conclusion that although Jesus was tested by every agency by which others are—sorrow, weariness, persecution, hostility—his sinless nature was incapable of responding to the temptation to sin (*Theology of Prepositions*, 5). For a defense of the translation adopted, see Vos, *PTR* 5 [1907] 583, who paraphrased χωρίς ἁμαρτίας as "without the result of sin in his case."

f The verb προσέρχεσθαι was used in the LXX for the approach to God in priestly service. The subjunctive mood in προσερχώμεθα is cohortative ("let us draw near"). The present tense emphasized that the opportunity to do so remains available (so F. Rienecker, *Linguistic Key*, 331).

g The gen in the expression "the throne τῆς χάριτος" is a gen of quality, i.e., a "throne characterized by grace." Such expressions are Hebraic; Turner describes it as a "septuagintalism," analogous to the common locution "the throne of glory" in the LXX (*Grammar*, 4:110). From a linguistic point of view, the expression may be classified as a "genitive-metaphor" for God's presence (Schenk, *NTS* 26 [1979–80] 248). Cf. NEB: "approach the throne of our gracious God"; TEV: "come forward to God's throne, where there is grace."

h The phrase τὰ πρὸς τὸν θεόν provides an example of the accusative of respect, which was frequent in classical usage but was almost entirely displaced in the Koine by the dative (cf. BDF §160; Moule, *Idiom-Book*, 33). The expression is resumed from 2:17.

i The verb προσφέρειν, which occurs nineteen times in Hebrews, never in Paul, and rarely elsewhere in the NT, has its source in the sacrificial vocabulary of the LXX.

j The intention of the τε καί construction is to distinguish as well as to connect: "*both* gifts *and* sacrifices for sins." The construction, which occurs also in 8:3; 9:9, carefully and accurately distinguishes two classes of offerings.

k The verb μετριοπαθεῖν, which occurs only here in the Gk. Bible, was coined from the adjective μετριοπαθής for use in the Peripatetic tradition in opposition to the Stoic word ἀπαθής, "indifferent" (so Moulton and Howard, *Grammar*, 2:284). It connoted the "golden mean" between indifference and sentimental indulgence. In Philo, Josephus, and Plutarch, it denotes "to restrain or moderate one's anger" (Yarnold, *VD* 38 [1960] 149–55). There is here no evidence of the specifically philosophical use of the word that is characteristic for Philo, who thought the state of μετριοπάθεια to be inferior to that of ἀπάθεια (*Concerning Abraham* 257; *Allegorical Interpretation of the Law* 3.129, 134, 140–44; *Moses* 195, discussed by Williamson, *Philo*, 25–30). The usage is closer to Jos., *Ant.* 12.128, where the term carries the positive nuance of clemency or compassion.

l In the expression τοῖς ἀγνοοῦσιν καὶ πλανωμένοις, the two ptcps share one article and may refer to a single class or category, i.e., "those who err through ignorance" (cf. Zerwick, *Biblical Greek* §184). The reference is to sins committed inadvertently (cf. Lev 4:2; 22:14 LXX: ἀγνοοῦντες; Heb 9:7, where the high priest's ministry is said to be for "the errors of the people [ἀγνοημάτων]").

m The verb ὀφείλει carries the connotation of moral obligation. The present tense is gnomic, indicating that which is always true (cf. Burton, *Moods*, 8).

n The prep περί is used here in the sense of ὑπέρ, meaning "on account of, because, for" (BDF §229[1]; cf. Zerwick, *Biblical Greek* §96). There is, in fact, no distinction in nuance between the phrase ὑπὲρ ἁμαρτιῶν, "for sins," in v 1 and περὶ ἁμαρτιῶν in v 3. The preps may be used interchangeably. Cf. Riesenfeld, *TDNT* 6:55; 8:512.

o The term τιμή, which usually means "honor," is used in Josephus to denote the "office" of high priest (*Ant.* 3.188–89).

p It is necessary to understand a second occurrence of λαμβάνει in the sense of "he receives it," according to Zerwick and Grosvenor (*Grammatical Analysis*, 662).

q The inf γενηθῆναι is used in an epexegetical sense; it defines more closely the content of the action denoted by the previous verb ἐδόξασεν (so Moule, *Idiom-Book*, 127). The translation seeks to make evident the parallelism of the initial segments of vv 4 and 5.

ʳ Hoskier called attention to the unique reading of P⁴⁶ (ἐπεύξ, "precentor," a leader of prayer and praise, for ἱερεύς, "priest") and argued for its originality (*Text*, 3–6). He failed to observe that ἐπεύξ, which was presumably derived from the verb ἐπεύχομαι, "to pray," occurs nowhere else in all extant Gk. literature. It is properly classified as "a startling error" by Beare (*JBL* 63 [1944] 382). Zuntz suggested that the scribe of P⁴⁶ may have been familiar with the Latin "P" and confused it with the Greek "P" (which is comparable to the letter "R") (*Text*, 253, n. 7).

ˢ The term τάξις here and in 5:10; 6:20; 7:11, 17 is commonly understood in the sense of "order" or "succession" (RSV: "after the order of Melchizedek"; NEB: "in the succession of Melchizedek"). In the strict sense of the term, however, there is no succession to Melchizedek (cf. 7:3, 8). Two priests, Melchizedek and Christ, do not make up a succession. Nor does the writer of Hebrews emphasize the idea of rank (cf. Moffatt, "with the rank of Melchizedek"). He uses the term τάξις to convey the same meaning as when it is said that Melchizedek is "like the Son of God" (7:3) or that Christ is "like Melchizedek" (7:15). For a review of the issues and a defense of the translation adopted, see P. Ellingsworth, "Just like Melchizedek," *BT* 28 (1977) 236–39.

ᵗ The expression ἐν ταῖς ἡμέραις τῆς σαρκὸς αὐτοῦ does not mean "in the days of his flesh," but "his flesh days." In Heb. as well as in Aram., a construct state combination tolerates the pronominal suffix only at the end (i.e., not with the governing noun, but with the governed noun); the suffix is related then to the whole expression. The construction passed into Gk. via the LXX. In v 7 the expression simply refers to the human experience of Jesus.

ᵘ On the assumption that if Jesus' prayers had been heard he would have been delivered from impending death, A. von Harnack conjectured that the text as it has been transmitted in all MSS is corrupt. Originally, he argued the negative particle οὐκ must have stood before the pass ptcp εἰσακουσθείς. The text, as reconstructed by Harnack, read, "he was not heard (and rescued) from his anxiety, although he was Son." Understandably, the assertion was found offensive on dogmatic grounds, and the negative particle was deleted from the text at a very early stage, according to Harnack (SPAW [1929] 69–72). This conjectural emendation was accepted, with some hesitation, by Windisch (43–44), and with a greater degree of confidence by Bultmann (*TDNT* 2:753) and F. Scheidweiler ("καίπερ nebst einem Exkurs zum Hebräerbrief," *Hermes* 83 [1955] 224–26). There is a broad consensus that the proposal is not only unnecessary but is actually subversive of the writer's intention.

ᵛ The phrase ἀπὸ τῆς εὐλαβείας is difficult because the meaning of both the prep ἀπό and the substantive εὐλάβεια has been disputed. Grammarians have tended to understand the ambiguous prep ἀπό in a causal sense (i.e., "because"), a usage that finds abundant illustration in the LXX (e.g., A. T. Robertson, *Grammar*, 580; BDF §210[1]; Turner, *Grammar*, 4:11). Mayser, however, insists that ἀπό indicates here in a genuine genitival function the point of departure for an event (*Grammatik*, 2:376). On this understanding, ἀπό does not mean "because," but "after," i.e., "he was heard after his experience of anguish." Andriessen noted that the writer uses ἀπό 23 times in Hebrews, and in no other instance does it bear a causal sense. If ἀπό is understood in the sense proposed by Mayser, it designates the moment when Jesus was heard, i.e., "he was heard after his agony" (*NRT* 96 [1974] 286–87; Andriessen and Lenglet, *Bib* 51 [1970] 208–12). More recently Andriessen has argued that the prep ἀπό is practically equivalent, as far as the sense goes, to that which immediately follows in v 8, the expression ἀφ᾽ ὧν. The two expressions form almost a chiasm: Jesus having been heard after suffering, learned from that which he suffered (*En lisant*, 13–15). The cogency of these proposals depends upon the determination of the meaning of εὐλάβεια.

The noun εὐλάβεια, which occurs in 5:7 and 12:28 (and not elsewhere in the NT), can mean "fear, anxiety" or "reverence, piety." If in v 7 εὐλάβεια connotes an emotion of fear felt by Jesus when faced with the prospect of impending death, ἀπό will mean "from" and the phrase will signify "he was heard (and rescued) from fear." This was the understanding of the lat (*exauditus a metu*; cf. Ambrose: *exauditus ab illo metu*, "he was heard [and rescued] from that fear") sa bo sy. It involves, however, a rather harsh ellipsis, which is unexpected in a writer so skillful. Moreover, he has already spoken of the "fear of death" in 2:15, where he wrote φόβος θανάτου, and not εὐλάβεια. It is difficult to perceive how Jesus could have rescued others from the fear of death (2:14–15) if he had himself been shaken by that fear.

The ptcp εὐλαβηθείς occurs in 11:7, where it signifies careful attentiveness within the context of a godly life. In 12:28 the noun εὐλάβεια connotes attentiveness to the divine will or godly reverence. This would seem to be the nuance of the term in v 7 as well. This understanding precludes the proposal that ἀπό means "from" or "after" and supports the translation "heard because of his godly fear" (cf. Jeremias, *ZNW* 44 [1951–52] 107–11; Rissi, *TZ* 11 [1955] 38; Lescow, *ZNW* 58 [1967] 227; Attridge, *JBL* 98 [1979] 90–93).

ᵂ A major consideration in A. von Harnack's proposal to emend the text of v 7 was the conviction that the clause καίπερ ὢν υἱός must qualify what precedes, and not what follows (SPAW [1929]71). The objections of Jeremias (*ZNW* 44 [1952–53] 108, n. 4) and Strobel (*ZNW* 45 [1954] 261, n. 30) that there are ample precedents in hellenistic Gk., and especially in the LXX, for placing such a clause before the principal clause to which it belongs (cf. Prov 6:8c LXX; 2 Macc 4:34; 3 Macc 5:32; 4 Macc 3:10; 4:13; 15:24; *T. Jos.* 10:5) were dismissed by F. Scheidweiler ("καίπερ nebst ein Exkurs zum Hebräerbrief," *Hermes* 83 [1955] 220–30). He argued that when καίπερ introduces a clause that is connected with what follows, it always has some other word before it that serves as a link with what precedes (e.g., 4 Macc 3:15, ὁ δὲ καίπερ, "But he, although feverish with thirst, reasoned that"; 15:11, ἀλλ᾽ ὅμως καίπερ, "Nevertheless, though so many considerations"). If Jeremias were correct, the formulation καὶ γὰρ καίπερ ὢν υἱός, "for even though he was Son," would have been expected. Scheidweiler concluded that, on the grounds of the syntactical use of καίπερ, any interpretation that severs "although he was Son" from what precedes is unlikely (225–26). There is no doubt that Scheidweiler has correctly identified dominant tendencies in the use of καίπερ. Nevertheless, the introduction of a protasis with καίπερ is not at all unusual even in classical Gk., according to H. Krämer (cited by Brandenburger, *NovT* 11 [1969] 220, n. 1; Krämer notes Homer, *Iliad* 2.270; Hesiod, *Theogony* 533; Pinder, *Isthmian Odes* 8.5; Thucydides 4.41.3; Xenophon, *Anabasis* 5.5.17–18; Aristotle, *Nicomachean Ethics* 2.2, p. 1104a, 10).

ˣ It is practically impossible to duplicate in translation the euphony in the expression ἔμαθεν ἀφ᾽ ὧν ἔπαθεν, "he learned from those things which he suffered." A dependence upon the phonetic similarity of different words for rhetorical effect is called *parechesis* (cf. Coste, *RSR* 43 [1955] 485). On the special meaning of πάσχειν in the sense of "to suffer death" in Hebrews, see above on 2:9.

ʸ The aor pass ptcp τελειωθείς could be temporal or causal. The decision to understand it in a temporal sense takes account of the finite verb ἐγένετο, which asserts that this occurrence belongs to the character of "once-for-all" time (cf. Maurer, "'Erhört wegen der Gottesfurcht,'" 283). In Hebrews, the use of the verb τελειοῦν follows the practice of the LXX translators of the Pentateuch; it means "to put someone in the position in which he can come, or stand, before God" (cf. Delling, *TDNT* 8:82, who cites Lev 21:10; Heb 7:19; 10:1). God has qualified the Son "to come before him" in priestly action. The ptcp could thus be translated, "and once qualified."

ᶻ The verb προσαγορεύειν contains the idea of a formal and solemn ascription of an honorific title (Moulton and Howard, *Grammar*, 2:399). The use of the verb with the meaning "to address, hail, salute" in the sense of an acclamation finds illustration in the papyri (MM 545).

Form/Structure/Setting

In 2:17 the writer announced that it was necessary for Jesus to be "like his brothers" so that he might become a merciful and faithful high priest in the service of God. In 3:1–6 he began to develop the aspect of the authority of Jesus as high priest on the ground of his faithfulness to God who appointed him. That authority stands behind the appeal for fidelity addressed to the community in 3:7–4:14. In 4:15–5:10 the writer takes up the assertion that Jesus is a "merciful high priest in the service of God." Thus the purpose of 3:1–5:10 as a major division is to consider the two relationships necessary to the exercise of priestly mediation, namely the relationship with God, in which Jesus proved faithful, and the relationship with men, in which he proved to be compassionate.

The order in which the subject announced in 2:17 is taken up in 3:1–5:10 corresponds to the first major division (1:5–2:18), where the writer presented the exalted position of the Son of God (1:5–14), and then his solidarity with others through suffering (2:5–18). The same order of presentation is evident in the third major division (7:1–10:18) as well. The priesthood of the glorified Christ is considered first, and only then the sacrificial aspects of his priestly office (8:1–10:18). Consistently, the point of departure for exposition is the present status of Christ as exalted Son and Priest, who addresses the community of faith with a sovereign authority from heaven. The writer then takes account of the humiliation and the suffering of death that was the prelude to Jesus' exaltation. That retrospective reflection allows the stress to fall on the fact that although Christ is the transcendent Son who is now enthroned in the Father's presence, he is related by experience to a humiliated and suffering community. The way that led to glory was that of complete solidarity with the human condition (cf. Vanhoye, *NTS* 23 [1976–77] 452–55).

Apart from a single exhortation to prayer (4:16), 4:15–5:10 is cast in the form of exposition. A smooth transition from the previous section is achieved in 4:15 with the repetition with only slight variation, of the same initial expression found in 4:14 (see *Comment* above). The apparent redundancy marks a shift, however, from exhortation to exposition and introduces a new unit of integrated thought. The writer now takes up a number of motifs introduced in 2:17–18: Jesus' solidarity with the people of God in their trials, his priestly compassion, his experience of testing through the suffering of death, and his ability to help those who are exposed to the ordeal of testing. The formulation of 4:15–16 recalls the announcement of these themes in 2:17–18 and prepares for the exposition of Jesus' appointment to the high priestly office in 5:1–10 (cf. A. Vanhoye, *La structure*, 105–7).

Although it is common to regard 5:1–10 as a self-contained unit (e.g., Gyllenberg, *SEÅ* 22–23 [1957–58] 141; Michel, 214), a relationship with 4:15–16 is established by the conjunction γάρ, "for," in 5:1 (Riggenbach, 123–24; Mora, *La Carta*, 162). Close examination demonstrates that the orientation of 5:1–10 is determined by the themes enunciated in 4:15–16. The description of the Levitical high priest in 5:1–4 is restricted to the note of priestly mercy (4:16, ἔλεος) and the capacity of the high priest to display compassion that results from his personal participation in the human situation (4:15). When attention is directed to Christ in 5:5–10, there is explicit reference to his solidarity with all those who experience distress and to his submission to testing and suffering (5:7–8), through which he became qualified for his priestly office (5:9–10). These emphases reinforce the statement in 4:15 and give it specific content (cf. Vanhoye, *NTS* 23 [1976–77] 446; Mora, *La Carta*, 165–71).

The literary structure of 4:15–5:10 is clear once it is recognized that 4:15–16 functions to announce the perspectives to be developed in 5:1–10. A concentric symmetry is given to the exposition:

    A   The old office of high priest (5:1)
       B   The solidarity of the high priest with the people (5:2–3)
         C   The humility of the high priest (5:4)
         C' The humility of Christ (5:5–6)
       B' The solidarity of Christ with the people (5:7–8)
    A' The new office of high priest (5:9–10)

The literary structure of 5:1–10 permits the writer to stress at this point Jesus' essential similarity to the high priest, even though he is acutely aware of the profound differences that separate the unique priesthood of Christ from the Levitical priesthood (cf. Schröger, *Verfasser*, 115; Vanhoye, *NTS* 23 [1976–77] 446–48; Mora, *La Carta*, 162–65). As a unit 4:15–5:10 lays the foundation for the great central exposition of Jesus' priesthood in 7:1–10:18, where the emphasis will be placed on his dissimilarity to the Levitical priesthood. The themes of that exposition are announced in 5:9–10, namely the high priesthood like that enjoyed by

Melchizedek (7:1–28), the qualification of Jesus for his office (8:1–9:28), and Jesus as the source of eternal salvation (10:1–18).

Several scholars have argued that a primary source for this section of the sermon was a primitive Christian hymn or creed (Schille, *ZNW* 64 [1955] 81–109; Rissi, *TZ* 11 [1955] 28–45; Friedrich, *TZ* 18 [1962] 95–115; Lescow, *ZNW* 58 [1967] 224–39; Brandenburger, *NovT* 11 [1969] 190–224). The abrupt introduction of the masculine relative pronoun ὅς at the beginning of v 7 and the characteristic participial style of vv 7–10 are common features in other NT passages where the presence of a liturgical fragment has been detected. Schille (84–87) observed that in vv 7–10 a series of words occur that are not found elsewhere in Hebrews (δέησις ["prayer"], ἱκετηρία ["entreaty"], κραυγή ["cry"], εἰσακουσθείς ["heard"]). Moreover, terms that do occur elsewhere in Hebrews appear here with a different nuance (σώζειν in the sense of "rescue" or "deliver" [cf. 7:25], θάνατος in the sense of "the realm of the dead" [cf. 2:9, 14–15; 7:23], εὐλάβεια in the possible but unlikely sense of "anxiety" [cf. 11:7; 12:28], τελειωθείς in the sense of "exalted" [cf. 9:15–16; 11:5]). Friedrich (104–7) noted, in addition, the number of anarthrous nouns and the doubling of expressions ("prayers and entreaties," "cries and tears"). Schille further contended that a different theology is expressed in vv 5–10 from that found elsewhere in Hebrews. Here it is stressed that Jesus had to experience anguish and suffering before God bestowed upon him the priestly office, which Jesus would not arrogate to himself during his earthly life. In opposition to this concept, he argued, the writer to the Hebrews held that Jesus was high priest at least from the time of his passion when he offered himself as a priestly sacrifice. Schille concluded that 5:5–10 did not originate with the writer, but was taken over by him, in large part, from the tradition. His reconstruction posited a primitive hymn of four strophes, each containing three lines, which celebrated Jesus as Son and Priest (*ZNW* 64 [1955] 84–109).

Schille's proposal was taken up and modified by subsequent writers, who tended to distinguish between the poetical arrangement of vv 7–10 and the more prosaic formulation of vv 5–6 (cf. Friedrich, 99–111; Rissi, 28–45; Lescow, 224–30). Friedrich's reconstruction, for example, called for a hymn of two strophes of three lines each, which celebrated the themes of Jesus' humiliation and exaltation. He drew the significant conclusion that the recognition of a very old Jewish-Christian "hymn of the high priest" behind vv 7–10 proves that the conception of Jesus as high priest was not the distinctive teaching of the writer of Hebrews, but a strand of the tradition that was deeply embedded in the faith and liturgy of the primitive Church (*TZ* 18 [1962] 109–11).

There are, nevertheless, difficulties with this hypothesis and conclusions based upon it. They begin to surface when a comparison is made between the several proposals for reconstructing the primitive source(s) purportedly borrowed from the tradition. Brandenburger, for example, separated vv 8–10 from v 7 on stylistic grounds; he argued that they represented two different traditions that were first brought together by the writer (*NovT* 11 [1969] 195–224; for a dissenting opinion, cf. Thurén, *NovT* 13 [1971] 136–46). Lescow (*ZNW* 58 [1961] 229–30) sought to refine his analysis to the point where he could recognize a hymn of two strophes of three lines each, and behind that an even older hymn of two strophes of two lines each:

Christ did not exalt himself
But he learned obedience from what he suffered

And became for all who obey him
The source of eternal salvation

This reconstruction has no greater claim to credence than any other; it is interesting primarily because it contains no reference to Christ as high priest. The contention of Schille and Friedrich that the conception of Jesus as high priest was the common property of the primitive Church cannot be verified on the basis of source-reconstruction.

The writer may have made use of early creedal and hymnic fragments in composing his sermon. It must be remembered, however, that he is a master of the intricate, disciplined, and yet lucid sentence (see 1:1–4; 2:2–4, 14–15; 3:12–15; 4:12–13). The exposition in 5:1–10 is introduced by a periodic sentence (vv 1–3) and is concluded with another periodic sentence (vv 7–10). The formulation in vv 7–10 is consistent with the individuality and stylistic creativity of the writer, who is ultimately responsible for the tight, continuous flow of 5:1–10 (so also Maurer, "'Erhört wegen der Gottesfurcht,'" 278).

Another observation has bearing upon this issue. Parallels from the Psalms, especially to v 7, have frequently been pointed out (cf. Ps 22[LXX 21]:3, 25; 31[LXX 30]:23; 39[LXX 38]:13; 69[LXX 68]:4). Strobel was the first to observe the relationship between vv 7–9 and Ps 116(LXX 114, 115). When he exhibited the extensive linguistic and conceptual parallels in a table, it became evident that most of the linguistic anomalies that had encouraged Schille and others to posit an early Christian hymn behind Heb 5:7–10 could be accounted for on the basis of Ps 116(LXX 114, 115) (Strobel, *ZNW* 45 [1954] 256; cf. Schröger, *Verfasser,* 121–22). As one of the psalms that was sung at the celebration of the Passover, it would have been familiar both to the writer and to his hearers. If it was the writer's intention to allude to Ps 116(LXX 114, 115), it is unnecessary to posit any other source for the formulation of vv 7–9. Having affirmed in vv 5–6 that Christ is high priest on the basis of Ps 110(LXX 109):4, he described the humiliation of Christ by means of a correspondingly significant word from the Psalms (Strobel, 255–63). Strobel's proposal has been found convincing by Schröger, who observed that if Ps 116 does stand behind v 7, the correctness of the reading καὶ εἰσακουσθείς, "and having been heard," is evident (cf. Ps 116[LXX 114]:1: ὅτι εἰσακούσεται κύριος τῆς φωνῆς τῆς δεήσεώς μου, "because the Lord heard the voice of my prayer") and the conjectural amendation proposed by Harnack (see *Notes* on 5:7) is invalid (Schröger, *Verfasser,* 122, n. 6). Schröger concluded that the writer of Hebrews formulated and developed the presentation of Jesus as high priest on the basis of a messianic interpretation of Pss 2, 110 (LXX 109), and 116 (LXX 114, 115) (*Verfasser,* 126–27).

Comment

It is commonly stated that the purpose of 4:15–5:10 is to demonstrate that the conditions required of any high priest were satisfied by Christ. In 5:1–4 two conditions are set forth: (1) he must be able to empathize with the frailty of those he serves (vv 1–3); and (2) he must be called by God (v 4). In a second paragraph (5:5–10) it is shown on the grounds of Scripture and the gospel tradition that Jesus fulfilled these conditions: (1) he was called by God (vv 5–6); and (2) after he had been exposed to the full range of human emotion and testing, he was installed as high priest (vv 7–10). The direction of the flow of thought is from Aaron to Christ.

It is questionable whether this scheme represents the writer's intention. It is evident that he made no attempt to develop the two paragraphs in parallel fashion. It is preferable to recognize that the brief review of the Levitical high priesthood in 5:1–4 stands in relationship to the priestly ministry of Jesus contemplated in 4:15–16. It is presented here in order to prepare for the contrast to be developed in detail between the Levitical priesthood and the unique priesthood of Christ at a later point in the sermon (7:1–10:18). The stress on inner disposition in 5:1–3 shows that the description of the Levitical high priest has been conformed to the representation of Christ in 4:15 (cf. 7:3). The direction of the flow of thought is not from Aaron to Christ but from Christ to Aaron and his successors. The entire section of 4:15–5:10 develops the assertion that Jesus is a merciful high priest in the service of God (2:17).

15 οὐ γὰρ ἔχομεν ἀρχιερέα μὴ δυνάμενον συμπαθῆσαι ταῖς ἀσθενείαις ἡμῶν, "For we do not have a high priest who is unable to feel our weaknesses with us." A possible objection that Jesus' exalted status as high priest in heaven implied his aloofness from the weariness and discouragement of the Church in a hostile world is anticipated in v 15. The writer resorts to a double negative (οὐ . . . μή) to assert forcefully that Jesus identifies himself with those who feel defenseless in their situation. His high priestly ministry of intercession is effective on their behalf. The special nuance of συμπαθῆσαι (see *Note* c) extends beyond the sharing of feelings (i.e., compassion). It always includes the element of active help (cf. 10:34; 4 Macc 4:25; 13:23; *T. Sim.* 3:6; *T. Benj.* 4:4). In this context the stress falls on the capacity of the exalted high priest to help those who are helpless (Schenk, *NTS* 26 [1979–80] 246–47, 251).

This capacity derives from Christ's full participation in humanity (cf. 2:17–18). The heavenly exercise of his office is based upon the accomplishments of his earthly ministry. The writer will not recognize any disjunction between the ministry that Christ performs in the state of his exalted glory from that of the state of his humiliation. The experience of sufferings and trials endured during his humiliation equipped him with empathy so that he is able to support the covenant people in their sufferings and temptations. The emphatic statement that he was "tested" κατὰ πάντα καθ᾽ ὁμοιότητα, "in every respect, in quite the same way as we are," implies that he was susceptible to all the temptations that are connected with the weaknesses inherent in the frailty of humanity (cf. Cullmann, *Christology*, 95). This was necessarily the condition for his full equipment with the fellow-feeling required for the discharge of the priestly ministry of helping. Suffering produced sympathy by endurance.

The analogy between the testing of Christ and that to which the hearers are exposed remains unimpaired by the qualifying phrase χωρὶς ἁμαρτίας, "only without the result of sin." It does not restrict the likeness of the testing but relates exclusively to its outcome, i.e., "but without the result of sin in his case" (Vos, *PTR* 5 [1907] 583; cf. Schenk, *NTS* 26 [1979–80] 252). This conclusion has been challenged by Buchanan, who contends that "this does not necessarily mean that [Jesus] never committed a moral offense in his life" nor that he was sinless prior to the crucifixion. Inasmuch as the writer presented Jesus as a high priest, he may have understood the death on the cross as an offering on the Day of Atonement to cleanse his own sins as well as those of the people. This would be consistent with 5:3 (8, 82, 130–31). Buchanan has been supported by Williamson, who asks, "How could Jesus in any sense save sinners if he had not fully shared himself in the human condition . . . including actual participation in the experience of sinning?" (*ExpTim* 86 [1974–75] 7). Appealing to 5:8, Williamson emphasizes that Jesus had to learn obedience by overcoming disobedience, a process that was not complete until the moment of his sacrificial death on the cross (4–8).

These arguments, we submit, are untenable. The expression καθ' ὁμοιότητα, "in quite the same way," in v 15 involves both similarity and distinction, excluding identity. The writer nowhere suggests that Jesus had to become identical to fallen humanity in order to redeem it. In fact, in 7:27 he denies that Jesus had to offer sacrifice "first for his own sins, and then for the sins of the people. He sacrificed for *their* sins once for all when he offered himself." In 9:14 it is affirmed that Jesus "offered himself *unblemished* to God." It is striking that when the writer speaks of Jesus' qualification for his priestly ministry he adds the proviso that he was without sin (cf. 7:26–28). "Without sin" is a comment concerning Jesus' faithfulness to the one who appointed him (3:2) and describes the issue of Jesus' temptations. It indicates why his provision of compassionate help is charged with unique virtue and efficacy (cf. Michaelis, *TDNT* 5:933–36; Seesemann, *TDNT* 6:33; Michel, 211–13; Peterson, "Examination," 326–31).

16 The encouragement offered in v 15 is complemented by an exhortation to persistent prayer. The force of the present tense of προσερχώμεθα is "let us again and again draw near to the throne of grace" (Schenk, *NTS* 26 [1979–80] 252). The source of the terminology is cultic. The "throne of grace" is the place of God's presence, from which grace emanates to the people of God. The only one who was permitted to "draw near" under the provisions of the Mosaic covenant was the high priest, who could approach the altar in the most holy place of the tabernacle once a year, on the Day of Atonement. If his ministry was acceptable, the altar of judgment became the place from which mercy was dispensed to the people (cf. Lev 16:2–34; Heb 9:5). In a bold extension of the language of worship the writer calls the community to recognize that through his high priestly ministry Christ has achieved for them what Israel never enjoyed, namely, immediate access to God and the freedom to draw near to him continually (7:19, 25; 9:8–12, 14; 10:1, 22; cf. Käsemann, "Hebräer 4:14–16," 304). They may draw near to God through prayer with the confidence that they will be graciously received.

The instruction to pray with παρρησία, "bold frankness," takes advantage of a development in the meaning of this word that first occurred in hellenistic Judaism. In secular Greek the term connotes the free open speech of citizens with one another, but it is never used in the context of prayer. But in hellenistic Judaism the range of the term was extended to apply to speech with God (e.g., Jos., *Ant.* 2.52; 5.38). Attridge has called attention to Philo's tractate, *Who Is the Heir?* 5, where in a comment on Gen 15:2–3 Abraham is described as coming before God with "courage and well-timed frankness" (παρρησία). This is precisely the attitude that the hearers of Hebrews are encouraged to adopt in speaking with God (91–92). Because they have a high priest who empathizes with them they can go with frankness to the throne of grace and receive timely help in their distress. The free right to approach God with bold frankness was given in the sacrifice of Christ (cf. W. C. van Unnik, "The Christian's Freedom of Speech in the New Testament," *BJRL* 44 [1961–62] 485). The promise that they will receive ἔλεος, "mercy," accompanied by sustaining χάρις, "grace," refers to closely allied and essential aspects of God's love. That love is outgoing in the provision of εὔκαιρον βοήθειαν, i.e., protective help that does not arrive too late, but at the appropriate time because the moment of its arrival is left to the judgment of God (cf. Delling, *TDNT* 3:462; Käsemann, "Hebräer 4:14–16," 304).

5:1 The consideration of the solidarity of the exalted heavenly high priest with those who are weak in 4:15–16 sets the tone for the exposition in 5:1–3. The connection of the new paragraph with the preceding verses is established by the conjunction γάρ, "for." The concern is with what is true of πᾶς ἀρχιερεύς, "every high priest." By an effective use of prepositional phrases the writer is able to insist on the solidarity of the Levitical high priest with those whom he represents. He is selected ἐξ ἀνθρώπων, "from among men," and is appointed ὑπέρ ἀνθρώπων, "on behalf of men," to represent them before God. The interest in the office of the high priest is sharply focused upon his ministry on the Day of Atonement when he offered the sacrifices for the cleansing of sin in the most holy place (cf. v 3). The writer states that he was installed ἵνα προσφέρῃ δῶρά τε καὶ θυσίας ὑπέρ ἁμαρτιῶν, "in order to offer both gifts and sacrifices for the purging of sins." The cultic term προσφέρειν, "to offer," is used with the special nuance "to accomplish the sacrifice" (Weiss, *TDNT* 9:67). Although it would be natural to distinguish between δῶρα, "gifts" (i.e., peace and cereal offerings), and θυσίαι, "sacrifices" (i.e., the sin and trespass offerings), in later statements in the OT all sacrifices pertain to the procuring of atonement and the removal of sin (cf. Ezek 45:15–17). The bloody offerings for the Day of Atonement are in the foreground of the discussion of the sacrificial ministry of the Levitical high priest here and elsewhere in Hebrews (cf. 7:27; 10:4, 12, 26).

2 The thought expressed in v 2 has no clear parallels in contemporary sources from Judaism. Philo, for example, resorted to a tortuous exegesis of Lev 16:17 in order to argue that the high priest's humanity was suspended when he discharged his duties in the most holy place on the Day of Atonement (cf. Stewart, *NTS* 14 [1967–68] 131–35, for a discussion of the texts). The emphasis on the inner disposition of the high priest and his awareness that he too is subject to weakness in v 2 is therefore remarkable. It was influenced by the writer's prior reflection on Jesus as high priest in 4:15, which enabled him to perceive what God intended priesthood to be (cf. W. Manson, *The Epistle to the Hebrews*, 107–8). The two verses, however, are not parallel. In 4:15 the writer stresses the high priest's relationship to the source of transgression, i.e., human frailty. Jesus is able to feel the weaknesses of others because he was exposed to testing even as they are. In 5:2 the accent is placed on the relationship of the Levitical high priest to transgressors; he is able to show forbearance and compassion because he knows his own limitations (cf. 7:28, "the law appoints as high priest men who are weak"). The verbs συμπαθῆσαι (4:15) and μετριοπαθεῖν (5:2) are not synonymous (see *Notes* c and k above). μετριοπαθεῖν means to restrain or moderate one's feelings, and so to deal gently and considerately with other (cf. Yarnold, *VD* 38 [1960] 149–55). Philo regarded this disposition as inferior to the Stoic quality of ἀπάθεια, "indifference" (cf. Williamson, *Philo*, 26–30). But it is clear that in this context it is regarded as a positive quality: an awareness of his own frailty and sin causes the high priest to moderate his justifiable displeasure and anger toward the sins of the people. His compassion, however, extended only to those who sinned through ignorance or error (cf. 9:7; Lev 4:2, 13, 22, 27; 5:2–4). Sins that were committed intentionally would entail exclusion from the congregation of Israel (cf. Num 15:30–31).

3 From its inception, the extraordinary dignity of the office of high priest was stressed (Exod 28:1–2; cf. Sir 45:6–13; 50:5–11). The writer deviates from this usual perspective in order to take up the particular orientation defined by 4:15–16 (Vanhoye, *NTS* 23 [1976–77] 447). He asserts that the high priest's oneness with other men and women in human weakness and need was kept alive by his continual obligation to make atonement offerings for himself as well as for others in Israel (cf. 7:27; 9:7). This is a distinctive interpretation of the provisions governing the high priest in the OT. Although his life had to be as morally blameless as personal discipline could achieve, and the regulations governing his life were stricter than those affecting an ordinary priest (cf. Lev 21), he remained fallible, and provision was made for an appropriate sacrifice in the event of his sin (Lev 4:3–12; 9:7). On the Day of Atonement he was required to make atonement for himself, for his immediate household, as well as for the congregation of Israel (Lev 16:6, 11, 15–17; cf. *m. Yoma* 4:2–5:7). In the time of the Second Temple the high priest customarily uttered three prayers on the Day of Atonement as he laid his hands of the sacrificial bull and goat: (1) for his own sins and those of his household (*m. Yoma* 3:8); (2) for his own sins, those of his household, and those of the Aaronic priests (*m. Yoma* 4:2); and (3) for the sins of the house of Israel (*m. Yoma* 6:2). Neither the OT nor contemporary Judaism encouraged the expectation of a high priest who was χωρὶς ἁμαρτίας, "without sin" (4:15; cf. Stewart, *NTS* 14 [1967–68] 126, 130–31).

4 The divine appointment of Aaron and the hereditary character of his office are clearly affirmed in the Pentateuch (Exod 28:1; Num 3:10; 18:1; cf. Sir 45:6–7a; Jos., *Ant.* 3.188–92). In stressing that the high priest does not receive his office from men, but from the call of God, just as Aaron did, the writer remains faithful to the point of view he has developed in vv 1–3. What his statement expresses directly is not the dignity associated with the office nor the grandeur of the divine call, but, on the contrary, the humility required of the high priest who is dependent upon the divine appointment for his office. His humility is consistent with his solidarity with the people in their weakness (cf. Vanhoye, *NTS* 23 [1976–77] 447).

5–6 In 3:1–6 the point of departure for the comparison between Jesus and Moses was their likeness: both were faithful to God who appointed them (3:1–2). Only then was Jesus' superiority to Moses asserted and vindicated (3:3–6a). A similar pattern is evident in the comparison between Aaron and the Christ. The stress falls initially on the continuity between Aaron and Jesus, who did not elevate themselves to the office of high priest, but were appointed by God. The parallel is established by means of consecutive comparative clauses: καθώσπερ καὶ Ἀαρών . . . οὕτως καὶ ὁ Χριστός, "just as Aaron also was . . . so also the Christ" (vv 4b–5a). The writer then asserts implicitly the discontinuity and the superiority of the Christ to Aaron with the citation of Ps 110:4, although he defers the interpretation of the text until 7:1–25 (cf. Kistemaker, *Psalm Citations*, 118; Vanhoye, *NTS* 23 [1976–77] 455).

The use of the official title ὁ Χριστός, "the Christ/the Anointed One" (cf. 9:28), already affirms the fact of divine appointment. The primary proof that Jesus displayed the humility required of his office and did not take for himself the honor of becoming high priest is provided on the basis of Scripture. The writer correctly interprets Ps 2:7 as a declaration of appointment, not of parentage. He had earlier cited this text to demonstrate that the decisive factor in the enthronement and acclamation of the Son was God's own witness (see *Comment* on 1:5; cf. Barth, "The Old Testament in Hebrews," 63). The quotation refers to the investiture of the Son with royal power and authority. In v 5 the quotation emphasizes God's declarative action.

The same emphasis is evident in the quotation of Ps 110:4. Both texts declare the decrees in accordance with which Jesus was installed in his office and invested with power. A conscious concern to associate the titles "Son" and "Priest" is apparent in the conjunction of the psalm quotations in vv 5–6. A correlation between Christ's sonship and priesthood was implied in the exordium to the sermon, when the priestly function of making "purification for sins" is ascribed to the transcendent Son (1:3), but here it is asserted explicitly. "Son" and "priest" are the primary models for the writer's christology. In 1:1–4:14 the representation of Jesus as the Son of God predominates; in 4:15–10:22 the primary focus is upon the titles "priest" or "high priest."

Hay (*Glory*, 114–45) has made the suggestive proposal that in 5:5–10 the writer deliberately restated the enthronement description in chap. 1 in order to link the titles of "Son" and "priest." The formal similarities between the two sections are impressive. The periodic sentence in 5:7–10, with its kerygmatic contrast of the period of Jesus' humiliation and his present exalted status, furnishes a striking parallel to the confession in 1:3–4. The divine oracles quoted in 5:5–6 are Ps 2:7 and Ps 110:4, whereas in 1:5–14 the initial quotation is drawn from Ps 2:7 and the final quotation from Ps 110:1. The general similarity of 5:5–10 and 1:3–13 is sufficient to imply that the writer understood Jesus to have been acclaimed as divine Son and priest concurrently at his ascension.

The primary function of the quotation of Ps 110:4 in v 6 is to prove that Jesus did not arrogate priesthood to himself but was directly called to the office by God. Jesus manifested the humility required of the Levitical priests. But a secondary function of the quotation is to introduce Ps 110:4 into the discussion as a testimony about Jesus. No other Christian writer of this period drew attention to Ps 110:4, but in Hebrews there are more references to Ps 110:4 than to any other biblical text. In addition to three direct quotations of the passage (5:6; 7:17, 21), there are eight allusions to it in chaps. 5, 6, and 7, and each of the allusions is distinctive in form and function (see especially Hay, "Chart 4: Early Christian Interpretation of Psalm 110:4," in *Glory*, 46–47). The primary reason for the emphasis on Ps 110:4 in Hebrews is that it supplied a scriptural basis for the writer's priestly christology. The text is introduced repeatedly to substantiate the argument that Jesus is a heavenly high priest. Subsequent to the NT era, Ps 110:4 was often cited by Christian writers as proof of Jesus' everlasting priesthood. The impact of Hebrews on this development is particularly evident, for example, in *Apost. Const.* 2.27.4 when the declaration of vv 5–6 is restated: Jesus did not thrust himself into priestly office but waited for the summons of his Father expressed in Ps 110:4 (Hay, *Glory*, 47–50).

7   The declaration in vv 7–10 is confessional in character, relating Christ's humiliation and exaltation to the theme of appointment to priesthood. Cast in rhythmic prose and abruptly introduced by the relative pronoun ὅς, "he who," which must refer back to ὁ Χριστός, "the Christ," in v 5a for an antecedent, the seam joining v 7 to v 6 has been visible to most interpreters. The declaration has commonly been regarded as an adaptation of an early Christian hymn or creed (see *Form/Structure/Setting* above). It is, nevertheless, formally consistent with other highly compressed statements for which the writer is undoubtedly responsible (e.g., 2:2–4; 3:12–15; 4:12–13; 5:1–3; 7:26–28), and it is anchored in its setting by the concluding allusion to Ps 110:4, which reiterates the theme of divine appointment.

The interpretation of v 7 is difficult because of ambiguities in the statement that cannot be resolved on purely linguistic or syntactical grounds (see *Form/Structure/Setting* above). A resolution of the problems can be achieved only from weighing contextual considerations. We may enumerate these:

(1)   The kerygmatic summary of Jesus' earthly ministry in v 7 provides content to the assurance that he participated fully in the human condition (2:14–18) and was tested in every respect like we are, in order to become a high priest who was capable of feeling what we feel (4:15). These moving words express how intensely Jesus entered the human condition, which wrung from him his prayers and entreaties, cries and tears. W. Manson has suggested that it was reflection on the character of Jesus as priest that made the writer more sensitive to this dimension in the story of Jesus than any other writer in the NT (*The Epistle to the Hebrews*, 109–10).

(2)   When the writer states that Jesus "offered" (προσενέγκας) prayers and entreaties, the use of a technical cultic term for offering sacrifice is deliberate (Maurer, "'Erhört wegen der Gottesfurcht,'" 279–81). He intends the parallel with the description of the Levitical high priest in v 1 to be recognized. Corresponding to the "gifts and sacrifices" that the high priest offers (προσφέρειν) for sins are the prayers and entreaties offered by Jesus. The use of προσφέρειν in connection with prayer and praise had already become established in contemporary Jewish sources (cf. *T. Levi* 3:8; *T. Gad* 7:2; Jos., *J. W.* 3.353). Jesus' prayers were a sacrificial offering (cf. Rasco, *Greg* 43 [1962] 734–44). The reference in v 7 is not to particular moments in his ministry but to the totality of Christ's high priestly service (so Maurer, 283–84).

(3)   The final clause of v 7, "and he was heard because of his godly fear," qualifies the immediately preceding participial clause, "having offered prayers and entreaties with fervent cries and tears." The assurance that "he was heard" is equivalent to stating that Jesus' offering was accepted by God (so Boman, *NTS* 10 [1963–64] 268; Rissi, *TZ* 11 [1955] 42–44; Maurer, 278–80, 284). The writer may have been thinking of the tradition that the high priest's offering was not always acceptable. So far, then, from being "an unfortunate parenthesis" that complicates the logic of v 7, as argued by Lescow (*ZNW* 58 [1967] 226–28), the affirmation "he was heard" is emphatic and essential to the writer's presentation of Jesus as a "great high priest" (4:14). The declaration in v 7 establishes a clear contrast to the statement in v 3 concerning the obligation of the Levitical high priest to offer sacrifice for his own sins as well as for those of the people. No such obligation was imposed upon the Christ. The decisive distinction between the Christ and the Levitical high priest, which is asserted with the qualification "only

without the result of sin" in 4:15, is articulated again in v 7 with the clause "having been heard because of his godly fear."

These considerations bring a degree of clarity to the text and demonstrate that certain common approaches to v 7 are untenable. The statement that Jesus "was heard" has frequently been considered in relationship to the description of God as "the one who was able to save him from death." That approach led naturally to the question, In what sense was Jesus heard, inasmuch as he was not rescued from impending death? (see, e.g., Bultmann, *TDNT* 2:753). The assumption is that "hearing" could consist only in Jesus' deliverance from death. One response to the question was the recognition that in the OT God is recognized as the one who is able to rescue life ἐκ θανάτου (i.e., "from the realm of death"; cf. Job 33:28, 30; Ps 30 [LXX 29]:4; Prov 23:4). Jesus was not kept from the experience of death, but death had no lasting dominion over him. He was led out of the realm of the dead through resurrection (13:20), and in that sense he was heard (Vos, *PTR* 5 [1907] 585; Friedrich, *TZ* 18 [1962] 104–5). Or alternatively, the object of the prayers of Jesus was glorification (cf. John 12:27; 17:5); his prayers were heard in the sense that he was exalted and seated at the Father's right hand (Jeremias, *ZNW* 44 [1951–53] 109–10; Attridge, *JBL* 98 [1979] 91). It is preferable to interpret the statement "he was heard" in reference to the context that speaks of sacrifice and to recognize that ὁ δυνάμενος σῴζειν αὐτὸν ἐκ θανάτου, "the one who was able to save him from death," is simply a traditional circumlocution for God (cf. Hos 13:14; Ps 32[MT 33]:19 LXX; Jas 4:12). It defines not the content of Jesus' prayers but the character of God as the Lord of life who acts for the accomplishment of salvation (Rissi, *TZ* 11 [1955] 39).

It is unnecessary to connect Jesus' prayers and entreaties with the Synoptic tradition of Gethsemane (e.g., Omark, *Int* 23 [1958] 40–41; Jeremias, *ZNW* 44 [1952–53] 109; Lescow, *ZNW* 58 [1967] 223–39; Maurer, "'Erhört wegen der Gottesfurcht,'" 279; Feuillet, *EV* 86 [1976] 49–53; Serra, *Serv* 4 [1970] 441–48) or with the agony of Golgotha (e.g., Andriessen, *NRT* 96 [1974] 287). In v 7 Jesus' passion is described in its entirety as priestly prayer, taking advantage of the expression of those psalms that were interpreted within the Christian communities in the light of Jesus' passion (cf. Dibelius, *TBl* 21 [1942] 8–9; Strobel, *ZNW* 45 [1954] 256–66; Rasco, *Greg* 43 [1962] 728–33). Variations on the double expression "prayers and entreaties" occur in the LXX (Job 40:27), Philo (*On the Cherubim* 47), and elsewhere in hellenistic sources (e.g., Isocrates, *Concerning Peace* 138; Polybius 3.112.8). References to "cries and tears" are not uncommon in hellenistic Jewish sources describing prayer in a setting of crisis (cf. 2 Macc 11:6; 3 Macc 1:16; 5:7, 25; Philo, *Questions on Genesis* 4.233). The proper background for understanding the description in v 7, according to Attridge (*JBL* 98 [1979] 90–93), is the tradition of prayer in hellenistic Judaism, as set forth in Philo's tractate *Who Is the Heir?* 1–29. Like Abraham, Jesus prayed with fervent cries (14), and like Moses, with deep emotion (19). Like Abraham, his prayers were accompanied by εὐλάβεια, a godly fear expressed in the recognition of God's sovereignty and submission to the divine will (22, 24–29). What distinguishes Hebrews from the hellenistic-Jewish tradition of effective prayer is the emphasis on the significance of the passion of Jesus.

8 The decision to relate the concessive clause καίπερ ὢν υἱός, "although he was the Son," to what follows (see *Note* w above) has significant bearing upon the interpretation of v 8. It indicates that the discussion of the obedience of the Christ is qualified by the affirmation that Jesus is inherently and intrinsically the Son of God, whose essential sonship is a fact wholly apart from his experience of suffering (cf. Longenecker, "The Obedience of Christ," 148–52). It is instructive to contrast the statement in v 8 with 12:5, where it is stated that "sons" are disciplined precisely because they are sons. In v 8 all the functions of "sons" are set aside by the conjunction καίπερ and the recognition that υἱός, "Son," is used concessively. Although Jesus was the eternal Son of God, he entered into a new dimension in the experience of sonship by virtue of his incarnation and sacrificial death.

The phrase ἔμαθεν ἀφ᾽ ὧν ἔπαθεν, "he learned from what he suffered," has a long history in Greek literature (Coste, *RSR* 43 [1955] 485–97; Dörrie, *Leid und Erfahrung*, 3–42). The two verbal roots μαθ-/παθ-, from the simple fact of their phonetic similarity, gave rise naturally to a variety of combinations for rhetorical effect. The play on words is relatively common in Philo (cf. Coste, 508–17), who applies it to the young and the foolish who must learn from what they endure (e.g., *On Flight and Finding* 138). From this perspective the application of the conventional proverb to Jesus is daring.

The parallels in Greek literature, however, are not the significant factor for understanding v 8. The crucial consideration is that in Hebrews the verb πάσχειν, which ordinarily means "to suffer," is used only of the passion of Jesus and takes on the nuance of "to die" (2:9, 10; 9:26; 13:12; cf. Rengstorf, *TDNT* 4:410–12; Michaelis, *TDNT* 5:917, 934–35). In v 8 the term ἔπαθεν, "he suffered [death]," has in view the unique redemptive sufferings of the Son in the discharge of his priestly office. By suffering in undeviating acceptance of the divine will as his own, Jesus honors God as sovereign and entrusts himself to him, confident that he will give him his office and dignity. The term ἔμαθεν, "he learned," carries a nuance developed in biblical Greek, where learning takes place in the reception of Scripture as the word of God (cf. Rengstorf, *TDNT* 4:408–9, 411). From Scripture, and especially from the Psalms, Jesus learned that his passion was grounded in the saving will of God and could not be severed from his calling. Thus in the declaration that Jesus "learned obedience from what he suffered," the term τὴν ὑπακοήν, "obedience," has a very specific meaning: it is *obedience* to the call to suffer death in accordance with the revealed will of God (cf. Vos, *PTR* 5 [1907] 584–85). Jesus freely accepted the suffering of death because Scripture, and through it God, appointed him to this sacrifice for the sake of his office.

The new element in the application of a pregnant pun to Jesus is not the learning of obedience (so Spicq, 2:117; Cullmann, *Christology*, 96–97), but its nature and manner as denoted by the expression ἀφ᾽ ὧν ἔπαθεν, "from what he suffered." The accent in the proverbial saying falls on ἔπαθεν, "he suffered [death]" (so Coste, *RSR* 43 [1955] 520; Rengstorf, *TDNT* 4:412). Consequently, the introductory clause καίπερ ὢν υἱός, "although he was Son," is to be understood in the light of the paradox that the transcendent Son was ordained to suffer death. He does not cling to the privileged status that his unique sonship implies but receives it from the Father only after he has suffered the humiliation of death on the cross (cf. 12:2). Jesus learned experientially what obedience entails through his passion in order to achieve salvation and to become fully qualified for his office as eternal high priest (2:10; 5:9–10).

9–10 In extremely concise style, Jesus' redemptive accomplishment and exaltation are expressed in vv 9–10. The temporal clause καὶ τελειωθείς, "and once made perfect," announces the validation by God of the perfect obedience that Jesus rendered as the priestly representative of the people. It reflects upon the sufferings by which he was brought to the goal appointed for him by God, through which he became a perfect high priest (cf. Vos, *PTR* 5 [1907] 580, 588–89; Meeter, *Heavenly High Priesthood*, 89–94). The LXX translators of the Pentateuch gave to the verb τελειοῦν a special cultic sense of consecration to priestly service (cf. Exod 29:9, 29, 33, 35; Lev 4:5; 8:33; 16:32; 21:10; Num 3:3), and this official conception stands behind τελειωθείς in v 9. It signifies that Jesus has been fully equipped to come before God in priestly action (cf. Delling, *TDNT* 8.83). Through his sufferings and the accomplishment of his redemptive mission, Jesus has been perfected by God as the priest of his people and exalted to the divine presence (cf. Klappert, *Eschatologie*, 54–57, who calls attention to the pattern of suffering and perfection in 2:10; 7:28). The acceptance of Jesus' sacrifice asserted with the participle εἰσακουσθείς, "he was heard," in v 7 is implied again in v 9 with the participle τελειωθείς (Maurer, "'Erhört wegen der Gottesfurcht,'" 283–84).

The result of this action is expressed with the main verb in v 9. Jesus has become (ἐγένετο) the source of eternal salvation for all those who obey him. The description of the community of faith as those who obey Jesus is appropriate to the stress on the radical obedience of Jesus in v 8. As the one who experienced the meaning of obedience in the suffering of death in response to the will of God, Jesus recognizes obedience in his followers and on their behalf carries out his priestly ministry of intercession (cf. Vos, 586). This affirmation repeats the theme of "timely help" from 4:16 and relates it to the fact of Christ's accomplished sacrifice. The salvation he provides is "eternal" not simply because it extends beyond time but because it is true, heavenly, and not human-made (9:23–24; cf. Williamson, *Philo*, 84–88).

The designation of Jesus by God as high priest like Melchizedek (v 10) was concomitant with the acceptance of his sacrifice. The divine acclamation confirms Jesus' qualification for his office. The primary function of the allusion to Ps 110:4 in v 10 is to reaffirm God's appointment of Jesus as high priest (vv 5–6). But the allusion also serves to connect Jesus' priesthood with his saving work (Hay, *Glory*, 46).

Explanation

In 4:15–5:10 the writer takes up the declaration that Jesus had to become "a merciful high priest in the service of God" (2:17). "Merciful" implies the capacity to understand and to help those dependent upon his ministry, and is related by the writer to Jesus' redemptive accomplishment. The emphasis is placed on Jesus' full humanity and his solidarity with those who are exposed to weakness and temptation (4:15). Because he was exposed to testing as they are, he knows experientially what humiliation entails. That the one who has this fellow-feeling with the people of God appears in the presence of God as their high priestly advocate invests his compassion and help with a quality that guarantees they will be able to endure their situation and obtain the salvation promised to them.

The orientation given to the exposition is intensely practical. The solidarity of the heavenly high priest with the community in its weakness provides a strong motivation for earnest prayer. The demand to draw near to the one who is thoroughly familiar with the human condition, who suffers with their suffering, and who is therefore qualified to mediate renewed strength (4:15–16) is an appeal to recognize the importance of prayer in the rhythm of Christian life. The writer knew the community was exposed to the pull of past loyalties and to the peril of renewed hostility (cf. 10:32–34; 12:1–4). To fulfill their Christian vocation they needed the different quality of experience provided by prayer. The depiction of prayer as priestly approach to the presence of God developed the insight that prayer creates a sanctuary in time when one may not be available in space. In the rhythm between exposure to pressure and tired resignation under spiritual conflict, they will find in prayer the refreshment that flows from openness to God's invincible mercy and sustaining grace and will receive the help that arrives at the right time.

Although the title "high priest" was introduced in 2:17, the designation is not clarified until 4:15–5:10. The development is supported by the use of formal elements of the OT. For the first time the writer establishes the spiritual basis for his high priestly christology and begins to compare the Levitical high priesthood and the unique priesthood of Jesus. The description of the high priesthood in 5:1–4 does not constitute a general definition of the Levitical institution. On the contrary, it is oriented wholly in a particular sense determined by the preceding verses (4:15–16), that of the solidarity of the priest with the people. In the Pentateuch it is stressed that the high priest is appointed *for God* (Exod 28:1, 3; 29:1); in Heb 5:1 the high priest is appointed *for men*. The writer adopts the OT form in a positive fashion to establish a parallel between the Levitical high priest and Jesus.

Aaron and Jesus are brought into direct comparison in 5:4–6. The basis of the comparison is the humility which both displayed in refusing to exalt themselves to the office of high priest, which could be received only by divine appointment. The point is made that Jesus' priestly ministry was effective because it was accomplished with authorization (5:5–6, 10).

The likeness of Jesus to Aaron, however, is shattered with the citation of Ps 110:4. The appeal to Melchizedek, who as the first priest mentioned in Scripture is the archetype of all priesthood, validates Jesus' priesthood as different from and superior to the Levitical priesthood. Christ enjoys a preeminence that removes him from the sphere of comparison with Aaron. He was "without sin" (4:15), and he is summoned to be "a priest forever" (5:6). His priestly task is to create an order of salvation that is valid forever (5:9), which has the effect of rendering the Aaronic institution obsolete.

The parallel between Aaron and Christ is infringed most sharply in the description of their respective priestly functions. In reference to the Levitical high priest, the writer mentions the cultic ministry of sacrifice on the Day of Atonement (5:1) and the extension of forbearance to those who are weak (5:2–3). In contrast to this, Christ's high priestly offering culminated in the surrender of his life to the suffering of death in perfect obedience to God's revealed will. This self-sacrifice is not only superior to the OT prototype. It represents an incomparably deeper and more radical identification with men and women in their weakness than was ever envisioned in the case of the Levitical high priest. The acceptance of Jesus' completed sacrifice is celebrated in the confessional affirmation that "he was heard" (5:7) and has been pronounced "qualified" to come before God in high priestly mediation (5:9). On this basis he has inaugurated a new, redemptive relationship between God and the human family that merits the perseverance of the community in faith and obedience.

III. The High Priestly Office of the Son (5:11–10:39)

Bibliography

Attridge, H. W. "The Uses of Antithesis in Hebrews 8–10." *HTR* 79 (1986) 1–9. **Black, D. A.** "The Problem of the Literary Structure of Hebrews: An Evaluation and a Proposal." *GTJ* 7 (1986) 163–77. **Bligh, J.** *Chiastic Analysis of the Epistle to the Hebrews.* 8–21. ———. "The Structure of Hebrews." *HeyJ* 5 (1964) 170–77. **Cladder, H.** "Hebr. 5,11–10, 39." *ZKT* 29 (1905) 500–524. **Descamps, A.** "La structure de l'Épître aux Hébreux." *RDT* 9 (1954) 251–58; 333–38. **Dussaut, L.** *Synopse structurelle de l'Épître aux Hébreux.* 54–115. **Gourgues, M.** "Remarks sur la 'structure centrale' de l'Épître aux Hébreux." *RB* 84 (1977) 26–37. **Gyllenberg, R.** "Die Komposition des Hebräerbriefs." *SEÅ* 22–23 (1957–58) 137–47. **Hillmann, W.** "Der Höhenpriester der künftigen Güter: Einführung in die Grundgedanken des Hebräerbriefes (4,14-10,31)." *BibLeb* 1 (1960) 157–78. **Nauck, W.** "Zum Aufbau des Hebräerbriefes." In *Judentum, Urchristentum, Kirche.* FS J. Jeremias. Ed. W. Eltester. BZNW 26 (1960) 199–206. **Rice, G. E.** "Apostasy as a Motif and Its Effect on the Structure of Hebrews." *AUSS* 23 (1988) 29–35. ———. "The Chiastic Structure of the Central Section of the Epistle to the Hebrews." *AUSS* 19 (1981) 243–46. **Songer, H. H.** "A Superior Priesthood: Hebrews 4:14–7:28." *RevExp* 82 (1985) 345–59. **Swetnam, J.** "Form and Content in Hebrews 1–6." *Bib* 53 (1972) 368–85. ———. "Form and Content in Hebrews 7–13." *Bib* 55 (1974) 333–48. **Thien, F.** "Analyse de l'Épître aux Hébreux." *RB* 11 (1902) 74–86. **Vanhoye, A.** "Discussions sur la structure de l'Épître aux Hébreux." *Bib* 55 (1974) 349–80. ———. "Les indices de la structure littéraire de l'Épître aux Hébreux." *SE* 2 (1964) 493–509. ———. "Literarische Struktur und theologische Botschaft des Hebräerbriefs." *SNTU* 4 (1979) 119–47; 5 (1980) 18–49. ———. *La structure littéraire.* 42–60, 115–82. ———. "Structure littéraire et thèmes théologiques de l'Épître aux Hébreux." In *Studiorum Paulinorum Congressus Internationalis Catholicus 1961.* AnBib 18. Rome: Biblical Institute, 1963. 175–81.

Introduction

The third and central division extends from 5:11–10:39. Both in terms of its length and subject matter, the writer ascribes to it a particular preeminence. It represents approximately two-fifths of the space allotted for the composition of the sermon. It is the only major division in which a preliminary exhortation related to the situation of the community prepares for the exposition in a formal way (5:11–6:20) and in which a concluding exhortation applies the insights developed to that situation (10:19–39). The writer's fundamental concern is to set forth distinctive features of the high priestly office of the Son. Three aspects of this subject were announced thematically in the description of Jesus' exaltation in 5:9–10. What was entailed in the declaration that Jesus "was made perfect" occupies the central place in the exposition and receives the fullest development (8:1–9:28). This unit is framed by two other sections that provide commentary on the significance of designating Jesus as "a high priest like Melchizedek" (7:1–28) and as "the source of eternal salvation" (10:1–18) (cf. Vanhoye, *La structure,* 42–60).

The beginning of a new division is indicated by the simple transition from exposition (4:15–5:10) to exhortation (5:11–6:20). The writer clearly enunciated his intention to discuss the subject announced in 5:9–10, since he states, "On this subject we have many things to say" (JB). Swetnam argued that it is more consonant with the nature of parenesis to follow an exposition, and that this is the normal procedure in Hebrews. Consequently, he connected 5:11–6:20 with the preceding unit (*Bib* 53 [1972] 385). In this instance, however, the exhortation serves to enlist the attention of the readers and appropriately appears before the exposition of what the writer regarded to be of the greatest importance, not after (so Vanhoye, *Bib* 55 [1974] 372). The exhortation clearly anticipates the discussion of Jesus' office as high priest and his sacrificial offering in 7:1–10:18. The end of the preliminary remarks is indicated by the declaration that Jesus has become "a high priest forever, like Melchizedek" (6:20). That affirmation constitutes a second announcement of one aspect of the subject (5:10), which is developed systematically in 7:1–28. The transition from the conclusion of the preliminary exhortation to the first section of exposition is achieved with the repetition of the proper name, "This Melchizedek" (7:1).

As a section, 7:1–28 contains a number of characteristic terms. The proper name Melchizedek occurs in 7:1, 10, 11, 15, 17, and not beyond this point. Other terms related to the announcement of the subject in 5:10 are taken up in the course of the exposition: "high priest" (7:26, 27, 28), "priest" (7:1, 3, 11, 14, 15, 17, 20, 21, 23), "priesthood" (7:11, 12, 24, and not elsewhere in the NT), "forever" (7:17, 21, 24, 28), and "like Melchizedek" (7:11, 17). These priestly categories are considered in relation to "the law" (7:5, 12, 16, 19, 28) and the appointment of "Levi" (7:5, 9; nowhere else in Hebrews) under the "Levitical" arrangement (7:11; nowhere else in the NT). The concentration of vocabulary bearing on the priestly office gives to the section its distinctive character (so Vanhoye, *La structure*, 42–43).

The exposition of Jesus' unique priesthood in 7:1–28 is summed up with an antithesis in v 28:

> For the law appoints as high priest men who are weak; but the word of the oath, which came after the law, appointed the Son, who has been made perfect forever.

The qualification in this verse, τετελειωμένον, "has been made perfect," is assigned the final position in the sentence for emphasis. It repeats the announcement of the subject in 5:9, καὶ τελειωθείς, "and once made perfect," and provides the point of transition to the central section of the exposition (8:1–9:28). The literary construction shows clearly that the writer conceived of the section which begins with 8:1 as a development of this announced theme. In 7:26–28 he describes the ideal high priest who meets the need of the community, "the Son who was perfected forever." Then in 8:1 he announces triumphantly, "we do have such a high priest." The declaration refers back to 7:26–28 and anticipates the exposition announced thematically in 7:28. The importance of the new unit is underscored for the community by designating it "the chief point" of the exposition (8:1) (cf. Vanhoye, *La structure*, 44, 134–35; *Bib* 55 [1974] 359).

The subject of the central section is the high priestly sacrifice that Jesus offered to God. Appropriately, the characteristic vocabulary of this unit consists of cultic terms: "To offer" (προσφέρειν: 8:3, 4; 9:7, 9, 14, 25, 28), "both gifts and sacrifices" (8:3; 9:9; elsewhere only 5:1), "sanctuary" (8:2; 9:1, 8, 12, 24, 25; elsewhere only 10:19; 13:11), "tent" (8:2, 5; 9:2, 3, 6, 8, 11, 21; elsewhere only 11:9; 13:10), "blood" (9:7, 12, 13, 14, 18, 19, 20, 21, 22, 25), and "covenant" (8:6, 8, 9, 10; 9:4, 15, 16, 17, 20). The unitary character of the vocabulary gives a distinctive color to the presentation in this section.

The argument is summed up in the declaration "so Christ was sacrificed once to take away the sins of many people; and he will appear a second time, not to bear sin, but to bring salvation to those who are waiting for him" (9:28 NIV). Once again, the crucial term σωτηρίαν, "salvation," is assigned the final, emphatic position. It calls to mind the statement in 5:9 that Jesus "has become the source of eternal salvation to all who obey him." The final clause in 9:28 repeats the announcement of the subject in 5:9 and marks the point of transition to the third section of the exposition, which is devoted to that aspect (10:1–18). The announcement of the subject to be developed immediately before the section that corresponds to it exhibits the writer's concern to assist his auditors to follow at an oral level the course of the exposition in the great central division of the sermon. His consistent practice in this regard (6:20; 7:28; 9:28) attests decisively that he is following a literary and rhetorical procedure designed to make clear the structure of the exposition (Vanhoye, *La structure*, 44, 160; *Bib* 55 [1974] 360).

In the final paragraph of the central section (9:23–28), the continual repetition of the sacrifices under the law is contrasted with the unique, singular character of the sacrifice of Christ. The third section develops the nature of the salvation provided by Christ by clarifying the reason for the superior efficacy of the sacrifice offered by Jesus. The characteristic terms are those associated with the sacrificial offering: "to offer" (προσφέρειν, 10:1, 2, 8, 11, 12), "offering" (προσφορά, 10:5, 8, 10, 14, 18, and not elsewhere in Hebrews), and "sacrifice" (10:1, 5, 8, 11, 12), and with the result of such an offering: "sanctification" (10:10, 14), "to perfect" (10:1, 14), "to purify" (10:2), "remission" (10:18), and "to take away sin" (10:4, 11; cf. also "sin," 10:2, 3, 6, 8, 12, 17, 18) (Vanhoye, *La structure*, 44). The argument is summed up and given closure with the striking declaration, "And when these [sins and lawless acts] have been forgiven, there is no longer any offering for sin" (10:18).

A change of literary genre marks the transition to the concluding exhortation (10:19–39), which applies the insights developed in the preceding sections to the community in its situation (cf. 9:12 with 10:19, for example). The verbal repetition of the noun παρρησία, "confidence," in vv 19 and 35 provides an *inclusio*, which marks off the opening and closing of the unit and prepares the auditors for the announcement of the subject to be developed in the fourth major division, patient endurance and saving faith, in 10:36–39.

It is instructive to observe the similarity in formulation between the final statement in the preliminary exhortation (6:19–20) and the initial statement in the concluding exhortation (10:19–20). The vocabulary and conception are similar, but there is a greater degree of precision in 10:19–20, which is able to take advantage of the completed exposition in 7:1–10:18. In reformulating the substance of 6:19–20 in 10:19–20, the writer repeats his appeal for confidence and unwavering adherence to the confession of the Church.

The structural parallelism between 5:11–6:20 and 10:19–39 has been recognized by several writers (cf. Thien, *RB* 11 [1902] 79; Descamps, *RDT* 9 [1954] 335; Vanhoye, *La structure*, 45, 173). It gives to the third major division a formal symmetry, which has bearing upon the interpretation of Hebrews:

a	Preliminary exhortation	(5:11–6:20)	
A	A priest like Melchizedek	(7:1–28)	(28 verses)
B	The single, personal sacrifice for sins	(8:1–9:28)	(41 verses)
C	The achievement of eternal salvation	(10:1–18)	(18 verses)
a'	Concluding exhortation	(10:19–39)	

The concentric symmetry has the effect of drawing attention to the central section (B), which is explicitly introduced as "the crowning affirmation" (8:1) and is given privileged treatment in terms of length. The placement of the exposition of Jesus' unique sacrifice in the center of the central division sufficiently indicates the importance that the writer ascribed to this aspect of his message. In this regard, thematic analysis confirms the results of purely literary analysis: the central theme of Hebrews is redemptive sacrifice (so Vanhoye, *La structure*, 59–60, 237–42, 247–51, 256–58).

A. The Third Warning: The Peril of Spiritual Immaturity (5:11–6:12)

Bibliography

Adams, J. C. "The Epistle to the Hebrews with Special Reference to the Problem of Apostasy in the Church to Which It Was Addressed." Dissertation, Leeds University, 1964. ———. "Exegesis of Hebrews VI. 1f." *NTS* 13 (1966–67) 378–85. **Albani, J.** "Hebr. v,11–vi,8: Ein Wort zur Verfasserschaft des Apollos." *ZWT* 47 (1904) 88–93. **Anderson, J. C.** "Repentance in the Greek New Testament." Dissertation, Dallas Theological Seminary, 1959. **Andriessen, P.** "La communauté des 'Hébreux,' était-elle tombée dans le relâchement?" *NRT* 96 (1974) 1054–66. ———. "L'Eucharistie dans l'Épître aux Hébreux." *NRT* 94 (1972) 269–77. ——— and **Lenglet, A.** "Quelques passages difficiles de l'Épître aux Hébreux (5,7.11; 10,20; 12,2)." *Bib* 51 (1970) 207–20. **Ballarini, T.** "Il peccato nell' epistola agli Ebrei." *ScC* 106 (1978) 358–71. **Barker, P. R. P.** "Studies in Texts: Hebrews 6:1f." *Th* 65 (1962) 282–84. **Barnhart, D.** "The Life of No Retreat: An Exegetical Study of Hebrews 6:1–12." *CentBibQ* 19 (1976) 16–31. **Campbell, A. G.** "The Problem of Apostasy in the Greek New Testament." Dissertation, Dallas Theological Seminary, 1957. **Carlston, C. E.** "Eschatology and Repentance in the Epistle to the Hebrews." *JBL* 78 (1959) 296–302. **Collins, B.** "Tentatur nova interpretatio Hebr. 5,11–6,8." *VD* 26 (1948) 144–51, 193–206. **Costanzo, J.** "Il Peccato e la sua Remissione nella Lettera agli Ebrei." Dissertation, Gregorian Pontifical University, Rome, 1964. **Coterill, D. R.** "The Concept of Maturity in Hebrews 5:11–14." Dissertation, Dallas Theological Seminary, 1971. **Cox, L. G.** "Let Us Go unto Perfection: Hebrews 6:1." *ASem* 18 (1964) 49–59. **Cruvellier, J.** "Impossible de ramener à la repentance! (à propos de deux passages difficiles de l'Épître aux Hébreux)." *EEv* 12 (1952) 135–40. **Custer, S.** "The Awfulness of Apostasy." *BV* 2 (1968) 15–20. **Delville, J. P.** "L'Épître aux Hébreux à la lumière du prosélytisme juif." *RevistCatT* 10 (1985) 323–68. **Dunham, D. A.** "An Exegetical Examination of the Warnings in the Epistle to the Hebrews." Dissertation, Grace Theological Seminary and College, 1974. **Dunn, J. D. G.** *Baptism in the Holy Spirit.* Philadelphia: Westminster, 1970. 205–11. **Dussaut, L.** *Synopse structurelle de l'Épître aux Hébreux.* 54–58. **Elliott, J. K.** "Is Post-Baptismal Sin Forgivable?" *BT* 28 (1977) 330–32. **Fernández, J.** "La teleíosis o perfección cristiana en la epístola a los Hebreos." *CB* 13 (1956) 251–59. **Goguel, M.** "La doctrine de l'impossibilité de la seconde conversion dans l'Épître aux Hébreux et sa place dans l'évolution du Christianisme." *AEPHE* (1931) 4–38. **Grundmann, W.** "Die νήπιοι in der urchristlichen Paränese." *NTS* 5 (1958–59) 188–205. **Gyllenberg, R.** "Zur Exegese von Hbr. 5,11–6,12. In *Commentationes philologicae*. FS I. A. Heikel. Ed. discipuli. Helsinki: Suomal. kirjall. kirjapaion osakleyhtiö, 1926. 73–82. **Hamm, D.** "Faith in the Epistle to the Hebrews: The Jesus Factor." *CBQ* 52 (1990) 270–91. **Hohenstein, H.** "A Study of Hebrews 6,4–8." *CTM* 27 (1956) 433–44, 536–46. **Hughes, P. E.** "Hebrews 6:4–6 and the Peril of Apostasy." *WTJ* 35 (1973) 137–55. **Kawamura, A.** "'Αδύνατον in Heb 6:4." *AJBI* 10 (1984) 91–100. **Kiley, M.** "Melchisedek's Promotion to *archiereus* and the Translation of *ta stoicheia tēs archēs*." SBLASP 25 (1986) 236–45. ———. "A Note on Hebrews 5:14." *CBQ* 42 (1980) 501–3. **Lang, W.** "L'Appel à la pénitence dans le christianisme primitif." *CMech* n.s. 29 (1959) 380–90. **Marshall, I. H.** *Kept by the Power of God: A Study of Perseverance and Falling Away.* London: Epworth, 1969. 132–54. ———. "The Problem of Apostasy in New Testament Theology." *PRS* 14 (1987) 65–80. **McCullough, J. C.** "The Impossibility of a Second Repentance in Hebrews." *BibTh* 20 (1974) 1–7. **Mora, G.** *La Carta a los Hebreos como Escrito Pastoral.* 11–48, 69–118. **Mugridge, A.** "Warnings in the Epistle to the Hebrews: An Exegetical and Theological Study." *RTR* 46 (1987) 74–82. **Nicole, R.** "Some Comments on Hebrews 6:4–6 and the Doctrine of the Perseverance of God with the Saints." In *Current Issues in Biblical and Patristic Interpretation.* FS M. C. Tenney. Ed. G. F. Hawthorne. Grand Rapids: Eerdmans, 1975. 355–64. **Oberholtzer, T. K.** "The Thorn-Infested Ground in Hebrews 6:4–12." *BSac* 145 (1988) 319–27. **Owen, H. P.** "The 'Stages of Ascent' in Hebrews V.11–VI.3." *NTS* 3 (1956–57) 243–53. **Perkins, R. L.** "Two Notes on Apostasy." *PRS* 15 (1988) 57–60. **Peterson, D. G.** "An Examination of the Concept of 'Perfection' in the 'Epistle to the Hebrews.'" Dissertation, University of Manchester, 1978. 305–25. ———. "The Situation of the 'Hebrews' (5:11–6:12)." *RTR* 35 (1976) 14–21. **Poschmann, B.** *Paenitentia Secunda: Die kirchliche Busse im ältesten Christentum bis Cyprian und Origenes.* Bonn: Hanstein, 1940. 38–52. **Proulx, P.** and **Schökel, L. A.** "Heb 6,4–6: εἰς μετάνοιαν ἀνασταυροῦντας." *Bib* 56 (1975) 193–209. **Rice, G. E.** "Apostasy as a Motif and Its Effect on the Structure of Hebrews." *AUSS* 23 (1985) 29–35. **Rigaux, B.** "La στερεὰ τροφή de l'Épître aux Hébreux." *NTS* 4 (1957–58) 257–62. **Rose, C.** "Verheissung und Erfüllung: Zum Verständnis von ἐπαγγελία im Hebräerbrief." *BZ* 33 (1989) 60–80. **Rowell, J. B.** "Exposition of Hebrews Six." *BSac* 94 (1937) 321–42. **Sabourin, L.** "'Crucifying Afresh for One's Repentance' (Heb 6:4–6)." *BTB* 6 (1976) 264–71. **Sailer, W. S.** "Hebrews Six: An Irony or a Continuing Embarrassment?" *EvJ* 3 (1985) 79–88. **Sauer, R. C.** "A Critical and Exegetical Re-examination of Hebrews 5:11–6:8." Dissertation, University of Manchester, 1981. **Schnackenburg, R.** "Typen der 'Metanoia' Predigt im Neuen Testament." *MTZ* 1 (1950) 1–13. **Solari, J. K.** "The Problem of *Metanoia* in the Epistle to the Hebrews." Dissertation, The Catholic University of America, 1970. **Spicq, C.** "La penitencia impossible." *CTom* 244 (1952) 353–68. **Sproule, J. A.** "Παραπεσόντας in Hebrews 6:6." *GTJ* 2 (1981) 327–32. **Thüsing, W.** "'Milch' und 'feste Speise' (1 Kor 3, 1f. und Hebr 5,11–6,3): Elementarkatechese und theologische Vertiefung im neutestamentlicher Sicht." *TTZ* 76 (1967) 233–46, 261–80. **Tongue, D. H.** "The Concept of Apostasy in the Epistle to the Hebrews." *TynBul* 5–6 (1960) 19–26. **Toussaint, S. D.** "The Eschatology of the Warning Passages in the Book of Hebrews." *GTJ* 3 (1982) 67–80. **Vanhoye, A.** "Héb 6:7–8 et le mashal rabbinique." In *The New Testament Age.* FS B. Reicke. Ed. W. C. Weinrich. Macon, GA: Mercer UP, 1984. 2:527–32. **Verbrugge, V. D.** "Towards a New Interpretation of Hebrews 6:4–6." *CTJ* 15 (1980) 61–73. **Vitti, A. M.** "Rursum crucifigentes sibi metipsis Filium Dei et ostentui habentes." *VD* 22 (1942) 174–82. **Weeks, N.** "Admonition and Error in Hebrews." *WTJ* 39 (1976) 72–80. **Williamson, R.** "The Eucharist and the Epistle to the Hebrews." *NTS* 21 (1974–75) 300–12. ———. *Philo and the Epistle to the Hebrews.* 23–25, 114–16, 118–22, 233–41, 245–63, 277–308. **Wuest, K. S.** "Hebrews Six in the Greek New Testament." *BSac* 119 (1962) 45–53. **Young, N. H.** "Is Hebrews 6:1–8 Pastoral Nonsense?" *Coll* 15 (1982) 52–57.

Translation

[11] *We have much to say about this subject, and it is hard to explain intelligibly,*[a] *since*[b] *you have become sluggish in understanding.*[c] [12] *In fact, although by this time you ought*[d] *to be teachers, you need someone to teach you*[e] *again the elementary truths of God's revelation; you are at the stage of needing*[f] *milk, and not solid food.* [13] *Anyone who lives on a diet of*[g] *milk is inexperienced with the teaching about righteousness, for he is an infant;* [14] *but solid food is for adults, who have their faculties trained by constant use*[h] *to distinguish between good and evil.*

[6:1] *So then, let us leave standing*[i] *the elementary Christian teaching,*[j] *and be carried forward*[k] *to the goal of spiritual maturity,*[l] *not laying again a foundation consisting of repentance*[m] *from works that lead to death and of faith in God,* [2] *the catechetical instruction*[n] *concerning cleansing rites*[o] *and laying on of hands, the resurrection of the dead and*[p] *eternal judgment.* [3] *And we will do this if, that is,*[q] *God allows.* [4] *For it is impossible*[r] *when those who have once*[s] *been brought into the light, and who have experienced*[t] *the gift from heaven, and who have received a share in the Holy Spirit,* [5] *and who have experienced the goodness of God's word*[u] *and the powers of the coming age,* [6] *and then have fallen away,*[v] *to restore them to repentance, because*[w] *to their loss*[x] *they are crucifying the Son of God again*[y] *and exposing him to public shame.* [7] *For the field which soaks up the frequent rain which falls upon it, and which yields a useful crop to those for whom it is cultivated, shares a blessing from God.* [8] *But if it produces thorns and thistles, it is useless, and a curse hangs over it;*[z] *in the end it will be burned over.*

[9] *But even though we speak like this, dear friends, in your case we remain sure*[aa] *of the better things which accompany your salvation.*[bb] [10] *For God is not so unjust as to overlook*[cc] *your work and the love which you demonstrated*[dd] *with regard to him*[ee] *when you served and continue to serve fellow Christians.*[ff] [11] *But we want each one of you to demonstrate the same earnest concern with regard to the realization of your hope until the end,* [12] *so that you will not become sluggish, but*[gg] *imitators of those who with faith and steadfast endurance inherit the promises.*

Notes

[a] In the construction λόγος καὶ δυσερμήνευτος λέγειν, which sounds classical, the inf λέγειν is complementary to the adj δυσερμήνευτος; its function is to explain the adjective: "and hard of interpretation to state," i.e., "hard to state intelligibly." So BDF §393(6); A. T. Robertson, *Grammar*, 1075; cf. Moffatt, "which it is hard to make intelligible to you."

[b] The translation of ἐπεί in a causal sense ("since, because") has been challenged by Andriessen (*NRT* 96 [1974] 1057–59; cf. Andriessen and Lenglet, *Bib* 51 [1970] 212–14). He finds in v 11 an elliptical use of the conj, which calls for the translation "otherwise" (cf. 9:26; 10:2). The ellipse implies a suppressed condition that must be supplied for the sense. He translates: "On this subject we have a detailed and difficult explanation to make. *Otherwise* you would have become sluggish of hearing." On this understanding, vv 11–12 express an unreal situation; i.e., the community is actually not sluggish or regressive.

Andriessen's proposal has been effectively countered by Peterson (*RTR* 35 [1976] 14–16). He points out that whenever ἐπεί is used with the sense of "otherwise" rather than "since," the context clearly indicates that an unreal or contrary-to-fact situation is implied. This is the case in Heb 9:26 and 10:2, which conform to a class of sentence that is logically conditional with an "implied protasis" (see Moule, *Idiom-Book*, 151). The presence of an adversative in the next clause (9:26, νυνὶ δέ, "But now") or sentence (10:3, ἀλλ᾽, "But") clearly indicates that the preceding statement is "unreal." An entirely different syntactical pattern is evident in the other contexts where ἐπεί is used (2:14; 4:6; 5:2; 6:13; 9:17; 11:11); in each of the verses the relevant clause represents a further positive statement in what may be described as a cumulative argument. The ἐπεί clause in v 11 belongs syntactically to the latter group of references, and not to the former. To make sense of the clause with the translation "otherwise," Andriessen had to ignore the force of γεγόνατε ("you have become"), which describes a state of affairs that the writer knows to be a present condition of the community, "with the perfect tense perhaps suggesting some definite point in the past when this began" (15).

More recently, Andriessen has put forward an alternative proposal (*En lisant*, 22–23) based on the free use of ἐπεί by the Greek Atticists to introduce an interrogative phrase when the response could only be negative. The presence of direct discourse in v 11 explains the free use of the conj, which should be translated "or": "We have to treat at greater depth this important subject and its difficult clarification, *or* will you have become slow to understand and have you, whom time has made teachers, a need that one teach you again the first elements of the oracles of God?" This new proposal equally ignores the pf tense of the predicate γεγόνατε.

ᶜ The expression νωθροί . . . ταῖς ἀκοαῖς could be translated "sluggish in hearing," or "hard of hearing" (so BAG 549). This nuance is suggested by the repeated emphasis on attentive hearing of the voice of God in Hebrews (2:1; 3:7–8, 15; 4:2, 7). The pl form ἀκοαῖς ("ears" as organs of hearing), however, denotes receptivity and understanding. Cf. JB, "so slow at understanding"; Zerwick and and Grosvenor, *Grammatical Analysis*, 663, "sluggish in receptivity."

ᵈ The second person pl subj of the concessive ptcp ὀφείλοντες is revealed by the verb ἔχετε, "you have."

ᵉ The articular inf in the gen (τοῦ διδάσκειν) is epexegetical to the noun χρείαν, "need"; it indicates what is needful (cf. Turner, *Grammar*, 3:141).

ᶠ The translation takes account of the pf tense of the verb γεγόνατε followed by the accusative and a present ptcp (χρείαν ἔχοντες): "you have become people needing" (Zerwick and Grosvenor, *Grammatical Analysis*, 663).

ᵍ The present ptcp μετέχων denotes partaking of something, but in this context "living on (a diet of)" (cf. BAG 515).

ʰ The term ἕξις can be interpreted either passively as a state ("condition, capacity") or actively as a process ("exercise, use"). Philo frequently uses the term in the first sense (e.g., *Allegorical Interpretation of the Law* 3.210: "as the result of a fixed state"); the Prologue to Sir 10, where ἕξις denotes skill acquired by practice, illustrates the second usage. H. Montefiore (101), who translated v 14, "But solid food is for mature men, who, in virtue of their condition, have had their perceptions trained to distinguish," has recently received fresh support from Kiley (*CBQ* 42 [1980] 501–3). He observed that the Middle Platonist philosopher Albinus (mid-second century A.D.) used ἕξις in the sense of a "characteristic state," which a child may acquire by learning. Similarly, the writer to the Hebrews praises "those, who on account of their characteristic state (as adults) have their senses trained to discern good and bad" (503). In the case of v 14, however, the immediate linguistic context must determine the translation. The presence of the ptcp γεγυμνασμένα, "trained," seems to require that ἕξις be interpreted in the active sense as "exercise, practice, long use." So R. Williamson, *Philo*, 118–21; cf. RSV: "by practice"; NEB: "by long use."

ⁱ The ptcp ἀφέντες does not imply contempt for or an abandonment of the elementary teaching (cf. Owen, *NTS* 4 [1957–58] 248–49, "omit the foundation"; 253, "he [the author] discards the substance of the θεμέλιος ['foundation'] altogether"). The use of the verb in 2:8 (cf. Matt 22:22, 25; 24:2; John 11:48; 14:27) shows that the word may signify "leave standing, let remain." The foundation with which they became acquainted a long time ago (5:12) is solid. The ptcp gains an imperatival force from the hortatory subjunctive φερώμεθα, "let us be carried forward."

ʲ In the expression τὸν τῆς ἀρχῆς τοῦ Χριστοῦ λόγον, "the elementary teaching of Christ," the gen τοῦ Χριστοῦ could be obj (i.e., the elementary teaching concerning Christ; cf. JB, NIV, "the elementary teaching(s) about Christ") or it could be subj (i.e., "Christ's initial teaching"). Adams (*NTS* 13 [1966–67] 381–84) has argued for the latter rendering, which yields the sense: "let us leave on one side Christ's original teaching, and let us advance towards maturity." He interprets the ptcp ἀφέντες to mean "leave behind," on the understanding that the community was preoccupied with the content of Christ's own teaching, but had failed to grasp the significance of his person and work (383). It seems preferable to interpret the phrase as an obj gen descriptive of Christian instruction. Cf. TEV: "the first lessons of the Christian message."

ᵏ EV have tended to ignore the passive voice in the hortatory φερώμεθα (e.g., RSV, NIV: "let us leave . . . and go on"; TEV: "let us go forward"). The pass implies the agency of God and conveys the thought of surrender to God's active influence, rather than personal striving for a goal (so Westcott, 145).

ˡ The translation of the term τελειότης is difficult. The term describes a goal rather than a process. The problem with translating this word with "maturity" is the implication that a state is being described that is achieved gradually by successive steps of development. What is described, however, is the accomplishment of God through Jesus Christ. The English "perfection" would be suitable only if it were clearly understood that perfection is the result of calling rather than of possession, of the action by God the Judge (cf. 10:14) rather than of a gradual transformation of character.

m The word μετανοίας is used as a gen of apposition or definition, which indicates the substance of which the preceding noun θεμέλιον, "foundation," consists, i.e., "consisting of repentance" (Turner, *Grammar,* 3:214–15).

n The translation reflects the reading διδαχήν (accusative), supported by P^{46} B the OL *d* and the Syriac Peshitta, rather than the gen διδαχῆς, which enjoys the strong support of good representatives of the major types of text (ℵ A C D I K P 33 81 614 1739 Byzantine Lectionaries it vg sy^h co arm). Although the support for διδαχήν is relatively slight, it is early and weighty. It is probable that the surrounding gen led to the alteration of the text to διδαχῆς in the remainder of the MS tradition (so Zuntz, *Text of the Epistles,* 93–94; Tasker, *NTS* 1 [1954–55] 186; Beare, *JBL* 63 [1944] 394; cf. BDF §168[2]; for the contrary opinion that the accusative διδαχήν is a later stylistic improvement introduced to avoid so many gen, see Metzger, *Textual Commentary,* 666). The significance of reading διδαχήν lies in the virtual equation of repentance from works that lead to death and faith in God with the catechetical instruction that undergirds baptism and laying on of hands, since διδαχήν is epexegetical of θεμέλιον, "foundation."

o It is difficult to determine whether the writer intended to refer to "baptisms" or "cleansing rites, ablutions" when he used the pl βαπτισμῶν (sg, βαπτισμός). The customary term for baptism in the NT is βάπτισμα. Although Josephus used the term βαπτισμός in reference to the baptism of John (*Ant.* 18.117), elsewhere in the NT (Mark 7:8; Heb 9:10) the term denotes ritualistic "washings," and not baptism. The translation reflects the conviction that the pl form βαπτισμῶν was chosen to suggest a comparison between Jewish and Christian cleansing rites. Cf. BDF §109(2); Adams, *NTS* 13 [1966–67] 383.

p The effect of the change in conj from τε to καί (τε . . . τε . . . καί . . .) is to link "resurrection" and "judgment" more closely together than the other aspects of the verse (BDF §444[4]).

q The translation seeks to express the force of the conj ἐάνπερ; the ptcp -περ used with conditional conj ἐάν emphasizes that the action is in spite of opposition, i.e., "if in spite of opposition God permits" (BDF §237).

r Grammatically, vv 4–6 constitute a long, complex sentence that begins emphatically with an adj as predicate (ἀδύνατον, "impossible") and carries an inf as complement in v 6 (ἀνακαινίζειν, "to renew, restore"). The statement is set forth by two blocks of well-differentiated ptcp, the first consisting of five aor with a definite article (vv 4–6*a*), and the second of two present ptcp without the definite article (v 6*b*). The adv ἅπαξ, "once," in v 4 and πάλιν, "again," in v 6 indicate the enunciation of the statement. The syntactical construction is open to different interpretations.

The translation reflects the commonly accepted interpretation, which associates the adj ἀδύνατον with the inf in v 6. The five aor ptcp introduced by the article supply the direct obj of the inf, while the phrase εἰς μετάνοιαν, "repentance," is the indirect obj, i.e., "it is impossible to renew to repentance those who once . . . because they are crucifying again."

A different interpretation has been proposed by Proulx and Schökel (*Bib* 56 [1975] 197–201), who make the phrase εἰς μετάνοιαν dependent not on the inf ἀνακαινίζειν (i.e., "to renew to repentance") but on the present ptcp ἀνασταυροῦντας (i.e., "crucifying . . . with a view to repentance"). They translate, "As for those who have once . . . and have fallen away, it is impossible to renew them again, crucifying for them a second time the Son of God and exposing him to shame that they might repent." Alternatively, they propose that it is possible that the functions of the principal and subordinate clauses have been inverted (cf. Zerwick, *Biblical Greek* §263). In that case, the translation would read: "It is impossible to crucify a second time the Son of God for one's own repentance, so making a mockery of him, in order to renew again those who have once . . ." (For a recapitulation in English of some of the lines of their argument, see Sabourin, *BTB* 6 [1976] 264–71).

s This is the first occurrence of the important term ἅπαξ, "once" (6:4; 9:7, 26, 27, 28; 10:2; 12:26, 27), which in Hebrews carries a qualitative rather than merely a numeric nuance. It connotes the sufficiency, validity, and permanance of what Christ has accomplished and is accomplishing. Cf. A. Winter, "ἅπαξ ἐφάπαξ im Hebräerbrief," Dissertation, Gregorian Pontifical University, Rome, 1960; Wikgren, *NTS* 6 [1959–60] 162: "As the sacrifice of Christ was an ἐφάπαξ ("once-for-all") event, so is the believer's participation in it."

t The use of the ptcp γευσαμένους here, and in v 5, reflects the common metaphorical usage of a verb meaning "to taste" throughout hellenistic Gk. in the sense of "to experience" (cf. Williamson, *Philo,* 305, for examples from Philo; Heb 2:9, "to experience death").

ᵘ In the expression καλὸν γευσαμένους θεοῦ ῥῆμα, the direct obj of the verb is virtually a substantival clause, i.e., "the goodness of God's word," not "the good word of God" (as in NASB, JB). Cf. Moule, *Idiom-Book*, 36; F. Zorell, "Notae lexicales in N. T.," *Bib* 1 (1920) 264–65.

ᵛ The aor ptcp παραπεσόντας could be conditional, i.e., "and if they have fallen away" (so RSV, NIV; cf. P. E. Hughes, *WTJ* 35 [1973] 150).

ʷ The present ptcp ἀνασταυροῦντας and παραδειγματίζοντας have been treated as causal ("because they are crucifying . . . and exposing to shame"), in accordance with the judgment of Moulton (*Grammar*, 1:230; cf. RSV, NEB, TEV, NIV). J. K. Elliott (*BT* 28 [1977] 330–32) takes the two ptcp in a contemporaneous, temporal sense rather than a causal sense, and translates, "it is impossible to bring them back again to repentance while they are crucifying the Son of God with their own hands and making mock of his death." On this understanding, the falling away is not irreversible. "Repentance is impossible only while those who sinned are still doing so" (331). But this is a truism, which vitiates the force of the statement. It is more appropriate to take the ptcp as causal than temporal in this context; they indicate why it is impossible to restore such people to repentance (cf. F. F. Bruce, 124).

ˣ The reflexive pronoun ἑαυτοῖς is used as a dative of disadvantage, i.e., "against themselves," or "to their loss" (A. T. Robertson, *Grammar*, 539; cf. BDF § 61, "to their own hurt").

ʸ The verb ἀνασταυροῦν is frequently synonymous in meaning with the simple form, with no sense of repetition (so Jos., *J. W.* 1.97; 2.75, 241, 253, 306; 5.449; *Ant.* 2.73; 6.374; 11.246; *Life* 420). But the presence of the phrase πάλιν ἀνακαινίζειν, "to restore again," just before the verb already supports the translation "to crucify a second time" (so Schneider, *TDNT* 7:583–84).

ᶻ For the compressed expression καὶ κατάρας ἐγγύς, Zerwick and Grosvenor (*Grammatical Analysis*, 665) suggest the translation "and it is threatened with a curse."

ᵃᵃ The writer's choice of the pf tense πεπείσμεθα conveys well his confidence in the members of the community, i.e., "we remain sure."

ᵇᵇ The phrase καὶ ἐχόμενα σωτηρίας is epexegetical of τὰ κρείσσονα, "the better things," explaining the sense in which that general descriptive term is meant.

ᶜᶜ The inf ἐπιλαθέσθαι is used in a free way to express a consecutive sense ("to the extent of forgetting") or result ("so as to forget"). Cf. BDF §391(4); Moulton, *Grammar*, 1:204, 210; Burton, *Moods and Tenses* §371.

ᵈᵈ The aor tense in ἐνεδείξασθε is in itself neutral; it can refer to one or many occasions. The aor ptcp διακονήσαντες, "when you served," suggests that a particular event may be in mind (cf. 10:32–34).

ᵉᵉ The prep phrase εἰς τὸ ὄνομα is ambiguous. It may qualify the love demonstrated in past and present service to the people of God as done "for God's sake" (cf. RSV, NEB); or it may qualify the love as shown for God himself, i.e., "for his name" (cf. NIV); or the phrase may reflect a formula found in hellenistic legal and commercial papyri, indicating that the deeds of love are dedicated to God. See R. G. Bratcher, "The 'Name' in Prepositional Phrases in the New Testament," *BT* 14 (1963) 74–75.

ᶠᶠ The translation reflects the familiar designation of the people of God as οἱ ἅγιοι (so TEV; RSV, "the saints"; NEB, NIV, "his people").

ᵍᵍ After the negative μή, δέ has the strong adversative force of ἀλλά as in 4:13 (so Turner, *Grammar*, 3:331).

Form/Structure/Setting

Although it is commonly recognized that 5:11–6:20 forms a literary unit within the structure of Hebrews, there has been no general agreement concerning its character or logical scheme. There has been a broad tendency to regard 5:11–6:20 as an abrupt parenetic digression that interrupts the exposition of Christ as high priest (e.g., Riggenbach, xxviii; Michel, 231; Kuss, 5; F. F. Bruce, 106; Buchanan, 100–101). This is the inevitable result of the failure to recognize the conclusion of a major division in 5:9–10, with the announcement of the subject to be treated in the central portion of the sermon. If a major division has been indicated at 4:14 (e.g., F. F. Bruce, lxiii, 84) or at 5:1 (e.g., Buchanan, 1, 84), it is natural to describe the writer as "turning aside" or "interrupting" his argumentation for further exhortation. It is preferable to regard the unit as a preliminary exhortation, which provides an appropriate preamble to the central exposition that follows in 7:1–10:18 (see *Introduction* to 5:11–10:39).

A consideration of the content of 5:11–6:20 appears to have been the primary factor in the common division of this unit into two sections, the first extending from 5:11 to 6:8, and the second from 6:9 to 6:20. Within this scheme, the severity with which the community is reproved in 5:11–6:8 is balanced by the encouragement extended in 6:9–20. The striking formulation of 6:8 is accordingly regarded as the conclusion to the first paragraph, while the change in tone and the reference to the perspectives of salvation in 6:9 are regarded as signaling the introduction of a new paragraph (so Riggenbach, 138; Michel, 230; Spicq, 2:141; Teodorico, 103–4; Collins, *VD* 26 [1948] 144–51, 193–206).

Unfortunately, this division is not supported by the literary indications in the text. The introduction and repetition of the colorful word νωθροί, "sluggish," in 5:11 and 6:12 is intentional and establishes an *inclusio*, which frames 5:11–6:12 as a literary unit. This word occurs only here in Hebrews, and nowhere else in the NT. Its literary function corresponds to the use of ἀπιστία in 3:12 and 3:19 to indicate the limits of a paragraph of comment on the biblical citation of Ps 95:7*b*–11 (see *Form/Structure/Setting* on 3:7–19). The writer's proven dependence upon literary procedures to enable his readers and auditors to follow the conceptual development of the sermon is the crucial consideration in determining the limits of this section (so Vanhoye, *La structure*, 115; Andriessen, *NRT* 96 [1974] 1055–56; Gyllenberg, "Zur Exegese," 73–82; Peterson, *RTR* 35 [1976] 14–15; Mora, *La Carta*, 18). The accuracy of this analysis is confirmed by the fact that 5:11–6:12 consists of exhortation. With 6:13 there is a change in literary genre. It is no longer appropriate to speak of exhortation, but rather of exposition of the firm character of the promises extended to those who remain faithful to God (Vanhoye, *La structure*, 121).

The recognition of the rhetorical function of νωθροί, "sluggish," in 5:11–6:12 has important bearing upon proposed source criticism of this unit. Kosmala (*Hebräer, Essener, Christen*, 17–31), for example, was convinced that the primitive text of Hebrews had been expanded by interpolations. To rid the present text of apparent contradictions, he proposed the deletion of 5:11*b*–14, and of 6:5, 6*b* as well. This proposal, which has no support in the MS tradition, is sufficiently refuted by an analysis of the literary structure of the text. The key term νωθροί, which establishes the *inclusio* in 5:11, would be affected by the deletion (Vanhoye, *La structure*, 115, n. 14).

The importance of this unit for determining the historical circumstances that occasioned the preparation of Hebrews has been generally appreciated. Mora, for example, who has investigated Hebrews as a document of early Christian pastoral care, regards 5:11–6:20 as "the key text for the interpretation of Hebrews" (*La Carta*, 18; cf. Peterson, *RTR* 35 [1976] 14–21; contrast Andriessen, *NRT* 96 [1974] 1054–66). Käsemann found in 5:11–6:12 a main support for the gnostic interpretation of Hebrews (*Das wandernde Gottesvolk*, 117–24). He pointed out that in gnosticism, as in the mystery religions, those who are about to receive the primary revelation (the λόγος τέλειος, i.e., the word for those who are "perfect") are questioned concerning their worthiness and the testing to which they have been exposed. On the basis of alleged parallels with the expression in *Barnabas* (1:5; 4:11; 5:4), Käsemann contended that 5:11–6:12 corresponds to this preliminary examination, while the instruction in 7:1–10:39 is the λόγος τέλειος itself. The decisive technical vocabulary of gnosticism, however, is absent from Hebrews, and even the expression λόγος τέλειος was coined by Käsemann himself. Moreover, the idea of growth or progressive initiation into perfection through successive stages of enlightenment is not present in 5:11–6:12. The writer acknowledges no intermediate stage between childhood and adulthood. He does not suggest that the lack of gnosis (esoteric "knowledge") within the community implies a lack of redemption or an inability to approach God (cf. 4:16). The writer is persuaded that "solid food" is not the privilege of a few initiates who have been exposed to deeper truths or have attained a higher level of existence, but is intended for all Christians (so Thüsing, *TTZ* 76 [1967] 233–34, 240–41). For the writer "solid food" represents Christian truth undergirded by a profound appreciation of Christ and his work of redemption. In 5:11–14 "milk" designates elementary instruction; in gnosticism it is the food of "the perfect" who have been initiated into the word of knowledge (cf. *Odes Sol.* 19). It is imperative, therefore, to avoid the gnostic hypothesis in the interpretation of 5:11–6:12 and to allow the text to determine its distinctive perspectives on the condition of the community.

Comment

It is commonly assumed on the basis of 5:11–6:3 that the community addressed had failed to mature in faith and understanding, and consequently required rudimentary instruction rather than the advanced exposition of Christ's priesthood and sacrifice presented in 7:1–10:18. The problem with this reconstruction of the situation is that it is not supported by the detail of the text. The biblical interpretation and the presentation of christology in 1:1–5:10 presuppose advanced Christian instruction and a level of understanding that corresponds to the adult consumption of solid food and not to a diet of milk. In addition, the writer shows no inclination to review with his hearers the foundational elements of the Christian faith. He clearly regarded the hearers as mature. He reminds them that they have ingested over a considerable period of time the instruction that qualified them to be the teachers of others (5:12). Consequently, the portrayal of them as infants who have to be nurtured with milk is not an actual description of some or of all of the members of the community. It is irony, calculated to shame them and to recall them to the stance of conviction and boldness consonant with their experience (6:4–5, 10) and hope (6:9–12). The community has deviated from its earlier course (cf. 10:32–34) by becoming sluggish in understanding (5:12). Their regression to infancy must represent a quite recent development. It was apparently an attempt to sidestep their responsibility in a world that persecuted them and held them in contempt, but it threatened their integrity. The purpose of 5:11–6:12 is to preserve the community from such aberration by reminding them of what they have experienced and what they possess through the gospel (cf. Riggenbach, 142–47, 158).

11a περὶ οὗ πολὺς ἡμῖν ὁ λόγος καὶ δυσερμήνευτος λέγειν, "We have much to say about this subject, and it is hard to explain intelligibly." To prepare the community for the development of the subject announced in vv 9–10, the writer formally declares his intention to treat it fully. In the expression περὶ οὗ it seems preferable to consider the relative pronoun οὗ as a neuter, having reference to the priesthood of Christ in its totality (i.e. "about this subject," JB; Spicq, 2:140), rather than as a masculine relative, which has for its antecedent "Melchizedek" in v 10 (i.e., "about him," NEB; Williamson, *Philo*, 278). It is the whole subject under discussion, and not simply the priesthood like Melchizedek's, that requires the skill of the writer and the attention of the community.

The rhetorical training of the writer is reflected in the wealth of literary vocabulary, idioms, and thought in vv 11–14. The discussion appears to have been aimed at a highly literate audience. As an educated person, the writer was familiar with the oratorical procedures used by speakers and writers to indicate a transition to an important subject. The expression πολὺς ὁ λόγος is a common literary phrase for "there is much to say" (e.g., Dionysius of Halicarnassus, *Roman Antiquities* 1.23.1; *First Letter to Ammaeus* 3; Lysias, *Against Pancleon* 11; Philo, *Who Is the Heir?* 133, 221). In these sources the idiom occurs in a context where a writer wishes to draw attention to the importance of the subject to be treated.

The adjective δυσερμήνευτος, "hard to explain," occurs only here in the Greek Bible. Among hellenistic writers it is used uniformly to describe a difficulty intrinsic to the material to be expounded and not extrinsic to it, i.e., a difficulty that derives from the complexity of the matter rather than the lack of skill in the writer or his audience. This is the case whether it is a question of dreams, of the colors of the light, of bitter or sweet flavors, of the course of the stars, of the nature of the soul, of the creation of the world, or of the resurrection (cf. Artemidorus, *On Dreams* 3.66; Diodorus Siculus, *World History* 2.52; Galen [ed. C. G. Kühn] 9.454; *Catalogus codicum astrologorum Graecorum* [ed. F. Cumont] 1.114.22–24; Philo, *On Dreams* 1.188; Origen, *On John* 1:21 [SC 157, 193], *Against Celsus* 5.59 [SC 150, 85], 4.37 [SC 136, 276]). This usage is consistent with the use of adjectives composed with the prefix δυσ-, which are employed in the LXX and the NT solely when the matter is difficult in itself (cf. Wis 17:1; Luke 11:46; 2 Pet 3:16). In view in v 11a is the important and profound theme announced in vv 9–10 (Andriessen, *NRT* 96 [1974] 1058; *En lisant*, 16–17).

11b   The reason it was necessary to alert the readers to the importance of the announced subject is that they have become νωθροὶ ταῖς ἀκοαῖς, "sluggish in understanding" or "hard of hearing," cf. Preisker (*TDNT* 4:1126). The choice of terms is significant in the context of v 9, where Jesus was designated "the source of eternal salvation for all who obey him" (τοῖς ὑπακούουσιν). Deafness or dullness in receptivity is a dangerous condition for those who have been called to radical obedience. The importance of responsible listening has been stressed repeatedly in the sermon (2:1, "we must pay the closest attention to what we have heard" [τοῖς ἀκουσθεῖσιν]; cf. 3:7b–8a, 15; 4:1–2, 7b). The charge of having become spiritually lethargic in v 11 resumes the challenges expressed in the previous hortatory sections and makes them more explicitly personal and relevant to the community (so Peterson, *RTR* 35 [1976] 15–16). What is implied is a lack of responsiveness to the gospel and an unwillingness to probe the deeper implications of Christian commitment and to respond with faith and obedience (cf. 2:1–4; 4:1–2). If this apathetic attitude was not checked, it would lead to spiritual inertia and the erosion of faith and hope.

12   The key to the interpretation of vv 12–14 is the recognition of the presence of irony. The rebuke administered in v 12 may be related to a tendency to withdraw from contact with outsiders and to the loss of certainty which this presupposes. This proposal is supported by the contention that they ought to be διδάσκαλοι, "teachers," which refers specifically to an ability to communicate the faith to others (cf. Spicq, 2:143). The correlative statement that "you need someone to teach you again the elementary truths of God's revelation" is normally taken to be the writer's considered judgment on the actual condition of the community. This understanding, however, is difficult to reconcile with his determination to respond to them as to mature Christians (cf. 6:1, 3). It is possible that the hearers themselves had expressed to the writer, or to someone else, a need for rudimentary instruction (cf. Nairne, *The Epistle of Priesthood*, 333; Peterson, *RTR* 35 [1976] 17). That would explain the slightly derogatory nuance in the expression τὰ στοιχεῖα, "mere rudiments" (where the notion of basic principles is strengthened by τῆς ἀρχῆς, rendered "elementary" above; cf. Delling, *TDNT* 7:687; NEB: "the ABC of God's oracles"), as well as the touch of sarcasm in the formulation of v 12*a*. The writer's response in v 12*b*, then, is ironical.

The source of the metaphors γάλακτος, "milk," and στερεᾶς τροφῆς, "solid food," was the assimilation of education to nurture in hellenistic popular philosophy. In the ethical tradition the distinction between those at an elementary stage of instruction and those who had attained an advanced stage was commonly expressed in the comparison of infants who require a diet of milk and adults who can enjoy solid food (for references to the Greek ethical tradition, see Thüsing, *TTZ* 76 [1967] 233–34; for a review of the relevant passages in Philo, Williamson, *Philo*, 280–85; cf. 1 Cor 3:1–3). The presence of this rhetorical convention in vv 12*b*–14 has been characterized as a "pedagogical device" with which the writer sought to convince the community that they need to make greater progress in their understanding of biblical theology or of the OT when interpreted in the light of the Christ-event. Williamson, for example, asserts that the writer "inherited an understanding of education in terms of food and the various *stages* of human development" (*Philo*, 285–86 [italics mine]; cf. 277–308), and H. P. Owen finds evidence in 5:11–6:3 for speaking of "stages of ascent" (*NTS* 3 [1956–57] 243–53). Although this manner of characterization is appropriate to Epictetus or Philo, it is inappropriate to Hebrews because there is no reference in the text to an intermediate stage between infancy and adulthood. In addressing the community the writer recognizes only an either/or. The idea of progressive stages, or of development and growth toward maturity, seems *not* to have been in his mind. This is not normal pedagogics, because it acknowledges no alternative except regression to infancy or adult acceptance of responsibility. With biting irony, the writer calls the community to acknowledge its maturity, which has both ethical and theological ramifications for responsible life in the world.

13–14 The interpretation of v 13 is contingent upon a proper understanding of the phrase ἄπειρος λόγου δικαιοσύνης, "inexperienced (or, unacquainted) with the teaching about righteousness," or "unskilled in the word of righteousness." The expresssion λόγος δικαιοσύνης, however, is unusually difficult and has called forth a variety of proposals, listed below:

(1) The genitive case of δικαιοσύνης is one of definition. The expression signifies "right speech" and is to be interpreted in the light of the immediate context, which refers to a νήπιος, an "infant." One who is an infant is incapable of speaking

correctly (Riggenbach, 144–45; Michel, 236–37) or of understanding the meaning of normal speech (Schrenk, *TDNT* 2:198; BDF §165).

(2) The expression should be interpreted in a manner consonant with the
concentration of ethical vocabulary in 5:11–14. The infant does not know "what
is right" (NEB); he lacks "a moral standard" or "a principle of righteousness."
Consequently, he is unskilled in ethical reasoning (T. H. Robinson, 67; Spicq,
2:144; Owen, *NTS* 3 [1956–57] 244). He requires "instruction regarding the will
of God" (Delling, *TDNT* 8:77). A variation on this proposal acknowledges that
the formulation was drawn from the ethical teachers, but what it refers to in Hebrews is "correct theology." The person described in v 13 is unskilled in making
the basic distinctions in exegesis and consequently was unprepared to engage in
the discussion of the larger problems of christology or Christian thought
(Williamson, *Philo*, 288–92, 299; Peterson, *RTR* 35 [1976] 20).

(3) The formulation is synonymous with the figurative expression "strong food"
in vv 12 and 14. It has specific reference to the instruction presented in 7:1–10:18
and is roughly equivalent to "the teaching of the Christian religion" (Gyllenberg,
"Zur Exegese," 77; Thüsing, *TTZ* 76 [1967] 239–40).

(4) The formulation connotes "the teaching about righteousness" that is
foundational to Christian faith, namely "the insistence on Christ as our righteousness" (P. E. Hughes, 191).

All these proposals, we suggest, are not based on a firm linguistic foundation.
They draw their primary support from the immediate or more distant context. It
may be preferable, therefore, to take account of a technical use of the formulation in the early second century that clearly links the phrase with martyrdom. In
calling for unceasing perseverance in Christian hope, Polycarp appeals to Christ
Jesus and says, "he endured everything. Therefore, let us become imitators of his
patient endurance and glorify him whenever we suffer for the sake of his name. I,
therefore, exhort you *to obey the word of righteousness* [πειθαρχεῖν τῷ λογῷ τῆς
δικαιοσύνης] and practice patient endurance to the limit—an endurance of which
you have had an object lesson not only in those blessed persons Ignatius, Zosimus,
and Rufus, but also in members of your own community as well as in Paul himself and
the other apostles" (*Phil.* 8.1–9.1). J. A. Kleist comments on the expression τῷ λογῷ
τῆς δικαιοσύνης: "Polycarp now shows that the great and paramount *lesson in holiness* which a Christian has received is to hold himself in readiness for martyrdom"
(ACW 1:193, n. 65 [italics mine]). Polycarp's use of the motifs of endurance to the
end and of imitation in a context referring to known martyrs as those who had
obeyed "the word of righteousness" is suggestive for the interpretation of Hebrews
(cf. Heb 6:11–12; 10:36; 13:7). If this is the proper linguistic context for interpreting v 13, it suggests that what was involved in the regression of the community was a
failure in moral character rather than in keen theological insight. The expression
ἄπειρος λόγου δικαιοσύνης acknowledges a basic moral weakness aggravated by
the fear of violent death (cf. 2:14–15). If the community had begun to avoid
contact with outsiders because they were unprepared for martyrdom, a social
setting is established for the rebuke of v 12, for the reference to the sharpening
of one's faculties in the arena of moral decision in v 14, and for the prospect of
crucifying the Son of God again and exposing him to public shame in 6:6.

In contrast to the child (v 13), the τέλειοι, "adults," are those who are prepared for στερεὰ τροφή, "solid food" (v 14). In this context, "solid food" must

have reference to the actual instruction about the high priestly office of Christ provided in 7:1–10:18, which makes explicit what was implied in the foundational truths entrusted to the community (so Thüsing, *TTZ* 76 [1967] 239–41, 275; see *Comment* on 6:1–2). The emphasis in v 14, however, falls on the further qualification of adults as those who have their spiritual faculties trained by experience to distinguish good from evil. The Stoics had used αἰσθητήριον as a technical term for an organ of sense; by metaphorical extension it acquired an ethical sense (e.g., Jer 4:19 LXX). The plural form speaks of a plurality of capacities for moral decision, which, through continual use (ἕξις), have developed into specific qualities (cf. Delling, *TDNT* 1:188; Williamson, *Philo*, 114–16). The formulation of v 14*b* seems to imply a capacity for spiritual discrimination and not simply moral discernment (Michel, 237). The period of time contemplated in v 12 (διὰ τὸν χρόνον, "by this time") has provided the community with the opportunity to achieve a condition of moral and spiritual maturity that makes them capable of sound discrimination. The play on words καλοῦ τε καὶ κακοῦ, "good and evil," evokes one strand of Jewish hope preserved in a Targumic comment on Gen 3:22: "Many people are to arise from the man, and from him will arise one people who will be capable of distinguishing between good and evil" (*Tg. Neof.* and *Tg. Ps-J.* Gen 3:22).

In the contrast posed in vv 13–14 it is significant that the writer alternates between the singular (νήπιος, "an infant") and the plural (τελείων, "adults"). It is v 14, with its description of a plurality of persons, that describes the community prior to its recent withdrawal and regression. In vv 11–14 the writer uses irony effectively to summon the house church to resume their status as adults with its attendant responsibilities.

6:1–2 The warning expressed in 5:11–14 finds an emphatic continuation in 6:1–12. The chapter break is both unwarranted and unfortunate. The initial word διό, "so then," shows distinctly that the writer did not consider the members of the house church to be infants requiring a diet of milk. Otherwise, a sound educational approach and pastoral concern would certainly have forced him to dwell on the primary instruction. In reality he knew that he could encourage them to be "carried forward to the goal of spiritual maturity" because they were prepared to receive solid food; they were experienced and exercised for distinguishing between what is wholesome and what is unwholesome (cf. Riggenbach, 158). A failure to appreciate the irony in 5:11–14 and the firm connection between these verses and 6:1 is evident when H. P. Owen, for example, speaks of "the violence of the διό" (*NTS* 3 [1956–57] 248).

When the writer urges his readers to "leave standing" (ἀφέντες, see *Note* i above) the elementary Christian teaching, he is not dismissing it but regarding it as so well established that the urgent need is for a fuller appreciation and application of that teaching. The writer is wholly optimistic about the community: a foundation has been laid (cf. 2:3–4) that need not, and cannot, be laid again (6:1, 4). The exhortation extended to the community in 6:1–12 is precisely a reminder of that solid foundation. The second clause in v 1 ("not laying again a foundation") clarifies in negative fashion the meaning of the positive injunction ("let us leave standing . . . and be carried forward"; cf. Peterson, *RTR* 35 [1976] 19). The movement to τὴν τελειότητα, "the goal of spiritual maturity," "perfection," does not call for a progress away from a simpler form or content of preaching but for a personal surrender to God's active influence within the community ("let us be carried forward [by God]"). In this context spiritual maturity implies receptivity and responsiveness to the received tradition (5:14), an earnest concern for the full realization of hope (6:11), unwavering faith and steadfast endurance (6:12).

There may be a difference between τὰ στοιχεῖα τῆς ἀρχῆς τῶν λογίων τοῦ θεοῦ, "the primary elements of the revelation of God," in 5:12 and τὸν τῆς ἀρχῆς τοῦ Χριστοῦ λόγον, "the primary word about Christ," in 6:1. The instruction mentioned ironically in 5:12 may have reference to a preliminary and insufficient teaching based upon the OT, without specific reference to Christ. The primary Christian teaching mentioned in 6:1 is described positively as a firm foundation for Christian life. This conclusion has been called into question on the ground that in none of the six items mentioned in 6:1–2 is there any reference to anything specifically Christian (e.g., Adams, *NTS* 13 [1966–67] 379–84; Weeks, *WTJ* 39 [1976] 74–76). Each of the six articles, however, is related to the high priestly christology developed in the subsequent chapters, which makes explicit the christological structure of the foundation. The call to repentance from dead works and faith in God is reviewed in 9:14 from the standpoint of the redemptive accomplishment of Jesus. There the "dead works" are defined as the external regulations associated with the Levitical priesthood in the earthly sanctuary (9:10). The discrimination between useless washings on the one hand and purification by the blood of Christ on the other (9:9–10, 19; 10:22), or between priests appointed by the imposition of hands according to the law, which in its weakness could not achieve the perfection of the people of God, and the high priest appointed by the oath of God and the power of an indestructible life (5:1 6, 7:5, 15–28) demonstrates the relationship between the foundational teaching and the advanced instruction provided in 7:1–10:18. Accordingly, in 6:1–2 the writer is not asking the community to discard one aspect of Christian instruction for another but to build upon the solid foundation already laid for them (Thüsing, *TTZ* 76 [1967] 233–46, 261–80; Peterson, *RTR* 35 [1976] 19).

Although the six articles of faith can be arranged in pairs that consider the knowledge and service of God, the cultus, and eschatology (so Thüsing, 243), acceptance of the variant reading διδαχήν, "the teaching," in v 2 calls for a different arrangement. The "catechetical instruction concerning cleansing rites and laying on of hands, the resurrection of the dead and eternal judgment" stands in apposition to "the foundation" of repentance from dead works and faith in God. This means that the laying of the foundation consisted in the provision of catechetical instruction (so Michel, 238; F. F. Bruce, 112). One implication of this interpretation is that repentance and faith were prompted, at least in part, by instruction that developed a distinctively Christian perspective on the articles of faith enumerated in v 2 (so Dunn, *Baptism*, 208).

3 The statement "and we will do this" has specific reference to the proposal put forward in v 1. At the same time it resumes the announcement made in 5:11*a* (so Vanhoye, *La structure*, 116). The writer is confident that those he has addressed in 5:11–6:2 will recognize that their regression and withdrawal from contact with others is untenable, despite the risks entailed in the resumption of a bold stance for Christ in a hostile world. The qualification, "if, that is, God allows," is not to be understood as merely a pious convention (Moffatt, 76; cf. Spicq, 2:149). The development of the christological structure of the foundational articles as well as

the attainment of the goal of spiritual maturity places both the writer and his audience in dependence upon the blessing of God (cf. vv 1a and 7).

4–6 The reason for the writer's resolve in v 3 becomes clear when it is linked to the warning in vv 4–6 by the conjunction γάρ (Solari, "The Problem of *Metanoia*," 75). The rich experience of the community provides the basis for the writer's confidence that he can proceed to develop his exposition of the high priestly office of Christ. They can be addressed in preaching and teaching because something has actually been done with and to them by God (vv 4–5). Yet the danger of apostasy was real, and not merely hypothetical, and called for the gravest possible warning (for a sketch of the history of the interpretation of 6:4–6, see Solari, 1–7).

The writer begins with an impressive list of positive statements. The ἀδύνατον, "impossible," which is placed emphatically at the beginning of the sentence, is created and conditioned by an event and by facts. A firm and vital relationship has been established between God and the community. The recital of what occurred with the reception of the gospel does not describe a succession of salvific events but the one event of salvation that is viewed from different aspects and manifestations (P. E. Hughes, *WTJ* 35 [1973] 143). Each of the positive statements is conditioned by the qualification ἅπαξ, "once," which conveys the notion of definitive occurrence (cf. Stählin, *TDNT* 1:382).

The experience of the power of the gospel (cf. 2:3–4) resulted in the saving illumination of their minds and hearts (cf. 10:32). A reference to baptism has sometimes been recognized in the term φωτισθέντας, "brought to the light" (e.g., Käsemann, *Das wandernde Gottesvolk*, 119; H. Montefiore, 108; Conzelmann, *TDNT* 9:355). Although the Syriac Peshitta translated the expression in v 4 "those who have once descended for baptism," it stands alone among the Syriac and other older versions in this understanding. The earliest usage of the verb φωτίζεσθαι and its cognate noun for baptism is found in Justin (*First Apology* 61.12; *Dial.* 39.2; 122.1–2, 6), and the description of baptism as illumination seems to have gained in popularity after this time. But prior to the middle of the second century there is no clear evidence that φωτίζειν means "to baptize." In the NT the term is used metaphorically to refer to spiritual or intellectual illumination that removes ignorance through the action of God or the preaching of the gospel (cf. John 1:9; Col 4:5; Eph 1:18; 2 Tim 1:10; Rev 18:1). What is signified is not simply instruction for salvation but the renewal of the mind and of life. In a parallel passage in Hebrews, the statement that corresponds to φωτισθέντας in v 4 is "we have received knowledge of the truth" (10:26). Illumination is not effected, but rather attested, by baptism (cf. Dunn, *Baptism*, 209–10).

What is denoted by ἅπαξ φωτισθέντας is described more fully by the clauses that follow. The verb γεύεσθαι, literally, "to taste," is appropriate to an experience that is real and personal (cf. Hughes, *WTJ* 35 [1973] 141). The two clauses introduced by the repeated participle γευσαμένους expose internal and external aspects of conversion. The "gift from heaven," which describes redemption as the free gift of God, and reception of the Holy Spirit were experienced by the congregation inwardly. The goodness of God's word and the endowment of members of the community with charismatic gifts (2:4) are what they heard and saw (so Dunn, *Baptism*, 209). Together, the clauses describe vividly the reality of the experience of personal salvation enjoyed by the Christians addressed. The Holy Spirit had not only formed the community but was bringing it to eschatological fulfillment.

The present period was already pervaded by the power of the coming age, which, through Christ, had made a profound inroad upon the community. Accordingly, in vv 4–5 the writer identifies the congregation as witnesses to the fact that God's salvation and presence are the unquestionable reality of their lives.

If those who have enjoyed a full and authentic Christian experience should then fall away, a renewal to repentance is impossible (v 6). Stylistically, the final aorist participle, παραπεσόντας, "fall away," stands out, in contrast to the previous four (which expressed the positive character of the experience of the community), as something unjustified and tragic (Proulx and Schökel, *Bib* 56 [1975] 196). The aorist tense indicates a decisive moment of commitment to apostasy. In the LXX, the term παραπίπτειν has reference to the expression of a total attitude reflecting delibrate and calculated renunciation of God (Ezek 20:27; 22:4; Wis 6:9; 12:2; cf. Michaelis, *TDNT* 6:171; P. E. Hughes, *WTJ* 35 [1973] 146–50). In Hebrews it is equivalent to the expression ἀποστῆναι ἀπὸ θεοῦ ζῶντος, "to fall away from the living God," in 3:12. Apostasy entailed a decisive rejection of God's gifts, similar to the rejection of the divine promise by the Exodus generation at Kadesh (3:7–4:2; cf. McCullough, *BibTh* 20 [1974] 2–3). In Hebrews the characteristic terms for sin that display contempt for God are compounds of παρα-, many of which occur nowhere else in the NT: παραδειγματίζειν, "to expose to public humiliation" (6:6), παραπικραίνειν, "to rebel" (3:16), παραπικρασμός, "rebellion" (3:8, 15), παραρρεῖν, "to drift away" (2:1), παραφέρειν, "to carry away" (13:9), and παρειμένος, "being listless" (12:12) (Proulx and Schökel, *Bib* 56 [1975] 198). The nuance in the participle παραπεσόντας in v 6 is brought out sharply by the present participles ἀνασταυροῦντας, "crucifying again [the Son of God]," and παραδειγματίζοντας, "exposing [him] to public humiliation," which express the odious consequences of the decision to spurn the gifts of God. Specific reference to "the Son of God" serves to remind the community sharply of its own baptismal confession (4:14). What is visualized by the expressions in v 6 is every form of departure from faith in the crucified Son of God. This could entail a return to Jewish convictions and practices as well as the public denial of faith in Christ under pressure from a magistrate or a hostile crowd, simply for personal advantage (cf. Mark 8:34–38; *Herm. Sim.* 8.8.2; 9.19.1).

The assertion "it is impossible to restore them to repentance" is parallel to the notion of laying again the foundation concerning repentance in v 1. There the primary word concerning Christ was the foundation, which had to be left standing and which could not be recast. This thought is reiterated precisely in v 6; it is impossible to seek to lay another foundation than the one that has been laid and is sustaining the people of God. In Jewish intertestamental and later literature, it is strongly emphasized that repentance was the gift of God (Wis 12:10: "You gave them a chance to repent"; Pr Man 8: "You have given me, a sinner, repentance"; cf. Acts 5:31; 11:18; *1 Clem.* 7:14). In the eschatological perspective of Hebrews, there is no other repentance than that provided by God through Jesus Christ. There is no salvation apart from the purification for sins accomplished by the divine Son in the final period of God's redemptive activity (1:1–3). The ἀδύνατον, which is used absolutely and without qualification in v 4, expresses an impossibility because the apostate repudiates the only basis upon which repentance can be extended (cf. Williamson, *Philo*, 249–51). To repudiate Christ is to embrace the "impossible."

7–8   The presence of γάρ, "for," establishes that vv 7–8 are an integral part of the argument in vv 4–6. The force of the γάρ may be causal or explanatory. Verbrugge (*CTJ* 15 [1980] 62–63) prefers a causal notion; the writer can make the assertion expressed in vv 4–6 *because* he knows that land which has been well watered by frequent rain and cultivated will face destruction if it produces only thorns and thistles instead of useful crops. It seems equally valid to regard the γάρ as having the force of further explanation. The agricultural illustration clarifies the appropriateness of the warning in vv 4–6. The recital of the blessings and advantages enjoyed by the community in vv 4–5 demonstrates that they are like land that receives frequent rain and is cared for by God (cf. Deut. 11:11–12). There is a firm basis for confidence that the community will share in further blessing from God (v 7*b*; cf. 13:7, 17). But if the Christian community should become apostate, it would be like a field which was well watered and cultivated, but which then produced only thorns and thistles (v 8). In the parable all interest is concentrated on the harvest, rather than on preliminary stages of growth. What is decisive is what is produced. The issue is usefulness or worthlessness. The initial advantage described is the same; it is only the final result that is different (cf. Williamson, *Philo*, 233–41).

The use of an agricultural illustration of this kind was common in antiquity (e.g., Plato, *Republic* 492A; Isa 5:1–7; 28:23–29; Ezek 19:10–14; cf. Matt 3:10; 7:16). The formulation of v 8 makes a clear allusion to Gen 3:17–18, where the growth of "thorns and thistles" is the consequence of the curse invoked by human disobedience. According to v 8, the sober consequence of apostasy would be the consigning of life to the curse that hangs over a field producing only thorns and thistles, whose "end" (τέλος) is to be set on fire. The significance of the imagery is driven home when subsequently in Hebrews fire is associated with the severity of the eschatological judgment that will consume the adversaries of God (10:27; 12:29; see 6:2; cf. Priesker, *TDNT* 2:331).

The motif of blessing (v 7) and curse (v 8) places the discussion firmly in a covenantal context. The promise of blessing is attached to obedience, but the curse sanction is invoked in opposition to apostasy and disobedience (cf. Deut 11:26–28). It is possible that in vv 7–8 the writer was thinking of the infamous cities of the Jordan plain, which were "well watered like the garden of the Lord" (Gen 13:10) but which were subsequently judged by God and were destroyed by fire (Gen 19:24). These cities were held up to the covenant people to illustrate the expectation of those who abandoned God and who expressed contempt for the covenant (Deut 29:22–25; cf. Verbrugge, *CTJ* 15 [1980] 65–66). The members of the congregation had experienced the blessing of God's salvation. Those who committed apostasy must expect the imposing of the curse sanctions of the covenant (cf. 10:29; Williamson, *Philo*, 246).

9   The optimism concerning the congregation expressed in vv 1–3 is reiterated impressively in v 9 ("we remain sure"). The basis of the writer's confidence is that a true work of God has taken place among them. Although it was necessary to warn them sternly of the consequences of apostasy because they had become unreceptive (5:11) and were withdrawing from contact with others (5:12), they nevertheless displayed indisputable evidence of God's blessing (2:4; 6:4–5, 7; cf. Ballarini, *ScC* 106 [1978] 368–71). The severity of vv 4–8 is softened when the writer addresses the community for the first (and only) time as ἀγαπητοί, "dear friends." In their case he remains sure of τὰ κρείσσονα, "the better things," where the article is significant and looks back on the better of the two options contemplated in vv 7–8. They are like the field described in v 7, which has already received the blessing of God and which will yet experience further blessing (so Vanhoye, *La structure*, 119–20; Andriessen, *NRT* 96 [1974] 1060; Peterson, *RTR* 35 [1976] 20–21). The expression καὶ ἐχόμενα σωτηρίας, "which accompany salvation," relates this firm expectation to God's activity on behalf of the redeemed community.

10–12 The writer's persuasion that the commitment displayed by the community was genuine was based on the recollection of their conduct in the past. If some particular occasion was in mind in v 10*a*, it is almost certainly to be identified with the events recalled in 10:32–34. At that time the members of the congregation had identified themselves with the stigma attached to the name of Jesus and had publicly demonstrated their love for him and for one another. When v 10*a* is read in the light of 10:32–34, the "work" that God will not forget must have reference to their boldness before their persecutors, their practical concern for those abused or imprisoned, and the cheerful acceptance of the seizure of their property. Their loyalty to Christ and to one another on that occasion was an experression of firm faith and compelling hope (cf. 10:34) as much as of love. In view of this, it seems that the words καὶ τῆς ἀγάπης, "and your love," are not epexegetical or explanatory of τοῦ ἔργου ὑμῶν, "your work," but identify the ultimate source of the motivation for their bold stance as love for God (cf. Peterson, *RTR* 35 [1976] 21).

The present participle διακονοῦντες, "continue to serve," in v 10*b* acknowledges that in some measure the exemplary service of fellow Christians that was the hallmark of the community in the past continued to find expression. Nevertheless, there are important hints in Hebrews that the expression of love within the congregation needed to be deepened and extended (cf. 10:24; 12:14*a*; 13:1, 3, 6). It would be unwise to distinguish sharply among the concepts of love (v 10), hope (v 11), and faith (v 12), as if the congregation were deficient only in hope and faith (Michel, 249–50). What the writer calls for is a renewal of their former zeal in every respect (cf. 10:22–24).

The admonition in vv 11–12 is addressed to each person in the house church (ἕκαστον ὑμῶν, "each one of you"; cf. 3:12, 13; 4:1, 11; 10:25; 12:15). They are all to display τὴν αὐτὴν . . . σπουδήν, "the same concern," for the realization of their hope, which they had displayed on that earlier occasion (cf. 10:34). What this implies is the ability to translate Christian conviction into action that will express the quality of hope that distinguishes the Church from other contemporary clubs and societies (cf. Bertram, *TDNT* 4:920). The clause ἄχρι τέλους, "until the end," reiterates the eschatological emphasis of 3:14; it evokes the parousia when hope will be fully realized (cf. 9:28).

The motivating concern behind the extended exhortation in 5:11–6:12 is expressed in a purpose clause in v 12; ἵνα μὴ νωθροὶ γένησθε μιμηταὶ δέ, "so that you will not become sluggish, but imitators." The unusual term νωθροί, "sluggish," "unreceptive," reflects back on the charge formulated in 5:11*b* and functions literarily to round off the hortatory section introduced at that point. The members of the house church have become sluggish and unreceptive (5:11*b*), but the renewal of the same earnest concern demonstrated in the past (6:11) will assure that they will not continue to be sluggish. The summons to be μιμηταί, "imitators," of those who were designated heirs to the promises of God prepares for the transition to 6:13–20. The theme of imitation recurs in 13:7, and in both instances faith is seen as steadfast persistence that pursues the divine promise (cf. Grässer, *Glaube*, 121–26). The qualification διὰ πίστεως καὶ μακροθυμίας, "through faith and steadfastness," is expanded in reference to include a plurality of figures, perhaps in anticipation of the development in 11:1–12:3. Originally, however, it was conventional terminology in Jewish tradition concerning Abraham (cf. *Jub.* 17:7; 19:1–9), and it is in this restricted sense that these terms are expounded in 6:13–15.

Explanation

Before the writer develops the theme of the high priestly office of the Son of God, it was necessary for him to address the fact that the community for whom he was writing had become sluggish and unreceptive to the claims of the gospel. They appeared to be unwilling to accept the deeper implications of faith and obedience. This had been implied earlier in the sermon (2:1–4; 4:1–2, 11), but it is now asserted explicitly. Dullness in understanding was a dangerous state for those who had been called to obedience (5:9, 11). The members of the house-church appear to have withdrawn from contact with outsiders and were no longer prepared to propagate their faith (5:12). They had regressed from a level of spiritual maturity attained over an extended period of years during which they had received ample instruction. These developments, which appear to be of relatively recent origin, were symptomatic of a serious erosion of faith and hope. They displayed a sharp deviation from the stance of boldness and mature commitment exhibited by the congregation on an earlier occasion (10:32–34). They may have been induced by the acute realization that commitment to Christ and the gospel entailed loss, and even martyrdom (5:13). The purpose of 5:11–14 is only indirectly to prepare the community for the core instruction in 7:1–10:18. The immediate intention is to shame them into recognizing that they are mature and must assume the responsibilities that accrue to a spiritually mature group of Christians in a hostile society.

The writer uses irony and sarcasm effectively when he speaks of infants who require a diet of milk (5:12–13). Yet this is not a factual description of the men and women he addressed. It is just a warning. What the writer actually believes his intended readers to be is expressed by the image of the adult, and this is confirmed by the solid food they have received, and continue to receive in the homily. The community is mature. The signs of regression they have displayed are an aberrational innovation that marred their integrity and imperiled their spiritual welfare. An act of deliberate apostasy would result in their permanent loss of all the benefits obtained for them by Christ. The appeal in 5:11–6:12 is an extended exhortation not to cast aside their hope but to hold it confidently until it is realized (6:11–12).

The writer remains optimistic about the congregation because he knows they have been established upon an unshakable foundation. The exhortation extended to the community is precisely a reminder of that solid foundation. The intention of the stern warning in 6:4–6, consequently, is positive. There the writer recalls for his audience what they possess and what they have experienced as the result of God's redemptive activity through Christ. God's presence and salvation are the undoubted reality of their lives. They have participated in the eschatological gifts of spiritual insight and renewal, the Holy Spirit, and the intrusion of the mighty deeds of the coming aeon into the present situation. If they were to withdraw from Christ in an act of apostasy, they would be witnesses against themselves. They are a well-watered and cultivated field capable of producing the useful harvest that God expects (6:7). They must not succumb to the temptation to become weary of being God's people in a world that rejects their witness and holds them in contempt. To repudiate Christ would entail unbelief and the radical disobedience that makes inevitable the imposing of the curse sanctions of the covenant (6:8). That we do not choose the impossible, but that we enjoy the perfection freely given to us in Christ, is the sum of 6:4–6. This calls for a renewal of the same earnest concern demonstrated on an earlier difficult occasion, when the community had openly identified itself with the stigma attached to the name of Christ and had given tangible expression to its love, hope, and faith.

The severity of the warning in 5:11–6:12 is thoroughly understandable. The writer addressed a situation that threatened to engulf and destroy his friends. If the tendency to drift from their commitment to the gospel and to become unreceptive to its implications for the claim of God upon their lives were not checked, they might flagrantly and contemptuously reject the efficacy of the sacrifice of Christ. The congregation needed to be reminded that there was only one sacrifice for sins (10:26) and one basis upon which repentance could be extended (6:6). Writing from a distance and dependent upon the performance of the written word alone, the writer had to address them in terms that would expose the peril of spiritual immaturity and recall them to their previous stance of confidence in their experience and expectations. Pastoral concern for his friends is evident in every line of this extended section. The writer makes use of biting irony, confident assurance, sharp warning, and warm encouragement to cajole the community into recognizing that they cannot turn back the clock and deny the reality of the eschatological salvation that they have experienced.

B. A Basis for Confidence and Steadfastness   (6:13–20)

Bibliography

Babel, R. *La foi d'Abraham dans le Nouveau Testament.* Paris: Gabalda, 1970. **Baird, W.** "Abraham in the New Testament: Tradition and the New Identity." *Int* 42 (1988) 367–79. **Cassien, J.** "Jésus le Précurseur (Hébr VI, 19–20)." *Th* 27 (1956) 104–22. **Colacci, M.** "Il Semen Abrahae alla luce del Vecchio e de Nuovo Testamento." *Bib* 21 (1940) 1–27. **Daniélou, J.** "Abraham dans la tradition chrétienne." *CSion* 5 (1951) 68–87. **Démann, P.** "La signification d'Abraham dans la perspective du Nouveau Testament." *CSion* 5 (1951) 44–67. **Derescon, K.** "De divino foedere cum patriarchis." *Anton* 27 (1957) 11–38. **Dyck, T. L.** "Jesus Our Pioneer." 96–103. **Eitrem, S.** "De Servatore mundi navis gubernature." *ConNT* 4 (1940) 5–8. **Ellingworth, P.** "Jesus and the Universe in Hebrews." *EvQ* 58 (1986) 337–50. ———. "Just Like Melchizedek." *BT* 28 (1977) 236–39. **Gehman, H. S.** "The Oath in the Old Testament: Its Vocabulary, Idiom and Syntax; Its Semantics and Theology in the Masoretic Text and the Septuagint." In *Grace upon Grace.* Ed. J. I. Cook. Grand Rapids: Eerdmans, 1975.

51–63. **Grässer, E.** *Der Glaube im Hebräerbrief.* 25–35, 115–17. **Grossouw, W.** "L'espérance dans le Nouveau Testament." *RB* 61 (1954) 508–32. **Hilgert, E.** *The Ship and Related Symbols in the New Testament.* Assen: Vangoram, 1962. 9–11, 19–25, 31–45, 133–36. **Hofius, O.** "Die Unabänderlichkeit des göttlichen Heilsratschlusse: Erwägungen zur Herkunft eines neutestamentlichen Theologumenon." *ZNW* 64 (1973) 135–45. ———. *Der Vorhang vor dem Thron Gottes.* 1–48, 84–96. **Jacobs, E.** "Abraham et sa signification pour la foi chrétienne." *RHPR* 42 (1962) 148–56. **Kennedy, C. A.** "Early Christians and the Anchor." *BA* 38 (1975) 115–24. **Kirsch, J. B.** "Ancre." *DACL* 1:2 (1907) 1999–2031. **Köster, H.** "Die Auslegung der Abraham-Verheissung in Hebräer 6." In *Studien zur Theologie der alttestamentlichen Überlieferung.* FS G. von Rad. Ed. R. Rendtorff and K. Koch. Neukirchen: Moers, 1961. 95–109. **Laub, F.** *Bekenntnis und Auslegung.* 244–46. **Lindeskog, G.** "The Veil of the Temple." *ConNT* 11 (1947) 132–37. **Mayer, G.** "Aspekte des Abrahambildes in der hellenistisch-jüdischen Literatur." *EvT* 32 (1972) 118–27. **Melbourne, B. L.** "An Examination of the Historical-Jesus Motif in the Epistle to the Hebrews." *AUSS* 26 (1988) 281–97. **Mora, G.** *La Carta a los Hebreos como Escrito Pastoral.* 205–7. **Nicolau, M.** "La esperanza en la Carta a los Hebreos." In *La esperanza en la Biblia* (XXX Semana Bíblica Española, 1972). 187–202. **Rice, G. E.** "The Chiastic Structure of the Central Section of the Epistle to the Hebrews." *AUSS* 19 (1981) 243–46. ———. "Hebrews 6:19: Analysis of Some Assumptions Concerning *ΚΑΤΑΠΕΤΑΣΜΑ.*" *AUSS* 25 (1987) 65–71. **Robinson, W.** "The Eschatology of the Epistle to the Hebrews: A Study in the Christian Doctrine of Hope." *Enc* 22 (1961) 37–51. **Rogers, C.** "The Covenant with Abraham and Its Historical Setting." *BSac* 127 (1970) 214–56. **Rose, C.** "Verheissung und Erfüllung: Zum Verständnis von *ἐπαγγελία* im Hebräerbrief." *BZ* 33 (1989) 60–80. **Schröger, F.** *Der Verfasser des Hebräerbriefes.* 127–30, 202–3. **Spicq, C.** "*Ἄγκυρα* et *πρόδρομος* dans Hébr. VI. 19–20." *ST* 3 (1949) 185–87. ———. "L'Épître aux Hébreux et Philon: Un cas d'insertion de la littérature sacrée dans la culture profane du Ier siècle (Hébr. V, 11–VI, 20 et le 'De sacrificiis Abelis et Caini' de Philon)." *ANRW* 25.4 (1987) 3602–18. **Swetnam, J.** *Jesus and Isaac.* 90, 184–88. **Teodorico, P.** "Metafore nautiche in Ebr. 2,1 e 6,19." *RivB* 6 (1958) 33–49. **Vernet, J. M.** "Cristo, él que abre el camino." *Sal* 47 (1985) 419–31. **White, H. E.** "The Divine Oath in Genesis." *JBL* 92 (1973) 165–79. **Williamson, R.** *Philo and the Epistle to the Hebrews.* 201–12.

Translation

[13] *When God made a promise*[a] *to Abraham, since he could swear by no one greater he swore by*[b] *himself,*[c] [14] *saying, "Yes,*[d] *I will certainly*[e] *bless you and give you numerous descendants."* [15] *And thus after steadfast endurance,*[f] *Abraham received the promise.* [16] *For men swear by someone greater than themselves, and the oath serves as confirmation and puts an end to all argument.* [17] *Because*[g] *God wanted to make especially plain*[h] *to the heirs of his promise the irrevocable character of his resolve, he confirmed it by means of an oath,* [18] *so that by two irrevocable facts in which it is impossible for God*[i] *to lie, we who had fled for refuge might have strong incentive to hold fast*[j] *to the hope which is placed in front of us.* [19] *We have this hope as an anchor for life,*[k] *safe and secure.*[l] *It enters*[m] *the inner sanctuary behind the curtain,* [20] *where Jesus has entered on our behalf*[n] *as forerunner, having become a high priest forever, just like Melchizedek.*[o]

Notes

[a] The aor ptcp *ἐπαγγειλάμενος* is temporal, expressing action contemporaneous with the main verb (Turner, *Grammar*, 3:80).

[b] A special use of the prep *κατά* with the verb of swearing gives the resultant meaning "he swore by himself" (Moule, *Idiom-Book*, 60).

ᶜ In literary Gk., a principal action is frequently expressed by a ptcp and a subordinate one by a main verb. Since the dominant idea in 6:13 is the promise, and the swearing of an oath was only an attendant circumstance, this may be a case of the transposition of ptcp and finite verb. If so, translate, "Swearing by himself (since he could swear by no one greater), God made a promise to Abraham, saying . . ." For the construction, see Zerwick, *Biblical Greek* §§263, 376, and the discussion of the relative importance of the ptcp and inf in the *Comment* on 6:6.

ᵈ The particle εἰ μήν (P⁴⁶ ℵ A B C D) is unique to Hebrews in the NT, but is well attested in the LXX and in the papyri as a particle of solemn affirmation or corroboration of an oath. Turner (*Grammar*, 3:366) proposes that it be translated "yes." (Cf. BDF §441[1]; A.T. Robertson, *Grammar*, 192–93, 1024, 1150.)

ᵉ In the LXX, the Heb. inf absolute was customarily translated by adding a cognate or related ptcp to a finite verb to provide emphasis and certainty to the expression (cf. Zerwick, *Biblical Greek* §§60, 369; BDF §442; Moule, *Idiom-Book*, 178).

ᶠ The ptcp μακροθυμήσας is to be understood as circumstantial, not causative. This follows from the use of the gen with διά in v 12 (διὰ πίστεως καὶ μακροθυμίας, "with faith and steadfast endurance"), which implies that the faith and patient endurance were the circumstances of the acquiring of the promises, not the cause (which would have been expressed by διά with the accusative [so Swetnam, *Jesus and Isaac*, 185]).

ᵍ The expression ἐν ᾧ introduces a causal clause, as in 2:18 (cf. Moule, *Idiom-Book*, 131–32; BDF §219[2]).

ʰ Although the adj περισσότερον is comparative in form, its meaning is emphatic and elative. In Koine Gk., there was a decline in the use of the superlative form, and the comparative was pressed into service to take its place (cf. BDF §60[1], and the use of the adv form περισσοτέρως in 2:1; 13:19). If the adj is regarded as comparative, it would be translated "more forcefully," "more convincingly."

ⁱ The writer ordinarily uses the noun θεός with the article (cf. vv 10, 13, 17), and the article τόν is attested in P⁴⁶ ℵ A C P 33 1739 and in citations in Eus, Did, Chr, and Cyr. The presence of the article would call for the translation "our God." Zuntz (*Text of the Epistles*, 130) urged that the absence of the article in B, D, and the majority of later authorities was correct and that the anarthrous θεόν functions in practice as a participial clause: "It is impossible for *one who is God* to lie."

ʲ The inf κρατῆσαι could express either purpose or result. Turner (*Grammar*, 3: 72) proposed to read the term as an ingressive aor, i.e., "begin to grasp" (cf. Zerwick, *Biblical Greek*, §250).

ᵏ The term ψυχή, which is sometimes translated "soul," is used of the whole person, as in 10:38, 39; 13:7.

ˡ In the Gk. text, as in the translation, the adj ἀσφαλῆ τε καὶ βεβαίαν are separated from the noun they qualify (viz., ἄγκυραν, "anchor") for the sake of emphasis (cf., A.T. Robertson, *Grammar*, 417–18).

ᵐ The syntax of the phrase καὶ εἰσερχομένην is debated. The translation reflects the judgment that the antecedent is ἐλπίδος, "hope," of which the relative ἥν in v 19 is the direct complement and εἰσερχομένην the third of three attributes of hope (so Cassien, *Th* 27 (1956) 109–10). Alternatively, the καί can be understood to explain "anchor," and then the ptcp εἰσερχομένην has a causal nuance: the anchor is safe and secure "because it enters" (so Hofius, *Vorhang*, 87, n. 226).

ⁿ It seems more natural to regard ὑπὲρ ἡμῶν, "on our behalf," as dependent upon the finite verb εἰσῆλθεν, "he has entered," rather than on πρόδρομος, "forerunner" (cf. 9:24, where the expression ὑπὲρ ἡμῶν must be attached to the verb). For a discussion of this issue, see Cassien, *Th* 27 (1956) 104–6.

ᵒ For the translation of the phrase κατὰ τὴν τάξιν Μελχισέδεκ, see *Note* s to 5:6.

Form/Structure/Setting

The introduction of a new literary unit in 6:13 is indicated by a simple change in genre. The writer turns from exhortation to an exposition of the reliability of the divine promise extended to Christians through the high priestly ministry of Christ. The transition from the previous unit is achieved smoothly by the repetition of catchwords introduced in 6:12. The appeal to imitate those who had acquired the promises of God through faith and steadfast endurance in 6:12 called for specification, and this is provided in 6:13–20 by reference to Abraham. He received the promise and God's confirming oath after having endured the most severe trial of his faith (vv 13–15; cf. Gen 22:1–18). The relevance of his firm faith, obedience, and patience to those who are now the heirs of God's promise is demonstrated in vv 16–20. God's promise and oath provide strong encouragement to hold firmly to the objective content of Christian hope (vv 16–18; cf. 6:11), which is defined in distinctly cultic terms (vv 19–20). The concluding reference to Jesus having become a high priest like Melchizedek (v 20) constitutes a fresh announcement of the subject announced previously in 5:10, and prepares for the development of this theme in 7:1–28 (cf. Vanhoye, *La structure*, 121–23).

There is a remarkable concentration of forensic language in 6:13–18. The determination to provide a commentary that explains and emphasizes the significance of God's oath in Gen 22:16 accounts for the context being permeated with technical legal expressions. The distinctive character of the vocabulary finds ample illustration in the LXX and in contracts preserved among the papyri. The use of ὅρκος for "oath" (vv 16–17), of ἀντιλογία for "legal dispute" (v 16), and of ὀμνύειν for "swear" (vv 13, 16) is well attested in the LXX (cf. MM 48, 448, 457 for examples from the papyri). The special use of κατά followed by a noun in the genitive to signify the guarantee of an oath (vv 13, 16) occurs both in the LXX (cf. Gen 22:16) and in legal papyri (MM 322). The oath cited in v 14 is introduced by εἰ μήν, which has the force of intensifying the juridical solemnity of an action (cf. Trites, *Witness*, 219). The verb μεσιτεύειν, which normally means "to mediate," is used in v 17 in the special and forensic sense of "to furnish a guarantee" (MM 399; cf. Oepke, *TDNT* 4:620). The verb ἐπιδεικνύναι, which ordinarily means "to show," carries the special nuance of "to give proof" (v 17; cf. Acts 18:28; MM 237). The formula εἰς βεβαίωσιν, "as confirmation," in v 16 is one that persisted for centuries as a technical expression for a legal guarantee in a transaction (MM 108). The term ἀμετάθετος, "irrevocable," was used in wills and contracts to signify a stipulation that could not be disregarded or annulled (MM 26). A recognition of these connotations adds considerably to the force of the encouragement extended to the congregation in 6:16–18.

A popular motif in the Jewish tradition transmitted through the hellenistic synagogues was that God confirmed his promise to Abraham with an oath (Gen 22:16). Strands of the tradition are preserved by Philo in several passages (*Allegorical Interpretation of the Law* 3.203–7; *On the Sacrifices of Abel and Cain* 91–96; *On Abraham* 273). Köster has compared these passages with Heb 6:13–20 and has identified an underlying common tradition ("Die Auslegung," 98–103; cf. Sowers, *Hermeneutics*, 70–71). Between Hebrews and the passages in Philo there are similarities in terminology as well as in the sequence of particular motifs. Köster isolated as two elements in the tradition used by Hebrews (1) the emphasis on the divine oath with which God assured Abraham, and (2) the paradigm of Abraham as the prototype of the person who trusts God. According to Köster, the writer of Hebrews was more conservative in the literal interpretation of the biblical text than Philo.

The parallel between Philo and Hebrews may indicate a common tradition of interpretation. Nevertheless, it is important not to exaggerate its significance. The degree of parallel must be evaluated in the light of the evidence for earlier or contemporary interpretation, which is visible in the structure of Philo's argument when he refers to views other than his own. Philo displays a considerable ambivalence on the question whether one could say that God swore an oath. In

Abraham 273 he appears to accept this fact without discussion. But in *Allegorical Interpretation* 3.203–7 he openly acknowledges that severe objections have been raised concerning the appropriateness of describing God as swearing an oath. In *Sacrifices* 91–96 he aligns himself with a large number of others who find the anthropomorphism of Gen 22:16 objectionable and concludes that it was a Mosaic concession to human weakness (cf. Williamson, *Philo*, 206–9; Moxnes, *Theology in Conflict*, 141–46). The fact that a similar point of view has been preserved in a fragment from an earlier commentary on the Pentateuch by the Alexandrian teacher Aristobulus (preserved in Eusebius, *Preparation for the Gospel* 13.12.9–16; cf. N. Walter, *Der Thoraausleger Aristobulos* [Berlin: Akademie, 1964] 141–48) suggests that it is this interpretation which comes closer to the traditional teaching of an Alexandrian "school." No such ambivalence is displayed in Hebrews. If the argument there reflects an underlying common tradition, it is apparent that Hebrews represents an independent adaptation of the tradition.

E. Käsemann has contended that the reference to Jesus' penetration behind the heavenly curtain in Heb 6:19–20 provides significant proof that Hebrews stands under the influence of gnostic interpretation (*Das wandernde Gottesvolk*, 135, 145–49). The source of the notion is "a gnostic school tradition which was preoccupied with the curtain between heaven and earth" (135). In this tradition the cosmic curtain was regarded as a hindrance to the heavenly journey of the soul from the *cosmos* to the *pleroma* (147). According to Käsemann, the writer's representations of Jesus as the savior who broke through the cosmic dividing wall shows dependence upon a gnostic redeemer-myth, which is also the source of the conception of Jesus as πρόδρομος, "forerunner" (81–82; cf. 79–82, 152–55).

Käsemann's proposal has been subjected to an incisive critique by Hofius (*Vorhang*, 24–48). His own investigation of the tradition of the heavenly curtain in older Jewish sources pointed not to gnosticism but to early Jewish Merkabah mysticism and speculation about the throne-chariot of God (4–27, 74–75). Hofius argues that Heb 6:19–20 provides the earliest evidence for the old Jewish conception of a heavenly curtain before the Throne of Glory. The element that appears to be decisive in refuting the interpretation of Käsemann is that in Hebrews there is no thought of the curtain as a hindrance to the people of God (84; Hofius calls attention to Rev 11:19; 15:5, where the inner sanctuary is described as "open"). A careful review of the primary sources to which Käsemann and others (e.g., Grässer, *Glaube*, 34, 112, n. 284) have appealed for support demonstrates that they fail to validate the gnostic hypothesis (Hofius, 89–94).

Comment

13–15   There is in Hebrews a sustained interest in Abraham (2:16; 6:13–15; 7:4–5; 11:8–19). The appeal to Abraham as the prototype of faithful endurance in vv 13–15 gives specific content to the exhortation in v 12. The occasion for the repetition and elaboration of God's earlier promise to Abraham (Gen 12:2–3; 15:5) and its confirmation with an oath was the obedience of the patriarch to the divine command to sacrifice his son Isaac (Gen 22:1–12). In response God reaffirmed his pledge to bless Abraham, reinforced by a promissory oath in which he named himself as the guarantor of his word (Gen 22:16; cf. White, *JBL* 92 [1973] 173). The account of the ᶜAqēdâ, the offering of Isaac, had a firm place in the liturgy both of the synagogue and the Church and would have been thoroughly familiar to the congregation (Werner, *The Sacred Bridge*, 79, 87–88, 123; cf. Swetnam, *Jesus and Isaac*, 23–75).

The declaration that God swore by himself (καθ' ἑαυτοῦ) because there was no one greater by whom he could swear (v 13) is made by Philo as well (*Allegorical Interpretation* 3.203). This is simply a logical deduction from the statement of the text "I swear by myself" (κατ' ἐμαυτοῦ, Gen 22:16 LXX). When the two writers comment on the purpose of the divine oath, however, they diverge. Philo concludes that God swore an oath to Abraham "to assist faith" (*Allegorical Interpretation* 3.204, 207), whereas the writer of Hebrews explains that the purpose of the oath was to prove how irrevocable was the resolve expressed in the divine promise (v 17). The notion that God swears by himself (cf. Exod 32:13; Isa 45:23; Jer 22:5; 49:13) signifies that he is bound to his word by his character. The divine oath provides the guarantee that excludes doubt and affirms the abiding validity of the promise.

The quotation of Gen 22:17 in v 14 differs both from the LXX and the MT. The result of the alteration of the LXX text, πληθυνῶ τὸ σπέρμα σου, "I will multiply your seed," to πληθυνῶ σε, "I will multiply you," is a promise consisting of two clauses with identical endings ("I will bless you and I will multiply you").With this modification the promise of blessing is sharply focused upon Abraham (Schröger, *Verfasser*, 128). According to Gen 22:17, the divine oath extended both to the promise of numerous descendants and to possession of the land. In specifying only the promise of numerous descendants, the writer of Hebrews prepares his hearers for his emphasis in 11:17–19, when he again refers to the ʿAqēdâ, and focuses on Abraham's concern for the posterity promised to him through Isaac (cf. Swetnam, *Jesus and Isaac*, 185).

Abraham received the definitive confirmation of the divine promise after having been severely tested both in faith and endurance (v 15; cf. Gen 22:1, 15–18). The fulfillment of the promise he had received from God (Gen 12:2; 15:5) depended upon Isaac. The steadfast trust in God's word of promise that he displayed when he was commanded to offer up his son is precisely the quality of commitment appropriate to those who are currently the heirs to the divine promise. The writer's stress on Abraham's patient endurance (μακροθυμήσας, v 15) gives specific content to the summons in v 12 to imitate those who "through trust and μακροθυμίας [patient endurance] acquired the promises." A number of commentators are prepared to find in the declaration ἐπέτυχεν τῆς ἐπαγγελίας an indication that Abraham "received what was promised," namely, the birth of his son Isaac or of his grandchildren Esau and Jacob (e.g., Michel, 251; Spicq, 2:160; Köster, "Die Auslegung," 103–4; cf. RSV, NEB, JB, NIV). The immediate context, however, points to the reception of the reinforced promise of numerous descendants after Isaac had been restored to him (Gen 22:15–17). The writer's exposition in vv 13–15 provides a biblical basis for the community to emulate the faith and endurance of Abraham in the certain expectation that they will receive what God has promised to them (cf. Swetnam, *Jesus and Isaac*, 90, n. 22, 184–85).

16 The fact that God swore an oath to Abraham is compared to the universal human practice of regarding an oath as final for confirmation (cf. Cicero, *Topica* 20.77; Philo, *On Noah's Work as a Planter* 82). By common definition, an oath is a definitive and binding confirmation of the spoken word and invalidates any contradiction of the statement made. In the OT it was prescribed that oaths should be taken in Yahweh's name (Deut 6:13; 10:20), and lying under oath was condemned as a violation of the Third Commandment (Exod 20:7; Deut 5:11; Zech

5:3–4; Wis 14:29–31; cf. Trites, *Witness*, 28–29, 219; Horst, "Der Eid im Alten Testament," *EvT* 17 [1957] 366–71). In practice, an oath involved the solemn calling upon God to ratify the unequivocal truthfulness of what was asserted or promised. Philo declares, "an oath is nothing else than to call God to bear witness in a disputed matter" (*On the Special Laws* 2.10). The writer may have had in mind the fact that Abraham himself swore by God and required others to do so (Gen 14:22; 21:23–24; 24:3).

17–18 Abraham remains in view through v 17; the statement that God ἐμεσίτευσεν ὅρκῳ, "guaranteed with an oath," the irrevocable character of the intention expressed in his promise has specific reference to Gen 22:16–17. But the focus of the exposition shifts sharply from the patriarch to Christians, who are designated οἱ κληρονόμοι τῆς ἐπαγγελίας, "the heirs of the promise" (cf. v 12). As those who have inherited the promises through Christ, they are to appreciate the relevance of the biblical account to them. What is recorded in Scripture is intended to strengthen them in their conviction that God's purpose for them is also unalterable. The sworn assurance of God is extended to them (cf. Michel, 252; Spicq, 2:165; Foerster, *TDNT* 3:785). The relevance to Christians of the oath sworn to Abraham lies in the proof that God is absolutely trustworthy in the act of promising (Köster, "Die Auslegung," 106). The unchanging purpose of God provides a strong reason for emulating the trust and steadfastness of Abraham.

On δύο πραγμάτων ἀμεταθέτων, "two irrevocable facts," rests the assurance of receiving the blessings that are the content of Christian hope and that are already prepared for the people of God (v 18a). Although the two items remain unspecified in the text, the reference is almost certainly to the promise of God and his oath (vv 13, 17; cf. Michel, 253; Kuss, 84; Köster, "Die Auslegung," 100; Hofius, *ZNW* 64 [1973] 135–36). F. Schröger, however, prefers to think of the declarative utterances of God in Ps 2:7 and Ps 110:4, which were brought together and applied to the Son of God in 5:5–6 (*Verfasser*, 128–29); E. Reisner (122) thinks of the two divine oaths that figure prominently in Hebrews, Gen 22:16 and Ps 110:4. In view of the context and the focus on the Christian community in vv 17–18, it would appear to be proper to regard the promise given to Abraham and confirmed with an oath as the type that is given to the community of the new covenant in Christ. B. Klappert has recognized the parallel in formulation between 6:13–20 and 7:19–21, which indicates that the promise of 6:16–20 is identical with the high priesthood introduced with an oath (*Eschatologie*, 27–28, 32; cf. Köster, "Die Auslegung," 105–8; Hofius, *Vorhang*, 85, n. 207). Christ is himself the eschatological word of promise (1:2), and his redemptive achievement has been confirmed with an unalterable oath (Ps 110:4; cf. Heb 5:6, 10; 6:20; 7:17, 21, 28).

The irrevocability of God's promise and oath is underscored by the relative clause "in which it is impossible for God to lie." This deduction is rooted in the OT, but is not derived from any single passage (cf. Num 23:19; 1 Sam 15:29; Ps 89 [LXX 88]:35; Isa 31:2). O. Hofius has demonstrated that in the OT there is a strong connection between God's word and oath and between his word and plan (*ZNW* 64 [1973] 137–39). He found the closest parallel to the statement in Hebrews in the interpretation of Num 23:19 in rabbinic texts, where the conviction concerning God's unchanging will is made to rest on his fidelity to the covenant (141–44). In Hebrews the thought of v 18 is resumed in the confessional formulation πιστὸς ὁ ἐπαγγειλάμενος, "he who promised is faithful" (10:23; cf. 11:11).

The definition of Christians as fugitives (οἱ καταφυγόντες, "those who had fled for refuge") is suggestive, but remains undeveloped. In the LXX the compound verb καταφεύγειν is used for fleeing from the avenger to the asylum of the cities of refuge (Deut 4:42; 19:5; Josh 20:9), but in the papyri the word is almost technical for suppliants fleeing or resorting to anyone for help (MM 334). Christians are fugitives who have sought asylum and ultimate deliverance from God. It was God's intention that they should have "a strong incentive to take hold of the hope set in front of them" (v 18b). The qualification of *hope* as something placed in front of the community (προκειμένης ἐλπίδος) defines hope as the objective gift that God extends to his people through Christ. In Hebrews, the word "hope" never describes a subjective attitude (i.e., "our hope," or "hopefulness") but always denotes the objective content of hope, consisting of present and future salvation (so Michel, 253; Grässer, *Glaube*, 32–33; Mora, *La Carta*, 205-6). In vv 18–20 the community is led to consider the character of hope as "promise" and "realization" (cf. v 11), as announcement and fulfillment (cf. 7:19). The writer declares that the eschatological redemptive hope of the Christian community has attained a double certainty through God's irrevocable promise and through the realization already achieved in Christ (Schierse, *Verheissung*, 200). The encouragement and consolation this offers to the congregation are powerful for resisting all assaults and temptations to waver in confidence (Schmitz, *TDNT* 5:797).

19–20 The literary use of the anchor as a nautical metaphor was widespread in the ancient world (cf. Wettstein, *Η ΚΑΙΝΗ ΔΙΑΘΗΚΗ*, 406–7; Hilgert, *The Ship*, 22, 135; Eitrem, *ConNT* 4 [1940] 6; Spicq, *ST* 3 [1949] 185–86). The source of the metaphor was the common experience of the maritime peoples of the Mediterranean basin that "the firm grip of the anchor's teeth holds the ships fast" (Virgil, *Aeneid* 6, ll. 3–5). In Greek literature the metaphor was used constantly to evoke the notion of stability provided by adherence to virtue, and especially to hope. The basis of the comparison is the security which firm anchorage provided for a ship (e.g., Epictetus, *Fragment* 30: "we ought neither to fasten our ship to one small anchor, nor our life to a single hope"; cf. Philo, *On Dreams* 1.277; Acts 27:29, 40). The nearly synonymous terms ἀσφαλῆ τε καὶ βεβαίαν, "firm and secure," were used to describe anything that had sufficient stability and firmness not to be moved (e.g., Wis 7:23; 3 Macc 5:3; 4 Macc 17:4). In Hebrews, βέβαιος is a favorite term for that which is assured (2:2; 3:6, 14; 6:19; 9:17). The pair of terms is appropriate to the metaphor (cf. Sextus Empiricus, *Against the Logicians* 2.374; Dio Chrysostom, *Orations* 74.24) and here qualifies the antecedent "hope." As a ship is held fast when at anchor, the life of the Christian is secured by hope that binds that life to Christ, who has entered the heavenly sanctuary (Hofius, *Vorhang*, 85–87).

The further qualification of hope as "having entered behind the curtain" where Christ has entered as high priest gives to the concept of hope a precise eschatological nuance. The notion that the participle εἰσερχομένην, "entering," qualifies ἄγκυραν, "anchor," so that it is the anchor that "has entered behind the curtain," accounts for so many commentators identifying the anchor with Jesus (Windisch, 59; Käsemann, *Das wandernde Gottesvolk*, 147, n. 3; Grässer, *Glaube*, 116, n. 302; Köster, "Die Auslegung," 106; Schröger, *Verfasser*, 151, 211; et al.). It seems preferable to recognize that the antecedent is the relative pronoun ἥν, which is itself the complement of the immediately preceding word ἐλπίδος, "hope" (so Kuss, 85; Michel, 253–54; Spicq, 2:165). That it is hope which penetrates behind the curtain is confirmed when the writer subsequently refers to "a new hope by which we draw near to God" (7:19). The objective content of the promised hope is the assurance that with the consummation of redemption the community may draw near to God in priestly service (so Hofius, *Vorhang*, 86; cf. Michel, 273). They have already been encouraged to "draw near" through prayer (4:16).

The curtain before the Throne of God is described in terms borrowed from the LXX, where τὸ ἐσώτερον τοῦ καταπετάσματος, "the inner sanctuary," signifies the inner curtain that separated the sanctuary of God from the holy place in the tabernacle (Lev 16:2, 12, 15; cf. Exod 26:31–35; Lev 21:23; 24:3; Philo, *Moses* 2.86.101; Jos., *Ant.* 8.75; Heb 9:3). This area could be entered by the high priest alone and then only on the occasion of the Day of Atonement (Lev 16:2). The representation of Jesus as having entered the heavenly sanctuary on our behalf (v 20) presupposes this cultic background. The expression ὑπὲρ ἡμῶν, "on our behalf," introduces the motif of the unique self-offering of the high priest Jesus as the ground of Christian certainty: Jesus is our eternal high priest who has opened for us the true presence of God (cf. 10:19–21). His presence behind the curtain is the firm pledge that we also shall pass through the curtain and enter within the inner sanctuary (10:19, 22; cf. Hofius, *Vorhang*, 88–89).

The designation of Jesus as πρόδρομος, "forerunner," is intriguing and has elicited a variety of proposals (cf. Bauernfeind, *TDNT* 8:235; Cassien, *Th* 27 [1956] 106–8; Spicq, *ST* 3 [1949] 186–87). The question of the derivation of the term, however, is still unanswered. The word rarely occurs in the singular in classical or hellenistic literary sources and has not been found in the papyri. In the plural the word πρόδρομοι designates advance military scouts or a corps moving ahead of the main army (Herodotus, 1.60; 4.121, 122; Arrian, *Anabasis* 1.12; Polybius, 12.20.7), advance ships of a fleet (Alciphron, *Letters* 1.14.1; cf. Livy, 36.41.7), early ripened fruit (Num 13:20; Isa 28:4), or heralds who announce the approach of a party (Herodotus, 7.203; 9.14). Julius Pollux defined the word in the singular in an athletic sense; it refers to the swiftest runner who breaks away from the group and wins the course (*Onomasticon* 3.30.148). The notion common to these references is that of precedence. πρόδρομος is a relative term, like "precursor" or "forerunner," implying a sequence. Only one proposal takes serious account of the immediate context. Cassien has suggested that the usage in Hebrews is explicated by the concluding phrase in v 20b (*Th* 27 [1956] 106–7). The writer makes the quality of "precursor," which he attributes to Jesus, dependent upon his high priestly ministry. Jesus is the πρόδρομος in that he has entered behind the curtain as our precursor in his office as high priest like Melchizedek. The assured character of God's promise is confirmed in the life, death, entry, and high priestly investiture of Jesus (cf. Bauernfeind, *TDNT* 8:235).

According to 5:7–10 Jesus was confirmed in his high priestly office after an earthly career of suffering and obedience. His ascension and priesthood go together. This same understanding is reflected in v 20, which indicates that Jesus entered the heavenly sanctuary through his death, which secures for the people of God the purification that enables them to draw near to God (cf. 10:14). The phrase "a high priest like Melchizedek" is thus joined to the saving work of Jesus in v 20, as in 5:10. This is striking precisely because in chap. 7 the phrase will be attached to Jesus' office but not his activity (Hay, *Glory*, 145–46). The concluding phrase also functions as a fresh announcement of the subject of 5:10, which prepares the hearer for the exposition of Jesus' high priestly office in 7:1–28.

Explanation

After he had exposed the peril of spiritual immaturity in 5:11–6:12, the writer felt constrained to affirm the utter reliability of God's word of promise to the congregation. The emphasis in 6:13–20 falls on the continuity of the new people of God with Abraham as heirs to the divine promise. The writer's optimism concerning the congregation is shown to be established upon the word of God as promise and oath. The new element that is introduced with the reference to the divine oath is the intensity of God's speaking. God's oath is his most holy and solemn declaration of the absolute truthfulness of his word and is given in order that the people of God may know that he will fulfill his promise. The word of promise confirmed with an oath reveals the irrevocable character of God's will and provides his people with strong encouragement to obey him with unwavering confidence.

God's unchanging purpose for his people does not exclude a history of human experience of his word. The writer's choice of Gen 22:16–17 as the text upon which he would comment is significant. The command to sacrifice Isaac (Gen 22:1) placed God's earlier promise to Abraham in jeopardy (Gen 12:2; 15:5). Abraham's obedience required firm trust and steadfastness. But in response the promise was reaffirmed and solemnized with the confirming oath. The history of the word of God proves that God cannot lie in what he has said he will do. Abraham's experience indicates that at certain moments in redemptive history God gave his word the form of an oath in order that the irrevocable character of his resolve might be recognized by those who have received his promise.

In 6:13–20 the writer depicts Abraham as a paradigm of trust and steadfast endurance. But he wanted to do more. He wished to describe God's promise and oath to Abraham as a type of the way in which God has acted with the Christian community. The promise to bless Abraham is a prefiguration of the salvation that God has given to the new people in Jesus. Abraham's experience with God was first and foremost a demonstration that God is faithful, that his words are reliable, and that he stands behind his promise. The promised salvation secured through the high priestly ministry of Jesus is certain because it is guaranteed by God. The present time is the time of sure and steadfast hope precisely because through his sacrificial death Jesus has entered the presence of God on behalf of his people and has made it possible for them to approach God in priestly service. As a unit, 6:13–20 serves to place the ensuing exposition of 7:1–10:18 under the aspect of an event of promise that is confirmed with an oath.

C. Melchizedek, the Royal Priest   (7:1–10)

Bibliography

Aptowitzer, V. "Malkizedek." *MGWJ* 70 (1926) 93–113. **Auberlen, C. A.** "Melchizedek's ewige Leben und Priestertum: Hebr. 7." *TSK* 30 (1857) 453–504. **Bamburg, C. C.** "Melchisedech." *EuA* 40 (1964) 5–21. **Bandstra, A. J.** "Heilsgeschichte and Melchizedek in Hebrews." *CTJ* 3 (1968) 36–41. **Bardy, G.** "Melchisédech dans la tradition patristique." *RB* 35 (1926) 469–

509; 36 (1927) 25–45. **Carmignac, J.** "Le document de Qumran sur Melkisédeq." *RevQ* 27 (1970) 343–78. **Carmona, A. R.** "La figura de Melquisedec en la literatura targúmica." *EstBib* 37 (1978) 79–102. **Casalini, N.** "Ebr 7,1–10: Melchisedek prototipi di Cristo." *SBFLA* 34 (1984) 149–90. ———. "Una *Vorlage* extra-biblica in Ebr 7,1–3? (Verifica delle ragioni letterarie dell' ipotesi)." *SBFLA* 34 (1984) 109–48. **Cockerill, G. L.** *The Melchizedek Christology in Heb. 7:1–28.* Ann Arbor: University Microfilms International, 1979. **Cominskey, J. P.** "The Order of Melchizedek." *TBT* 27 (1966) 1913–18. **Déaut, R. le.** "Le titre de 'Summus Sacerdos' donné à Melchisédech est-il d'origine juive?" *RSR* 50 (1962) 222–29. **Delcor, M.** "Melchizedek from Genesis to the Qumran Texts and in the Epistle to the Hebrews." *JSJ* 2 (1971) 115–35. **Demarest, B.** "Hebrews 7:3, A *Crux Interpretum* Historically Considered." *EvQ* 49 (1977) 141–62. ———. *A History of Interpretation of Hebrews 7,1–10 from the Reformation to the Present.* BGBE 19. Tübingen: Mohr, 1976. **Dey, L. K. K.** *The Intermediary World and Patterns of Perfection.* 185–214. **Ellingworth, P.** "'Like the Son of God': Form and Content in Hebrews 7,1–10." *Bib* 64 (1983) 255–62. **Emerton, J. A.** "The Riddle of Genesis 14." *VT* 21 (1971) 403–39. ———. "Some False Clues in the Study of Genesis 14." *VT* 21 (1971) 24–47. **Fabris, R.** "La lettera agli Ebrei e l'Antico Testamento." *RivB* 32 (1984) 237–52. **Feuillet, A.** "Une triple préparation du sacerdoce du Christ dans l'Ancien Testament (Melchisédec, le Messie du Ps 110, le Serviteur d'Is 53): Introduction à la doctrine sacerdotale de l'Épître aux Hébreux." *Div* 28 (1984) 103–36. **Fisher, L. R.** "Abraham and His Priest-King." *JBL* 81 (1962) 264–70. **Fitzmyer, J. A.** "Further Light on Melchizedek from Qumran Cave 11." *JBL* 86 (1967) 25–41. ———. "Now this Melchizedek . . . (Heb. 7,1)." *CBQ* 25 (1963) 305–21. **Friedländer, M.** "La sect de Melchisédech et l'Épître aux Hébreux." *REJ* 5 (1882) 1–26, 188–98; 6 (1883) 187–99. **Gammie, J. G.** "Loci of the Melkizedek Tradition of Genesis 14:18–20." *JBL* 90 (1971) 385–96. **Gianotto, C.** *Melchisedek e la sua tipologia: Tradizioni giudaiche, cristiane e gnostiche (sec. II a.C.-sec. III d. C.).* Supplementi alla Rivista Biblica 12. Brescia: Paideia, 1984. **Hay, D. M.** *Glory at the Right Hand.* 28–29, 134–50, 152–53. **Horbury, W.** "The Aaronic Priesthood in the Epistle to the Hebrews." *JSNT* 19 (1983) 43–71. **Horton, F. L., Jr.** *The Melchizedek Tradition: A Critical Examination of the Sources to the Fifth Century A.D. and in the Epistle to the Hebrews.* SNTSMS 30. Cambridge: Cambridge UP, 1976. **Hunt, I.** "Recent Melchizedek Study." In *The Bible in Current Catholic Thought.* Ed. J. L. McKensie. New York: Herder and Herder, 1962. 21–33. **Jérôme, F. J.** *Das geschichtlichen Melchisedech-Bild und seine Bedeutung im Hebräerbrief.* Freiburg: Caritatisdruckerei, 1920. **Jonge, H. J. de.** "Traditie en exegese: de hogepriester-christologie en Melchizedek in Hebreeën." *NedTTs* 37 (1983) 1–19. **Jonge, M. de** and **Woude, A. S. van der.** "11Q Melchizedek and the New Testament." *NTS* 12 (1965–66) 301–26. **Kennedy, G. T.** *St. Paul's Conception of the Priesthood of Melchisedech: An Historico-Exegetical Investigation.* Washington, DC: Catholic University, 1951. **Kirkland, J. R.** "The Incident at Salem: A Re-examination of Genesis 14:18–20." *StudBibTh* 7 (1977) 3–23. **Kobelski, P. J.** *Melchizedek and Melchireša͟ᶜ.* CBQMS 10. Washington, DC: The Catholic Biblical Association of America, 1980. **Lang, G. H.** "Melchizedek." *EvQ* 31 (1959) 21–31. **Laub, F.** *Bekenntnis und Auslegung.* 31–41, 236–43. **Longenecker, R. N.** "The Melchizedek Argument of Hebrews: A Study in the Development and Circumstantial Expression of New Testament Thought." In *Unity and Diversity in New Testament Theology.* FS G. E. Ladd. Ed. R. Guelich. Grand Rapids: Eerdmans, 1978. 161–85. **Mackay, C.** "The Order of Melchizedek." *CQR* (1944) 175–91. **Marshall, J. L.** "Melchizedek in Hebrews, Philo and Justin Martyr." *SE* 7 (1982) 339–42. **McCullough, J. C.** "Melchizedek's Varied Role in Early Exegetical Tradition." *ThRev* 1 (1978) 52–66. **Meeter, H. H.** *The Heavenly High Priesthood of Christ.* 56–85. **Milik, J. T.** "*Milkî-sedeq* et *Milkî-rešaᶜ* dans les anciens écrits juifs et chrétiens." *JJS* 23 (1972) 95–144. **Neal, M.** "Melchizedek and Christ (Hebrews 7)." *BV* 2 (1968) 21–27. **Panosian, E. M.** "Hebrews: 'Neither Beginning of Days Nor End of Life.'" *BV* 2 (1968) 9–14. **Paul, M. J.** "The Order of Melchizedek (Ps 110:4 and Heb 7:3)." *WTJ* 49 (1987) 195–211. **Pearson, B. A.** "The Figure of Melchizedek in the First Tractate of the Unpublished Coptic-Gnostic Codex IX from Nag Hammadi." In *Proceedings from the XIIth International Congress of the International Association for the History of Religions.* Ed. C. J. Bleeker, G. Widengren, E. J. Sharpe.

Leiden: Brill, 1975. 200–208. **Petuchowski, J. J.** "The Controversial Figure of Melchizedek." *HUCA* 28 (1957) 127–36. **Rábanos, R.** "Sacerdocio de Melquisedec, sacerdocio de Aarón y sacerdocio de Cristo." *CB* 13 (1956) 264–75. **Rusche, H.** "Die Gestalt des Melchisedek." *MTZ* 6 (1955) 230–52. **Schröger, F.** *Der Verfasser des Hebräerbriefes.* 130–44, 156–59, 258–59. **Sen, F.** "La nueva figùra de Melquisedec (11QMelch)." *CB* 29 (1972) 93–107. **Sheehan, J. F. X.** "Melchisedech in Christian Consciousness." *ScEc* 18 (1966) 127–38. **Simon, M.** "Melchisédech dans la polémique entre juifs et chrétiens et dans la légende." *RHPR* 17 (1937) 58–93. **Smith, R. H.** "Abraham and Melchizedek (Gen. 14:18–20)." *ZAW* 77 (1965) 129–53. **Soubigou, L.** "Le chapitre VII de l'Épître aux Hébreux." *ATh* 7 (1946) 69–82. **Spicq, C.** "Melchisédech et l'Épître aux Hébreux: La sacerdoce de la nouvelle alliance." *EV* 87 (1977) 206–8. **Stork, H.** *Die sogenannten Melchisedekianer mit Untersuchung ihrer Quellen auf Gedankengehalt und dogmengeschichtliche Entwicklung: Historische Studien zum Hebräerbrief.* FGNK 8/12. Leipzig: Deichert, 1928. **Theissen, G.** *Untersuchungen zum Hebräerbrief.* 13–33, 130–52. **Thompson, J. W.** "The Conceptual Background and Purpose of the Midrash in Hebrews VII." *NovT* 19 (1977) 209–23. **Verme, M. del.** "La 'prima decima' guidaica nella pericope di Ebrei 7,1–10." *Hen* 8 (1986) 339–63. ———. "La 'prima decima' nel giudaismo del Secondo Tempio." *Hen* 9 (1987) 5–38. **Watson, J. K.** "Melkisédec et le Fils de Dieu." *CCER* 30 (1982) 49–60. **Willi, T.** "Melchisedek: Der alte und der neue Bund im Hebräerbrief im Lichte der rabbinischen Tradition über Melchizedek." *Judaica* 42 (1986) 158–70. **Williamson, R.** *Philo and the Epistle to the Hebrews.* 20–23, 103–9, 434–49. **Woude, A. S. van der.** "Melchisedek als himmlische Erlösergestalt in den neugefundenen eschatologischen Midraschim aus Qumran Höhle XI." *OTS* 14 (1965) 354–73. **Wuttke, G.** *Melchizedek, der Priesterkönig von Salem: Eine Studie zur Geschichte der Exegese.* BZNW 5. Giessen: Töpelmann, 1927. **Yadin, Y.** "A Note on Melchizedek and Qumran." *IEJ* 15 (1965) 152–54. **Zimmermann, H.** *Das Bekenntnis der Hoffnung.* 79–99, 145–53.

Translation

[1]*Now this Melchizedek was king of Salem and priest of God Most High.*[a] *He met Abraham as he was returning from the defeat of the kings*[b] *and blessed him,* [2]*and Abraham allotted him a tenth share of everything. Translated, his name means first "king of righteousness"; then*[c] *also "king of Salem" means "king of peace."* [3]*His father, mother, and line of descent are unknown,*[d] *and there is no record of his birth or of his death, but having been made to resemble the Son of God, he remains a priest continuously.*[e]

[4]*Consider how great*[f] *a man this must have been to whom the patriarch*[g] *Abraham gave a tenth of the choicest spoils of war.* [5]*Now the descendants of Levi who receive the priestly office*[h] *have a commandment in accordance with the law to exact a tenth from the people— that is to say, their brothers—although their brothers are descended from Abraham.* [6]*This man, however, did not trace his descent from them, yet he collected a tenth from Abraham and blessed*[i] *him who had the promises.* [7]*(Now unquestionably, the person of lesser status*[j] *is blessed by the one of greater status.)* [8]*In the one case, mortal men*[k] *exact a tenth, but, in the other case, one to whom witness is borne that he lives.*[l] [9]*And one might almost say*[m] *that even Levi, who received the tenth,*[n] *paid the tenth through Abraham,* [10]*because Levi was still in the body of his ancestor when Melchizedek met Abraham.*

Notes

[a] 7:1–3 is another example of a majestic periodic sentence which has been broken up in translation out of respect for English style. The main clause of the sentence is "This Melchizedek . . . remains

a priest continuously." For other examples of artistic periods, see 1:1–4; 2:2–4, 14–15; 3:12–15; 4:12–13; 5:1–3, 7–10.

ᵇ MS 460 adds, "when he pursued the foreigners and rescued Lot with all the prisoners of war," a clear example of a homiletical gloss suggested by the Gen narrative.

ᶜ The expressions πρῶτον μέν . . . ἔπειτα δέ are designations of enumeration which separate one thought from another in a series so that they may be easily distinguished (A. T. Robertson, *Grammar*, 1153).

ᵈ The triad ἀπάτωρ, ἀμήτωρ, ἀγενεαλόγητος consists of terms that occur nowhere else in the Gk. Bible. The key to the translation is provided in the final word, which appears to have been coined by the writer because it is found elsewhere in Gk. literature only with reference to this passage. It denotes "without priestly genealogy," in reference to the absence of a genealogical record as the basis of Melchizedek's priesthood (cf. v 6). In the papyri, as in Plutarch, the word ἀπάτωρ does not mean "fatherless" but "father unknown" (LSJ 181; MM 54–55). The term ἀμήτωρ does not occur in the papyri but shares this special sense by association. The Syriac Peshitta translation is instructive: "whose father and mother were not entered in genealogies." See further Cockerill, *Melchizedek Christology*, 42–50.

ᵉ The expression εἰς τὸ διηνεκές is a classical phrase, which in the NT occurs only in Hebrews (7:3; 10:1, 12, 14). It denotes "uninterruptedly, perpetually, continuously" (Moule, *Idiom-Book*, 164).

ᶠ The interrogative pronoun πηλίκος is used as a term of exclamation (Turner, *Grammar*, 3:50). In conjunction with the oratorical imperative "consider," it introduces a conversational style that contrasts sharply with the majestic description of Melchizedek in vv 1–3.

ᵍ The Gk. text displays an unusual word order, which appears to have been designed to enlist the hearers' attention: "to whom Abraham gave a tenth of the choicest spoils of war—the patriarch!" (Turner, *Grammar*, 4:107).

ʰ The word ἱερατεία denotes the priestly office, in contrast to the more abstract ἱερωσύνη (vv 11–12, 24), which refers to the institution of the priesthood (cf. Schrenk, *TDNT* 3:247–48, 251).

ⁱ Grammarians describe the pf tense of the verbs in vv 6, 9, 11, 16, 20, 23 as "narrative perfects," which occur in the NT when the OT is being expounded. The pf tense denotes that the event stands recorded in the Scripture and could therefore be regarded as qualifying a past but still relevant event. Cf. Moule, *Idiom-Book*, 14–15; Turner, *Grammar*, 3:70.

ʲ The articular form of the neuter adj τὸ ἔλαττον is used of persons if the emphasis is on quality, as here (Zerwick, *Biblical Greek* §141; BDF §§61[1], 138[1]).

ᵏ In the anarthrous construction ἀποθνῄσκοντες ἄνθρωποι, which is virtually adjectival, the present tense of the ptcp is frequentative, i.e., it refers to an action that recurs from time to time. It, therefore, means "men who are to die, mortal men" (Moulton, *Grammar*, 1:114).

ˡ The expression μαρτυρούμενος ὅτι ζῇ is described by Moule as "a bold and rather unusual way" of declaring "it is attested that he is alive" (*Idiom-Book*, 104–5).

ᵐ The literary phrase ὡς ἔπος εἰπεῖν, which occurs only here in the NT, is a rather imprecise qualifying phrase used to limit a startling declaration or to soften a sweeping statement (cf. Williamson, *Philo*, 103–9).

ⁿ The attributive ptcp ὁ . . . λαμβάνων is here equivalent to an explanatory relative clause (Burton, *Moods and Tenses* §426).

Form/Structure/Setting

The presentation of Melchizedek in 7:1–10 assumes the form of homiletical midrash, in which the exposition of Scripture determines the structure of the argument. The unit exhibits five characteristics of this distinctive form: (1) the point of departure for interpretation is the OT text; (2) the exposition is homiletical in character; (3) the writer is attentive to the analysis of the details of the text; (4) the text is made relevant to the current situation through interpretation; and (5) the point of interest is the narrative account, not merely the characters themselves (Fitzmyer, *JBL* 86 [1967] 305). The clear allusion to Ps 110:4 in the description of Christ as the heavenly high priest in 6:20 sets the stage for the midrash that follows. In 7:1–10 the writer introduces Gen 14:17–20 to identify the Melchizedek of Ps 110:4 (vv 1–3) and to exhibit the basis in history for the superiority of his priesthood over the Levitical priesthood (vv 4–10).

G. Cockerill has argued that there are structural, terminological, and conceptual signs that 7:1–25 may once have been an independent midrash. He has demonstrated that 7:4–25 is a tightly knit and balanced structural unit based on 7:1–3 and has sought to show that the function of 7:26–28 was to relate 7:1–25 to the exposition in 8:1–10:18. It is certain that the christological tradition in 7:1–25 is distinct from the traditions that may have been used in 2:17–18; 3:1; 4:15–16 and 8:1–10:18. The most serious structural difficulty in the way of regarding 7:1–25 as an independent midrash is that the dominant text of the midrash, Ps 110:4, is not cited at the beginning. The fact that the verse has been quoted already at 5:6, however, may explain why it was not formally introduced at this point. The significant place that 7:1–25 assumes in the central division of Hebrews indicates that its thought, though differing from other traditions used in the homily, was congenial to the writer. Cockerill is prepared to suggest the midrash was prepared by the writer himelf on some occasion previous to the composition of Hebrews (*Melchizedek Christology*, 290–307).

The basis of the midrash in 7:1–10 is the hermeneutical principle of *gĕzêrâ šāwâ*, that is, if two separate passages of Scripture contain the same word, the verbal analogy provides a sufficient reason for explaining one text in the light of the other (cf. Heb 1:5; 3:7–4:11; 13:5–6). The dominant text in 7:1–10 is Gen 14:17–20, but in chap. 7 as a whole Gen 14:17–20 is subordinated to Ps 110:4 (cf. Schröger, *Verfasser,* 156–59; Michel, 256). Two other interpretive principles also are found in the midrash. The principle that even the silence of Scripture was charged with significance was recognized both in rabbinic (cf. Str-B 3:694–96) and in Alexandrian exegesis (cf. Philo, *The Worse Attacks the Better* 178; *On Drunkenness,* 68–70; *On the Virtues* 200; *On Flight and Finding* 60; *On the Confusion of Tongues* 12). This understanding informs the statement in v 3 and in v 8. It was also agreed that what applies in a lesser case applies in a greater one (cf. Heb 2:1–3; 9:13–14; 10:28–29; 12:9, 25). Consistent with this principle, Abraham is exalted in v 4, and the Levitical priests in v 5, in order that Melchizedek may be more highly exalted (Schröger, *Verfasser,* 258–59). The exegesis presupposes that an antecedent revelation is the pledge of a future eschatological fulfillment. In 7:1–10 the revelation in Ps 110:4 is understood to have confirmed the eschatological implications of Gen 14:17–20 (Michel, 255–59).

The allusion to Ps 110:4 in 6:20 is transitional, leading to the exposition of Christ's high priestly office in 7:1–28. The opening words in 7:1 clearly refer to the announcement of the subject in 6:20 and serve to introduce the new unit. The structure of the chapter confirms the writer's carefully conceived plan: 7:1–10 provides an interpretation of Gen 14:17–20, and 7:11–28 directs attention to the significance of each phrase in Ps 110:4. The limits of the first section are confirmed literarily by an *inclusio* established between vv 1 and 10 by the repeated statement that Melchizedek met Abraham. The point is interesting, because in Gen 14:17 it is stated that Abraham was met by the king of Sodom. The specification that it was Melchizedek who met the patriarch is consistent with the context but was not necessary to the writer's argument. It serves, however, both literarily and conceptually to facilitate the exposition.

The verses of 7:1–10 are linked internally by the train of thought as well as by grammatical construction. The fact of the meeting, the conferring of the blessing, and the giving of the tithe are taken up in inverse order in two paragraphs, providing the section with a balanced symmetry:

	Vv 1–3		*Vv 4–10*
A	The meeting (v 1*a*)	C'	The tithe (v 4)
B	The blessing (v 1*b*)	B'	The blessing (v 6)
C	The tithe (v 2)	A'	The meeting (v 10)

The two paragraphs are complementary: vv 1–3 introduce the enigmatic person of Melchizedek; vv 4–10 explore the significance of his encounter with Abraham (cf. Vanhoye, *La structure,* 125–27; Cockerill, *Melchizedek Christology,* 16–20).

There have been a variety of proposals that the opening sentence (vv 1–3), which is a well-rounded period, preserves a fragment of a traditional poem or hymn. Michel regarded v 3 as a brief poem of four lines (259), while Zimmermann considered the entire sentence to be hymnodic (*Hohepriester-Christologie,* 13, 15). Schille's proposal was almost as inclusive, assigning vv 1*a,* 2*b,* 3*a, b, d* to the hymn (*ZNW* 46 [1955] 84). He theorized that the writer transferred to Melchizedek an early Christian hymn in honor of Christ. Theissen has lent his support to these proposals, but finds additional lines to the hymn in the remainder of the chapter (vv 1*a,* 3*a, b, d,* 16*b,* 25, 26*b, c, d*). He posited a hellenistic-Jewish hymn about Melchizedek, which originally had nothing to do with Christ (*Untersuchungen,* 20–28). The hymn hypothesis has recently been reviewed by Cockerill (307–27), who has posed the question of criteria for detecting a traditional hymn in chap. 7 (309–16). He finds sufficient ground for regarding v 3*a, b, d* as hymnic in origin. But even this limited proposal appears to be unlikely. The source of v 3*d* is clearly Ps 110:4, a text that the writer has introduced previously (5:6, 10; 6:20); v 3*b* is an interpretation of this text, and v 3*a* is composed from predicates based on an interpretation of Gen 14:18–20 (cf. Schröger, *Verfasser,* 142). Considering the writer's skill in composing artistic periods, it seems preferable to assign to him sole responsibility for the formulation of 7:1–3 (see *Comment* on 5:7–10).

The task of ascertaining the conceptual background for the treatment of Melchizedek in 7:1–10 is complicated by the variety of traditions associated with Melchizedek in literary sources broadly contemporaneous with Hebrews. There was undoubtedly an interest in Melchizedek in the apocalyptic tradition. Unfortunately, in all four of the extant Ethiopic MSS of *Jubilees* there is an obvious lacuna at the beginning of 13:25, just at the point where the reader would expect a recounting of the main events in Gen 14. When the account is resumed, there is reference to the right of the priests to receive tithes and mention of Abraham's conversation with the king of Sodom (*Jub.* 13:25*b*–29). The fact that Melchizedek met Abraham appears to have been suppressed by copyists, since there is no such lacuna anywhere else in the entire text (cf. Longenecker, "Melchizedek Argument," 164–65).

A different strand of the apocalyptic tradition has been preserved at Qumran. In 1QapGen xxii.13–17 there is a simple paraphrase of the biblical text, but in a fragmentary text known as 11QMelch, Melchizedek appears as a heavenly figure who executes eschatological judgment upon Belial and his band of perverse spirits (van der Woude, *OTS* 14 [1965] 356–73; for subsequent reconstructions of the text, see Fitzmyer, *JBL* 86 [1967] 25–41; Milik, *JJS* 23 [1972] 95–144). Although the precise tenor of the document is debated because of its fragmentary condition, it is recognized by nearly all interpreters that Melchizedek occupied an exalted status in the apocalyptic expectations of first-century sectarian Judaism.

11QMelch is a midrash on three different sets of texts: (1) Lev 25:13 and Deut 15:2 (ll. 1–9a); (2) Pss 82:1–2 and 7:8–9 (ll. 9b–15a); and (3) Isa 52:7 (ll. 15b–26). An allusion to Lev 25:9 in l. 26 indicates that the dominant text is Lev 25:13, but Isa 61:1 is also important, for in each of the three sections allusions to this unquoted passage are used to interpret the texts that are cited in the midrash (ll. 4, 6, 9, 13, 18). The text of ll. 1–9a presupposes a periodization of history in terms of Jubilee years, the last of which will bring atonement and eschatological deliverance. This final Jubilee is designated "the year of Melchizedek." The theme of salvation in the proclamation of deliverance to the captives, which is confirmed by the theme of the judgment of Belial and the spirits of his lot, is developed in ll. 9b–15a. These lines are crucial for understanding the conception of Melchizedek in this document. He is clearly God's agent of judgment and almost certainly is an angel who is exalted above the hosts of heaven (cf. de Jonge and van der Woude, *NTS* 12 [1965–66] 304; Fitzmyer, *JBL* 86 [1967] 31, 34; Delcor, *JSJ* 2 [1971] 133–34; for a radically different proposal, Carmignac, *RevQ* 27 [1970] 353, 358, 367–68). Though difficult to interpret because of their fragmentary state, ll. 15b–26 appear to declare that Melchizedek is king, or that he reigns (see further, Horton, *Melchizedek Tradition*, 60–82, 167–70; Demarest, *History*, 120–28; Cockerill, *Melchizedek Christology*, 367–70, 412–67, 519–44).

Some scholars are convinced that the writer of Hebrews developed his argument with an awareness of the significance of Melchizedek at Qumran (e.g., de Jonge and van der Woude, *NTS* 12 [1965–66] 301–26; Yadin, *IEJ* 15 [1965] 152–54; Longenecker, "Melchizedek Argument," 173–79; cf. Fitzmyer, *JBL* 86 [1967] 31, 41). It must be recognized, however, that in 11QMelch there is no explicit association of Melchizedek and priesthood, nor is there any demonstrable connection between 11QMelch and the biblical texts that mention Melchizedek, Gen 14:18–20 and Ps 110:4. There is no direct connection between 11QMelch and its tradition concerning Melchizedek and the conception developed in Heb 7:1–25, where the biblical passages concerning Melchizedek and the notion of priesthood are the controlling ideas (so also Cockerill, 458–61).

Philo refers to Melchizedek in five passages (*Allegorical Interpretation of the Law* 3.79, 82; *On the Preliminary Studies* 99; *On Abraham* 235; and the brief fragment discovered by R. Harris; unfortunately, the extant text of the *Questions and Answers on Genesis* has nothing between Philo's comments on Gen 10:8–9 and Gen 15:7). Of the five passages, the first three alone are relevant to the question of the conceptual framework for Philo's treatment of Melchizedek. Philo displays no real interest in the details of the account in Gen 14:18–20 except insofar as they provide material for his allegorical exegesis or reinforce his conclusions. His handling of the text exhibits a general application of various patterns of interpretation that occur elsewhere in his works. For him, Melchizedek is primarily a symbol of "the right principle" (ὁ ὀρθὸς λόγος) (*Allegorical Interpretation* 3.79) in an individual. In contrast to Hebrews, where Melchizedek is associated with Christ's high priesthood and sonship on the basis of Ps 110:4, Philo does not allegorize Melchizedek as the cosmological Logos, nor as the Logos as high priest (λόγος ἀρχιερεύς), and he never cites Ps 110:4. Although a few interpreters have argued that the conceptual framework exhibited in Heb 7 finds its closest analogies in

Philo (e.g., Moffatt, 91–92; Spicq, 2:182, 207; Thompson, *NovT* 19 [1977] 222), it is generally recognized that at this point Philo has exerted no influence upon the thought and language of Hebrews (cf. Williamson, *Philo*, 434–37, 445–49; Rusche, *MTZ* 6 [1955] 238–44; Cockerill, *Melchizedek Christology*, 211, 371, 388–94, 412).

In the Targumic tradition Melchizedek is identified as Shem, Noah's son, and it is specified that he served God "at that time" (*Tg. Ps.-J.* Gen 14:18; see especially Carmona, *EstBib* 37 [1978] 79–102). The qualification of Melchizedek's service is consistent with the rabbinic notion that the priesthood was transferred to Abraham and his posterity at the meeting recorded in Gen 14:18–20 because Melchizedek proved to be unworthy of his office. According to this tradition the Levitical priesthood is the legitimate successor to the priesthood forfeited by Melchizedek. In rabbinic literature the primary interest in Gen 14:18–20 centers on the greatness of Abraham, to whom the words of Ps 110:4 were applied by R. Ishmael as early as A.D. 135. (*b. Ned.* 326; cf. Aptowitzer, *MGWJ* 70 [1926] 93–113; Wuttke, *Melchizedek*, 18–27; Petuchowski, *HUCA* 28 [1957] 127–36; Horton, *Melchizedek Tradition*, 114–30, 160). Josephus refers briefly to Melchizedek as the first priest of God and asserts that he built a temple in Jerusalem and that he persuaded Abraham to accept gifts from the king of Sodom (*Ant.* 1.180–91; *J. W.* 6.438). There is no mention of Melchizedek nor of the events of Gen 14 in *Biblical Antiquities* of Pseudo-Philo.

There has been a persistent interest in the Melchizedek speculation in certain gnostic circles. A century ago Friedländer postulated that Heb 7 was a polemical response to a pre-Christian gnostic Melchizedekian sect (*REJ* 5 [1882] 193–94), and Wuttke found traces of pre-Christian gnosticism behind the formulation of Heb 7:2*b*–3 (*Melchizedek*, 3–17, 27–32). In the absence of solid evidence, however, such proposals found relatively little support (cf. Bardy, *RB* 35 [1926] 501–9; Stork, *Die sogenannten Melchisedekianer*, 25–35, 75, 81). Käsemann was persuaded that a gnostic *anthropos* or "primal man" myth had influenced the high priestly christology of Hebrews. He sought to demonstrate that in late Jewish tradition Melchizedek was identified with Michael and Elijah, who were the recurring manifestations of the primal Adam (*Das wandernde Gottesvolk*, 124–40). The evidence for this contention, however, is slender. Theissen, for example, rejects Käsemann's thesis of a late Jewish tradition that identified the gnostic primal man with the eschatological high priest as an untenable scholarly construction. He attempted to show that the interpretation of Melchizedek in Philo and Hebrews is dependent upon a common or similar gnostic speculation about Melchizedek (*Untersuchungen*, 143–52). His argument, however, is seriously flawed (see Cockerill, *Melchizedek Christology*, 398–99, n. 111). The new fragmentary Melchizedek text in Codex IX from Nag Hammadi (NHC IX.1) is representative of one strand of Christian gnosticism, which developed its speculation on the basis of Gen 14:18 and Ps 110:4 (see especially Pearson, "Figure of Melchizedek," 200–208). It fails to lend any support, however, to the proposals of Käsemann or Theissen (cf. Cockerill, 372–412).

In Hebrews Melchizedek is not a redeemer, and he performs no saving act. He is a historical figure who serves as a precedent for a priesthood not based on lineage or law. It is possible that the writer of Hebrews was aware of and stood critically against some of the traditions concerning Melchizedek, but it is now impossible to specify which traditions the writer may have known. His devlopment of Melchizedek is essentially independent from extrabiblical ideas. It is derived from Gen 14:17–20, which has been approached typologically from the perspective of Ps 110:4.

Comment

The presentation on Melchizedek is an integral part of the "subject which is difficult to explain intelligibly" (5:11). The writer's main concern in 7:1–28 is to delineate the nature of Jesus' priestly office and prove that it is superior to the Levitical priesthood. The basis of his argument is a reflection on Ps 110:4 and God's oath to establish an eternal priesthood like that of Melchizedek. In 7:1–10 the writer explores this theme in dependence upon selected elements in Gen 14:17–20, which are used freely to clarify who Melchizedek was and the nature of his priesthood. He uses the incident of Melchizedek's meeting with Abraham to show the priority of Melchizedek over the Levitical priests. The comparison is primary to the demonstration in 7:11–28 that the priest "like Melchizedek" is superior to the Levitical priests. In the Genesis narrative and Ps 110:4, the writer finds the unmistakable implication that the Levitical priesthood will be replaced by the eternal priesthood foreshadowed and prefigured in the person of Melchizedek. The object of interest throughout the midrash is not Melchizedek but the one to whom a priesthood like his was promised in the psalm oracle.

1–3 In the opening sentence the writer addresses two questions: (1) who was Melchizedek and (2) what significance is to be attached to his brief and enigmatic appearance to Abraham in primal history? It might be expected that he would argue, as did Philo (*Allegorical Interpretation* 3.79) and Josephus (*J. W.* 6.438), that as the first priest mentioned in Scripture Melchizedek was the archetype of all priesthood (cf. Horton, *Melchizedek Tradition,* 152–60). The writer's determination to present Christ as an eternal priest "like Melchizedek" may have been influenced by some such consideration, but it is not articulated in the text of Hebrews. Rather, the explanatory particle γάρ, "now," introduces a terse recital and interpretation of selected features of the narrative in Gen 14:17–20. The material is drawn from the LXX, although the writer substitutes the spelling Ἀβραάμ, "Abraham," for the LXX spelling Ἀβράμ, "Abram," an orthographic variation attested elsewhere in the NT and the Apostolic Fathers.

The name and titles of Melchizedek (v 1a) are taken directly from Gen 14:18. The further qualification that he was "the one meeting Abraham as he was returning from the defeat of the kings," however, is a paraphrase of Gen 14:17, where the words refer to the king of Sodom. The attribution of ὁ συναντήσας, "the one meeting," to Melchizedek helped to focus the argument on the central figure in the account (Cockerill, *Melchizedek Christology,* 203). In vv 1b–2a the writer paraphrases the incidents from Genesis that he selects for comment: Abraham's allotment of a tenth of the plunder to Melchizedek and Melchizedek's blessing of Abraham. Both details supported the writer's point that Melchizedek was superior to Abraham (vv 4–10). The fact that Melchizedek brought out bread and wine and ministered to Abraham's needs (Gen 14:18) is not mentioned, possibly because that circumstance might be construed as implying that Abraham was actually superior to Melchizedek (Williamson, *Philo,* 445). The name and the two titles of Melchizedek are interpreted in the same order in which they are given in v 1a (v 2b). Finally, in v 3 the writer takes account of the fact that, unlike other significant historical figures in Genesis, Melchizedek is introduced without genealogy and without reference to his birth or death, and develops the implications of this silence for the significance of Melchizedek's priesthood (cf. Demarest, *History of Interpretation,* 131–32; Cockerill, 22).

Unlike the Hebrew kings, Melchizedek represented the tradition of sacral kingship; he united in his person the dual honors of royalty and priesthood. In the description provided in Gen 14:18, his office as king of Salem is mentioned first (for a review of OT scholarship on Gen 14:18–20, see Kirkland, *StudBibTh* 7 [1977] 3–23). The city-state of Salem has been identified traditionally as Jerusalem (Ps 76:2; Jos., *Ant.* 1.180; 1QapGen xxii.13; *Tg. Neof.* Gen 14:18; cf. L. H. Vincent, "Abraham à Jérusalem," *RB* 58 [1951] 360–71; P. Winter, "Note on Salem-Jerusalem," *NovT* 2 [1957] 151–52). This identification, however, is debated, and a strong case can be made for locating Salem at ancient Shechem (cf. Kirkland, 5–11). Hebrews shows no concern to equate Salem with Jerusalem but simply records the statement of fact.

Melchizedek is introduced as "priest of God Most High," who in Genesis is presumed to be the God of Abraham. In Hebrews the designation presupposes the fact that in Judaism and early Christianity "God Most High" was a common ascription emphasizing the transcendent dignity of God (e.g., Philo, *Allegorical Interpretation* 3.82; Mark 5:7 par.; Acts 7:48; 16:17; *1 Clem.* 59:3; cf. T. Hanlon, "The Most High God of Genesis 14:18–20," *Scr* 11 [1959] 110–18). The only priestly action recorded of Melchizedek is his blessing of the patriarch in the name of God Most High (Gen 14:19–20a; Heb 7:1b). In recognition of Melchizedek's priesthood, Abraham gave him a tenth of the booty that had been recovered from the defeated kings. The finite verb ἐμέρισεν, "he allotted," is substituted for the verb ἔδωκεν, "he gave," in the LXX text to emphasize the fact that Abraham paid a tithe (Moffatt, 91–92; Cockerill, *Melchizedek Christology,* 31). In Gen 14:20b it is not specified who gave the tithe to whom, but in the tradition no doubt is left that it was Abraham who paid the tithe to Melchizedek (Philo, *Harris Fragment; On the Preliminary Studies* 99; Jos., *Ant.* 1.181; 1QapGen xxii.17; *Pirqe R. El.* 27).

The expression πρῶτον μέν, "first," in v 2b marks the division between the detail cited from Genesis concerning Melchizedek and the interpretation of the material. In vv 2b–3 the identity of Melchizedek is explained in terms of the designations provided in v 1. The etymological interpretation of Melchizedek's Hebrew name and titles are natural ones, and similar interpretations occur independently in Philo (*Allegorical Interpretation* 3.79) and Josephus (*Ant.* 1.180; cf. Fitzmyer, *CBQ* 25 [1963] 311–13). The writer may have recognized in Melchizedek's character as "king of righteousness" and "king of peace" a prefiguration of the promised Messiah (cf. Zimmermann, *Hohepriester-Christologie,* 13), but nothing is made of these notions. All interest is concentrated on the priesthood of Melchizedek, which is interpreted in v 3. The impression conveyed by v 2b is that the writer gave a brief interpretation of "Melchizedek" and the title "king of Salem" only for the sake of completeness (Cockerill, *Melchizedek Christology,* 34–35, 38).

A correct understanding of v 3 is essential to a proper appreciation both of the uniqueness of Melchizedek and of the priest "like him." Yet the four declarations in this verse are by no means self-evident in the biblical text. The range of critical opinion prompted by the detail of the writer's statement is an indication of its difficulty. J. W. Thompson is representative of those who have interpreted v 3 in the light of hellenistic metaphysical speculation and who understand the predicates concerning Melchizedek as literally true about him. He argues that the distinctive expression has a long history in Greek metaphysics and piety: the descriptive term ἀπάτωρ, "without father," and ἀμήτωρ, "without mother," for example, are well known as divine predicates in hellenistic sources (e.g., Julius Pollux, *Onomasticon* 3.26; cf. Schrenk, *TDNT* 5:1021–22). According to Thompson, they are employed by the writer to support his claim that Melchizedek is "a divine figure" (*NovT* 19 [1977] 211), a heavenly being who is not a part of the world of sense-perception (212–14; cf. Wuttke, *Melchizedek*, 3–13; Windisch, 59–63; Käsemann, *Das wandernde Gottesvolk*, 116–56; de Jonge and van der Woude, *NTS* 12 [1965–66] 318–26; Dey, *Intermediary World*, 190–91, 210–11; Cockerill, *Melchizedek Christology*, 62–64, 189–90). On the other hand, Demarest is representative of those who insist that if the statements of v 3 are interpreted in a strictly literal sense, Melchizedek would appear "as a supra-human figure whose priesthood would encroach upon the eternal priesthood of Christ" (*History of Interpretation*, 9; cf. Westcott, 173; Riggenbach, 179; Meeter, *Heavenly High Priesthood*, 64; Kuss, 55; F. F. Bruce, 133–38). These diametrically opposed points of view concerning the writer's intention reflect different estimates of the element in v 3 that is crucial. According to the first approach, the crucial statement is v 3*b* ("having neither beginning of days nor end of life"), which indicates that the writer is developing a hellenistic mythological concept of a supra-human figure endowed with a mysterious heavenly origin. According to the second approach, the significant element is the third term in v 3*a* ("without genealogy"), in the light of which the other declarations are to be interpreted. The writer is developing the essentially Jewish notion that Melchizedek is representative of no priestly ancestry, and that for all of his greatness the non-Levitical priest bears a scandalous relation to the Mosaic Law (cf. Cockerill, 38–41).

In deciding between alternative approaches it is imperative to recognize that v 3 is a polished example of condensed reference. The writer secures the maximum of meaning with a strict economy in expression (Rendall, *EvQ* 27 [1955] 214). He presents a concise summary of points that neither have to be established nor explained. The formulation is more illustrative than argumentative. The highly compressed style is calculated to prompt a search for interpretive links between the OT record and the distinctive clauses of the verse. The primary purpose of the statement is not to establish a factual point but to exhibit the radical difference that existed between the priesthood of Melchizedek and the more familiar Levitical line of priests. In this context, the silence of the Genesis narrative concerning Melchizedek's parents or line of priestly descent was significant because of the contrast it posed with the Levitical priesthood, where recorded line of descent was required for accession to the priestly office (Exod 28:1; Lev 21:13–15; Num 3:10; 18:1; Ezra 2:61–63; Neh 7:63–65).

The first clause consists of an alpha-privative (ἀ) triad. The key to its interpretation is provided by the third term ἀγενεαλόγητος, "without recorded descent," which amplifies the meaning of the first two words and indicates that v 3*a* concerns priestly qualification and not miraculous birth (Soubigou, *ATh* 7 [1946] 71;

Horton, *Melchizedek Tradition*, 162). There is no hint in the argument that unfolds in vv 4–10 that the writer regarded Melchizedek in mythological terms. He presents the royal priest of God Most High as a historical personage in primal history. Melchizedek is ἀπάτωρ, "without father," and ἀμήτωρ, "without mother," because no mention is made of his father, mother, or line of descent in Genesis. Philo offers a similar interpretation of the biblical text when he twice uses ἀμήτωρ to describe Sarah precisely because her mother is not mentioned in the biblical text (*On Drunkenness* 61; *Who Is the Heir?* 62). The silence of Scripture concerning Melchizedek's parents and family line is stressed by the writer to amplify the concept of the uniqueness of his priesthood, and not as a proof of that uniqueness (cf. Horton, 159–60). It implies that Melchizedek's priesthood was not established upon the external circumstances of birth and descent. It was based on the call of God and not on the hereditary process by which the Levitical priesthood was sustained (cf. 5:5–6; 7:14). Without a recorded priestly genealogy, Melchizedek could not have qualified for Levitical priesthood. Nevertheless, this man was priest of God Most High, and Abraham recognized his dignity (cf. Demarest, *History of Interpretation*, 133–34; Cockerill, *Melchizedek Christology,* 49–50).

Exploiting the silence of the Genesis account concerning Melchizedek's birth or death, the writer declares in the second clause (v 3*b*) that the priesthood of Melchizedek had no beginning and no end. Michel remarks that "the priest without priestly origin also had no Scriptural limitation to his life and work" (263). He required neither priestly ancestry nor succession to authorize his unique and unending priesthood, which shows the unrestricted quality of his life. Melchizedek's sudden appearance and equally sudden disappearance from recorded history evoked the notion of eternity, which was only prefigured in Melchizedek but was realized in Christ. Consequently, Melchizedek foreshadows the priesthood of Christ at that point where it is most fundamentally different from the Levitical priesthood (cf. Spicq, 2:209; Demarest, *History of Interpretation*, 134–35).

The transition from the negative predicates of v 3*a*, *b* to the positive assertions in v 3*c*, *d* is effected by the adversative particle δέ, "but." The third clause (v 3*c*) discloses that the events in Genesis have been read from the perspective of the eschatological reality they prefigured; Melchizedek has been assimilated to the Son of God. This implies that the predicates applied to Melchizedek have been colored by the writer's conception of the eternal Son. Spicq describes the person of Melchizedek as a mirror in which the writer found reflected essential aspects attributed by Ps 110:4 to the promised eternal priest (2:189). That explains why the description of Melchizedek in v 3 appears singularly stylized. The perfect passive participle ἀφωμοιωμένος is an example of a "divine passive" ("having been made [by God] to resemble"); the term presupposes God's appointment of Melchizedek as an illustration of the higher priesthood that the writer finds in the OT record. The formulation in v 3*c* appears to assume the subordination of Melchizedek to the eternal Son (Horton, *Melchizedek Tradition*, 156). He possesses a prophetic, but not saving, significance.

The final clause transcends the warrants of the text in Genesis by endowing Melchizedek with a perpetual priesthood. In a strict sense, the conclusion that he remains a priest continually is a logical deduction from the assertion in v 3*b*. The formulation of v 3*d* demonstrates the impact of Ps 110:4 upon the interpretation of Gen 14:18–20. The expression εἰς τὸ διηνεκές, "continually without interruption," is a refinement of the phrase εἰς τὸν αἰῶνα, "forever," in Ps 110:4. It indicates how precisely the writer understood the ascription of eternity predicated on the priest "like Melchizedek." The most obvious source for the notion of the perpetuity of Melchizedek's priesthood in v 3 is the writer's confidence in the eternal priesthood of Christ (Soubigou, *ATh* 7 [1946] 71; Horton, *Melchizedek Tradition*, 170; cf. Cockerill, *Melchizedek Christology*, 484, 490). The writer finds that the eternal character of the priesthood of the one "like Melchizedek" was already implied in Gen 14, where Melchizedek does not take up his priestly service from a predecessor and remains a priest without successor. The silence of the record invests Melchizedek with an intransmissible, and therefore continuous, priesthood, which foreshadows the eternal and final character of the priesthood of Christ (Michel, 263; Demarest, *History of Interpretation*, 134–36). The writer uses the term μένει, "he remains," which evokes the notion of eternity, in an eschatological sense. The implication that Melchizedek "remains" a priest continually permits a measure of understanding of Christ as the abiding, eternal priest. The "eternal" nature of the Melchizedek priesthood is its distinguishing feature. It is the one element above all others that interests the writer as he prepares to present Christ as the high priest "like Melchizedek" (cf. Meeter, *Heavenly High Priesthood*, 65; Spicq, 2: 210; Hay, *Glory*, 147; et al.).

The Gen 14 narrative thus implies the kind of priesthood that was intended by God to displace the Levitical priesthood, namely the service of an eternal priest who exercises his priesthood continuously. It anticipates the appearance of a high priest who does not have any successor because he does not require one (Williamson, *Philo*, 439–40). The use of the incident in the Valley of the Kings maintains redemptive-historical categories of thought and provides a historical basis for the superiority of the priest like Melchizedek. Positive use is made of Melchizedek in v 3 to point to the eternity of the new priest. Subsequently, every clause of v 3 will become important to the argument developed in 7:1–28 (v 3*a* is used in vv 5–6, 13–14; v 3*b* in vv 8, 15–16, 24, 28; v 3*c* in vv 15–16; and v 3*d* in vv 22–25; see especially Cockerill, *Melchizedek Christology*, 63–64, 187–90).

4 The point to be proven in vv 4–10 is that Melchizedek is a priest who was superior to the Levitical priests. Basic to the argument is Abraham's payment of a tithe to him (v 2*a*; Gen 14:20), which provides historical verification for the greatness of the Salemite priest. The fact that Melchizedek blessed Abraham is also introduced in a supplementary way. In the course of the argument the writer develops two contrasts between Melchizedek and the Levitical priesthood that make effective use of the description of Melchizedek in v 3*a*, *b*. In the first (vv 5–6*a*), use is made of the predicates in v 3*a*; the second (v 8) depends upon the enigmatic assertion of v 3*b* for its point. It is evident throughout the paragraph that the writer treats the meeting recorded in Gen 14:17–20 as an actual historical incident. The "historicity" of the events is important to his argument (Cockerill, *Melchizedek Christology*, 23, 65–66, 211).

The theme of the new paragraph is announced homiletically by an oratorical imperative, "consider how great a man this must have been." The key word in this section is πηλίκος, a correlative pronoun used here in an exclamatory sense, "how great!" But the greatness of Melchizedek is emphasized in other ways. Abraham's allotment of a tenth of everything to Melchizedek (v 2*a*) is further

defined in v 4 by specifying that it was a tenth of the spoils of war. The term
ἀκροθινίων, denoting the best or choicest of the spoils, appears to have been chosen to sharpen the impression of Melchizedek's exalted stature. According to Philo,
what Abraham gave Melchizedek were τὰ τοῦ πολέμου ἀριστεῖα, "the weapons of
war" (*Harris Fragment*; text in Moffatt, 91). The term ὁ πατριάρχης, "the patriarch," which is placed at the end of the sentence for emphasis, serves to underscore
the stature of Abraham as the progenitor of Israel (4 Macc 7:19; 16:23; Acts 7:8–
9; cf. Riggenbach, 186). But Abraham is exalted in v 4 only to emphasize the
exalted status of Melchizedek even more.

The designation of Abraham as "patriarch" is important to the argument that
follows: it is because Abraham is the patriarch of the race that a comparison can
be made between the Levitical priesthood and Melchizedek through him. The
ancestor embodies, symbolizes, and represents the whole group of his descendants. Abraham is not simply an individual, but a representative figure in this
context. By using the term "patriarch," the writer prepares for the conclusion of
vv 9–10 that Levi paid a tithe to Melchizedek through his father (πατήρ), Abraham
(Cockerill, *Melchizedek Christology*, 66).

5–6a The first contrast between Melchizedek and the Levitical priests is set
forth within a μέν . . . δέ construction ("Now on the one hand . . . but on the
other"). The exalted status of the Levitical priests is stressed in v 5 so that when
Melchizedek is compared with them in v 6 he will appear to be all the greater.
The use of the present tense throughout v 5 probably represents the present of
general statement, but there is no indication here, or elsewhere in Hebrews, that the
Levitical priesthood has ceased to function (Cockerill, *Melchizedek Christology*, 66).

The comparison is focused upon the identity of the two priesthoods and the
authority by which they collected tithes. The ground of the comparison with
Melchizedek is the term τὴν ἱερατείαν, "priestly office." The Levitical priests were
to receive tithes for their service in the priestly office (Num 18:21–24; cf. Luke
1:9). The expression ἐκ τῶν υἱῶν Λευί, "those belonging to the sons of Levi," is
basic to the comparison because it connects the Levitical priests with Abraham
and emphasizes their physical descent, a factor to be used later in the argument
in vv 9–10. The statement that these priests collect tithes on the ground of an
ordinance in the Mosaic law comes from LXX usage, where ἀποδεκατοῦν is used
of the collecting of tithes (1 Sam 8:15, 17; Neh 10:37) and where ἐντολή denotes
the specific command and νόμος the law as the sum of the commandments (e.g.,
Exod 16:18; 24:12; Josh 22:5; Sir 35:24; cf. Schrenk, *TDNT* 2:546). The distinction between ἐντολή and νόμος in the LXX is maintained in Hebrews, where each
time ἐντολή occurs it is used in association with νόμος (7:5, 16–18; 9:19; cf. Schrenk,
TDNT 2:553; Gutbrod, *TDNT* 4:1078). Cockerill has made the point that law in
Hebrews is seen in terms of priesthood and sacrifice, and consequently the expression κατὰ τὸν νόμον in v 5 denotes "according to the Levitical religious system"
(*Melchizedek Christology*, 68, 105–7). The writer stresses in v 5 that the particular
ordinance by which those priests who descended from Levi and Abraham exacted the tithe depended on the total legal system of authority. By contrast,
Melchizedek is identified as "one not tracing his descent from them" (v 6a) who
did not require the law to authorize his reception of a tithe (Cockerill, 67–69).

The impact of the comparison is strengthened by a contrast between those
from whom tithes were received. Those from whom the Levitical priests collect

tithes are defined as "the people," and "their brothers" or equals (v 5*b*). According to the Pentateuch, the people paid the tithes to the Levites, who then paid a tithe of that amount to the priests (Lev 18:21; Num 18:26–28). This practice continued to be in force as late as the period of the restoration following the Exile (Neh 10:38–39). There is evidence, however, that in the period contemporary with Hebrews the priests themselves collected the tithe from the people (cf. Jos., *Life* 80; *Ant.* 20.181, 206–7). The writer does not contest the Levitical claim to the tithe, but he presents Melchizedek as one whose claim was recognized not by those who were his equals but by the patriarch Abraham himself (Michel, 264). Such was the exalted status of this man. The implication to be drawn from this comparison is that since the Levitical priests as well as those from whom they exacted the tithe were descendants of Abraham, Melchizedek must be superior to the Levitical priests (cf. vv 9–10).

In this first contrast, Abraham's allotment of a tenth of everything to Melchizedek is seen in the light of the fact that Melchizedek was ἀγενεαλόγητος, "without recorded descent" (v 3*a*). In contrast to the legal priests, for whom paternal descent from Aaron (Exod 28:1; Num 3:10; 18:1) and maternal descent from a pure Israelite (Lev 21:7; Ezek 44:2) was mandatory, Melchizedek exercised a priestly role on the basis of divine appointment and innate worth (cf. Cockerill, *Melchizedek Christology*, 71). The description of Melchizedek in v 6*a* describes him as without legal qualification for the priesthood and adumbrates the picture of the promised messianic priest as one who was descended from the nonsacerdotal tribe of Judah (vv 13–14; cf. Demarest, *History of Interpretation*, 134).

6*b*–7 The impression of Melchizedek's superiority to Abraham, and by implication to the Levitical priesthood, is intensified in v 6*b*. The clause amplifies the simple statement in v 1*b* that Melchizedek blessed Abraham by identifying the patriarch as the one "who had the promises." In the immediate context a contrast is implied between Abraham, who received the divine promise (v 6*b*), and the Levitical priests, who possessed the law (v 5). The theologically significant term ἐπαγγελία, "promise," in Hebrews has the connotation of effectiveness and certainty: what God has promised, he will accomplish (6:13–18; 10:23). The expression νόμος, "law," on the other hand, has the connotation of ineffectiveness (7:19*a*, 28*a*). In this manner the contrast between Melchizedek and the Levitical priests is heightened because they collected tithes according to the law, but Melchizedek blessed Abraham, who had himself received the divine promise that God would surely bless him (6:13–14; cf. Cockerill, *Melchizedek Christology*, 71–72).

The significance of Melchizedek's priestly act of blessing is explained parenthetically in v 7. The adverbial phrase χωρὶς δὲ πάσης ἀντιλογίας, "now unquestionably," is common in the papyri when a writer wishes to stress the certainty of what he is saying (MM 48). Here it qualifies the general statement of principle that the less prominent person is blessed by the more prominent (τὸ ἔλαττον ὑπὸ τοῦ κρείττονος εὐλογεῖται). The comparative term κρείττων/κρείττονος, "better, more prominent, greater," is frequently used by the writer in making value judgments (see on 1:14; 7:19, 22; 8:6; 9:23; 11:40). In Judaism there was a tradition of discussing the relative greatness of the leading figures in primal history (Str-B 1:249–50, 774). The writer assumes that the issue of the relative greatness of Melchizedek and Abraham is decided in Gen 14:18–20 in favor of the priest of God Most High (cf. Cockerill, *Melchizedek Christology*, 73–74, 79–80).

8 The second contrast between Melchizedek and the Levitical priests is drawn in v 8. The basis of the comparison remains that both the Levitical priests and the priest of Salem received tithes. The emphasis, however, has shifted from the question of qualification (v 3*a*, 5–6*a*) to that of the relative duration of their respective ministries.

The two halves of the verse are set in sharp contrast by the construction καὶ ὧδε μέν . . . ἐκεῖ δέ . . . . , "in the one case . . . but in the other . . . ." In v 8*a* the participle ἀποθνῄσκοντες, "mortal," is placed before the noun it modifies to characterize the Levitical priests who receive tithes as mortal men. Those who are appointed to priestly service by the law are subject to death and so have a series of successors. Although the term δεκάτας, "tithes," and the appropriate form of λαμβάνειν, "to receive," are not repeated in v 8*b*, they are implied. It is this fact which justifies the application of the extraordinary ascription ὅτι ζῇ, "that he lives," to Melchizedek. As the clause stands, all the emphasis falls on the startling assertion that Melchizedek is "one to whom witness is borne that he is alive." The term μαρτυρούμενος, "witness is borne," almost certainly has reference to Scripture (cf. v 17; 10:5). In this context the declaration must refer back to v 3, which the writer considered to be exegetically established on the basis of Ps 110:4 and Gen 14:18–20. Scripture announces of Melchizedek only his living and the administration of a priesthood that is free from temporal limitation (cf. Schröger, *Verfasser*, 143; Cockerill, *Melchizedek Christology*, 74–78; Demarest, *History of Interpretation*, 136).

The basis of Melchizedek's superiority to the Levitical priests in this second contrast is the "eternity" of Melchizedek predicated in v 3*b*, which has in view the perpetuation of his priestly office. The importance of this aspect of the argument will become clear in vv 15–16, where it is applied to the messianic priest. So far as the record of Scripture is concerned, Melchizedek has no end of life and his unique priesthood has no successor. But what is true of Melchizedek in a limited and literary sense is true absolutely of the one who serves his people as high priest in the presence of God (F. F. Bruce, 141–42).

9–10 The climax of the argument is reached in v 9 and qualified in v 10. It specifies the implication of the first contrast between Melchizedek and the Levitical priests (vv 5–6*a*) by deducing the deeper significance of the fact that Abraham allotted a tithe to Melchizedek (Cockerill, *Melchizedek Christology*, 23–24, 78). The literary phrase ὡς ἔπος εἰπεῖν, "one might almost say," was frequently used when a writer broke off the train of his thought and, not wishing to treat his theme more fully, would summarize as succinctly as possible what he had to say. Here it indicates the writer clearly recognized his statement that Levi had paid a tithe to Melchizedek was not literally true, because at the moment in primal history when Abraham met Melchizedek Levi was as yet unborn. Nevertheless, the statement that Levi had himself paid the tithe was true in an important sense, indicated by the expression δι' Ἀβραάμ, "through Abraham," which immediately follows. The corporate solidarity that bound Israel to the patriarch implied that Levi was fully represented in Abraham's action. Therefore, Levi's status relative to Melchizedek was affected by Abraham's relationship to that personage. Consequently, the superiority of Melchizedek over the Levitical priesthood is not merely theoretical but has a basis in history (cf. Riggenbach, 190–91; Williamson, *Philo*, 107–9; Cockerill, *Melchizedek Christology*, 78–80).

The assertion in v 9 is justified and explained in v 10, as shown by the explanatory conjunction γάρ, "because." Although Levi was as yet unborn when Melchizedek met Abraham, the tithe Abraham gave to Melchizedek was a gesture that anticipated the subordination of Levi and the Levitical priesthood to the priesthood like Melchizedek's that would be inaugurated at God's appointed time.

Explanation

In chap. 7 the writer expounds the new and profound concept of the priesthood of Christ implicit in the oracle of Ps 110:4, a christological theme found nowhere else in the NT. In preparation for the explication of the high priest who would arise after "the likeness of Melchizedek," he concerns himself in 7:1–10 with the ancient priestly model who prefigured the messianic priest. A proper appreciation of the conceptions embodied in the radically new priesthood of Christ (7:11–28) depends upon a correct understanding of the excellence of Melchizedek and his priesthood. The writer's use of Melchizedek is positive. An understanding of Christ's eternal priesthood will be gained from a consideration of selected features of the perpetual priesthood of Melchizedek. He regards Melchizedek not as a type to be fulfilled, but as a witness to the higher priesthood he finds foreshadowed in the OT. Melchizedek serves as a precedent for a superior priesthood based on a character apart from line of descent and ordained by God apart from law. He represents an exception to the common interpretation of priesthood in the OT in that he anticipates the ultimate displacement of the Levitical priesthood. The "typical" significance of Melchizedek lies in the timeless nature of his office as priest without successor. The motif of the "eternity" of Melchizedek and of the priesthood he exercises constitutes the prominent theme of 7:1–10.

The basis of the exposition is an exegesis of Gen 14:17–20 in the light of the interpretation implied in Ps 110:4. The writer's analysis shows deep respect for the detail of the biblical text. Inasmuch as the presentation of any fact always entails a certain degree of interpretation, he could conceive of the Genesis narrative as already implying a germinal interpretation in the form of the presentation. Consequently, even the silence of Scripture is significant. The portrayal of a royal priestly figure who is devoid of parentage, descent, and commencement and termination of life evokes the notion of a priest who continues in his office forever. His superiority to the patriarch Abraham and to the Levitical priests descended from him is deduced from the detail of Genesis, which establishes a historical basis for the superiority of Melchizedek's priesthood.

The use that is made of Melchizedek in 7:1–10 is thoroughly christological. He has no independent significance in Hebrews; he is introduced only for the sake of the Son (7:3*c*). His function is not soteriological but prophetic. Although Melchizedek stands outside the mainstream of redemptive history, he illustrates those prophecies of the OT that pointed to the deficiency of the old order and to the superiority and sufficiency of the coming new age. This persuasion explains why the writer understands Melchizedek from the perspective of Ps 110:4. The use made of Melchizedek as a witness to the unique priestly office of the eternal Son is singular in Hebrews, for nowhere else does the writer focus upon an event in primal history to explain an oracle that he found fulfilled in Christ. Conversely,

Melchizedek derives his significance from the Son. It is only in the perspective of the eternal Son that the "eternal" character of Melchizedek and his priesthood becomes evident. Melchizedek bears the eternal character of the Son, but it is the Son who remains primary. Accordingly, christology, and not speculation, is the determining factor in the portrayal of Melchizedek in 7:1–10.

D. Jesus, Eternal Priest Like Melchizedek (7:11–28)

Bibliography

Andriessen, P. *En lisant l'Épître aux Hébreux.* 26–31. **Auberlen, C. A.** "Melchizedek's ewige Leben und Priestertum: Hebr. 7." *TSK* 30 (1857) 453–504. **Brooks, W. E.** "The Perpetuity of Christ's Sacrifice in the Epistle to the Hebrews." *JBL* 89 (1970) 205–14. **Cockerill, G. L.** *The Melchizedek Christology in Heb. 7:1–28.* Ann Arbor: University Microfilms International, 1979. **Cominskey, J. P.** "The Order of Melchizedek." *TBT* 27 (1966) 1913–18. **Culpepper, R. H.** "The High Priesthood and Sacrifice of Christ in the Epistle to the Hebrews." *ThEduc* 32 (1985) 46–62. **Demarest, B.** "Priest after the Order of Melchizedek: A History of Interpretation of Hebrews 7 From the Era of the Reformation to the Present." Dissertation, University of Manchester, 1973. [published as *A History of Interpretation of Hebrews 7, 1–10 from the Reformation to the Present.* BGBE 19. Tübingen: Mohr, 1976.] **Dey, L. K. K.** *The Intermediary World and Patterns of Perfection.* 185–214. **Dussaut, L.** *Synopse structurelle de l'Épître aux Hébreux.* 58–64. **Ellingworth, P.** "Jesus and the Universe in Hebrews." *EvQ* 58 (1986) 337–50. ———. "Just like Melchizedek." *BT* 28 (1977) 236–39. ———. "The Unshakable Priesthood: Hebrews 7:24." *JSNT* 23 (1985) 125–26. **Fabris, R.** "La lettera agli Ebrei e l'Antico Testamento." *RivB* 32 (1984) 237–52. **Gayford, S. C.** "The Aorist Participles in Heb. 1:3; 7:27; 10:12." *Th* 7 (1923) 282. **Gordon, V.** "Studies in the Covenantal Theology of the Epistle to the Hebrews in the Light of Its Setting." Dissertation, Fuller Theological Seminary, 1979. 157–234. **Hay, D. M.** *Glory at the Right Hand.* 130–34, 146–50, 152–53. **Hollander, H. W.** "Hebrews 7:11 and 8:6: A Suggestion for the Translation of *nenomothetētai epi.*" *BT* 30 (1979) 244–47. **Horbury, W.** "The Aaronic Priesthood in the Epistle to the Hebrews." *JSNT* 19 (1983) 43–71. **Hunt, I.** "Recent Melchizedek Study." In *The Bible in Current Catholic Thought.* Ed. J. L. McKensie. New York: Herder and Herder, 1962. 21–33. **Jonge, H. J. de.** "Traditie en exegese: de hogepriester-christogie en Melchizedek in Hebreeën." *NedTTs* 37 (1983) 1–19. **Kennedy, G. T.** *St. Paul's Conception of the Priesthood of Melchisedech: An Historico-Exegetical Investigation.* Washington, DC: Catholic University, 1951. **Kistemaker, S.** *The Psalm Citations in the Epistle to the Hebrews.* 116–24. **Kögel, J.** "Der Begriff τελειοῦν im Hebräerbrief im Zusammenhang mit dem neutestamentlichen Sprachgebrauch." In *Theologische Studien.* FS M. Kähler. Leipzig: Deichert, 1905. 35–68. **Lach, S.** "Les ordonnances du culte Israélite dans la lettre aux Hébreux." In *Sacra Pagina: Miscellanea Biblica Congressus Internationalis Catholici de Re Biblica.* Ed. J. Coppens, A. Descamps, and E. Massaux. Paris: Gabalda, 1952. 2:390–403. **Laub, F.** *Bekenntnis und Auslegung.* 31–41, 236–43. **Lehne, S.** *The New Covenant in Hebrews.* JSNTSup 44. Sheffield: JSOT, 1990. **Loader, W. R. G.** "Christ at the Right Hand— Ps. CX.1 in the New Testament" *NTS* 24 (1977–78) 199–217. ———. *Sohn und Hoherpriester.* 39–49, 142–48, 151–60, 203–22. **Lorimer, W. L.** "Hebrews VII, 23f." *NTS* 13 (1966–67) 386–87. **Marshall, J. L.** "Melchizedek in Hebrews, Philo and Justin Martyr." *SE* 7 (1982) 339–42. **Mauchline, J.** "Jesus Christ as Intercessor." *ExpTim* 64 (1952–53) 355–60. **McCullough, J. C.** "Melchizedek's Varied Role in Early Exegetical Tradition." *ThRev* 1 (1978) 52–66. **Meeter, H. H.** *The Heavenly High Priesthood of Christ.* 86–112, 181–203. **Melbourne, B. L.** "An Examination of the Historical-Jesus Motif in the Epistle to the Hebrews." *AUSS* 26 (1988) 281–97. **Neal, M.**

"Melchizedek and Christ (Hebrews 7)." *BV* 2 (1968) 21–27. **Nomoto, S.** "Herkunft und Struktur der Hohenpriestervorstellung im Hebräerbrief." *NovT* 10 (1968) 10–25. **Olson, S. N.** "Wandering but Not Lost." *WW* 5 (1985) 426–33. **Parsons, M. C.** "Son and High Priest: A Study in the Christology of Hebrews." *EvQ* 60 (1988) 195–215. **Paul, M. J.** "The Order of Melchizedek (Ps 110:4 and Heb 7:3)." *WTJ* 49 (1987) 195–211. **Peterson, D. G.** "An Examination of the Concept of 'Perfection' in the 'Epistle to the Hebrews.'" Dissertation, University of Manchester, 1978. 174–222, 326–38. **Plessis, P. J. du.** *ΤΕΛΕΙΟΣ: The Idea of Perfection in the New Testament.* 212–33. **Rábanos, R.** "Sacerdocio de Melquisedec, sacerdocio de Aarón y sacerdocio de Cristo." *CB* 13 (1956) 264–75. **Schlosser, J.** "La médiation du Christ d'après l'Épître aux Hébreux." *RevScRel* 63 (1989) 169–81. **Schröger, F.** *Der Verfasser des Hebräerbriefes.* 144–59, 203, 206, 225–29. **Seeberg, A.** "Versuch einer neuen Erklärung von Hebr 7,27." *JDT* 3 (1894) 364–74. **Silva, M.** "Perfection and Eschatology in Hebrews." *WTJ* 39 (1976) 60–71. **Songer, H. S.** "A Superior Priesthood: Hebrews 4:14–7:28." *RevExp* 82 (1985) 345–59. **Soubigou, L.** "Le chapitre VII de l'Épître aux Hébreux." *ATh* 7 (1946) 69–82. **Spicq, C.** "La perfection chrétienne d'après l'Épître aux Hébreux." In *Bibliothèque de la Faculté Catholique de Théologie de Lyon* 5. FS J. Chaine. Ed. G. Villepelet. Lyon: Facultés Catholiques, 1950. 337–52. **Stott, W.** "The Conception 'Offering' in the Epistle to the Hebrews." *NTS* 9 (1962–63) 62–67. **Tetley, J.** "The Priesthood of Christ in Hebrews." *Anvil* 5 (1988) 195–206. **Theissen, G.** *Untersuchung zum Hebräerbrief.* 13–33, 130–52. **Thompson, J. W.** "The Conceptual Background and Purpose of the Midrash in Hebrews VII." *NovT* 19 (1977) 209–23. **Torm, F.** "Om τελειοῦν: Hb." *SEÅ* 5 (1940) 116–25. **Vanhoye, A.** "La parfait grand prêtre (He 7,23–27)." *AsSeign* 93 (1965) 15–31. **Watson, J. K.** "Melkisédec et le Fils de Dieu." *CCER* 30 (1982) 49–60. **Williamson, R.** *Philo and the Epistle to the Hebrews.* 81–83, 129–30, 177–80, 441–43, 447. **Zimmermann, H.** *Das Bekenntnis der Hoffnung.* 100–110. **Zorn, R.** "Die Fürbitte im Spätjudentum und im Neuen Testament." Dissertation, Göttingen, 1957. **Zwemer, S. M.** "Melchizedek and Aaron." *EvQ* 23 (1951) 164–70.

Translation

[11] *If, then, perfection had been attainable*[a] *through the Levitical priesthood (for the people received regulations concerning the Levitical priesthood*[b]*), what need would there still have been for a different kind of priest to arise "like Melchizedek" and not one designated*[c] *"like Aaron"*[d]*?* [12] *(For whenever the priesthood is altered,*[e] *there is necessarily also an alteration of law.)* [13] *The one*[f] *about whom these things were said belongs to a different tribe, from which no one ever officiated at the altar.*[g] [14]*For it is perfectly clear*[h] *that our Lord was descended from Judah, in relation to which tribe Moses said nothing concerning priests.* [15] *And it is still more obvious*[i] *that if, as said before, according to the likeness of Melchizedek a different priest arises,*[j] [16] *he does so not by virtue of a legal ordinance concerning physical descent,*[k] *but by virtue of the power of an indestructible*[l] *life,* [17] *for he has witness borne to him as follows:*

"You are a priest forever
    like Melchizedek."

[18] *Now there was the annulment*[m] *of a former commandment, because of its weakness and uselessness* [19] *(for the law perfected nothing), but the introduction of the better hope*[n] *through which we are drawing near to God.*

[20] *And insofar as*[o] *it was not without the swearing of an oath*[p] *(for others*[q] *became priests without the swearing of an oath,* [21] *but he became a priest with the swearing of an oath through the one who said to him,*

"The Lord has sworn
    and he will not change his mind,
You are a priest forever"),

²²*just so far Jesus has become the guarantor* ʳ *of a better covenant.* ²³*Now on the one hand, these many* ˢ *have become priests, because they were prevented by death from continuing in office,* ᵗ ²⁴*but on the other hand that one, because he continues forever, has a priesthood which is permanent.* ᵘ ²⁵*And so he is able to save absolutely* ᵛ *those who approach God through him, because he continually lives in order to intercede for them.*

²⁶*Now such a high priest was precisely* ʷ *appropriate for us, one who is devout, guileless, and undefiled; having been separated from sinners,* ˣ *he became exalted even higher than the heavens.* ʸ ²⁷*He does not need to offer sacrifices daily,* ᶻ *like those other high priests, first for his own sins, and then for the sins of the people. For he sacrificed for their sins* ᵃᵃ *once for all when he offered himself.* ²⁸*For the law appoints men* ᵇᵇ *as high priests affected by weakness, but the word sworn on oath, which came after the law, appoints as high priest* ᶜᶜ *the Son who has been made perfect forever.* ᵈᵈ

Notes

ᵃ The εἰ μὲν οὖν . . . ἦν construction is characteristic of a contrary-to-fact, or "unfulfilled," condition (εἰ followed by the verb in the ind; Zerwick, *Biblical Greek* §313–14; BDF §§360[4], 447[3]). Such constructions occur with relative frequency in Hebrews (4:8; 7:11; 8:4, 7; 11:15).

ᵇ The import of the prep ἐπί in the expression ἐπ᾽ αὐτῆς νενομοθέτηται has been understood in three ways: (1) the law was given *on the basis* of the Levitical priesthood (so NEB, JB, TEV, NIV; BDF §234[8]); (2) the law was given *under* (or, *through*) the Levitical priesthood (RSV); (3) the law was given *in association with* the Levitical priesthood (Hughes, 256). The verb in the pass, which in the NT occurs only in Hebrews (7:11; 8:6), means "to be regulated by law" (BAGD 541–42). This form occurs elsewhere with the prep ἐπί followed by the gen (as in Heb 7:11) or by the dative (as in Heb 8:6) with the nuance "regulations have been laid down by the law *in the case of* (or, *concerning*)" (e.g., Philo, *On the Special Laws* 2.35, "These are the regulations laid down by law concerning people [ἐπ᾽ ἀνθρώπων]; but concerning animals [ἐπὶ δὲ κτήνων] we have the following regulations [νομοθετεῖται]"; *On the Special Laws* 1.235, "regulations concerning sins of ignorance have been laid down [νομοθετήσας ἐπὶ τοῖς ἀκουσίοις]"). The translation reflects this idiomatic usage: the people have received regulations concerning the genealogical descent of the Levitical priests (so Hollander, *BT* 30 [1979] 244–47, Dey, *Intermediary World*, 194, n. 6).

These variant proposals assume that the personal pronoun αὐτῆς finds its antecedent in ἱερωσύνης, "priesthood." Recently Andriessen has argued that the personal pronoun should be related to the more distant term τελείωσις, "perfection." He translates the parenthesis, "For it is in view of that (i.e., perfection) that the law was given to the people" or "for it is in view of the perfection that the people were subjected to the law" (*En lisant*, 26–30; cf. Michel, 269).

ᶜ The determination whether the negative particle οὐ is to be connected with the inf λέγεσθαι, "to be designated," will inevitably make a difference in the translation. If καὶ οὐ does not regulate the inf λέγεσθαι but the concept κατὰ τὴν τάξιν Ἀαρών, "like Aaron," then the inf governs the entire clause (so BDF §429; cf. Riggenbach, 194, n. 31). There are grammarians who think there is some connection with the inf here (e.g., A. T. Robertson, *Grammar*, 1155, 1175; cf. Moffatt, 96). The translation is based on the judgment that λέγεσθαι is intended to stand in contrast to the inf ἀνίστασθαι, "to arise"; for that reason, the negative should go with λέγεσθαι (so also Cockerill, *Melchizedek Christology*, 87, n. 213).

ᵈ The phrase κατὰ τὴν τάξιν Ἀαρών does not occur elsewhere and was probably formulated by the writer in dependence upon the phrase κατὰ τὴν τάξιν Μελχισέδεκ, cited from Ps 110:4. The translation "like Aaron" reflects the decision to translate the older biblical phrase "like Melchizedek" (cf. Ellingworth, *BT* 28 [1977] 236–39; Cockerill, *Melchizedek Christology*, 103).

ᵉ The gen absolute construction μετατιθεμένης . . . τῆς ἱερωσύνης may be taken circumstantially ("whenever the priesthood is altered"; BAG 515 [2] or conditionally ("if the priesthood is altered"; A. T. Robertson, *Grammar*, 1022–23, 1129).

ᶠ The demonstrative pronoun οὗτος is implied at the beginning of the sentence (A. T. Robertson, *Grammar*, 721).

ᵍ It is impossible to produce an English translation which is true to the rhetorical and literary skill of the writer. He is so sensitive to the fact that the homily will be read aloud that he achieves an aural effect when he introduces the two clauses of this verse with similar sounding prep phrases ($\dot{\epsilon}\phi$' $\ddot{o}\nu$ . . . $\dot{a}\phi$' $\dot{\eta}_S$ . . . , "about whom . . . from which . . ."). The rhetorical concern for sound becomes a factor in determining the text in v 13. The presence in v 13*a* of the well attested $\mu\epsilon\tau\dot{\epsilon}\sigma\chi\eta\kappa\epsilon\nu$ (pf tense: "belongs") favors the adoption in v 13*b* of the reading $\pi\rho\sigma\dot{\epsilon}\sigma\chi\eta\kappa\epsilon\nu$ (pf tense: "officiated"), which has the support of ℵ B D Ψ and the majority text. The resulting paronomasia between the two similar sounding perfects is consonant with the literary style of the writer. Although the variant $\pi\rho\sigma\dot{\epsilon}\sigma\chi\epsilon\nu$ (aor tense) has early support (P[46] A C 33 81 1739) and suits the sense of the text equally well, it does not reflect the writer's characteristic concern for phonetic effectiveness.

[h] Examples from the papyri and inscriptions indicate that the prefix $\pi\rho\sigma$- in $\pi\rho\dot{o}\delta\eta\lambda\sigma_S$ is intensive rather than temporal: "perfectly clear," "evident" (MM 538).

[i] It is possible that the adv $\pi\epsilon\rho\iota\sigma\sigma\dot{o}\tau\epsilon\rho\sigma_S$ should be taken in its emphatic and elative sense: "It is especially clear" (BDF §60[3]; cf. Turner, *Grammar*, 3:29).

[j] The particle $\epsilon\dot{\iota}$ is used with the present ind to refer to a present reality, "as said before" (BDF §372[1]; Turner, *Grammar*, 3:115). The statement, which assumes the truth of the "if"-clause, looks back to v 11.

[k] The prep $\kappa\alpha\tau\dot{\alpha}$ with the accusative here is used in a transferred sense, and denotes "by virtue of [a law]" (Moule, *Idiom-Book*, 59). The translation of the qualifying phrase $\dot{\epsilon}\nu\tau\sigma\lambda\dot{\eta}_S$ $\sigma\alpha\rho\kappa\dot{\iota}\nu\eta_S$ recognizes the reference to the law relating selection to physical descent (so RSV, JB, NIV). Peterson prefers to interpret the expression as a gen of content: "the law consisting in the carnal commandment" ("Examination," 183; cf. BDF §167; Gutbrod, *TDNT* 4:1078).

[l] The term $\dot{\alpha}\kappa\alpha\tau\dot{\alpha}\lambda\nu\tau\sigma_S$ is a rare word. In the LXX it occurs only in 4 Macc 10:11, where it has reference to "indestructible" or "endless" sufferings.

[m] The word $\dot{\alpha}\theta\dot{\epsilon}\tau\eta\sigma\iota_S$ was used technically as a legal term in the papyri for the cancellation or annulment of a legal decree. Cockerill prefers to translate the phrase $\dot{\alpha}\theta\dot{\epsilon}\tau\eta\sigma\iota_S$ . . . $\gamma\dot{\iota}\nu\epsilon\tau\alpha\iota$, "(a former commandment) becomes invalid" (*Melchizedek Christology*, 91).

[n] There is an ellipsis at this point that should probably be filled with the words "did bring perfection." The full sense of the verse could be paraphrased: "Now the law made nothing complete, but the introduction of the better hope did bring completion, through which hope we are drawing near to God."

[o] It is difficult to render into English the complex sentence in vv 20–22. The writer develops a comparison in vv 20*a* and 22 governed by the relative and correlative expression $\kappa\alpha\theta$' $\ddot{o}\sigma\sigma\nu$ . . . $\kappa\alpha\tau\dot{\alpha}$ $\tau\sigma\sigma\sigma\hat{\nu}\tau\sigma$ . . . , "in so far as . . . just so far. . . ." A lengthy parenthesis (vv 20*b*–21) explains the first half of the comparison (A. T. Robertson, *Grammar*, 435, 966–67). Since there is no comparative in the relative clause (v 20*a*) of this comparison, Robertson (966–67) thinks it should be translated causally: "Since he was not made priest without an oath, Jesus has become the surety of a better covenant." This interpretation renders the sense of the passage well in translation. Nevertheless, the writer's use of the relative-correlative construction that normally denotes a comparison is understandable because the idea he has in mind is comparative. This fact is demonstrated by the parenthesis of vv 20*b*–21, which is connected to v 20*a* by the explanatory conj $\gamma\dot{\alpha}\rho$, "for." The writer is fond of parenthetical construction and has used it in vv 11, 12, 19, 20*b*–21.

[p] The ellipsis in v 20*a* should probably be completed with $\dot{\iota}\epsilon\rho\epsilon\dot{\nu}_S$ $\gamma\dot{\epsilon}\gamma\sigma\nu\epsilon\nu$, "he became priest," on the basis of the parenthesis (so Westcott, 188; Riggenbach, 202). Other interpreters, however, have argued that it should be filled from the preceding verse: "And it was not without an oath that this better hope was introduced" (so Moffatt, 98; Kuss, 64; Lenski, 233–34; Ketter, 53).

[q] In vv 20, 21, 23, and 24, the expression $\sigma\dot{\iota}$ $\mu\dot{\epsilon}\nu$ . . . $\dot{o}$ $\delta\dot{\epsilon}$ . . . is used to denote the contrast between the Levitical priests and Jesus, instead of repeating the nouns (BDF §250).

[r] The term $\dot{\epsilon}\gamma\gamma\nu\sigma_S$ was used in the papyri in legal and promissory documents with the meaning "a guarantor," or one who guarantees the payment of another's debt (MM 179; BAG 213; cf. Cockerill, *Melchizedek Christology*, 124–25).

[s] The comparative form $\pi\lambda\epsilon\dot{\iota}\sigma\nu\epsilon_S$ is used here for the positive, i.e., "many" (Turner, *Grammar*, 3:30). The contrast developed is between the "many" (v 23) and the "one" (v 24).

[t] Examples from the papyri indicate that $\pi\alpha\rho\alpha\mu\dot{\epsilon}\nu\epsilon\iota\nu$ by itself means "to remain in office" or to continue in an occupation (MM 487–88). An alternative proposal is to supply $\tau\hat{\eta}$ $\dot{\iota}\epsilon\rho\omega\sigma\dot{\nu}\nu\eta$ from v 24: "they were prevented by death from remaining in their priesthood" (so Hauck, *TDNT* 4:578).

[u] There has been a persistent tendency to find in the predicate adj $\dot{\alpha}\pi\alpha\rho\dot{\alpha}\beta\alpha\tau\sigma\nu$ the intransitive meaning "without a successor," or "untransmitted" (cf. Moffatt, 99; Spicq, 2:197; Strathmann, 112; Ketter, 53, 56–57; TEV: "does not pass on to someone else"). In contrast to the succession of former priests (v 23), Jesus' priesthood is nontransferable. Lorimer has even conjectured that the writer originally wrote, or "meant to write," $\dot{\alpha}\mu\epsilon\tau\dot{\alpha}\beta\alpha\tau\sigma\nu$, "without a successor." He attributes the

corruption of the text to the presence of παρα[μένειν], "to continue in office," in v 23 (*NTS* 13 [1966–67] 386–87). There is no textual support for Lorimer's conjecture, and the active sense of the term ἀπαράβατον is not attested linguistically elsewhere. The term is used broadly in hellenistic Gk. but always in the pass sense of "unchangeable," "permanent," "inviolable" (Simpson, *EvQ* 18 [1946] 187–88). If the term is taken in this common sense, it fits the context well (so BAGD 80; Michel, 276; Schneider, *TDNT* 5:742–43; Demarest, "Priest," 14–15, 339; Cockerill, *Melchizedek Christology*, 130, 133–34; et al.).

Moule has called attention to a delicate subtlety in placing ἀπαράβατον in a predicate position relative to the article. The article suggests that it is known that Jesus possesses a priesthood: it is "his known (or, assumed) priesthood." But the predicate adj has the effect of a relative clause, thus throwing the emphasis on the fact that he possesses a priesthood "which is permanent" (*Idiom-Book*, 109, 186).

ᵛ The debate concerning the nuance in the phrase εἰς τὸ παντελές is already reflected in the ancient versions. The Vulgate, Syriac, and Coptic versions lend their support to a temporal sense ("for all time," "forever"; so RSV, TEV, NASB); the Armenian version understands the phrase in a qualitative sense ("completely"; so NIV; cf. JB, "utterly certain"). The choice of the term "absolutely" (so NEB) is meant to imply that both ideas are contained and expressed by the same phrase (so Michel, 276; Delling, *TDNT* 8:66–67; P. E. Hughes, 269; Cockerill, *Melchizedek Christology*, 135–36).

ʷ At this point the conj καί functions to emphasize the finite verb ἔπρεπεν. Both Zuntz (*Text of the Epistles*, 211) and A. T. Robertson (*Grammar*, 1181) suggest the translation "precisely." Other instances of emphatic καί occur in Heb 11:19-20.

ˣ The translation presupposes that v 26c is to be understood in relation to the following clause; the consequence of Christ's exaltation was that he was taken from the midst of a sinful world. For the proposal that v 26c is to be understood in relation to the preceding clause (v 26b) and to be translated "different from sinful men," see BAG 898; Peterson, "Examination," 196–97, 201.

ʸ The translation fails to bring out the fact that vv 26–28 constitute another instance of the periodic sentence, which is characteristic of artistic prose (see 1:1–4; 2:2–4, 14–15; 3:12–15; 4:12–13; 5:1–3, 7–10; 6:4–6; 7:1–3). The sentence has been broken up in translation out of consideration for English style.

ᶻ The expression καθ' ἡμέραν means "day by day" or "daily." Yet the double sacrifice of the high priest, first for his own sins and then for the sins of the people, was the central feature of the great Day of Atonement ritual, which the writer knew to be a yearly event (9:7, 25; 10:1, 3). The proposal to interpret καθ' ἡμέραν as "on every day on which he had to offer" (Str-B 3:698) would resolve the crux, but this is not the most natural rendering of the expression. Turner has proposed that καθ' ἡμέραν is a Semitism, reflecting a Heb. or Aram. construction on which the term "day" signifies "the Day [of Atonement]." On this understanding, the expression would be translated "on one Day each year," or "on every Day of Atonement" (*Grammar*, 4:111–12). There are strong objections, however, to this proposal. It seems better to render the expression idiomatically and to defer to the commentary the discussion of the exegetical problem in v 27.

ᵃᵃ The expression τοῦτο γὰρ ἐποίησεν could be translated "for he did this," with the implication that Jesus sacrificed for his own sins as well as for the sins of the people when he offered himself on the cross (so Buchanan, 130–31). But the analogy with the offerings of the Aaronic high priests breaks down in the light of the preceding statements concerning the sinlessness of Jesus (4:15; 7:26). The translation reflects the writer's insistence that Jesus did not have any need to make a personal offering for sin. Accordingly, the inexact expression τοῦτο, "this," has reference only to the preceding clause, introduced by ἔπειτα, "then for the sins of the people," and not to the entire statement concerning the double sacrifice. (So also Peterson, "Examination," 198–99, 328–29.)

ᵇᵇ The anarthrous nouns ἀνθρώπους, "men," and υἱόν, "son," emphasize the comparative quality of each and prepare the reader to grasp the ensuing contrasts drawn between those who are men and the one who is the Son (A. T. Robertson, *Grammar*, 794[2]).

ᶜᶜ It seems necessary to complete the second part of the verse by the words "appoints as high priest" to sustain the parallel with v 28a. The circumstantial "forever" is to be attached to "high priest" and not to "Son," as in the formulation of the oath (cf. 5:6, 10; 6:20; 7:17, 21, 24; cf. Andriessen, *En lisant*, 30–31).

ᵈᵈ The key term τετελειωμένον, "has been made perfect," has been placed at the end of the sentence for emphasis. A. T. Robertson (*Grammar*, 418) speaks of "the emphatic climax" in reference to its position.

Form/Structure/Setting

Within the structure of the homily, 7:1–28 is clearly defined as a literary unit. The reference to "the Son of God" in v 3 prepares for the climactic reference to the "Son" in v 28. The entire chapter is concerned with the Son as priest, or high priest, "like Melchizedek," who is superior to the Levitical priests. The fact that v 28 summarizes and concludes the comparison of Jesus as Son with the Levitical priesthood, a subject that occupies the writer in a preparatory way in 7:1–10 and directly in 7:11–28, is of special importance (Vanhoye, *La structure*, 125; Cockerill, *Melchizedek Christology*, 16–20).

The form of the exposition is homiletical midrash (see *Form/Structure/Setting* on 7:1–10). Fitzmyer considered 7:1–28 a midrash on Gen 14:18–20, into which the writer introduced Ps 110:4 in a supplementary way in vv 11, 15, 17, 21, 28 ("'Now this Melchizedek . . .' [Heb 7, 1]," *CBQ* 25 [1963] 305–6). The use made of the OT in 7:1–28 is certainly midrashic in character, but the dominant text is Ps 110:4, not Gen 14:18–20. In 7:1–10, Ps 110:4 is interpreted on the basis of Gen 14:17–20, but the Genesis text plays no role in the second half of the chapter. The importance of Ps 110:4 to the writer's argument, however, becomes explicit in 7:11–28, where the oracle is expounded in detail (cf. Sowers, *Hermeneutics*, 123–24; Cockerill, *Melchizedek Christology*, 16–18).

The function of Melchizedek in 7:1–10 is essentially prophetic: in an enigmatic way he bears witness to the insufficiency of the Levitical priesthood and anticipates the coming of an eternal priest who would be "like" him. He is not a type of Christ, but an illustration of the subordination of the Levitical priesthood to a higher priestly ideal (see *Explanation* on 7:1–10). But in 7:11–28 the writer engages in a typological exegesis of the OT. Goppelt's analysis of the elements in a "typological" interpretation of the OT is helpful: (1) this form of interpretation discerns a relationship between persons, acts, events, or institutions; (2) it holds that this relationship was established by God in the course of redemptive history; and (3) the earlier events are types of the more perfect, and greater, later events. The eschatological aspect of typological interpretation is preserved by Goppelt when he insists that the later events are the fulfillment of the earlier (*Typos*, 18–19; cf. Cockerill, *Melchizedek Christology*, 236–38).

In 7:11–28 the writer presents the Levitical priesthood as a type which was fulfilled by the priesthood of Christ. The inability of the Levitical institution to attain the goal of perfection and Christ's corresponding ability to do so are demonstrated in 7:11–28 through the interpretation of Ps 110:4 as an oracle announcing the establishment of a new eternal priesthood on the basis of the oath of God. The argument from context that the word of the oath came subsequent to the promulgation of the law (v 28) preserves the redemptive-historical perspective so important to typological exegesis. The writer clearly recognizes the validity of the OT priesthood: Aaron was called by God (5:4), but from the perspective of the event of Christ only as a foreshadowing of a new and superior priesthood announced in the OT itself. The fulfillment of the oracle in the Christ-event demonstrates the superiority of the new arrangement over the old. The form of the exposition in 7:11–28 is thus clearly defined as typological exegesis, in contrast to the form of the midrash in 7:1–10.

This analysis of form assumes the validity of Vanhoye's division of 7:1–28 into two main parts, 7:1–10 and 7:11–28 (*La structure*, 125). His understanding of the structure of 7:1–28 is supported by the detail of the argument: the consideration of Ps 110:4 in the light of Gen 14:17–20 in 7:10 shifts to the direct consideration of Ps 110:4 in 7:11–28 and is accompanied by the shift from proving the superiority of Melchizedek to the Levitical priests to demonstrating the superiority of the priest "like Melchizedek" to the Levitical priests (Riggenbach, 191). From a purely formal point of view, the reference to τελείωσις, "perfection," in v 11 finds a complement in the theologically significant word τετελειωμένον, "has been perfected," in v 28. The link between these terms, however, is no more than verbal, since 7:11–19 concerns the failure of the law and the Levitical priesthood to achieve the perfection of the people of God and v 28 concerns the perfecting of the Son. The two expressions announce the movement of the argument from its beginning to its conclusion: "perfection" was not achieved through the old priests, but the Son "has been perfected forever."

Vanhoye's subsequent separation of 7:11–19 from 7:20–28 takes account of this difference in perspective, which is confirmed by literary considerations. The words τελείωσις, "perfection," and ἐτελείωσεν, "perfected," in 7:11 and 19 respectively establish an *inclusio*, which is reinforced by the reference to "the law" in each case. Similarly, the verbal repetition of the rare word ὁρκωμοσία, "oath," in 7:20 and 7:28 forms another instance of *inclusio*. The shift in perspective in the two subdivisions reflects the distinctive use made of Ps 110:4. In 7:11–19 the writer opposes the name of Melchizedek to that of Aaron to develop the theme that a change in priesthood was prompted by the insufficiency of the Levitical priesthood. In 7:20–28 Melchizedek is not mentioned directly, but the writer seizes on the concepts of "oath" and "eternity" to demonstrate the superiority of the new priesthood. The concluding verses (vv 26–28) summarize the chapter as a whole by restating the major themes (cf. Vanhoye, *La structure*, 129–36; Peterson, "Examination," 175–76; Cockerill, *Melchizedek Christology*, 24–29). They also constitute a significant announcement of the subject and themes to be treated in the central section of Hebrews (cf. A. Vanhoye, "La structure centrale de l'Épître aux Hébreux [Hébr 8:1–9:28]," *RSR* 47 [1959] 44–56; J. Bligh, "The Structure of Hebrews," *HeyJ* 5 [1964] 173).

Although 7:1–28 is firmly embedded in its context, Cockerill has argued that 7:1–25 shows many signs of structural, terminological, and conceptual independence from the rest of Hebrews. He has proposed that this unit may once have been an independent midrash, which may have been prepared by the writer sometime prior to the composition of the homily (*Melchizedek Christology*, 277–307; see *Form/Structure/Setting* on 7:1–10). Cockerill has demonstrated that 7:4–25 is a well-balanced structural unit based on 7:1–3, in which vv 20–25 balance vv 4–10. Characteristic of this unit is a particular style of argument by comparison, which is advanced in a close, tight manner. In 7:4–10 the writer develops two comparisons (vv 5–6, 8) and draws the significance of the first for his reader (vv 9–10). In 7:11–19 he moves from Melchizedek to Christ in preparation for the development of two more contrasts in 7:20–25 (vv 20–21, 23–24), the christological significance of which is emphasized (vv 22, 25). The concluding reference to the present and future ministry of intercession on behalf of the redeemed community in 7:25 is a natural outcome of the argument for the superiority of Christ based on his eternity, and could serve as a fitting climax to an independent midrash based on Ps 110:4 (192–96).

Linguistically, 7:1–25 exhibits a concentration of distinctive terms employed to express the concept of the eternally existent one as priest and the concept of his priestly work as intercession. These notions, which find little or no mention elsewhere in Hebrews, call attention to the conceptual peculiarity of 7:1–25. The concepts of "law" and of the "new covenant" are crucial to the exposition in 7:1–10:18, but the way in which νόμος, "law," and διαθήκη, "covenant," are used underscores the distinctiveness of 7:1–25. In 7:1–25 the concept of law is closely related to the ordinance of priestly descent. The basis for the rejection of the old law and for the finality of the new covenant is the oath of God and the eternity of the Son. In 8:1–10:18 the rejection of the law and the finality of the new covenant are based on the once-for-all self-sacrifice of Christ and his entrance into the heavenly sanctuary (*Melchizedek Christology,* 297–301, 303–5). Cockerill concludes that, linguistically and conceptually, 7:1–25 has little more in common with other passages in Hebrews that develop Christ's ministry as priest than a common use of cultic terminology and a similar eschatological outlook.

The purpose of 7:1–25 was to develop the theme of the sonship of Christ in terms of priesthood. The focus on Melchizedek, who is not mentioned after 7:17, and the development of a "Melchizedek christology" is unique to 7:1–25. Cockerill has shown that 7:26–28 functions only to relate this distinctive tradition to the priestly traditions developed in 8:1–10:18 (*Melchizedek Christology,* 288–90, 306–7). Although it cannot be proven that 7:1–25 existed as an independent midrash, the evidence would appear to justify the conclusion that at the very least 7:1–25 represents a christological tradition distinct from the priestly traditions developed in 8:1–10:18.

Windisch had suggested, without elaborate argumentation, that the source of 7:26–28 was a concise liturgical hymn (67–69). Michel gave more precise reasons for locating a hymn fragment in 7:26. He appealed to the work of the classicist E. Norden, who carefully distinguished between hellenistic and oriental styles of predication (*Agnostos Theos,* 143–207). Characteristic of the hellenistic style is a third-person predication; the person is not addressed directly. Titles of honor and participles that are attributive, or predicative, are accumulated, but they are expressed without the definite article. Parallelism is not characteristic of the hellenistic style of predication, as it is of the oriental. On the basis of these criteria Michel identified a four-line hymn in v 26 that reflects the hellenistic style of predication. He pointed especially to the three anarthrous adjectives in v 26*b,* followed by the two attributive participial phrases in v 26*c, d* (278; cf. Nomoto, *NovT* 10 [1968] 12; Buchanan, 127–28). Theissen, however, showed conclusively that the first line of v 26 reflects the hand of the writer, and limited the hymnic fragment to v 26*b–d* (*Untersuchung,* 20–28; cf. Cockerill, *Melchizedek Christology,* 289, 321–25). He was impressed that the content of v 26*b–d* is completely different from anything in 7:1–25. It does not celebrate the eternity of the high priest, but his cultic-moral purity and his triumphant exaltation.

Even this limited suggestion is difficult to accept considering that v 26*a* clearly presupposes the argument of 7:1–25 and v 27 in turn depends on the formulation of v 26*b–d* (cf. Peterson, "Examination," 195, n. 79). It is striking that the series of proposals concerning the detection of liturgical fragments in Hebrews concentrates on segments of artistic prose and the use of the periodic sentence (see *Comment* on 1:2*b*–4; 5:7–10; 7:3). This is the case here as well, where 7:26–28 is a periodic sentence. Such sentences should be recognized as an integral element in the literary signature of this writer.

Comment

In 7:11–28 the consideration of Gen 14:17–20 is left behind. The focus of concern is no longer the superiority of Melchizedek over the Levitical priests, but the superiority of the priest "like Melchizedek." Attention is directed to Ps 110:4, and its phraseology is allowed to dictate the course of the argument. Virtually every phrase of the oracle is probed for its christological significance: "like Melchizedek" (vv 11–14); "forever" (vv 15–19), "the Lord has sworn and will not change his mind" (vv 20–22), "forever" (vv 23–25; cf. Hay, *Glory,* 46–47, 146; Cockerill, *Melchizedek Christology,* 18–19).

The main purpose of 7:11–19 is to substantiate the insufficiency of the Levitical priesthood and the system based on it. The fact that Ps 110:4 proclaimed the appointment of a different kind of priest implied an essential weakness in the existing order. The projected change in priesthood also implied a change in the law regulating the Levitical institution. The context for the categorical declaration that the Levitical system has been replaced by a better hope is the demonstration that Christ is a priest of superior quality "like Melchizedek" and that this exaltation signals the inauguration of the better priesthood announced in the psalm citation (vv 16–19). In 7:20–28 the permanence and effectiveness of the new priesthood are expounded. The superiority of the new priesthood is illustrated in terms of the solemn oath with which it was established (vv 20–22), in terms of the unending duration of its tenure (vv 23–25), and in terms of the character, achievement, and status of the Son as the eternal and final high priest (vv 26–28).

11   The resumption of the train of thought that was interrupted after 6:20 is announced by the expression μὲν οὖν, which is equivalent to an inferential particle ("then," "therefore"). The writer returns to Ps 110:4 and the concept of Jesus who "became a high priest forever like Melchizedek." The dramatic question posed rhetorically in v 11 is a deduction from Ps 110:4: the Levitical priesthood must not have been sufficient, because the oracle proclaimed a new priest "like Melchizedek" and not "like Aaron." In an attempt to indicate more particularly the inadequacy of the Levitical priesthood, the writer specifies its inability to secure τελείωσις, "perfection." This term, which occurs only here in Hebrews, poses for the first time the concept of perfection as applied to the people of God, rather than to Christ. The introduction of a new concept, tantalizing in its brevity, in anticipation of a fuller development of the theme at later points in the homily is quite typical for the writer (Peterson, "Examination," 180–81).

Delling has argued that the primary influence upon the writer's use of the vocabulary of "perfection" is the LXX, which employs the word τελείωσις with a broad range of meanings found in extrabiblical Greek. He contends strongly for the cultic associations of the noun in v 11, which must be related to the use of the cognate verb τελειοῦν in v 19. There, according to Delling, "perfection" consists in being able to "draw near to God." The old Levitical system could not enable the worshiper to approach God because its sacrifices were impotent actually to cleanse him from sin (cf. 9:9; 10:1). This imperfection was underscored by the declaration in Ps 110:4 of a need for a different kind of priest (*TDNT* 8:79–86; cf. Käsemann, *Das wandernde Gottesvolk,* 82–90; du Plessis, *ΤΕΛΕΙΟΣ,* 229; Michel, 269, n. 2; Cockerill, *Melchizedek Christology,* 85–87).

A cultic interpretation of τελείωσις, however, is not supported by the context. The writer does not absolutely deny to the people of the old covenant the possibility of "drawing near to God" (note 10:1; 11:6). The significant difference characterizing the new people of God, according to v 19, is the "better hope by which we draw near to God." Preisker remarks: "The certainty of the actualization of the drawing near is now stronger and surer and more complete than in the OT and later Judaism" (*TDNT* 2:331). In v 11 the writer intends to contrast the failure of the Levitical priesthood to bring τελείωσις to the people of God and the accomplishment of Jesus in this regard. These considerations indicate that the more usual nuance of "fulfillment" or "completion" is more appropriate to the context. It is also consonant with the writer's sustained concern with God's declared intention to bring humanity to its appointed goal of a right relationship with himself. Contemplated in a hypothetical way in v 11 is the possibility of the present realization of God's purposes for the human family through the Levitical priesthood. The writer denies that perfection could be achieved through the Levitical system, as Silva remarks, "not because there was anything intrinsically wrong with it, but because in the divine arrangement it was designed as a shadow, anticipating the substance. The substance, therefore, far from opposing the shadow is its *fulfillment*—this is perfection" (*WTJ* 39 [1976] 68). The concept of τελείωσις is thus eschatological: the fulfillment of the promises of the new covenant in the priestly ministry of Christ makes possible an access to God and relationship with him that was not possible under the former covenant (cf. Riggenbach, 191–93; Peterson, "Examination," 187–88, 217–22).

The term Λευιτικός, "Levitical," is a rare word. Its only occurrence in the LXX is on the title page of the book of Leviticus, where the writer undoubtedly saw the term. Philo used the adjective of the biblical book (*Allegorical Interpretation* 2.105; *Who Is the Heir?* 251) or of the tribe of Levi (*On Flight and Finding* 87, 93; *On the Change of Names* 2; *On the Preliminary Studies* 98.132; *Moses* 2.170). In the light of the discussion about Levi in Heb 7:5–10, the use of the word in v 11 emphasizes the genealogical requirement of the Levitical priesthood (Williamson, *Philo*, 129–30).

The parenthetical statement that "the people received regulations concerning the Levitical priesthood" is basic to the argument (on the meaning of the expression ἐπ᾽ αὐτῆς νενομοθέτηται, see above, *Note* b). It establishes a context for the clear allusion to Ps 110:4 in v 11c and anticipates the premise expressed in v 12, that a change in the priesthood necessarily implies a change in the law. The immediate context shows that the reference is to the Mosiac law, which is seen from the perspective of the sacrificial regulations that governed the cultic community (vv 13, 16; cf. Windisch, 66). The new priest does not receive his office from the designation of the Levitical ordinance concerning physical descent from Aaron, but does "arise" in accordance with the oracle proclaiming ἕτερον ἱερέα, "a different kind of priest," "like Melchizedek."

12 In expanding upon v 11 (the conjunction γάρ, "for," is explanatory), the writer makes use of the present tense of general statement (Riggenbach, 195, n. 32). His deduction is parenthetical to the main argument. This becomes apparent when in vv 13–14 he clarifies in what sense a priest has arisen who may be described as ἕτερος, "different in kind," and οὐ κατὰ τὴν τάξιν ᾿Ααρών, "not 'like Aaron.'" The weakness of the Mosaic law as an arrangement by which the people were related to God is associated in the writer's thinking with the weakness of the priesthood that it regulated (cf. v 28). The law provided prescriptions only on the subject of the Levitical priests; it could not foresee anything concerning the appearance of any other priest, especially of one attached to the tribe of Judah. The supersession of the Levitical cultus envisioned in the psalm oracle implicitly involved the setting aside of the Mosaic law, which the writer perceived in terms of priesthood and sacrifice (cf. Peterson, "Examination," 181–82; Andriessen, *En lisant*, 28).

13–14   The writer clarifies how the new priest announced in Ps 110:4 is different from the priests of Aaron's line in vv 13–17. He first develops the negative side of the argument, explaining how he is "not like Aaron" in vv 13–14. Then in vv 15–17 he points out the superior quality of the new priest by explaining how he is "like Melchizedek" (Riggenbach, 197).

Continuing the main argument, the writer declares that the one about whom the new priesthood was prophesied came from a non-Levitical tribe. The perfect tense of the finite verb μετέσχηκεν in the phrase "belongs to a different tribe" expresses both a historical and an official condition of fact. It accentuates the incompatibility, resulting from the fact of descent, between the one proclaimed in the oracle and the priesthood when viewed in the light of the conditions of validity prescribed in the Mosaic law (Spicq, 2:192). The initial expression ἐφ' ὅν, "the one about whom," finds its antecedent in the phrase ἕτερον . . . ἱερέα, "a different kind of priest," in v 11, while the general term ταῦτα, "these things," refers back to the allusion to Ps 110:4 in that verse. Just as Melchizedek proved to be ἀγενεαλόγητος, "without recorded [priestly] descent" (v 3a), the new priest lacks legal qualification (Cockerill, *Melchizedek Christology*, 92–93). The significance of this fact is indicated in v 13b: no one from this tribe ever officiated at the altar (θυσιαστήριον, with reference to the altar of burnt offering in the inner forecourt of the tabernacle or temple; cf. Lev 16:7–9, 18). There was no precedent for priestly performance. In v 13 the writer is commenting on the wording of Ps 110:4, but he is clearly thinking of the prophecy as historically fulfilled in Jesus.

The two clauses of v 14 provide confirmation for the two clauses of v 13 and identify Jesus as the one about whom the oracle was formulated. The appeal to the tradition, πρόδηλον γάρ, "for it is perfectly clear," presupposes the historical verification of the factual statement in v 13a: the priest acclaimed in Ps 110:4 could not trace his descent to the priestly tribe. The prepositional phrase ἐξ Ἰούδα, "from Judah," which denotes origin from the tribe of Judah, is placed first in the clause for emphasis. The allusion to the common historical tradition that Jesus belonged to the tribe of Judah (cf. Matt 1:2–3; 2:6; Luke 3:33; Acts 2:29–36; 12:23; Rom 1:3; 2 Tim 2:8; Rev 5:5; 22:16) reinforced the fact that he was not "from Levi." It verified that the priesthood of Jesus does not depend on physical descent but on a radically new arrangement. The use of the unusual term ἀνατέταλκεν, "was descended," to indicate that Jesus was descended from Judah may convey the hint of a royal messianic reference. There is no evidence in classical Greek, the LXX, or the papyri for the use of ἀνατέλλειν to denote descent from a certain family. The verb is used in the LXX, however, for the rising of a star or the sprouting of a branch in contexts that have been traditionally recognized as messianic (e.g., Num 24:17; cf. Jer 23:5; see Schlier, *TDNT* 1:351–53; Buchanan, 123–24; Cockerill, *Melchizedek Christology*, 96–97). The designation of Jesus as "our Lord" sounds distinctly confessional

(Michel, 271). It recalls the reference to Jesus as "the Lord" in 2:3 and anticipates the closing doxology with its reference to "our Lord Jesus" (13:20).

The argument of the second clause, that when Moses gave the law he said nothing concerning priests in relation to this tribe, develops the thought of v 13*b*. The tribe of Judah was not appointed to priestly service. The conjunction of prepositional phrases ($\epsilon\dot{l}s$ $\dot{\eta}\nu$ $\phi\nu\lambda\dot{\eta}\nu$/$\pi\epsilon\rho\dot{l}$ $\dot{l}\epsilon\rho\dot{\epsilon}\omega\nu$, "in relation to which tribe/ concerning priesthood") has the effect of emphasizing the contrast between "this tribe" and "priesthood" under the Mosaic economy (cf. Cockerill, *Melchizedek Christology*, 95–99).

15–17 In preparation for describing the superior quality of the new priest, the writer intensifies his language: $\kappa\alpha\dot{l}$ $\pi\epsilon\rho\iota\sigma\sigma\dot{o}\tau\epsilon\rho\sigma\nu$ $\ddot{\epsilon}\tau\iota$ $\kappa\alpha\tau\dot{\alpha}\delta\eta\lambda\dot{o}\nu$ $\dot{\epsilon}\sigma\tau\iota\nu$, "and it is still more obvious." He has been explaining the meaning of the oracle of Ps 110:4 from v 11, making clear that the whole Levitical system of approach to God is ineffective and that the law that regulated its priesthood has been superseded (cf. Moffatt; Cockerill, *Melchizedek Christology*, 99–101). In vv 13–14 the writer points out the negative implication of the promised priest being "like Melchizedek": he does not possess Levitical qualification. Then in vv 15–17 he explains the positive significance of the new priest being "like Melchizedek": he possesses a unique quality of life. The manner in which the biblical phrase $\kappa\alpha\tau\dot{\alpha}$ $\tau\dot{\eta}\nu$ $\tau\dot{\alpha}\xi\iota\nu$ $M\epsilon\lambda\chi\iota\sigma\dot{\epsilon}\delta\epsilon\kappa$, "like Melchizedek," is understood becomes clear when it is paraphrased by an equivalent expression in v 15*b*: $\kappa\alpha\tau\dot{\alpha}$ $\tau\dot{\eta}\nu$ $\dot{o}\mu\sigma\iota\dot{o}\tau\eta\tau\alpha$ $M\epsilon\lambda\chi\iota\sigma\dot{\epsilon}\delta\epsilon\kappa$, "according to the likeness of Melchizedek." The word $\dot{o}\mu\sigma\iota\dot{o}\tau\eta s$ denoted "likeness," "the same as," or "similarity" from pre-Socratic times (Schneider, *TDNT* 5:189). The writer thus understands the term $\tau\dot{\alpha}\xi\iota s$ in its derived meaning as "character" or "quality." The oracle has reference to a priest whose quality would be like Melchizedek as he is described in Gen 14:18–20 and in Ps 110:4. The promise was fulfilled in Christ who *is* actually what Melchizedek *was* symbolically, an eternal priest who exercises his priestly prerogatives in a nonlegal, universal ministration (Demarest, "Priest," 335–36; Ellingworth, *BT* 28 [1977] 236–39; see *Comment* on 7:3; 8).

The arrangement of the clauses in vv 15–16 exhibits the writer's skill in using syntax to enhance the rhetorical impact of his statement. V 15*a* contains the unfinished apodosis of a conditional sentence. The protasis (or, "if"-clause) follows in v 15*b*. Only then is the apodosis completed by means of the two-part relative clause in v 16. Taking account of this disjunction, the complete apodosis reads: "And it is still more obvious that he does so not by virtue of . . . , but by virtue of . . ." (vv 15*a*, 16). By separating the two halves of the apodosis the writer achieves a tension in his statement that is unrelieved until the listener hears the triumphant reference to the "power of an indestructible life," supported by the citation of Ps 110:4 in v 17.

The relative pronoun $\ddot{o}s$, "he," refers to the closest antecedent in v 15*b*, $\dot{l}\epsilon\rho\epsilon\dot{v}s$ $\ddot{\epsilon}\tau\epsilon\rho\sigma s$, "a different priest." The purpose of the relative clause is to define the way in which the promised priest is like Melchizedek, giving first the negative ($\sigma\dot{v}$) and then the contrasting positive aspect of the matter ($\dot{\alpha}\lambda\lambda\dot{\alpha}$, "but"). The negative expression $\sigma\dot{v}$ $\kappa\alpha\tau\dot{\alpha}$ $\nu\dot{o}\mu\sigma\nu$ $\dot{\epsilon}\nu\tau\sigma\lambda\dot{\eta}s$ $\sigma\alpha\rho\kappa\dot{l}\nu\eta s$, "not by virtue of a legal ordinance concerning physical descent," is complementary to the negative phrase in v 11, $\sigma\dot{v}$ $\kappa\alpha\tau\dot{\alpha}$ $\tau\dot{\eta}\nu$ $\tau\dot{\alpha}\xi\iota\nu$ $\dot{\mathcal{A}}\alpha\rho\dot{\omega}\nu$, "not 'like Aaron.'" The law here is perceived in terms of the ordinance regarding legal descent and certain standards of bodily qualification and ritual purity (Michel, 272). Like Melchizedek, Christ could not have been declared a priest on the basis of the Mosaic law, where the priesthood was implicated with and dependent upon fleshly descent (Michel, 272–72; Peterson, "Examination," 183–84; Cockerill, *Melchizedek Christology*, 104–8).

The positive description ἀλλὰ κατὰ δύναμιν ζωῆς ἀκαταλύτου, "but by virtue of the power of an indestructible life," further defines the corresponding expression in v 11, κατὰ τὴν τάξιν Μελχισέδεκ, "like Melchizedek." In contrast to νόμος, "law," δύναμις, "power," in Hebrews connotes effectiveness. It expresses God's activity and the intrusion of eschatological reality upon the present (see *Comment* on 2:4; 6:5). The characterization of "power" in v 16 by the qualitative genitives ζωῆς ἀκαταλύτου, "of indestructible life," offers a striking definition of the meaning of the phrase εἰς τὸν αἰῶνα, "forever," in Ps 110:4, which is cited in v 17. It designates the eternity of the new priest from the perspective of his postresurrection existence. As an explanation of the phrase "according to the likeness of Melchizedek" in v 15*b*, the climactic clause in v 16*b* draws upon the striking statements ascribing "eternity" to Melchizedek in 7:3*b* and 7:8. Cockerill remarks: "We learn that to be a priest like Melchizedek is to be a priest by virtue of the power of an indestructible life" (*Melchizedek Christology*, 110).

The term ἀκατάλυτος, "indestructible," which occurs elsewhere in the Greek Bible only in 4 Macc 10:11, appears to have been carefully chosen. It was well suited to acknowledge that although Jesus' human life had been exposed to κατάλυσις, "destruction," through crucifixion, his life was not destroyed by the death suffered on the cross. The phrase δύναμιν ζωῆς ἀκαταλύτου describes the new quality of life with which Jesus was endowed by virtue of his resurrection and exaltation to the heavenly world, where he was formally installed in his office as high priest (Demarest, "Priest," 337–38; Peterson, "Examination," 185–86). The author refers to an objective event in which Christ participated, rather than to a quality which belonged to him inherently. The power of life that the resurrection conferred upon Jesus demonstrated that his priesthood is not limited by the temporal, transitory character of the old priesthood based on physical descent; it is undergirded by a power that overcame mortality and corruption, and consequently is beyond the reach of mortality and corruption (Grundmann, *TDNT* 2:305). The acknowledgment that Jesus is a priest "like Melchizedek" implies that he is priest by virtue of his resurrection (cf. Manson, *The Epistle to the Hebrews*, 116; Williamson, *Philo*, 82, 442, 447).

The formula μαρτυρεῖται γὰρ ὅτι, "for he has witness borne that," introduces the quotation of Ps 110:4 to support the assertion that Jesus possesses a life that can never be destroyed. By emphasizing the "witness"-character of the citation, the writer indicates that the biblical text has been read in the light of its eschatological fulfillment. The quotation proves why Jesus' life qualifies him as a priest. It indicates that an authentic priesthood independent of the Levitical order exists and that it is characterized as a perpetual priesthood. In the context of v 16*b*, the phrase εἰς τὸν αἰῶνα, "forever," has the connotation of "unending." Williamson holds that the central place of Ps 110 in the argument of Hebrews results from the writer's firm conviction that the resurrection provided absolute proof of Jesus' indestructible life (*Philo*, 447). Accordingly, it was Easter faith that drew attention to the relevance of Ps 110:4 for the distinctive christology in 7:1–25.

18–19 The argument begun in v 11 is brought to a conclusion in vv 18–19. In v 11 the writer deduced from Ps 110:4 that the prophecy of a new priesthood showed the old to be insufficient. In v 12 he implied that a change in the priesthood would necessitate a change in the law by which it was regulated. The subsequent demonstration that Jesus is the eschatological priest acclaimed in Ps 110:4, who holds his office by virtue of a superior qualification, permitted the writer to assert categorically that the old priesthood and law have been replaced by the new arrangement announced in the psalm oracle. The Levitical priesthood and law have been superseded by the new and "better hope" based on the superior quality of the new priest (cf. Cockerill, *Melchizedek Christology*, 24–25, 113). The climax to the argument is expressed by means of a contrast, introduced by a μέν . . . δέ construction ("on the one hand . . . but on the other," vv 18, 19*b*). In all such constructions the emphasis is invariably on the δέ clause (Riggenbach, 200). The writer takes up the notion of the μετάθεσις, "alteration, change," of the law from v 12, and explains it negatively in v 18 (the "annulment" of the old) and then positively in v 19*b* (the "introduction" of the new).

The dramatic change in God's manner of relating to his people is defined in v 18. The term ἀθέτησις, "annulment," is a stronger term than μετάθεσις, "alteration" (v 12). Its force is brought out in the papyri, where it assumes a technical legal sense for the annulment of a decree or the cancellation of a debt (MM 12). The use of a legal term in v 18 is appropriate to the argument, which concerns the law. The "former commandment" has primary reference to the particular ordinance regulating the priesthood mentioned in v 16. The writer views the whole OT law under the aspect of the priesthood and sacrifice (cf. Windisch, 66; in Hebrews the law is "the sum of the sacrificial regulations for the ancient cultic community"). The descriptive term προαγούσης, "former, previous in time," in the expression "former commandment," is not incidental to the argument. It is in the light of the subsequent eschatological fulfillment that this previous, transitory ordinance based on physical descent has been abrogated. With the promulgation of Ps 110:4, God announced his intention to set aside the whole Levitical system because it had proven to be ineffective in achieving its purpose. Its "weakness" (ἀσθενής) inheres not in the law or its purpose, but in the people upon whom it depends for its accomplishment (see *Comment* on 4:15; 5:2; 7:28). Its "uselessness" (ἀνωφελής) derives from the fact that the law regulated the approach to God in a cultic sense and was able to cleanse only externally (9:9–10, 13, 23; 10:14). Both terms are summarized by the sharp parenthetical comment in v 19*a*, which is translated by Kögel, "nothing was brought to its appointed end" ("Der Begriff," 60). The finite verb ἐτελείωσεν draws its force from the use of the cognate noun τελείωσις in v 11. The law did not bring the eschatological fulfillment intended by God. The particular concern in v 19*a* is the failure to bring the people into a right relationship with God through the cleansing of the conscience or heart (see *Comment* on 9:14). The institutions of priesthood, sacrifice, and atonement were not able to achieve a definitive arrangement of the relationship to God (cf. Riggenbach, 201; Michel, 273; Peterson, "Examination," 186–87, 220–22).

The positive half of the conclusion is drawn in v 19*b*: although the law proved to be ineffective, it has been replaced by an effective hope. The force of the μέν . . . δέ construction is to emphasize the initial expressions ἀθέτησις, "annulment," and ἐπεισαγωγή, "introduction." A former commandment has been declared invalid: a better hope has been introduced. The word ἐπεισαγωγή is used by Josephus with the idea of replacement (*Ant.* 11.196: the new wife brought in replaces the old), and this notion seems to be present in v 19*b* as well. The term κρείττων, "better," is the characteristic word for the new redemptive arrangement in Hebrews (see *Comment* on 7:22; 8:6; 9:23). It signifies the established, certain character of the reality introduced by Christ, which leads the people to the goal appointed by God (Michel, 273). The hope now extended to the people is κρείττων by virtue of its effectiveness, which is guaranteed by God's fidelity (6:18; 10:23). It concerns what the law and its priesthood had failed to realize and could only point forward to in a symbolic way, namely, direct and lasting access to God. Through this "better hope" the new people of God have secured the assurance of a quality of access to and a relationship with God that were not possible under the Levitical institution.

In the LXX of Exodus, Leviticus, and Ezekiel, the expression ἐγγίζειν τῷ θεῷ, "to draw near to God," is used of those who approach God in a state of cultic purity (e.g., Exod 3:5; 24:2; Lev 10:3); it is used particularly of a priest who enters the sanctuary for sacrificial duty (Exod 19:22; Lev 21:21; Ezek 40:46; 42:13; 43:19; 44:13; 45:4). Outside these books it is used more generally of a worshiper who approaches God or who directs his thoughts toward God in prayer (Ps 31[MT 32]:6; 33[MT 34]:19[18]; 144[MT 145]:18; 148[MT 149]:14; Hos 12:6; Zeph 3:2; Isa 29:13; 58:2; Jdt 8:27). This more general use of ἐγγίζειν to denote a drawing near to God in prayer serves as a caution against reading a particular cultic meaning into its usage here. In Hebrews the "drawing near" certainly has a future aspect (see *Comment* on 6:18–20), but it also occurs in the present and is indispensable for receiving help that is needed in a time of stress or crisis (see *Comment* on 4:16). The accent in the present passage falls upon the certainty of the "drawing near," which is the legacy of the Christian as the result of the absolute effectiveness of the priesthood of Christ (Preisker, *TDNT* 2:331; Cockerill, *Melchizedek Christology*, 118–20).

20–22   The pastoral implications of the conclusion reached in vv 18–19 are more fully drawn out in 7:20–25. This unit is closely tied to the demonstration in 7:11–19 that Christ is the superior priest who has replaced the old priesthood by the repetition of the connective καί, "and," at the beginnning of v 20 and v 23. In 7:20–22 and 7:23–25 the writer takes up a phrase from Ps 110:4 to contrast the new priest like Melchizedek with the old priesthood in some particular aspect. In 7:20–22 he interprets the clause "the Lord has sworn and will not change his mind"; in 7:23–25 he explores the significance of the clause "you are a priest forever." Each of these two smaller units denotes a further benefit that the new arrangement is able to bring to the community because of its superior priest. The first benefit, outlined in vv 20–22, is that the new covenant has a guarantor who assures its effectiveness, both for the present and for the future. This is so because the eschatological priest was established in his office by an oath, while the old priesthood was not (cf. Cockerill, *Melchizedek Christology*, 26–27, 121–22).

The syntactical structure of vv 20–22 is complex. The comparison introduced in v 20*a* is completed in v 22. The comparative expressions καθ᾽ ὅσον . . . κατὰ τοσοῦτο . . . , "in so far as . . . just so far . . . ," direct attention to the relationship between the divine oath and the "guarantor" of the better covenant: the divine oath stands behind the guarantor and supports him in his mission. The basis for the comparison is detailed in a lengthy parenthesis (vv 20*b*–21), which is connected to v 20*a* by the explanatory γάρ, "for." The writer develops parenthetically a contrast between the new priest, whose appointment was validated by God's solemn oath, and the Levitical priesthood, which was based on the law without the benefit of a divine oath (cf. v 28). This contrast expresses forcefully that the difference between Jesus and the Levitical priest is not one of degree (lesser and greater) but of kind, demonstrating that Jesus is the eschatological priest of the new age (Michel, 274; Cockerill, *Melchizedek Christology*, 127–28).

The initial statement that Jesus became a priest οὐ χωρὶς ὁρκωμοσίας, "not without the swearing of an oath" (v 20a), anticipates the exegetical deduction from Ps 110:4 that is drawn in v 21. It asserts categorically that the new priesthood is a divine institution unconditionally validated by God's solemn oath. The divine oath verifies the absolute reliability of the priesthood of Christ, upon which the hopes of the Christian community are anchored (6:18–20). The achievement of its purpose is assured (cf. Schneider, *TDNT* 5:183–84; Thompson, *NovT* 19 [1971] 218–29). The previous exposition of God's word of promise to Abraham that was confirmed with an oath in 6:13–18 demonstrated that the divine oath is the impregnable guarantee that excludes all doubt and gives to faith assurance of the promise. The function of the oath is to characterize the promise as final, eternal, and unchangeable. The writer now demonstrates that the promise extended to the community in 6:16–20 is identical with the eschatological priesthood introduced with an oath in Ps 110:4 (Klappert, *Eschatologie*, 32; cf. Trites, *Witness*, 220).

The distinctive way in which the citation of Ps 110:4 is introduced in v 21 accentuates the immediacy of God's word to his Son. When the writer introduced Ps 110:4 in the course of the homily, he treated the quotation as a word spoken directly by God to the Son and fulfilled in him (5:6a; cf. 1:6, 7, 10). This point is sustained in v 21. Emphasizing that Jesus became a priest μετὰ ὁρκωμοσίας, "with the swearing of an oath," the writer refers to God as the one who addressed Jesus in the words of Ps 110:4. The formal decree of installation was prefaced with a solemn oath. The finality of the oath is strengthened by the provision that the Lord "will not change his mind," thus guaranteeing the utter reliability of the promise (cf. Cockerill, *Melchizedek Christology*, 128–29, 224–26). The institution of the eternal priest is inviolable. In v 17 the acclamation "you are a priest forever" was still qualified by the significant phrase "like Melchizedek." The absence of this qualifying reference to the ancient priestly predecessor in the form of the citation in v 21, together with the introduction of the personal name "Jesus" in v 22, permits all interest to be concentrated upon the eschatological realization of the promise (Demarest, "Priest," 11). As elsewhere in Hebrews, the personal name "Jesus" is deferred to the final position in the sentence for dramatic emphasis (see *Comment* on 2:9).

Because God's oath stands behind the appointment of the eschatological priest, Jesus can guarantee that the goals announced in the new covenant will be achieved (v 22). The qualitative description of the new covenant as κρείττονος διαθήκης, "better covenant," recalls the use of the expression κρείττονος ἐλπίδος, "better hope," in v 19. It marks the first occurrence of the theologically significant term διαθήκη, "covenant," in Hebrews. The writer's usage presupposes the LXX, where διαθήκη was given a particular nuance. In the papyri, and in hellenistic Greek generally, the term means "testament" or "will." But the translators of the LXX introduced this common term to express the unilateral character of God's sovereign and gracious disposition toward Israel. It receives the connotation of "covenant" or "sovereign arrangement," and this nuance was maintained in the OT Apocrypha and Pseudepigrapha (cf. Behm, *TDNT* 2:124–34). In v 22 the writer views the διαθήκη from the cultic point of view; it denotes the arrangement God has established for those who approach him. The new covenant (cf. 8:8–10; 9:15–20) can be described as "better" because it is effective: the approach to God is guaranteed by Jesus in his office as eternal priest (cf. 7:19; 13:20).

In relationship to the covenant, Jesus is designated ἔγγυος, "guarantor." The choice of the term, which occurs only here in the NT, is purposeful. In the papyri it can denote a bond, a collateral, or some form of material guarantee that a debt will be paid or a promise fulfilled. But it may also refer to an individual who offers his own life as the guarantor of another person (see especially Sir 29:15–17). In this personal sense, the ἔγγυος assumes a weightier responsibility than the μεσίτης, "mediator" (cf. 8:6; 9:15; 12:24). The "mediator" steps into the gap between two parties, but the "guarantor" stakes his person and his life on his word (cf. Michel, 275). Through his death, exaltation, and installation as heavenly priest, Jesus provides security that the new and better covenant will not be annulled. God's new work of salvation, which had its beginning in the proclamation of Jesus (2:3), will necessarily be followed by its completion (Preisker, *TDNT* 2:329; cf. Oepke, *TDNT* 4:618–20). Jesus has become the ἔγγυος who offers himself as the pledge that this obligation will be fulfilled.

23–25   The new priesthood of Jesus brings to the people of the new covenant another benefit. This becomes evident in reflection on the clause, "You are a priest forever" (Ps 110:4). Since Jesus exercises an eternal and final priesthood, he is able to mediate an eternal and ultimate salvation. In vv 23–24 the comparison between the old priesthood and the new priest is developed in the form of a chiasmus that sharply contrasts the temporal character of the one and the perpetuity and finality of the other. The benefit to the community that results from the superiority demonstrated in the contrast is described in v 25 (cf. Cockerill, *Melchizedek Christology*, 27, 129).

In vv 23–24 the main emphasis appears to rest on the contrast between the "many" and the "one": οἱ μὲν πλείονες . . . ὁ δέ, "on the one hand these many . . . but on the other hand that one." The fact that there were many priests under the Levitical arrangement is important to the writer's argument. In Hebrews multiplicity signifies incompleteness, imperfection, and inconclusiveness (e.g., 1:1; 10:1–4; cf. Michel, 276; Thompson, 200). According to Josephus (*Ant.* 20.227) a total of eighty-three high priests was installed from the inception of the Aaronide priesthood to the cessation of temple worship in A.D. 70. In v 23 the writer is not merely thinking of the succession of high priests. The direction of his thought is indicated more precisely by the causal clause in v 23b: the reason there were many priests is that every one of them was prevented from continuing in office by the simple fact of death. Consequently, the continuity of the Levitical priesthood was repeatedly disrupted. The verb παραμένειν is rare in the LXX, but it is used by Josephus of priests continuing in office (*Ant.* 2.309; 9.27, cf. Hauck, *TDNT* 4:578, n. 3). According to Exod 40:15 LXX, Aaron and his sons had been appointed to the priesthood εἰς τὸν αἰῶνα, "forever," but this unlimited expression is immediately qualified by the phrase εἰς τὰς γενεὰς αὐτῶν, "in their respective generations" (cf. Num 25:13 LXX). The Levitical priesthood was perpetuated only because provision had been made for a succession of priests to exercise the ministry.

By way of contrast, Jesus has been invested with an eternal and final priesthood (v 24). The reason he is the paramount ministrant of an eternal priesthood is provided in a causal clause in v 24a: διὰ τὸ μένειν αὐτὸν εἰς τὸν αἰῶνα, "because he continues forever." Juxtaposing the two causal clauses (v 23b/v 24a) in the chiastic structure of vv 23–24 emphasizes the temporal character of the many priests and the permanence of the one. The choice of the infinitive μένειν, "to continue," appears to be theologically significant. In the LXX μένειν signifies God's continuing life in contrast to limited human existence (e.g., θεὸς μένων καὶ ζῶν εἰς γενεὰς γενεῶν ἕως τοῦ αἰῶνος, "God continuing and living from generation to generation forever," Dan 6:27 LXX; cf. Hauck, *TDNT* 4:575–76). In v 24a μένειν, together with εἰς τὸν αἰῶνα, "forever," recalls the striking declaration concerning Melchizedek in 7:3d ("he continues as priest without interruption"). What is true of Melchizedek in a literary and symbolic way attains its definitive realization in the priest of the new covenant (cf. Cockerill, *Melchizedek Christology*, 132, n. 361). The predication "he continues forever" implies Christ's participation in the life of God.

In v 16 the writer had declared that Christ was a priest "by virtue of the power of an indestructible life." He now provides a further explanation of that statement. Because he continues forever, he has a priesthood that is ἀπαράβατον, "permanent" (see above, *Note* u). In contrast to the Levitical priests, whose ministries were continually disrupted by death, there is no temporal limitation to the ministry of a priest who lives forever. The eternity of the Son (v 24a) qualifies him to exercise a ministry that is permanent and final. The unequivocal statement that nothing can infringe upon Christ's priesthood includes the subsidiary notion that it passes to no successor (Demarest, "Priest," 338–39).

The inferential particle ὅθεν, "and so," at the beginning of v 25 indicates that the conclusion reached is a logical deduction from the argument in vv 23–24. The writer frequently uses this particle to indicate the practical implications of his christological reflections for the life of the community (cf. 2:17; 3:1; 8:3; 9:18). His intention is to strengthen a community that has lacked certainty. In v 25 he specifies the further benefit of Christ's eternal priesthood that he is able to save εἰς τὸ παντελές, "absolutely" (see *Note* v above). Faith and hope are solidified through an awareness of the finality and duration of Christ's priestly ministry on behalf of his people (cf. Thompson, *NovT* 19 [1977] 221). The designation of those for whom Christ cares continually as τοὺς προσερχομένους, "those who approach [God]," which makes use of an equivalent expression for the description of the community in v 19, is appropriate to the cultic imagery in the context. In the LXX the Greek expressions προσέρχεσθαι, "to approach," and ἐγγίζειν, "to draw near," are used interchangeably for the approach to God in worship (cf. Schneider, *TDNT* 2:683–84).

The scope of Christ's priestly ministry is suggested by the infinitives σώζειν, "to save," and ἐντυγχάνειν, "to intercede." In Hebrews "salvation" is presented as a future eschatological inheritance (1:14; 5:9; 9:28). There is, nevertheless, a definite sense in which the community has already begun to participate in salvation as a result of the obedience and sacrificial death of Christ and his subsequent exaltation (cf. 2:3–4; 6:4–5, 9). The present tense of σώζειν reflects the current experience of the community and suggests that Jesus' support is available at each critical moment. He has a sustained interest in the welfare of his people. The perfection and eternity of the salvation he mediates is guaranteed by the unassailable character of his priesthood.

The conjunctive participial phrase in v 25*b*, πάντοτε ζῶν εἰς τὸ ἐντυγχάνειν ὑπὲρ αὐτῶν, "he continually lives in order to intercede for them," can be understood in two ways. It appears to be causal, supplying a further reason for the ability of the exalted priest to save absolutely (BDF §418[1]). It could also be modal, indicating the manner in which he is able to save (BDF §418[5]). The clause expresses the active, representative ministry of Christ throughout the course of the present age. The adverbial clause πάντοτε ζῶν, "he continually lives," is an inference drawn from Ps 110:4. It asserts emphatically that Jesus' capacity for effectively acting on behalf of his people is unlimited. He is able to meet every need of the Christian.

The form of his uninterrupted ministry is indicated by the purpose phrase εἰς τὸ ἐντυγχάνειν ὑπὲρ αὐτῶν, "in order to intercede for them." The verb ἐντυγχάνειν with ὑπέρ followed by the genitive means "to approach on behalf of someone"; when the one approached is God the expression frequently comes to mean "to pray" (cf. Wis 8:21; 16:28; Philo, *Moses* 1.173). With his exaltation to heaven, Jesus became the permanent intercessor for his people. His ministry involves an active advocatory role in the presence of God on behalf of the oppressed (cf. Murray, "The Heavenly, Priestly Activity of Christ," 44–58). The direct result of his intercessory activity is the sustaining of the people and the securing of all that is necessary to the eschatological salvation mentioned in the previous clause.

The term ἐντυγχάνειν is used in reference to a heavenly intercessor also in Rom 8:34, in a passage that appears to belong to the tradition (cf. Nomoto, *NovT* 10 [1968] 12–13; Loader, *NTS* 24 [1977–78] 205–6). The ministry of intercession is there associated with Jesus' death, resurrection, ascension, and session at God's right hand. Michel has suggested that Rom 8:34 and Heb 7:25 may preserve variant forms of an early Christian confession that regarded the exalted Christ as the "Advocate of the community" (276). Similar ideas cluster in 1 John 2:1 (see O. Betz, *Der Paraklet* [Leiden: Brill, 1963] 60–64, 149–59). Alongside this heavenly advocate, Melchizedek has no place.

It is unnecessary to agree with Hay that the idea of eternal intercession in v 25 is a "foreign element" in the theology of Hebrews, which is only imperfectly fused with the writer's understanding of Jesus' death as a priestly sacrifice (*Glory*, 132, 149–50). Hay senses a tension between the active character of intercession and the passive character of Christ's death. The concept of Christ's death as a high priestly sacrifice, however, is not developed as a major argument until chap. 9. Prior to that point, the notion of high priest is consistently linked with Christ's readiness to assist those who are severely tested (2:18; 4:14–16). Much is made of his presence at God's right hand and his continual intercession, which provides certainty that the people of God will be able to obtain the promised salvation. Thus, 7:25 is not a "foreign element" in the writer's theology but reflects the perspective of the pivotal exhortation on perseverance and prayer in 4:14–16. In 10:19–21 Christ's present intercessory ministry is seen to be a direct consequence of his sacrifice, which provides a ground for boldness in approaching God. The concept of an intercessory ministry in 7:25 is appropriate to the context. As representative of the people in their approach to God, it was the task of the high priest to intercede. In point of fact, the final clause of v 25 is a miniature of the argument in 7:1–25: the Son's indissoluble life is the basis of his uninterrupted priestly intercession (cf. Loader, *NTS* 24 [1977–78] 205–6; Peterson, "Examination," 192–94; Cockerill, *Melchizedek Christology*, 301, 321).

26 The argument in 7:11–25 is aptly summarized in the final paragraph of chap. 7. On the basis of Ps 110:4, the writer has been showing that the promised exalted priest supersedes the old priesthood and that he is effective where the Levitical priests were not. The exposition is brought to a conclusion in vv 26–28 with a majestic statement concerning Jesus' character, achievement, and status as high priest. The change in these verses from ἱερεύς, "priest," to ἀρχιερεύς, "high priest," is explained by the simple literary consideration that the writer is moving beyond the warrant of Ps 110:4. In 7:11–25 the use of ἱερεύς was dictated by dependence upon the prophetic oracle announcing the "priest like Melchizedek." The resumption of the designation ἀρχιερεύς (cf. 2:17; 3:1; 4:14–15; 5:5, 10; 6:20) signals the writer's readiness to reach back and take up motifs introduced in earlier sections of the homily. The writer moves beyond Ps 110:4 to prepare for the subsequent discussion of the sacrifice of Christ and the heavenly sanctuary that follows in 8:1–10:18 (cf. Demarest, "Priest," 346–47; Cockerill, *Melchizedek Christology*, 27–29, 148, 260).

The initial statement indicates the writer's concern to apply what he has to say to his hearers in their situation τοιοῦτος γὰρ ἡμῖν καὶ ἔπρεπεν ἀρχιερεύς, "Now such a high priest was precisely appropriate to us" (v 26a). In the NT the dominant tendency is for the demonstrative τοιοῦτος, "such [a high priest]," to refer to what precedes, and this clearly is the case in Heb 11:14; 12:3; and 13:6. It is, therefore, reasonable to hold that there is at least some degree of reference to the discussion of the eternity and effectiveness of the exalted priest in 7:11–25 (so Michel, 278). When the demonstrative is followed by a correlative, however, τοιοῦτος refers to what follows (as in 8:1). The demonstrative in v 26a is followed by the relative ὅς, "he," in v 27, which has correlative force. The primary reference of v 26a, therefore, would appear to be what follows: the high priest who is appropriate to the community is precisely the one who offered himself (so also F. F. Bruce, 156–57; Cockerill, *Melchizedek Christology*, 148–50). On this understanding, v 26a is the controlling statement for vv 26–27. The description of the kind of high priest who fits the circumstances of the community and who is able to meet all their needs proceeds from the cross of Christ (cf. Michel, 278–79).

The three adjectives added in v 26b to fill out the description of the high priest refer to his personal character. Although it is difficult to distinguish the particular nuance of each term, all three are probably to be understood from a cultic and priestly perspective and to be interpreted in relationship to the LXX. The word ὅσιος, "devout," appears in Hebrews only here. In the LXX it describes those whose relationship to God and to others reflects fidelity to the covenant (Pss 12:1; 18:26; 32:6; 79:1–2; 132:9, 16; 149:1–2). The term resumes the motif of Jesus' obedient relationship to the Father demonstrated through the experiences of his earthly life (5:7–8). As one who was consecrated to the service of God (10:5–10), he was qualified religiously to be the true high priest (cf. Hauck, *TDNT* 5:492; Spicq, 2:200). The word ἄκακος, "guileless, pure, innocent," is used in the LXX predominantly with a passive and moral significance. It was an appropriate term for denoting the moral qualification of Jesus to be high priest. It signifies not only that Jesus was guileless in his relationship with other people, but that he was not touched by evil (Moffatt, 101; Grundmann, *TDNT* 3:482; F. F. Bruce, 156). The term ἀμίαντος, "undefiled," denotes cultic purity (2 Macc 14:26; 15:34; Jos., *J. W.* 6.99). Elsewhere it is almost always applied to things, not to a person, but in two passages Philo applies the term directly to the high priest, as in Heb 7:26 (*On Flight and Finding* 118; *On the Special Laws* 1.113). In v 26*b* the cultic imagery is used figuratively to express the qualification of this high priest to enter the presence of God (Hauck, *TDNT* 4:647). The three terms are not descriptive of static moral qualities but of dispositions demonstrated by the incarnate Son in spite of his complete involvement in the life of common humanity. Taken together, these three adjectives describe the sinlessness of the high priest (Michel, 279; Spicq, 2:201). In contrast to the Levitical high priest, of whom there was demanded only ritual purity (Lev 21:11) and bodily integrity (Lev 21:17), the high priest appropriate to the Christian community was qualified by spiritual and moral perfection.

The two participial phrases that follow (v 26*c, d*) are also in apposition to ἀρχιερεύς, "high priest." It has been argued that the phrase κεχωρισμένος ἀπὸ τῶν ἁμαρτωλῶν, "having been separated from sinners" (v 26*c*) is to be understood in relationship to the preceding adjectives; the phrase reflects the high priest's moral separateness from sinners. He is "different from sinful humanity" (cf. Buchanan, 128; Peterson, "Examination," 196–97, 201). A comparative study of the linguistic usage of the verb χωρίζειν in the passive ("to be separated, severed, divided"), however, lends little support to this proposal. In the later books of the LXX, especially 1 Esdras, Ezra, and Nehemiah, the passive of χωρίζειν followed by ἀπό, "separated from," is an idiom denoting local separation (of the Israelites from the people around them, e.g., 1 Esdr 7:13; 9:7; Ezra 9:1; Neh 9:2). In the passive, χωρίζειν can also have a second meaning, denoting "separated" in the sense of "different from." However, when χωρίζειν implies mere difference or "distinction," it is rarely, if ever, followed by the preposition ἀπό. In point of fact, this connotation occurs only once in the LXX (3 Macc 2:25), never in Philo, and never in the NT, with the possible exception of this passage. The evidence suggests that the idiom κεχωρισμένος ἀπό in v 26*c* denotes local separation and that the perfect tense of the verb is used to express the state of having been separated (Cockerill, *Melchizedek Christology*, 163–69). The clause affirms that Jesus' life among sinners ceased with his ascension. He has left the sphere characterized by testing, hostility, and suffering and has been exalted to the sphere of God. His separation assumes his moral perfection, but the emphasis falls upon his actual entrance before the divine presence, where he accomplishes the ministry of intercession. The phrase is descriptive of the majesty of the high priest and is to be related to the phrase that follows (cf. Riggenbach, 209; Michel, 280).

Like v 26*c*, the phrase in v 26*d* focuses on the sphere of Christ's high priestly ministry. The expression ὑψηλότερος τῶν οὐρανῶν, "higher than the heavens," has specific reference to the place of God's throne. Similar spatial imagery is found in certain apocalyptic sources (e.g., *Asc. Isa.* 7–8) which refer to a visionary journey through a number of heavens to reach the presence of God in "the heaven above all heavens" (cf. Traub, *TDNT* 5:527–28; Bertram, *TDNT* 8:609). In v 26*d* the writer has made use of a spatial metaphor to denote the highest possible exaltation. The phrase resumes the motif of the high priest who "has passed through the heavens" to gain access to the presence of God (see *Comment* on 4:14).

Jesus enjoys direct, unhindered access to God, which enables him to fulfill his high priestly ministry on behalf of his people. Although Jesus' exaltation to the right hand of God removes him in a quasi-spatial sense from his Church, it by no means implies a remoteness from his brothers and sisters or a lack of involvement in their struggles (cf. Michel, 279–81; Cockerill, *Melchizedek Christology*, 170–72).

27 The description of the personal character and exalted sphere of ministry of the high priest in v 26 is carried forward in v 27 by reflection upon his singular achievement. The connection between the two statements is established by the correlative phrase at the beginning of v 27, ὃς οὐκ ἔχει καθ᾽ ἡμέραν ἀνάγκην . . . θυσίας ἀναφέρειν, "he does not need to offer sacrifices daily," which refers back to the demonstrative τοιοῦτος, "such a one," in v 26. The appropriate high priest is the one whose unique offering of himself put an end to the whole system of Levitical sacrifices. He was able to make the definitive sacrifice because he was the sinless high priest described in v 26. A comparison between the eschatological high priest and the high priests of Aaron's line is only implied in v 26, but in v 27 it is made explicit. The measure of the superiority of the new high priest is that he has offered himself as the final sacrifice. In 7:11–25 the demonstration of the superiority and finality of the new priest over the established legal priesthood was based on Ps 110:4 and the promise of a priest "like Melchizedek." The formulation of v 27 indicates how far the writer has moved beyond that line of argument, for Melchizedek has no connection with sacrifice (Cockerill, *Melchizedek Christology*, 172–73).

The unique surrender of Christ's life is considered under the image of sacrifice: ἑαυτὸν ἀνενέγκας, "he offered himself." In the LXX the verb ἀναφέρειν is a technical term meaning "to offer a sacrifice, to make an offering" (Weiss, *TDNT* 9:60–61). The writer presents Christ as performing an essentially high priestly function when he offered his life to God (Zimmermann, *Hohepriester-Christologie*, 15). The perfection of his sacrifice matches the spiritual and moral perfection of the high priest who is simultaneously the unblemished offering (cf. 9:14). Since he offered the perfect sacrifice, both the necessity and the possibility of perpetuating a sacrificial ministry, as other priests do, are excluded. It is this striking realization that invites the contrast between the one sacrifice of Christ and the many sacrifices of the Levitical high priests (for a related contrast between the "one" and the "many," see *Comment* on 7:23–24). The fact that Christ offered himself ἐφάπαξ, "once and for all," signifies the completeness of his sacrifice. In the NT ἐφάπαξ is a technical term for the definitiveness and uniqueness of the death of Christ and the redemption it secured (9:12; 10:10; cf. Stählin, *TDNT* 1:383–84). In v 27 this term acquires its force from comparison with the temporal expression καθ᾽ ἡμέραν, "daily," which qualifies the sacrificial ministry of the Levitical high priests and connotes incompleteness and ineffectiveness.

The basis for the comparison between Christ and the Levitical high priests in v 27 is the prescription for sacrifice on the Day of Atonement. Only on that occasion was it prescribed that the high priest should make an atonement first for his own sins and then for those of the people (Lev 16:6–10; see *Comment* on 5:3). The writer appears to have regarded the double sacrifice of the Day of Atonement as decisive for the typology he is developing (cf. 9:7). The specification καθ᾽ ἡμέραν in v 27a, however, is problematical. The double sacrifice was not offered "daily" but once each year (Exod 20:30; Lev 16:1–33). Moreover, the writer was fully aware of the fundamental difference between the annual sacrifices offered by the high priest on the Day of Atonement (9:7, 25; 10:1, 3) and the daily offerings of the ordinary priests (10:11, καθ᾽ ἡμέραν, "day by day"). A variety of proposals have been made to resolve this crux. We pass them under review.

(1) It is possible that the procedure on the Day of Atonement has been generalized, so that the writer has interpreted all of the daily sacrifices in the light of the atonement ritual (cf. Riggenbach, 209–15; Michel, 282–83; F. F. Bruce, 157–58; Cockerill, *Melchizedek Christology,* 175–77, n. 488). The daily sacrifices, which were offered in the morning and again in the evening, consisted of a lamb and appropriate cereal and drink offerings on behalf of the whole nation (Exod 29:38–46; Num 28:3–10) and the cereal offering for the high priest, which is designated in the LXX θυσία, "sacrifice" (Lev 6:9–23; cf. Jos., *Ant.* 3.257: "the [high] priest also, of his own charge, offered a sacrifice, and he did that twice each day"). These two offerings were closely associated in the old synagogue liturgy, but the offering for the people preceded the offering for the high priest, in contradiction to the order of v 27 (see *m. Yoma* 7:3; *Taʿan.* 4:6; cf. Philo, *Who Is the Heir?* 174).

(2) The writer had in mind the daily involvement of the high priest in the sacrificial ritual of Judaism. If the reference was to the offering that the priest must make when he committed unintentional sin (Lev 4:2–18), or to some other daily offerings in which the high priests were involved (Lev 6:12–23), it would not have been difficult to interpret the daily sacrifices in the light of the Day of Atonement (Williamson, *Philo,* 177–79).

(3) The reference is not to the law as prescribed in the Pentateuch but to the tradition that Aaron had to offer daily sacrifice for himself and the people (Sir 45:14, "his sacrifices shall be wholly burned twice each day continually"). Although Philo undoubtedly knew that the high priest did not actually officiate every day, he makes a similar statement when he says the high priest "day by day offers prayers and sacrifices and asks for blessings" (*On the Special Laws* 3.131; cf. Lach, "Les ordonnances," 392–93).

The continual obligation of the high priest to make an atonement offering for himself as well as for the people served to emphasize the ineffectiveness of the Levitical high priests. The writer regarded the purpose of all sacrifice as atonement (see *Comment* on 5:1). The point of the contrast in v 27 is that atonement was achieved fully and perfectly only through the definitive sacrifice when the sinless Son of God offered himself for the sins of the people. This notion will be developed more fully in 9:11–14; 10:1–15.

28 The profound difference between the two priesthoods is detailed in a concluding contrast summarizing the argument of the entire chapter. The writer's appreciation of the rhetorical effectiveness of forceful antithesis is particularly evident here (cf. Nomoto, *NovT* 10 [1968] 16): (1) the basis of the Levitical institution was ὁ νόμος, "the law," but that of the new priesthood was ὁ λόγος τῆς ὁρκωμοσίας, "the word of the sworn oath," which was promulgated subsequent to the law; (2) the old priesthood consisted of ἄνθρωποι, "men," but the new priest is υἱός, "the Son"; (3) the old priests are characterized as ἔχοντας ἀσθένειαν, "affected by weakness," but the new priest as τετελειωμένον, "has been made perfect." These three antitheses restate the lines of the argument expounded in the preceding verses.

The first antithesis recalls the argument that the law was ineffective in establishing a priesthood that could attain God's intended goal for his people (vv 11–19). As a result, God swore an oath to establish a radically different priesthood to supersede the Levitical institution (vv 20–22). The notion of supersession affirmed in v 22 is implied in v 28 by the phrase τῆς μετὰ τὸν νόμον, "which came after the law." The oracle in Ps 110:4 was fulfilled when the promised priest appeared and vindicated his high priestly status on the basis of a perfect and final sacrifice.

The second antithesis recalls the argument contrasting the many priests who were prevented by death from remaining in office with the one priest of the new covenant who continues forever. The mortality of the old priests contrasts sharply with the eternity and eschatological finality of the new priest (vv 23–25). The particular aspect of Jesus' priesthood guaranteed by the oath, which the writer emphasizes, is its permanency: he is a priest εἰς τὸν αἰῶνα, "forever." This aspect shows Jesus' essential likeness to Melchizedek in vv 3, 8, and the fundamental difference with the priesthood of the Levites.

The third antithesis goes beyond the range of argument in vv 11–25 and is related to vv 26–27. The law appointed to the high priestly office men who by virtue of the limitations common to human nature were subject to imperfection and sin. In this context, the term ἀσθένεια, "weakness," is almost equivalent to "sin" (5:2; cf. Stählin, *TDNT* 1:492; Michel, 283–84). The weakness of the Levitical high priests is openly displayed in the obligation to offer sacrifice repeatedly for their own sin, as well as for those of the people (5:3; 7:27; 9:7). The perfection of the new priest is exhibited and is fully accomplished in the offering of himself once for all as the sufficient sacrifice for the transgressions of the people. His own sinlessness (4:15; 7:26) required of him no sin offering and assured the unconditional efficacy of his atoning death (cf. Demarest, "Priest," 340–44; Peterson, "Examination," 174, 197–201; Cockerill, *Melchizedek Christology*, 179–80).

The emphasis in v 28 falls on the concluding statement that the word sworn on oath appoints as high priest υἱὸν εἰς τὸν αἰῶνα τετελειωμένον, "the Son who has been made perfect forever." The formulation directs attention to the vocation of Jesus and announces the complete realization of the objectives of his high priesthood (cf. Kögel, "Der Begriff," 64). The participle τετελειωμένον does not repeat, but presupposes, the consecration that is expressed in the verb καθιστάνειν, "to appoint or ordain to the priesthood." The perfecting of Christ as Son entails the perfecting of his quality as mediator and his compliance with the divine mandate of an eternal ministry of intercession in the heavenly sanctuary.

The "vocational" understanding of Christ's perfection in 2:10 and 5:9 establishes a context for interpreting the significance of the related phrase in v 28. In 2:10 and 5:9 the emphasis falls on Jesus' perfecting through sufferings. Read against this background, the perfect passive participle in v 28 implies that a lifetime of human experience punctuated by testing, humiliation, and the affliction of death is now behind Jesus (Riggenbach, 214–15). The concluding phrase in v 28 recalls the obedience of Christ in life and death, which was acknowledged in his exaltation to heavenly dignity and power. The concept of Christ as "perfect" in Hebrews corresponds to the death and exaltation motif in the apostolic preaching (2:10; 5:9; 7:28; 12:2; cf. Klappert, *Eschatologie*, 34, 57; Silva, *WTJ* 39 [1976] 66–67). The eschatological exaltation of Christ, in fulfillment of the divine promises, constitutes the concrete designation of perfection.

In the context of chap. 7, Jesus' perfecting as Son is also related to his becoming an eternal priest "like Melchizedek." He authenticated the priestly character of his mission through a series of events that culminated in the offering of himself as an unblemished sacrifice. His subsequent exaltation obtained for him unhindered access to the presence of God, which is the fundamental qualification for the exercise of a perpetual priesthood. The expression εἰς τὸν αἰῶνα, "forever," emphasizes the continual effectiveness of his priestly intercession. The verb τελειοῦν, "to perfect," is accordingly best understood in a dynamic sense as referring to the whole process by which Jesus was personally prepared and vocationally qualified for his continuing ministry in the presence of God. In v 28 that ministry is contemplated as an accomplished fact of singular importance to the stability of the community addressed (cf. du Plessis, *ΤΕΛΕΙΟΣ*, 221; Peterson, "Examination," 201–9, 215, 328; Cockerill, *Melchizedek Christology*, 181–84).

Explanation

A comparison between the Levitical high priesthood and the unique priesthood of Christ was introduced in 5:1–10. When Aaron and Christ were brought into direct comparison, the basis of the comparison was the humility both displayed in refusing to exalt themselves to the office of high priest, which could be received only by divine appointment (5:4–6). The validity of the OT priesthood resides in its authorization. The likeness of Jesus to Aaron, however, was shattered with the citation of Ps 110:4. The appeal to Melchizedek proved that Jesus' priesthood was different from and superior to the Levitical priesthood. The one who is summoned to be "a priest forever" enjoys a preeminence that removes him beyond the sphere of comparison with Aaron. The parallel between Aaron and Christ was infringed most dramatically when the writer described their respective priestly functions. In reference to the Levitical high priest, mention was made of the cultic ministry of sacrifice on the Day of Atonement (5:1, 3) and the extension of forbearance to those who are weak (5:2). By way of contrast, Christ's high priestly offering culminated in the surrender of his life in perfect obedience to God (5:7–9). This self-sacrifice represented an incomparably more profound and more radical identification with men and women in their weakness than was ever envisioned in the case of the Levitical high priest.

In 7:11–28 the comparison between the Levitical high priesthood and the unique priesthood of Christ is resumed. The writer turns directly to Ps 110:4 and its designation of a new eternal priest "like Melchizedek" and not "like Aaron." The interpretation of the oracle as a solemn decree of appointment spoken by God to the Son established a basis for a series of intricate comparisons between the new priesthood based on divine oath and the old Levitical priesthood based on the law. These comparisons demonstrate the superiority and finality of the Son's eternal priesthood. On the basis of the oracle in Ps 110:4, the writer deduces that the old priesthood, sacrifices, and covenant have been replaced by the new priest and the covenant he secured with his sacrifice.

While developing these comparisons, the writer is careful not to dissolve redemptive history into timeless categories. It is crucial to his argument for the superiority of the priest like Melchizedek that the oracle proclaiming a new act of God was promulgated after the law (7:11–19, 28). That God announced a different and superior priesthood in the OT was itself indicative that the Levitical priesthood had been insufficient and was obsolete. Its inability to achieve the goal of "perfection" implied its abrogation (7:11–12, 19). The use made of this concept is radical. The old order of salvation suffered from inherent weakness and has been completely set aside. It has been replaced by the eschatological priesthood of Jesus, which is endowed with a life impervious to death (7:13–17). The new priesthood is qualitatively different from the old because it is a fully effective priesthood (7:18–19).

The exposition of Ps 110:4 made it possible for the writer to connect the tradition about the Son with the priesthood and "eternity" predicated of Melchizedek. The use made of Melchizedek is thoroughly christological. His qualitatively different priesthood anticipated an eschatological priesthood based not on legal prescription but on divine appointment. The new priest is installed in his office by the oath of God. The timeless character of Melchizedek's priesthood pointed to the eternity and finality of the new priest. The priesthood of Christ is not described in terms of absolute eternity but in terms of its perpetual and final character (7:16, 24–25). It is as the possessor of a perpetual priesthood that the Son is "like Melchizedek." The argument for the eschatological superiority of the new priest is actually completed by v 25. The positive use made of Melchizedek supports a "Melchizedek christology."

There is an intensely practical orientation to the exposition of Ps 110:4. The members of the community appear to have doubted the ability of God to act decisively in the present on their behalf. The writer's concern was to help his audience realize the reality of God's final action in Christ and of Christ's present ability to help them face the realities of their circumstances. He had to assist them to grasp anew the significance of their confession that Jesus is the Son of God. By interpreting sonship in terms of priesthood, he was able to show the members of the community how the Son is able to save them in the present and to the end. His exercise of a ministry of advocacy on their behalf assured them of final and complete salvation (7:24–25). The main purpose of the Melchizedek christology of 7:1–25 was to prove the effectiveness of the Son's eternal priesthood. It provided a fresh and insightful perspective from which to grasp the meaning of the confession that Jesus is the Son of God.

The development of the Melchizedek christology was motivated by the writer's pastoral concern for the community. But it could not be the sole basis for the presentation of high priestly christology in Hebrews, since Melchizedek has nothing to do with sacrifice. For that reason, in 7:26–28 the writer moves beyond the warrant of Ps 110:4 to speak of the sinless character and sacrificial death of the new high priest. Particularly significant is the allusion to the action of the high priest on the Day of Atonement, which establishes a context for interpreting the death of Christ in priestly terms as atoning sacrifice. The sacrificial ministry of the Levitical priesthood was a type, which was fulfilled by the priesthood of Christ. These verses touch upon themes that are fully developed only in the exposition that follows (8:1–10:18). They affirm that the high priest who is appropriate to the community is the one whose singular offering of himself put an end to the whole Levitical system of sacrifice. The perfection and definitiveness of his sacrifice were the consequences of the spiritual and moral perfection of his life. The description of the high priest who fits the circumstances of the community proceeds not from Ps 110:4 but from the cross.

The fundamental qualification for the exercise of a fully effective, perpetual priesthood is one of continual access to the presence of God. The exalted status of the new high priest who was vocationally qualified for an uninterrupted ministry of advocacy in the heavenly sanctuary provides the assurance that the objectives of his perpetual priesthood will be completely realized.

E. Sanctuary and Covenant (8:1–13)

Bibliography

Attridge, H. W. "The Uses of Antithesis in Hebrews 8–10." *HTR* 79 (1986) 1–9. **Beavis, M. A.** "The New Covenant and Judaism." *TBT* 22 (1984) 24–30. **Bell, W. E.** "The New Covenant." Dissertation, Dallas Theological Seminary, 1963. **Blumenthal, A. von.** "τύπος und παράδειγμα." *Hermes* 63 (1928) 391–414. **Brandt, W.** "Die Wortgruppe λειτουργεῖν im Hebräerbrief und bei Clemens Romanus." *JTSB* 1 (1930) 145–76. **Cody, A.** *Heavenly Sanctuary and Liturgy.* 9–46, 77–107, 151–55. **Coppens, J.** "La nouvelle alliance en Jérémie 31, 31–34." *CBQ* 25 (1963) 12–21. **D'Angelo, M. R.** *Moses in the Letter to the Hebrews.* 201–58. **Dequeker, L.** "Het Nieuwe Verbond bij Jeremia, bij Paulus en in de Brief aan de Hebreeën." *Bijdragen* 33 (1972) 234–61. **Devescovi, U.** "Annotozioni sulla dottrina di Geremia circa la nuovo alleanza." *RevistB* 8 (1960) 102–28. **Dunkel, F.** "Expiation et Jour des expiations dans l'épître aux Hébreux." *RevRéf* 33 (1982) 63–71. **Dussaut, L.** *Synopse structurelle de l'Épître aux Hébreux.* 66–72. **Ellingworth, P.** "Jesus and the Universe in Hebrews." *EvQ* 58 (1986) 337–50. **Estève, H. M.** *De caelesti meditatione sacerdotali Christi iuxta Hebr. 8.3–4.* Madrid: Consejo superior de investigaciones cientificas, 1949. **Fabris, R.** "La lettera agli Ebrei e l'Antico Testamento." *RivB* 32 (1984) 237–52. **Fischer, J.** "Covenant, Fulfilment and Judaism in Hebrews." *ERT* 13 (1989) 175–87. **Gourgues, M.** "Lecture christologique du Psaume CX et fête de la Pentecôte." *RB* 83 (1976) 5–24. ———. "Remarques sur la 'structure centrale' de l'Épître aux Hébreux: À l'occasion d'une réédition." *RB* 84 (1977) 26–37. **Hofius, O.** *Der Vorhang vor dem Thron Gottes.* 50–60, 67–69. **Hollander, H. W.** "Hebrews 7:11 and 8:6: A Suggestion for the Translation of *nenomothetētai epi.*" *BT* 30 (1979) 244–47. **Horbury, W.** "The Aaronic Priesthood in the Epistle to the Hebrews." *JNST* 19 (1983) 43–71. **Hughes, P. E.** "The Blood of Jesus and His Heavenly Priesthood in Hebrews: Part III. The Meaning of 'The True Tent' and 'The Greater and More Perfect Tent.'" *BSac* 130 (1973) 305–14. **Hurst, L. D.** "The Background and Interpretation of the Epistle to the Hebrews." Dissertation, Oxford University, 1981. 24–29, 32–34, 37–41, 67–68. [Published as *The Epistle to the Hebrews: Its Background of Thought.* SNTSMS 65. Cambridge: Cambridge UP, 1989.] ———. "How 'Platonic' are Heb viii.5 and ix.23f.?" *JTS* 34 (1983) 156–68. **Johnsson, W. G.** "The Cultus of Hebrews in Twentieth-Century Scholarship." *ExpTim* 89 (1978) 104–8. **Kaiser, W. C.** "The Old Promise and the New Covenant: Jeremiah 31:31–34." *JETS* 15 (1972) 11–23. **Laub, F.** *Bekenntnis und Auslegung.* 203–7. **Lee, E. K.** "Words Denoting 'Pattern' in the New Testament." *NTS* 8 (1961–62) 166–73. **Lehne, S.** *The New Covenant in Hebrews.* JSNTSup 44. Sheffield: JSOT, 1990. **Lempp, W.** "Bund und Bundeserneuerrung bei Jeremias." Dissertation, Tübingen, 1955. **Lohfink, N.** *Die niemals gekündigte Bund: Exegetische Gedanken zum christlich-jüdischen Gespräch.* Freiburg/Basel/Vienna: Herder, 1989. **Luz, U.** "Der alte und der neue Bund bei Paulus und im Hebräerbrief." *EvT* 27 (1967) 318–36. **MacRae, G. W.** "Heavenly Temple and

Eschatology in the Letter to the Hebrews." *Semeia* 12 (1978) 177–99. **Martin-Achard, R.** "La nouvelle alliance selon Jérémie." *RTP* 12 (1962) 172–96. ———. "Quelques remarques sur la nouvelle alliance chez Jérémie (Jérémie 31, 31–34)." BETL 33. Louvain, 1974. 141–64. **McCullough, J. C.** "The Old Testament Quotations in Hebrews." *NTS* 26 (1979–80) 364–67. **McNicol, A. J.** "The Relationship of the Image of the Highest Angel to the High Priest Concept in Hebrews." Dissertation, Vanderbilt University, 1974. 54–113, 148–71, 189–92. **Michaud, J. P.** "Le passage de l'ancien au nouveau, selon l'Épître aux Hébreux." *ScEs* 35 (1983) 33–52. **Moule, C. F. D.** "Sanctuary and Sacrifice in the Church of the New Testament." *JTS* n.s. 1 (1950) 29–41. **Nomoto, S.** "Herkunft und Struktur der Hohenpriestervorstellung im Hebräerbrief." *NovT* 10 (1968) 10–25. **Omanson, R. L.** "A Superior Covenant: Hebrews 8:1–10:18." *RevExp* 82 (1985) 361–73. **Peterson, D. G.** "An Examination of the Concept of 'Perfection' in the 'Epistle to the Hebrews.'" Dissertation, University of Manchester, 1978. 222–27. ———. "The Prophecy of the New Covenant in the Argument of Hebrews." *RTR* 38 (1979) 74–81. **Pretorius, E. A. C.** "*Diathēkē* in the Epistle to the Hebrews." *Neot* 5 (1971) 37–50. **Roark, D. M.** "The New Covenant." *ThEduc* 32 (1985) 63–68. **Rose, C.** "Verheissung und Erfüllung: Zum Verständnis von ἐπαγγελία im Hebräerbrief." *BZ* 33 (1989) 60–80. **Sabourin, L.** "Liturge du sanctuaire et de la tente véritable (Héb. VIII.2)." *NTS* 18 (1971–72) 87–90. ———. "Sacrificium et liturgia in Epistula ad Hebraeos." *VD* 46 (1948) 235–58. **Schierse, F. J.** *Verheissung und Heilsvollendung.* 26–59. **Schlosser, J.** "La médiation du Christ d'après l'Épître aux Hébreux." *RevScRel* 63 (1989) 169–81. **Schreiber, R.** "Der neue Bund im Spätjudentum und Urchristentum." Dissertation, Tübingen, 1956. **Schröger, F.** *Der Verfasser des Hebräerbriefes.* 159–68. **Sharp, J. R.** "Philonism and the Eschatology of Hebrews: Another Look." *EAJT* 2 (1984) 289–98. **Spicq, C.** "La théologie des deux alliances dans l'Épître aux Hébreux." *RSPT* 33 (1949) 15–30. **Teodorico, P.** "Il sacerdozio celeste di Cristo nella lettera agli Ebrei." *Greg* 39 (1958) 310–34. **Unnik, W. C. van.** "Ἡ καινὴ διαθήκη—a Problem in the Early History of the Canon." *SP* 1 (1961) 212–27. **Vanhoye, A.** "De 'aspectu' oblationis Christi secundum Epistulam ad Hebraeos." *VD* 37 (1959) 32–38. ———. "La structure centrale de l'Épître aux Hébreux (Héb. 8/1–9/28)." *RSR* 47 (1949) 44–60. ———. "Le Dieu de la nouvelle alliance dans l'Épître aux Hébreux." In *La notion biblique de Dieu.* BETL 41. Ed. J. Coppens. Louvain, 1976. 315–30. **Vuyst, J. de.** "*Oud en nieuw Verbond*" in de Brief aan de Hebreeën. Kampen: Kok, 1964. 92–216. **Williamson, R.** *Philo and the Epistle to the Hebrews.* 123–29, 142–60. ———. "Platonism and Hebrews." *SJT* 16 (1963) 415–24. **Wolmarans, J. L. P.** "The Text and Translation of Hebrews 8:8." *ZNW* 75 (1984) 139–44.

Translation

^{1}*Now the crowning affirmation*[a] *to what we are saying*[b] *is this: We do have such a high priest, who has taken his seat at the right hand of the throne of the Majesty*[c] *in heaven,* ^{2}*the ministering priest*[d] *of the sanctuary, of the true tabernacle,*[e] *which the Lord pitched, not man.*

^{3}*Every high priest is appointed to offer both gifts and sacrifices; this being the case, this one too had necessarily to have something to offer.*[f] ^{4}*So if he had been on earth, he would not be a priest,*[g] *since there are those who offer*[h] *the gifts prescribed by the law.* ^{5}*They serve a sanctuary that is a shadowy suggestion*[i] *of the heavenly sanctuary, even as Moses was admonished by God*[j] *when he intended*[k] *to erect the tabernacle: "Look," (he says),*[l] *"you must make everything according to the pattern*[m] *shown to you on the mountain."*

^{6}*In fact,*[n] *the ministry which he has attained*[o] *is as superior to theirs as the covenant of which he is the mediator is superior to the old one, seeing that*[p] *this covenant has been drawn up on the basis of*[q] *better promises.* ^{7}*For if that first covenant had been irreproachable, there would have been no occasion sought for a second.*[r] ^{8}*For God finds fault when he says to them:*[s]

"The time is coming," declares the Lord,
    "when[t] I will establish a new covenant
with the house of Israel
    and with the house of Judah.
9   *It will not be like the covenant*
        I made with their forefathers
    at the time when[u] I took them by the hand
        to lead them out of Egypt,
because they did not remain faithful to my covenant,
    and I turned away from[v] them," declares the Lord.
10 *"This is the covenant I will make with the house of Israel*
        after that time," declares the Lord.
"I will put my laws in their minds
    and inscribe them on their hearts.
I will be their God,
    and they will be my people.
11 *No longer shall another person teach[w] his fellow-citizen,[x]*
        or a man his brother, saying, 'Know the Lord,'
because they will all know me,
    from the least of them to the greatest.
12 *For I will be gracious toward their iniquities*
        and will never again[y] remember their sins."
13 *In that he says[z] "new," he treated the first covenant as obsolete, and what is obsolete*
and outdated will soon disappear.

Notes

[a] The word κεφάλαιον was used metaphorically by Gk. writers with several shades of meaning. It denoted (1) the "main" or "chief point" in an argument, the "gist" or essential point of view in a question; (2) a "summary," "résumé," or brief "recapitulation" of the main points of a subject; or (3) the "crowning affirmation" in a discussion, the "crowning example" of something, its "completion" or final stage. The second of these nuances is excluded in 8:1 since the writer does not summarize what he has been saying, but in 8:1–2 he passes to a new point. Most commentators and translations show a preference for the first shade of meaning (BAGD 429; MM 342; cf. RSV, NEB, NASB, NIV). The translation given above is based on the conviction that the new affirmation that Christ exercises his priestly ministry in the heavenly sanctuary (8:2) is the "crowning affirmation" to the foregoing argument. For a defense of this translation, see Field, *Notes,* 227–28; W. Manson, 122–23; and especially Williamson, *Philo,* 123–29.

[b] The special nuance in the prep ἐπί with the dative, in the expression ἐπὶ τοῖς λεγομένοις, would appear to be "in addition to [what we are saying]." This accords with classical usage (cf. BAG 286; BDF § 235[3]; A.T. Robertson, *Grammar,* 605).

[c] The gen τῆς μεγαλωσύνης denotes the majesty of God, so that "of the Majesty" is to be taken as an equivalent of the divine name, as in 1:3. It is instructive to compare the formulation in 8:1 with the parallel statement in 12:2, "he has taken his seat at the right hand of the throne of God [τοῦ θρόνου τοῦ θεοῦ]." Cf. Schmitz, *TDNT* 3:161, n. 7; Hofius, *Vorhang,* 59, n. 65, 74, n. 141.

[d] The word λειτουργός has here a cultic sense as in the LXX. It contemplates the priesthood of Christ from the perspective of the high priestly ministry performed in the heavenly sanctuary (cf. Strathmann, *TDNT* 4:230).

[e] The expression καὶ τῆς σκηνῆς τῆς ἀληθινῆς is almost certainly epexegetical to τῶν ἁγίων, "the sanctuary." Cf. NEB ("the real sanctuary, the tent pitched by the Lord") and NIV ("the sanctuary, even the true tent"). That a hendiadys is intended by "the sanctuary καί the true tabernacle" seems obvious from the sg number of the pronoun ἥν in the relative clause that follows, ἣν ἔπηξεν ὁ κύριος, "which

the Lord pitched" (so Riggenbach, 220–31; Moffatt, 105; Spicq, 2:234; Michel, 288; P.E. Hughes, 289). For a contrary opinion, see Hofius, *Vorhang*, 59–60, who appeals to Lev 16:16, 20, 33 as a basis for distinguishing between τὰ ἅγια (the most holy place within the sanctuary) and σκηνὴ ἀληθινή (the heavenly sanctuary in its totality). Other writers argue on the basis of 9:11–12 that a distinction should be made between the σκηνή, "tabernacle," through which Jesus passed, and τὰ ἅγια, "the sanctuary," which he entered in 8:2 (so Andriessen, "Das grössere und volkommenere Zelt [Hebr 9:11]," *BZ* 15 [1971] 87–88; Vanhoye, "Par la tente plus grande et plus parfait . . . [Heb 9:11]," *Bib* 46 [1965] 4; Sabourin, *NTS* 18 [1971] 87–90). There is, however, no common agreement among these writers as to the theological significance of the distinction. For a defense of the position taken in this commentary, that a distinction must be made in 9:11–12, but that such a distinction is inappropriate in 8:2, see Peterson, "Examination," 223–24.

[f] Vanhoye (*VD* 37 [1959] 32–35) has called attention to the fact that the writer consistently uses the present tense (with its iterative "aspect") when referring to the constantly reiterated sacrifices of the Levitical priesthood, and the aor tense (with its once-only "aspect") when referring to the definitive sacrifice offered by Christ. To bring out the nuance of the aor tense of προσενέγκῃ in 8:3, Vanhoye translates: "Hence for this priest too the necessity of having something to offer (at a particular moment of time)."

[g] The construction εἰ . . . ἦν . . . οὐδ' ἂν ἦν signals a second-class conditional sentence that expresses an unreal (contrary-to-fact) or unfulfilled condition (see on 4:8; cf. Zerwick, *Biblical Greek*, §§313–14; BDF §360[4]). The same construction appears in v 7 (εἰ . . . ἦν . . . οὐκ ἂν ἐζητεῖτο, "if . . . had been . . . there would not be sought").

[h] The ptcp is used in a gen absolute construction ὄντων τῶν προσφερόντων and is causal. The present tense of the ptcp is frequentative; i.e., it expresses that which occurs repeatedly (cf. Zerwick and Grosvenor, *Grammatical Analysis*, 670).

[i] It seems preferable to treat the expression ὑποδείγματι καὶ σκιᾷ as a hendiadys (with Moffatt, 105: "a shadowy outline"; or Schlier, *TDNT* 2:33: "a shadowy reflection") rather than as the conjunction of distinct terms ("a copy and a shadow": RSV, NEB, TEV, NIV). The writer's intention is to underscore that the tabernacle erected by Moses and its ritual were only an impf reflection of the heavenly original. For a defense of the translation of ὑπόδειγμα as "suggestion," see Lee (*NTS* 8 [1961–62] 167–69), who holds that the idea of "suggestion" is characteristic of the noun in the NT. In 8:5 it connotes "a *glimpse* as distinct from a vision, a partial *suggestion* as distinct from a complete expression, a *shadow* as distinct from the reality of heaven" (168).

[j] The pf tense of κεχρημάτισται is to be recognized as a "narrative perfect," used in explaining the OT (see *Note* i on 7:6; cf. 7:9, 11, 13, 16, 20, 23): "he was admonished." The qualification that Moses was admonished "by God" treats the pass voice of the verb as a case of the "divine passive" (see *Note* c on 2:2).

[k] When the verb μέλλειν is used with the present inf (in this instance, ἐπιτελεῖν), it denotes an intended action (so BAG 502).

[l] The use of the impersonal φησίν, with God as the unexpressed subj, is typical of Jewish-Gk. phraseology, according to Turner, *Grammar*, 4:108.

[m] The common meaning of τύπος is "offprint," or "copy," the image made by a seal on wax. The writer, however, revises its meaning by pairing it with ἀντίτυπος, "copy" (9:24), so that τύπος is to be understood as analogous to the pattern in the seal, and ἀντίτυπος to the impression made by the seal (cf. D'Angelo, *Moses*, 208, 224–25).

[n] The particle νυνὶ (δέ) is logical rather than temporal.

[o] It is common to intrude the official name "Christ" (RSV) or the personal name "Jesus" (NEB, TEV, NIV) in v 6, but it seemed appropriate to preserve the distinctive character of the exposition, which makes use of a demonstrative pronoun in v 3 (τοῦτον, "this one") and of third person sg in v 6 (τέτυχεν, "he attained"). The writer has carefully avoided an explicit designation of Jesus. After an extended absence of personal reference, the reappearance of the name "Christ" in 9:11 is rhetorically dramatic (cf. Vanhoye, *La structure*, 139–40).

[p] The pronoun ἥτις has a causal sense (cf. Zerwick, *Biblical Greek* §215; A. W. Argyle, "The Causal Use of the Relative Pronouns in the Greek New Testament," *BT* 6 [1955] 165–69).

[q] In the expression ἐπὶ . . . νενομοθέτηται, ἐπί with the dative has the meaning "on the basis of" or "in accordance with" (so BDF §235[2]; Gutbrod, *TDNT* 4:1090). Moffatt (107) rightly suggests that the pass νενομοθέτηται implies that God is ὁ νομοθετῶν, "the one who draws up, or enacts," as in Ps 83:7 LXX. For an alternate proposal to translate ἐπί with the dative as "concerning," see Hollander,

BT 30 [1979] 244–47. Hollander translates v 6*b*: "For this covenant includes regulations concerning better promises." The details of the text quoted in vv 8–12, however, would appear to favor the translation "on the basis of" rather than "concerning."

ʳ See *Note* g above. The use of a second-class conditional sentence indicates that the first covenant was open to reproach.

ˢ The translation reflects a critical decision based on text and syntax. Although the MS tradition is quite evenly divided between the accusative αὐτούς (ℵ* A D* I K P ψ 33 81 it vg co) and the dative αὐτοῖς (P⁴⁶ ℵᶜ B Dᶜ 614 1739 byz Lect Or *alia*), there are good reasons for adopting αὐτοῖς as the primitive reading. It enjoys early and impressive support. If αὐτοῖς is taken with the verb λέγει, "he says," instead of with μεμφόμενος, "finding fault," the logical connection with the preceding verse is sustained. God found fault not simply "with them" (i.e., the people) but with the first covenant (so also P.E. Hughes, 298–99, n. 19).

ᵗ At this point καί expresses a temporal designation and means "when" (BDF §442[4]; Zerwick, *Biblical Greek* §455*d*).

ᵘ For this translation of the temporal expression ἐν ἡμέρᾳ, see BAG 348; BDF §423(5).

ᵛ The idiom ἀμελεῖν τινός denotes "to overlook, neglect, pay no attention to, or have no concern for someone." Zerwick and Grosvenor propose the translation "I lost interest in them" (*Grammatical Analysis*, 671).

ʷ The translation reflects the adoption of the sg reading of P⁴⁶ (διδάξῃ ἕτερος), which appears to be primitive. All other extant MSS have suffered corruption through assimilation to the LXX, which reads διδάξωσιν ἕκαστος, "they shall teach every one." See Beare, *JBL* 63 (1944) 386–87.

ˣ The reading πολίτην is strongly attested by P⁴⁶ ℵ A B D K L most minuscules itᵈ·ᵉ syᵖ·ʰ cop arm. The variant reading πλησίον, "neighbor" (JB, NIV), is read by P 81 104 326 436 629 630 1985 it vg syʰᵐᵍ aeth, bringing the citation into conformity with the LXXᴬ text.

ʸ The use of οὐ μή with the aor subjunctive expresses emphatic denial here (cf. Turner, *Grammar*, 3:96).

ᶻ Although the articular inf with the prep ἐν is usually temporal ("while"), it occasionally appears in a sense not purely temporal. Here ἐν τῷ λέγειν could be translated "in saying" or "in that he says" (BDF §404[3]).

Form/Structure/Setting

A new stage in the argument is clearly indicated in 8:1–2. Previously the writer has focused on Jesus' appointment as high priest and his vocational qualification for the exercise of a fully effective ministry (5:6–10; 6:20; 7:11–28). He now calls attention to Jesus as high priestly ministrant in the heavenly sanctuary and underscores the significance of this concept by designating it the "crowning affirmation" to the preceding argument (8:1). The unit introduced in 8:1–2 consists entirely of exposition. Its limits are indicated by an *inclusio:* corresponding to the statement in 8:3 that every high priest is appointed to offer (προσφέρειν) gifts and sacrifices is the complementary declaration that Christ was offered (προσενεχθείς) once to take away the sins of the people in 9:28. These limits are confirmed by the observation that the theme of Christ's entrance into the heavenly sanctuary, which is announced in 8:1–2, is actually developed in 9:11–28. The new unit extends from 8:1–9:28 and constitutes the central section within the compositional structure of the sermon. Its place at the center indicates the importance that the writer ascribed to this facet of his message (cf. Vanhoye, *RSR* 47 [1949] 44–60; *La structure*, 138–61).

The transition to the central section was carefully prepared. The description of the high priest who is appropriate to the Christian community in 7:26–28 is presupposed in the triumphant announcement, "We do have such a high priest," in 8:1. The contrast drawn in 7:27 between the Levitical high priests, who were obliged to make repeated offerings for sins, and Jesus, whose single offering brought an end to the Levitical arrangement, is resumed. It is also amplified in the distinction between those who offer gifts and sacrifices on earth (8:3–5; 9:9) and the eschatological high priest whose redemptive sacrifice was presented in heaven (8:3, 6; 9:14, 25, 28). The solemn appointment of the Son as high priest who has "been made perfect forever" asserted in 7:28 is taken up and expounded in terms of the definitive sacrifice that Christ offered to God when he entered the heavenly sanctuary (8:1–2; 9:11–28). The topics announced thematically in 7:26–28 are taken up and developed in the course of the exposition in 8:1–9:28.

In his analysis of the central section, Vanhoye found an accumulation of literary indications of a tightly unified structure. He appealed to various compositional elements as the basis for dividing and subdividing 8:1–9:28. He demonstrated that the function of 8:1–2 was to introduce the section and to anticipate the development of Christ's ministry in 9:11–28. He then argued that the section should be divided into two units, the first of which extends from 8:3 to 9:10. This unit is essentially negative in cast and exposes the deficiency and displacement of the old arrangement. The second unit, extending from 9:11 to 9:28, is positive in its evaluation of the effectiveness of Christ's sacrifice. Within the first unit he was able to distinguish three paragraphs marked off by distinctive vocabulary or phrases, to which correspond three paragraphs in the second unit as well. Vanhoye's analysis can be summarized schematically in the following table:

8:1–9:10
	Introduction	8:1–2
A	The earthly sanctuary and its ministry	8:3–6
B	The first covenant	8:7–13
C	Worship under the old arrangement	9:1–10

9:11–28
C'	Worship under the new arrangement	9:11–14
B'	The new covenant	9:15–23
A'	The heavenly sanctuary and its ministry	9:24–28

The corresponding parallelism of the six sections, arranged in concentric symmetry, confirms to Vanhoye's satisfaction that he has uncovered the compositional scheme for the central section (*RSR* 47 [1949] 46–56; *La structure,* 139–61).

Although it is not necessary here to respond in detail to this analysis (for a detailed critique see Gourgues, *RB* 83 [1976] 28–31), issue must be taken with Vanhoye's contention that the first unit in the central section extends from 8:1 to 9:10. When analyzing the course of the exposition, it is imperative to take into account a fundamental difference between 8:1–13 and 9:1–10. In 8:1–13 the writer draws attention to Jesus' ministry to heighten the contrast with the Levitical arrangement under the old covenant. The argument proceeds by comparison. In 9:1–10 the writer concentrates narrowly upon the arrangement of the tabernacle and its provision for ministry. The component of comparison is not introduced until 9:11. In the light of this difference, it seems preferable to treat 8:1–13 and 9:1–10 as separate units. The presentation of Jesus as priestly ministrant and mediator of a "better covenant" in 8:1–13 establishes a context for the discussion of cultic worship and covenant in 9:1–10 and 9:11–28 respectively. From this perspective, 8:1–13 is a transitional passage to the exposition that follows (cf. Hay, *Glory,* 87, 151; Kuss, *MTZ* 7 [1956] 263). The conceptual unity of 8:1–13 is exhibited in the following outline proposed by M. Gourgues (*RB* 83 [1976] 31):

A	Christ, the ministering priest	8:1–5
	1. A new ministry	8:1–2
	2. which is set in opposition to the old	8:3–5
B	Christ, the mediator of the new covenant	8:6–13
	1. The new ministry is associated with a better covenant	8:6
	2. which is set in opposition to the old	8:7–13

In this case, considerations of content must take precedence over merely formal indications of literary structure.

Comment

In 7:11–28 the writer drew attention to certain deficiencies in the Levitical arrangement. Among these were the mortality of the ministering priests (7:23) and the necessity of repeated sacrifices for sins, both of the priests and the people (7:27). Two further weaknesses of the Levitical arrangement are demonstrated on the basis of Scripture in 8:1–13. First, the contrast between the heavenly and earthly tabernacle is introduced to supplement the distinction between the new and the old. Levitical priests serve only a shadowy suggestion of the heavenly sanctuary in which Christ exercises his ministry. To the degree that the earthly sanctuary with its ministry only imperfectly corresponds to the ministry conducted in the presence of God, it is marked by deficiency. Secondly, the covenant under which the Levitical arrangement was instituted has been treated by God as obsolete. The mediation of the new covenant demonstrates the eschatological superiority of Christ's ministry and the divine intention to replace the old arrangement with another that is eschatologically new.

1–2 Having established the eschatological superiority of the high priesthood of Christ, the writer proceeds to relate his high priesthood to the themes of sanctuary and covenant. His rhetorical training is evident in the initial phrase, κεφάλαιον δὲ ἐπὶ τοῖς λεγομένοις, "Now the crowning affirmation to what we are saying." The expression is calculated to draw the attention of the community to the significance of the new affirmation with which the foregoing argument is crowned. The exposition in 8:1–9:28 adds important considerations to the preceding chapters, and κεφάλαιον must be attached to what follows (see above, *Note* a; cf. Spicq, 2:233). The writer's statement in 8:1–2 is the summit of his case. The "crowning affirmation" is not simply that Christians have a high priest who has taken his seat at God's right hand (v 1) but that he is the ministering priest in the heavenly sanctuary (v 2).

The assertion τοιοῦτον ἔχομεν ἀρχιερέα, "we do have such a high priest," points back, at least in some measure, to the parallel expression in 7:26–27 (cf. Michel, 287). In the construction τοιοῦτον . . . ὅς, "such a one . . . who," however, the relative pronoun ὅς has correlative force, so that τοιοῦτον refers primarily to what follows (see *Comment* on 7:26; cf. Cockerill, *Melchizedek Christology*, 151). Christians have as their high priest one who has taken his seat at the right hand of God in heaven.

In 7:28 the writer drew together the concepts of priesthood and sonship; in 8:1 he unites the themes of priesthood and heavenly session. Jesus' session at God's right hand is linked with his priestly office only in 8:1 and at 10:12–13. The phrasing ὃς ἐκάθισεν ἐν δεξιᾷ τοῦ θρόνου τῆς μεγαλωσύνης ἐν τοῖς οὐρανοῖς, "who has taken his seat at the right hand of the Majesty in heaven," recalls the formulation in 1:3, where the writer alluded to Ps 110:1 to assert the exaltation of the incarnate Son to a position of supreme honor. The session at God's right hand is invoked here not for its connotation of transcendent dignity but for its implication that Jesus exercises a heavenly office. The primary allusion is to Ps 110:1, but the writer may have intended a secondary allusion to Zech 6:13 LXX, where the one who is seated at God's right hand is the anointed priest: καὶ ἔσται ὁ ἱερεὺς ἐκ δεξιῶν αὐτοῦ, "and the priest shall be at his right hand" (cf. Synge, *Hebrews and the Scriptures*, 25). That Jesus was the ministering priest in the celestial sanctuary was a crucial consideration in the writer's argument for the superiority of Jesus to the Levitical priesthood. The formulation in v 1 attests that he based this conviction on the wording of Ps 110:1. In v 4 he will acknowledge that apart from the heavenly session asserted in Ps 110:1, Jesus would not be a priest at all. Ps 110:1 is thus an essential ingredient in the two-sanctuary reasoning elaborated in 8:1–5 (Hay, *Glory*, 87, 151; cf. Gourgues, *A la droite de Dieu*, 114–18).

The high priest is identified as τῶν ἁγίων λειτουργός, "the ministering priest of the sanctuary." The term λειτουργός is here virtually equivalent to ἀρχιερεύς, "high priest," but emphasizes the cultic rather than the official aspect of the office. It implies activity (cf. 7:25), and not merely status. The expression τῶν ἁγίων is used, as often in the LXX, to refer to the sanctuary in general (cf. 9:1), without any reference to the distinction between the inner and outer shrines (cf. 9:2–3; so Moffatt, 104; Michel, 287–88; P. E. Hughes, 281, n. 54). Cody has shown that the concept of a heavenly sanctuary corresponding to the earthly sanctuary had become common currency in Judaism (*Heavenly Sanctuary*, 9–46; cf. McNicol, "Relationship," 54–113). He holds that the theme as it is presented in Hebrews reflects direct dependence upon the OT (Exod 25:9, 40; 26:30; 27:8; Num 8:4) and shows more in common with the rabbinic and Jewish apocalyptic literature (cf. *T. Levi* 3:4–8; 5:1; *2 Apoc. Bar.* 4:3–6; *4 Ezra* 7:26; 8:52; 13:36) than it does with Philo (see the helpful table in Cody, 35–36). In one important respect, however, the writer shares with Philo a notion which is not reflected in the Palestinian Jewish literature and which was influenced by a current from the Greek philosophical tradition, namely, that only what is heavenly is of lasting value (Cody, *Heavenly Sanctuary*, 36).

The further description of the heavenly sanctuary as "the true tabernacle [καὶ τῆς σκηνῆς τῆς ἀληθινῆς] which the Lord pitched, not man," anticipates the contrast of v 5, where Moses, not God, is to be regarded as the builder of the earthly tabernacle (cf. 9:11, 24). The formulation in v 2 reflects an adaption of Num 24:5–6 LXX, where it is said that the Lord pitched the tents (σκηναί) of Jacob. The plural is here changed to the singular in reference to the sanctuary (Michaelis, *TDNT* 7:376). The adjective ἀληθινή is used with the meaning "that which truly is" or "that which is eternal" (cf. Bietenhard, *Das himmlische Welt*, 125–30, 136, n. 2). "True" implies genuine, of effective value, and the expression "true tabernacle" is used in contrast not to what is false but to what is symbolical and imperfect (Cody, *Heavenly Sanctuary*, 151).

The fact that the sanctuary in which Christ carries out his work of salvation is in heaven identifies the place of his ministry with a transcendent order, which derives immediately from God, without human, earthly intermediary. The writer used the terminology of the heavenly sanctuary and the true tabernacle as spatial expressions for the session at God's right hand, as the collocation of the two ideas in 8:1–2 shows (cf. Nomoto, *NovT* 10 [1968] 17–19, who argues that the contrast between the earthly and heavenly sanctuary is not an expression of Alexandrian metaphysics, but the writer's way of presenting the typological relation between the old and new covenants; the heavenly liturgy is the eschatological reality that the OT institutions only foreshadowed, and the relationship between the two sanctuaries is basically a *temporal* one). The point emphasized in v 2 is that the possibility of access to God through a Levitical and earthly arrangement no longer exists because of their intrinsic inadequacy. Access is possible only through the ministering priest who serves in the heavenly sanctuary.

3–4 The concept of priesthood logically entails the concept of sacrifice. This point was made earlier in 5:1, where it was stated that every high priest is appointed "in order to offer gifts and sacrifices for sins." Although the qualification "for sins" does not appear in v 3, the writer regarded all sacrifice in terms of the procuring of atonement and the removal of sin (see *Comment* on 5:1; cf. 9:9, 10:11). The thought of 5:1 is repeated here to specify that it was necessary for "this man also to have something to offer." Johnsson has observed that "in such a statement we look straight into the heart of the cult, as it were" (*ExpTim* 89 [1978] 106). It serves to underscore the importance of cultus in the total argument of Hebrews. In v 3 the writer is thinking of Jesus' presentation of himself as a sin offering (cf. 7:27), but the nature of his offering is not stated until 9:14. In actuality, Jesus' priesthood could never have been contained within the Levitical sacrificial system. The law regulated all that concerns the earthly priesthood, and by this law Jesus was excluded from the priestly office (see *Comment* on 7:13–14). The writer declares emphatically that the priesthood of Jesus is not an earthly priesthood, but a priesthood in the heavenly realm. Although he was vocationally qualified for the office of high priest on earth, his actual priestly ministry of sacrifice and intercession is associated with his entrance into a transcendent heavenly realm.

5 The Levitical priests performed their ministry in a sanctuary that was sanctioned by God, but which only imperfectly and incompletely reproduced what Moses had seen. Although Moses was shown a "model" to follow, as a human-made sanctuary (9:24), the tabernacle that he erected was inferior to the sanctuary in which Christ performs his ministry (cf. 9:1, where the Mosaic tabernacle is called "an earthly sanctuary," and the antonym is clearly ἐπουράνιος, "heavenly," as in 8:5). The descriptive phrase ὑποδείγματι καὶ σκιᾷ, "a shadowy suggestion," implies that the tabernacle was a rough reminiscence intended to suggest the idea of the original and to train the people of God to appreciate eventually the heavenly reality itself (Lee, *NTS* 8 [1961–62] 167–69). The fact that it was only a copy of the heavenly reality consigns the earthly sanctuary to the realm of the changing and transitory, which has only limited validity because it must ultimately pass away (cf. Cody, *Heavenly Sanctuary*, 17–21, 154–55; Goppelt, *Typos*, 196–205).

The argument in v 5 is substantiated by the quotation of Exod 25:40 (cf. Acts 7:44), which implies that Moses was shown some sort of "model" that could be reproduced on earth. The LXX term τύπος, which translates the MT תבנית, "building," "construction," connotes something more objective than oral instruction. The citation deviates from the LXX^A text at two points: the writer adds the word πάντα, "everything," and he alters the verb from the perfect participle δεδειγμένον to an aorist, δειχθέντα, "shown." The oracle was drawn from a context containing instruction concerning the erection of the tabernacle, its furnishings, and the consecration of its priests (Exod 25–31). Four passages imply that the instructions given to Moses included illustrations (Exod 25:9 [LXX 25:8], 39–40; 26:30; 27:8; cf. Num 8:4). The choice of Exod 25:40 seems to have been influenced by the presence of the term τύπος, "pattern, model, illustration," which attests the "shadowy" character of the earthly sanctuary and its liturgy. D'Angelo has argued that the revision of the oracle by the addition of πάντα, "everything," was an exegetical device to extend the interpretation of the oracle by placing the other three verses at the service of the writer. This applies especially to Exod 25:8 LXX, where Moses was admonished to make πάντα according to the paradigm. D'Angelo suggests that the writer's ultimate intention was to include the whole context (Exod 25–31), since he had determined to treat not only the tabernacle but also its ministry as a foreshadowing of things to come (see *Comment* on 10:1). With the addition of πάντα, Exod 25:40 was adapted into an exegetical principle, according to which all the features of the cult become clues to the heavenly liturgy accomplished by Christ (D'Angelo, *Moses*, 205–22).

The distinction between the material world and the heavenly world and the contrast between shadow and reality might appear to make unavoidable the conclusion that in v 5 the writer has been influenced by the classical dualism of Plato, mediated to him by Philo or by the influence of an Alexandrian education (cf. Moffatt, xxxiii; Héring, 10; T. H. Robinson, 108; Sower, *Hermeneutics*, 107). R. Williamson, however, has demonstrated that the resemblance to Platonism is merely verbal. The crucial consideration is that the writer presents Jesus as one who, at a particular point in history, lived a full and authentic human life and entered into the celestial sanctuary after the completion of his work on earth, the climax of which was his sacrificial death on the cross in perfect obedience to the will of God. This perspective introduces a dramatic temporal and historical aspect into the contrast developed in 8:1–5 that is antithetical to the serene and unhistorical metaphysics of Plato. The contrast developed is not simply between an earthly copy and a heavenly archetype but between a historical situation in the past and one that succeeded it *in time*. During the former situation, marked by the ministry of the Levitical priests, there was no entrance into the real, heavenly presence of God; full entrance into the eternal presence of God was made possible only with the life and redemptive accomplishment of Jesus. The celestial sanctuary became the scene of an effective priesthood only from the moment of Christ's exaltation. For the writer of Hebrews, the temporal contrast was decisive: the ministry of the Levitical priests in the tabernacle was antecedent to the ministry exercised in the heavenly sanctuary. It foreshadowed the definitive sacrificial work of Christ that was accomplished centuries later, "in these last days" (1:2). The categories of time and history are inextricably bound up with the thought of v 5 in a way that is inconsistent with Platonism

(Williamson, *SJT* 16 [1963] 415–24, especially 418–19; id., *Philo*, 142–46, 157–59, 557–65). The distinction between "earthly" and "heavenly" in 8:1–5 is eschatological rather than philosophical.

6 The expression νυνὶ δέ, "in fact," introduces a declaration set in opposition to the contrary-to-fact condition developed in v 4 ("So if he had been on earth, he would not be a priest"; the particle μέν, "on the one hand," in v 4 anticipates the particle δέ, "on the other hand," in v 6). Jesus' securing of a different and superior ministry sharply displays the untenability of the hypothesis that Jesus would not even be a priest (Vanhoye, *La structure*, 142). The truth is that the sacrificial ministry of the Levitical priests foreshadowed only superficially the definitive priestly ministry of Christ in his death and entrance into the presence of God. In the statement διαφορωτέρας τέτυχεν λειτουργίας, "he has attained a superior ministry," the perfect tense of the verb affirms that Jesus has attained, and now possesses, a more excellent ministry than that of the Levitical high priests. In classical Greek the verb λειτουργεῖν and its cognates had no religious content, but Hebrews reflects the LXX, where the verb and its substantive were given a cultic nuance and were used for divine service only. Jesus' ministry is superior because it is effective (cf. Strathmann, *TDNT* 4:226–28).

The measure of that superiority is expressed with a comparison based on Jesus' entrance into the heavenly sanctuary as the mediator of a superior covenant. In Hebrews the theologically significant word μεσίτης, "mediator," is always associated with the new covenant (8:6; 9:15; 12:24; cf. 7:22). The new covenant required a new mediator. By his life of perfect obedience and his death, Jesus inaugurated the new covenant of Jer 31:31–34. His entrance into the heavenly sanctuary guarantees God's acceptance of his sacrifice and the actualization of the provisions of the superior covenant he mediated. The new covenant is superior because it is based on better promises. This significant point is made by repeating twice the qualitative term "better" (κρείττονος and κρείττοσιν), each time in an emphatic position in its phrase. Although the promises of the new covenant are not expressed in cultic terms and are silent concerning a new priesthood and sacrifice, the subsequent development shows the extent to which these promises have influenced the writer's theology. The link between the themes of priesthood and covenant promise is provided in 10:15–18, where the basis of the forgiveness pledged in the new covenant is shown to be the accomplishment of Christ as high priest (so Peterson, "Examination," 227, n. 39).

7–8a Vanhoye has observed that the introductory and concluding verses (vv 7–8a, 13) to the extensive citation of Jer 31:31–34 stress the imperfect and provisional character of "that first" covenant (ἡ πρώτη ἐκείνη [διαθήκη]) concluded at Sinai. The writer directs the attention of the community to the blame contained within the oracle itself (see vv 8–9) and defers to a later point in the exposition his treatment of the positive implications of the "better promises" (v 6) associated with the new covenant (10:15–18). In this setting, the citation of Jer 31:31–34 serves the fundamentally negative purpose of exposing the defective character of the old covenant (*La structure*, 143–44). Only in v 7 is the new covenant described as δεύτερα, "second," in relation to the description of the Sinaitic covenant as ἡ πρώτη, "the first." The type of reasoning displayed in v 7 parallels the argument concerning the ineffectiveness of the Levitical arrangement in 7:11–19.

The treatment of the two covenants in vv 7–8*a* exhibits the eschatological outlook of the writer. At the level of historical events, the covenant mediated by Moses had developed faults on the human side and has been replaced by a better arrangement. The supersession of the old covenant was not due simply to the unfaithfulness of the people to the stipulations of the covenant. It occurred because a new unfolding of God's redemptive purpose had taken place, which called for new covenant action on the part of God. That God took the initiative in announcing his intention to establish a new covenant with Israel (v 8*a*) indicates that he fully intended the first covenant to be provisional (cf. R. A. Harrisville, *The Concept of Newness in the New Testament* [Minneapolis: Augsburg, 1960] 48–53). Thus God finds fault (μεμφόμενος) with the Mosaic covenant, and not simply with the people (see above, *Note* s). The writer's use of the present tense in the verb λέγει, "he says," makes the quotation contemporary with the readers.

8*b*–12 The prophetic word of censure and promise found in Jer 31(LXX 38):31–34 is quoted in full in substantial agreement with the LXX^A text. There are, however, a number of notable variants from the critically established text (see E. Nestle, *Das Buch Jeremia greichisch und hebräisch* [Stuttgart: Kohlhammer, 1934] 69). It has been argued that the deviations from the LXX text have interpretive significance (K. J. Thomas, "The Old Testament Citations in Hebrews," *NTS* 11 [1964–65] 310–13; cf. Schröger, *Verfasser,* 162–68). Specifically, Thomas asserts that the expressions συντελέσω . . . διαθήκην καινήν, "I will establish . . . a new covenant" (v 8), and τὴν διαθήκην ἣν ἐποίησα, "the covenant which I made" (v 9), reflect an idiomatic usage in Jeremiah (cf. Jer 41:8, 15, 18 LXX), which indicates that the new covenant will be kept, whereas the old covenant was broken. Apart from the question whether the first hearers would have recognized the significance of the subtle distinction in formulation detected by Thomas, his analysis will not sustain critical scrutiny (see the objections posed by McCullough, *NTS* 26 [1979–80] 364–67). The variation is, in fact, a stylistic change, as are the other variants from the LXX text. It is possible that these stylistic alterations reflect liturgical usage of the oracle in the early Church (so Kistemaker, *Psalm Citations,* 40–42).

Jer 31(LXX 38):31–34 is the only passage in the OT that promises the future establishment of a definitive relationship with God that is described as qualitatively "new." The central affirmation of the new covenant is the pledge of the presence of the law in the hearts of believers as the gift of God (v 10). The mention of such a gift occurs nowhere else in the OT (the closest parallel is Jer 24:7: God will give his people a new heart capable of knowing him). The quality of newness intrinsic to the new covenant consists in the new manner of presenting God's law and not in newness of content. The people of God will be inwardly established in the law and knowledge of the Lord. The emphasis falls on the interior quality of the human response to God through the new covenant (cf. Coppens, *CBQ* 25 [1963] 16–20; van Unnik, *SP* 1 [1961] 166–67, 171).

The new covenant thus brings to its consummation the relationship between God and his people, which is at the heart of all covenant disclosure from Abraham onward (cf. v 10*c*). The relationship between God and his people, which was the intention of the covenant concluded at Sinai but which was broken by the past failure of Israel to observe the conditions of the relationship established by God (v 9), will be restored. Redemptive grace reaches its zenith in the full and final

realization of this promise through Christ. The inauguration of the new covenant
with the entrance of the eschatological high priest into the heavenly sanctuary
(v 6) indicates the privileged status of the Christian community. In this immediate context it is possible that the writer applied directly to Jesus Christ the promise
that it will be unnecessary to instruct someone γνῶθι τὸν κύριον, "know the Lord"
(cf. 2:3; 7:14; 13:20, where "Lord" designates Jesus). When a second, abbreviated
citation from the same prophecy concludes the central exposition of the work of
Christ (10:16–17), it is clear that the oracle was vital to the writer's theological
understanding (cf. Peterson, *RTR* 38 [1979] 74–81).

13 At this point the writer shows no interest in the promises attached to the
new covenant. He focuses all attention upon the implications of the key word of
the cited text, καινήν, "new" (cf. v 8). The argument that by designating the covenant "new" God declared the covenant concluded at Sinai to be unserviceable
and outmoded (πεπαλαίωκεν, "obsolete, antiquated") carries the corollary that
God himself has canceled its validity. He intends to make no further use of the
old covenant and the forms through which it operated to achieve his redemptive
purpose for his people (cf. de Vuyst, *"Oud en nieuw Verbond,"* 254–55; Seesemann,
TDNT 5:720). Consequently, the old arrangement is on the point of disappearing. The principle that a new act of God makes the old obsolete (cf. 7:11–12)
reflects an eschatological outlook that perceives the Mosaic and Levitical institutions as fulfilled and superseded by Christ.

Explanation

The elaboration of the significance of Christ's redemptive accomplishment
exhibits the profound influence of the outlook and vocabulary of the OT cultus
on the writer's expression. In 8:1–5 the primitive Christian confession of Jesus
as the one who has taken his seat at God's right hand is reinterpreted in the
light of the theme of heavenly sanctuary and liturgy. The development of this
theme, which dominates the argument in 8:1–9:28, is clearly the central and
most distinctive aspect of the writer's interpretation of the saving work of Christ.
The high priestly ministry in the heavenly sanctuary becomes a pregnant metaphor from redemptive history with which to elucidate the session at God's right
hand and the intercession on behalf of the people of God as the result of the
eschatological work of salvation. By means of a typological interpretation of
the OT, the writer asserts that Christ has achieved what the sacrificial action of the
high priest on the great Day of Atonement only foreshadowed. His entrance
into the heavenly sanctuary, which is the true tabernacle where he has unrestricted access to the eternal presence of God, demonstrates the eschatological
superiority of his priestly service to the ministry of the Levitical high priests.
The priestly ministry of Christ in the celestial sanctuary is of capital importance
in the thought of Hebrews.

The writer's concept of a heavenly realm, where sacrificial liturgy and priesthood are perfectly expressed, is difficult. Its source is biblical. On the basis of
Exod 25:40 and related passages, the writer deduced an axiological perspective
(that is, making a value judgment) concerning heaven and earth. Viewed cosmo-
logically, heaven and earth constitute an integral whole. But viewed axiologically,
heaven, as the "place" of God's presence, transcends earth as the source of all

reality and value. God's presence in heaven made it appropriate to qualify the perfectly real as "heavenly." In the polarity between heaven and earth, the perfection of the heavenly realm can be sharply contrasted with the relative imperfection of the earthly realm as reality to shadow. The earthly tabernacle and its priestly ministry were valid and real only because of the heavenly validity and reality to which they corresponded, in which they participated, and to which they referred. The fact that they were only a "shadowy suggestion" of the corresponding reality in heaven implied that they possessed only limited usefulness and validity. For the writer, an axiological consideration of heaven and earth was decisive in the evaluation of the elements that specify the sanctuary, and through the sanctuary the liturgy or ministry associated with it on the two planes of reality.

The modality that distinguishes the sanctuary that really matters from those earthly structures that have only a limited usefulness and validity is that of heavenliness. It is heavenliness that specifies the sanctuary Christ entered. The heavenliness of the sanctuary also has bearing on the priest officiating in it and the liturgy accomplished by him. "Heavenly" in Hebrews has an axiological meaning based on the notion of heaven as the source of reality and the place of salvation perfectly realized. A salvation that is heavenly is a real, perfect salvation that is consummated in the immediacy of God's presence. In 8:1–5 the category of the heavenly adds the dimension of axiological dignity to the reality of the salvation secured through Christ. In the development of this concept the writer does not lose sight of a temporal and historical perspective. Christ's entrance into the heavenly sanctuary is presented as something eschatologically new, which replaces the old arrangements because he has fully achieved their intention.

The comparison between Jesus' priestly ministry and the ministry of those who served the earthly tabernacle is sharpened by the description of Jesus as the mediator of a new and superior covenant. Reflection on God's intention to establish a new covenant and the extensive citation of Jer 31:31–34 serves to exhibit the imperfect and provisional character of the old covenant and its institutions (8:6–13). Corresponding to the axiological evaluation of the theme of sanctuary is the redemptive-historical evaluation of the theme of covenant. The mediation of the new covenant, in contrast to the old, has provided access to the "heavenly sanctuary," the "true tabernacle," and the "superior priestly ministry." The adjectives "heavenly," "true," and "superior" speak of the perfection of the salvation mediated through Christ.